19e

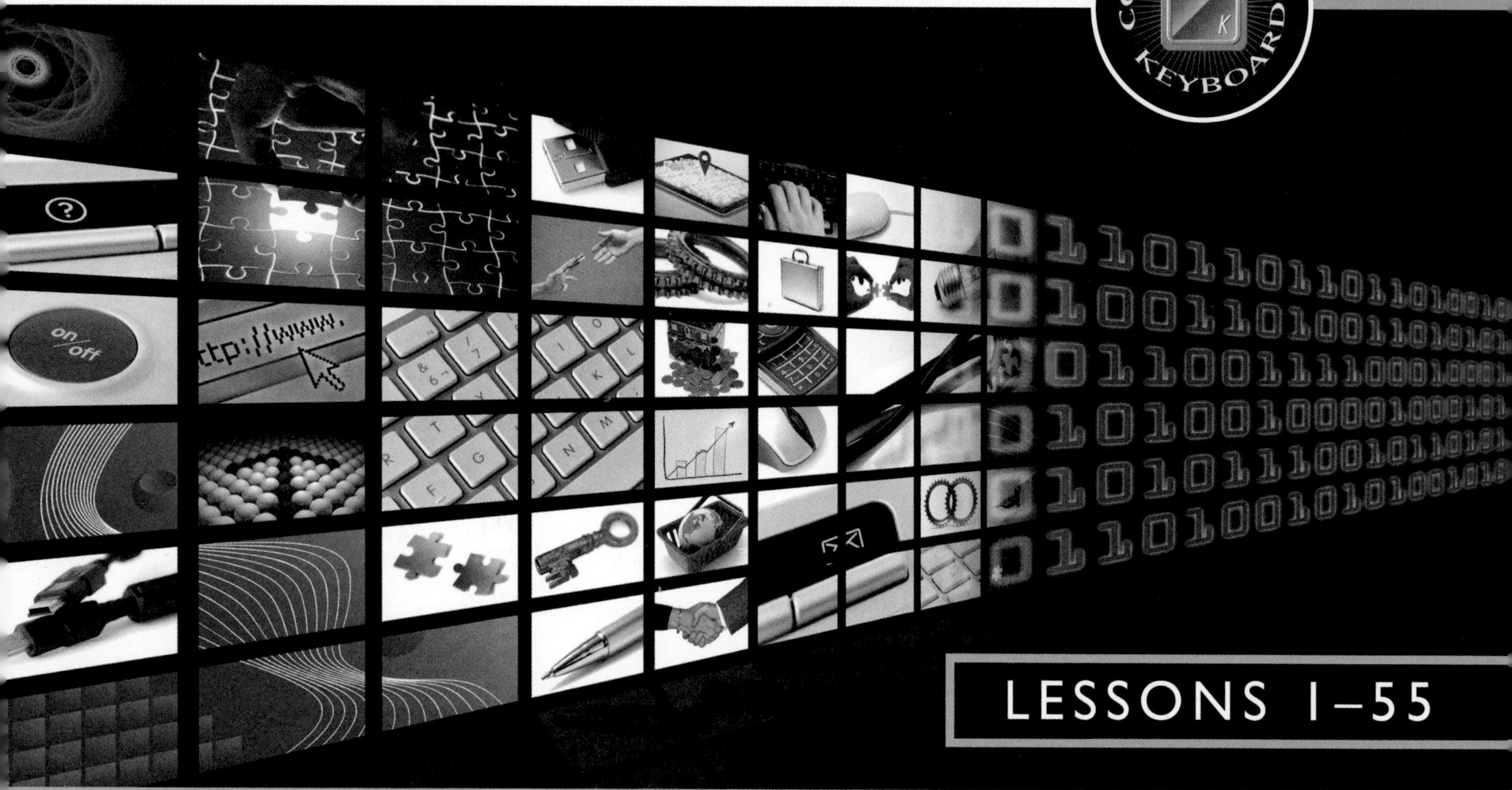

LESSONS 1–55

Keyboarding & Word Processing Essentials

Microsoft® Word 2013

+ **Susie H. VanHuss**, Ph.D., Distinguished Professor Emeritus, University of South Carolina
+ **Connie M. Forde**, Ph.D., Mississippi State University
+ **Donna L. Woo**, Cypress College, California
+ **Vicki Robertson**, Southwest Tennessee Community College

Australia • Brazil • Japan • Korea • Mexico • Singapore • Spain • United Kingdom • United States

SOUTH-WESTERN
CENGAGE Learning

Keyboarding and Word Processing Essentials, Lessons 1-55, Nineteenth Edition

Susie H. VanHuss, Connie M. Forde, Donna L. Woo, Vicki Robertson

SVP Global Product Management, Research, School & Professional: Frank Menchaca

Vice President/Editor-in-Chief: Karen Schmohe

Sr. Developmental Editors: Dave Lafferty, Karen Caldwell

Consultant: Catherine Skintik

Sr. Market Development Manager: Mark Linton

Sr. Content Project Manager: Martha Conway

Marketing Coordinator: Elizabeth Murphy

Sr. Media Editor: Mike Jackson

Sr. Editorial Assistant: Debra Roark

Technical Reviewers: Gayle Statman, Amy Cole

Manufacturing Planner: Charlene Taylor

Production Service: PreMediaGlobal

Sr. Art Director: Michelle Kunkler

Cover and Internal Designer: Imbue Design

Cover and Special Page Images:
© Luis Francisco Cordero/Shutterstock;
© Jezper/Shutterstock.com;
© Joe Belanger/Shutterstock.com;
© Kostsov/Shutterstock.com;
© 3d Brained/Shutterstock.com

Rights Acquisition Director: Audrey Pettengill

Rights Acquisitions Specialist, Text and Image: Deanna Ettinger

Permissions Researcher, Image and Text: PreMediaGlobal

ISBN-13: 978-1-133-58894-8

ISBN-10: 1-133-58894-8

South-Western
5191 Natorp Boulevard
Mason, OH 45040
USA

Cengage Learning is a leading provider of customized learning solutions with office locations around the globe, including Singapore, the United Kingdom, Australia, Mexico, Brazil, and Japan. Locate your local office at:
www.cengage.com/global

Cengage Learning products are represented in Canada by Nelson Education, Ltd.

For your course and learning solutions, visit **www.cengage.com**

Purchase any of our products at your local college store or at our preferred online store **www.cengagebrain.com**

Printed in the United States of America
1 2 3 4 5 6 7 17 16 15 14 13

Commands by Module

Lesson	Commands
Module 3 Word 2013 Essentials	
26	Launch Word
	New Folder
	Save, Save As
	Open
	Close
	New
	Print
	Exit
27	Fonts
	Mini Toolbar
28	Alignment
	Show Hide
	Line and Paragraph Spacing
	Quick Access Toolbar
29	Bullets and Numbering
	Navigation (Scroll bars, Slider, View)
	Spelling and Grammar
	Help
	Define
	Thesaurus
30	Clipboard: Cut, Copy, Paste
	Format Painter
	Center Page
Module 4 Memos and Letters	
32	Date and Time
	Vertical Page Position
33	Remove Space After Paragraph
34	Envelopes
35	Left Tab

Lesson	Commands
Module 5 Tables	
38	Insert Table
39	Table Tools—Layout
41	Table Tools—Design
Module 6 Reports	
43	Themes and Style Sets
	Styles
	Footnotes
44	Margins
	Find and Replace
45	Page Number
	Line and Page Breaks
	Insert File
	Symbols and Special Characters
46	Header
	Save as Template
	Hanging Indent
Module 7 Graphics	
50	Pictures; Format Pictures
	Page Borders
51	SmartArt
	Shapes
	WordArt
52	Columns

See Appendix F: Command Summary, for a detailed list of commands, the path, and button for each command.

The Power of Word 2013...Starts Here!

LEARN . . . DISCOVER

Touch Keyboarding

Word 2013 Essentials

Document Design

Communication Skills

Web Apps

Windows 8 Basics

Discover the POWER of *College Keyboarding, 19th edition* print and digital solutions for *Microsoft Word 2013.*

College Keyboarding, 19e, L1–110 combines easy-to-use tools with a proven track record of ensuring classroom and workplace success.

Keyboarding Pro DELUXE Online (KPDO) provides the tools to master document skills for use in school, career, and personal situations.

NEW to this Edition

- Coverage of *Word 2013* and *Windows 8*
- Direct correlation with the web-based ***Keyboarding Pro DELUXE Online (KPDO)*** to build, apply, and assess skills
- Six new keyboarding review lessons increase confidence and performance
- Two new MLA and APA lessons give greater emphasis to academic reports
- Thirteen new projects at the end of selected modules for additional reinforcement
- Two new modules on Web Apps for realistic exposure to the SkyDrive and cloud computing
- Three new modules are projects that apply critical thinking and reinforce word processing skills
- Restructured employment module underscores the impact and use of social media sites and resume tracking systems

KPDO

Keyboarding Pro™

DELUXE Online

Stephen Coburn/Shutterstock.com

The Power of Keyboarding... Starts Here!

Ready, Set, Key!

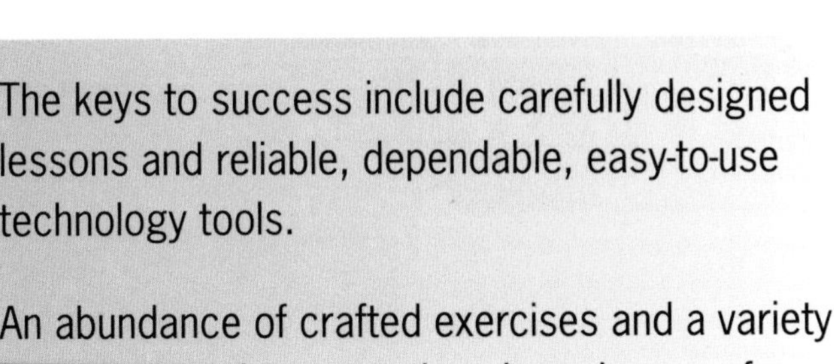

The keys to success include carefully designed lessons and reliable, dependable, easy-to-use technology tools.

An abundance of crafted exercises and a variety of relevant software routines keep lessons fun and help build a strong foundation.

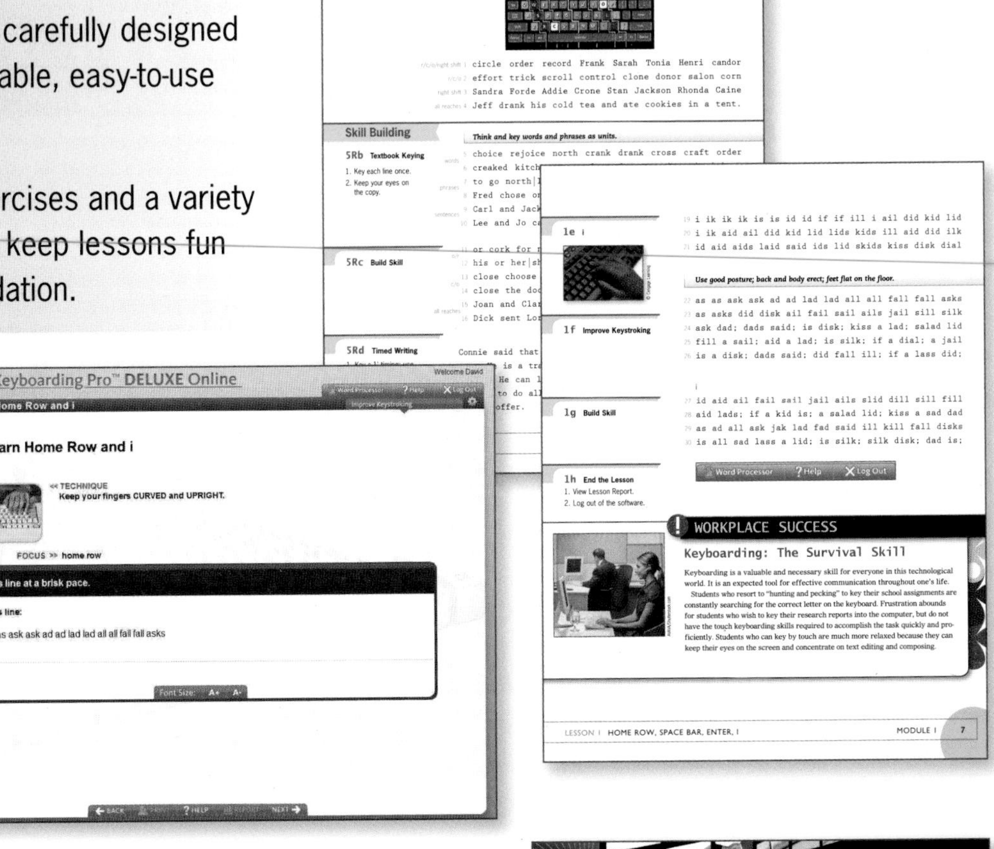

KPDO--Online and Better than Ever

Keyboarding Pro DELUXE Online (KPDO) is an easy-to-use web-based program designed to be used with *College Keyboarding 19e.*

- Textbook directions correlate with *KPDO*
- Relevant, engaging routines that work
- Abundance of Skill Building
- Meaningful, easy-to-use reports

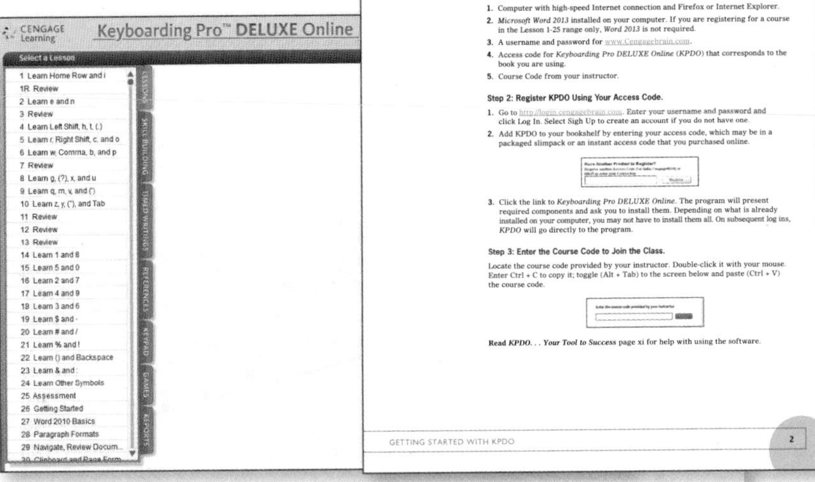

LESSONS | SKILL BUILDING | TIMED WRITINGS | REFERENCES | KEYPAD | GAMES | REPORTS

Accelerate Learning—Follow the Path of Word 2013

Follow Microsoft's path **(Tab/Group/Command)** to learn the main steps of each new command. Once the path is before you, the steps to successfully learning new concepts are easy.

Each new command is immediately applied within a short drill and then reinforced in **Apply It.**

Data files provide immediate opportunities to practice the new command quickly.

Learn and Reinforce with New Commands, Drills, and Apply It

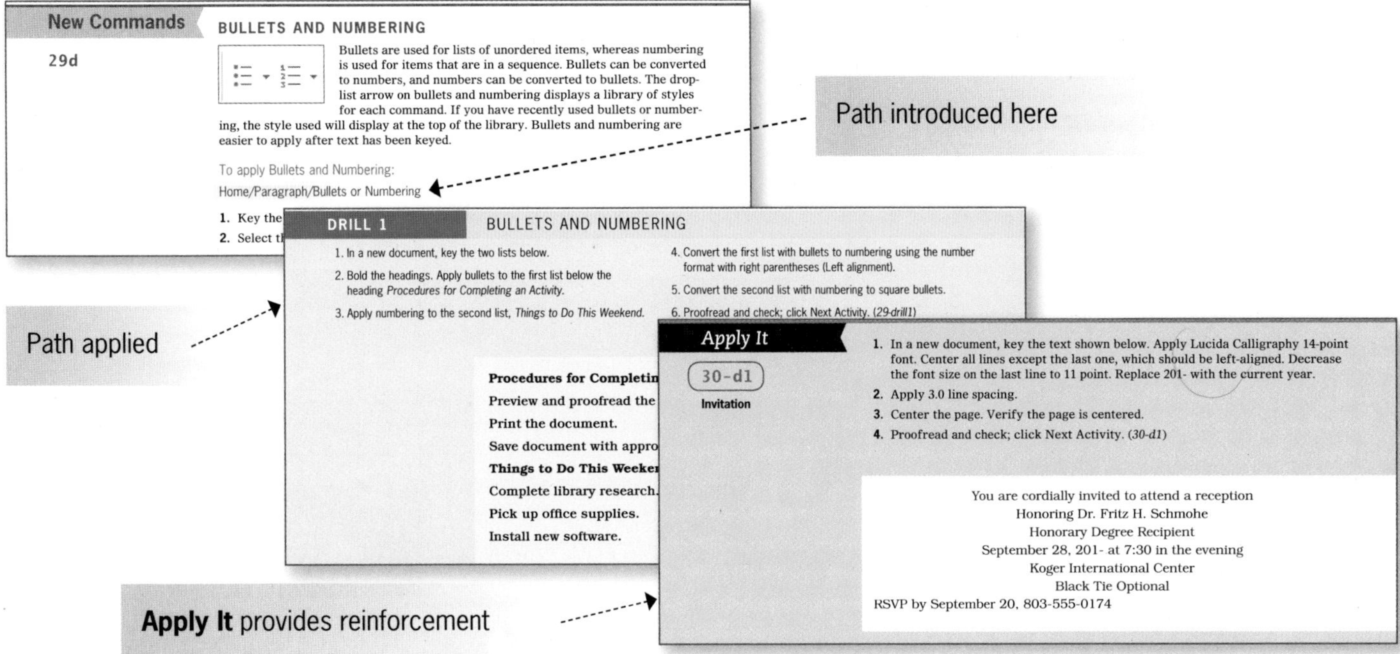

Ensure Success with QuickChecks, Discover, and Tips

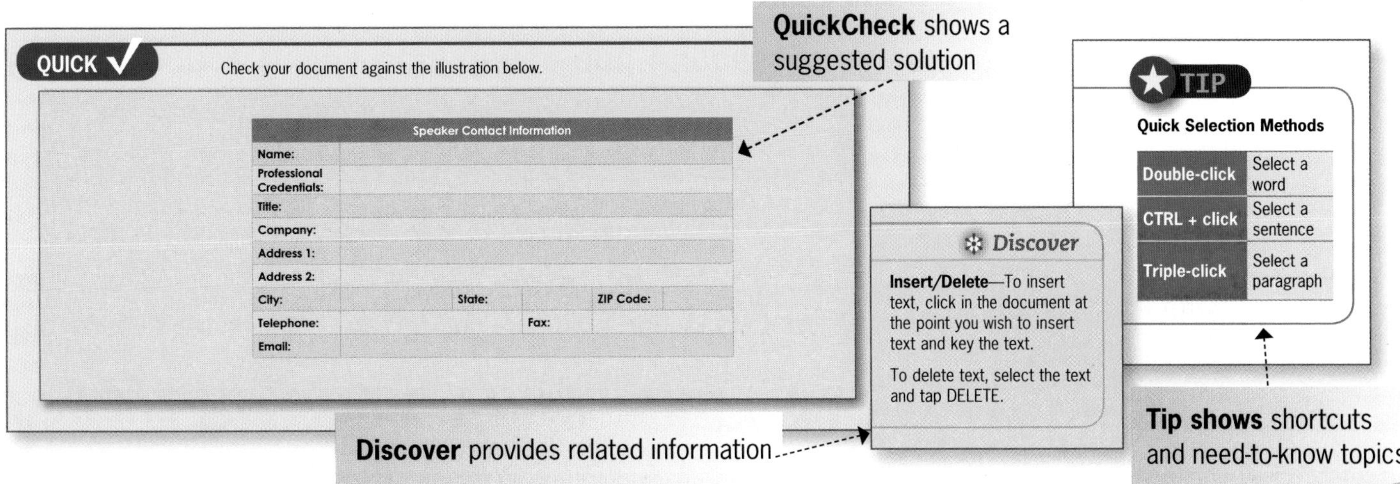

Always Relevant, Fresh, and New

The lessons are updated with an abundance of new documents and additional practice on *Microsoft Word 2013*.

Productivity tools are applied from the start: Styles, Table Styles, Themes, and more.

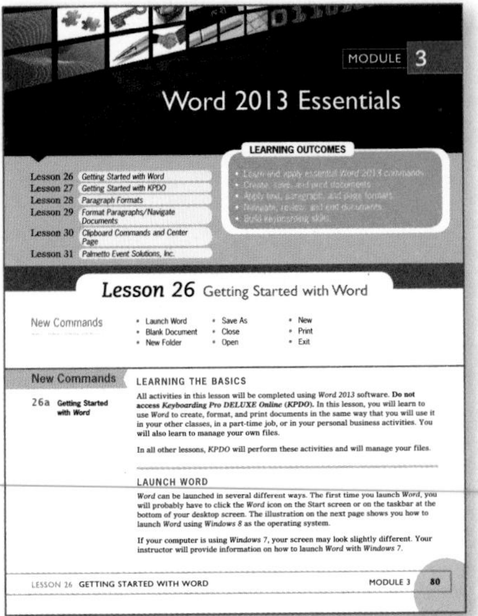

Extra Practice Builds Confidence and Success

Skill Builders in the text, Skill Building Drills in *KPDO*, Textbook Keying, and Timed Writings provide extra practice to strengthen accuracy and techniques.

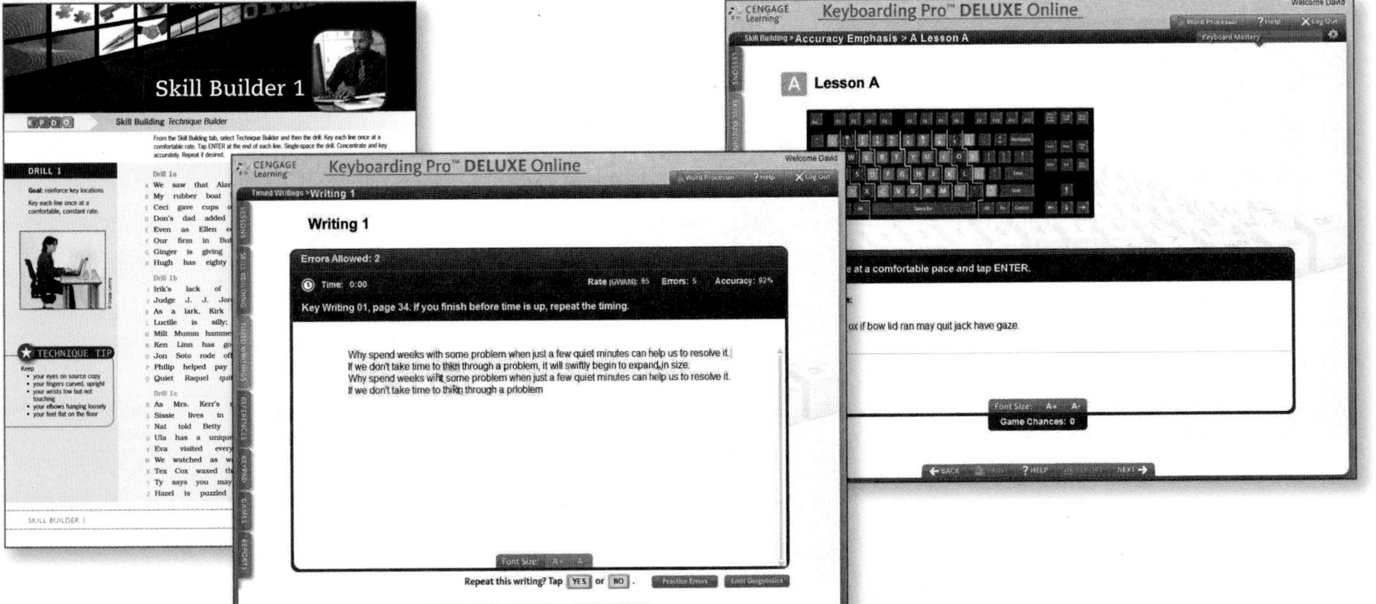

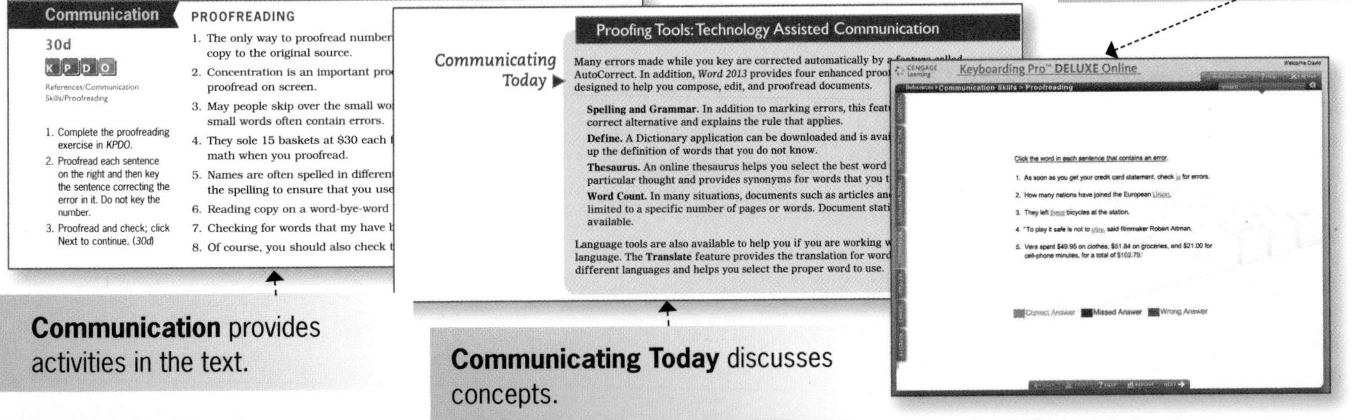

KPDO has related **Communications** activities.

Communication provides activities in the text.

Communicating Today discusses concepts.

Powerful Tools . . . Working for You

College Keyboarding 19e provides the tools students need to develop expertise in keyboarding, document formatting, and essential word processing skills using *Microsoft Word 2013*. When coupled with *Keyboarding Pro DELUXE Online (KPDO)*, students can work at home or school with ease.

TEXT/KPDO PAC BUNDLE ISBNS: 9781581759549 9781285576329 9781285576282 9781285576336

Keyboarding Pro DELUXE Online (KPDO)—Customizable

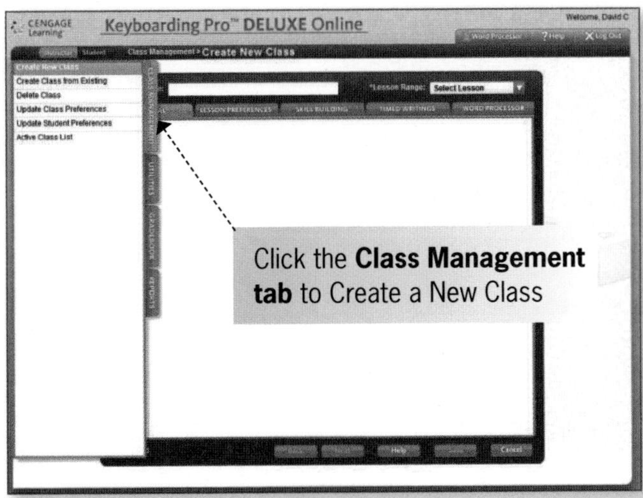

Instructor Main Screen—Create New Class

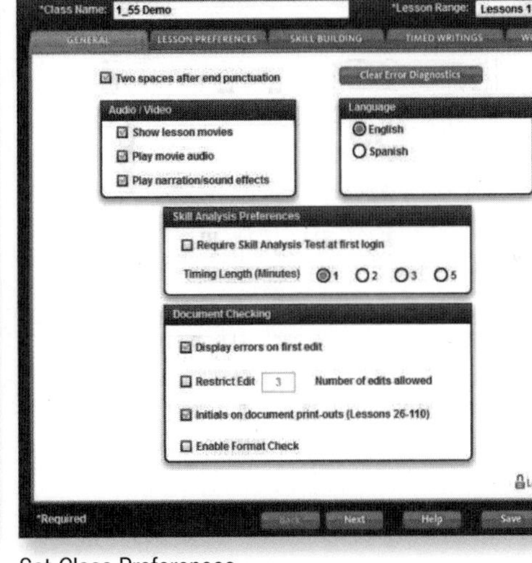

Set Class Preferences

Set Preferences for general, lessons, skill building, timed writings, and the word processor

- Customizable class preferences
- Gradebook to track progress on timed writings, daily assignments, tests, and more
- Quick toggle to student *Word* documents
- Reference tools for Communication Skills, Document Formats, and more
- Document checking of keystrokes with optional format checking

www.collegekeyboarding.com

www.cengagebrain.com

New Content and Changes in Lessons 1–55

Modules 1–2

New Content and Changes in Both Modules of Level 1
Developing Keyboarding Skill, Lessons 1–25, Skill Builders 1 and 2

- Six new review lessons were added – four lessons review alphabetic reaches in Module 1 and two lessons review numbers and symbols in Module 2.
- Many drill lines were revised and keying tips placed above them to emphasize basic skills.
- Modified and added timed writings triple-controlled at the easy level of difficulty in Module 1 and at the low-average level of difficulty in Module 2 to build confidence and gradually increase skill.
- Materials are formatted using one space after colons and after periods to conform to current business usage.
- Many exercises are repositioned to align them in the same sequence as *KPDO*.

Modules 3–9

New Content and Changes in All Modules in Level 2
Essentials—Formatting Business Documents, Lessons 26–55, Skill Builder 3

- Learning load reduced by focusing on most frequently used commands rather than all commands required for certification.
- New project added at the end of each module, *Palmetto Event Solutions*, Inc., enabling students to apply word processing and document formatting skills in a real-world business setting. Linking learning to career goals is a key factor in student retention in the first year of a program.
- Materials are formatted using one space after colons and after periods to conform to current business usage.
- A new feature, *Communicating Today*, was added to each module that focuses on trends and current practices in business communication.
- In addition to communication reviews, all modules and all projects now include composing at the keyboard activities to enhance communication skills required for workplace success.
- Model documents have been shortened to increase the number of formatting jobs and build formatting skills.
- Assessments have been reorganized to provide instructors with flexibility in using projects for review or for authentic assessments in addition to the tests provided on the IRCD. A module assessment and practice test are provided on the IRCD for each module. Each assessment in the textbook covers two modules to allow more time for project-based learning.
- All timed writings in Lessons 26–55 are now triple-controlled at the average level of difficulty to provide a consistent measure of difficulty on all timed writings used for grading purposes.
- A new module, *Web Apps*, was added to introduce students to cloud computing by working on the SkyDrive to upload, view, share, and edit documents using the *Word Web App*.

Module 3

New Content and Changes Specific to Individual Modules
Word 2013 Essentials, Lessons 26–31

- *Microsoft Word 2013* commands necessary to use *Word* as a standalone application are introduced in Lesson 26. Students launch *Word 2013* from the taskbar or the Start screen and learn to create, save, and print a document. (26)
- Steps for creating, saving, and checking *Word* documents in *KPDO* are presented in a logical order with drills and applications that reinforce learning. (27)
- Thesaurus, Define (as a Dictionary App), and Word Count are included with the other Proofing tools; Autocorrect and Translate are omitted. (29)
- **Communicating Today** features discuss the Proofing Tools that assist writers, including AutoCorrect and Translate. (29) Editing challenges when use the clipboard commands (cut, copy, and paste) are discussed. (30)
- Orientation, Margins, and Indent are delayed until later modules.

Module 4	Memos and Letters, Lessons 32–37
	Formatting email is addressed with memos, including the common business practice of attaching a memo to an email so that coworkers have a more permanent record. (32)
	SHIFT + ENTER is presented as a more efficient way of removing space after a paragraph instead of the line spacing command. (33)
	Business Letters – Then and Now discussed in **Communicating Today**; reading letters online and retaining hyperlinks are becoming the new norm. (34)

Module 5	Tables, Lessons 38–42
	Inserting and Deleting Rows/Columns and Merge and Split Cells are covered in a separate lesson. (40)
	Manual formatting by shading, changing borders, and line styles is omitted; Table Styles are emphasized.
	The versatility of using tables for creating page layout and organizing data is highlighted in **Communicating Today**. (41)

Module 6	Reports, Lessons 43–49
	Unbound reports apply the default Office theme; however, the Title style is no longer followed by a divider line in *Word* 2013.
	Multiple-page reports apply symbols, special characters, and Insert File as well as page numbers. (45)
	New lesson addresses the academic MLA Report style, which is double-spaced and has a running head on each page. References are shown as internal citations and listed on the Works Cited page. Student creates an MLA template to use each time a report is keyed. (46)
	New lesson covers the academic report in APA style with internal citations and a Bibliography page. The report and bibliography are double-spaced. Student creates an APA template to use each time a report is keyed. (47)
	Section breaks and Cover page are moved to Advanced Word Processing (71). Go To is introduced in Module 18 with Bookmarks. (101)
	A case for users to take advantage of Styles is emphasized in **Communicating Today**. (43)

Module 7	Graphics, Lessons 50–53
	Pictures are inserted using the Pictures command to insert pictures from your computer and the Online Pictures command to insert images from Microsoft Clip Art, your SkyDrive, or Flickr. (50)
	Shapes and Character Spacing are not covered. Paragraph borders and Drop Cap are presented in Advanced Word Processing.
	Communicating Today addresses the value of color and graphics in electronic documents. (51)

Module 8	Palmetto Event Solutions, Inc., Lessons 54–55
	New comprehensive project applies the document formats and word processing commands presented in Lessons 26–53.

Module 9	Web Apps
	New module that includes concepts of setting up an account on SkyDrive with Microsoft Live, uploading, viewing, and sharing documents on SkyDrive, creating and editing *Word* documents using the *Word Web App*.
	Ten new activities with step-by-step directions integrate concepts.

	Reference Guide
	Numeric Keypad drills for use within *KPDO*.
	Windows 8 overview and activities.

New/Modified Commands in Word 2013 Taught in Level 2

Command	Description
Word Launch Pin to Taskbar	*Word* is launched from the Start screen which replaces the Start button. Pin to the Task Bar enables students to access *Word* easily.
Status Bar	Now includes Word Count on the left side and the Document Views on the right now include Read Mode, Print Layout, and Web Layout.
Save As	Save As now defaults to the SkyDrive. You have to select the place (your Computer or Flash Drive/Removable Disk) that you wish to save the document.
Close on File Menu	Closes the *Word* document, but does not exit *Word*.
Collapsible Ribbon Pin	Ribbon collapses to show only the Tabs and provide more space to view the document. Pin keeps the Ribbon open to display all commands.
Line and Paragraph	The new *Word 2013* default is 1.08 line spacing and 8 points after paragraph.
Read Mode	Provides a digital book when you open a document that takes you back to the last page you read before closing it. Also marks changes made since you last read it.
Define	Now provided by a Dictionary App. Word Count has been added.
Table Styles	Table Styles are now divided into three clearly identified main groups: Plain, Grid, and List; these identifiers make it easier for users to locate various styles.
Design Tab	This new tab contains the Themes, Document Formatting Styles, and Page Background commands. Office remains the default style but is accompanied by a different Document Formatting Style than Office 2010 style. Document styles include line spacing, space after paragraph, color, and other stylistic elements that can be selected for each theme. Preview designs has been eliminated and new designs added.
Navigation Tools and Options	Navigation tools and options have been added and improved.
Page Number, Header, and Footer Styles	Some styles have been eliminated and new ones were added.
Online Pictures	Clip Art has been eliminated as a separate command and is now a part of Online Pictures, which inserts images from Clip Art on Office.com, Bing Image Search, SkyDrive, and Flickr, a photosharing social media site.
Live Layout	Live layout displays Wrap Text options and how the document would look when a picture or other objects are inserted in a document.
Page Borders	Commands for Page Borders are now on the new Design tab.
SmartArt	Office.com has been eliminated as a category of designs and minor changes have been made in the SmartArt graphics.
SkyDrive	SkyDrive and the *Word Web App* are integrated closely with *Word*. Commands have been added and many features have been upgraded.

Welcome to *Keyboarding Pro DELUXE Online (KPDO)*, a web-based, easy-to-use, tutorial software for learning the alphabetic and number keys, numeric keypad, and document processing with *Word 2013*. You are about to tap into the best digital solution available for keyboarding and word processing instruction; enjoy and learn. The essential information about *KPDO* is covered below.

WHAT DO I NEED TO GET STARTED?

- Computer with high-speed Internet connection
- Firefox or Internet Explorer browser
- *Microsoft Word 2013* installed on your computer. If you are registering for a course in the Lesson 1–25 range, *Word 2013* is not required.
- A username and password for www.cengagebrain.com.
- Access code for *KPDO* that corresponds to the book you are using. You can purchase this at cengagebrain.com or through your bookstore.
- Course Code from your instructor.

INSTALLING THE *KPDO* TOOLS

The first time you access *KPDO*, the program will check your computer for various components to make sure your computer is configured to run the software. Depending on what is already installed on your computer, you may not have to install all the components. On subsequent log ins, the student portal will display as soon as you click the link from your bookshelf.

For step-by-step help with installing the program, go to the *KPDO* student companion site.

Microsoft Visual Studio Tools for Office Version 4

Flash Player

KPDO Plug-in

KPDO Word Add In

INSTRUCTIONS FOR LOGGING INTO *KPDO*

See page 2, Getting Started with *KPDO*, steps 2 and 3.

WELCOME SCREEN

Read the Welcome screen to get a quick overview of the software. Return to the Welcome page by clicking the product name in gray. Use the **Skill Analysis** button at the bottom of the screen to test your current skill by taking the timed writing. If the Skill Analysis is required, you will not be able to go into the lessons until you take the timing. Key at a controlled pace that is comfortable and concentrate on keying accurately. Results display in the Skill Analysis report.

NAVIGATING *KPDO*

Left Navigation Bar

Lessons, Skill Building, Timed Writings, References, Keypad, Games, Reports— These tabs at the left side will take you to lessons and various activities. Tabs and menus display for each option. Once you make a selection, the left navigation menu closes so that you can view your activity in a full screen.

When you select a lesson, *KPDO* opens to the first activity. The other activities associated with that lesson appear in a drop-down menu at the right. This menu collapses; simply click it when you want to navigate between activities.

Top Navigation Bar

The top navigation bar lists your name and includes access to important features.

Word Processor—A *Windows* word processor that enables you to create documents or key drills and timed writings.

Log Out—Saves your work and closes your *KPDO* session and returns you to the Cengage dashboard. Log Out of the software each time you exit the program.

Preferences—You may be able to customize some preferences, depending on whether your instructor has locked them.

Bottom Navigation Bar

Some screens have buttons at the bottom of the screen. The buttons are specific to the screen you are viewing. They will enable/disable based upon your current activity.

WORKING WITH *WORD* DOCUMENTS

Beginning in Lesson 27, you will launch *Word* directly in *KPDO* to complete all word processing documents. The Document Options box presents these options.

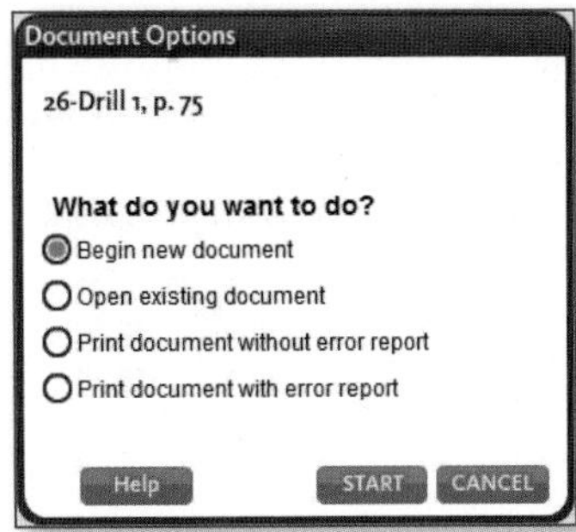

Begin new document—Creates a new document or **pass**.

If you begin the document again, results will be replaced with the new pass. Some documents require opening a document from an earlier lesson. Many activities automatically open a prerecorded data file; files are identified with an icon in the textbook.

Open existing document—Opens the saved document for editing.

Revising a document creates an **edit**. The Total Time on Document reported represents the total time of all edits of a single pass.

Print document without error report—Opens the *Word* document for printing. Errors and the header are not displayed.

Print document with error report—Displays the document in checked format.

Creating a *Word* Document in *KPDO*

1. From the Document Options dialog box, select Begin new document and select OK.
2. *Word* opens with the *KPDO* Student tab displayed; four commands are available.

   Save and Close—Saves the document and returns to the Lesson menu.

   Check Document—Checks your completed document, reports errors, and displays results. Documents must be 90% complete before the document can be checked. If it is not, you will receive a message to save the document or continue.

   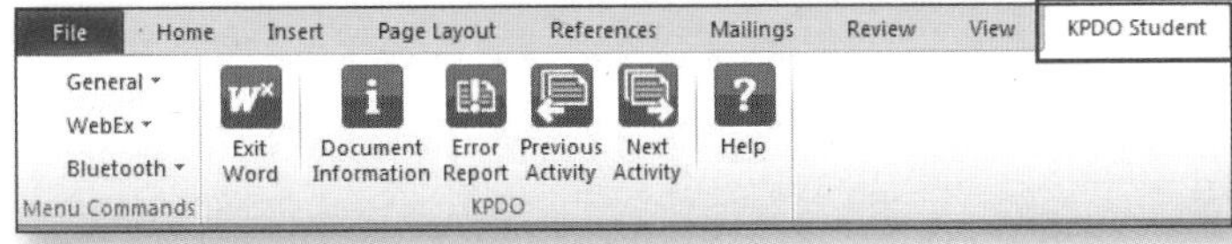

   Document Information—Displays the activity name and page number.

   Help—Provides access to global help.
3. The Insertion point is positioned in the document and ready for you to begin. To access any *Word* command, select the tab you need and the ribbon displays.
4. After creating and proofreading the document, select Check Document from the *KPDO* Student tab.

TIMED WRITINGS

Timed Writings are keyed from the textbook. They appear in some lessons, and they are available from the Timed Writing tab. Results are reported on the Last 40 Timed Writings report. If the results meet the accuracy requirement set by your instructor, they appear on the Best Timed Writing Report. Error Diagnostics tracks the errors by row, finger, and type of reach on each timing. To improve accuracy on the type of reach you are making most frequently, see Drill Practice on the Skill Building tab. For best results when keying timed writings, focus on the words you are keying, keep calm, and concentrate.

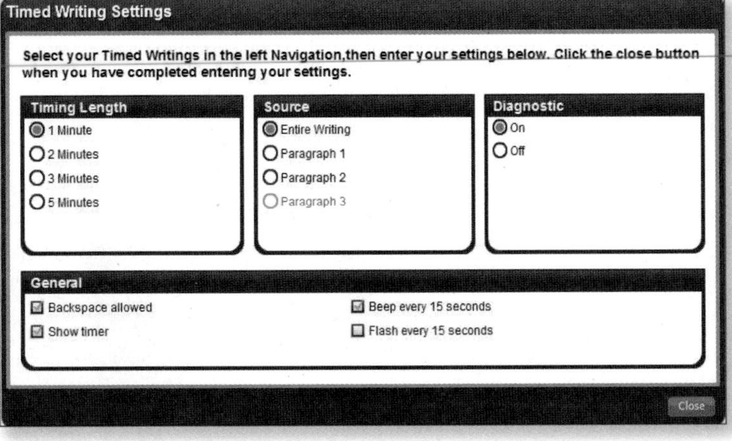

REFERENCES

The References tab includes tutorials to review Document formats, Communication Skills, videos to reinforce posture, and more.

Welcome to KPDO

- Summary Lessons 1-25
- Numeric Keypad
- Keypad Timed Writings
- Skill Analysis
- Skill Building - Accuracy
- Skill Building - Speed
- Technique Builder
- Drill Practice
- Best Timed Writings
- Last 40 Timed Writings
- Cumulative Error Diagnostics
- Summary Lessons 26-110
- WORD 2013 Documents
- Production Tests
- Lesson Report - Lessons 1-55
- Lesson Report - Accuracy
- Lesson Report - Speed
- Lesson Report - Numeric Keyp...
- Gradebook
- ▼ Performance Graphs

KEYPAD

The Keypad lessons and timed writings will help you build a strong foundation in 10-key skills. Extra Keypad Practice drills are in Appendix A of your textbook.

REPORTS

The Report tab shown at the left displays a variety of reports for reviewing your lesson results, skill building lessons and activities, and timed writings. Many of the reports hyperlink, giving greater detail; go ahead and dig deeper into the results.

DATA FILES

Many *Word* applications utilize a data file or prerecorded file. *KPDO* opens this file automatically when you access the activity. Occasionally, you will be directed to **insert** a data file. In order to insert the file, you must download the data file from the student companion website or at www.collegekeyboarding.com. The files are zipped; simply download to a location on your computer and unzip the file.

LEVEL 1

Developing Keyboarding Skill

Learning Outcomes

Keyboarding

+ Key the alphabetic and numeric keys by touch.
+ Develop good keyboarding techniques.
+ Key fluently—at least 25 words per minute.
+ Develop reasonable accuracy.

Communication Skills

+ Develop proofreading skills.
+ Apply proofreaders' marks and revise text.

Project Setting

Activity 9

Upload and Edit Letter

internship completed

1. Open the *internship completed* data file on your computer and upload it to a new folder on your SkyDrive.
   a. Click Save As and select your SkyDrive as the place.
   b. Click Browse and then click New Folder in the Save As dialog box that displays. Key the folder name **Module 9 Palmetto Project**.
   c. Then save the file in the new folder; name the file **Activity 9**.
2. Open the document on your SkyDrive and edit the letter in the *Word Web App*. Include the current date, your name and address formatted properly, and your first name in the salutation.
3. Click Save on the Quick Access Toolbar to save the document.

Activity 10

Upload Form and Compose Memo

palmetto memo form

1. Upload the *palmetto memo form* data file and save it to the Module 9 Palmetto Project folder; name it **Activity 10**.
2. Open it on your SkyDrive. Select Edit in Word.
3. Complete the memo heading to your instructor from you. Use the current date and the subject **Internship Completed**.
4. Compose the memo from the information shown below. Format the table attractively using a style that fits with the theme and logo of Palmetto Event Solutions.
5. Proofread and edit the memo carefully; then share the folder with your instructor.
   a. Click the Module 9 Palmetto Project folder and then click Share on the blue bar above the files pane.
   b. Key your instructor's email in the Send link to box. Add a message if desired.
   c. Click Share.

- Write a paragraph describing your experience with the Palmetto Event Solution projects and what you liked about them. Indicate that you are sharing the letter from Mr. Garrett Russell.
- Key the sentence above the table, the table, and the sentence below the table.

You requested that I summarize my experiences both quantitatively in a table and qualitatively to describe the value derived from the experience.

Office	Number of Jobs	Estimated Time
Hilton Head, South Carolina	5	8 hours
Portland, Oregon	4	5 hours
Las Cruces, New Mexico	8	11 hours
Newport, Rhode Island	4	6 hours
Kansas City, Missouri	7	9 hours

Please note that I completed two different projects in two of the cities—Las Cruces and Hilton Head.

- Add a paragraph or two about the value of this practical experience in a real job setting.

Getting Started with KPDO

Step 1: What Do I Need to Get Started?

1. Computer with high-speed Internet connection and Firefox or Internet Explorer.
2. *Microsoft Word 2013* installed on your computer. If you are registering for a course in the Lesson 1-25 range only, *Word 2013* is not required.
3. A username and password for www.Cengagebrain.com.
4. Access code for *Keyboarding Pro DELUXE Online* (*KPDO*) that corresponds to the book you are using.
5. Course Code from your instructor.

Step 2: Register KPDO Using Your Access Code.

1. Go to http://login.cengagebrain.com. Enter your username and password and click Log In. Select Sign Up to create an account if you do not have one.
2. Add *KPDO* to your bookshelf by entering your access code, which may be in a packaged slimpack or an instant access code that you purchased online.

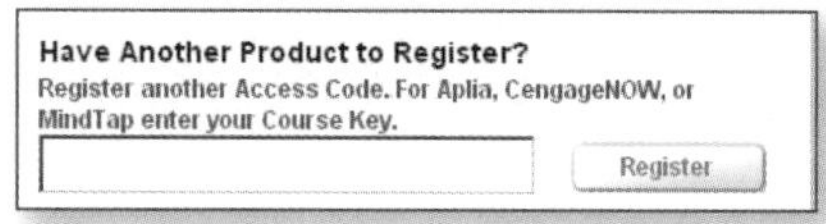

3. Click the link to *Keyboarding Pro DELUXE Online*. The program will present required components and ask you to install them. Depending on what is already installed on your computer, you may not have to install them all. On subsequent log ins, *KPDO* will go directly to the program.

Step 3: Enter the Course Code to Join the Class.

Locate the course code provided by your instructor. Double-click it with your mouse. Enter Ctrl + C to copy it; toggle (Alt + Tab) to the screen below and paste (Ctrl + V) the course code.

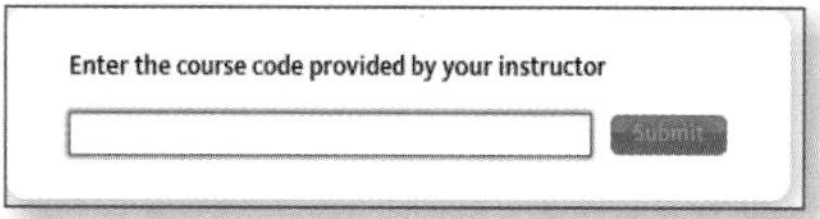

Read *KPDO. . . Your Tool to Success* page xi for help with using the software.

Fundraising Committee

Each year five volunteers agree to handle the fundraising for the scholarship. This year our volunteers exceeded their goals significantly. The following table provides the results.

Celebration for Volunteers

The volunteers were honored at a special dinner recognizing their outstanding work for setting a record both on the number of donors and on the total amount raised. At the request of the volunteers, Chef Pat once again prepared the four-course dinner featuring his special crown pork roast.

Fundraiser	Number of Donors	Amount Raised
Susie	78	$146,750
John	43	96,520
Peter	38	74,925
Alden	56	62,750
William	64	59,250
Total	279	$440,195

5. Apply Title style to the title and Heading 1 to the headings.
6. Format the table as follows:
   a. Center and bold the headings in row 1.
   b. Align data in column A at the left, in column B at the center, and in column C at the right.
7. Save the document using the Save command on the Quick Access Toolbar.
8. Then click Save As to download the document to your computer. Create a new folder named **Module 9 Solutions**. Close the *Web Apps* document.

Activity 8

Edit in Word from SkyDrive

To apply commands that are not part of the *Word Web App*, select Edit in Word. The *Word Web App* does not contain the commands needed for Activity 8.

1. On your computer, open *Activity 7* from the Module 9 Solutions folder and save it to the SkyDriveModule 9 Web Apps folder; name it **Activity 8**.
2. From the SkyDrive, open *Activity 8* in the Module 9 Web Apps folder and edit it. Click Edit in Word.
3. Apply Ion theme. Click in the table and apply List Table 3 – Accent 1.
4. Insert a row above the first row, merge the cells, and key **Endowed Scholarship**.
5. Increase height of rows 1 and 2 to 0.3" and apply Center Align.
6. Save the document.

Warmup

1. Open *KPDO*.
2. Click the Word Processor button in the upper-right corner.
3. Key the paragraph using wordwrap (do not tap ENTER at the end of lines). Repeat if desired.
4. Click the Close button in the upper-right corner to close the Word Processor; do not save it.

Good keyboarding skills are essential for almost all careers today. The time spent learning to key quickly and accurately is time well spent. Use good posture and good techniques to get you started on the right track. Then work diligently to achieve your speed and accuracy goals. Good keyboarding skills will save you time in preparing assignments for all of your classes. Also your work will impress your instructors.

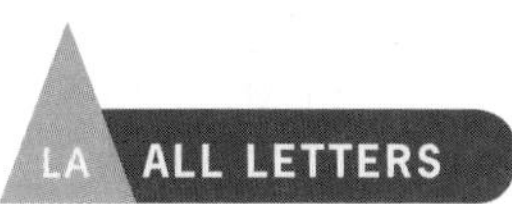

Timed Writing

1. Click the Timed Writings tab.
2. Choose Pretest.

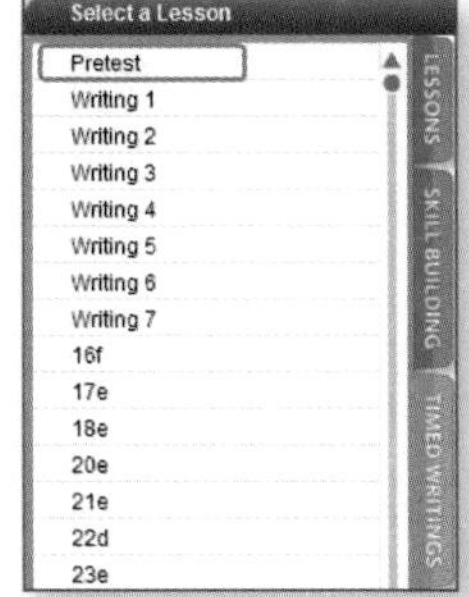

3. Choose 3' as the length; click Close.
4. Tap TAB to begin. Key from the textbook. Use wordwrap.
5. Repeat the timing for 3'.
6. Your results will be displayed in the Timed Writing Report.

Learning to key is just the first step toward developing a very meaningful career skill. The next step is to build both speed and accuracy. With basic keyboarding skills, you will be able to present information in an attractive format that is quite easy to read. You will also be able to develop your communication skills at the same time.

The next big step is to learn word processing. The software most often used in business organizations is Word, which is much more sophisticated than the basic word processor you used for your warmup. With Word you will be able to create attractive letters, memos, reports, and many other types of documents used in business.

One of the exciting things about working diligently to develop a skill is that you have the opportunity to set very specific goals and challenge yourself to meet them. Nothing is more motivating than being able to accomplish the goals that we set for ourselves. The incremental goals that you meet each day will result in major progress by the end of the course.

CREATE A DOCUMENT USING THE WORD WEB APP

You can create a *Word* document using the *Word Web App*. Remember that you will have limited commands available. However, the commands that are available are exactly the same ones you have been using in *Word* on your computer.

To create a document using the *Word Web App*:

1. Use your browser to access your SkyDrive.
2. Click the folder you wish to use to store your document, or create a new folder if you do not have an appropriate folder to use.
3. Click Create on the blue bar near the top of the screen and select Word document to display the New Microsoft Word document name box.
4. Key the name of the document and click Create.
5. A new document will open in the *Word Web App*.
6. Key, format, and edit the document using the available commands.

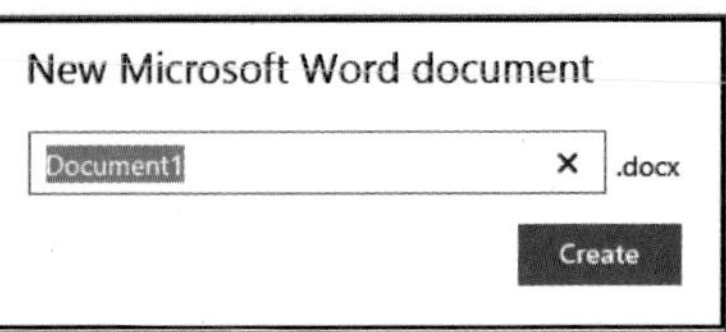

Apply It

Activity 7

Report with Table

1. Access SkyDrive and click Module 9 Web Apps folder.
2. Click Create on the blue bar near the top of the screen. Select Word Document.
3. Key **Activity 7** in the document name box and click Create to open a blank document.
4. Tap ENTER three times and key the following document. Then apply the formats listed below the document.

Volunteer Celebration

Our Fifth Annual Endowed Scholarship Fundraising Campaign was very successful. The model of naming the scholarship in honor of a community leader proved to be very successful once again.

Model Success Factors

Several primary factors are responsible for its success:

Many potential donors believe that providing a needy student with a scholarship is a worthy cause, and they are willing to support worthy causes.

Endowing a scholarship makes it a gift that keeps giving. The funds raised are invested in the Foundation's portfolio, and only the interest is used to fund the scholarship each year. Usually 4 to 5 percent of the total fund (principal plus interest) is used each year. Therefore, a scholarship is granted every year in perpetuity.

Friends and family of the community leader being honored often support the scholarship simply because they want to honor that particular person.

(continued)

MODULE 1

Alphabetic Keys

Lessons 1–10 *Alphabetic and Basic Punctuation Keys*

Lessons 11–13 *Review*

LEARNING OUTCOMES

- Key the alphabetic keys by touch.
- Key using proper techniques.
- Key at a rate of 14 *gwam* or more.

Lesson 1 Home Row, Space Bar, Enter, I

Standard Plan *For Using KPDO*

1. From the Lessons tab, select the lesson (Lesson 1).
2. Follow the directions on screen. Repeat the exercise for reinforcement or continue.
3. To end a lesson, view the Lesson Report.
4. Click the Log Out button in the upper-right corner.

5. Use these directions for all lessons.

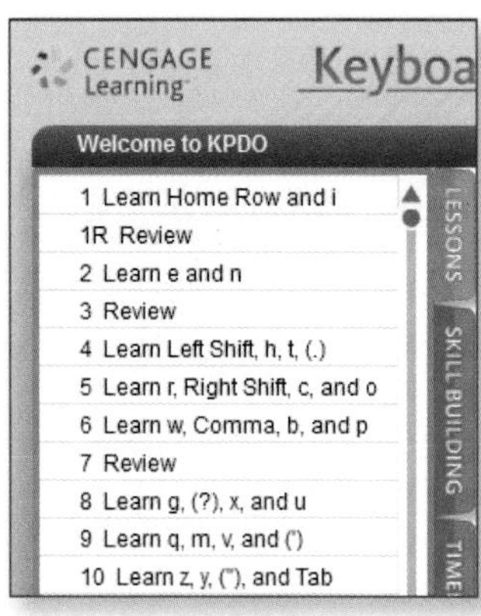

To find text in a document on SkyDrive:

1. Click Find above the open document and key the search information.

2. Click the search icon. The results display.

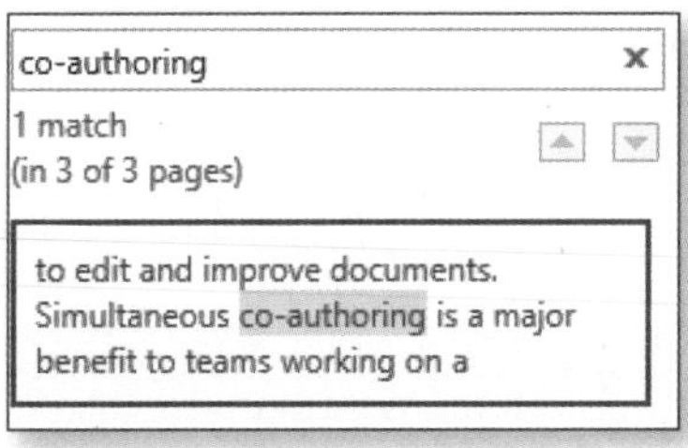

Apply It

Activity 5

Find Text in a Document

1. Use Find to check and ensure that *co-authoring* was covered in the document.
2. Click Find and key **co-authoring** in the Search box. Then click the search icon.
3. Use the results that display to verify that the topic was matched.

To edit a document on SkyDrive:

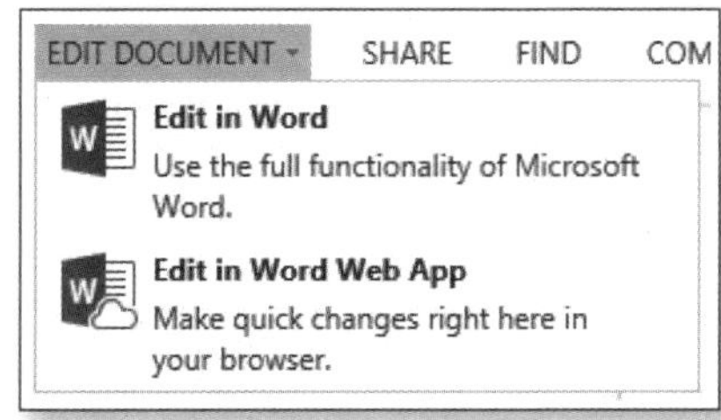

1. Click Edit Document.
2. Select the option you wish to use to edit the document. If the edits are easy to make, select Edit in Word Web App. If they are complex, select Edit in Word, which opens the Word application on your computer.

Apply It

Activity 6

Compose Closing Paragraph

In this activity, you will edit the document using the *Word Web App*.

1. Click Edit Document and then click Edit in *Word Web App*.
2. At the end of the document, key the heading **Summary** and apply Heading 1 style.
3. Use the information below and the information in the Overview to compose a summary paragraph. Save (will save as *Activity* 2).
4. Proofread and edit your paragraph carefully using the commands on the Ribbon; then share your document with your instructor.

- Begin with one or two sentences indicating that SkyDrive is a place to store documents on the Web and to work with Web-based Office applications. Name the applications.
- Point out that you can edit using the web apps or the applications on your computer.
- End with a sentence or two about the three services that complement the desktop version of the software.

STANDARD PLAN For Learning New Keyreaches

1. Find the new key on the illustrated keyboard. Then find it on your keyboard.
2. Watch your finger make the reach to the new key a few times. Keep other fingers curved in home position. For an upward reach, straighten the finger slightly; for a down reach, curve the finger a bit more.
3. Use these directions for learning all new keyreaches.

New Keys

1a Learn Home Row

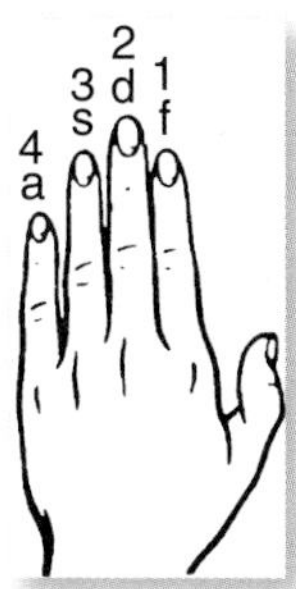

HOME-ROW POSITION

1. Drop your hands to your side. Allow your fingers to curve naturally. Maintain this curve as you key.
2. Lightly place your left fingers over the **a s d f** and the right fingers over the **j k l ;**. You will feel a raised element on the **f** and **j** keys, which will help you keep your fingers on the home-row position. You are now in home-row position.

© Cengage Learning, Courtesy of Meg Shanahan

© Cengage Learning

Note the curve of your fingers when your arms are hanging loosely at your side. Maintain this same curve when you place your hands on the home row.

To share a document on SkyDrive:

1. Click Share above the open document.

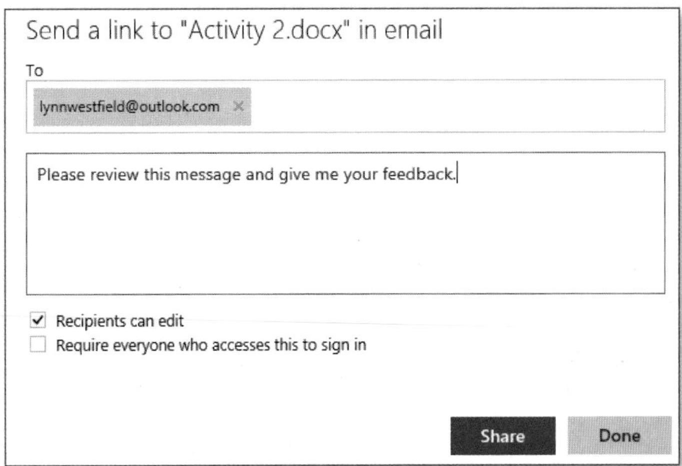

2. Send a link by email to one or more reviewers. Key the person's email address and include a message if desired.
3. Click Share.

Apply It

Activity 3

Share a Document on SkyDrive

1. Share the document with your instructor or one of your classmates who has an Outlook.com email address or a Microsoft Live Account.
2. Click Share above the open document.
3. Key the person's email address in the To box.
4. Key the following message in the Message box:

   Please review this document and give me your feedback.
5. Click Share.

To add a comment on SkyDrive:

1. Click Comments above the open document.
2. The Comments box with your name displays.
3. Select the text that applies and key the comment.
4. Click Post to send your comment.

Apply It

Activity 4

Add a Comment

1. Post a comment on the shared document. The person with whom you shared the document texted you and asked you to post the following comment on the document.
2. Click Comments above the open document.
3. Select the heading *Overview of SkyDrive* and then click New Comment.
4. Key the comment below your name in the Comments box.

   I read the Overview, and I think it is really helpful. The only suggestion I have is to add a closing summary.
5. Click Post.

1b Learn Space Bar and ENTER

SPACE BAR AND ENTER

Tap the Space Bar, located at the bottom of the keyboard, with a down-and-in motion of the right thumb to space between words.

© Cengage Learning

Enter Reach with the fourth (little) finger of the right hand to ENTER. Tap it to return the insertion point to the left margin. This action creates a **hard return**. Use a hard return at the end of all drill lines. Quickly return to home position (over ;).

© Cengage Learning

```
1 j jj f ff k kk d dd l ll s ss ; ;; a aa jkl; fdsa
2 a aa ; ;; s ss l ll d dd k kk f ff j jj fdsa jkl;
```

1c Practice Home Row

```
3 ff  jj  ff  jj  fj  fj  fj  dd  kk  dd  kk  dk  dk  dk
4 ss  ll  ss  ll  sl  sl  sl  aa  ;;  aa  ;;  a;  a;  a;
5 fj  fj  dk  dk  sl  sl  a;  fjdk  sla;  fjkd  ls;a
6 fff  jjj  fjf  fff  jjj  fjf  fjf  jfj  jfj  fjf
7 ddd  kkk  dkd  ddd  kkk  dkd  dkd  kdk  kdk  dkd
8 sss  lll  sls  sss  lll  sls  sls  lsl  lsl  sls
9 aaa  ;;;  a;a  aaa  ;;;  a;a  a;a  ;a;  ;a;  a;a
10 f  j  d  k  s  l  a  ;  ;  a  l  s  k  d  j  f
11 ff jj dd kk ss ll aa ;; jj ff kk dd ll ss aa ;;
12 fff  jjj  ddd  kkk  sss  lll  aaa  jjj  ;;;  fjdk  sla;
```

Keep your eyes on the textbook as you key each line.

1d Textbook Keying

1. Key each line once. Tap ENTER at the end of each line.
2. Click Stop to end the exercise.

```
13 a  a;  al  ak  aj  s  s;  sl  sk  sj  d  d;  dl  dk  dj
14 j  ja  js  jd  jf  k  ka  ks  kd  kf  l  la  ls  ld  lf
15 a;  sl  a;sl  dkfj  a;sl  dkfj  a;sl  dkfj  asdf  jk
16 a;  sl  a;sl  dk  fj  dkfj  a;sl  dkfj  fjdk  a;a
17 f  ff  j  jj  d  dd  k  kk  s  ss  l  ll  a  aa  ;  ;;  fj
18 afj;  a  s  d  f  j  k  l  ;  asdf  jkl;  fdsa  jkl;
```

Review the illustration on the previous page as you work on these activities.

CREATING A FOLDER

You can create folders on the SkyDrive or from your computer.

To create a folder on the SkyDrive:

1. In the opening screen, click the down arrow on Create on the blue bar at the top of the screen.
2. Click Folder from the drop-list to display the new folder.
3. Key the desired folder name.

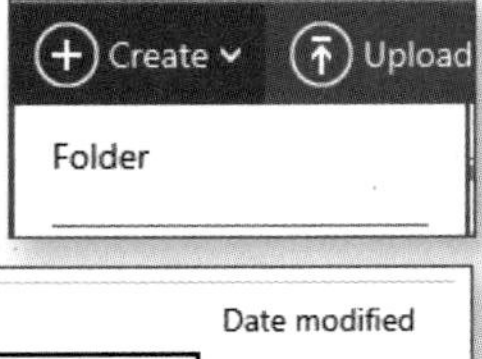

Name ↑ Date modified

New folder

Apply It

Activity 1

Access SkyDrive and Create a New Folder

1. Go to https://skydrive.live.com and sign in to SkyDrive. If you do not have a Microsoft Live account, click Sign up now and create one.
2. Create a new folder in your files.
3. Key the name **Module 9 Web Apps**.
4. Minimize the SkyDrive.

SAVE A FILE

You can save documents on your computer to the SkyDrive.

To save a file on the SkyDrive:

1. With the document you wish to save open, click the File menu and Save As.
2. Click your SkyDrive and then click the Browse button.
3. Locate the folder in which you want to save the document or create a new folder.
4. Key the file name and click Save.

Apply It

Activity 2

Save Document to SkyDrive

overview of skydrive

1. With *Word* open on your computer, open the data file *overview of skydrive*.
2. Read the document carefully. This document is designed to help you understand what the SkyDrive is and how you will be using it in this module.
3. Save the document in the Module 9 Web Apps folder that you set up on your SkyDrive in Activity 1. Name the file **Activity 2**. Note that you may have to click Files in the left pane if you do not see the folder. Close the document.

WORKING WITH A DOCUMENT ON SKYDRIVE

Click the document that you saved on the SkyDrive to open it in the *Word Web App*. The four commands that can be used to work with a document display above the open document.

Module 9 Web Apps ▸ Activity 2.docx

EDIT DOCUMENT ▾ SHARE FIND COMMENTS

1e i

© Cengage Learning

19 i ik ik ik is is id id if if ill i ail did kid lid

20 i ik aid ail did kid lid lids kids ill aid did ilk

21 id aid aids laid said ids lid skids kiss disk dial

1f Improve Keystroking

Use good posture; back and body erect; feet flat on the floor.

22 as as ask ask ad ad lad lad all all fall fall asks

23 as asks did disk ail fail sail ails jail sill silk

24 ask dad; dads said; is disk; kiss a lad; salad lid

25 fill a sail; aid a lad; is silk; if a dial; a jail

26 is a disk; dads said; did fall ill; if a lass did;

1g Build Skill

i

27 id aid ail fail sail jail ails slid dill sill fill

28 aid lads; if a kid is; a salad lid; kiss a sad dad

29 as ad all ask jak lad fad said ill kill fall disks

30 is all sad lass a lid; is silk; silk disk; dad is;

1h End the Lesson

1. View Lesson Report.
2. Log out of the software.

WORKPLACE SUCCESS

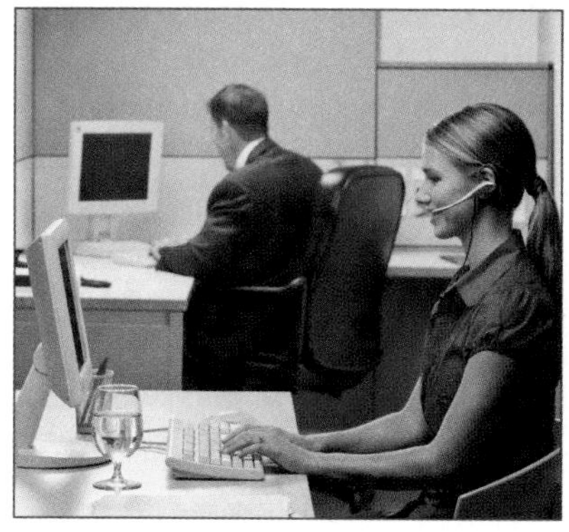
AVAVA/Shutterstock.com

Keyboarding: The Survival Skill

Keyboarding is a valuable and necessary skill for everyone in this technological world. It is an expected tool for effective communication throughout one's life.

Students who resort to "hunting and pecking" to key their school assignments are constantly searching for the correct letter on the keyboard. Frustration abounds for students who wish to key their research reports into the computer, but do not have the touch keyboarding skills required to accomplish the task quickly and proficiently. Students who can key by touch are much more relaxed because they can keep their eyes on the screen and concentrate on text editing and composing.

Access SkyDrive

Once you have obtained your Microsoft Live ID, you can access the SkyDrive by going to https://skydrive.live.com and sign in with your email address and password. To simplify accessing your SkyDrive from your browser after you have signed in, add it to Favorites to set a bookmark for it. You can also access the SkyDrive from the File menu on a *Word* document. Note the opening screen that displays from the browser (you may have different file folders):

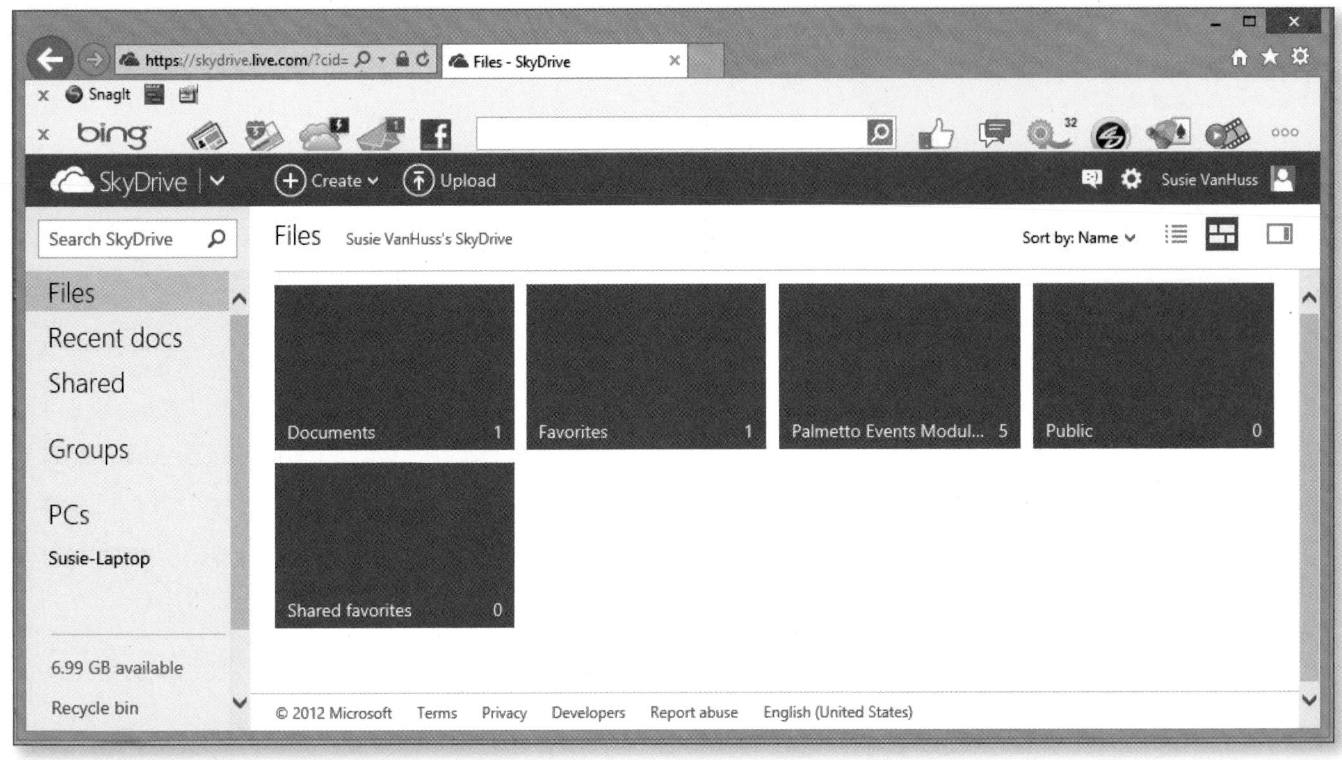

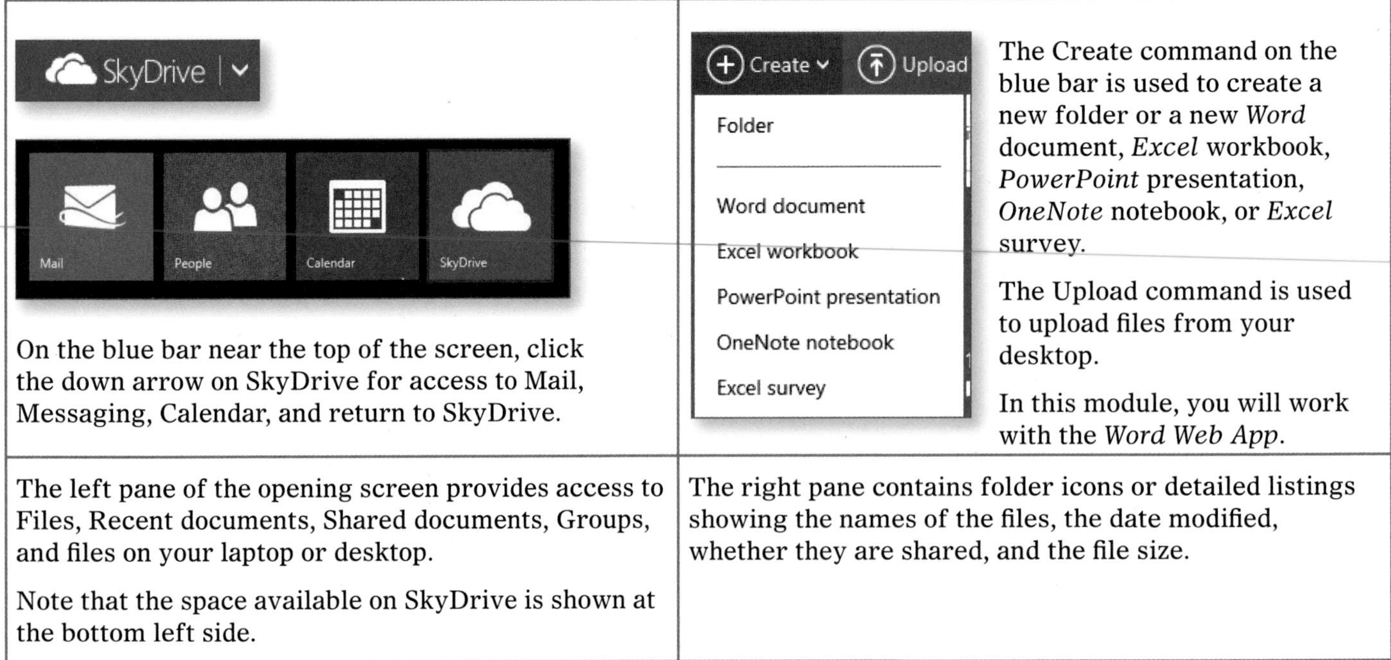

On the blue bar near the top of the screen, click the down arrow on SkyDrive for access to Mail, Messaging, Calendar, and return to SkyDrive.	The Create command on the blue bar is used to create a new folder or a new *Word* document, *Excel* workbook, *PowerPoint* presentation, *OneNote* notebook, or *Excel* survey. The Upload command is used to upload files from your desktop. In this module, you will work with the *Word Web App*.
The left pane of the opening screen provides access to Files, Recent documents, Shared documents, Groups, and files on your laptop or desktop. Note that the space available on SkyDrive is shown at the bottom left side.	The right pane contains folder icons or detailed listings showing the names of the files, the date modified, whether they are shared, and the file size.

Lesson 1R Review

Warmup *Lesson 1Ra Warmup*

Fingers curved and upright

```
1  ff dd ss aa ff dd ss aa jj kk ll ;; fj dk sl a; a;
2  fj dk sla; fjdk sla; a;sl dkfj fjdk sla; fjdk sla;
3  aa ss dd ff jj kk ll ;; aa ss dd ff jj kk ll ;; a;
4  if a; as is; kids did; ask a sad lad; if a lass is
```

Skill Building

1Rb Textbook Keying

1. Key each line once.
2. Click Stop to end the exercise.

Move fingers without moving your hands; eyes on textbook.

```
5  f  j  fjf  jj  fj  fj  jf  dd  kk  dd  kk  dk  dk  dk
6  s  ;  s;s  ;;  s;  s;  s;  aa  ;;  aa  ;;  a;  a;  a;
7  fj  dk  sl  a;  fjdk  sla;  jfkd  lsa;  ;a  ;a  ;s
8  f  j  fjf  d  k  dkd  s  l  sls  a  ;  fj  dk  sl  a;a
9  a;  al  aka  j  s  s;  sl  sk  sj  d  d;  dl  dk  djd
10 ja  js  jd  jf  k  ka  ks  kd  kf  l  la  ls  ld  lfl
```

1Rc Improve Keystroking

```
11 f fa fad s sa sad f fa fall fall l la lad s sa sad
12 a as ask a ad add j ja jak f fa fall; ask; add jak
13 ik ki ki ik is if id il ij ia ij ik is if ji id ia
14 is il ill sill dill fill sid lid ail lid slid jail
15 if is il kid kids ill kid if kids; if a kid is ill
```

Build Skill and Game

When you finish the lesson, log out of *KPDO*.

Use the game to showcase your skills.

MODULE 9

Web Apps

LEARNING OUTCOMES

- Set up an account and use SkyDrive.
- Upload, view, and edit documents on SkyDrive.
- Create and edit *Word* documents using the *Word Web App*.
- Share folders and documents.

Web Apps

Palmetto Event Solutions, Inc.

New Commands

GETTING STARTED WITH OFFICE WEB APPS

In Module 9 you use *Word*, the SkyDrive, and the *Word Web App*. You will not launch nor use *KPDO* in this module. You need to do two things to use the SkyDrive and Office Web Apps.

1. Download and install the SkyDrive software to your computer if that was not done in the *Office* installation process.
2. Establish a free Microsoft Live account. Note you will already have a Microsoft Live account if you have an Outlook.com email account, an Xbox account, or a Windows phone.

Hotmail accounts have been replaced by the free Outlook.com email accounts. If you have a Hotmail email address, you can continue to use it, but you cannot get a new Hotmail account.

To download the SkyDrive desktop app for Windows:

Download now

1. Open a *Word* document and click File. If the Download button appears, click Download now and install the SkyDrive desktop app. -or-
2. If you see your name with SkyDrive such as shown at the right, you may already have the app and a Microsoft Live account.

SkyDrive

Microsoft account What's this?

someone@example.com

Password

Keep me signed in

Sign in

Can't access your account?

Sign in with a single-use code

Don't have a Microsoft account? Sign up now

To get a Microsoft Live account:

1. Click Sign up for Microsoft Live account during the installation process.

   -or-

2. Go to https://skydrive.live.com and click Sign up now.
3. Complete the short form that displays. Note you may use your current email address and password or you may get an Outlook.com address and password.

Lesson 2 E and N

K P D O **Warmup** *Lesson 2a Warmup*

1 ff dd ss aa ff dd ss aa jj kk ll ;; fj dk sl a; a;
2 fj dk sl a; fjdk sla; a;sl dkfj dk sl a; fjdk sla;
3 aa ss dd ff jj kk ll ;; aa ss dd ff jj kk ll ;; a;
4 if a; as is; kids did; ask a sad lad; if a lass is

New Keys

2b E and N

e Reach *up* with *left second* finger.

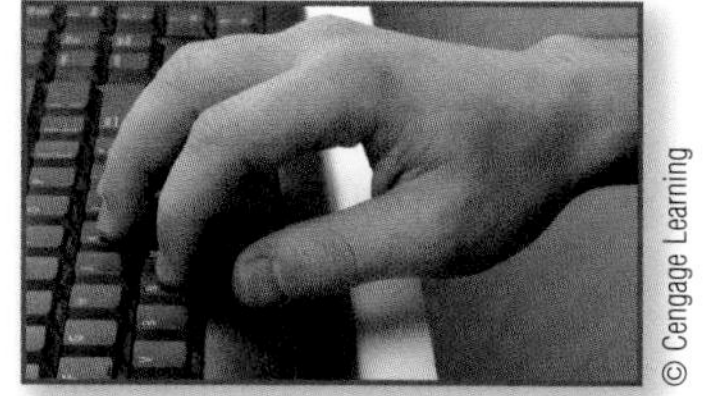

n Reach *down* with *right first* finger.

e

5 e ed ed led led lea lea ale ale elf elf eke eke ed
6 e el el eel els elk elk lea leak ale kale led jell
7 e ale kale lea leak fee feel lea lead elf self eke

n

8 n nj nj an an and and fan fan and kin din fin land
9 n an fan in fin and land sand din fans sank an sin
10 n in ink sink inn kin skin an and land in din dink

2c All Reaches Learned

11 den end fen ken dean dens ales fend fens keen knee
12 if in need; feel ill; as an end; a lad and a lass;
13 and sand; a keen idea; as a sail sank; is in jail;
14 an idea; an end; a lake; a nail; a jade; a dean is

8-d7

Compose Memo

palmetto memo form

Please draft a memo for me to Jennifer Anderson in our Northwest Office. Be sure to include the recommendations we agreed on. My handwritten notes are shown below for your reference.

RB

1. Compose the memo; use subject **Wexford Information Requested**.
2. Read the report you printed in 8-d5 for reference in composing this memo. The report will be attached to the email along with this memo when it is sent to Jennifer Anderson.
3. Tell her that you have obtained the information about the Wexford Conference Center that she requested, and you think Wexford is ideal for her client.
4. Things to point out include how easy Julie Anders, the director, is to work with; the great facilities; and how cost-effective it will be. Include the options, but recommend the 80 percent room guarantee with all meals at Wexford if they have a need for that many rooms.
5. Note that the A/V situation is state-of-the-art (see report).
6. Remember the notes are rough and unorganized. Organize your thoughts, write complete sentences, and edit your memo very carefully. Check to see that you included all information requested. Remember to use the report for information as needed.
7. Proofread and check; click Exit *Word*. Click Log out to exit *KPDO*. (*8-d7*)

Information based on client's estimate of 75 to 90 rooms needed.

Options:

- *Guarantee 70% rooms get 50% discount—A/V, media and equipment needed and use of Oak Room & computer lab. 80%—A/V free.*
- *80% all rooms plus all meals for participants; entire facility limited to your group except remaining residence rooms.*
- *Best food deals—buffet in dining room best breakfast & lunch; combination of themed buffets and seated dinners night meals. Outdoor recpts—especially gazebo area super if weather OK.*

Julie Anders will provide negotiated room rate by email tomorrow. Might get suites for senior managers at same rate as room with 80% guar. Also requested discounted rates golf and tennis for one afternoon; menus for food selection and pricing.

Skill Building

2d Textbook Keying

1. Key each line once.
2. Keep your eyes on the textbook copy.

Reach with little finger; tap* ENTER*; return to home key.

15 if a lad;
16 is a sad fall

17 if a lass did ask
18 ask a lass; ask a lad

19 a;sldkfj a;sldkfj a;sldkfj
20 a; sl dk fj fj dk sl a; a;sldkfj

21 ik ik if if is is kid skid did lid aid laid said
22 ik kid ail die fie did lie ill ilk silk skill skid

2e Improve Keystroking

i

23 ik ik ik if is il ik id is if kid did lid aid ails
24 did lid aid; add a line; aid kids; ill kids; id is

n

25 nj nj nj an an and and end den ken in ink sin skin
26 jn din sand land nail sank and dank skin sans sink

e

27 el els elf elk lea lead fee feel sea seal ell jell
28 el eke ale jak lake elf els jaks kale eke els lake

2f Build Skill

29 dine in an inn; fake jade; lend fans; as sand sank
30 in nine inns; if an end; need an idea; seek a fee;
31 if a lad; a jail; is silk; is ill; a dais; did aid
32 adds a line; and safe; asks a lass; sail in a lake

Keep your eyes on copy; key words at a steady pace.

2g Textbook Keying

Key each line once.

33 send land skin faded sand kind line nine sale fail
34 dense sales lakes jaded likes jails salad kale inn
35 lad likes kale; lass likes silk; add a fee; is ill
36 kids in a lake; if in need; ask a lass; lad is ill

2h End the Lesson

Log out of *KPDO*.

Log Out

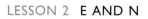

3. Key and format the following table; place it below the paragraph in which it is referenced in the report. Key a dash between price ranges.

Lunch buffet in dining room	$10.00
Lunch in a separate meeting room	$12.00–$18.50
Theme buffet in the evening	$20.00
Seated dinners in the dining room	$25.50–$75.00
Indoor and outdoor receptions	$15.50–$50.00

   a. Size column A 4.5" wide and column B 2" wide.
   b. Add a row above row 1 and merge the cells; increase row height to 0.4".
   c. Key the table title **Meal Charges Per Person**; apply 16-point font.
   d. Apply Grid Table 4 – Accent 1 table style. Apply Align Center format to the title and Align Center Left to the remaining cells.
   e. Apply 0.3" row height to the rows with data.
   f. In the Table Style Options group on the Design tab, remove the check from the first column.

4. Print a copy of this report; you will use it in *8-d7*.
5. Proofread, check, and click Next Activity. (*8-d5*)

8-d6

Newsletter

pen
new office

If Heading 3 is not displayed in the Styles group on the Home tab, click Heading 2. Note that Heading 3 will then display.

Format the open pen data file as follows:

1. Use the keywords *tablet computer with pen* to find an image of a tablet computer with a pen and insert it. Size it 1" high and 1" wide. Position in Top Left with Square Text Wrapping. See the illustration at the right.
2. Insert Fill – Black, Text 1, Outline – Background 1, Hard Shadow – Accent 1 WordArt (second icon in bottom row). Select the text and key **The Pen—Kansas City News**. Reduce the font size to 28 point. Position in Top Right with Square Text Wrapping.
3. Select the text and apply two-column format.
4. Apply Heading 3 format to each of the headings.
5. Insert the *new office* picture from the data files. Size it 1.5" high. Position in Bottom Right with Square Text Wrapping. Then drag it to the center of the column.
6. Proofread, check, and click Next Activity. (*8-d6*)

The Newsletter Committee has written the articles for The Pen; please format so we can send it to Hilton Head.
RB

The Pen—Kansas City News

Warmup *Lesson 3a Warmup*

home 1 ad ads lad fad dad as ask fa la lass jak jaks alas
n 2 an fan and land fan flan sans sand sank flank dank
i 3 is id ill dill if aid ail fail did kid ski lid ilk
all 4 ade alas nine else fife ken; jell ink jak inns if;

Skill Building

3b Textbook Keying

Key each line once.

Lines 5–8: Think and key words. Make the space part of the word.

Lines 9–12: Think and key phrases. Do not key the vertical rules separating the phrases.

easy words

5 if is as an ad el and did die eel fin fan elf lens
6 as ask and id kid and ade aid eel feel ilk skis an
7 ail fail aid did ken ale led an flan inn inns alas
8 eel eke nee kneel did kids kale sees lake elf fled

easy phrases

9 el el|id id|is is|eke eke|lee lee|ale ale|jill jak
10 is if|is a|is a|a disk|a disk|did ski|did ski|is a
11 sell a|sell a|sell a sled|fall fad|fall fad|fad is
12 sees a lake|sees a lake|as a deal|sell sled|a sale

3c Improve Keystroking

home row: fingers curved and upright

13 jak lad as lass dad sad lads fad fall la ask ad as
14 asks add jaks dads a lass ads flak adds sad as lad

upward reaches: straighten fingers slightly; return quickly to home position

15 fed die led ail kea lei did ale fife silk leak lie
16 sea lid deal sine desk lie ale like life idea jail

double letters: stroke double letters at a steady, unhurried pace

17 fee jell less add inn seek fall alee lass keel all
18 dill dell see fell eel less all add kiss seen sell

8-d5

Report with Table

wexford facilities

Prepare a draft of the following report:

> Our Northwest Regional VP requested a report on the Wexford Center for a three-day leadership seminar for one of her Portland clients. I talked with her today, and she agreed Wexford is the best choice for her client.
>
> RB

1. Apply the following formats in the open document:
   a. Apply Title style to the title; decrease the font size to fit on one line.
   b. Apply Heading 1 style to all headings except for the specific meeting and training rooms that follow the meeting facilities paragraph.
   c. Apply Heading 2 to the meeting and training rooms listed.
   d. Number the pages at the top of the page using Plain Number 3. Do not number the first page.
2. Key Insert #1 after the paragraph below the Guest Accommodations heading and Insert #2 after the paragraph below the Summit and Lakeview Rooms. Apply Heading 1 format to the headings in Insert #2.

Insert #1

In addition to the on-site fitness center, extensive fitness and recreational facilities are available at the nearby Oak Park SportsPlex. Guests can access tennis, swimming, golf, walking trails, and a host of other activities with less than a five-minute ride on the free Wexford shuttle.

Insert #2

Outdoor Functions

The patios and large gazebo area provide excellent venues for receptions and picnics when the weather is appropriate for outdoor functions. Large climate-controlled tents can also be rented for special functions.

Food Service

The Wexford dining room provides full breakfast and lunch buffets for residential guests and for conference functions that do not have group meals for participants. Chef Pat receives rave reviews for the theme buffets he offers in the evening. The Wexford lounge is open daily from 5:00 p.m. until 11:00 p.m.

Meals are competitively priced. The following table shows the meal prices per person. Prices shown in ranges vary depending on the menu selection.

The chef requests that the number of participants for meal events be confirmed at least 24 hours in advance.

(continued)

3d Build Skill

19 and and land land el el elf elf self self ail nail

20 as as ask ask ad ad lad lad id id lid lid kid kids

phrases: think and key as phrases

21 if if|is is|jak jak|all all|did did|nan nan|elf elf

22 as a lad| ask dad| fed a jak| as all ask| sales fad

23 sell a lead|seal a deal|feel a leaf|if a jade sale

24 is a|is as if|a disk|aid all kids|did ski|is a silk

3e Textbook Keying

Key each line once.

Tap Space Bar with down-and-in motion.

reach review

25 ea sea lea seas deal leaf leak lead leas flea keas

26 as ask lass ease as asks ask ask sass as alas seas

27 sa sad sane sake sail sale sans safe sad said sand

28 le sled lead flee fled ale flea lei dale kale leaf

29 jn jn nj nj in fan fin an; din ink sin and inn an;

30 de den end fen an an and and ken knee nee dean dee

3f Timed Writing

Key lines 31–34 for 1'. If you finish before time is up, repeat the lines.

31 el eel eld elf sell self el dell fell elk els jell

32 in fin inn inks dine sink fine fins kind line lain

33 an and fan dean elan flan land lane lean sand sane

34 sell a lead; sell a jade; seal a deal; feel a leaf

Game

Log out when you finish the lesson.

Showcase your keyboarding skills in the game.

8-d4

Table

Prepare the following budget to present to Ms. Miguel for approval.

1. Tap ENTER three times, and key the table shown below; then apply the following formats.
2. Add a column between columns B and C and key the following data: **Unit Cost, $24.50, 65.75, 250.00, 4.25,** and **3.75.**
3. Insert a row above the column heads; merge all cells in the row. Set the row height at 0.5". Key the table title **Pre-Grand Opening Celebration Budget** using 16-point font.
4. Apply Grid Table 4 – Accent 1. Apply Align Center to Table title.
5. Change the row height of rows 2–8 to 0.3". Apply Align Center and bold to the column heads.
6. Align text in the columns as follows—A: Align Center Left, B: Align Center, C and D: Align Center Right.
7. Preview, proofread, and check; click Next Activity. (*8-d4*)

Description	Quantity/Number	Estimated Cost
Food/beverage	120	$2,940.00
Floral arrangements	4	263.00
Decorations	1	250.00
Party favors	125	531.25
Invitations/mailing	150	562.50
Total cost		$4,546.75

QUICK ✓

Check your document against the illustration below.

Pre-Grand Opening Celebration Budget			
Description	**Quantity/Number**	**Unit Cost**	**Estimated Cost**
Food/beverage	120	$24.50	$2,940.00
Floral arrangements	4	65.75	263.00
Decorations	1	250.00	250.00
Party favors	125	4.25	531.25
Invitations/mailing	150	3.75	562.50
Total cost			$4,546.75

Lesson 4 Left Shift, H, T, Period

Warmup *Lesson 4a Warmup*

home row 1 al as ads lad dad fad jak fall lass asks fads all;
e/i/n 2 ed ik jn in knee end nine line sine lien dies leis
all reaches 3 see a ski; add ink; fed a jak; is an inn; as a lad
easy 4 an dial id is an la lake did el ale fake is land a

New Keys

4b Left Shift and h

left shift Reach *down* with *left fourth* (little) finger; shift, tap, release.

h Reach to *left* with *right first* finger.

left shift

5 J Ja Ja Jan Jan Jane Jana Ken Kass Lee Len Nan Ned
6 and Ken and Lena and Jake and Lida and Nan and Ida
7 Inn is; Jill Ina is; Nels is; Jen is; Ken Lin is a

h

8 h hj hj he he she she hen aha ash had has hid shed
9 h hj ha hie his half hand hike dash head sash shad
10 aha hi hash heal hill hind lash hash hake dish ash

4c All Reaches Learned

11 Nels Kane and Jake Jenn; she asked Hi and Ina Linn
12 Lend Lana and Jed a dish; I fed Lane and Jess Kane
13 I see Jake Kish and Lash Hess; Isla and Helen hike

4d Textbook Keying

Key the drill once. Strive for good control.

14 he she held a lead; she sells jade; she has a sale
15 Ha Ja Ka La Ha Hal Ja Jake Ka Kahn La Ladd Ha Hall
16 Hal leads; Jeff led all fall; Hal has a safe lead
17 Hal Hall heads all sales; Jake Hess asks less fee;

8-d2

Memo

palmetto memo form

1. Prepare the following memo:
   a. Use the information provided below to complete the heading on the memo.
   b. Use Find and Replace to locate *contract* each time it is used and replace it with **agreement**.
2. Proofread and check; click Next Activity. (*8-d2*)

> *This memo will be distributed to Haley Edwards, Jackson Moore, Lance Davis, and Cristina Kulchar with a copy to Karl Metze.*
>
> *RB*

To: Senior Executives | Subject: Miguel Contract

Miguel Enterprises accepted the Palmetto Event Solutions proposal to manage the grand opening and marketing of the new Miguel Emporium. Elena Miguel called me today to indicate that she had signed the contract without any modifications whatsoever, and she was having it hand delivered to us today.

Ms. Miguel also requested that our senior staff, as well as the Miguel Enterprises senior account manager, meet with her next Tuesday at 10:30 a.m. in our offices. Please plan to attend this important session, which will take place in the Board Room.

Marlene Delhomme, who is no longer with us, was the account manager responsible for the last two Miguel events. Karl Metze has been assigned as the senior account manager for the Miguel account. Please work with Karl on the proposed plan that we will present at the meeting.

c   Karl Metze

8-d3

Invitation

invitation
miguel logo

Format the invitation as follows:

1. In the open document, center each line except the *rsvp*, which should be left-aligned.
2. Apply Lucida Calligraphy 16-point font and Dark Red standard color; use 2.5 line spacing.
3. Remove the space after the paragraph on each line, and change orientation to landscape.
4. Use the Insert Picture command to insert the company logo, *miguel logo*, at the top of the page. Change the size of the logo to 1" high, and use Center alignment on the Home tab to position the logo.
5. Proofread and check; click Next Activity. (*8-d3*)

> *Please format the draft invitation Sarah created. It is saved as <u>invitation</u> in the data files.*
>
> *RB*

4e t and . (period)

t Reach *up* with *left first* finger.

. (period) Reach *down* with *right third* finger.

t

18 t tf tf aft aft left fit fat fete tiff tie the tin
19 tf at at aft lit hit tide tilt tint sits skit this
20 hat kit let lit ate sit flat tilt thin tale tan at

Space once after a period.

. (period)

21 .l .l l.l fl. fl. L. L. Neal and J. N. List hiked.
22 Hand J. H. Kass a fan. Jeff did. Hank needs ideas.
23 Jane said she has a tan dish; Jed and Lee need it.

4f Improve Keystroking

24 I did tell J. K. that Lt. Lee had left. He is ill.
25 tie tan kit sit fit hit hat; the jet left at nine.
26 I see Lila and Ilene at tea. Jane Kane ate at ten.
27 tf .l hj ft ki de jh tf ik ed hj de ft ki l. tf ik
28 elf eel left is sis fit till dens ink has delt ink
29 he he heed heed she she shelf shelf shed shed she
30 it is if id did lit tide tide tile tile list list

Skill Building

4g Build Skill

31 he has; he had; he led; he sleds; she fell; he is
32 it is; he hit it; he is ill; she is still; she is
33 Hal and Nel; Jade dishes; Kale has half; Jed hides
34 Hi Ken; Helen and Jen hike; Jan has a jade; Ken is

4h End the Lesson

Log out of *KPDO*.

Do not prepare envelopes. In this office, most documents are distributed as attachments to email. Documents will be distributed after Ms. Barnett adds her electronic signature or initials.

KANSAS CITY OFFICE

You will report to Ms. Rachel Barnett, the Midwest Regional Vice President. She follows the SOPs and often leaves directions on yellow sticky notes. Check each document to make sure you have used or done the following:

- Ion theme for all documents.
- Use the Kansas City letterhead and the standard memo form for all letters and memos. Use block letter style with open punctuation.
- Note the standard for bulleting items has been changed. Use the new square bullet style with Dark Red, Accent 1 color.
- Unless directed otherwise, use the salutation *Dear + personal title and last name*, such as Dear Ms. Miguel.
- Unless otherwise directed, use: **Sincerely** | **Rachel C. Barnett** | **Regional Vice President** for the closing lines. Position the name and title on two lines; do not use a title on any documents sent to Palmetto Event Solutions offices.
- Provide an appropriate subject line for memos and emails if one is not provided.
- Use the current date unless instructed otherwise.
- Add your reference initials, attachment notation, and copy notations as needed.
- Ensure that all documents are error-free. Use proofing tools and then edit, proofread, and correct errors. Verify dates and numerical data against the source.

8-d1

Letter

palmetto letterhead - kansas city

1. Prepare the following letter for Ms. Barnett with all necessary letter parts.
2. Proofread and check; click Next Activity. *(8-d1)*

Send the letter to:
Ms. Elena T. Miguel, President
Miguel Enterprises, Inc.
One Ward Parkway
Kansas City, MO 64114-2601

Ms. Barnett does not put the name of the attachment on the letter because it will be displayed on the email used to transmit the letter and attachment. Just key *Attachment* to call attention to it.

Thank you for accepting our proposal to manage the grand opening and marketing of your new gift shop, Miguel Emporium. We are very pleased to have the opportunity to work with you on another new store opening.

The senior staff of Palmetto Event Solutions, Inc. would be happy to meet with you next Tuesday at 10:30 a.m. in our offices as you requested. Prior to that meeting, we will prepare a proposed plan for the grand opening event. As we discussed, we will build on the same model that we used on your previous store openings.

Please sign the attached agreement and return one copy to us. We look forward to helping you make this a memorable event.

Lesson 4R Review

Warmup Lesson 4Ra Warmup

home row 1 sad lad hall lad sale ask jak add aka fall fad ha;

review 2 H. Le Ki J. tan tin hit at tat nat hat nit Lt. hid

all reaches 3 Jed is in sales; Kate ate fish. Hank hit his head.

easy 4 sit dial and land fit then half din hand lend disk

Skill Building

4Rb Textbook Keying

Key the drill once.

Think and key words and phrases.

words 5 slain tent Kent lent tea Jill Ned fed said laid he

phrases 6 he fakes | she hikes | his lead is safe | she and I fish

sentences 7 Nan is ill; Ed is at the lake; Jake is at the Inn.

sentences 8 Jed Hess did ski. Kit and I fished. Tina ate fish.

sentences 9 Hank ate his salad. Jane has the disk in the tent.

sentences 10 Ed said that Nate left the lake and is at the Inn.

4Rc Build Skill

11 shelf lead jiff lead sand find dine kind fend tent

12 kale sake takes deal tended salad jaded dined left

13 if I sell it; seek a deal; find a tent; at the Inn

14 He asked Ann; I need a fan; Ed sells jade and land.

15 Linda likes to hike; Dan likes to eat at the lake.

4Rd Timed Writing

1. Take two 1' timed writings. If you finish before time is up, begin again.
2. Use wordwrap.
3. When you are finished, log out.

Log Out

Wordwrap: Text within a paragraph moves automatically from one line to the next; tap ENTER only to begin a new paragraph.

Use wordwrap

Janet sat in the tent, and then she fished at the (4, 8) lake. Eddie and his dad did find the disk in the tent (12, 16, 20) at the lake. Helen and the dean ate a salad at the (24, 28) Inn. Then she asked the dean if he had a keen idea. (32, 36, 40) She said the dean did have a keen idea. (44, 48)

MODULE 8

Palmetto Event Solutions, Inc.

Lessons 54–55 *Palmetto Event Solutions, Inc.*

LEARNING OUTCOMES

- Apply keying, formatting, and word processing skills.
- Work independently with few instructions.

Warmup *Lesson 54a Warmup*

Skill Building

54b Timed Writing

Key two 3' timed writings. Strive for control.

Voting is a very important part of being a good citizen. However, many young people who are eligible to vote choose not to do so. When asked to explain or justify their decision, many individuals simply shrug their shoulders and reply that they have no particular reason for not voting. The explanation others frequently give is that they just did not get around to going to the polls.

A good question to consider concerns ways that we can motivate young people to be good citizens and to go to the polls and to vote. Some people approach this topic by trying to determine how satisfied people who do not vote are with the performance of their elected officials. Unfortunately, those who choose not to vote are just as satisfied with their elected officials as those who voted.

One interesting phenomenon concerning voting relates to the job market. When the job market is strong, fewer young people vote than when the job market is very bad. They also tend to be less satisfied with their elected officials. Self-interest seems to be a powerful motivator. Unfortunately, those who do not choose to vote miss the point that it is in their best interest to be a good citizen.

Project Setting

PALMETTO EVENT SOLUTIONS, INC.

In this project, you are an executive assistant in the Kansas City office. This experience gives you an opportunity to apply the document formatting and word processing skills that you learned in Modules 3–7. Review the SOPs that are summarized on the next page, and apply them to your work.

Special instructions for non-KPDO users:

Set up a folder named Palmetto Event Solutions. Save each document as 8-d + the document number. (*8-d1*, *8-d2*, *8-d3*, etc.)

Lesson 5 R, Right Shift, C, O

Warmup *Lesson 5a Warmup*

home keys 1 a; ad add al all lad fad jak ask lass fall jak lad

t/h/i/n 2 the hit tin nit then this kith dint tine hint thin

left shift/. 3 I need ink. Li has an idea. Hank hit it. I see Kate.

all reaches 4 Jeff ate at ten; he left a salad dish in the sink.

New Keys

5b r and Right Shift

© Cengage Learning

r Reach *up* with *left first* finger.

© Cengage Learning

right shift Reach *down* with *right fourth* finger; shift, tap, release.

r

5 r rf rf riff riff fir fir rid ire jar air sir lair

6 rf rid ark ran rat are hare art rant tire dirt jar

7 rare dirk ajar lark rain kirk share hart rail tart

left shift

8 D D Dan Dan Dale Ti Sal Ted Ann Ed Alf Ada Sid Fan

9 and Sid and Dina and Allen and Eli and Dean and Ed

10 Ed Dana; Dee Falk; Tina Finn; Sal Alan; Anna Deeds

5c All Reaches Learned

11 Jane and Ann hiked in the sand; Asa set the tents.

12 a rake; a jar; a tree; a red fire; a fare; a rain;

13 Fred Derr and Rai Tira dined at the Tree Art Fair.

5d Textbook Keying

Key each line once.

14 ir ir ire fir first air fair fire tire rid sir

15 fir jar tar fir flit rill till list stir dirt fire

16 Renee is ill. Fred read to her. Ed Finn left here.

17 All is still as Sarah and I fish here in the rain.

18 I still see a red ash tree that fell in the field.

19 Lana said she did sail her skiff in the dark lake.

Day Three Highlights

On this day, you go back in time about 2,000 years to visit the ancient city, Pompeii. It is often called the forgotten city because the volcano Mount Vesuvius erupted and buried residences, temples, artwork, and many other objects. You will have a full-day tour to visit the ruins and excavations as well as the surrounding areas.

Day Four Highlights

On this day, you select the surrounding city or town from a number of options that you would like to tour. Our staff will provide you with information about the many alternatives and will arrange your transportation to the desired destination.

Day Five Highlights

You can relax, swim, golf, play tennis, visit the spa, shop, or do whatever you would like as you prepare for your departure. Our final evening is a memorable banquet and gala with the award presentations followed by dancing.

Remove Space Before Paragraph

Home/Paragraph/Line and Paragraph Spacing

1. Position the insertion point in the heading.
2. Click Remove Space Before Paragraph.

3. Select the text and format it in two equal-width columns. Insert a Continuous section break at the end of the second column to balance the columns.
4. Apply Heading 1 format to each of the headings; then remove the space before each of the headings.
5. Key the title, **Amalfi Coast—Here We Come** at the second paragraph marker above the Continuous section break; apply 28-point Heading font.
6. Apply Text Effects: Fill – Dark Red, Accent 1, Shadow. Center the title.
7. Insert *the isle of capri boat trip* data file; size it 2.5" high. Position in Middle Center with Square Text Wrapping.
8. Proofread and check; click Next Activity. (*53-d3*)

53-d4

Compose

 palmetto memo form

Several employees have suggested that it would be nice to have an electronic employee newsletter with information supplied by each office. You talked with Mr. Sutton about it and he asked you to compose a memo to be sent to all Palmetto executive assistants.

1. Tell them about the suggestion and ask them to discuss it with their colleagues to determine the level of interest.
2. List questions that would need to be answered and ask everyone to share their thoughts on each question. The following examples are just to help you get started.
   a. What types of information would be included? Business activities and results from each office? Information about employees and their families? Company news? Tips for being more effective, etc.
   b. Who would report news from each office? Who would coordinate and distribute it?
   c. How often? How long would it be? What would it be named?
3. Edit, proofread, and check; exit *Word*. (*53-d4*)
4. Click Log out to exit *KPDO*.

Learn More:

www.cengagebrain.com

5e c and o

© Cengage Learning

c Reach *down* with *left second* finger.

© Cengage Learning

o Reach *up* with *right third* finger.

c

20 c c cd cd cad cad can can tic ice sac cake cat sic
21 clad chic cite cheek clef sick lick kick dice rice
22 call acid hack jack lack lick cask crack clan cane

o

23 o ol ol old old of off odd ode or ore oar soar one
24 ol sol sold told dole do doe lo doll sol solo odor
25 onto door toil lotto soak fort hods foal roan load

Skill Building

5f Improve Keystroking

o/r
26 or or for for nor nor ore ore oar oar roe roe sore
27 a rose|her or|he or|he rode|or for|a door|her doll

e/n
28 en en end end ne ne need need ken ken kneel kneels
29 lend the|lend the|at the end|at the end|need their

c/o
30 ch ch check check ck ck hack lack jack co co cones
31 the cot|the cot|a dock|a dock|a jack|a jack|a cone

all reaches
32 Carlo Rand can call Rocco; Cole can call Doc Cost.
33 Trina can ask Dina if Nick Corl has left; Joe did.
34 Case sent Carole a nice skirt; it fits Lorna Rich.

5g Build Skill

i/t
35 is is tis tis it it fit fit tie tie this this lits
36 it is|it is|it is this|it is this|it sits|tie fits

all reaches
37 Jack and Rona did frost nine of the cakes at last.
38 Jo can ice her drink if Tess can find her a flask.
39 Ask Jean to call Fisk at noon; he needs her notes.

Begin new paragraph →

I also encourage you to add an extra day to the length of the retreat and devote it to an intensive seminar entitled Upscale Corporate Marketing. This past quarter, our marketing team worked with a marketing consultant focusing on using an upscale, in-home event for senior executives of our top ten clients. We experimented with one event that produced very interesting results that we would like to share at the retreat. The setting for the event is shown below.

53-d3

Newsletter

isle of capri boat trip

You are working with Mason James, the senior event planning manager in the Newport office, on a reward trip for one of your major clients, Market Trust Insurance Company. This is the third time the Newport team has planned the annual reward trip. This is an all-expense paid trip for the 25 CEOs and their spouses of insurance companies that provide Market Trust the most revenue for the previous year. Your job is to prepare a one-page newsletter providing a few trip highlights that will be emailed to each attendee one week before their departure to get participants excited about the trip. They will have a complete packet of information when they arrive at the resort.

1. Apply Narrow margins. Turn Show/Hide on. Tap ENTER three times.
2. Key the newsletter shown below. Then follow directions to format the document.

One week from today you will arrive at the five-star Palazzo Ravello on the cliffs of the medieval town of Ravello for five exciting days on the Amalfi Coast of Italy! The spectacular view from your balcony high above the Mediterranean is simply breathtaking. Luxurious rooms with exquisite furnishings; impeccable service; a rooftop sun terrace; gym; spa; outdoor pool; three restaurants including a world-renowned, highly rated fine dining restaurant; and many other amenities await you.

Day One Highlights

Your first day is designed to be a relaxing one. You can have a delightful lunch on the Cliff Terrace overlooking the Mediterranean or at the Grille near the pool. A ten-minute walk will bring you to the Town Square with shops featuring hand-painted china and a variety of other art objects as well as a panoramic view of the area. The day ends with a reception and dinner so that you will have the opportunity to meet all of the President's Award Trip winners.

Day Two Highlights

Get your camera ready for a sightseeing boat trip around the Amalfi Coast and to the Isle of Capri. Bring your bathing suit if you want to swim in the Mediterranean near one of the famous grottos on the mountainous side of the island or at the Isle of Capri beach. You will have a sightseeing tour in a convertible and a delightful lunch. In the evening, transportation will be provided to some of the local dinner and entertainment places.

(continued)

Warmup *Lesson 5Ra Warmup*

r/c/o/right shift 1 circle order record Frank Sarah Tonia Henri candor

r/c/o 2 effort trick scroll control clone donor salon corn

right shift 3 Sandra Forde Addie Crone Stan Jackson Rhonda Caine

all reaches 4 Jeff drank his cold tea and ate cookies in a tent.

Skill Building

Think and key words and phrases as units.

5Rb Textbook Keying

1. Key each line once.
2. Keep your eyes on the copy.

words
5 choice rejoice north crank drank cross craft order
6 creaked kitchen store lost frost train rained horn

phrases
7 to go north|I left at noon|reach up|he trusted her
8 Fred chose one|Connie cooked|Daniel ate fried food

sentences
9 Carl and Jack left for a short train ride at noon.
10 Lee and Jo can cook for their friends in the tent.

5Rc Build Skill

o/r
11 or cork for nor sore tore rote lore snore ore core
12 his or her|she rode|at the door|she tore her skirt

c/o
13 close choose color cork corn coal ocean cold scorn
14 close the door|choose a color|for a dock|cook corn

all reaches
15 Joan and Clark selected a nice color for the dock.
16 Dick sent Lori a nice skirt and Frank a red shirt.

5Rd Timed Writing

1. Key a 1' timing; use wordwrap—do not return at the end of the line. If you finish before time is up, begin again.
2. Key a 1' timed writing at a slower but fluent pace.

wordwrap

Connie said that her son can cook for her friends at noon. He is a trained chef and likes to cook for others. He can locate and choose the food. Harold offered to do all of the dishes. I think that is also a nice offer.

53-d1

Organization Chart

A client who is considering a proposal for a project that Mr. Straton submitted has requested an organization chart showing the Senior Management Team. Abbreviate Vice President (VP) on the chart. Note from the Quick Check that you will need to add additional shapes.

1. Insert a SmartArt Name and Title Organization chart from the Hierarchy category, and include the members of the Senior Management Team:
   a. **Garrett Russell, President and CEO**
   b. **Ellen Miller, Executive Assistant**
   c. **Jennifer Anderson, Northwest Regional VP**
   d. **Rachel Barnett, Midwest Regional VP**
   e. **Aydyn Ellison, Chief Financial Officer**
   f. **Willie Straton, Northeast Regional VP**
   g. **Carlos Torres, Southwest Regional VP**
2. Size the chart 3.5" high and 6.5" wide; position it in the Top Center with Square Text Wrapping.
3. Proofread and check; click Next Activity.

Compare your document to the one shown below.

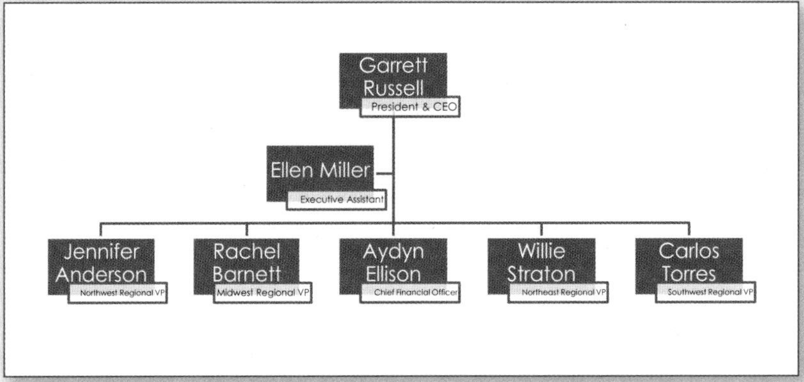

53-d2

Memo with Graphics

Prepare the memo below for Mr. Straton; he will attach it to an email to the Senior Management Team.

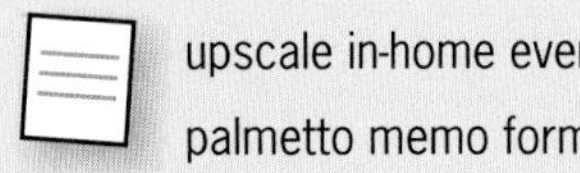

upscale in-home event

palmetto memo form

1. Use the current date and subject line: **Senior Management Team Retreat.**
2. Tap ENTER after the last paragraph and insert the *upscale in-home event* picture from the data files. Size it 3.5" high and apply Center from the Home tab.
3. Proofread and check; click Next Activity.

The past two Senior Management Team Retreats were held in Portland and Hilton Head. Please consider letting the Northeast Region host this year's Senior Management Team Retreat on Goat Island. Goat Island, as most of you know, is a gorgeous and historic island located in the Newport Harbor.

(continued)

Warmup *Lesson 6a Warmup*

home row	1	`ask a lad; a fall fad; had a salad; ask a sad jak;`
o/t	2	`to do it; to toil; as a tot; do a lot; he told her`
c/r	3	`cots are; has rocks; roll cot; is rich; has an arc`
all reaches	4	`Holt can see Dane at ten; Jill sees Frank at nine.`

New Keys

6b w and , (comma)

w Reach *up* with *left third* finger.

, (comma) Reach *down* with *right second* finger.

w

5 `w ws ws was was wan wit low win jaw wilt wink wolf`
6 `sw sw w sow ow now now row row own own wow wow owe`
7 `to sew; to own; was rich; was in; is how; will now`

, (comma)

8 `k, k, k, irk, ilk, ask, oak, ark, lark, jak, rock,`
9 `skis, a dock, a fork, a lock, a fee, a tie, a fan,`
10 `Joe, Ed, and I saw Nan, Ann, and Wes in a new car.`

6c All Reaches Learned

11 `Win, Lew, Drew, and Walt will walk to West Willow.`
12 `Ask Ho, Al, and Jared to read the code; it is new.`
13 `The window, we think, was closed; we felt no wind.`

Good posture builds an attitude of preciseness.

6d Textbook Keying

Key each line once.

14 `walk wide sown wild town went jowl wait white down`
15 `a dock, a kit, a wick, a lock, a row, a cow, a fee`
16 `Joe lost to Ron; Fiji lost to Cara; Don lost to Al`
17 `Kane will win; Nan will win; Rio will win; Di wins`
18 `Walter is in Reno; Tia is in Tahoe; then to Hawaii`

Lesson 53 Palmetto Event Solutions, Inc.

Learning Outcomes

- Apply keying, formatting, and word processing skills.
- Prepare documents with columns and graphics.
- Work independently with few specific instructions.

Warmup *Lesson 53a Warmup*

A ALL LETTERS

Skill Building

53b Timed Writing

Key two 3' timed writings.

Most people today realize that they cannot count on their employer or on the government to provide for their retirement. They must plan for their own future. Young people who are healthy and are not concerned about retirement often do not consider the value of the benefits when they compare job offers they have. They tend to focus more on the salary they will earn.

Most companies provide some type of health benefits. The portion that the employee has to pay tends to vary widely, however. Therefore, it is wise to analyze the quality, the type of coverage provided, and the cost of the benefits to the employee. A lower salary with benefits paid by the company may produce more net income than a higher salary with high benefit costs to the employee.

To recruit bright young people who are likely to change jobs many times, companies set up portable savings plans that defer taxes on income. The company matches a certain percentage of the savings to provide incentives for the employee to contribute to the plan. Usually the plan vests in less than five years, and employees can take the entire amount with them when they leave.

Project Setting

PALMETTO EVENT SOLUTIONS, INC.

For the project in this module, you will be preparing documents for Willie Straton, our Northeast Regional Vice President in Newport, Rhode Island. You will use the Newport letterhead and the standard memo form. You may wish to review the SOPs for Palmetto Events Solutions and the *About Us* section on pages 117 and 118. All documents are to be reviewed by Mr. Straton before they are sent to the recipients. Do not prepare envelopes or emails to transmit the documents at this time.

As you work through each job and after all jobs are completed, make sure that you have used or done the following:

- Correct letterhead or the memo form for letters and memos.
- Block letter style for letters.
- Ion theme for all documents.
- Previewed and proofread documents carefully.

6e b and p

b Reach *down* with *left first* finger.

p Reach *up* with *right fourth* (little) finger.

b

19 bf bf bf biff fib fib bib bib boa boa fib fibs rob
20 bf bf bf ban ban bon bon bow bow be be rib rib sob
21 a dob, a cob, a crib, a lab, a slab, a bid, a bath

p

22 p; p; pa pa; pal pal pan pan pad par pen pep paper
23 pa pa; lap lap; nap nap; hep ape spa asp leap clap
24 a park, a pan, a pal, a pad, apt to pop, a pair of

Skill Building

6f Improve Keystroking

all reaches learned

25 Barb and Bob wrapped a pepper in paper and ribbon.
26 Rip, Joann, and Dick were all closer to the flash.
27 Bo will be pleased to see Japan; he works in Oslo.

reach review

28 ki kid did aid lie hj has has had sw saw wits will
29 de dell led sled jn an en end ant hand k, end, kin

s/w

30 ws ws lows now we shown win cow wow wire jowl when
31 Wes saw an owl in the willow tree in the old lane.

b/p

32 bf bf fib rob bid ;p p; pal pen pot nap hop cap bp
33 Rob has both pans in a bin at the back of the pen.

6g Build Skill

34 to do|can do|to bow|ask her|to nap|to work|is born
35 for this|if she|is now|did all|to see|or not|or if

all reaches

36 Dick owns a dock at this lake; he paid Ken for it.
37 Jane also kept a pair of owls, a hen, and a snake.

38 Blair soaks a bit of the corn, as he did in Japan.
39 I blend the cocoa in the bowl when I work for Leo.

8. Insert an Alternating Flow SmartArt graphic (second icon in the second row) from the Process category.
    a. Click in the line below the Continuous section break and change the column format to one column.
    b. Size the entire graphic 2.5" high and 6.0" wide.
    c. Position it in the Bottom Center with Square Text Wrapping.
    d. Key the text shown below in the SmartArt text pane.
9. Proofread and check; click Next Activity. *(52-d1)*

Architectural Plans
    Contract 6/25
    Approved 3/3
Next Steps
    Groundbreaking 3/18
    Cornerstone Club 3/18
Grand Opening
    Construction contract 6/15
    Completion 12 to 15 months

Check your document against the illustration below. (Photo may vary.)

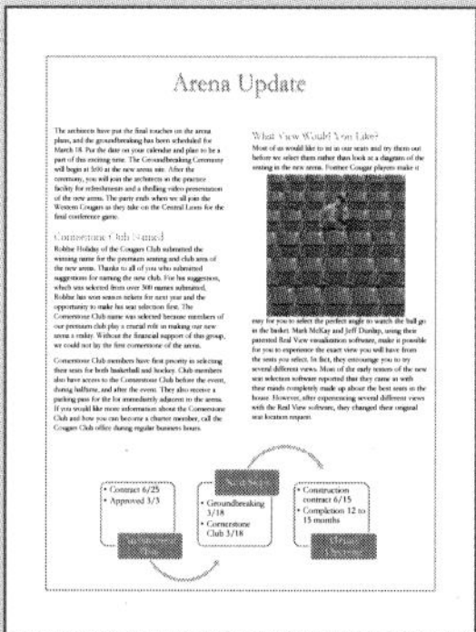

52-d2

Composition

cornerstone club memo form

1. Use the following information to compose a memo to Robbie Holiday from Jeff Crane inviting him to represent the Cornerstone Club at the groundbreaking ceremony. Date it March 5, 201-; add an appropriate subject line. Ask him to confirm his acceptance.
    a. Five people will participate in the ceremony; use the Arena Update for time, date, site, and other information as needed.
    b. Shovels and hardhats will be provided.
    c. Media will be present and may interview participants. Business attire is requested.
2. Edit and proofread to ensure that you used complete sentences and well-formed paragraphs.
3. Proofread and check; click Next Activity. *(52-d2)*

Lesson 7 Review

Warmup *Lesson 7a Warmup*

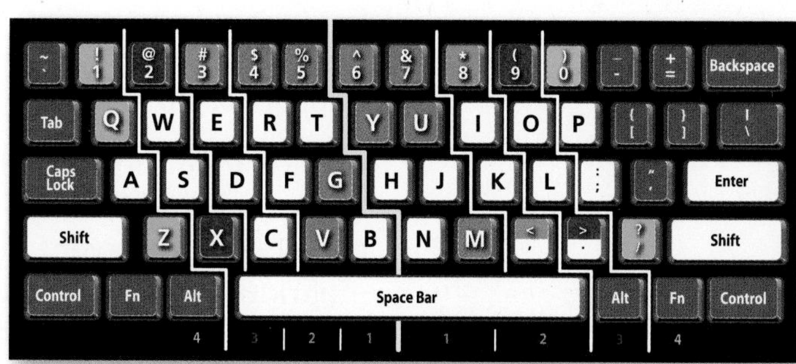

all 1 We often can take the older jet to Paris and back.
home 2 a; sl dk fj a;sl dkfj ad as all ask fads adds asks
1st row 3 Ann Bascan and Cabal Naban nabbed a cab in Canada.
3rd row 4 Rip went to a water show with either Pippa or Pia.

7b Improve Keystroking

5 ad la as in if it lo no of oh he or so ok pi be we
6 an ace ads ale aha a fit oil a jak nor a bit a pew
7 ice ades born is fake to jail than it and the cows
8 Ask Jed. Dr. Hand left at ten; Dr. Crowe, at nine.

Skill Building

7c Textbook Keying

Key each line once.

Keep your eyes on the textbook copy as you key.

9 ws ws was was wan wan wit wit pew paw nap pop bawl
10 bf bf fb fb fob fob rib rib be be job job bat back
11 p; p; asp asp pan pan ap ap ca cap pa nap pop prow
12 Barb and Bret took an old black robe and the boot.
13 Walt saw a wisp of white water renew ripe peppers.
14 Pat picked a black pepper for the picnic at Parks.

7d Build Skill

15 Jake held a bit of cocoa and an apricot for Diane.
16 Dick and I fish for cod on the docks at Fish Lake.
17 Kent still held the dish and the cork in his hand.
18 Ask far as I know, he did not read all of the book.

Cornerstone Club Named

Robbie Holiday of the Cougars Club submitted the winning name for the premium seating and club area of the new arena. Thanks to all of you who submitted suggestions for naming the new club. For his suggestion, which was selected from over 300 names submitted, Robbie has won season tickets for next year and the opportunity to make his seat selection first. The Cornerstone Club name was selected because members of our premium club play a crucial role in making our new arena a reality. Without the financial support of this group, we could not lay the first cornerstone of the arena.

Cornerstone Club members have first priority in selecting their seats for both basketball and hockey. Club members also have access to the Cornerstone Club before the event, during halftime, and after the event. They also receive a parking pass for the lot immediately adjacent to the arena. If you would like more information about the Cornerstone Club and how you can become a charter member, call the Cougars Club office during regular business hours.

What View Would You Like?

Most of us would like to sit in our seats and try them out before we select them rather than look at a diagram of the seating in the new arena. Former Cougar players make it easy for you to select the perfect angle to watch the ball go in the basket. Mark McKay and Jeff Dunlap, using their patented Real View visualization software, make it possible for you to experience the exact view you will have from the seats you select. In fact, they encourage you to try several different views. Most of the early testers of the new seat selection software reported that they came in with their minds completely made up about the best seats in the house. However, after experiencing several different views with the Real View software, they changed their original seat location request.

3. Select the text and format it into two equal-width columns. Note that a Continuous section break is positioned above the columns.
4. Apply Heading 1 to both headings.
5. Apply a Green – Accent 1, 1½-point box border.
6. Insert Fill – Green – Accent 1, Shadow WordArt.
   a. Size WordArt 0.8" high.
   b. Key the title **Arena Update**.
   c. Position in the Top Center with Square Text Wrapping. Note that it should be between the top border and the Continuous section break.
7. Position the picture described in the following steps after the third line under the last heading.
   a. Search for clip art in Online Pictures using *stadium seats* as the keywords.
   b. Insert the clip shown on the next page; apply Top and Bottom Text Wrap.
   c. Size it 2.75" high and drag to the center of the column.

(continued)

You must have either a blank paragraph marker or an unselected title for the system to add a Continuous section break above the columns.

7e Textbook Keying

Key each line once.

Words: key as single unit; phrases: say and key fluently; sentences: work for fluency.

words 19 a an pan so sot la lap ah own do doe el elf to tot
phrases 20 if it|to do|it is|do so|for the|he works|if he bid
sentences 21 Jess ate all of the peas in the salad in the bowl.

words 22 bow bowl pin pint for fork forks hen hens jak jaks
phrases 23 is for|did it|is the|we did a|and so|to see|or not
sentences 24 I hid the ace in a jar as a joke; I do not see it.

words 25 chap chaps flak flake flakes prow prowl work works
phrases 26 as for the|as for the|and to the|to see it|and did
sentences 27 As far as I know, he did not read all of the book.

7f Timed Writing

1. Take two 1' timed writings. If you finish before time is up, begin again.
2. Use wordwrap; do not tap ENTER at the ends of the lines.
3. End the lesson.

Goal: 12 *gwam*

wordwrap

gwam 1'

It is hard to fake a confident spirit. We will do 10
better work if we approach and finish a job and 19
know that we will do the best work we can and then 29
not fret. 31

| 1 | 2 | 3 | 4 | 5 | 6 | 7 | 8 | 9 | 10 |

7g Word Processor Timer

Word Processor

1. Review the Standard Plan for Using the Word Processor Timer.
2. Key the timed writing from the textbook in 7f following the directions in the textbook.

STANDARD PLAN for Using the Word Processor Timer

You can check your speed in the Word Processor using the Timer. 

1. In the Word Processor, click the Timer button on the status bar.
2. The Timer begins once you start to key and stops automatically.
3. To save the timing, click the File menu and Save As. Use your initals (*xx*), the exercise number, and number of the timing as the filename. Example: *xx-7f-t1* (your initials, exercise 7f, timing1).
4. Click the Timer button again to start a new timing.
5. Each new timing must be saved with its own name.

7h Word Processor

1. In the Word Processor, key each line once for fluency.
2. Set the Timer for 30". Take two 30" writings on each line. Do not save the timings.

Goal: Reach the end of the line before time is up.

28 Dan took her to the show.
29 Jan lent the bowl to the pros.
30 Hold the wrists low for this drill.
31 Jessie fit the black panel to the shelf.
32 Patrick cooked breakfast for Jill and her friends.

DRILL 3 REMOVE LINE AND ADD GRAPHICS

1. Open *52-drill2* and remove the line between the columns.
2. Search for an appropriate clip for training from Online pictures using the keywords *business people on computers*. Size it 1.8" high and position it in the Middle Center with Square Text Wrapping.
3. Apply an Orange – Accent 2 thick and thin box page border. See Quick Check below.
4. Preview and check; click Next Activity. (*52-drill3*)

Check your document against the illustration below. Photo may vary.

Productivity Enhancement Program

The Executive Committee's new Productivity Enhancement Program resulted in standardizing all computer software applications for the company in all locations. The Training and Development Team, at the request of the Executive Committee, developed a training program designed to help all employees learn how to integrate applications available in the standardized suite and to use electronic mail and the Internet.

The Productivity Enhancement Program specifies that each employee must develop in-depth skill in at least two applications, basic skill in the other applications, and be able to produce a compound document—that is, a document that includes elements from multiple software applications in the suite. Employees must also be able to use electronic mail. The Productivity Enhancement Program specifies that most internal documents will be distributed electronically.

To meet the needs of all employees, the Training and Development Team structured the Integrating Computer Applications training program in three phases.

Assessment provides employees who already have developed skill in an application to demonstrate that competence without taking the training module. Two levels of assessments—basic skill and in-depth skill—are available for each application. Each computer-administered and scored assessment contains three versions.

An employee who does not successfully complete the assessment in three tries or who elects not to take the assessment option must take the training module for that application. Assessments are also used at the conclusion of training modules.

Development follows assessment. Two options are available for developing skill in the various applications. Employees may sign up for regular training classes or may elect to use the new computer-based training programs (CBT) to develop the skill. The advantage of using the CBT program is that it can be completed at your own workstation. A combination of both instructor-led training and the CBT program may be the best alternative for most employees. An assessment must be completed at the end of each training session to demonstrate the level of skill attained on each software application.

Integration is the final phase of the program. The integration program accomplishes two objectives—teaching employees how to prepare documents that use objects from the various applications in the suite and standardizing the format for frequently used documents. Detailed information about the integration phase will be provided at least three weeks prior to the training.

Apply It

52-d1

Newsletter

1. Apply Organic theme and Narrow margins.
2. Tap ENTER four times; then key the newsletter as it is shown. Do not format as you key.

The architects have put the final touches on the arena plans, and the groundbreaking has been scheduled for March 18. Put the date on your calendar and plan to be a part of this exciting time. The Groundbreaking Ceremony will begin at 5:00 at the new arena site. After the ceremony, you will join the architects in the practice facility for refreshments and a thrilling video presentation of the new arena. The party ends when we all join the Western Cougars as they take on the Central Lions for the final conference game.

(continued)

Lesson 8 G, Question Mark, X, U

Warmup *Lesson 8a Warmup*

all 1 Dick will see Job at nine if Rach sees Pat at one.
w/b 2 As the wind blew, Bob Webber saw the window break.
p/, 3 Pat, Pippa, or Cap has prepared the proper papers.
all 4 Bo, Jose, and Will fed Lin; Jack had not paid her.

New Keys

8b g and ? (question mark)

g Reach to *right* with *left first* finger.

? Left SHIFT; reach *down* with *right fourth* finger.

Question mark: The question mark is followed by one space.

g

5 g g gf gaff gag grog fog frog drag cog dig fig gig
6 gf go gall flag gels slag gala gale glad glee gals
7 golf flog gorge glen high logs gore ogle page grow

? (question mark)

8 ? ?; ?; ? ? Who? When? Where? Who is? Who was she?
9 Who is here? Was it she? Was it he? Did Pablos go?
10 Did Geena? Did he? What is that? Was Joe here too?

8c All Reaches Learned

11 Has Ginger lost her job? Were her June bills here?
12 Phil did not want the boats to get here this soon.
13 Loris Shin has been ill; Frank, a doctor, saw her.

8d Textbook Keying

1. Key each line once.
2. Keep your eyes on the textbook copy.

reach review
14 ws ws hj hj tf tf ol ol rf rf ed ed cd cd bf bf p;
15 wed bid has old hold rid heed heed car bed pot pot

g
16 gf gf gin gin rig ring go gone no nog sign got dog
17 to go|to go|go on|go in|go in|to go in|in the sign

?
18 ?; ?;? who? when? where? how? what? who? It is he?
19 Is she? Is he? Did I lose Paul? Is Gabe all right?

To format equal-width columns:

Page Layout/Page Setup/Columns

1. Select the text you want to format in columns; click Columns and select the desired number of columns from the options that display.
2. To balance columns on a page, click at the end of the columns and insert a Continuous section break.

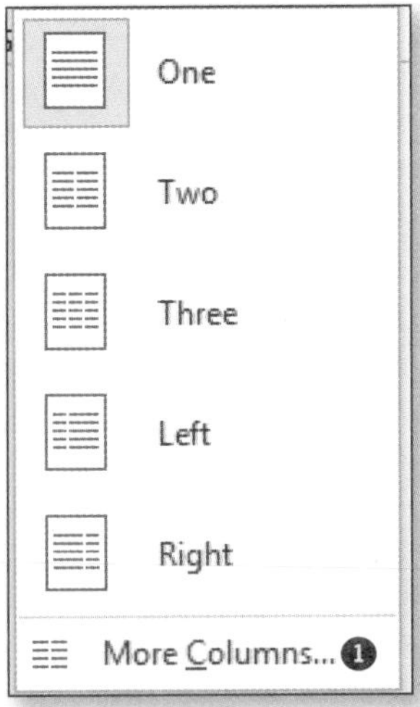

DRILL 1 COLUMNS

1. In the open document, select the title and apply Fill – Orange, Accent 2, Outline – Accent 2 Text Effect from the Font group on the Home tab.
2. Select the text, click Columns, and select Three.
3. Preview the document and then revise the column structure; select the text again and click Two columns.

Page Layout/Page Setup/Breaks

4. Add a Continuous section break at the end of the columns to balance them.
5. Proofread and check; click Next Activity. (*52-drill1*)

To add a line between columns:

Page Layout/Page Setup/Columns

1. From the number of column options, click More Columns ❶ to display the Columns dialog box.
2. Click Line between ❷. To remove the line, remove the check from the box.

DRILL 2 LINE BETWEEN COLUMNS

1. Open *52-drill 1* and add a line between the columns.
2. Preview and check; click Next Activity. (*52-drill2*)

New Keys

8e x and u

© Cengage Learning

x Reach *down* with *left third* finger.

© Cengage Learning

u Reach *up* with *right first* finger.

Concentrate on correct reaches.

x

20 x x xs xs ox ox lox sox fox box ex hex lax hex fax
21 sx six sax sox ax fix cox wax hex box pox sex text
22 flax next flex axel pixel exit oxen taxi axis next

u

23 u uj uj jug jut just dust dud due sue use due duel
24 uj us cud but bun out sun nut gun hut hue put fuel
25 dual laud dusk suds fuss full tuna tutus duds full

Skill Building

8f Improve Keystroking

Think and key phrases.

26 Paige Power liked the book; Josh can read it next.
27 Next we picked a bag for Jan; then she, Jan, left.
28 Is her June account due? Has Jo ruined her credit?
29 nut cue hut sun rug us six cut dug axe rag fox run
30 out of the sun|cut the action|a fox den|fun at six
31 That car is not junk; it can run in the next race.

8g Timed Writing

1. Take two 1' timed writings. If you finish before time is up, begin again. (The dot above various words equals 2 *gwam*; each number is another 4 *gwam*.)
2. Use wordwrap; do not tap ENTER at the end of lines.
3. Log out of *KPDO*.

Goal: 14 *gwam*

wordwrap

How a finished job will look often depends on how we feel about our work as we do it. Attitude has a definite effect on the end result of work we do.

Tap ENTER once

When we are eager to begin a job, we relax and do better work than if we start the job with an idea that there is just nothing we can do to escape it.

Lesson 52 Documents with Columns

New Commands

- Equal-Width Columns
- Balance Columns
- Revise Column Structure
- Line between Columns
- Format Banner

KPDO **Warmup** *Lesson 52a Warmup*

Skill Building

52b Textbook Keying

1. Key each line once, concentrating on using good keying techniques.
2. Repeat the drill if time permits.

1st finger

1 Freddie just gave a friend that nice ring for her fifth birthday.
2 Ginger and Gretchen recently found three cute bunnies in my yard.

2nd finger

3 David decided to compete as a place kicker for the football team.
4 Cecilia and Kit decided to kill time playing on the deck at noon.

double letters

5 Jarrett cheerfully killed millions of bugs near the pool at noon.
6 All planning committees have four dinner meetings with key staff.

New Commands

52c

COLUMNS OF EQUAL WIDTH

Text formatted in multiple columns on a page is easier to read. The text flows down one column and then to the top of the next column. The heading on a document with multiple columns, called a banner or masthead, usually spans multiple columns. Newsletters, flyers, brochures, and programs are typically formatted in columns. Columns may be of equal or varying widths. Columns may be formatted before or after text is keyed, but generally, it is easier to format text in columns after it has been keyed. Columns are usually balanced or forced to end at approximately the same point on the page.

Productivity Enhancement Program

The Executive Committee's new Productivity Enhancement Program resulted in standardizing all computer software applications for the company in all locations. The Training and Development Team, at the request of the Executive Committee, developed a training program designed to help all employees learn how to integrate applications available in the standardized suite and to use electronic mail and the Internet.

The Productivity Enhancement Program specifies that each employee must develop in-depth skill in at least two applications, basic skill in the other applications, and be able to produce a compound document—that is, a document that includes elements from multiple software applications in the suite. Employees must also be able to use electronic mail. The Productivity Enhancement Program specifies that most internal documents will be distributed electronically.

To meet the needs of all employees, the Training and Development Team structured the Integrating Computer Applications training program in three phases.

Assessment provides employees who already have developed skill in an application to demonstrate that competence without taking the training module. Two levels of assessments—basic skill and in-depth skill—are available for each application. Each computer-administered and scored assessment contains three versions.

An employee who does not successfully complete the assessment in three tries or who elects not to take the assessment option must take the training module for that application. Assessments are also used at the conclusion of training modules.

Development follows assessment. Two options are available for developing skill in the various applications. Employees may sign up for regular training classes or may elect to use the new computer-based training programs (CBT) to develop the skill. The advantage of using the CBT program is that it can be completed at your own workstation. A combination of both instructor-led training and the CBT program may be the best alternative for most employees. An assessment must be completed at the end of each training session to demonstrate the level of skill attained on each software application.

Integration is the final phase of the program. The integration program accomplishes two objectives—teaching employees how to prepare documents that use objects from the various applications in the suite and standardizing the format for frequently used documents. Detailed information about the integration phase will be provided at least three weeks prior to the training.

Lesson 8R Review

Warmup Lesson 8Ra Warmup

reach review 1 Jack is glad about the response to the fundraiser.
p 2 The local paper printed their public opinion poll.
b 3 Four babies babbled as big bears rode brown bikes.
easy 4 The newest prices were not given to her and to me.

Skill Building

8Rb Textbook Keying

1. Key each line once.
2. Keep your eyes on the copy.

Move fingers up and down without moving your hands.

home row
5 add hash shall slash salads flags alfalfa fall ask
6 A fresh salad dish was added for staff and guests.

third row
7 tire wrote rewrite ripe proper papers trip picture
8 A reporter edited the newspaper stories with ease.

1st/2nd fingers
9 returned guest changes kicked tonight flight drink
10 Ed kept doing kind deeds for the children in need.

8Rc Timed Writing

1. Take two 1' timed writings. If you finish before time is up, begin again.
2. Use wordwrap; do not tap ENTER at the ends of the lines.

gwam 1'

Luck comes to those who are prepared for it. Think 10
about what is needed to be where one should be in a 21
decade. What will it take? Will it take additional 31
education or perhaps just other experience? One sets 41
a large goal and then works through a series of other 52
lesser goals to get there. One needs to be able to 62
know what success looks like as one finishes one of 73
the goals to get to the next one. If one does it 83
well, people will think it was all luck. 91

| 1 | 2 | 3 | 4 | 5 | 6 | 7 | 8 | 9 | 10 |

8Rd Enrichment

Word Processor

1. In the Word Processor, key two 30" timings on each line. Try to increase your speed the second time.
2. Log out of *KPDO*.

We use the web and work online.
We shop online and use social networks.
The web helps us as we work and share data.
While working online, we need to keep our data safe.

Compare your document to the illustration shown below.

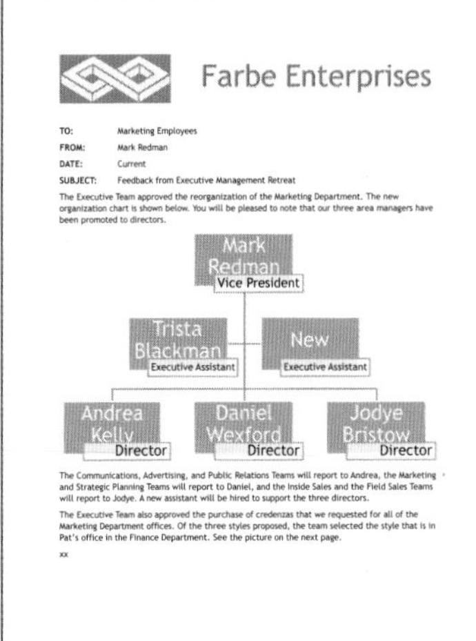

Farbe Enterprises

TO: Marketing Employees

FROM: Mark Redman

DATE: Current

SUBJECT: Feedback from Executive Management Retreat

The Executive Team approved the reorganization of the Marketing Department. The new organization chart is shown below. You will be pleased to note that our three area managers have been promoted to directors.

The Communications, Advertising, and Public Relations Teams will report to Andrea, the Marketing and Strategic Planning Teams will report to Daniel, and the Inside Sales and the Field Sales Teams will report to Jodye. A new assistant will be hired to support the three directors.

The Executive Team also approved the purchase of credenzas that we requested for all of the Marketing Department offices. Of the three styles proposed, the team selected the style that is in Pat's office in the Finance Department. See the picture on the next page.

xx

51-d3

Announcement with Online Picture, WordArt, and Border

1. Turn on Show/Hide. Apply Integral theme and Landscape orientation.
2. Apply Moderate margins.
3. In Online Pictures, search for *4th of July* clip art, and select the clip (or similar) shown at the left. Crop the black border from all sides, and resize 2" high.
4. Insert WordArt Fill – White, Outline – Accent 2, Hard Shadow – Accent 2.
   a. Select text and replace with **Fourth of July Celebration**; apply Red from Standard Colors Text Fill.
   b. Size the WordArt 1.5" high and 7" wide.
   c. Apply Transform Stop Text Effects (second icon under Warp).
   d. Position in Top Right with Square Text Wrapping.
5. Tap ENTER three times below the clip and apply 36-point font size. Key the text shown below. Justify the text.
6. Apply a thick and thin page border, using Blue from the Standard Colors.
7. Proofread and check; click Exit *Word*.
8. Click Log out to exit *KPDO*. (*51-d3*)

QUICK ✓

Fourth of July Celebration

Pack your lawn chairs or blankets and bring the entire family to join your friends and neighbors for the annual Fourth of July celebration at City Park. Music and festivities begin at 7:30 p.m. and end with a spectacular fireworks display at 10:30.

Pack your lawn chairs or blankets and bring the entire family to join your friends and neighbors for the annual Fourth of July celebration at City Park. Music and festivities begin at 7:30 p.m. and end with a spectacular fireworks display at 10:30.

Lesson 9 Q, M, V, Apostrophe

Warmup *Lesson 9a Warmup*

all letters 1 Lex gripes about cold weather; Fred is not joking.

space bar 2 Is it Di, Jo, or Al? Ask Lt. Coe, Bill; She knows.

easy 3 We did rush a bushel of cut corn to the six ducks.

easy 4 He is to go to the Tudor Isle of England on a bus.

New Keys

9b q and m

q Reach *up* with *left fourth* finger.

m Reach *down* with *right first* finger.

q

5 q qa qa quad quad quaff quant queen quo quit quick

6 qa qu qa quo quit quod quid quip quads quote quiet

7 quite quilts quart quill quakes quail quack quaint

m

8 m mj mj jam man malt mar max maw me mew men hem me

9 m mj ma am make male mane melt meat mist amen lame

10 malt meld hemp mimic tomb foam rams mama mire mind

9c All Reaches Learned

11 Quin had some quiet qualms about taming a macaque.

12 Jake Coxe had questions about a new floor program.

13 Max was quick to join the big reception for Lidia.

9d Textbook Keying

1. Key each line once; keep your elbows at your side.
2. Keep your eyes on the textbook copy.

m/x

14 me men ma am jam am lax, mix jam; the hem, six men

15 Emma Max expressed an aim to make a mammoth model.

q/u

16 qa qu aqua aqua quit quit quip quite pro quo squad

17 Did Quin make a quick request to take the Qu exam?

g/n

18 fg gn gun gun dig dig nag snag snag sign grab grab

19 Georgia hung a sign in front of the union for Gib.

Apply It

51-d1

Memo Form with Graphics

 farbe logo

Recolor

Picture Tools Format/Adjust/Color

1. Click the drop-list arrow on Color to display the color options.
2. Click the desired color.

1. Apply Facet theme style to a new document and insert the *Farbe logo* from the data files.
2. Farbe now distributes its documents electronically and wants to recolor the logo color to Green – Accent Color1 Light.
3. Insert Fill-Green – Accent 1, Shadow WordArt to the right side of the logo; select the text and key **Farbe Enterprises**; apply Cool Slant Bevel Text Effects (last bevel on first row).
4. Size the WordArt 1" high and 4.2" wide.
5. Key the memo headings as shown in the Quick Check on the next page.
6. Preview, proofread, check, and click Next Activity. (*51-d1*)

51-d2

Document with Graphics

 credenza

1. Open *51-d1* and key the memo shown below, inserting the SmartArt Name and Title Organization chart where noted.
2. Click in the top shape and add another Assistant shape. Use the Text Pane to key the names in the organization chart. Click in the Title boxes to key the titles. In the second Assistant shape, use **New** as the name.
3. Use In Line with Text wrapping and size the organization chart 3.8" high by 6.5" wide.
4. Tap ENTER after the reference initials and insert the *credenza* picture from the data files. Size it 5" high and position at Top Center with Square Text Wrapping. Compress the picture, accepting the defaults.
5. Proofread and check; click Next Activity. (*51-d2*)

Marketing Employees | Mark Redman | Current date | Feedback from Executive Management Retreat

The Executive Team approved the reorganization of the Marketing Department. The new organization chart is shown below. You will be pleased to note that our three area managers have been promoted to directors.

(Insert Name and Title Organization Chart here. Key the names and titles shown below in the chart.)

Mark Redman Vice President | Trista Blackmon Executive Assistant | New Executive Assistant | Andrea Kelly Director | Daniel Wexford Director | Jodye Bristow Director

The Communications, Advertising, and Public Relations Teams will report to Andrea, the Marketing and Strategic Planning Teams will report to Daniel, and the Inside Sales and the Field Sales Teams will report to Jodye. A new assistant will be hired to support the three directors.

The Executive Team also approved the purchase of credenzas that we requested for all of the Marketing Department offices. Of the three styles proposed, the team selected the style that is in Pat's office in the Finance Department. See the picture on the next page.

xx

9e v and ' (apostrophe)

© Cengage Learning

v Reach *down* with *left first* finger.

© Cengage Learning

' Reach to the *right* with the *right fourth* finger.

Apostrophe: The apostrophe shows (1) omission (as Rob't for Robert or it's for it is) or (2) possession when used with nouns (as Joe's hat).

v

20 v vf vf vie vie via via vim vat vow vile vale vote
21 vf vf ave vet ova eve vie dive five live have lave
22 cove dove over aver vivas hive volt five java jive

' (apostrophe)

23 '; '; it's it's Rod's; it's Bo's hat; we'll do it.
24 We don't know if it's Lee's pen or Norma's pencil.
25 It's ten o'clock; I won't tell him that he's late.

Skill Building

9f Improve Keystroking

26 It's Viv's turn to drive Iva's van to Ava's house.
v/? 27 Qua, not Vi, took the jet; so did Owen. Didn't he?
28 Wasn't Vada Baxter a judge at the post garden show?
29 Viola said she has moved six times in five months.
30 Does Dave live on Vines Avenue? Must he leave now?
q/? 31 Did Viv vote? Can Paque move it? Did Valerie quit?
32 Didn't Raquel quit Carl Quent after their quarrel?

9g Timed Writing

1. Take a 1' timing on each paragraph. If you finish before time is up, start the paragraph again. The dots equal 2 words. Use wordwrap.
2. Finish the lesson; log out of *KPDO*.

wordwrap

The questions of time use are vital ones; we miss so much just because we don't plan. If we structure our week, we save time for those extra premium things we long to do.

List the tasks to be done for the week and then place importance on each one. Complete the tasks in order of importance.

Compare your document to the illustration shown below.

Happy Birthday to You!

Communication

CAPITALIZATION

51d

References/Communication Skills/Capitalization

1. Review the capitalization rules and examples in *KPDO.*
2. Key the sentences, correcting all capitalization errors. Use the Numbering command to number the sentences.
3. Proofread and check; click Next Activity to continue. (*51d*)

1. according to one study, the largest ethnic minority group online is hispanics.
2. the american author mark twain said, "always do right; this will gratify some people and astonish the rest."
3. the grand canyon was formed by the colorado river cutting into the high-plateau region of northwestern arizona.
4. the president of russia is elected by popular vote.
5. the hubble space telescope is a cooperative project of the european space agency and the national aeronautics and space administration.
6. the train left north station at 6:45 this morning.
7. the trademark cyberprivacy prevention act would make it illegal for individuals to purchase domains solely for resale and profit.
8. consumers spent $7 billion online between november 1 and december 31, 201-, compared to $3.1 billion for the same period in 2010.
9. new students should attend an orientation session on wednesday, august 15, at 8 a.m. in room 252 of the perry building.
10. the summer book list includes *where the red fern grows* and *the mystery of the missing baseball.*

Communicating Today

Electronic Document Distribution

Electronic document distribution is a key factor leading to the increased use of color and graphics in business documents today especially in small businesses. Previously, small businesses limited the use of color and graphics because they did not have the graphic arts staff or the budget to create effective color graphics. Although the cost of color printing has declined dramatically, it still costs significantly more than black-and-white printing. When documents are distributed electronically, printing costs are eliminated.

SmartArt and color digital pictures make it easy to create effective graphics that simplify complex concepts. Color and SmartArt not only make documents more interesting; used effectively, they help make documents more understandable.

Lesson 9R Review

Warmup *Lesson 9Ra Warmup*

all reaches 1 Quij produces both fine work and excellent volume.

g/? 2 Did he go? Where is Gianna? Did George go golfing?

b/p 3 Paul has pictures of bears, bats, pigs, and bison.

easy 4 Paige is to go in a taxi to the address we stated.

Skill Building

Work for smoothness, not speed.

9Rb Textbook Keying

1. Key each line once.
2. Keep your eyes on the copy.

Apostrophe 5 I'll she'll o'clock we're didn't she's isn't don't

6 one's job; Donnel's, gov't, it's time; p's and q's

7 Spell out it's, doesn't, can't, gov't, and she'll.

q 8 netiquette queue quench quad FAQ quotes quit quest

9 Quen asked a question; eat a quince; make it quick

10 Quotes on quotas of useful equipment are required.

v 11 voice invert evoke vital prove event vacuum valid

12 improve best speed; strive high; have clear vision

13 Dev found five favorite websites for French class.

9Rc Timed Writing

1. Take two 1' timings on paragraph 1. If you finish before time is up, begin again.
2. Take a 2' timing on both paragraphs.
3. Log out of *KPDO* when you are finished.

Goal: 13 *gwam*

wordwrap	*gwam* 1'	2'
Drill practice is a good thing to do to help with	10	5
speed and control. To get the most out of practice,	20	10
use the drills that help with the most common	30	15
problems. Finger and row drills are often used. Work	40	20
is often needed with the first, second, third, and	50	25
fourth fingers and rows. Work on the use of the shift	61	31
for capital letters as needed.	67	34
Work with double letters and letters next to each	10	39
other, as these letters often cause problems in	20	43
words. Spacing can also be a major concern, so	29	48
practice in the use of the space bar will help. Be	39	53
sure to review the required drills, and work on what	50	59
seems to help the most.	54	61

1'	1	2	3	4	5	6	7	8	9	10
2'	1		2		3		4		5	

To insert WordArt:

Insert/Text/WordArt

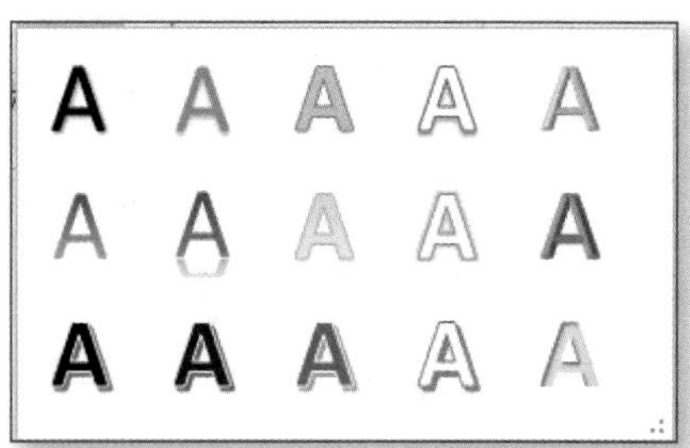

1. Click WordArt to display the WordArt gallery.
2. Preview and select the desired option.
3. Select the text in the text box that displays and replace it with your text.
4. Size and position the WordArt as desired.

WordArt can be formatted using the tools on the Drawing Tools Format tab.

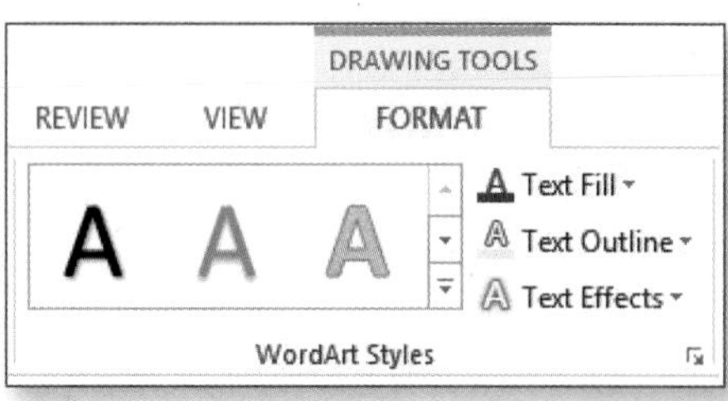

- *Styles*—can be changed to any style in the gallery.
- *Text Fill*—used to add color or change the color of the interior of the letters.
- *Text Outline*—used to change the color, style, or weight of the lines of the exterior border of the letters.
- *Text Effects*—add depth or emphasis to text. See Text Effects and Transform options below.

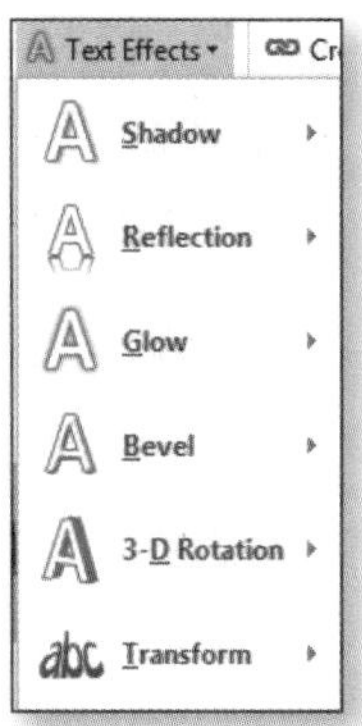

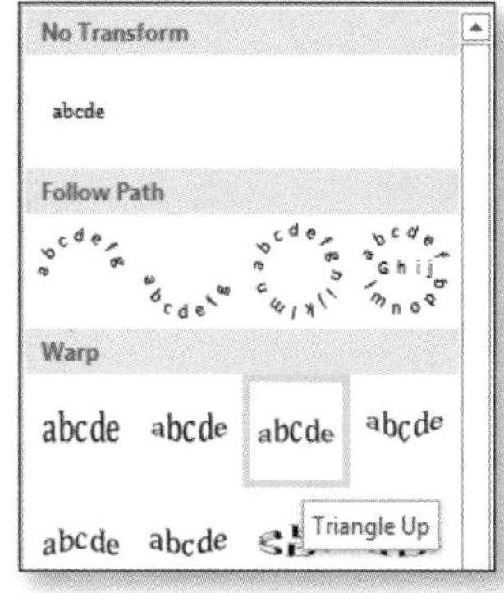

To apply WordArt formats:

Drawing Tools Format/WordArt Styles/Text Fill, Text Outline, Text Effects, or WordArt Styles

1. To change to a new WordArt style, preview and click the desired style.
2. To change Text Fill, Text Outline, or Text Effects, select the text, click the appropriate drop-list arrow, and select the desired color, line, or effect.

DRILL 3 WORDART

1. Display the WordArt gallery and select Fill – Black Text 1, Outline – Background 1, Hard Shadow – Background 1, and key **Happy Birthday to You!**
2. Select the text and apply Dark Red Standard Color fill.
3. Apply text effects: Art Deco Bevel (last icon) and Triangle Up Transform.
4. Size 1.5" high and 5.5" wide, and position in Top Center with Square Text Wrapping.
5. Compare your document to the Quick Check on the next page.
6. Preview and click Next Activity. (*51-drill3*)

Lesson 10 Z, Y, Quotation Mark, Tab

Warmup *Lesson 10a Warmup*

all letters	1	Quill owed those back taxes after moving to Japan.
spacing	2	Didn't Vi, Max, and Quaid go? Someone did; I know.
q/v/m	3	Marv was quite quick to remove that mauve lacquer.
easy	4	Lana is a neighbor; she owns a lake and an island.

New Keys

10b Learn z and y

© Cengage Learning

z Reach *down* with *left fourth* finger.

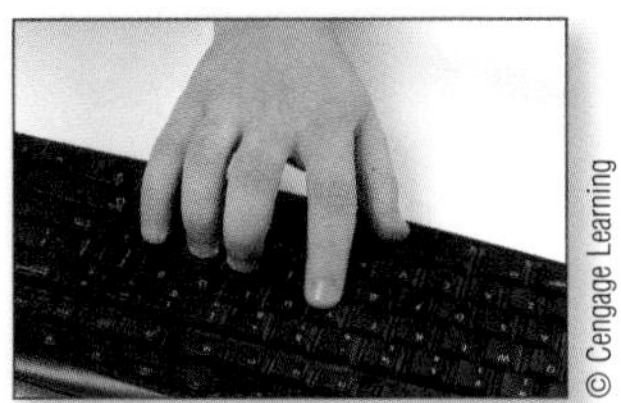

© Cengage Learning

y Reach *up* with *right first* finger.

Curve the little finger tightly to reach down and in for the z key.

z

5 za za zap zap zing zig zag zoo zed zip zap zig zed
6 doze zeal zero haze jazz zone zinc zing size ozone
7 ooze maze doze zoom zarf zebus daze gaze faze adze

y

8 y yj yj jay jay hay hay lay nay say days eyes ayes
9 yj ye yet yen yes cry dry you rye sty your fry wry
10 ye yen bye yea coy yew dye yaw lye yap yak yon any

10c All Reaches Learned

11 Did you say Liz saw any yaks or zebus at your zoo?
12 Relax; Jake wouldn't acquire any favorable rights.
13 Has Zack departed? Alex, Joy, and I will go alone.

10d Textbook Keying

Key each line once.

	14	Cecilia brings my jumbo umbrella to every concert.
direct reach	15	John and Kim recently brought us an old art piece.
	16	I built a gray brick border around my herb garden.
	17	sa ui hj gf mn vc ew uy re io as lk rt jk df op yu
Adjacent reach	18	In Ms. Lopez' opinion, the opera was really great.
	19	Polly and I were joining Walker at the open house.

ADD SHAPES

Each SmartArt diagram offers a few shapes by default. You can add more shapes by tapping ENTER after the last entry or from the SmartArt Tools Design tab.

To add shapes to SmartArt:

SmartArt Tools Design/Create Graphic/Add Shape

TIP

The options available on the Add Shape list depend on the type of diagram you are working with.

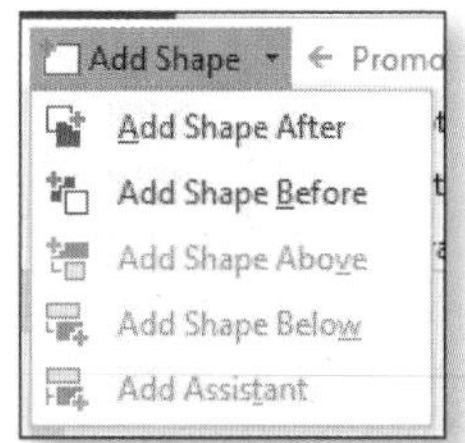

1. Click in the shape before or after which you want to add another shape.
2. Follow the path to add a shape, or click the drop-list arrow and select an option from the Add Shape options.
3. Repeat the process until you have as many shapes as you need in the layout.

DRILL 2 ADD SHAPES

1. Apply Organic theme and key **Effective Decision Making**; apply Title style and tap ENTER twice.
2. Insert a Block Cycle from the SmartArt Cycle category; add a shape after the last shape.
3. Key the text in the text pane.
4. Compare to the Quick Check and click Next activity. (*51-drill2*)

Identify decision to be made
Determine options
Analyze options
Select best option
Implement option
Evaluate decision

Compare your document to the illustration shown below.

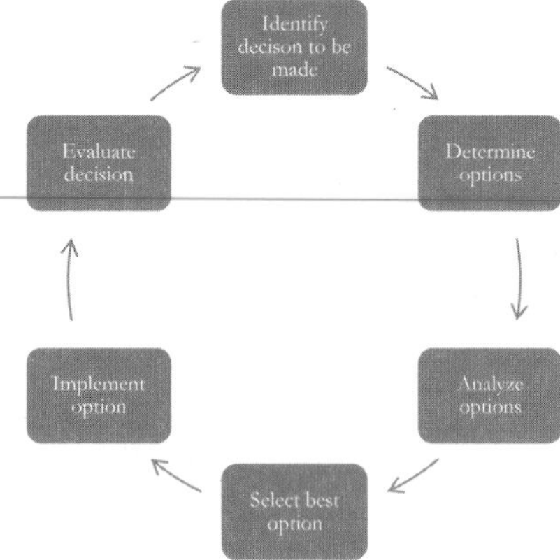

WORDART

WordArt adds special effects to text to make it more interesting. It is typically used in announcements, flyers, newsletters, and other casual documents.

New Keys

10e Learn " (quotation mark) and TAB

© Cengage Learning

" Shift; then reach to the *right* with the *right fourth* finger.

© Cengage Learning

TAB Reach *up* with *left fourth* finger.

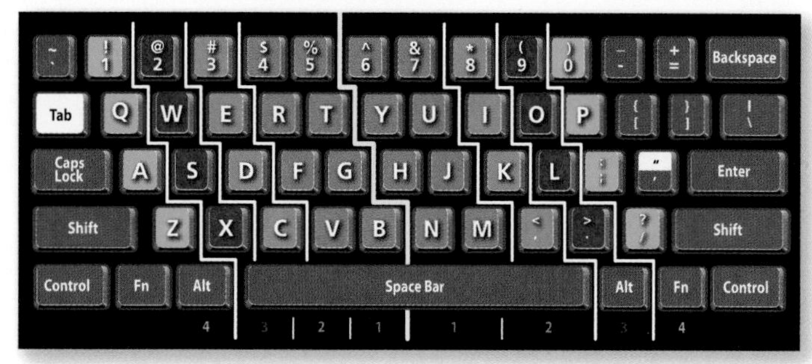

" (quotation mark)

20 ": ": " " "web" "media" "videos" I like "texting."

21 "I am not," she said, "going." I just said, "Why?"

TAB key

22 The tab key is used for indenting paragraphs and aligning columns.

23 Tabs that are set by the software are called default tabs, which are usually a half inch.

Skill Building

10f Textbook Keying

Key each line once. Tap TAB to indent each paragraph. Use wordwrap, tapping ENTER only at the end of each paragraph.

24 The expression "I give you my word," or put another
25 way, "Take my word for it," is just a way I can say, "I
26 prize my name; it clearly stands in back of my words."
27 I offer "honor" as collateral.

tab 28 Tap the tab key and begin the line without a pause to maintain fluency.

29 She said that this is the lot to be sent; I agreed with her.

30 Tap Tab before starting to key a timed writing so that the first line is indented.

10g Timed Writing

1. Take two 1' timed writings. If you finish before time is up, begin again.
2. End the lesson and log out of *KPDO*.

Goal: 15 *gwam*

wordwrap *gwam* 1'

Tab → All of us work for progress, but it is not 9
always easy to analyze "progress." We work hard for 19
it; but, in spite of some really good efforts, we may 29
fail to get just exactly the response we want. 39

Tab → When this happens, as it does to all of us, it 9
is time to cease whatever we are doing, have a quiet 20
talk with ourselves, and face up to the questions 29
about our limited progress. How can we do better? 39

| 1 | 2 | 3 | 4 | 5 | 6 | 7 | 8 | 9 | 10 |

If desired, apply a document theme so that the SmartArt layout will use the appropriate colors of the theme.

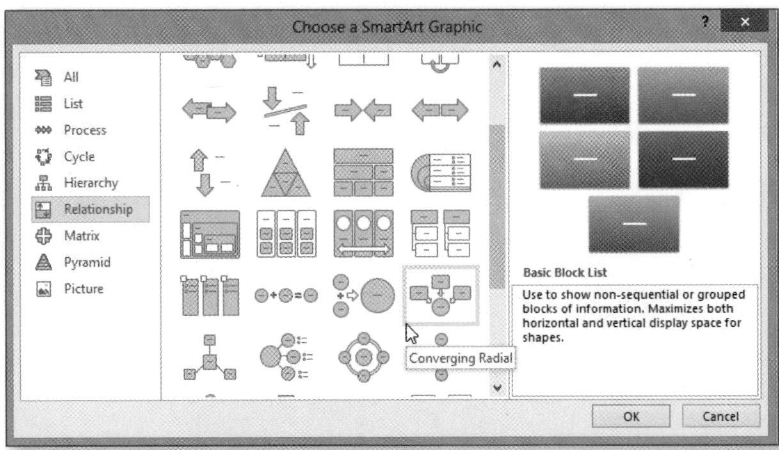

The Text Pane options adjust to match each layout. If the text pane is not displayed, follow the path and click Text Pane.

SmartArt Tools Design/ Create Graphic/Text Pane

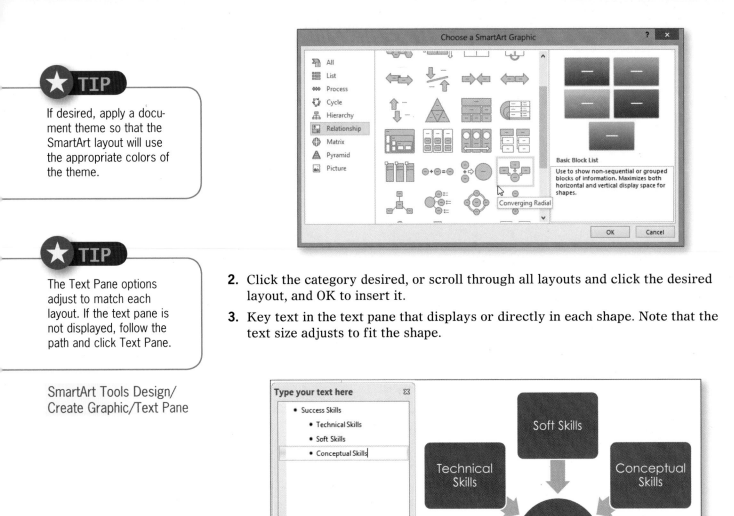

2. Click the category desired, or scroll through all layouts and click the desired layout, and OK to insert it.
3. Key text in the text pane that displays or directly in each shape. Note that the text size adjusts to fit the shape.

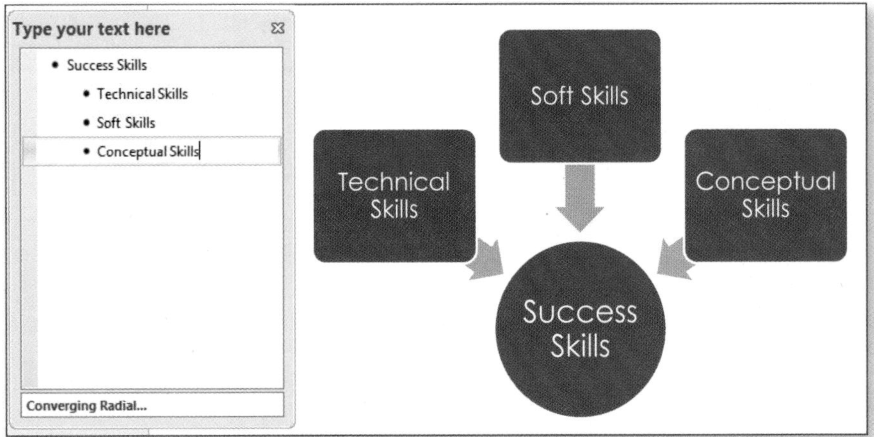

DRILL 1 SMARTART

1. In a new document, apply Ion theme and insert a SmartArt Converging Radial from the Relationship category.
2. Key the text shown at the right in the shapes using the Text pane.
3. Compare your solution to the illustration above; click Next Activity. (*51-drill1*)

Success Skills
    Technical Skills
    Soft Skills
    Conceptual Skills

Lesson 11 Review

Warmup *Lesson 11a Warmup*

alphabet 1 Zeb had Jewel quickly give him five or six points.

" (quote) 2 Can you spell "chaos," "bias," "bye," and "their"?

y 3 Ty Clay may envy you for any zany plays you write.

easy 4 Did he bid on the bicycle, or did he bid on a map?

Skill Building

11b Improve Keystroking

Work for smoothness, not speed.

5 za za zap az az maze zoo zip razz zed zax zoa zone

6 Liz Zahl saw Zoe feed the zebra in an Arizona zoo.

7 yj yj jy jy joy lay yaw say yes any yet my try you

8 Why do you say that today, Thursday, is my payday?

9 xs xs sax ox box fix hex ax lax fox taxi lox sixes

10 Roxy, you may ask Jay to fix any tax sets for you.

11 qa qa aqua quail quit quake quid equal quiet quart

12 Did Enrique quietly but quickly quell the quarrel?

13 fv fv five lives vow ova van eve avid vex vim void

14 Has Vivi, Vada, or Eva visited Vista Valley Farms?

11c Build Skill

Key balanced-hand words quickly and as phrases to increase speed.

15 is to for do an may work so it but an with them am

16 am yam map aid zig yams ivy via vie quay cob amend

17 to do is for an may work so it but am an with them

18 for it|for it|to the|to the|do they|do they|do it

19 Pamela may go to the farm with Jan and a neighbor.

20 Rod and Ty may go by the lake if they go downtown.

Lesson 51 SmartArt and WordArt

New Commands

- Insert SmartArt
- SmartArt Design Tools
- SmartArt Layout Tools
- Add Text to SmartArt
- Add Shapes
- Insert WordArt
- Format WordArt

KPDO **Warmup** *Lesson 51a Warmup*

Skill Building

51b Textbook Keying

1. Key each line once, concentrating on using good keying techniques.
2. Repeat the drill if time permits.

1st row
1 Max, Zam, and a local man saw an amazing cave on a long bus ride.
2 Janna came back home six times to visit the bat caves at the zoo.

3rd row
3 We wrote Terry to try to get a quote; Perry tried to get a quote.
4 Perry peeped at Terry's quote; were you there with Perry or Pete?

home row
5 Kala was glad Alyssa sold a glass flask at a gala sale in Dallas.
6 Jack Hall's dad was in Dallas at a glass sale; a sad lad saw him.

one hand
7 Jimmy saw him carve a great pumpkin; John deserved better awards.
8 Nikki saved a million as a minimum reserve on debt; Jimmy agreed.

balanced hand
9 Jamale Rodney, a neighbor, and Sydney may go to the lake by auto.
10 Bud got the tub of big worms to go to the dock to fish with them.

New Commands

51c

SMARTART

SmartArt consists of predesigned diagrams that help to simplify complex concepts. Note in the SmartArt graphic dialog box that SmartArt layouts are grouped into eight categories. You can view all of the layouts or the layouts in one category.

To insert and add text to SmartArt:
Insert/Illustrations/SmartArt

1. Position the insertion point where you want to add the graphic, and click SmartArt to open the Choose a SmartArt Graphic dialog box shown on the next page. Categories of SmartArt are listed on the left, layouts for each category display in the center, and the preview and description of the appropriate use appear in the right pane.

(continued)

11d Textbook Keying

Key each line once.

Key smoothly without looking at fingers.

```
      21 Make the return snappily
      22 and with assurance; keep
enter 23 your eyes on your source
      24 data; maintain a smooth,
      25 constant pace as you key.
```

© Cengage Learning

When spacing, use a down-and-in motion.

```
space bar 26 us me it of he an by do go to us if or so am ah el
          27 To enter the website, key "Guest" as the password.
```

Press Caps Lock key to toggle on or off.

```
caps lock 28 Use ALL CAPS for items such as TO, FROM, or SUBJECT.
          29 Did Kristin mean Kansas City, MISSOURI, or KANSAS?
```

11e Timed Writing

1. Take two 1' timed writings. If you finish before time is up, begin again. The dot above words represents 2 *gwam*.
2. End the lesson.

Goal: 16 *gwam*

wordwrap

	gwam 1'	2'
Have we thought of communication as a kind	8	4
of war that we wage through each day?	16	8
When we think of it that way, good language	24	12
would seem to become our major line of attack.	34	17
Words become muscle; in a normal exchange or in	43	22
a quarrel, we do well to realize the power of words.	53	27

11f Game

Use the game to showcase your skills.

11g Enrichment

1. Click the Skill Building tab from the main menu and choose Technique Builder; select Drill 1a.
2. Key Drill 1a from page 37. Key each line once, striving for good accuracy.
3. The results will be listed on the Skill Building Report.

   - b. Size the clip 2.4" high and use the Center command on the Home tab to center it.
6. Insert the *closed for work focus* and the *open for interaction* picture data files on the line below the last paragraph.
   - a. Compress both pictures; accept the defaults.
   - b. Size both pictures 2.4" high and apply Square Text Wrapping.
   - c. Position the *closed for work focus* picture on the left and the *open for interaction* picture on the right.
7. Number the pages on the top of the page using Plain Number 3. Do not show the number on the first page.
8. Preview and proofread the document carefully. Check the position of the photos against the illustration below.
9. Check and select Next Activity. (*50-d1*)

50-d2

Document with Page Border

1. Open *50-d1* and apply a box page border.
2. Use a single line style with Dark Blue – Accent 1 theme color and 1-point line width.
3. Apply to the whole document.
4. Preview, check, and exit *Word.*
5. Click Log out to exit *KPDO*. (*50-d2*)

The illustration on the left shows *50-d1* page 1 (photo may vary); the one on the right shows *50-d2* page 2 (with the border).

Open vs. Closed Office Environments

Finding the Right Balance

For several decades, the trend has been to move from the traditional closed office to an open office environment. Rather than continuing the debate on which is better, searching for a workable balance may be a better approach. Obviously, both settings have advantages and disadvantages. The right balance would maximize the advantages and minimize the disadvantages of each.

Closed Office

Employees often think of the closed office as the power or image office. Clearly, offices with walls and a door offer more privacy, fewer interruptions, and better noise control. At the same time, they are more expensive and are not as conducive to open communication and teamwork.

Open Office

Employees often call it *Cubicle Village* because of the large number of cubicles and lack of walls and doors. Defining what the open office looks like is difficult because the look varies widely. Most people think of the open office as being in a setting similar to the illustration below.

The advantages are putting more people in less space at a lower cost and making employees more accessible to each other, thereby enabling open communication and enhancing team work.

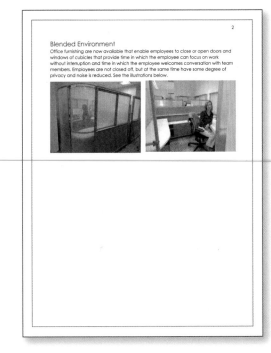

2

Blended Environment

Office furnishing are now available that enable employees to close or open doors and windows of cubicles that provide time in which the employee can focus on work without interruption and time in which the employee welcomes conversation with team members. Employees are not closed off, but at the same time have some degree of privacy and noise is reduced. See the illustrations below.

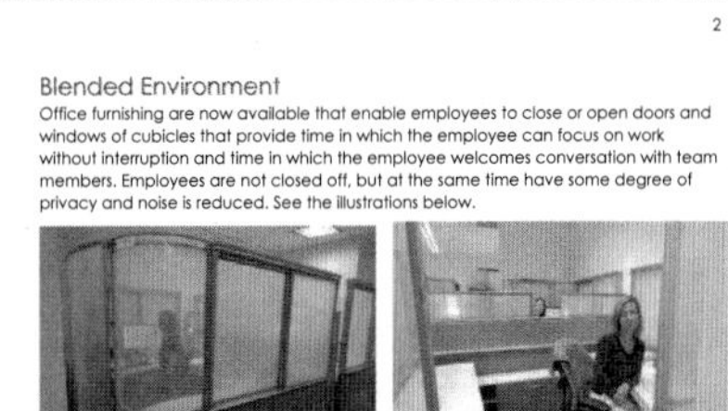

Warmup *Lesson 12a Warmup*

alphabet	1	Jack won five quiz games; Brad will play him next.
q	2	Quin Racq quickly and quietly quelled the quarrel.
z	3	Zaret zipped along sizzling, zigzag Arizona roads.
easy	4	Did he hang the sign by the big bush at the lake?

Skill Building

12b Improve Keystroking

b/f	5	bf bf fab fab ball bib rf rf rib rib fibs bums bee
	6	Did Buffy remember that he is a brass band member?
z/y	7	za za zag zig zip yj yj jay eye day lazy hazy zest
	8	Liz amazed us with the zesty pizza on a lazy trip.
q/u	9	qa qa quo qt. quit quay quad quarm que uj jug quay
	10	Where is Quito? Qatar? Boqueirao? Quebec? Quilmes?
v/m	11	vf vf valve five value mj mj ham mad mull mass vim
	12	Vito, enter the words vim, vivace, and avar; save.
all	13	I faced defeat; only reserves saved my best crews.
	14	In my opinion, I need to rest in my reserved seat.
all	15	Holly created a red poppy and deserves art awards.
	16	My pump averages a faster rate; we get better oil.

Keep fingers curved and body aligned properly.

12c Textbook Keying

Key each line once.

de/ed	17	ed fed led deed dell dead deal sled desk need seed
	18	Dell dealt with the deed before the dire deadline.
ol/lo	19	old tolls doll solo look sole lost love cold stole
	20	Old Ole looked for the long lost olive oil lotion.
op/po	21	pop top post rope pout port stop opal opera report
	22	Stop to read the top opera opinion report to Opal.
we/ew	23	we few wet were went wears weather skews stew blew
	24	Working women wear sweaters when weather dictates.

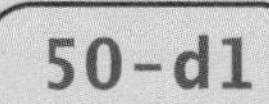

Apply It

50-d1

Document with Graphics

closed for work focus
open for interaction

1. Tap ENTER three times and key the title.
2. Key the report shown below and then apply the formats listed after the report.

Open vs. Closed Office Environments

Finding the Right Balance

For several decades, the trend has been to move from the traditional closed office to an open office environment. Rather than continuing the debate on which is better, searching for a workable balance may be a better approach. Obviously, both settings have advantages and disadvantages. The right balance would maximize the advantages and minimize the disadvantages of each.

Closed Office

Employees often think of the closed office as the power or image office. Clearly, offices with walls and a door offer more privacy, fewer interruptions, and better noise control. At the same time, they are more expensive and are not as conducive to open communication and teamwork.

Open Office

Employees often call it *Cubicle Village* because of the large number of cubicles and lack of walls and doors. Defining what the open office looks like is difficult because the look varies widely. Most people think of the open office as being in a setting similar to the illustration below.

The advantages are putting more people in less space at a lower cost and making employees more accessible to each other, thereby enabling open communication and enhancing teamwork.

Blended Environment

Office furnishings are now available that enable employees to close or open doors and windows of cubicles that provide time in which the employee can focus on work without interruption and time in which the employee welcomes conversation with team members. Employees are not closed off, but at the same time have some degree of privacy and noise is reduced. See the illustrations below.

3. Apply the Slice theme.
4. Apply Title style to the title, Subtitle style to the subtitle, and Heading 1 to the three headings. Decrease the title font size to fit on one line.
5. Use the Online Pictures command and the keywords *busy cubicles* to search for clip art illustrating an office. See the Quick Check on the next page.
   a. Tap ENTER after the first paragraph under the *Open Office* heading and insert the clip that is located.

(continued)

12d Textbook Keying

Key each line once.

Keep hands quiet; do not bounce. Keep fingers curved and upright.

25 a for we you is that be this will be a to and well
26 as our with I or a to by your form which all would
27 new year no order they so new but now year who may

28 This is Lyn's only date to visit their great city.
29 I can send it to your office at any time you wish.
30 She kept the fox, owls, and fowl down by the lake.

31 Harriette will cook dinner for the swimming teams.
32 Annette will call at noon to give us her comments.
33 Johnny was good at running and passing a football.

12e Timed Writing

1. Take a 2' timed writing. If you finish before time is up, begin again.
2. Use wordwrap.
3. End the lesson.

Goal: 16 *gwam*

Copy Difficulty

What factors determine whether copy is difficult or easy? Research shows that difficulty is influenced by syllables per word, characters per word, and percent of familiar words. Carefully controlling these three factors ensures that speed and accuracy scores are reliable—that is, increased scores reflect increased skill.

In Level 1, all timings are easy. Note "E" inside the triangle at left of the timing. Easy timings contain an average of 1.2 syllables per word, 5.1 characters per word, and 90 percent familiar words. Easy copy is suitable for the beginner who is mastering the keyboard.

E ALL LETTERS

	gwam 2'	
There should be no questions, no doubt, about	5	35
the value of being able to key; it's just a matter	10	40
of common sense that today a pencil is much too slow.	15	45
Let me explain. Work is done on a keyboard	19	49
three to six times faster than other writing and	24	54
with a product that is a prize to read. Don't you	29	59
agree?	29	60

2' | 1 | 2 | 3 | 4 | 5 |

12f Enrichment

1. Click the Skill Building tab, and choose Technique Builder; select Drill 1b.
2. Key Drill 1b from page 37. Key each line once, striving for good accuracy.
3. The results will be listed on the Skill Building Report.
4. Log out of *KPDO*.

PAGE BORDER

Page borders can be formatted using a variety of settings, styles, colors, and line widths. They can be applied to the whole document or to various sections of the document.

TIP

Note that the line color displayed is determined by the theme colors, or you can select a standard color.

To apply a page border:

Design/Page Background/Page Borders

1. Click Page Borders to display the Borders and Shading dialog box.
2. Make sure the Page Border tab is active.
3. Choose the desired setting, style, color, and width.
4. In the Apply to box, choose the desired option.

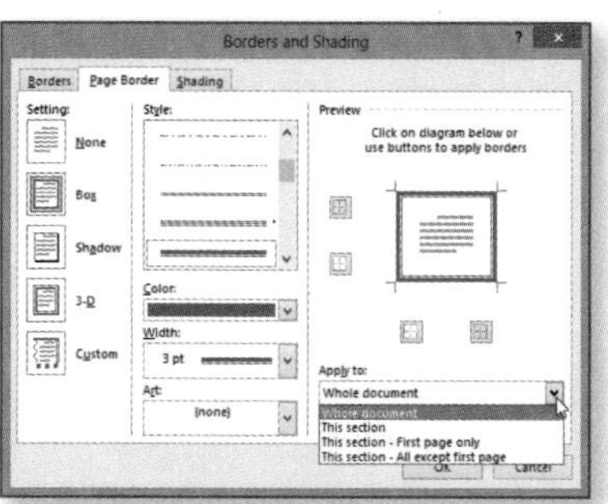

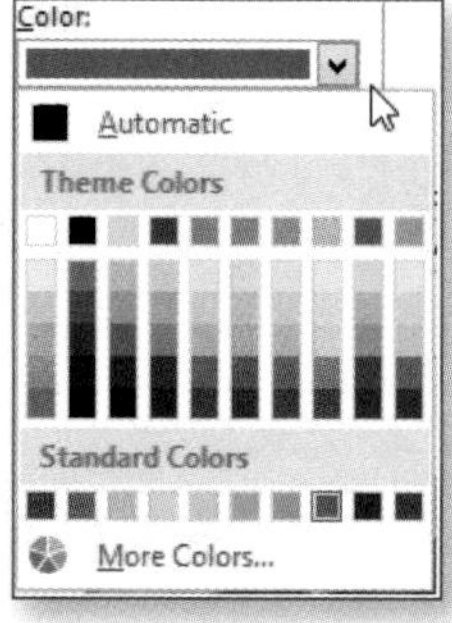

DRILL 5 PAGE BORDERS

1. Open *50-drill4* and apply a Box page border.
2. Choose the thick-and-thin line style, 3 pt. width shown in the illustration above.
3. Choose Standard Blue color.
4. Apply to the whole document.
5. Preview and select Next Activity. (*50-drill5*)

WORKPLACE SUCCESS

Elena Elisseeva/Shutterstock.com

Positive Attitude

What makes a successful employee? Employers say that "soft skills" are critical. A positive attitude is generally one of the top five soft skills required. Why? Because it enhances performance. People with positive attitudes tend to be problem solvers. They view problems as challenges with opportunities and find ways to solve them.

Self-confidence is also linked to a positive attitude. If you think you can do something, you are quite likely to do it. Workers with a poor self-image are more likely to look for faults than strengths.

Another important reason for developing a positive attitude is that other employees prefer to work with individuals who have a positive attitude. Most companies require employees to work on teams; thus, having a positive attitude enhances teamwork and contributes to the success of the team.

Lesson 13 Review

Warmup *Lesson 13a Warmup*

alphabet 1 Bev quickly hid two Japanese frogs in Mitzi's box.

shift 2 Jay Nadler, a Rotary Club member, wrote Mr. Coles.

, (comma) 3 Jay, Ed, and I paid for plates, knives, and forks.

easy 4 Did the amendment name a city auditor to the firm?

Skill Building

13b Textbook Keying

Key each line once.

Key short, familiar words as units.

5 is to for do an may work so it but an with them am

6 Did they mend the torn right half of their ensign?

7 Hand me the ivory tusk on the mantle by the bugle.

Key more difficult words by letter.

8 only state jolly zest oil verve join rate mop card

9 After defeat, look up; gaze in joy at a few stars.

10 We gazed at a plump beaver as it waded in my pool.

Use variable speed; your fingers will feel the difference.

11 it up so at for you may was but him work were they

12 It is up to you to get the best rate; do it right.

13 Sami greeted reporters as stars got ready at home.

13c Improve Keystroking

14 Pat appears happy to pay for any supper I prepare.

15 Knox can relax; Alex gets a box of flax next week.

16 Vi, Ava, and Viv move ivy vines, leaves, or stems.

17 It's a question of whether they can't or won't go.

18 Did Jane go? Did she see Sofia? Who paid? Did she?

19 Ms. E. K. Nu and Lt. B. A. Walz had the a.m. duty.

20 "Who are you?" he asked. "I am," I said, "Jayden."

21 Find a car; try it; like it; work a price; buy it.

ONLINE PICTURES

The Online Pictures command is used to access digital pictures and illustrations from sources other than your computer and your computer network. Note that some of the sources require you to set up an account if you do not already have one.

The free *Microsoft Live* account for your SkyDrive gives you access to Microsoft Web Apps.

The free Flickr account from Yahoo gives you access to the photo-sharing social media site. You can also access Flickr from a Facebook account.

To insert online pictures:

Insert/Illustrations/Online Pictures

1. Click Online Pictures to display the Online Pictures options. If you have used previous versions of *Word*, you will notice that Clip Art is now an online option.
2. Key the keywords in the search box to search for the desired clip or other picture.
3. Select the desired clip and double-click it or click Insert to insert the clip.

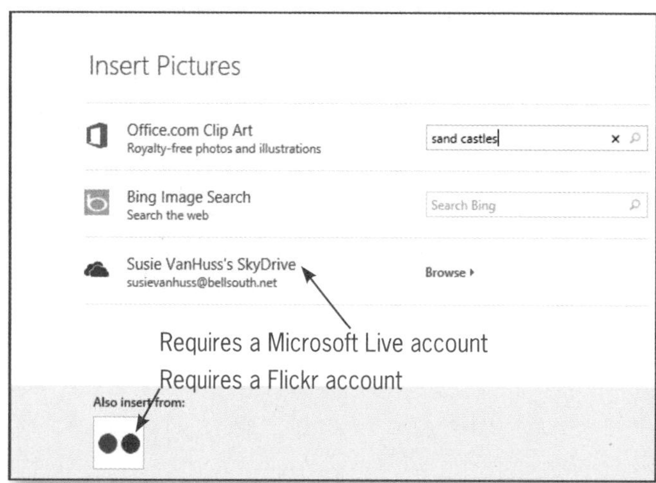

Note: You can format clip art and other online pictures and illustrations using the commands on the Picture Tools Format tab.

DRILL 4 INSERT AND FORMAT ONLINE PICTURES

1. In a new document, search *Office.com* clip art for *sand castles.*
2. Select the first picture shown above in the search results and insert it.
3. Size the picture 2.5" high, and apply Square Text Wrapping.
4. Move the picture to the right side of the page.
5. Crop the top of the picture to just above the flag.
6. Position the picture in the Middle Center with Square Text Wrapping.
7. Preview and check; click Next Activity. (*50-drill4*)

13d Textbook Keying

Key each line once.

© Cengage Learning

© Cengage Learning

Keep hands and arms still as you reach up to the third row and down to the first row.

t 22 at fat hat sat to tip the that they fast last slat
r 23 or red try ran run air era fair rid ride trip trap
t/r 24 A trainer sprained an arm trying to tame the bear.

m 25 am me my mine jam man more most dome month minimum
n 26 no an now nine once net knee name ninth know never
m/n 27 Many men and women are important company managers.

o 28 on or to not now one oil toil over only solo today
i 29 it is in tie did fix his sit like with insist will
o/i 30 Joni will consider obtaining options to buy coins.

a 31 at an as art has and any case data haze tart smart
s 32 us as so say sat slap lass class just sassy simple
a/s 33 Disaster was averted as the steamer sailed to sea.

e 34 we he ear the key her hear chef desire where there
i 35 it is in tie did fix his sit like with insist will
e/i 36 An expression of gratitude for service is desired.

13e Timed Writing

1. Take two 2' timed writings. If you finish before time is up, begin again.
2. End the lesson; log out of *KPDO*.

Goal: 16 *gwam*

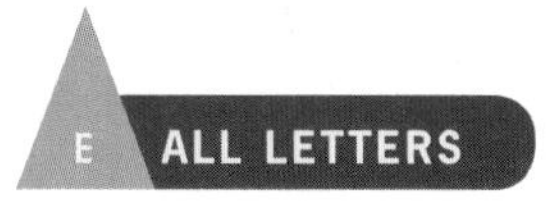

wordwrap	*gwam* 2'
Some people think that the first impression made	5
in the first few seconds is the best method to find	10
out what a person is like. Think of meeting friends	15
for the first time. Was this true of them? In some	20
cases, one might be correct in judging a person in a	26
few seconds. However, in most cases, one will find	31
that it takes more than the first meeting to know	36
what a person is like. But the first time meeting a	41
person could give some idea, often if a person does	46
not show good qualities. For example, one might see	51
poor speaking skills, improper dress, and poor	56
personal traits when meeting a person for the first	61
time.	62

2' | 1 | 2 | 3 | 4 | 5 |

To compress a picture:

Picture Tools Format/Adjust/Compress Pictures

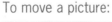

Compressing the picture reduces the file size; note that for email you can reduce the size even smaller.

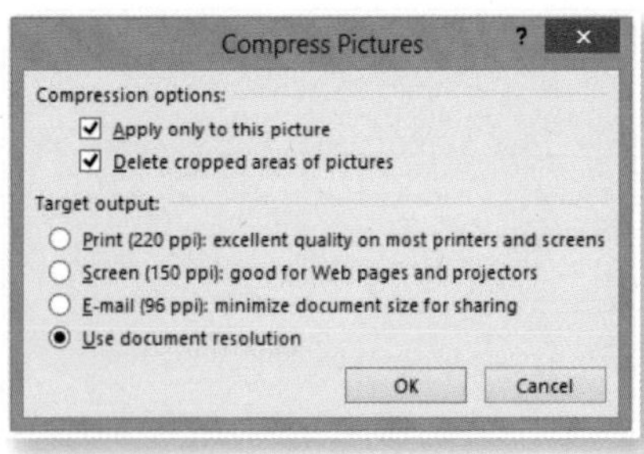

1. Select the picture and click Compress Pictures to display the Compress Pictures dialog box.
2. Note the options that are available; then click OK to accept the defaults.

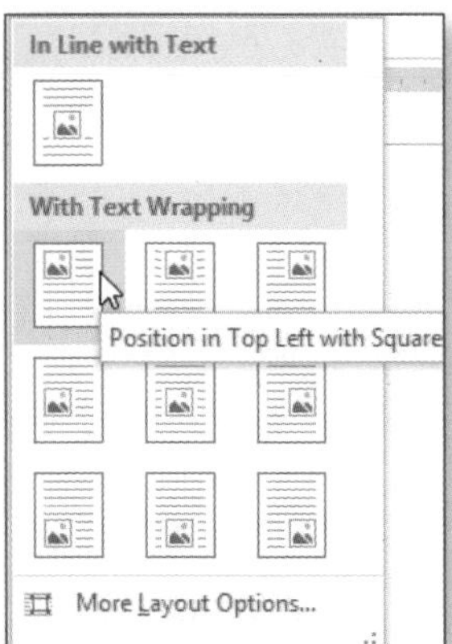

To move a picture:

Picture Tools Format/Arrange/Position

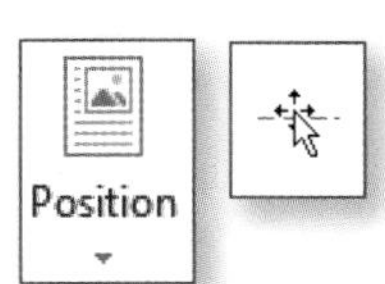

Pictures may be moved with the Position command or by dragging them with the mouse.

1. To position a picture, select the picture and click Position to display the position options.
2. Select the desired position as shown to the right. -or-
3. To move a picture with the mouse, select it and hover over the picture until the mouse turns to a four-headed arrow. Then drag the picture to the desired position.

Note that the default for wrapping text is In Line with Text as shown by the red arrow in the illustration.

To wrap text:

Picture Tools Format/Arrange/Wrap Text

Wrap Text determines how text wraps around a selected object, such as a picture. Wrap Text can be applied by using the Layout Options button that displays when a picture is selected or by using the Wrap Text command.

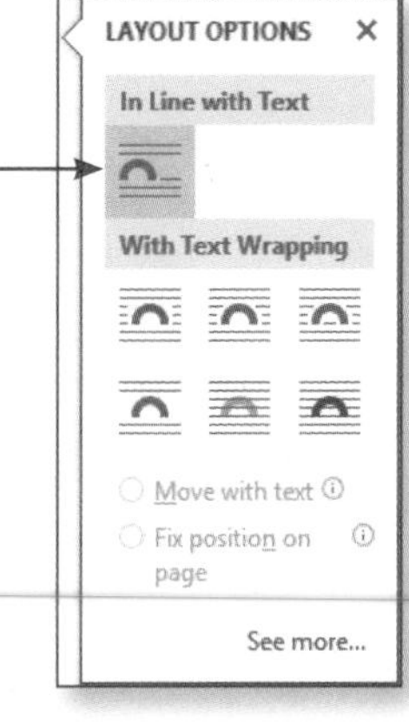

1. Select the picture and then click Layout Options button or the Wrap Text drop-list arrow to display the options.
2. Select the desired option, such as Square or Tight as shown on the right.

DRILL 3 FORMAT PICTURE

format pictures

1. With *format pictures* data file open, read the information in the document, and then complete the five numbered steps.
2. Preview and check; click Next Activity. (*50-drill3*)

StockLite/Shutterstock.com

Skill Builder 1

Skill Building *Technique Builder*

From the Skill Building tab, select Technique Builder and then the drill. Key each line once at a comfortable rate. Tap ENTER at the end of each line. Single-space the drill. Concentrate and key accurately. Repeat if desired.

DRILL 1

Goal: reinforce key locations

Key each line once at a comfortable, constant rate.

© Cengage Learning

TECHNIQUE TIP

Keep
- your eyes on source copy
- your fingers curved, upright
- your wrists low but not touching
- your elbows hanging loosely
- your feet flat on the floor

Drill 1a

A We saw that Alan had an alabaster vase in Alabama.
B My rubber boat bobbed about in the bubbling brook.
C Ceci gave cups of cold cocoa to Rebecca and Rocco.
D Don's dad added a second deck to his old building.
E Even as Ellen edited her document, she ate dinner.
F Our firm in Buffalo has a staff of forty or fifty.
G Ginger is giving Greg the eggs she got from Helga.
H Hugh has eighty high, harsh lights he might flash.

Drill 1b

I Irik's lack of initiative is irritating his coach.
J Judge J. J. Jore rejected Jeane and Jack's jargon.
K As a lark, Kirk kicked back a rock at Kim's kayak.
L Lucille is silly; she still likes lemon lollipops.
M Milt Mumm hammered a homer in the Miami home game.
N Ken Linn has gone hunting; Stan can begin canning.
O Jon Soto rode off to Otsego in an old Morgan auto.
P Philip helped pay the prize as my puppy hopped up.
Q Quiet Raquel quit quoting at an exquisite marquee.

Drill 1c

R As Mrs. Kerr's motor roared, her red horse reared.
S Sissie lives in Mississippi; Lissa lives in Tulsa.
T Nat told Betty not to tattle on her little sister.
U Ula has a unique but prudish idea on unused units.
V Eva visited every vivid event for twelve evenings.
W We watched as wayworn wasps swarmed by the willow.
X Tex Cox waxed the next box for Xenia and Rex Knox.
Y Ty says you may stay with Fay for only sixty days.
Z Hazel is puzzled about the azure haze; Zack dozes.

To size pictures:

Picture Tools Format/Size/Height or Width Arrows

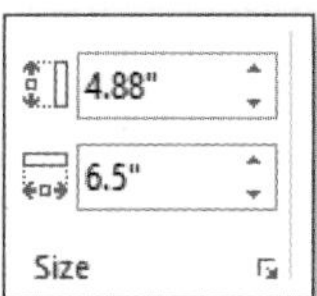

Pictures can be sized or cropped. Cropping removes unwanted portions of the picture. The file size of a picture can be reduced by compressing it.

1. To change the size of a picture, select it and use the height or width arrows to increase or decrease the size. -or-
2. Select the picture, position the mouse over the sizing handles; when the pointer turns to a double-headed arrow, drag to the size desired.

You can drag the square handle on the side of a picture or other graphic to size the image, but you will distort its size. Always drag a corner handle to maintain the clip's proportion.

To crop pictures:

Picture Tools Format/Size/Crop

1. To crop one side of a picture, click Crop and drag the cropping handle on the side inward. The cropping line will illustrate what will be cut off.
2. To crop the same amount on two sides, press CTRL while you drag the handle.
3. To finish, click off the picture.

DRILL 2 SIZE PICTURE

1. Open *50-drill1*; size the picture to 2.5" high.
2. Crop the picture to focus only on the sand castles as shown above.
3. Click off the picture to finish it; then size it to 2" high.
4. Preview and check; click Next Activity. (*50-drill2*)

DRILL 2

Goal: strengthen up and down reaches

Keep hands and wrists quiet; fingers well curved in home position; stretch fingers up from home or pull them palmward as needed.

home position

1 Hall left for Dallas; he is glad Jake fed his dog.
2 Ada had a glass flask; Jake had a sad jello salad.
3 Lana Hask had a sale; Gala shall add half a glass.

down reaches

4 Did my banker, Mr. Mavann, analyze my tax account?
5 Do they, Mr. Zack, expect a number of brave women?
6 Zach, check the menu; next, beckon the lazy valet.

up reaches

7 Prue truly lost the quote we wrote for our report.
8 Teresa quietly put her whole heart into her words.
9 There were two hilarious jokes in your quiet talk.

DRILL 3

Goal: strengthen individual finger reaches

1st finger

1 Bob Mugho hunted for five minutes for your number.
2 Juan hit the bright green turf with his five iron.
3 The frigates and gunboats fought mightily in Java.

2nd finger

4 Dick said the ice on the creek had surely cracked.
5 Even as we picnicked, I decided we needed to diet.
6 Kim, not Mickey, had rice with chicken for dinner.

3rd/4th finger

7 Pam saw Roz wax an aqua auto as Lex sipped a cola.
8 Wally will quickly spell Zeus, Apollo, and Xerxes.
9 Who saw Polly? Pax Zais saw her; she is quiet now.

DRILL 4

Goal: strengthen special reaches

Emphasize smooth stroking. Avoid pauses, but do not reach for speed.

adjacent reaches

1 Falk knew well that her opinions of art were good.
2 Theresa answered her question; order was restored.
3 We join there and walk north to the western point.

direct reaches

4 Barb Nunn must hunt for my checks; she is in debt.
5 In June and December, Irvin hunts in Bryce Canyon.
6 We decided to carve a number of funny human faces.

double letters

7 Anne stopped off at school to see Bill Wiggs cook.
8 Edd has planned a small cookout for all the troop.
9 Keep adding to my assets all fees that will apply.

| 1 | 2 | 3 | 4 | 5 | 6 | 7 | 8 | 9 | 10 |

New Commands

50c

LEARNING ABOUT GRAPHICS

Many different types of graphics can be used to enhance documents. Typically, graphics are used in documents such as announcements, invitations, flyers, brochures, reports, and newsletters. However, they can be used in virtually any type of document to enhance the document and to clarify or simplify concepts. For example, a picture may convey a concept that would take many words to describe adequately. It is important to use graphics strategically and not to overuse them. The overuse of graphics can be distracting to the reader.

PICTURES

Word provides two different commands to insert pictures based on the source of the picture. The Pictures button enables you to insert pictures from your computer or other computers on your network. The Online Pictures button enables you to insert pictures from Microsoft Clip Art, from web searches, your SkyDrive, or from Flickr—a photo-sharing social media site.

To insert pictures from your computer:

Insert/Illustrations/Pictures

1. Click at the position you wish to insert a picture and then click Pictures to display the Insert Pictures dialog box.
2. Browse through your files of digital pictures and select the one you wish to insert.
3. Double-click the picture or click the Insert button at the bottom of the dialog box to insert it.

Note that the size of the picture varies, but it is usually large.

DRILL 1 INSERT PICTURE

sand castles

1. In a new document, insert the *sand castles* picture from your data files.
2. Preview and check; click next activity. (*50-drill1*)

FORMAT PICTURES

Pictures are formatted using the tools on the Format tab that displays when you select a picture. These tools are used in a similar manner to the way you used Table tools in Module 5. Note that when you click the Picture Tools Format tab, the Ribbon displays with four groups of commands used to format pictures: Adjust, Picture Styles, Arrange, and Size. Remember you must select a picture before you apply any format.

DRILL 5

Goal: improve troublesome pairs

Use a controlled rate without pauses.

1 ad add did does dish down body dear dread dabs bad
d/k 2 kid ok kiss tuck wick risk rocks kayaks corks buck
3 Dirk asked Dick to kid Drake about the baked duck.

4 deed deal den led heed made needs delay he she her
e/i 5 kit kiss kiln kiwi kick kilt kind six ribs kill it
6 Abie had neither ice cream nor fried rice in Erie.

7 fib fob fab rib beg bug rob bad bar bed born table
b/v 8 vat vet gave five ever envy never visit weave ever
9 Vic and Bev gave five very big baby beds to a vet.

10 aft after lift gift sit tot the them tax tutu tyro
t/r 11 for far ere era risk rich rock rosy work were roof
12 In Toronto, Ruth told the truth about her artwork.

13 jug just jury judge juice unit hunt bonus quiz bug
u/y 14 jay joy lay you your only envy quay oily whey body
15 Willy usually does not buy your Yukon art in July.

DRILL 6

Goal: fluency

1 Dian may make cocoa for the girls when they visit.
2 Focus the lens for the right angle; fix the prism.
3 She may suspend work when she signs the torn form.
4 Augment their auto fuel in the keg by the autobus.
5 As usual, their robot did half turns to the right.
6 Pamela laughs as she signals to the big hairy dog.
7 Pay Vivian to fix the island for the eighty ducks.

DRILL 7

Goal: eyes on the copy

Option: In the Word Processor, set the Timer for Variable and then either 20" or 30". Choose a *gwam* goal that is two to three words higher than your best rate. Try to reach your goal.

	words 30"	20"
1 Did she make this turkey dish? **ENTER**	12	18
2 Blake and Laurie may go to Dubuque.	14	21
3 Signal for the oak sleigh to turn right.	16	24
4 I blame Susie; did she quench the only flame?	18	27
5 She turns the panel dials to make this robot work.	20	30

MODULE 7

Graphics

Lesson 50 *Pictures and Online Pictures*
Lesson 51 *SmartArt and WordArt*
Lesson 52 *Documents with Columns*
Lesson 53 *Palmetto Event Solutions, Inc.*

LEARNING OUTCOMES

- Learn and apply essential *Word 2013* commands.
- Create documents with pictures, clip art, SmartArt, WordArt, and borders.
- Create documents with equal-width columns and graphics.
- Build keyboarding skills.

Lesson 50 Pictures and Online Pictures

New Commands

- Insert Pictures
- Picture Tools Format
- Size Pictures
- Crop Pictures
- Compress Pictures
- Wrap Text
- Position Pictures
- Insert Online Pictures
- Page Borders

Warmup *Lesson 50a Warmup*

Skill Building

50b Timed Writing

1. Key a 1' timed writing on each paragraph; work to increase speed.
2. Key a 3' timed writing on both paragraphs.

Most of us know that having a good professional image can help us to create a good first impression when we meet people. The same general principle applies to the letters, memos, reports, and other documents that we prepare and send to our business associates, clients, or customers. The way that a document appears when the recipient opens it and looks at it makes either a good or a bad first impression.

The quality and the organization of the content are very important when a document is examined in detail, but they are not the factors that create the first impression. The general appearance does that. The judicious use of color and certain types of graphics can create a good visual impact, but using too much color or the wrong type of color or graphic can do just the opposite.

Any timed writing in the book can be completed using the Timed Writing feature.

TO USE THE TIMED WRITING FEATURE:

1. From the Timed Writings tab, select the timed writing.
2. Select the source and the timing length. For example,
   - Select Paragraph 1 and 1'. Key paragraph 1; if you finish before time is up, repeat the same paragraph. Always use wordwrap when keying timed writings.
   - Select Paragraph 2 and 1'. Key paragraph 2; repeat the same paragraph if you finish before time is up.
   - Select Entire Writing and 2'. Try to maintain your 1' rate. If you finish before time is up, start over, beginning with paragraph 1.
3. Timings save automatically.
4. The Timed Writing Report displays the results of the last 40 timed writings and the best 3 timings at each timing length (1', 2', 3').

Goal: build staying power

1. Key each paragraph as a 1' timing. Use wordwrap.
2. Key a 2' timing on both paragraphs. Use wordwrap.

Writing 1: 18 *gwam* — *gwam* 2'

Why spend weeks with some problem when just a few quiet 6
minutes can help us to resolve it. 9

If we don't take time to think through a problem, it will 15
swiftly begin to expand in size. 18

Writing 2: 20 *gwam*

We push very hard in our quest for growth, and we all think 6
that only excellent growth will pay off. 10

Believe it or not, one can actually work much too hard, 16
be much too zealous, and just miss the mark. 20

Writing 3: 22 *gwam*

A business friend once explained to me why he was often 6
quite eager to be given some new project to work with. 11

My friend said that each new project means he has to 16
organize and use the best of his knowledge and his skill. 22

Writing 4: 24 *gwam*

Just don't let new words get away from you. Learn how to spell 6
and pronounce new words and when and how to use them with skill. 13

A new word is a friend, but frequently more. New words 19
must be used lavishly to extend the size of your word power. 25

2' | 1 | 2 | 3 | 4 | 5 | 6 |

49-d2

Leftbound Report

study

1. Key the remainder of the report shown below and format as a leftbound report.
2. Apply the Retrospect theme. Format the title and side headings with the appropriate style. Tap ENTER twice after the title.
3. Key the table below, placing it in the report below the paragraph that describes Table 1; apply the Grid Table 6 Colorful – Accent 3. Merge the cells as shown. Center the headings as shown. Insert a right tab at the approximate center of columns B–E to align the numbers in the approximate center of the column.
4. Choose the open circle bullet for the bulleted list.
5. Insert the second content footnote as marked in the report.
6. Number the pages at the top right using the Accent Bar 2 page number style.
7. Proofread the document. Check the test and close. Click Exit Word. *(49-d2)*
8. Click Log out to exit *KPDO*.

Table 1 Comparison of Adherence of Dress Code Policy to Absenteeism and Tardiness				
	Absenteeism		Tardiness	
	Male	Female	Male	Female
Adhered to policy	2%	2%	1%	0%
Did not adhere to policy	25%	30%	12%	10%

The findings clearly verify our review of the business literature that employees who dress more professionally are absent fewer days and are on time for work more often.

Recommendations

Although complete adherence to the dress code was not found, the findings of the study do show that the compliance to our policy (89%) is much better than companies included in the NABASW Study.[2] However, because the findings in our company show a correlation between absenteeism and tardiness, this subcommittee respectfully submits the following recommendations.

- Consider employing an image consultant to teach employees what is appropriate business casual and to plan the best business attire to project the image of our company.
- Prepare online materials that more clearly explain the areas of the dress code that appeared in the study as violations.

In summary, the current dress code is fulfilling the company philosophy to provide a comfortable work environment and to project a positive corporate image. Professional development is recommended in selected areas.

Footnote text:

[2] Study of 500 companies revealed that 80 percent of the companies reported a 60 percent level of compliance by employees to established company dress policy.

Note: The dot above text represents two words.

Writing 5: 26 ***gwam*** *gwam* 2'

We usually get the best results when we know where 5
we are going. Just setting a few goals will help us quietly 12
see what we can do. 13

Goals can help measure whether we are moving at a good 19
rate or dozing along. You can expect a goal to help you find 25
good results. 26

Writing 6: 28 ***gwam***

To win whatever prizes we want from life, we must plan to 6
move carefully from this goal to the next to get the maximum 12
result from our work. 14

If we really want to become skilled in keying, we must 19
come to see that this desire will require of us just a little 26
patience and hard work. 28

Writing 7: 30 ***gwam***

Am I an individual person? I'm sure I am; still, in a 5
much, much bigger sense, other people have a strong voice in 12
thoughts I think and actions I take. 15

Although we are each a unique person, we work and 21
play in organized groups of people who just do not expect us to 26
dismiss their rules of law and order. 30

2' | 1 | 2 | 3 | 4 | 5 | 6 |

Warmup *Lesson 49a Warmup*

Apply It

Table

1. Key the table shown below. Apply Grid Table 5 Dark – Accent 6 style to the table.
2. Insert a row at the beginning of the table. Key the title **Occupational Health and Safety Department Survey**. Merge the cells and center the title.
3. Change row height of row 1 to 0.4" and click Align Center to center the text vertically and horizontally in the row.
4. Proofread and correct any errors; click Continue. (*49-d1*)

Safety and health is a primary concern in every operation at Areorbit Corporation, and our goal is to be in compliance with the state's job safety and health laws and regulations. A summary of the annual safety report is shown below. The necessary adjustments are being made to produce a safer working environment.

Safety Standard	Madison Facility	Central Park Facility
Adequate lighting in hallways and stairwells.	Pass	Pass
Aisles and passageways are sufficiently wide for easy movement and should be kept clear at all times.	Pass	Pass
Temporary electrical cords that cross aisles are taped or anchored to the floor.	Pass	Electrical cord to coffee maker needs to be anchored in kitchen.
Adequate lighting is provided during night hours.	Two exterior lights need to be replaced in front of the building.	Pass
Floor surfaces are even; no bulges in carpet that can cause tripping hazards.	Stretch carpet in employee lounge to eliminate bulges.	Pass
Signs leading to exits are posted and are easily visible in the dark.	Pass	Light needs to be replaced in exit sign 7.

MODULE 2

Figure and Symbol Keys

Lessons 14–18 *Figure Keys*
Lessons 19–24 *Symbol Keys*
Lesson 25 *Assessment*

LEARNING OUTCOMES

- Key the numeric keys by touch.
- Use symbol keys correctly.
- Build keying speed and accuracy.
- Apply correct number expression.
- Apply proofreaders' marks.

Lesson 14 I and 8

Warmup *Lesson 14a Warmup*

New Keys

14b 1 and 8

© Cengage Learning

1 Reach *up* with *left fourth* finger.

© Cengage Learning

8 Reach *up* with *right second* finger.

Abbreviations: Do not space after a period within an abbreviation, as in Ph.D., U.S., C.O.D., a.m.

The digit "1" and the letter "l" have separate values; do not interchange.

1

1 1 1a a1 1 1; 1 and a 1; 1 add 1; 1 aunt; 1 ace; 1 arm; 1 aye
2 1 and 11 and 111; 11 eggs; 11 vats; Set 11A; May 11; Item 11
3 The 11 aces of the 111th Corps each rated a salute at 1 p.m.

8

4 8 8k k8 8 8; 8 kits; ask 8; 8 kites; kick 8; 8 keys; spark 8
5 OK 88; 8 bags; 8 or 88; the 88th; 88 kegs; ask 88; order 888
6 Eight of the 88 cars score 8 or better on our Form 8 rating.

7 She did live at 818 Park, not 181 Park; or was it 181 Clark?
8 Put 1 with 8 to form 18; put 8 with 1 to write 81. Use 1881.
9 On May 1 at 8 a.m., 18 men and 18 women left Gate 8 for Rio.

14c All Figures Learned

48-d3

Letter

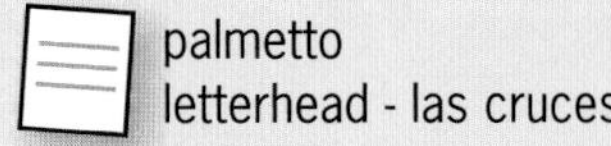
palmetto
letterhead - las cruces

Much communication will be necessary between Mr. Torres and Mr. Romero, the president of Southwest Culinary Association. Prepare the following letter.

1. Include all necessary letter parts. Address to **Mr. Jason Romero, President | Southwest Culinary Association | P.O. Box 3759 | Oklahoma City, OK 73101-3759**. Date the letter **January 15, 201-**.
2. Proofread and check; click Next Activity. (*48-d3*)

Our office is very pleased to be working with you on event planning for the Southwest Culinary Association Convention to be held in San Antonio on February 1-4. We distributed the Request for Proposals yesterday to the lists provided by Ms. Janet Wiseman, the treasurer of your association.

Next we are focusing our attention on sponsorships for the following major events:

1. Board dinner on March 31
2. Opening reception on February 1
3. Morning and afternoon coffee breaks on February 2 and 3
4. Wine and cheese reception on February 3

Event proposal forms are attached for each of the events listed above. Please complete the forms and return by email to me at conference201@palmettoeventsolutions.com. Your return of these forms by next Monday will be greatly appreciated. Our goal is to solicit at least two sponsors for each event, and this information is valuable to us as we plan our campaign.

Thank you for your valuable input in our event planning.

48-d4

Compose Letter

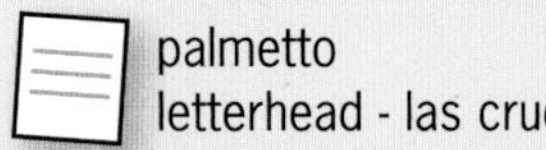
palmetto
letterhead - las cruces

Mr. Torres has asked you to compose a draft of the letter to be emailed to the presenters whose proposals are being accepted for the Southwest Culinary Association Convention. Date the letter May 31 and key on the Southwest letterhead. The following details are important to include.

1. Congratulate the presenter for having a proposal accepted for the convention.
2. Explain that the assignment of day, time, and room are not complete and will be emailed within the month.
3. Attach the speaker form you prepared earlier and ask the speaker to complete and return to you by June 15. Also request a brief biographical sketch to be used in the convention program and by the session facilitator who will introduce the speaker.
4. End with a gracious thank-you for their willingness to speak at the convention.
5. Proofread and check; click Exit Word. (*48-d4*) Click Log out to exit *KPDO*.

Learn More:
www.cengagebrain.com

Skill Building

14d Textbook Keying

Key each line once.

Work for fluency as you key these high-frequency words.

10 a an it been copy for his this more no office please service
11 our service than the they up was work all any many thank had
12 business from I know made more not me new of some to program
13 such these two with your about and have like department year
14 by at on but do had in letter most now one please you should
15 their order like also appreciate that there gentlemen letter
16 be can each had information letter may make now only so that
17 them time use which am other been send to enclosed have will
18 Please thank the department staff for the excellent program.
19 Therefore, send the information as they are very interested.
20 She sent a receipt and an invoice for the payment due today.
21 Our board and president are happy about the new tax service.
22 We appreciate the excellent help received from every office.
23 Please return the attached form prior to the second meeting.

14e Improve Keystroking

figures

24 Our 188 trucks moved 1881 tons on August 18 and December 18.
25 Send Mary 181 No. 188 panes for her home at 8118 Oak Street.
26 The 188 men in 8 boats left Docks 1 and 18 at 1 p.m., May 1.
27 pop was lap pass slaw wool solo swap Apollo wasp load plaque
28 Was Polly acquainted with the skillful jazz player in Texas?
29 The computer is a useful tool; it helps you to perform well.

14f Enrichment

1. Key these lines in the game.
2. Log out of *KPDO* when completed.

30 Did their form entitle them to the land?
31 Did the men in the field signal for us to go?
32 I may pay for the antique bowls when I go to town.
33 The auditor did the work right, so he risks no penalty.
34 The man by the big bush did signal us to turn down the lane.

48-d2

Speaker Form

A speaker form will be sent to presenters of proposals that were accepted for the convention program.

1. Create the table below as a 2 × 10 table. Split the cells in rows 8 and 9 into 5 columns, then merge row 9 as shown.
2. Select the entire table and change the height of the table rows to 0.3".
3. In row 1, change the text to Align Center; for text in rows 2–10, change text to Align Center Left.
4. Proofread and check; click Next Activity. (*48-d2*)

SPEAKER CONTACT INFORMATION				
Name:				
Professional Credentials:				
Title:				
Company:				
Address 1:				
Address 2:				
City:		State:		ZIP Code:	
Telephone:		Fax:		
Email:				

QUICK ✓

Check your document against the illustration below.

Speaker Contact Information					
Name:					
Professional Credentials:					
Title:					
Company:					
Address 1:					
Address 2:					
City:		State:		ZIP Code:	
Telephone:		Fax:			
Email:					

Lesson 15 5 and 0

Warmup *Lesson 15a Warmup*

New Keys

15b 5 and 0

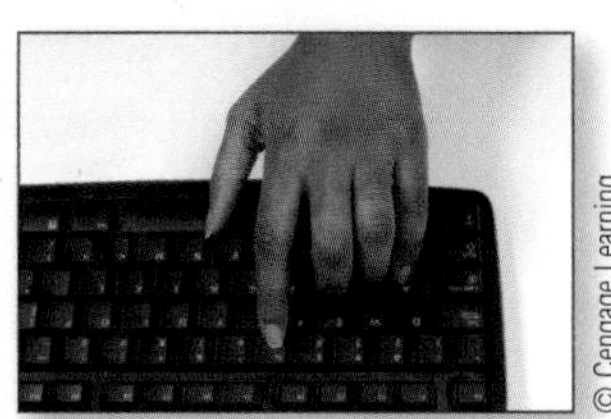

5 Reach *up* with *left first* finger.

0 Reach *up* with *right fourth* finger.

5

1 5 5f f5 5 5; 5 fans; 5 feet; 5 figs; 5 fobs; 5 frus; 5 flaws
2 5 o'clock; 5 a.m.; 5 p.m.; is 55 or less; buy 55; 5 and 5 is
3 Call Line 555 if 5 fans or 5 bins arrive at Pier 5 by 5 p.m.

0

4 0 0; ;0 0 0; skip 0; plan 0; left 0; is below 0; I scored 0;
5 0 degrees; key 0 and 0; write 00 here; the total is 0 or 00;
6 She laughed at their 0 to 0 score; but ours was 0 to 0 also.

15c All Figures Learned

7 I keyed 550 pages for Invoice 05, or 50 more than we needed.
8 Pages 15 and 18 of the program listed 150, not 180, members.
9 On May 10, Rick drove 500 miles to New Mexico in car No. 08.

Skill Building

15d Textbook Keying

Key each line once.

Watch the copy, not the hands.

10 Read pages 5 and 8; duplicate page 18; omit pages 50 and 51.
11 We have Model 80 with 10 meters or Model 180 with 15 meters.
12 After May 18, French 050 meets in room 15 at 10 a.m. daily.

13 Barb Abver saw a vibrant version of her brave venture on TV.
14 Call a woman or a man who will manage Minerva Manor in Nome.
15 We were quick to squirt a quantity of water at Quin and West.

Session Descriptions

Convention participants will choose from four types of convention sessions. In preparing the proposal, use the following information to select the most appropriate type of session for the proposed session content.

Type	Length	Room Setup	Audience Size
Lecture (L)	60 minutes	Tables	50
Roundtable (RT)	60 minutes (20 minutes per rotation)	Roundtables	8 per table
Hands-on Computer Workshop (W)	90 minutes	Lab with 20 laptop computers	20
Demonstrations (D)	60 minutes	Theater seating in teaching kitchen	100

Submission Information and Deadlines

Email proposals to Carlos Torres carlos.torres@palmettoeventsolutions.com by May 15 at 5 p.m. If you have questions, please call Carlos Torres at 505.555.0152.

Guidelines

The proposal must be no more than four single-spaced pages and must include the following information:

1. Cover Page that includes the title of presentation, type of session (Lecture, Roundtable, Hands-on Computer Workshop, or Demonstration), names of all presenters, and contact information for all presenters (company name, mailing address, email address, and telephone numbers)
2. Title of Presentation with description of presentation for program (limit to 50 words)
3. Purpose of Presentation and Justification for Acceptance
4. Topical Outline

Notification

Authors of accepted proposals will be notified on June 15.

15e Textbook Keying

Key each line once.

Build confidence—trust yourself to make the right reach.

pu/nv

16 pumps impulse campus invoices convey envy puck public canvas
17 Computer's input on environmental canvass confirms decision.

mb ey rk

18 embarked number climb eye obeying park remark thumb attorney
19 Ambitious people gambled money on unusual pieces of artwork.

tl ru pt

20 subtle apt capture excerpt adult abrupt brittle forums drug
21 Ruth opts to be greatly optimistic about seven new recruits.

ob rg un

22 objective lobster organize urge bounce tribunal global surge
23 Marge's hunger for mobile action targets frequent traveling.

15f Timed Writing

1. Take two 1' timed writings. If you finish before time is up, begin again.
2. Use wordwrap; do not tap ENTER at the end of lines.
3. End the lesson.

wordwrap

gwam 1'

I thought about Harry and how he worked for me in my 11
family insurance business for 10 years; how daily at 8 he 23
parked his old car in the company lot; then, he left exactly 35
at 5. Every day was almost identical for him. 44

In a quiet way, he did an outstanding job, requesting 56
little attention. So I never recognized his thirst for travel. 68
I didn't expect to find all those travel brochures near his 80
workplace. 82

1' | 1 | 2 | 3 | 4 | 5 | 6 | 7 | 8 | 9 | 10 | 11 | 12 |

Communication

15g Enrichment

1. Go to the Word Processor.
2. Compose one paragraph that describes travel that you have done or perhaps that you wish to take. Include at least two attractions you visited or hope to visit while on this trip. Use proper grammatical structure. Do not worry about keying errors at this time.
3. Save the document as *xx-travel*. (Replace *xx* with your initials.)
4. Log out of *KPDO*.

Project Setting

PALMETTO EVENT SOLUTIONS, INC.

For the project in this module, you will be preparing documents for Carlos Torres, the regional vice president in the Southwest office in Las Cruces. The Southwest office was recently contracted to coordinate events for the Southwest Culinary Association Convention to be held in San Antonio next year. You have been assigned exclusively to this project.

As you work through each job, make sure you do the following:

- Use Southwest letterhead for all letters and the block letter style with open punctuation.
- Key **Mr. Torres** as the author of all letters and format the signature line as follows: **Sincerely | Carlos Torres | Regional Vice President**. Letters are generally emailed as attachments unless otherwise directed. Items attached to the letter would be considered attachments.
- Apply the Ion theme for all documents.
- Apply the Grid Table 4 – Accent 5 table style for all tables.
- Use the Accent Bar 2 page number style for all reports.

48-d1

Request for Proposals

Prepare the Request for Proposals below as an unbound report.

1. Apply the Title style to the title and Heading 1 style to side headings.
2. Format the table appropriately and number the pages.
3. Proofread and check; click Next Activity. (*48-d1*)

Request for Proposals

The purpose of this Request for Proposals (RFP) is to solicit speakers for the Southwest Culinary Association Convention to be held on February 1-4, 201-, in San Antonio, Texas, at the San Antonio Hotel. Approximately 2,000 members, exhibitors, and guests are expected to attend this annual convention.

The Southwest regional office of Palmetto Event Solutions, Inc. is the official event planner of this conference and will oversee the RFP and the final selection program presenters. Send all questions to the following address before May 1:

Mr. Carlos Torres

Regional Vice President

Palmetto Event Solutions, Inc.

590 S. Solano Drive

Las Cruces, NM 88001-3290

575.555.0152

Press SHIFT + ENTER for these short lines.

The conference speakers will be carefully selected individuals who have expertise in the current trends and issues, use of cutting edge technology needed by today's chefs, and a showcase of best practices in the field.

(continued)

Lesson 16 2 and 7

Warmup *Lesson 16a Warmup*

New Keys

16b 2 and 7

© Cengage Learning

2 Reach *up* with *left third* finger.

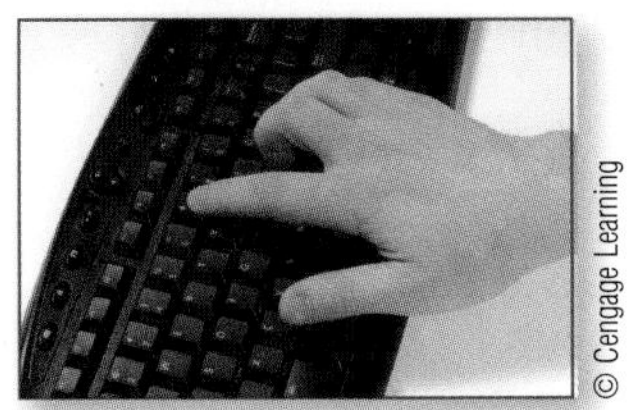

© Cengage Learning

7 Reach *up* with *right first* finger.

2

1 2 2s s2 2 2; has 2 sons; is 2 sizes; was 2 sites; has 2 skis
2 add 2 and 2; 2 sets of 2; catch 22; as 2 of the 22; 222 Main
3 Exactly at 2 on April 22, the 22nd Company left from Pier 2.

7

4 7 7j j7 7 7; 7 jets; 7 jeans; 7 jays; 7 jobs; 7 jars; 7 jaws
5 ask for 7; buy 7; 77 years; June 7; take any 7; deny 77 boys
6 From May 7 on, all 77 men will live at 777 East 77th Street.

16c All Figures Learned

7 I read 2 of the 72 books, Ellis read 7, and Han read all 72.
8 Tract 27 cites the date as 1850; Tract 170 says it was 1852.
9 You can take Flight 850 on January 12; I'll take Flight 705.

Skill Building

16d Textbook Keying

Key each line once. Keep fingers curved and relaxed; wrists low.

3rd/4th

10 pop was lap pass slaw wool solo swap apollo wasp load plaque
11 Al's quote was, "I was dazzled by the jazz, pizza, and pool."

1st/2nd

12 bad fun nut kick dried night brick civic thick hutch believe
13 Kim may visit her friends in Germany if I give her a ticket.

3rd/1st

14 cry tube wine quit very curb exit crime ebony mention excite
15 To be invited, petition the six executive committee members.

Lesson 48 Palmetto Event Solutions, Inc.

Warmup *Lesson 48a Warmup*

Skill Building

48b Textbook Keying

caps
1 James Carswell plans to visit Austin and New Orleans in December.
2 Will Peter and Betsy go with Mark when he goes to Alaska in June?
3 John Kenny wrote the book *Innovation and Timing—Keys to Success.*

double letters
4 Jeanne arranges meeting room space in Massey Hall for committees.
5 Russell will attend to the bookkeeping issues tomorrow afternoon.
6 Todd offered a free book with all assessment tools Lynette sells.

balanced hand
7 Jane, a neighbor and a proficient auditor, may amend their audit.
8 Blanche and a neighbor may make an ornament for an antique chair.
9 Claudia may visit the big island when they go to Orlando with us.

48c

Timed Writing

1. Key a 1' timing on each paragraph; work to increase speed.
2. Key a 3' timing on all paragraphs.

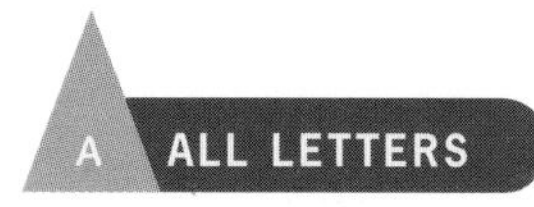

Whether any company can succeed depends on how well it fits into the economic system. Success rests on certain key factors that are put in line by a management team that has set goals for the company and has enough good judgment to recognize how best to reach these goals. Because of competition, only the best-organized companies get to the top.

A commercial enterprise is formed for a specific purpose: that purpose is usually to equip others, or consumers, with whatever they cannot equip themselves. Unless there is only one provider, a consumer will search for a company that returns the most value in terms of price; and a relationship with such a company, once set up, can endure for many years.

Thus our system assures that the businesses that manage to survive are those that have been able to combine successfully an excellent product with a low price and the best service—all in a place that is convenient for the buyers. With no intrusion from outside forces, the buyer and the seller benefit both themselves and each other.

16e Improve Keystroking

16 line 8; Book 1; No. 88; Seat 11; June 18; Cart 81; date 1881
17 take 2; July 7; buy 22; sell 77; mark 27; adds 72; Memo 2772
18 feed 5; bats 0; age 50; Ext. 55; File 50; 55 bags; band 5005
19 I work 18 visual signs with 20 turns of the 57 lenses to 70.
20 Did 17 boys fix the gears for 50 bicycles in 28 racks or 10?

16f Textbook Keying

Key each line once.

Think and key the words and phrases as units rather than letter by letter.

words: *think, say,* and *key* words

21 is do am lay cut pen dub may fob ale rap cot hay pay hem box
22 box wit man sir fish also hair giant rigor civic virus ivory
23 laugh sight flame audit formal social turkey bicycle problem

phrases: *think, say,* and *key* phrases

24 is it|is it|if it is|if it is|or by|or by|or me|or me|for us
25 and all|for pay|pay dues and|the pen|the pen box|the pen box
26 such forms|held both|work form|then wish|sign name|with them

easy sentences

27 The man is to do the work right; he then pays the neighbors.
28 Sign the forms to pay the eight men for the turkey and hams.
29 The antique ivory bicycle is a social problem for the chair.

16g Timed Writing

1. Take two 2' timed writings. If you finish before time is up, begin again. Use wordwrap.
2. End the lesson; log out of *KPDO.*

Goal: 16 *gwam*

	gwam 2'	3'
When choosing a password, do not select one you have	6	4
already used. Create a new one quite often, perhaps every	11	8
three to four weeks. Be sure to use a combination of both	17	11
letters and numbers.	19	13
Know your password; do not record it on paper. If you	25	17
must write it down, be sure the password is not recognized.	31	21
Don't let anyone watch you key. Just position yourself away	37	24
from the person or key a few extra strokes.	41	27

Apply It

47-d1

APA Template

1. In a new document, click No Spacing style and change line spacing to 2.0.
2. Change to 12-point Times New Roman font.
3. Double-click in the header section and change to 12-point Times New Roman font. Key **TITLE OF PAPER** at the left margin. Tap TAB twice and insert page number. Close the Header & Footer.
4. Key **Title of Paper** at 1" and center.
5. Proofread and check; click Next Activity. *(47-d1)*

47-d2

APA Report

1. In the open document *(47-d1)*, key the APA report shown on pages 201–202 using the template with the APA formatting already applied. Do not key the Bibliography page.
2. Double click in the header and change *TITLE OF PAPER* to **WRITING A SCHOLARLY REPORT**. Close the header.
3. In the title line, replace *Title of Paper* with **Writing a Scholarly Report**.
4. Click Increase Indent once to indent the long quotation 0.5" from the left margin.
5. Check that side headings are not alone at the bottom of the page. Use the Keep with next command if needed.
6. Proofread and check; click Next Activity. *(47-d2)*

47-d3

Bibliography

1. In the open document *(47-d2)*, position the insertion point at the end of the report. Press CTRL + ENTER to begin a new page.
2. Begin at 1" and key the bibliography shown below. DS and format the references in hanging indent style.
3. Proofread and check; click Exit Word. *(47-d3)*
4. Click Log out to exit KPDO.

Bibliography

Capitalize only the first word and proper nouns in book titles and journal titles.

Millsaps, J. T. (2014). *Report writing handbook: An essential guide.* Columbus: Wellington Books.

Quattlebaum, S. (2014). Apply reference styles correctly. *The Quarterly Reference Journal*, 27(1), 35-42.

Italicize journal name and volume number.

Warmup *Lesson 17a Warmup*

New Keys

17b 4 and 9

4 Reach *up* with *left first* finger.

9 Reach *up* with *right third* finger.

4

1 4 4f f4 f f f; if 4 furs; off 4 floors; gaff 4 fish; 4 flags
2 44th floor; half of 44; 4 walked 44 flights; 4 girls; 4 boys
3 I order exactly 44 bagels, 4 cakes, and 4 pies before 4 a.m.

9

4 9 91 l9 9 9 9; fill 9 lugs; call 9 lads; Bill 9 lost; dial 9
5 also 9 oaks; roll 9 loaves; 9.9 degrees; sell 9 oaks; Hall 9
6 Just 9 couples, 9 men and 9 women, left at 9 on our Tour 99.

17c All Figures Learned

7 4 feet; 4 inches; 44 gallons, 444 quarts, 4 folders, 44 fads
8 Lucky 99; 999 leaves; 9 lottery tickets; 9 losers; 9 winners
9 Memo 94 says 9 pads, 4 pens, and 4 ribbons were sent July 9.
10 Study Item 17 and Item 28 on page 40 and Item 59 on page 49.
11 Within 17 months he drove 85 miles, walked 29, and flew 490.

Skill Building

17d Textbook Keying

Key each line once.

Keep hands quiet as you reach to the top row; do not bounce.

12 My staff of *18* worked *11* hours a day from May *27* to June *12*.
13 There were *5* items tested by Inspector *7* at *4* p.m. on May *8*.
14 Please send her File *10* today at *8*; her access number is *97*.
15 Car *947* had its trial run. The qualifying speed was *198* mph.
16 The estimated total score? *485*. Actual? *390*. Difference? *95*.

INTERNAL CITATIONS IN APA STYLE

1. When cited information is paraphrased, the last name of the author(s) and the publication year of the paraphrased material are shown in parenthesis. Example: *Podcasts are effectively used by distance faculty (Crawford, 2014).*
2. When the author(s) names are used in the text, the publication year is keyed after the author name(s). Example: *According to Crawford (2014), podcasts are effectively used by distance faculty.*
3. When the citation is a direct quote, the page number appears in parenthesis after the quote. Example: *Crawford (2014) said, "Faculty are uploading podcast lectures" (p. 134).*
4. Long quotations of 40 words or more are indented 0.5" from the left margin and DS. Tap ENTER once before and after the long quotation. See the example below.

Probably no successful enterprise exists that does not rely upon the ability of its members to communicate for its success. Shaefer (2014) adds:

> Make no mistake, both written and verbal communication are the stuff upon which success is built in all types of organizations. Both forms deserve careful study by any business that wants to grow. Successful businesspeople must read, write, speak, and listen with skill. Often professional development in these areas is needed. (p. 28)

17e Improve Keystroking

first finger

17 buy them gray vent guy brunt buy brunch much give huge vying

18 Hagen, after her July triumph at tennis, may try volleyball.

19 Verna urges us to buy yet another of her beautiful rag rugs.

second finger

20 keen idea; kick it back; ice breaker; decide the issue; cite

21 Did Dick ask Cecelia, his sister, if she decided to like me?

22 Suddenly, Micki's bike skidded on the Cedar Street ice rink.

third/fourth finger

23 low slow lax solo wax zip zap quips quiz zipper prior icicle

24 Paula has always allowed us to relax at La Paz and at Quito.

25 Please ask Zale to explain who explores most aquatic slopes.

17f Timed Writing

Take a 2' timing on all the paragraphs. Repeat the timing. Use wordwrap.

	gwam 2'	3'
Many experts believe stress affects the mind as well as	6	4
the body. However, they are not quite sure just how much	11	8
damage can be caused. This may be because people deal with	17	12
stress in several different ways. Some learn to either shrug	23	16
it off or else put little thought to it.	27	19
Coping with stress is difficult but if one is willing to	34	23
make an effort, it can be handled easily. One way to deal	39	27
with stress is having a good diet as well as regular exercise.	46	31
Another way is to become involved with enjoyable activities	52	35
such as writing, painting, or running. Last, but certainly not	58	39
least, have a positive thought process, a great zest for life,	64	43
and a big cheerful smile.	67	45

17g Enrichment

1. From the Skill Building tab, choose Technique Builder; Drill 2.
2. Key Drill 2 from page 38. Key each line once, striving for good acuracy.
3. The results will be listed on the Skill Building Report.
4. Log out of *KPDO*.

Running head → WRITING A SCHOLARLY REPORT 2

a hanging indent in both MLA and APA, but be cautious of the differences in the formatting of authors' names and book and article titles" (p. 40).

Summary

Experienced writers understand the importance of selecting credible resources, documenting references, and applying the exact reference style required in the report. Learning to document your references accurately is an important step toward becoming an experienced writer.

WRITING A SCHOLARLY REPORT 3

Bibliography

Millsaps, J. T. (2014). *Report writing handbook: An essential guide*. Columbus: Wellington Books.

Quatttlebaum, S. (2014). Apply reference styles correctly. *The Quarterly Reference Journal, 27*(1), 35-42.

APA Report Style

Lesson 18 3 and 6

Warmup *Lesson 18a Warmup*

New Keys

18b 3 and 6

3 Reach *up* with *left second* finger.

6 Reach *up* with *right first* finger.

Note: Ergonomic keyboard users will use *left first* finger to key 6.

3

1 3 3d d3 3 3; had 3 days; did 3 dives; led 3 dogs; add 3 dips
2 we 3 ride 3 cars; take 33 dials; read 3 copies; save 33 days
3 On July 3, 33 lights lit 33 stands holding 33 prize winners.

6

4 6 6j 6j 6 6; 6 jays; 6 jams; 6 jigs; 6 jibs; 6 jots; 6 jokes
5 only 6 high; on 66 units; reach 66 numbers; 6 yams or 6 jams
6 On May 6, Car 66 delivered 66 tons of No. 6 shale to Pier 6.

18c All Figures Learned

7 At 6 p.m., Channel 3 reported the August 6 score was 6 to 3.
8 Jean, do Items 28 and 6; Mika, 59 and 10; Kyle, 3, 4, and 7.
9 Cars 56 and 34 used Aisle 9; Cars 2 and 87 can use Aisle 10.

18d Textbook Keying

Key each line once.

word response: *think* and *key* words

10 he el id is go us it an me of he of to if ah or bye do so am
11 Did she enamel emblems on a big panel for the downtown sign?

stroke response: *think* and *key* each stroke

12 kin are hip read lymph was pop saw ink art oil gas up as mop
13 Barbara started the union wage earners tax in Texas in July.

combination response: vary speed but maintain rhythm

14 upon than eve lion when burley with they only them loin were
15 It was the opinion of my neighbor that we may work as usual.

Running head on each page with title of page and page number

1"

Writing a Scholarly Report

Title

Preparing a thorough and convincing scholarly report requires excellent research, organization, and composition skills as well as extensive knowledge of documenting referenced materials. The purpose of this report is to present the importance of documenting a report with credible references and the techniques for creating accurate citations.

Well-Cited References

1"

For a report to be believable and accepted by its readers, a thorough review of related literature is essential. The background information is an important part of the report and shows integrity of the report.

Good writers must learn quickly how to evaluate many printed and electronic references located to support the theme of any report being written. Those references judged acceptable are then cited in the report. One writer shares this simple advice:

Long quotation indented 0.5"

> Today writers can locate a vast number of references in very little time. Electronic databases and Web pages . . . provide a multitude of information. The novice writer will be quick to include all these references in a report without verifying their credibility. Writers check electronic sources as well. (Millsaps, p. 12)

Correct Styles Applied

The *MLA Handbook for Writers of Research Papers* and the *Publication Manual of the American Psychological Association* are two popular style manuals. Knowing the required styles for the manuscript being produced is critical. For example, a running head with the paper title and page number is required in APA while MLA requires the last name of the author and the page number. Quattlebaum (2014) writes, "Be sure to check that the reference list is formatted as

1"

APA Report Style

18e Improve Keystroking

long reaches

16 ce cede cedar wreck nu nu nut punt nuisance my my amy mystic
17 ny ny any many company mu mu mull lumber mulch br br furbish
18 Cecil received a large brown umbrella from Bunny and Hunter.

number review

19 set 0; push 4; Car 00; score 44; jot 04; age 40; Billet 4004
20 April 5; lock 5; set 66; fill 55; hit 65; pick 56; adds 5665
21 Her grades are 93, 87, and 100; his included 82, 96, and 54.

18f Timed Writing

Key two 3' writings. Use wordwrap.

Jim West/Alamy

gwam 3'

I am something quite precious. Though millions of people 4
in other countries might not have me, you likely do. I am very 8
powerful. I choose the new president every four years. I 12
decide if a tax should be levied or repealed. I even decide 16
questions of war and peace. I was acquired with great expense; 20
however, I am free to all citizens. But sadly enough, I am 24
often ignored; or, still worse, I am just taken for granted. I 28
can be lost, and in certain circumstances I can even be taken 33
away. What am I? I am your right to vote. Don't take me 36
lightly. Exercise your right to vote at every election; 40
consider it an opportunity and a privilege. 43

3' | 1 | 2 | 3 | 4 |

Communication

18g Composition

1. Go to the Word Processor. Compose two paragraphs, each having about three sentences, in which you introduce yourself to your instructor. Use proper grammatical structure. Disregard keying errors at this time.
2. Save the document as *xx-profile*; replace *xx* with your initials. You will edit this document later.

Lesson 47 Reports in APA Style

Warmup *Lesson 47a Warmup*

Document Design

47b

APA REPORT STYLE

Study the guidelines shown below for an academic report formatted in APA style. Refer to the full-page model on pages 201–202 and always check the *Publication Manual of the American Psychological Association* and your teacher's instructions.

- Use 12-point Times New Roman font.
- Use 1" margins (top, bottom, left, and right).
- DS paragraphs and indent 0.5".
- DS long quotations of 40 or more words and indent 0.5" from the left margin.
- Key a running head in ALL CAPS at the top of each page that includes the title of paper (limited to 50 characters) at the left margin and page number aligned at the right.
- Center the report title and capitalize all main words.
- Include a complete alphabetical listing of all references cited in the report and label it **Bibliography**; DS.

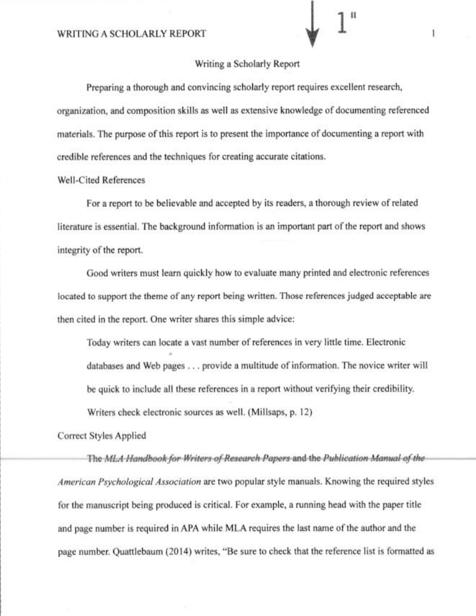

WRITING A SCHOLARLY REPORT 1

Writing a Scholarly Report

Preparing a thorough and convincing scholarly report requires excellent research, organization, and composition skills as well as extensive knowledge of documenting referenced materials. The purpose of this report is to present the importance of documenting a report with credible references and the techniques for creating accurate citations.

Well-Cited References

For a report to be believable and accepted by its readers, a thorough review of related literature is essential. The background information is an important part of the report and shows integrity of the report.

Good writers must learn quickly how to evaluate many printed and electronic references located to support the theme of any report being written. Those references judged acceptable are then cited in the report. One writer shares this simple advice:

> Today writers can locate a vast number of references in very little time. Electronic databases and Web pages . . . provide a multitude of information. The novice writer will be quick to include all these references in a report without verifying their credibility. Writers check electronic sources as well. (Millsaps, p. 12)

Correct Styles Applied

The *MLA Handbook for Writers of Research Papers* and the *Publication Manual of the American Psychological Association* are two popular style manuals. Knowing the required styles for the manuscript being produced is critical. For example, a running head with the paper title and page number is required in APA while MLA requires the last name of the author and the page number. Quattlebaum (2014) writes, "Be sure to check that the reference list is formatted as

Page 1

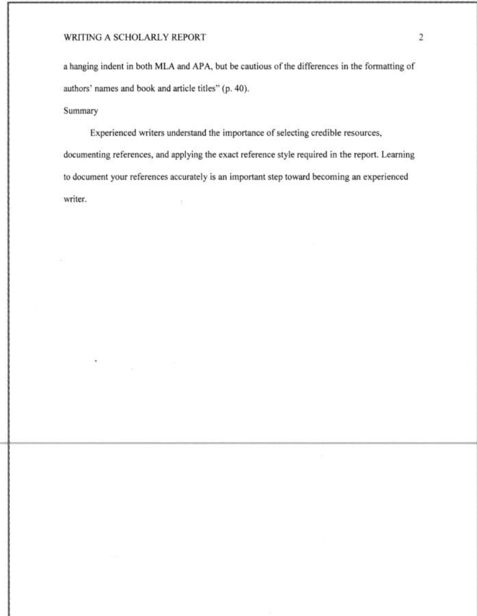

WRITING A SCHOLARLY REPORT 2

a hanging indent in both MLA and APA, but be cautious of the differences in the formatting of authors' names and book and article titles" (p. 40).

Summary

Experienced writers understand the importance of selecting credible resources, documenting references, and applying the exact reference style required in the report. Learning to document your references accurately is an important step toward becoming an experienced writer.

Page 2

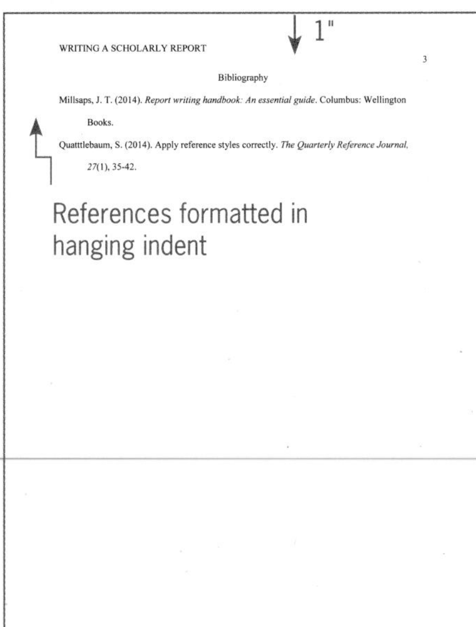

WRITING A SCHOLARLY REPORT 3

Bibliography

Millsaps, J. T. (2014). *Report writing handbook: An essential guide*. Columbus: Wellington Books.

Quattlebaum, S. (2014). Apply reference styles correctly. *The Quarterly Reference Journal, 27*(1), 35-42.

Bibliography Page

Warmup *Lesson 18Ra Warmup*

Skill Building

18Rb Textbook Keying

Key each line once; work for fluency.

1 Jake may pay the sixty men for eighty bushels of blue forks.
2 We used software versions 1.01, 2.6, 7.2, 8.3, 8.5, and 9.4.
3 The big box by the lake held fish, duck, apricot, and a map.
4 Adding 123 and 345 and 567 and 80 and 62 and 5 totals 1,182.
5 Lana and Jay and Ken paid to sit by the lake to fish at six.
6 We can see you at 6:30, 7:30, 8:45, 9:00, or 12:15 tomorrow.

18Rc Timed Writing

Key a 3' timing on all paragraphs. Repeat.

gwam 3'

You want to be known as a person of good character. If 4
someone says that you have character, it usually means that 8
you are honest, have integrity, and are reliable and 12
responsible. On the other hand, if you lie, cheat, or steal, 16
or are lazy, you will be known as a person with poor 19
character. If others say that you are quite a character, it 23
usually means that you have good character. 26

You will be judged by your actions and expressions. What 30
you say and do to others affects how others will respond to 34
you. You need to be considerate of others and conscientious in 38
your work. Others will respect and trust you and want you 42
involved in their activities. 44

3' | 1 | 2 | 3 | 4 |

Communication

18Rd Number Expression

1. From the Reference tab, click Communication Skills; select Number Expression.
2. Complete the pretest; click Report to review your results.

18Re Enrichment

Word Processor

1. In the Word Processor, take a 30" timing on the first line; repeat the line as many times as possible.
2. Take a 30" timing on the second line. Try to maintain the same speed as the first line.

7 Come work with us on this new job next month.
8 Jo will be 44 years 2 months and 24 days old.

9 I see you need some help with the new assignments.
10 I will be 44 years 2 months and 24 days old today.

11 Sixteen of us can come and help you today and tomorrow.
12 Order 99 cookies; at least have 33 sugar and 39 ginger.

13 Tell us how you want the work done; we will finish it today.
14 We must deliver order 6688 for 88 chairs and 66 tables by 6.

Apply It

46-d1

MLA Template

1. In a new document, click No Spacing style and change line spacing to 2.0.
2. Change to 12-point Times New Roman font.
3. Key the following heading at 1":

   Student's Full Name

   Instructor's Full Name

   Name of Assignment
4. Tap ENTER after *Name of Assignment and* insert the current date using the MLA-required date format (9 September 2012); click option to update automatically.
5. Double-click in the header section and change to 12-point Times New Roman font.
6. Click Align Right and key **LName**, space one time, and insert Page number command (Insert/Header & Footer/Page Number/Current Position. Click Plain Number). Close the Header & Footer.
7. Proofread and check; click Next Activity. (*46-d1*)

46-d2

MLA Report

Increase Indent

Home/Paragraph/ Increase Indent or Decrease Indent

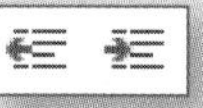

1. In the open document (*46-d1*), with the MLA formatting already applied, key the MLA report shown on pages 197–198.
2. Highlight the long quotation and click Increase Indent twice to indent it 1" from the left margin. Key a space after each period in the ellipsis.
3. Click Decrease Indent twice to return the insertion point back to the left margin.
4. Double-click in the header and change *LName* to **Watson**.
5. Edit the information at the top of page 1 with Watson's information.
6. Check that side headings are not alone at the bottom of the page. Use the Keep with next command if needed.
7. Proofread and check; click Next Activity. (*46-d2*)

46-d3

Works Cited Page

Page Break

Insert/Pages/Page Break

Shortcut: CTRL + ENTER

To remove a manual page break, position insertion point at the beginning of the page break (with Show/Hide on) and tap DELETE.

1. In the open document (*46-d2*), position the insertion point at the end of the report. Press CTRL + ENTER to begin a new page.
2. Key the works cited shown below with hanging indent formatting. Try the shortcut, CTRL + T.
3. Proofread and check; click Exit Word. (*46-d3*)
4. Click Log out to exit *KPDO*.

Works Cited

Millsaps, John Thomas. *Report Writing Handbook: An Essential Guide.* Columbus: Wellington Books, 2014. Print.

Quattlebaum, Sarah. "Apply Reference Styles Correctly." *The Quarterly Reference Journal* 27.1 (2014): 35-42. Print.

Lesson 19 $ and – (hyphen), Number Expression

Warmup *Lesson 19a Warmup*

19b Learn $ and -

$ Shift; then reach *up* with *left first* finger.

- (hyphen) Reach *up* with *right fourth* finger.

- = hyphen
- - = dash
Do not space before or after a hyphen or a dash.

$

1 $ $f f$ $ $; if $4; half $4; off $4; of $4; $4 fur; $4 flats
2 for $8; cost $9; log $3; grab $10; give Rolf $2; give Viv $4
3 Since she paid $45 for the item priced at $54, she saved $9.

- (hyphen)

4 - -; ;- - - -; up-to-date; co-op; father-in-law; four-square
5 pop-up foul; big-time job; snap-on bit; one- or two-hour ski
6 You need 6 signatures--half of the members--on the petition.

19c All Symbols Learned

7 I paid $10 for the low-cost disk; high-priced ones cost $40.
8 Le-An spent $20 for travel, $95 for books, and $38 for food.
9 Mr. Loft-Smit sold his boat for $467; he bought it for $176.

Skill Building

19d Improve Keystroking

10 Edie discreetly decided to deduct expenses in making a deal.
11 Working women wear warm wool sweaters when weather dictates.
12 We heard very rude remarks regarding her recent termination.
13 Daily sudden mishaps destroyed several dozens of sand dunes.
14 Beverley voted by giving a bold beverage to every brave boy.

Last Name + one space and Page Number command → Watson 2

for the manuscript being produced is critical. For example, a running head with the paper title and page number is required in APA while MLA requires the last name of the author and the page number. Quattlebaum (2014) writes, "Be sure to check that the reference list is formatted as a hanging indent in both MLA and APA, but be cautious of the differences in the formatting of authors' names as well as the capitalization of book and article titles" (40).

Summary

Experienced writers understand the importance of selecting credible resources, documenting references, and applying the exact reference style required in the report. Learning to document your references accurately is an important step toward becoming an experienced writer.

MLA Report Style

19e Textbook Keying

1. Key each line once.
2. When keying easy words and phrases:
   - Think and key words and phrases rather than letter by letter.
   - Make the space part of the word.

easy words

15 am it go bus dye jam irk six sod tic yam ugh spa vow aid dug
16 he or by air big elf dog end fit and lay sue toe wit own got
17 six foe pen firm also body auto form down city kept make fog

easy phrases

18 it is | if the | and also | to me | the end | to us | if it | it is | to the
19 if it is | to the end | do you wish | to go to | for the end | to make
20 lay down | he or she | make me | by air | end of | by me | kept it | of me

easy sentences

21 Did the chap work to mend the torn right half of the ensign?
22 Blame me for their penchant for the antique chair and panel.
23 She bid by proxy for eighty bushels of a corn and rye blend.

19f Textbook Keying

1. Review the Number Expression Guidelines 1–4 in the Reference Guide. Then key sentences 24–29.
2. Key lines 30–35. Decide whether the circled numbers should be keyed as figures or as words and make needed changes.

Key numbers without watching your fingers.

24 **Six** or **seven** older players were cut from the **37**-member team.
25 I have **2** of **14** coins I need to start my set. Christen has **9**.
26 Of **nine** **24**-ton engines ordered, we shipped **six** last Tuesday.
27 Shelly has read just **one-half** of about **forty-five** documents.
28 The **six** boys sent well over **two hundred** printed invitations.
29 **One** or **two** of us will be on duty from **two** until **six** o'clock.

30 Jan will come by at (4) o'clock to pick up the (3) girls.
31 Lauren and Paul invited (200) guests to the reception.
32 We have (3) more days to finish (2/3) of the plan.
33 Tish sent (7) (24)-pound boxes and (10) (3)-ounce envelopes.
34 I deposited (15) quarters, (10) dimes, and (4) nickels in the ATM.
35 A quorum was established; (7) of the (12) members voted.

19g Enrichment

1. From the Timed Writings tab, choose Writing 2.
2. Set the timing length for 1'.
3. Locate Writing 2 on page 40 and key it twice. Strive to increase speed by 2 gwam the second time.
4. Log out of *KPDO*.

1"

Last Name + one space and Page Number command

Watson 1

Daniel Watson

Dr. Caroline Kennedy

Assignment 1

14 February 2013 1

Writing a Scholarly Report

1" Preparing a thorough and convincing scholarly report requires excellent research, organization, and composition skills as well as extensive knowledge of documenting referenced materials. The purpose of this report is to present the importance of documenting a report with credible references and the techniques for creating accurate citations. 1"

Well-Cited References

For a report to be believable and accepted by its readers, a thorough review of related literature is essential. This background information is an important part of the report and shows integrity of the report.

Good writers must learn quickly how to evaluate many printed and electronic references located to support the theme of any report being written. Those references judged acceptable are then cited in the report. Millsaps shares this simple advice:

Long quotation indented 1"

> Today writers can locate a vast number of references in very little time. Electronic databases and Web pages . . . provide a multitude of information. The novice writer will be quick to include all these references in a report without verifying their credibility. Writers check electronic sources as well. (Millsaps 12)

Correct Styles Applied

The *MLA Handbook for Writers of Research Papers* and the *Publication Manual of the American Psychological Association* are two popular style manuals. Knowing the required styles

1"

MLA Report Style

Lesson 20 # and /

Warmup *Lesson 20a Warmup*

New Keys

20b Learn # and /

Shift; then reach *up* with *left second* finger.

/ Reach *down* with *right fourth* finger.

 # = number sign, pounds
/ = diagonal, slash

#

1 # #e e# # # #; had #3 dial; did #3 drop; set #3 down; Bid #3
2 leave #82; sold #20; Lyric #16; bale #34; load #53; Optic #7
3 Notice #333 says to load Car #33 with 33# of #3 grade shale.

/

4 / /; ;/ / / /; 1/2; 1/3; Mr./Mrs.; 1/4/12; 22 11/12; and/or;
5 to/from; /s/ William Smit; 2/10, n/30; his/her towels; 6 1/2
6 The numerals 1 5/8, 3 1/4, and 60 7/9 are “mixed fractions.”

20c All Symbols Learned

7 Invoice #737 cites 15 2/3# of rye was shipped C.O.D. 4/6/14.
8 B-O-A Company’s Check #50/5 for $87 paid for 15# of #3 wire.
9 Our Co-op List #20 states $40 for 16 1/2 crates of tomatoes.

Skill Building

20d Build Skill

Strive to maintain your speed on the second line in the pair.

10 She did the key work at the height of the problem.
11 Form #726 is the title to the island; she owns it.

12 The rock is a form of fuel; he did enrich it with coal.
13 The corn-and-turkey dish is a blend of turkey and corn.

14 It is right to work to end the social problems of the world.
15 If I sign it on 3/19, the form can aid us to pay the 40 men.

16 Profit problems at the firm may cause it to take many risks.
17 Dale discovered that Invoice #238 for $128.83 is dated 8/15.

INTERNAL CITATIONS IN MLA STYLE

The last name of the author(s) and the page number of the cited material are shown in parentheses within the body of the report (Crawford 134). When the author's name is used in the text to introduce the quotation, only the page number appears in parentheses: *Crawford said, "Faculty are uploading podcast lectures to their distance website" (134).*

Short, direct quotations of three lines or fewer are enclosed within quotation marks. Long quotations of four lines or more are indented 1" from the left margin and DS. Tap ENTER once before and after the long quotation.

> According to Estes, "Successful business executives have long known the importance of good verbal communication" (29).

Short Quotation

> Probably no successful enterprise exists that does not rely upon the ability of its members to communicate for its success. Shaefer adds:
>
> > Make no mistake, both written and verbal communication are the stuff upon which success is built in all types of organizations. Both forms deserve careful study by any business that wants to grow. Successful businesspeople must read, write, speak, and listen with skill. Often professional development in these areas is needed. (p. 28)

Long Quotation

WORKS CITED PAGE IN MLA STYLE

References cited in the report are listed at the end of the report in alphabetical order by authors' last name. Study the guidelines and the model shown below.

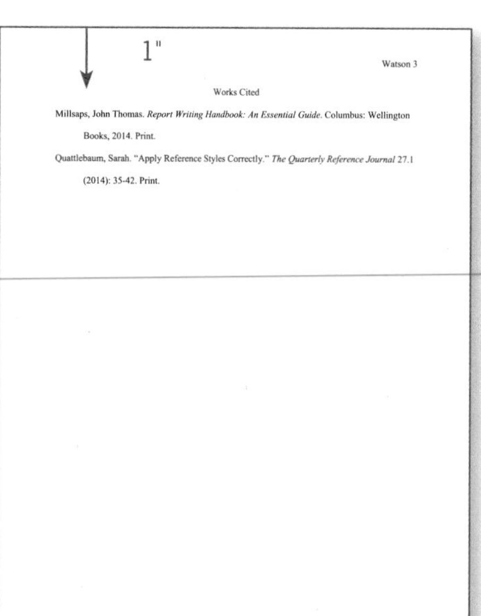

Watson 3

Works Cited

Millsaps, John Thomas. *Report Writing Handbook: An Essential Guide*. Columbus: Wellington Books, 2014. Print.

Quattlebaum, Sarah. "Apply Reference Styles Correctly." *The Quarterly Reference Journal* 27.1 (2014): 35-42. Print.

- Begin the references on a new page (insert manual page break at the end of the report).
- Center the title at the top of the page (1") with main words capitalized.
- Double-space the references. DS is 2.0 line spacing.
- Format references with hanging indent.
- Number the reference page at the top right of the page using same format as the report.

20e Textbook Keying

Key each line once. Notice the difference in the rhythm of your keying.

one hand
18 lip ere him bat lion date pink face pump rear only brag fact
19 at my; oh no; add debt; extra milk; union agreed; act faster

balanced hand
20 so it is|now is the|do so when|sign the forms|is it downtown
21 He may wish to go to town with Pamela to sign the amendment.

combination
22 was for|in the case of|they were|to down|pink bowls|wet rugs
23 They were to be down in the fastest sleigh if you are right.

20f Timed Writing

1. Key a 1' timing on each paragraph; work to increase speed.
2. Key a 3' timing on all paragraphs.

	gwam 1'	3'
Most people want to be socially acceptable. In some	11	4
cases, the need for attention can lead to difficulties. Some	23	8
of us think that the best way to get attention is to try a new	36	12
style, or to look quixotic, or to be different somehow.	47	16
Perhaps we are looking for nothing much more than acceptance	59	20
from others of ourselves just the way we now are.	68	23
There is no question about it; we all want to look our	12	27
best to impress other people. How this is achieved may mean	24	31
that we try something new, or perform things differently.	35	34
Regardless, our basic objective is to continue to build	46	38
character with zeal from our raw materials, you and me.	57	42

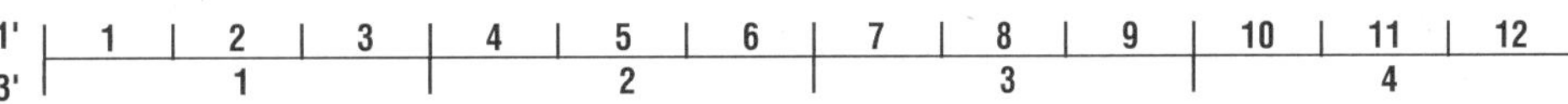

Communication

20g Number Expression

1. Review Number Expression in the Reference Guide.
2. In the Word Processor, key sentences 24–27 below. Do not use bold.
3. Key sentences 28 and 29, applying the rules correctly.

24 Ask **Group 2** to read **Chapter 7** of **Book 11** (**Shelf 19, Room 5**).
25 All **six** of us live at **One Bay Lane**, not at **142--59th Street**.
26 At **8 a.m.** the owners decided to close from **12 noon** to **1 p.m.**
27 Ms. Han leaves **June 3**; she returns the **14th or 15th of July**.
28 The 16 percent discount saves $123.50. The tax was 75 cents.
29 Jim poured 3 six-liter jars of oil into the 9 gallon barrel.

Document Design

46c

MLA REPORT STYLE

Study the guidelines shown below for an academic report formatted in MLA style. Refer to the full-page model on pages 197–198 and always check the *MLA Handbook for Writers of Research Papers* and your teacher's instructions.

- Use 12-point Times New Roman font.
- Use 1" margins (top, bottom, left, and right).
- DS paragraphs and indent 0.5".
- DS long quotations of 40 or more words and indent 1" from the left margin.
- Key heading information beginning at 1"; include full name, instructor's name, assignment name, and current date.
- Center the report title and capitalize all main words.
- Place page numbers at the top right of every page. Include the writer's last name and the page number (Last Name 1).
- Include a complete alphabetical listing of all references cited in the report and label it **Works Cited;** DS.

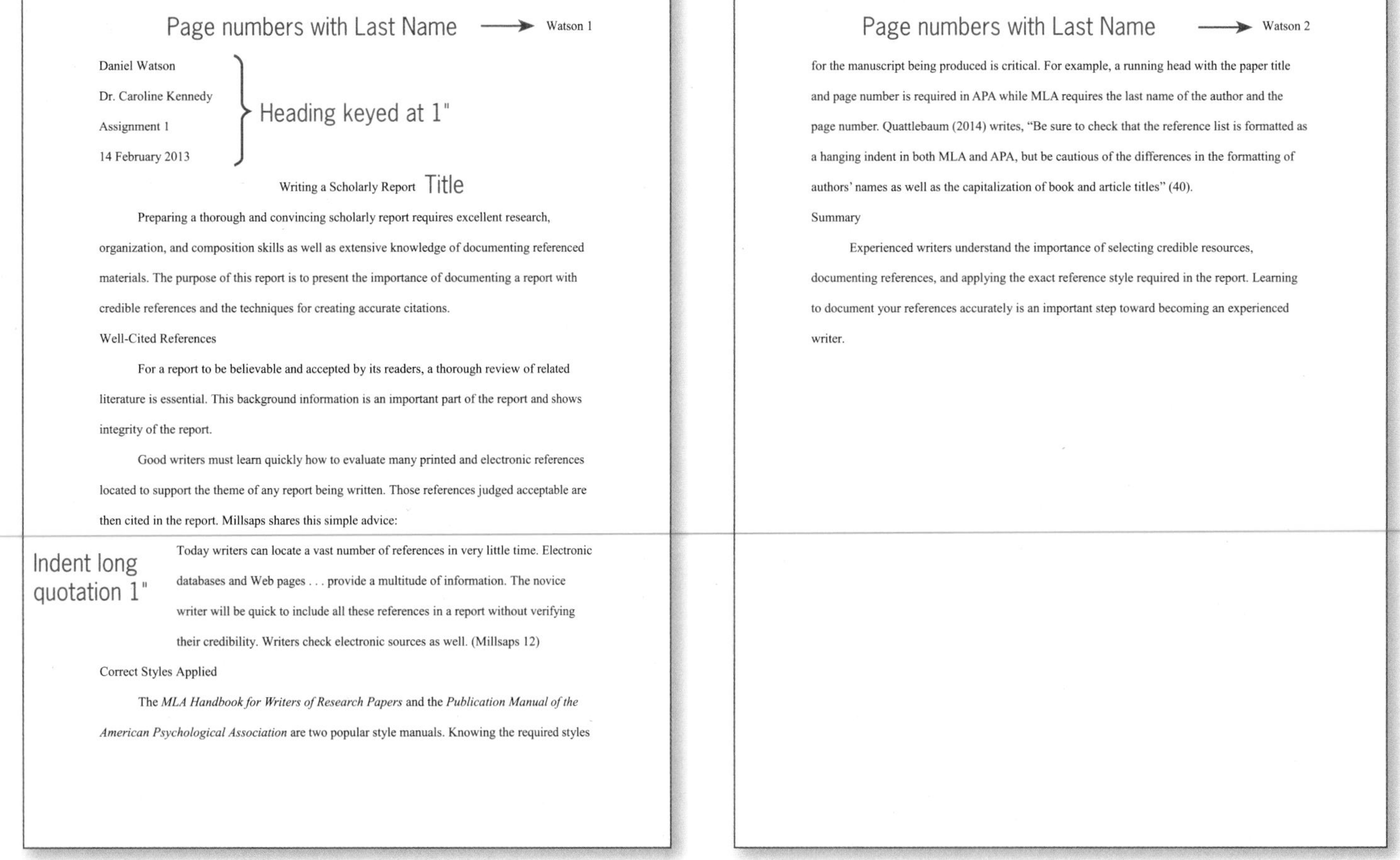
Page numbers with Last Name → Watson 1

Daniel Watson
Dr. Caroline Kennedy
Assignment 1
14 February 2013

Heading keyed at 1"

Writing a Scholarly Report Title

Preparing a thorough and convincing scholarly report requires excellent research, organization, and composition skills as well as extensive knowledge of documenting referenced materials. The purpose of this report is to present the importance of documenting a report with credible references and the techniques for creating accurate citations.

Well-Cited References

For a report to be believable and accepted by its readers, a thorough review of related literature is essential. This background information is an important part of the report and shows integrity of the report.

Good writers must learn quickly how to evaluate many printed and electronic references located to support the theme of any report being written. Those references judged acceptable are then cited in the report. Millsaps shares this simple advice:

Indent long quotation 1"

Today writers can locate a vast number of references in very little time. Electronic databases and Web pages . . . provide a multitude of information. The novice writer will be quick to include all these references in a report without verifying their credibility. Writers check electronic sources as well. (Millsaps 12)

Correct Styles Applied

The *MLA Handbook for Writers of Research Papers* and the *Publication Manual of the American Psychological Association* are two popular style manuals. Knowing the required styles

Page numbers with Last Name → Watson 2

for the manuscript being produced is critical. For example, a running head with the paper title and page number is required in APA while MLA requires the last name of the author and the page number. Quattlebaum (2014) writes, "Be sure to check that the reference list is formatted as a hanging indent in both MLA and APA, but be cautious of the differences in the formatting of authors' names as well as the capitalization of book and article titles" (40).

Summary

Experienced writers understand the importance of selecting credible resources, documenting references, and applying the exact reference style required in the report. Learning to document your references accurately is an important step toward becoming an experienced writer.

Lesson 21 % and !

Warmup *Lesson 21a Warmup*

New Keys

21b % and !

% Shift; then reach *up* with *left first* finger.

% = percent sign: Use % with business forms or where space is restricted; otherwise use the word "percent." Space once after the exclamation point!

- Do not space between a figure and the % or $ sign.
- Do not space before or after the dash.

%

1 % %f f% % %; off 5%; if 5%; of 5% fund; half 5%; taxes of 5%
2 7% rent; 3% tariff; 9% F.O.B.; 15% greater; 28% base; up 46%
3 Give discounts of 5% on rods, 50% on lures, and 75% on line.

! reach up with the left 4th finger

4 ! !a a! ! ! !; Eureka! Ha! No! Pull 10! Extra! America! Yea!
5 Attention! Now! Ready! On your mark! Get set! Go! Good show!
6 We need it now, not next week! I am sure to lose 50% or $19.

21c All Symbols Learned

7 The ad offers a 10% discount, but this notice says 15% less!
8 He got the job! With Loehman's Supermarket! Please call Mom!
9 Bill #92-44 arrived very late from Zyclone; it was paid 7/4.

21d Improve Keystroking

all symbols

10 As of 6/28, Jeri owes $31 for dinner and $27 for cab fare.
11 Invoice #20--it was dated 3/4--billed $17 less 15% discount.
12 He deducted 2% instead of 6%, a clear saving of 6% vs. 7%.

combination response

13 Look at my dismal grade in English; but I guess I earned it.
14 Kris started to blend a cocoa beverage for a shaken cowhand.
15 Jan may make a big profit if she owns the title to the land.

DRILL 2 SAVE AS TEMPLATE

chart

File/Save As

1. In the open document, replace (*Student's name*) with **Sophia Johnson.**

   KPDO: Your document will be saved as a *Word* file and not as a template.

2 Proofread and check; click Next Activity. (*46-drill2 Keyboarding progress template*)

HANGING INDENT

Hanging indent places the first line of a paragraph at the left margin and indents all other lines to the first tab. It is commonly used to format bibliography entries, glossaries, and lists. Hanging indent can be applied before or after text is keyed.

SHORTCUT

CTRL + T; then key the paragraph; or select the paragraphs to be formatted as hanging indents and press CTRL + T.

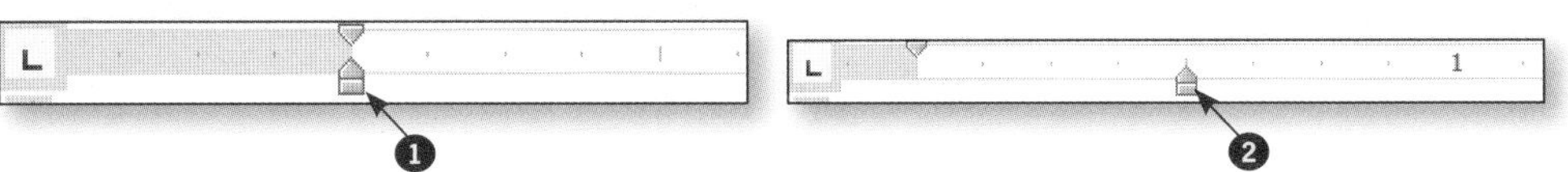

To create a hanging indent:

1. From the Horizontal Ruler, click on the Hanging Indent marker ❶.
2. Drag the Hanging Indent marker ❷ to the position where the indent is to begin.
3. Key the paragraph. Note that the second and subsequent lines are indented beginning at the marker.

DRILL 3 HANGING INDENT

glossary

1. In the open document, select all the glossary entries and format them with a hanging indent. **Hint:** Use the shortcut CTRL + T.
2. Proofread and check; click Next Activity. (*46-drill3*)

21e Textbook Keying

Key each line once.

1st finger

16 by bar get fun van for inn art from gray hymn July true verb

17 brag human bring unfold hominy mighty report verify puny joy

18 You are brave to try bringing home the van in the bad storm.

2nd finger

19 ace ink did cad keyed deep seed kind Dick died kink like kid

20 cease decease decades kick secret check decide kidney evaded

21 Dedre likes the idea of ending dinner with cake for dessert.

3rd finger

22 oil sow six vex wax axe low old lox pool west loss wool slow

23 swallow swamp saw sew wood sax sexes loom stew excess school

24 Wes waxes floors and washes windows at low costs to schools.

4th finger

25 zap zip craze pop pup pan daze quote queen quiz pizza puzzle

26 zoo graze zipper panzer zebra quip partizan patronize appear

27 Czar Zane appears to be dazzled by the apple pizza and jazz.

21f Timed Writing

1. Key a 1' timing on each paragraph.
2. Key a 3' timing on both paragraphs.

	gwam 1'	3'
Teams are the basic unit of performance for a firm. They	12	4
are not the solution to all the problems and needs of the	24	8
organization. However, they can perform at a higher rate	35	12
compared to other groups. Their support has great impact on	47	16
changes that are crucial to a firm.	54	18
Teams are not established just by joining people together	13	22
in a group. Team members should have a clear purpose and they	25	26
should also work with each other to reach a common goal. In	37	30
order to make a quality working plan, the team must maximize	49	38
their time and their abilities. They need to learn how to help	62	39
one another and make an effort to coordinate the tasks.	73	42

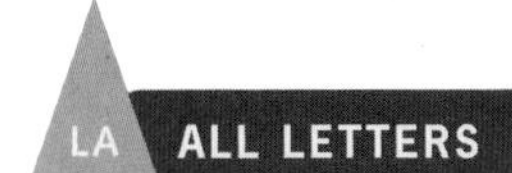

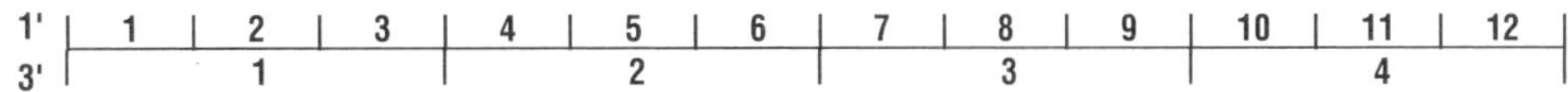

21g Enrichment

Take two 1' writings; the last number you key is your approximate *gwam.*

Reach for numbers with a minimum of hand movement.

1 and 2 and 3 and 4 and 5 and 6 and 7 and 8 and 9 and 10 and 11 and 12 and 13 and 14 and 15 and 16 and 17 and 18 and 19 and 20 and 21 and 22 and 23 and 24 and 25 and 26 and 27 and

SAVE AS TEMPLATE

A template is a set of predefined styles for a particular type of document. The purpose of a template is to reuse a document's formatting while easily changing the content. Templates are available for numerous types of documents and others can be downloaded from the Microsoft website. However, when existing documents are unique, it is useful to save them as a template.

By default, templates are saved to the Templates folder within the program. In a classroom environment, you will want to save templates you create to a USB memory device (flash drive) or another location.

To save a document as a template:

File/Save As

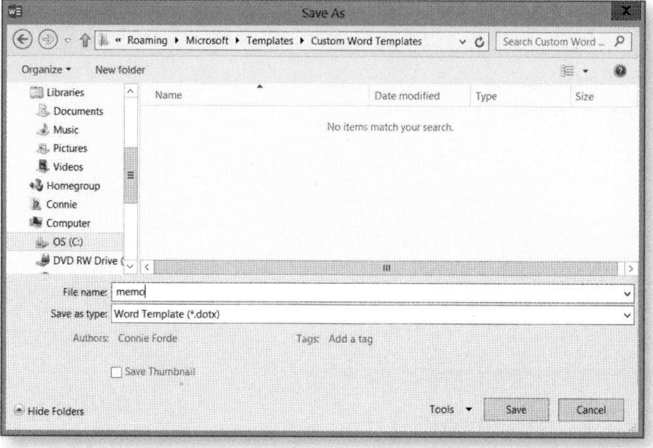

1. Click the File tab and then Save As. Click Computer and Browse. The Save As dialog box displays.
2. *Save to a USB memory device (flash drive):* Select Computer and browse to the flash drive.

   -or-

   Save to a hard drive: By default the software will save to the Templates folder or browse to the desired location.
3. In the File name box, key an appropriate template name such as **my memo**.
4. In the Save as type box, click the down arrow and select Word Template. Click Save. The extension *.dotx* is assigned automatically.

To use the template:

File/New

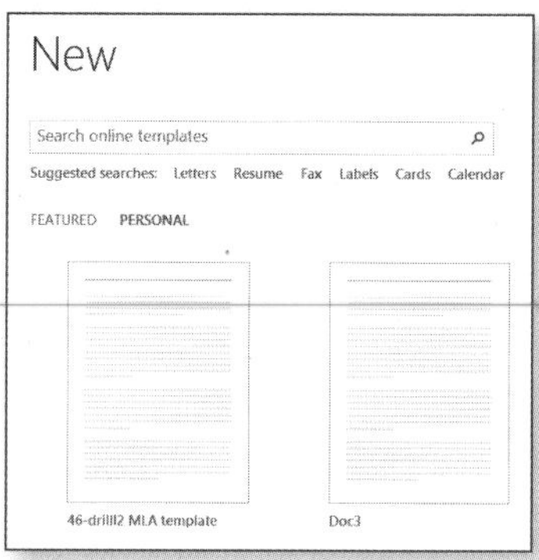

From a flash drive: Click the File tab and select New. From the Available Templates pane, browse to locate the desired template. Click OK.

-or-

From a hard drive: Click the File tab and select New. From the Available Templates pane, choose My templates; browse to locate the desired template. Click OK.

Lesson 22 (and) and Backspace Key

Warmup *Lesson 22a Warmup*

New Keys

22b (and)

(Shift; then reach *up* with the *right third* finger.

) Shift; then reach *up* with the *right fourth* finger.

( ) = parentheses
Parentheses indicate off-hand, aside, or explanatory messages.

1 ((l l((; (; Reach from l for the left parenthesis; as, ((.
2)); ;))); Reach from ; for the right parenthesis; as,)).

( )

3 Learn to use parentheses (plural) or parenthesis (singular).
4 The red (No. 34) and blue (No. 78) cars both won here (Rio).
5 We (Galen and I) dined (bagels) in our penthouse (the dorm).

22c All Symbols Learned

6 The jacket was $35 (thirty-five dollars)--the tie was extra.
7 Starting 10/29, you can sell Model #49 at a discount of 25%.
8 My size 8 1/2 shoe--a blue pump--was soiled (but not badly).

Skill Building

22d Textbook Keying

Key each line once.

Build confidence—trust yourself to make the correct reach.

9 Jana has one hard-to-get copy of her hot-off-the-press book.
10 An invoice said that "We give discounts of 10%, 5%, and 3%."
11 The company paid bill 8/07 on 5/2/14 and bill 4/9 on 3/6/14.
12 The catalog lists as out of stock Items #230, #710, and #13.
13 Ellyn had $8; Sean, $9; and Cal, $7. The cash total was $24.
14 A representative from the 16th District (Tom Law) will come.
15 The oldest family member (May Gray) will attend the reunion.

Lesson 46 Reports in MLA Style

New Commands

- Header
- Save As Template
- Hanging Indent

Warmup *Lesson 46a Warmup*

New Commands

46b

HEADER

A header contains text that is keyed in the top margin of the page. In this lesson you will create a header for an MLA report that displays on all pages.

To insert a header with text and page number:

Insert/Header & Footer/Header

1. Display the Built-in gallery of Header styles. Click the Blank style.
2. Tap the TAB key twice to place the insertion point at the far-right position. Key the desired text followed by a space.
3. From the Header & Footer group, click the Page Number drop-list arrow and choose Current Position. Choose the Plain Number style.

To edit a header:

Insert/Header & Footer/Header

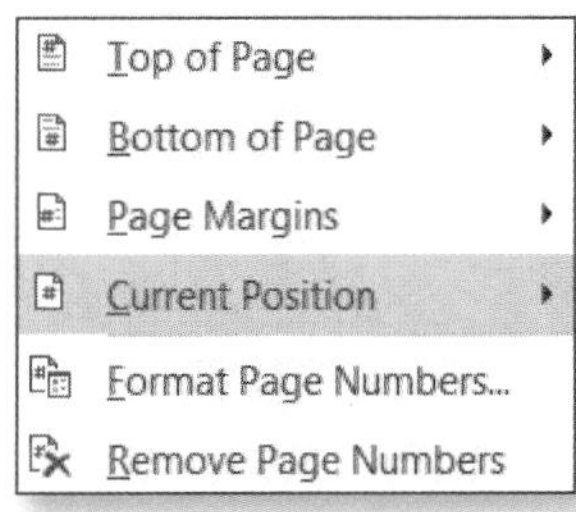

To edit a header, click Edit Header. An alternate method is to double-click in the header section of the document. To move to the text of the document, double-click in the document—not the header.

To remove a header, click Remove Header.

DRILL 1 HEADER

1. Double-click in the header section. Change to 12-point Times New Roman font.
2. Click the Align Right command and key **LNAME**. Tap the Space Bar and insert the Page Number command as shown above.
3. Proofread and check; click Next Activity. (*46-drill1*)

22e Timed Writing

1. Take two 3' timings on both paragraphs.
2. End the lesson.
3. Go to the Word Processor and complete 22f.

	gwam 3'
It is our obligation to preserve the planet and hand it	4
down to our children and grandchildren in a better condition	8
than when we first found it. We must take extra steps just to	12
make the quality of living better. Unless we change our ways	16
and stop damaging the environment, the world will not be a	20
good place to live.	22
To help save our ozone layer, we should not use any	25
products that may have harmful gas in them. There are many	29
simple and easy ways to clean the air such as planting more	33
trees and reusing materials. Also as important is the proper	37
disposal of our garbage in order to stop our water from	41
getting more and more polluted.	43

3' | 1 | 2 | 3 | 4 |

22f Backspace Key

Word Processor

1. Key sentences 16–21 in the Word Processor; use the BACKSPACE key to correct errors.
2. Key the numbers correctly in sentences 22–26. Refer to the Number Expression section in the Reference Guide.
3. Proofread and correct errors.
4. Save as *xx-22f* (your initials–22f). Print and close the document.

Use the Backspace key effectively.

16 You should be interested in the special items on sale today.
17 If she is going with us, why don't we plan to leave now?
18 Do you desire to continue working on the memo in the future?
19 Did the firm or their neighbors own the autos with problems?
20 Juni, Vec, and Zeb had perfect grades on weekly query exams.
21 Jewel quickly explained to me the big fire hazards involved.

22 All 7 contracts must be signed before 3 o'clock p.m.
23 Purchase 2 16-gigabyte USB flash drives; they are on sale.
24 Jim poured 3 six-liter jars of oil into the 9 gallon barrel.
25 My last computer project is approximately 1/2 complete.
26 The 16 percent discount saves $123.50. The tax was 75 cents.

Communication

22g Proofreading

1. From the Reference tab, click Communication Skills; select Proofreading.
2. Complete the pretest; click Report to review your results. Review the rules and complete the exercises and posttest.

Top right 0.5"

2

- Be sure to use the online thesaurus, spelling, and grammar features of the word processing software.
- Bookmark widely accepted online desk references and style manuals for easy use.
- Use the Show/Hide command to show the ¶ marks and other hidden formatting symbols.

1.5" These simple steps will assist you in your goal to create well-written and attractive reports. The next step is to practice, practice, and practice. 1"

Multiple-Page Report

Lesson 23 & and : (colon), Proofreaders' Marks

Warmup *Lesson 23a Warmup*

New Keys

23b & and : (Colon)

& Shift; then reach *up* with *right first* finger.

: (colon) Left shift; then tap key with *right fourth* finger.

& = ampersand: The ampersand is used only as part of company names.

Colon: Space once after a colon except when used within a number for time.

& (ampersand)

1 & &j j& & & &; J & J; Haraj & Jay; Moroj & Jax; Torj & Jones
2 Nehru & Unger; Mumm & Just; Mann & Hart; Arch & Jones; M & J
3 Rhye & Knox represent us; Steb & Doy, Firm A; R & J, Firm B.

: (colon)

4 : :; ;: : : :; as: for example: notice: Dear Sir: Gentlemen:
5 In stock: 10:30; 7:45; Age: Address: Read: Cell: Attachment:
6 Space once after a colon, thus: Telephone: Home Address: To:

23c All Symbols Learned

7 Consider these companies: J & R, Brand & Kay, Upper & Davis.
8 Memo #88-829 reads as follows: "Deduct 15% of $300, or $45."
9 Bill 32(5)--it got here quite late--from M & N was paid 7/3.

Skill Building

23d Textbook Keying

Key each line once.

10 *Jane may work with an auditing firm if she is paid to do so.*
11 *Pam and eight girls may go to the lake to work with the dog.*
12 *Clancy and Claudia did all the work to fix the sign problem.*
13 *Did Lea visit the Orlando land of enchantment or a neighbor?*
14 *Ana and Blanche made a map for a neighbor to go to the city.*
15 *Sidney may go to the lake to fish with worms from the docks.*
16 *Did the firm or the neighbors own the auto with the problem?*

About 2" (Tap ENTER 3 times.)

Title → # Report Writing and Technology ↓2

Being able to communicate effectively in a clear, concise, and logical manner continues to be one of the most demanded work skills. Employees who practice effective revision skills are far ahead of their counterparts who have had the mind-set that the first draft is the final draft. This report details excellent procedures for revising a report draft, explaining effective technology tools that make the process easier. The result is a more professional and accurate final product.

Heading 1

Revising the Draft ↓1

After a first draft of a report is completed, the writer is ready to refine or polish the report. The writer must be objective when revising the report draft and cultivate an attitude for improving the report by always considering the draft as a process.

1.5" 1"

First, read the draft for content. This might mean rewriting sections of the report or adding information to areas that appear weak in this review. In this evaluative review, the writer may realize that one section would fit more logically after another section.

When the writer is satisfied with the content, it is time to verity that all style rules have been followed. For example, check all headings to ensure they are "talking" headings. Do the headings describe the content of the section? Also, be sure all headings are parallel. If the writer chooses the side heading Know Your Audience, other side headings must also begin with a verb. Note that the side headings in this report are parallel, with both beginning with a gerund.

Ensuring Correct and Attractive Formats

The effective writer understands the importance of using technology to create an attractive document that adheres to correct style rules. Here are a few examples of how to use technology to create a professional final document. ↓1

- Select attractive headers and footers from the built-in design galleries to provide page numbers and other helpful information to the reader.
- Suppress headers, footers, and page numbering on the title page and on the first page of the report.
- Invoke the Widow/Orphan control feature to ensure that no lines display alone at the bottom or top of a page. Use the Keep with next command to keep side headings from appearing alone at the bottom of the page.
- Take advantage of automatic features, such as a table of contents and citations.
- Use styles to format tables and charts.

Multiple-Page Report

23e Improve Keystroking

double letters

17 Do Bennett was puzzled by drivers exceeding the speed limit.
18 Bill needs the office address; he will cut the grass at ten.
19 Todd saw the green car veer off the street near a tall tree.

figures and symbols

20 Invoice #84 for $672.90, plus $4.38 tax, was due February 3.
21 Do read Section 4, pages 60–74 and Section 9, pages 198–225.
22 Enter as follows: (a) name, (b) address, and (c) cell phone.

23f Timed Writing

Take two 3' timings. Use wordwrap.

	gwam 3'
Is how you judge my work important? Does your honest	4
opinion or feedback really matter? It does, of course; I hope	8
you appreciate the effort and recognize some basic merit in	12
it. We all expect to get credit for the hard work we put forth	16
and the good work we conclude. After all, we are all working	20
together to accomplish the goals of the company.	23
As a human being, I want approval for the ideas	27
presented, things written, and tasks completed. I always look	31
forward to your evaluations so I can learn more and continue	35
to grow. My work does not define me, but it shows my abilities	39
and skills. Through my work, I am my very own unique self.	43

3' | 1 | 2 | 3 | 4 |

Communication

23g Edit Text

Word Processor

1. In the Word Processor, key your name, class, and **23g** at the left margin. Then key lines 23–28, making the revisions as you key. Use the BACKSPACE key to correct errors.
2. Proofread and correct errors.
3. Save as *xx-23g*.

Symbol	Meaning	Symbol	Meaning
___	Italic	○ sp	Spell out
~~	Bold	¶	Paragraph
Cap or ═	Capitalize	#	Add horizontal space
^	Insert	/ or lc	Lowercase
	Delete		Close up space
	Move to left		Transpose
	Move to right	stet	Leave as originally written

```
23 We miss 50% in life's rowards by refusingto new try things.
24 do it now--today--then tomorrow's load will be 100% lighter.
25 Satisfying work--whether it pays $40 or $400-is the pay off.
26 Avoid mistakes:  confusing a #3 has cost thousands.
27 Pleased most with a first-rate job is the person who did it.
28 My wife and/or me mother will except the certifi cate for me.
```

Apply It

45-d1

Multiple-Page Report

 writing

Discover

Insert a File

Insert/Text/Object

1. Click the arrow next to Object.
2. Click Text from File.
3. Select the desired file and click Insert.

1. Key the first paragraph of the leftbound two-page report shown on the next two pages. Apply the appropriate style for the title of the report. Tap ENTER two times after title.
2. Insert the data file *writing* below the first PARAGRAPH. **Note:** Be sure to position the insertion point where you want the text to appear before inserting the file.
3. Apply the appropriate style for the side headings.
4. In the last bulleted item, delete the word *paragraph* and insert the ¶ mark from the Special Characters tab of the Symbol dialog box.
5. Use the Page Number command to number the pages at the top right. Select the Plain Number 3 number style. Click Different First Page to suppress the page number on the first page.
6. Preview the document to verify page numbers and that side headings are not left alone at the bottom of the page.
7. Proofread and check; click Next Activity. (*45-d1*)

45-d2

Edit Report

1. From the open document (*45-d1*), change the leftbound report to an unbound report. Apply the Facet document theme.
2. Position the insertion point on page 2 of the report. Change the page number style to Accent Bar 2.
3. Key the following as the last item in the bulleted list. Insert the symbols from the Wingdings font or the Special Characters tab.
   - **Use a wide array of symbols to provide a fresh and up-to-date appearance, such as ❶,** **, ©, or ®.**
4. Proofread and check; click Exit Word. (*45-d2*)
5. Click Log out to exit *KPDO*.

WORKPLACE SUCCESS

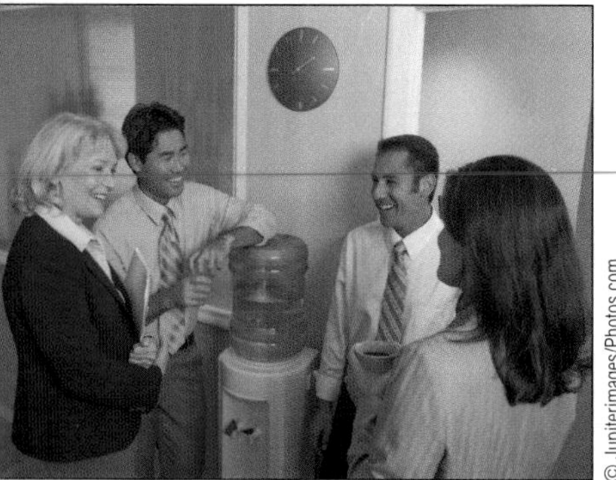

© Jupiterimages/Photos.com

Integrity

Integrity is synonymous with the word *honesty* and is confronted by employees in the workplace daily. Think about these rather common situations where integrity is clearly a choice:

- Arriving at work ten minutes late and then drinking coffee and chatting with coworkers for ten more minutes
- Talking with relatives and friends throughout the day
- Leaving work early regularly for personal reasons
- Presenting a report to the supervisor as original work without crediting the proper individuals for thoughts and ideas in the report
- Presenting a report that was completed at the last minute and that includes facts and figures that have not been verified as accurate

In all situations, ask the question, "Am I being honest?"

Lesson 24 Other Symbols

Warmup *Lesson 24a Warmup*

New Keys

24b Textbook Keying

@ * + =

@	at
*	asterisk
+	plus sign (use a hyphen for minus and x for "times")
=	equals

Be confident—watch the copy, not the hands.

@ shift; reach *up* with *left third* finger to @

1 @ @s s@ a a; 24 @ .15; 22 @ .35; sold 2 @ .87; were 12 @ .95

2 You may contact Calvin @: CEP@rpx.com or fax @ 602.555.0101.

3 E-mail Al ajj@crewl.com and Matt mrw10@scxs.com by 9:30 p.m.

* shift; reach *up* with *right second* finger to *

4 * *k k8* * *; aurelis*; May 7*; both sides*; 250 km.**; aka*

5 Note each *; one * refers to page 29; ** refers to page 307.

6 Use *.* to search for files; the * looks for all characters.

\+ shift; reach *up* with *right fourth* finger to +

7 + ;+ +; + + +; 2 + 2; A+ or B+; 70+ F. degrees; +xy over +y;

8 The question was 8 + 7 + 51; it should have been 8 + 7 + 15.

9 My grades on the tests and final exam are B+, C+, B+, and A.

= reach *up* with *right fourth* finger to =

10 = =; = = =; = 4; If 14x = 28, x = 2; if 8x = 16, then x = 2.

11 Change this solution (where it says "= by") to = bx or = BX.

12 Key the formula =(a2+b2)*d5/4 in the formula bar; tap Enter.

45c

References/Document Formats/
Multiple-Page Report

MULTIPLE-PAGE REPORT

Because reports are often longer than one page, page numbers are required for ease in reading the report. Remember when formatting a multiple-page document, insert page numbers on all pages except the first page.

Traditionally, page numbers are positioned at the top right of the page. However, in lengthy and more formal documents such as annual reports or manuals, attractive headers and footers are designed. The applications that follow will include the Simple gallery of page number designs. Advanced headers and footers will be presented later.

Study the illustration below, noting specifically the position of page numbers. Review the callouts to reinforce your understanding of report formats.

To format a multiple-page report with page numbers at the top right:

1. Insert page numbers at the upper-right corner in the header position (0.5").
2. Suppress the page number on the first page.
3. Protect side headings that may be separated from the related paragraph with the Keep with next command. **Note:** When styles are applied to side headings, Keep with next is automatically applied, and side headings will not display alone at the bottom of a page.

Report Writing and Technology

Being able to communicate effectively in a clear, concise, and logical manner continues to be one of the most demanded work skills. Employees who practice effective revision skills are far ahead of their counterparts who have had the mind-set that the first draft is the final draft. This report details excellent procedures for revising a report draft, explaining effective technology tools that make the process easier. The result is a more professional and accurate final product.

Revising the Draft

After a first draft of a report is completed, the writer is ready to refine or polish the report. The writer must be objective when revising the report draft and cultivate an attitude for improving the report by always considering the draft as a process.

First, read the draft for content. This might mean rewriting sections of the report or adding information to areas that appear weak in this review. In this evaluative review, the writer may realize that one section would fit more logically after another section.

When the writer is satisfied with the content, it is time to verity that all style rules have been followed. For example, check all headings to ensure they are "talking" headings. Do the headings describe the content of the section? Also, be sure all headings are parallel. If the writer chooses the side heading Know Your Audience, other side headings must also begin with a verb. Note that the side headings in this report are parallel, with both beginning with a gerund.

Ensuring Correct and Attractive Formats

The effective writer understands the importance of using technology to create an attractive document that adheres to correct style rules. Here are a few examples of how to use technology to create a professional final document.

- Select attractive headers and footers from the built-in design galleries to provide page numbers and other helpful information to the reader.
- Suppress headers, footers, and page numbering on the title page and on the first page of the report.
- Invoke the Widow/Orphan control feature to ensure that no lines display alone at the bottom or top of a page. Use the Keep with next command to keep side headings from appearing alone at the bottom of the page.
- Take advantage of automatic features, such as a table of contents and citations.
- Use styles to format tables and charts.

Header position, right side

2

- Be sure to use the online thesaurus, spelling, and grammar features of the word processing software.
- Bookmark widely accepted online desk references and style manuals for easy use.
- Use the Show/Hide command to show the ¶ marks and other hidden formatting symbols.

These simple steps will assist you in your goal to create well-written and attractive reports. The next step is to practice, practice, and practice.

Skill Building

24c Improve Keystroking

double letters
13 feel pass mill good miss seem moons cliffs pools green spell
14 Assets are being offered in a stuffy room to two associates.

balanced hand
15 is if of to it go do to is do so if to the to sign it vie to
16 Pamela or Jen may also go to town with Blanche if she works.

24d Timed Writing

Take two 3' timings.
Use wordwrap.

	gwam 3'
Why do we resist change so much? Do you think perhaps it	4
is because it requires more time and effort learning new	8
things and making difficult decisions? Is it also because we	12
are set in our ways, afraid to take chances and dislike being	16
told what to do? Besides, what is the point of trying to	20
improve something that works just fine?	22
We know change can and does extend new areas of	26
enjoyment, areas we might never have known existed. If we stay	30
away from all change, we could curtail our quality of life.	34
People who are open to change are more zealous and more	38
productive than those who aren't. They are also better at	42
coping with the hardships and challenges that life often	46
brings.	46

3' | 1 | 2 | 3 | 4 |

Communication

24e Composition

1. In the Word Processor, open the file *xx-profile* that you created in Lesson 18.
2. Position the insertion point at the end of the last paragraph. Tap ENTER twice.
3. Key an additional paragraph that begins with the following sentence:
   Thank you for allowing me to introduce myself.
4. Finish the paragraph by adding two or more sentences that describe your progress and satisfaction with keyboarding.
5. Correct any mistakes you have made. Click Save to resave the document. Print.
6. Mark any mistakes you missed with proofreaders' marks. Revise the document and save. Submit to your instructor.

24f Edit Copy

1. In the Word Processor, key your name, class, and date at the left margin on separate lines.
2. Key each line, making the corrections marked with proofreaders' marks.
3. Proofread and correct errors using the BACKSPACE key.
4. Save as *xx-24f*.

```
17 Ask Group 1 to read Chater 6 of Book 11 (Shelf 19,Room 5).
18 All 6 of us live at One Bay road, not at 126-56th Street.
19 AT 9 a.m. the owners decided to close form 12 noon to 1 p.m.
20 Ms. Vik leaves June 9; she r eturns the 14 or 15 of July.
21 The 16 per cent discount saves 115.  A stamp costs 44 cents.
22 Elin gave $300,000,000; our gift was only 75 cents.
```

SYMBOLS AND SPECIAL CHARACTERS

Symbols and special characters that are not on your keyboard can be inserted using the Symbol command. Different types of symbols can be inserted depending on the font selected. Some symbols are scientific or mathematical and are generally located on the Symbols font. Other symbols are decorative and are generally located on the Wingdings font.

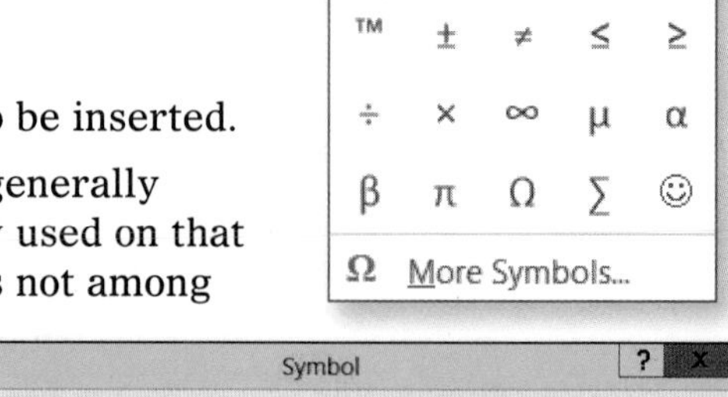

To insert symbols:
Insert/Symbols/Symbol

1. Click in the document where the symbol is to be inserted.
2. Display the gallery of symbols. The gallery generally contains the symbols that have been recently used on that computer. If the symbol you want to insert is not among the options, click More Symbols to display the Symbol dialog box.
3. Make sure the Symbols tab is selected and then check the Font box for the appropriate font. If Symbol (or the font you want to use) is not displayed, click the drop-list arrow and scroll to the desired font and select it.
4. Scroll down to locate the desired symbol and select it.
5. Click Insert and Close.

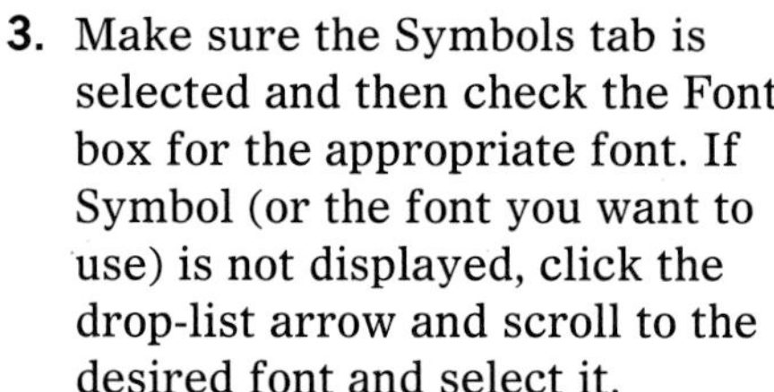

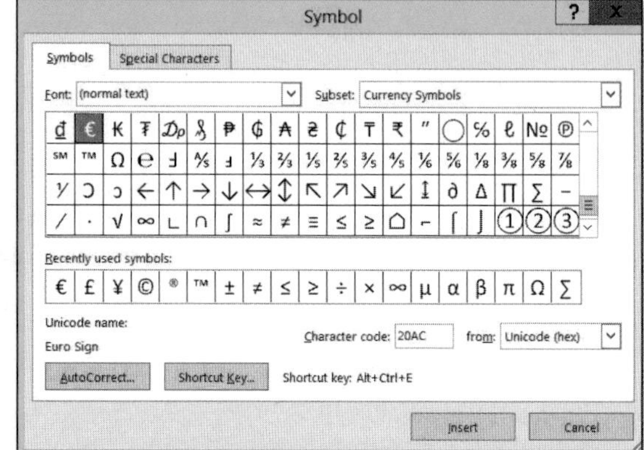

Special characters not located on the keyboard are located on the Special Characters tab. Examples include the em dash, nonbreaking hyphen, registered, trademark, and paragraph characters.

To insert special characters:
Insert/Symbols/Symbol

1. Click in the document where the special character is to be inserted.
2. Click the Special Characters tab in the Symbol dialog box.
3. Select the special character desired; click Insert and then click Close.

DRILL 2 SYMBOLS AND SPECIAL CHARACTERS

1. Apply Verdana 16-point font.
2. Insert these symbols; do not key the description or the parentheses. Tap ENTER after each symbol.

   Plus or minus symbol (±) from the Symbol font

   Smiley face (☺) from the Wingdings font

   Checkbox (☑) from the Wingdings 2 font
3. Key the text below and insert the special characters; do not key the description of the character in parenthesis. Tap ENTER after each character.

   Farbe Microfiber™ (Trademark)
   § (Section)
   ¶ (Paragraph)
4. Proofread and check; click Next Activity. (*45-drill2*)

Lesson 24R Review

Warmup *Lesson 24Ra Warmup*

Skill Building

24Rb Textbook Keying

Key each line once; work for fluency.

1 E-mail invoice #397 to gmeathe@skd.org; the $7 will be paid.
2 Jane and Ken may go to town to handle the pale and sick dog.
3 The answers to pop quiz #12 are: (1) a, (2) c, (3) b, (4) c.
4 Uncle Jeff rented a burgundy minivan for three days a month.
5 Check #42 was sent on 6/15 for the amount of $89 as payment.
6 Zale played amazing pop jazz on a saxophone and a xylophone.
7 L & D Bank pays 7% interest on savings accounts, 10% on CDs.

24Rc Timed Writing

1. Key a 1' timing on each paragraph; work to increase speed.
2. Key a 3' timing on all paragraphs.

	gwam 1'	3'
Do you find yourself forgetting the names of people that	12	4
you have known for quite some time? Did you put something down	25	8
and a few minutes later were not able to find it again? Memory	37	12
lapses like these are normal, and there are things you can do	50	17
to prevent them from happening as often. Just a few simple	62	21
lifestyle changes can easily help improve your emory.	72	24
Everyone can take steps to better their memory; it will	12	28
take both time and practice. It is important to get enough	24	32
sleep and to eat properly. Exercise both the mind and the	36	36
body. Read, write, and do puzzles each day to help develop	47	44
your memory. Make time for family and friends and have a good	60	48
time with them.	63	49

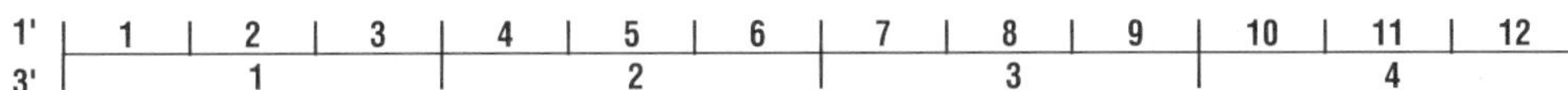

24Rd Enrichment

Word Processor

1. Key the paragraphs in the Word Processor, making revisions as you key.
2. Key your name and 24Rd below the paragraph.
3. Save as *xx-24Rd*.

Any one who expects someday to find an ~~excellent~~ *great* job should *begin now to* learn the value of accuracy. To be worth any thing ~~completed~~ *final* work must *be* ~~accurate~~ *correct*, without ~~any~~ question. ~~Naturally~~ *Of course,* we realize that the *human* aspect of the work equation raises always the chance of errors; *but* we should ~~know~~ *understand* that those same ~~mistakes~~ *errors* can be found and fixed. Every job completed should carry at least 1 *sp* stamp; the stamp of ~~approval~~ *true pride* in work that is ~~outstanding~~ *exemplary*.

LINE AND PAGE BREAKS

Pagination or breaking pages at the appropriate location can easily be controlled using two features: Widow/Orphan control and Keep with next.

Widow/Orphan control prevents a single line of a paragraph from printing at the bottom or top of a page. A check mark displays in this option box indicating that Widow/Orphan control is "on" (the default).

Keep with next prevents a page break from occurring between two paragraphs. Use this feature to keep a side heading from being left alone at the bottom of a page.

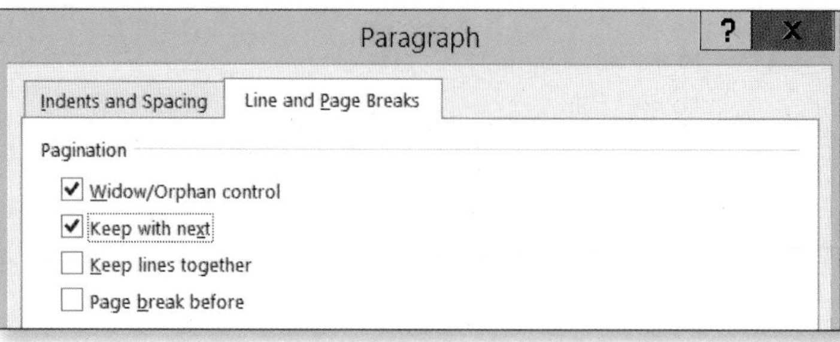

To use Keep with next:

Home/Paragraph/Dialog Box Launcher

1. Select the side heading and at least two lines of the paragraph that follow it.
2. Display the Paragraph dialog box.
3. From the Line and Page Breaks tab, select Keep with next.

DRILL 1 PAGE NUMBERS

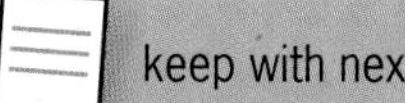

Insert/Header & Footer/Page Number

1. Add page numbers positioned at the top of page at the right. Do not print a page number on the first page.
2. Select the side heading at the bottom of the page along with the entire address and the 9:00 entry. Apply Keep with next so the side heading moves to page 2.
3. Preview to verify that the page number appears on page 2 only and that the side heading appears on page 2.
4. Proofread and check; click Next Activity. (*45-drill1*)

Itinerary for Thomas Stevens
October 22-25, 201-

Wednesday, October 22 Orange County to Detroit

1:30 p.m.	Leave Orange County Airport, Central Airlines, Flight 710; dinner. Arrive O'Hare International Airport, Chicago, at 8:34 p.m.
9:15 p.m.	Leave Chicago, Central Airlines, Flight 326; arrive Detroit Metropolitan Airport, Detroit at 10:05 p.m. Mid-size car reserved at A-1 Car Rental (Confirmation #5610). Reservations at Fairlane Cadillac Hotel (Confirmation #71325) 900 Michigan Avenue, Dearborn, MI (313.555.0197)

Thursday, October 23 Studebaker Motor Headquarters

	710 Michigan Avenue
	Dearborn, MI 48126-0710
	313.555.0143
8:00 a.m.	Breakfast with Jennifer Wright and John Daniels of Phoenix, Inc. Meet in hotel lobby at 7:50 a.m.
9:00 a.m.	Meeting with Walter Dodd, Manager, Process Engineering, regarding commitment to new model requirements.
10:00 a.m.	Meeting with Susana Lee, Head Engineer, Front-end Electrical, regarding wiring.
11:30 a.m.	Lunch with Joseph Mucholli, Project Coordinator.
2:00 p.m.	Meeting with all Project Coordinators on Raleigh Project.
7:00 p.m.	Dinner with Laura Mays, Vice President of Automotive Assembly Division.

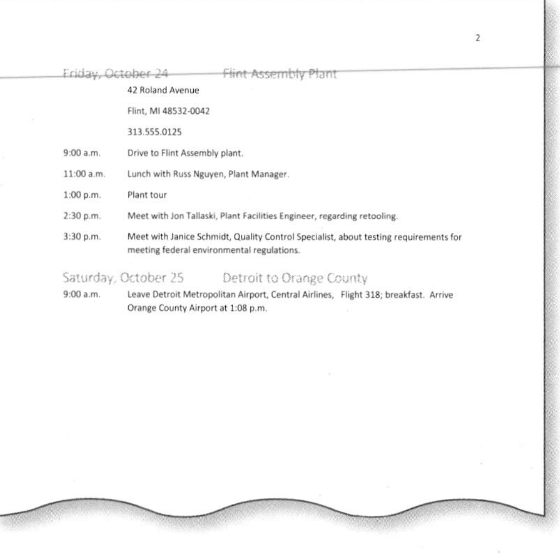

2

Friday, October 24 Flint Assembly Plant

	42 Roland Avenue
	Flint, MI 48532-0042
	313.555.0125
9:00 a.m.	Drive to Flint Assembly plant.
11:00 a.m.	Lunch with Russ Nguyen, Plant Manager.
1:00 p.m.	Plant tour
2:30 p.m.	Meet with Jon Tallaski, Plant Facilities Engineer, regarding retooling.
3:30 p.m.	Meet with Janice Schmidt, Quality Control Specialist, about testing requirements for meeting federal environmental regulations.

Saturday, October 25 Detroit to Orange County

9:00 a.m.	Leave Detroit Metropolitan Airport, Central Airlines, Flight 318; breakfast. Arrive Orange County Airport at 1:08 p.m.

Lesson 25 Assessment

Warmup *Lesson 25a Warmup*

Skill Building

25b Improve Keystroking

n/y
1 deny many canny tiny nymph puny any puny zany penny pony yen
2 Jenny Nyles saw many, many tiny nymphs flying near her pony.

b/r
3 bran barb brim curb brat garb bray verb brag garb bribe herb
4 Barb Barber can bring a bit of bran and herbs for her bread.

c/e
5 cede neck nice deck dice heck rice peck vice erect mice echo
6 Can Cedric erect a decent cedar deck? He erects nice condos.

n/u
7 nun gnu bun nut pun numb sun nude tuna nub fun null unit gun
8 Eunice had enough ground nuts at lunch; Uncle Launce is fun.

25c Textbook Keying

Key each line once.

9 is if he do rub ant go and am pan do rut us aid ox ape by is
10 it is|an end|it may|to pay|and so|aid us|he got|or own|to go
11 Did the girl make the ornament with fur, duck down, or hair?

12 us owl rug box bob to man so bit or big pen of jay me age it
13 it|it is|time to go|show them how|plan to go|one of the aims
14 It is a shame they use the autobus for a visit to the field.

25d Timed Writing

Key two 3' writings. Strive for accuracy. Use wordwrap.

Goal: 3', 19–27 *gwam.*

Build confidence—trust your reach instincts.

gwam 3'

The term career can mean many different things to 4
different people. As you know, a career is more than just an 8
occupation. It includes the jobs an individual has over time. 12
It also involves how the work life affects the other parts of 16
our life. There are as many types of careers as there are 20
people. 20

Almost every person has a career of some kind. A career 24
can help us attain unique goals, such as having a stable 28
livelihood or a rewarding vocation. The kind of career you 32
have will affect your life in many ways. For example, it can 36
determine where you live, the money you make, and how you feel 40
about yourself. A good choice can thus help you realize the 44
life you want. 45

3' | 1 | 2 | 3 | 4 |

Lesson 45 Multiple-Page Reports

New Commands

- Page Number
- Line/Page Breaks
- Insert File
- Symbols
- Special Characters

Warmup *Lesson 45a Warmup*

New Commands

45b

PAGE NUMBERS

Multiple-page documents, such as reports, require page numbers. The Page Number command automatically inserts the correct page number on each page. Page numbers may be positioned in the header position (0.5" from top of page) or in the footer position (bottom of page). To prevent the number from printing on the first page, you can modify the page layout on the first page.

To insert page numbers:
Insert/Header & Footer/Page Number

1. Display a list of page number positions and formatting options.
2. Click an option such as Top of Page ❶ to display a gallery of page number styles.
3. Click the down scroll arrow to browse the various styles ❷. **Note:** To remove page numbers, click Remove Page Numbers ❸ .

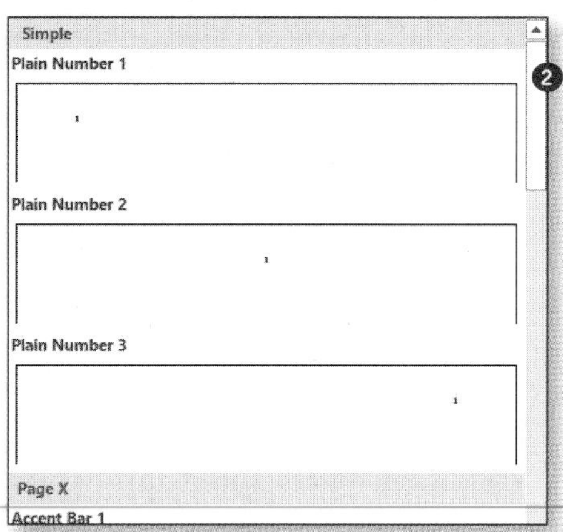

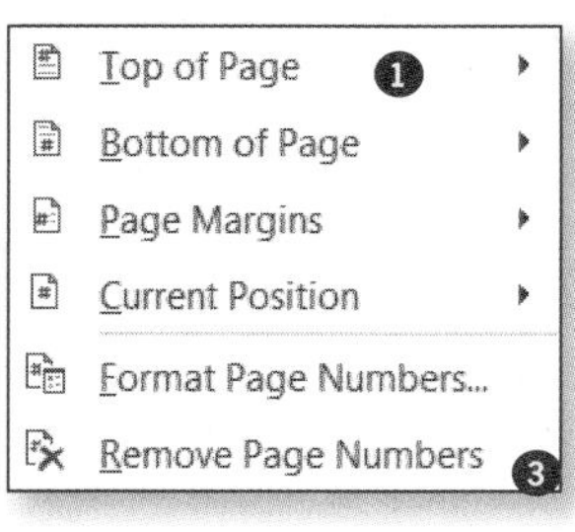

Double-click in the body of the document to close the header. Double-click in the header area to open the header.

To remove the page number from the first page:
Header & Footer Tools/Design/Options/Different First Page

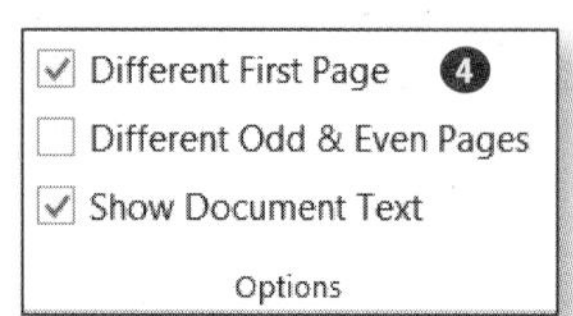

When the page number is inserted, the Header & Footer Tools Design conceptual tab displays. On the Design tab from the Options group, click Different First Page ❹. The page number does not display on the first page.

Option: Select Different First Page from the Layout tab of the Page Setup dialog box (Page Layout/Page Setup/Dialog Box Launcher).

25e Figure Check

Word Processor

In the Word Processor, key two 3' writings at a controlled rate. Save the timings as xx-25e-t1 and xx-25e-t2. Use wordwrap.

Goal: 3', 14–16 *gwam.*

gwam 3'

Do people read the stock market pages in the news? Yes; 4
at approximately 9 or 10 a.m. each morning, I know lots of 8
excited people who do that. Some people still like to have the 12
paper delivered to their home each morning. Others like the 16
convenience of reading the news on their computer or their 20
cell phone. Nevertheless, we can't wait to obtain the first 24
stock report each day. 26

Some people take the stock market very seriously. They 30
watch their stocks carefully and note the rise and fall of 34
each stock. Most investors like to be able to "buy at 52 and 38
sell at 60." Some would like to receive a dividend of 7 or 8 42
percent on their stocks. Regardless, each morning we zip 45
immediately to the stock report to see how the market is 49
doing. When the stock is down, we quickly purchase more shares 53
and keep them until they increase in value. The stock market 58
is an important and vital part of our life. 60

3' | 1 | 2 | 3 | 4 |

Communication

25f Edit Copy

1. In the Word Processor, key your name, class, and date at the left margin.
2. Key the paragraphs and make the corrections marked with proofreaders' marks. Use the BACKSPACE key to correct errors.
3. Check number expressions.
4. Save as *xx-25f.*

Last week the healthy heart foundation relased the findings of a study that showed exercise diet and ~~if individuals don't~~ smoke are the major controllable factors that led to a healthy heart. Factors such as heredity can not be controlled. The study included 25 to 65 ~~year old~~ males ~~as well as~~ females.

The study also showed that just taking a walk ~~benefits our health.~~ Those who walked an average of 2 to 3 hours a week were more then 30 percent less likely to have problems than those who did no exercise.

25g Proofread and Edit

1. In the Word Processor, open *xx-24Rd.*
2. Turn to page 70 and proofread your document with Writing 11.
3. Make corrections as needed. Save as *xx-25g.* Print.

Learn More:
www.cengagebrain.com

Apply It

44-d1

Leftbound Report

1. Key the model leftbound report shown on the previous page. Change the left margin to 1.5". Tap ENTER three times to position the title at about 2". Tap ENTER twice.
2. Apply appropriate styles to the title and side headings.
3. Key the table and apply the Grid Table 6 Colorful – Accent 1 style. Size the columns attractively and center the table horizontally. Click in the paragraph below the table and apply Add Space Before Paragraph to adjust the spacing after the table.
4. Proofread and check; click Next Activity. (*44-d1*)

REVIEW

Add Space Before Paragraph

Home/Paragraph/Line and Paragraph Spacing/Add Space Before Paragraph

44-d2

Edit Report

brochure

1. Format as a leftbound report. Apply the Retrospect document theme.
2. Key the paragraph shown below as the last paragraph. Apply Heading 1 style to the side heading.
3. Search for the word *photos* and replace with **photographs**.
4. Search for all occurrences of italics and replace them with no italic.
5. Search for all occurrences of bold and replace them with no bold except the side headings. **Hint:** Click the No Formatting button in the Find and Replace dialog box before you begin the new search. Click Find Next to review each replacement.
6. Click PAGES in the Navigation pane. Search for the word *readability*. Which page displays as a result of your search?
7. Click HEADINGS (*readability* is displayed in the search box). Which heading is displayed in yellow to indicate readability is discussed under that heading in the document?
8. Proofread and check; click Exit Word. (*44-d2*)
9. Click Log out to exit *KPDO*.

TIP

Replace Font Attribute (Italic)

Find what:

1. Click Format and then Font.
2. Under Font style, click Italic.

Replace with:

1. Click Format and then Font.
2. Under Font style, click Not italic.

Summary Apply Heading 1 style

Remember to plan your page layout with the three basic elements of effective page design. Always include sufficient white space to give an uncluttered appearance. Learn to add bold when emphasis is needed, and do consider your audience when choosing typestyles. Finally, use typestyles to add variety to your layout, but remember, no more than two typestyles in a document.

Skill Builder 2

Skill Building *Technique Builder*

Select the Skill Building tab from the Main menu and then Technique Builder. Select the drill and follow the directions in the book.

DRILL 8

Opposite Hand Reaches

Key each line once and DS between groups of lines. Key at a controlled rate; concentrate on the reaches.

i/e

1 ik is fit it sit laid site like insist still wise coil light
2 ed he ear the fed egg led elf lake jade heat feet hear where
3 lie kite item five aide either quite linear imagine brighter
4 Imagine the aide eating the pears before the grieving tiger.

w/o

5 ws we way was few went wit law with weed were week gnaw when
6 ol on go hot old lot joy odd comb open tool upon money union
7 bow owl word wood worm worse tower brown toward wrote weapon
8 The workers lowered the brown swords toward the wood weapon.

DRILL 9

Proofreaders' Marks

Key each line once and DS after each sentence. Correct the sentence as edited, making all handwritten corrections. Do not key the numbers.

- Capitalize
- Change letter
- Close up space
- Delete
- Insert
- Lowercase
- Space
- Transpose

1. When a writer create the preliminary version of a document, they are concentrating on conveying the intended ideas.
2. This ver sion of a prelpminary document is called a rough.
3. After the draft is created the Writer edits/refines the copy.
4. Sometimes proofreader's marks are used to edit the draft.
5. The changes will them be make to the original.
6. After the changes have been made then the Writer reads the copy.
7. Edit ing and proofreading requires alot of time and effort.
8. An attitute of excellance is reqiured to produce error free message.

DRILL 10

Proofreading

Compare your sentences in Drill 9 with Drill 10. How did you do? Now key the paragraph for fluency. Concentrate on keying as accurately as possible.

When a writer creates the preliminary version of a document, he or she is concentrating on conveying ideas. This preliminary version is called a rough draft. After the draft is created, the writer edits or refines the copy. Proofreaders' marks are used to edit the rough draft. The editing changes will be made to the original. Then the writer reads the copy again. Editing requires a lot of time and effort. An attitude of excellence is required to produce an error-free message.

About 2" (Tap ENTER three times.)

Title → # Identify Your Audience and Purpose

Title style ↓ 2

Effective presenters realize the need to prepare for a successful presentation. Two areas of extensive preparation are the development of a thorough audience analysis and identification of a well-defined presentation purpose. ↓ 1

Side heading → ## Audience Analysis

Heading 1 style

The presenter must conduct a thorough audience analysis before developing the presentation. A listing of common audience demographics is shown in the table below. ↓ 1

Audience Profile	
Age	Gender
Education	Ethnic group
Marital status	Geographic location
Group membership	Vested interest in topic

1.5"

1"

Given sufficient time, the presenter will research each of these areas carefully. Additionally, interviews with program planners and organization leaders will provide insight into the needs, desires, and expectations of the specific audience. ↓ 1

Many successful presenters find it useful to arrive early to the presentation and greet participants as they enter the meeting room. Often presenters may begin the presentation with one or two directed questions to understand the profile and demeanor of the audience. Knowing the audience is an important first step in preparing a successful presentation.

↓ 1

Purpose of the Presentation

After initially analyzing the audience profile well in advance, the presenter has a clear focus on the needs of the audience and then writes a well-defined purpose of the presentation. With a clear focus, the presenter confidently conducts research and organizes a presentation that is on target. The presenter remembers to state the purpose in the introduction of the presentation to assist the audience in understanding the well-defined direction of the presentation.

Leftbound Report

Assess Skill Growth:

1. Select the Timed Writings tab from the Main menu.
2. Select the writing number such as Writing 8.
3. Select 3' as the length of the writing. Use wordwrap.
4. Repeat the timing if desired.

Word Processor Option:

1. Key 1' writings on each paragraph of a timing. Note that paragraphs within a timing increase by two words.
   Goal: to complete each paragraph
2. Key a 3' timing on the entire writing.

gwam 1' | 3'

Writing 8

Any of us whose target is to have success in our professional 12 4
work will understand that we must learn how to work in harmony 25 8
with others whose paths may cross ours daily. 34 11

We will, unquestionably, work for, with, and beside people, just 13 15
as they will work for, with, and beside us. We will judge them, 25 20
as most certainly they are going to be judging us. 35 23

A lot of people realize the need for solid working relations and 13 27
have a rule that treats others as they, themselves, expect to be 26 32
treated. This seems to be a sound, practical idea for them. 37 35

Writing 9

I spoke with one company visitor recently; and she was very much 13 4
impressed, she said, with the large amount of work she had noted 26 9
being finished by one of our front office workers. 36 12

I told her how we had just last week recognized this very person 13 16
for what he had done, for output, naturally, but also because of 26 21
its excellence. We know this person has that "magic touch." 38 25

This "magic touch" is the ability to do a fair amount of work in 13 29
a fair amount of time. It involves a desire to become ever more 26 34
efficient without losing quality--the "touch" all workers should 39 38
have. 40 38

Writing 10

Isn't it great just to untangle and relax after you have keyed a 13 4
completed document? Complete, or just done? No document is 25 8
quite complete until it has left you and passed to the next step. 38 13

There are desirable things that must happen to a document before 13 17
you surrender it. It must be read carefully, first of all, for 26 22
meaning to find words that look right but aren't. Read word for 39 26
word. 40 26

Check all figures and exact data, like a date or time, with your 13 31
principal copy. Make sure format details are right. Only then, 26 35
print or remove the work and scrutinize to see how it might look 39 39
to a recipient. 42 40

DRILL 2 NAVIGATION

speeches

Home/Editing/Find

1. Click the Find button to display the Navigation pane.
2. Display all occurrences of the word *speeches* and replace with **presentations**.
3. Display all occurrences of the word *objective*. Click on the last occurrence and replace with **goal**.
4. Display all occurrences of the word *confident*. Click Options and select Find whole words only. Replace the one occurrence with **assured**.
5. Find *audience* and highlight each occurrence in yellow.
   Hint: Be sure to set the Highlight button in the Font group on the Home tab to yellow.
6. Key **discussion** in the Search box. Click PAGES to browse the pages where this word occurs.
7. Click HEADINGS to display the headings where the word *discussion* occurs. Click on the second heading and then the third heading to move in the report.
8. Click the Magnifying Glass button and click Tables to go to the table in the report.
9. Proofread and check; click Next Activity. (*44-drill2*)

Document Design

LEFTBOUND REPORT

44e

References/Document Formats/Reports

Reports prepared with binders are called leftbound reports. The binding takes 0.5" of space. Study the illustration below and the full model on page 183 and note the 1.5" left margin required for leftbound reports. Review the other report formats that are the same for unbound and leftbound reports.

Theme: Use the default Office theme.

Left margin: 1.5"

Right margin: 1"

Bottom margin: Approximately 1"; last page may be deeper

Font: 11 point for body of report

Title: ❶

- Position at about 2".
- Capitalize the first letter of all main words and apply Title style. Tap ENTER two times.

Side headings: ❷

- Capitalize the first letter of all main words and apply Heading 1 style.

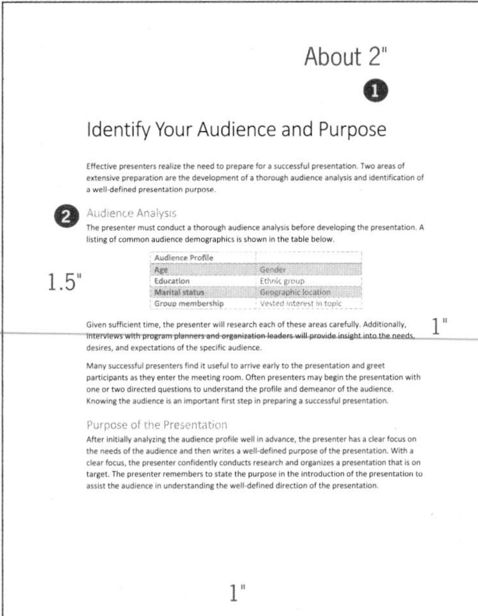

Identify Your Audience and Purpose

Effective presenters realize the need to prepare for a successful presentation. Two areas of extensive preparation are the development of a thorough audience analysis and identification of a well-defined presentation purpose.

Audience Analysis

The presenter must conduct a thorough audience analysis before developing the presentation. A listing of common audience demographics is shown in the table below.

Audience Profile	
Age	Gender
Education	Ethnic group
Marital status	Geographic location
Group membership	Vested interest in topic

Given sufficient time, the presenter will research each of these areas carefully. Additionally, interviews with program planners and organization leaders will provide insight into the needs, desires, and expectations of the specific audience.

Many successful presenters find it useful to arrive early to the presentation and greet participants as they enter the meeting room. Often presenters may begin the presentation with one or two directed questions to understand the profile and demeanor of the audience. Knowing the audience is an important first step in preparing a successful presentation.

Purpose of the Presentation

After initially analyzing the audience profile well in advance, the presenter has a clear focus on the needs of the audience and then writes a well-defined purpose of the presentation. With a clear focus, the presenter confidently conducts research and organizes a presentation that is on target. The presenter remembers to state the purpose in the introduction of the presentation to assist the audience in understanding the well-defined direction of the presentation.

Writing 11 *gwam* 3'

Anyone who expects some day to find a great job should 4
begin now to learn the value of accuracy. To be worth anything, 8
final work must be correct, without question. Of course, we 12
realize that the human aspect of the work equation always raises 16
the chance of errors; but we should understand that those same 20
errors can be found and fixed. Every completed job should carry 24
at least one stamp; the stamp of true pride in work that is exemplary. 29

Writing 12

No question about it: Many of the personal problems we face 4
today arise from the fact that we have never been very wise 8
consumers. We have not used our natural resources well; as a result, 13
we have jeopardized much of our environment. We excused our 17
actions because we thought that our stock of most resources had no 21
limit at all. So, at last, we are beginning to realize just how indiscreet 26
we were; and we are taking steps to rebuild our world. 30

Writing 13

When I see people in top jobs, I know I am seeing people who 4
sell. I am not just referring to employees who work in a retail outlet; I 9
mean all people who put extra effort into convincing others to 13
recognize their best qualities. They, themselves, are what they sell; 18
and the major tools they use are their appearance, their language, and 22
their personality. They look great, they talk and write well; and, with 27
much self-confidence, they meet you eye to eye. 30

3' | 1 | 2 | 3 | 4 |

To group search results by pages:

1. Click PAGES below the Search document box ❶. Only pages that contain results will display.
2. Click the desired page ❷ to go to that heading in the document.
3. Click x ❸ to end your search and display all your pages.

discussion
1 result
HEADINGS PAGES RESULTS
2

Note: For other searches, click the Magnifying Glass button to search for Graphics, Tables, Equations, Footnotes/Endnotes, or Reviewers.

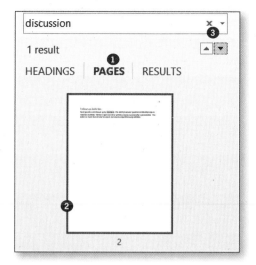

To replace text:

Home/Editing/Replace

1. Display the Find and Replace dialog box.
2. Key the text you wish to locate in the Find what box.
3. Key the replacement text in the Replace with box.
4. Click Find Next to find the next occurrence of the text. Click Replace to replace one occurrence or Replace All to replace all occurrences of the text.

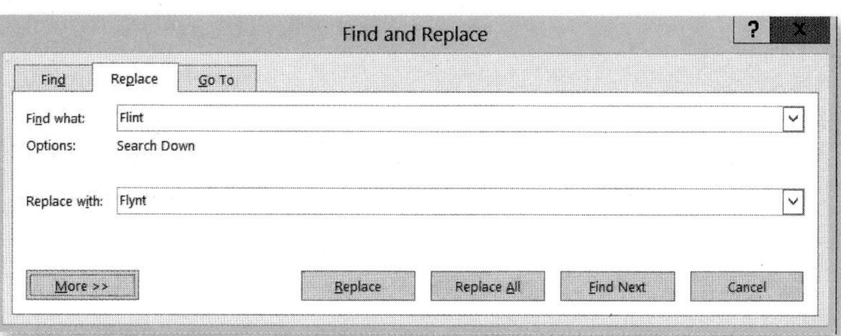

To find text and apply a format such as highlight:

Home/Editing/Replace

1. Display the Find and Replace dialog box.
2. Key the text you wish to locate in the Find what box.
3. Click More to display additional options.
4. Click in Replace with and then click Format ❹ and select the desired format. ❺

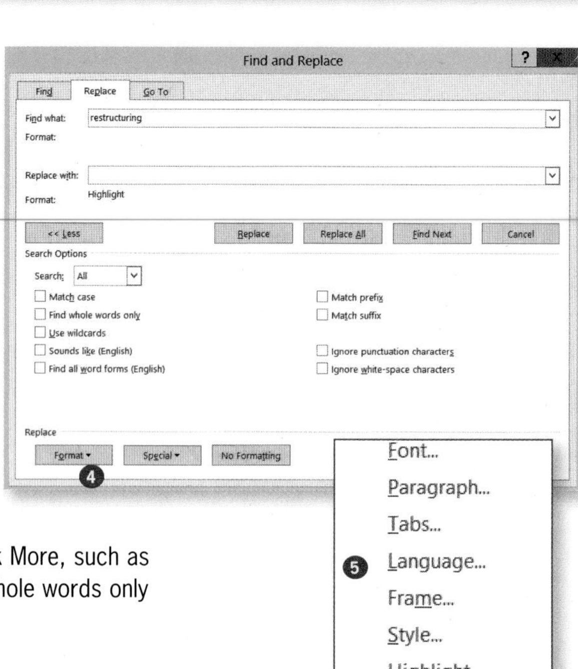

Note the search options available when you click More, such as Match case or Find whole words only. Finding whole words only prevents you from finding letters within a word.

Writing 14

	gwam 1'	3'
What do you expect when you have the opportunity to travel	12	4
to a foreign country? Quite a few people realize that one of the real	26	9
joys of traveling is to get a brief, but revealing glimpse of how	39	13
foreigners think, work, and live.	45	15
The best way to enjoy a different culture is to learn as much	12	19
about the country being visited and its culture as you can before you	26	24
leave home. Then you can concentrate on being an informed guest	39	28
rather than trying to find local people who can meet your needs.	52	32

Writing 15

	gwam 1'	3'
What do you enjoy doing in your free time? Health experts tell us	13	4
that far too many people choose to be lazy rather than to be	25	8
active. The unpleasant result of that misguided decision shows up in	39	13
our weight.	41	14
Working to control what we weigh is difficult, and seldom can	12	18
it be accomplished quickly. However, it is extremely important if our	26	22
weight exceeds what it should be. Part of the problem results from	39	27
the amount and type of food we eat.	46	29
If we desire to appear fit, we should include exercise as a	12	33
substantial component of our weight loss program. Walking at least	25	37
thirty minutes each day at a very fast rate can make a major	37	41
difference in our appearance and in the way we feel.	48	45

Writing 16

	gwam 1'	3'
Doing what we enjoy doing is quite important; however,	11	4
enjoying what we have to do is equally important. As you ponder	23	8
both of these concepts, you may feel that they are the same, but they	37	12
are quite different.	41	14
If we could do only those things that we prefer to do, the	12	18
chances are that we would do them exceptionally well. Generally, we will	26	22
take more pride in doing those things we thoroughly enjoy	37	26
doing, and we will not stop until we get them done correctly.	50	30
We realize, though, that we cannot restrict the tasks and	11	34
responsibilities that we must do just to those that we prefer to do.	25	39
Therefore, we need to build an interest in and an appreciation of all	39	43
the tasks that we must do in our positions.	48	46

1'	1	2	3	4	5	6	7	8	9	10	11	12
3'		1			2			3			4	

FIND AND REPLACE

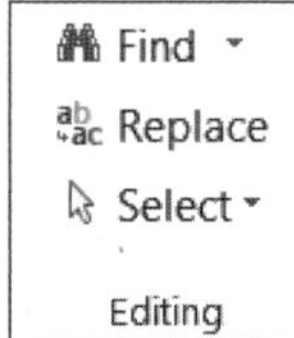

Locating text, headings, footnotes, graphics, page breaks, comments, formatting, and other items within a document quickly is an essential skill when working with long documents such as reports.

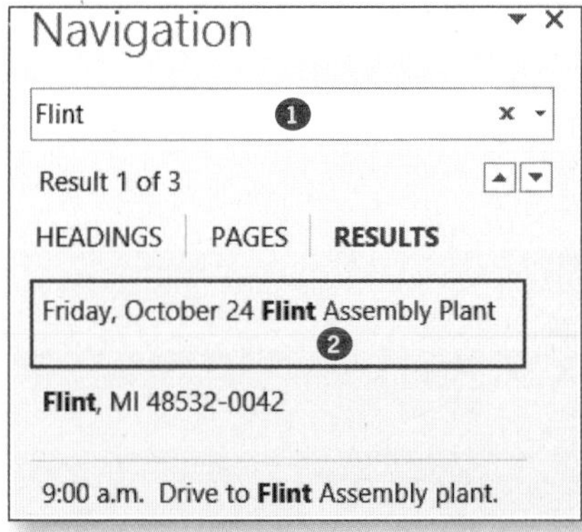

To find text:

Home/Editing/Find

1. Display the Navigation pane on the left side of the screen.
2. Key the text to be located in the search box ❶. The matches display below the search box. Click each match ❷ to go to the location in the document.

To display other find options:

Click the Magnifying Glass button ❸. Click Options. The Find Options dialog box displays. Review the various find options to determine its usefulness in a search.

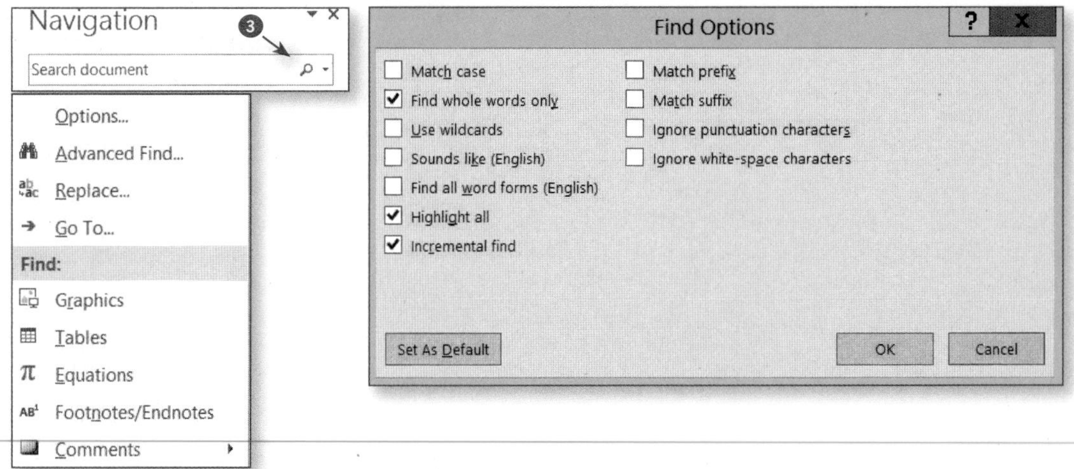

To group search results by headings:

1. Click HEADINGS below the Search document box ❹. Headings that contain text with the search results display in yellow.
2. Click the desired heading ❺ to go to that heading in the document.

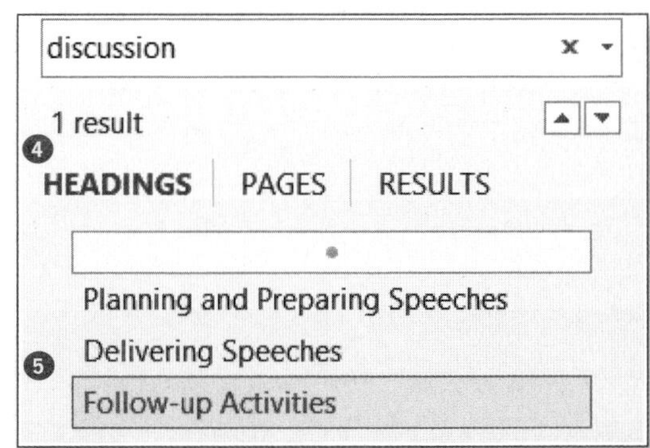

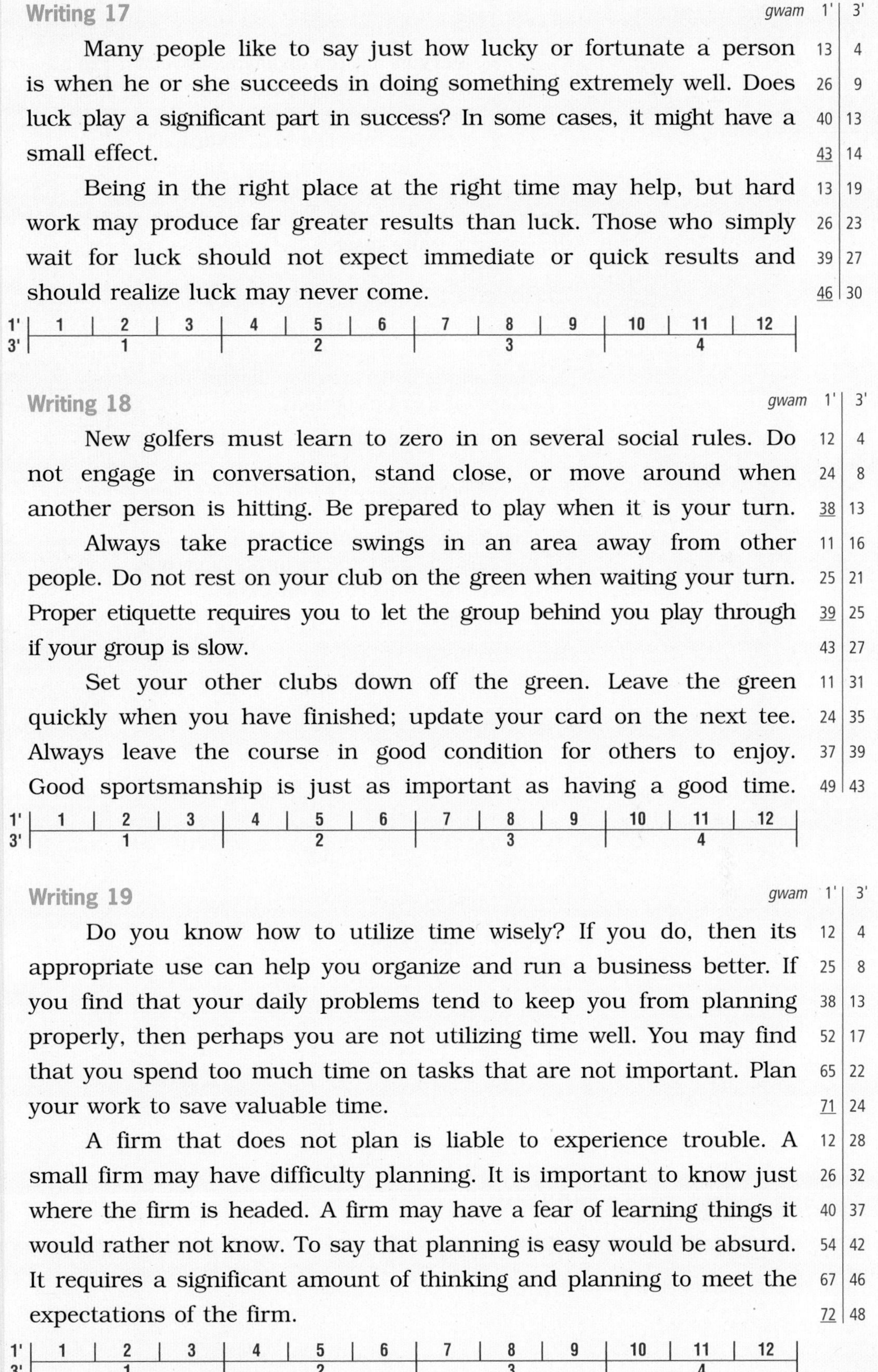

Writing 17

gwam 1' | 3'

Many people like to say just how lucky or fortunate a person 13 | 4
is when he or she succeeds in doing something extremely well. Does 26 | 9
luck play a significant part in success? In some cases, it might have a 40 | 13
small effect. 43 | 14

Being in the right place at the right time may help, but hard 13 | 19
work may produce far greater results than luck. Those who simply 26 | 23
wait for luck should not expect immediate or quick results and 39 | 27
should realize luck may never come. 46 | 30

1' | 1 | 2 | 3 | 4 | 5 | 6 | 7 | 8 | 9 | 10 | 11 | 12
3' | 1 | 2 | 3 | 4

Writing 18

gwam 1' | 3'

New golfers must learn to zero in on several social rules. Do 12 | 4
not engage in conversation, stand close, or move around when 24 | 8
another person is hitting. Be prepared to play when it is your turn. 38 | 13

Always take practice swings in an area away from other 11 | 16
people. Do not rest on your club on the green when waiting your turn. 25 | 21
Proper etiquette requires you to let the group behind you play through 39 | 25
if your group is slow. 43 | 27

Set your other clubs down off the green. Leave the green 11 | 31
quickly when you have finished; update your card on the next tee. 24 | 35
Always leave the course in good condition for others to enjoy. 37 | 39
Good sportsmanship is just as important as having a good time. 49 | 43

1' | 1 | 2 | 3 | 4 | 5 | 6 | 7 | 8 | 9 | 10 | 11 | 12
3' | 1 | 2 | 3 | 4

Writing 19

gwam 1' | 3'

Do you know how to utilize time wisely? If you do, then its 12 | 4
appropriate use can help you organize and run a business better. If 25 | 8
you find that your daily problems tend to keep you from planning 38 | 13
properly, then perhaps you are not utilizing time well. You may find 52 | 17
that you spend too much time on tasks that are not important. Plan 65 | 22
your work to save valuable time. 71 | 24

A firm that does not plan is liable to experience trouble. A 12 | 28
small firm may have difficulty planning. It is important to know just 26 | 32
where the firm is headed. A firm may have a fear of learning things it 40 | 37
would rather not know. To say that planning is easy would be absurd. 54 | 42
It requires a significant amount of thinking and planning to meet the 67 | 46
expectations of the firm. 72 | 48

1' | 1 | 2 | 3 | 4 | 5 | 6 | 7 | 8 | 9 | 10 | 11 | 12
3' | 1 | 2 | 3 | 4

New Commands

44d

MARGINS

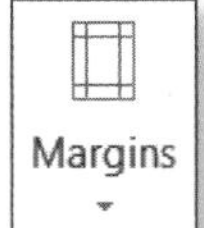

Margins are the distance between the edge of the paper and the text of a document. The default margins referred to as "Normal" are 1" top, bottom, right, and left. To fit more information on a page, select Narrow margins or select Wide margins to increase the white space.

To change margin settings:

Page Layout/Page Setup/Margins

1. Click on the down arrow to display the gallery of margins options.
2. Click the desired margins option.

To set custom margins not listed in the gallery:

3. Click Custom Margins ❶. From the Margins tab, click the up or down arrows to increase or decrease the default settings ❷.
4. Apply margins to the Whole document ❸ unless directed otherwise. Click OK.

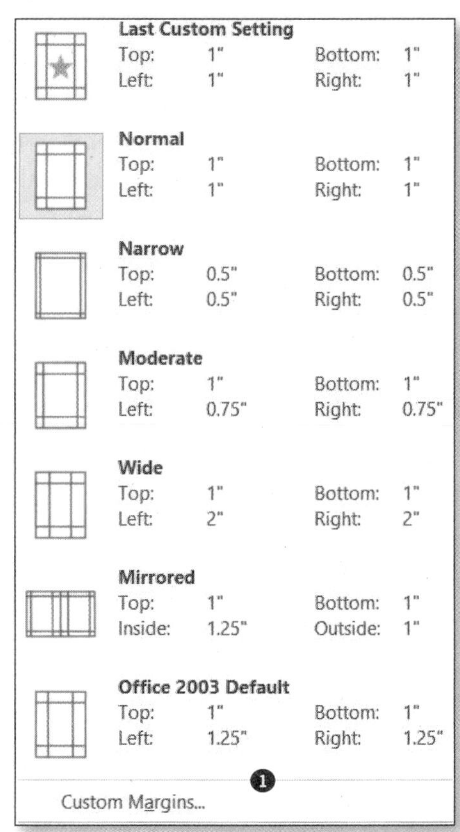

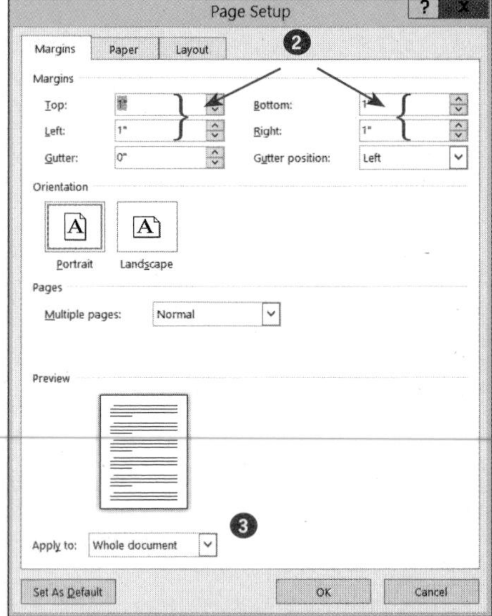

DRILL 1 MARGINS

custom margins

Page Layout/Page Setup/Margins/Custom Margins

1. In the open document, apply Wide margins.
2. Apply Narrow margins.
3. Change the left, right, and top margins to 1.5". Apply margin settings to the whole document.
4. Proofread and check; click Next Activity. (*44-drill1*)

Writing 20

1' | 3'

If asked, most people will agree that some people have far 13 4
more creative skills than others, and they will also say that 25 8
these skills are in great demand by most organizations. A follow-up 38 13
question is in order. Are you born with creative skills or can you 52 17
develop them? There is no easy answer to that question, but 64 21
it is worth spending a good bit of time pondering. 74 25

If creative skills can be developed, then the next issue is 13 29
how can you develop these skills. One way is to approach each 25 33
task with a determination to solve the problem and a refusal to 38 37
accept failure. If the normal way of doing a job does not work, 50 41
just keep trying things never tried before until you reach a good 63 46
solution. This is called thinking outside the box. 73 49

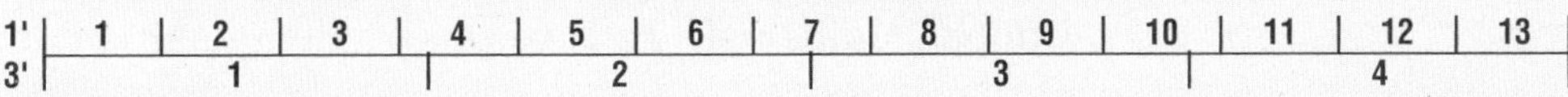

Writing 21

1' | 3'

Figures are not as easy to key as many of the words we use. 12 4
Balanced-hand figures such as 16, 27, 38, 49, and 50, although 24 8
fairly easy, are slower to key because each one requires longer 37 12
reaches and uses more time per stroke. 44 15

Figures such as 12, 45, 67, and 90 are even more difficult 12 19
because they are next to one another and each uses just a single 24 23
hand to key. Because of their size, bigger numbers such as 178, 37 27
349, and 1,220 create extra speed losses. 45 30

Skill Transfer

1. Set the Timer for 2'. Take a 2' writing on paragraph 1.
2. Set the Timer for 2'. Take a 2' writing on paragraph 2.
3. Take 2 or more 2' writings on the slower paragraph.

Writing 22

1' | 2'

Few people are able to attain financial success without some kind 13 7
of planning. People who realize the value of wise spending and 25 13
saving are those who set up a budget. A budget will help them to 38 19
determine just how much they can spend and how much they 49 25
can save so that they will not squander their money recklessly. 62 31

Keeping records is a ~~crucial~~ vital part of ~~a~~ budget(ing). ~~Complete~~ A detailed 11 37
record~~s~~ of (all) income and expen~~ses~~(ditures) over a period of ~~a number of~~ several 23 42
months ~~can~~ will help ~~to~~ determine what bills, (like utilities) ~~as water~~ or rent, are 35 49
~~static~~ fixed and which are flexible. To get the most out of your 47 54
income, ~~pay~~ focus attention ~~to~~ on the items that ~~you~~ can ~~modify~~ be changed. 58 60

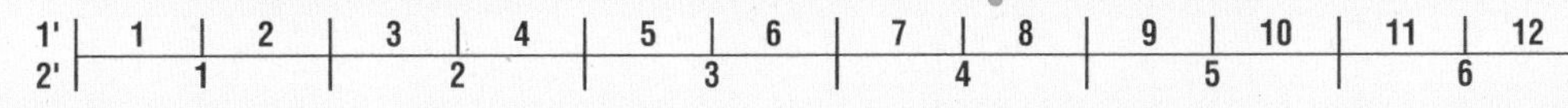

Lesson 44 Leftbound Reports

New Commands

- Margins
- Find and Replace

Warmup *Lesson 44a Warmup*

Skill Building

44b Textbook Keying

first row

1 Take the Paz exit; make a right turn; then the street veers left.

2 Stop by and see the amateur videos of Zoe at six o'clock tonight.

3 I made an excellent pizza with leftover bread, cheese, and beef.

home row

4 Dallas shall ask Sal to sell fake flash fads; Sal sells all fads.

5 A small fast salad is all Kallas had; Dallas adds a dash of salt.

6 Dallas saw all flasks fall; alas Dad adds a fast fake hall flask.

third row

7 We used thirty pails of yellow powder; Wesley threw the rest out.

8 I should go to the store with Paul to get eggs for the apple pie.

9 Did you see the request for Sy to take the test with your sister?

Communication

44c

References/Communication Skills/Number Expression

1. Review the Number Expression exercise in *KPDO* before completing this activity.
2. Key the numbered list at the right single-spaced; correct any number expression errors as you key.
3. Proofread and check; click Next Activity. (*44c*)

NUMBER EXPRESSION

1. Address the letter to 1 Elm Street and postmark by April 15th.
2. The retirement reception will be held on the 1st of May in Room Twelve at 5 o'clock.
3. Program participants included fifteen supervisors, five managers, and two vice presidents.
4. 12 boxes arrived damaged and about 2/3 of the contents were crushed.
5. The manager reported that 85% of the project was complete, with 9 days remaining until the March 15th due date.
6. The presiding officer called the meeting to order at two p.m. and requested that the 2 50-page reports be distributed.
7. Nearly 10 million people visited the virtual museum this year.
8. Jim lives at nine 21st Street and works on 6th Avenue.

Skill Builder 3

LESSON A

Skill Building *Accuracy Emphasis*

1. Select the Skill Building tab, Accuracy Emphasis, and then Assessment 1.

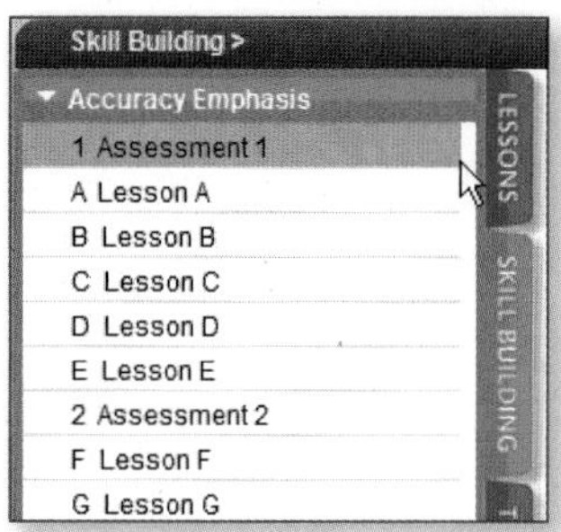

2. Key the timing from the screen for 3'; work for control.
3. Complete Lesson A or the first lesson you have not completed in either Speed Emphasis or Accuracy Emphasis as suggested by the software.
4. Your results will be summarized in the Skill Building Report.

Timed Writings

Writing 23

1. Key a 1' writing on each paragraph. (Remember to change the source in the Timed Writing Settings dialog box.) Compare your *gwam* on the two paragraphs.
2. Key additional 1' writings on the slower paragraph.

	gwam 1'	3'
The most valuable employees stand a greater chance of	11	4
maintaining their job in hard economic times. There are many	23	8
qualities which distinguish an excellent employee from other workers.	37	12
In the first place, they remain focused and keep their minds on the	51	17
tasks at hand. Good employees think about the work they perform and	64	21
how it relates to the total success of the project. They act as team	78	26
leaders and guide the project to completion.	87	29
Second, good workers have the ability to work consistently and	14	33
fully realize every goal. Many people in the workplace perform just	27	38
bits and pieces of a job. They begin one thing, but allow themselves	41	42
to be quickly distracted from the work at hand. Many people are good	55	47
starters, but fewer are also good finishers.	64	50

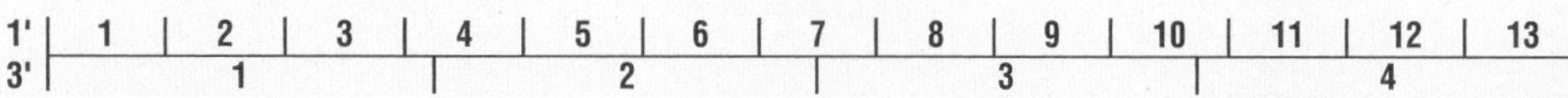

Apply It

43-d1

Unbound Report

1. Key the model report on the previous page. Tap ENTER three times to position the title at about 2". Use default side margins. Key a dash in line two of the report after *13.02*.
2. Capitalize the first letter of all main words in the title; tap ENTER twice after the title. Then select the title and apply Title style.
3. Select the side headings and apply Heading 1 style. Tap ENTER once after the side heading.
4. Insert the footnote in the first paragraph.
5. Apply square bullets to the list.
6. Proofread and check; click Next Activity. (*43-d1*)

43-d2

Edit Report

1. In the open document (*43-d1*), apply Integral theme.
2. Change the word *appropriate* in the first paragraph to *effective*.
3. Key the word **Communication** before the word *Preferences* in the second heading.
4. In the footnote, change the revision date to 9/2/2014.
5. Delete the last paragraph and replace with the following text:

   Contact the General Administration Office with questions.
6. Insert a footnote after the word *Office* in the last sentence just added. Key the footnote text below:

   Anne Holifield, Information Officer, extension 6932, AHolifield@sa.com

7. Select the bulleted list and change to numbers. Reorder the items as shown below and make the one correction shown.
8. Proofread and check; click Exit Word. (*43-d2*)
9. Click Log out to exit *KPDO*.

4 ~~1.~~ Write clear, concise sentences, avoiding clichés, slang, redundancies, and wordiness.

5 ~~2.~~ Avoid emoticons and text message jargon or acronyms.

6 ~~3.~~ Break the message into logical paragraphs, sequencing in an appropriate order. ~~White space is important in email messages as well as printed documents, so be sure to add extra space between paragraphs.~~

2 ~~4.~~ Limit email messages to one idea per message, and preferably limit to one screen.

3 ~~5.~~ Always include a subject line that clearly defines the email message.

1 ~~6.~~ Consider carefully the recipients of the email; do not waste your colleagues' valuable time by sending or copying unnecessary emails.

7. Spell-check email messages carefully; verify punctuation and content accuracy.

8. Check the tone of the message carefully. If angry, wait at least one hour before clicking the Send button. Review the message, modify if needed, and then send the message.

LESSON B

Skill Building *Accuracy Emphasis*

1. Select the Skill Building tab and choose either Speed Emphasis or Accuracy Emphasis as recommended in Assessment 1. Complete Lesson B.
2. Your results will be summarized in the Skill Building Report.

Skill Building *Technique Builder*

DRILL 11

Balanced-Hand

Key each line once, working for fluency.

1 to today stocks into ti times sitting until ur urges further tour
2 en entire trend dozen or order support editor nd and mandate land
3 he healthy check ache th these brother both an annual change plan
4 nt into continue want of office softer roof is issue poison basis

5 Did Pamela sign the title to the big lake mansion by Lamb Island?
6 Rick is to pay the eight men and women if they do the work right.
7 My time for a land bus tour will not change until further notice.
8 I am to blame for the big problem with the maid; I can handle it.

KPDO

Timed Writings

1. Key a 1' writing on each paragraph. Compare your *gwam*.
2. Key additional 1' writings on the slower paragraph.

Writing 24

	gwam 1'	3'
Most of us have, at some time or another, recognized an annoying	14	5
problem and had valid reasons to complain. The complaint may have	27	9
been because of a defective product, poor customer services, or	40	13
perhaps growing tired of talking to voice mail. However, many of us	54	18
feel that complaining to a business firm is an exercise in futility	67	22
so we do not bother. Instead, we just remain quiet, write it off as a	81	27
bad experience and continue to be taken advantage of.	92	31
Today, more than at anytime in the past consumers are taking some	13	35
steps to let their feelings be known—and with a great amount of	26	39
success. As a result, firms are becoming more responsive to	38	43
the needs of the consumer. complaints from customers alert firms	51	48
to produce or service defect and there by cause action to be taken	64	52
for their benefit.	68	53

1' | 1 | 2 | 3 | 4 | 5 | 6 | 7 | 8 | 9 | 10 | 11 | 12 | 13 |
3' | 1 | 2 | 3 | 4 |

About 2" (Tap ENTER three times.)

Title Style

Title →

AUP 13.02 Email Acceptable Use Policy ↓2

To encourage acceptable, consistent, and appropriate use of email, Sudduth and Associates has adopted AUP 13.02—Email Acceptable Use Policy.[1] To reap full benefit of this means of communication, follow the basic guidelines regarding message content and communication preferences. ↓1

Side Heading →

Message Content

Heading 1 Style

1"

Although perceived as informal documents, email messages are business records and archived as a part of the official records of Sudduth and Associates. Follow these effective communication guidelines: ↓1

Bulleted list →

- Write clear, concise sentences, avoiding clichés, slang, redundancies, and wordiness.
- Avoid emoticons and text message jargon or acronyms.
- Break the message into logical paragraphs, sequencing in an appropriate order. White space is important in email messages as well as printed documents, so be sure to add extra space between paragraphs.
- Limit email messages to one idea per message, and preferably limit to one screen.
- Always include a subject line that clearly defines the email message.
- Consider carefully the recipients of the email; do not waste your colleagues' valuable time by sending or copying unnecessary emails.
- Spell-check email messages carefully; verify punctuation and content accuracy.
- Check the tone of the message carefully. If angry, wait at least one hour before clicking the Send button. Review the message, modify if needed, and then send the message. ↓1

Preferences

Although email is a common means of communication, other methods include face-to-face communication, telephone, voice mail, and instant messaging. It is important to realize that each person has preferred methods of communication, and the method will vary depending upon the message content. To accomplish tasks more effectively, be aware of individuals' preferred channels of communication and use those channels if appropriate for the business purpose.

Remember that effective communication is essential to be successful in reaching the goals of Sudduth and Associates. Apply these important email acceptable use guidelines as directed in AUP 13.02.

---

[1] Adopted 1/15/2009; revised 6/30/2014

Unbound Report

LESSON C

Skill Building *Accuracy Emphasis*

Select the Skill Building tab, the appropriate emphasis, and then Lesson C. Your results will be summarized in the Skill Building Report.

Skill Building *Technique Builder*

DRILL 12

Balanced-Hand

Key each line once for fluency.

1 an anyone brand spans th their father eighth he head sheets niche
2 en enters depends been nd end handle fund or original sport color
3 ur urban turns assure to took factory photo ti titles satin still
4 ic ice bicycle chic it item position profit ng angle danger doing

5 I want the info in the file on the profits from the chic bicycle.
6 Hang the sign by the lake not by an island by six or eight today.
7 Did Vivian, the widow, pay for eight flair pens, and eight gowns?
8 When did Viviana go to the firm to sign the title to the emblems?

Timed Writings

1. Take a 1' writing on each paragraph.
2. Take a 3' writing on both paragraphs.

Writing 25

	gwam 1'	3'
Practicing basic health rules will result in good body condition.	14	5
Proper diet is a way to achieve good health. Eat a variety of foods each	29	10
day, including some fruit, vegetables, cereal products, and foods rich	43	14
in protein, to be sure that you keep a balance. Another part of a good	57	19
health plan is physical activity, such as running.	67	22
Running has become quite popular in this country. Some people	13	27
run for the joy of running, others run because they want to maximize	27	31
the benefits that can be gained by running on a regular basis. Some	41	36
of the benefits include weight loss, improved heart health, improved	55	41
bone health, and improved mood. Running is one of the most effective	68	45
forms of exercise that will help achieve ideal body weight.	80	49

1' | 1 | 2 | 3 | 4 | 5 | 6 | 7 | 8 | 9 | 10 | 11 | 12 | 13 |
3' | 1 | 2 | 3 | 4 |

Document Design

43d

References/Document Formats/Reports

UNBOUND REPORT FORMAT

Reports prepared without binders are called unbound reports. Unbound reports may be attached with a staple or paper clip in the upper-left corner. Often reports are attached to an email. Study the illustration below to learn to format a one-page unbound report. A full-page model is shown on page 176. In this module you will generally use the default Office theme.

AUP 13.02 Email Acceptable Use Policy ❶

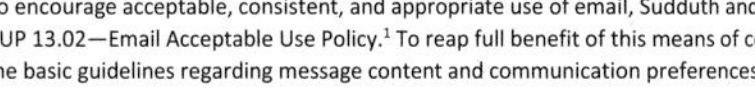

To encourage acceptable, consistent, and appropriate use of email, Sudduth and Associates has adopted AUP 13.02—Email Acceptable Use Policy.[1] To reap full benefit of this means of communication, follow the basic guidelines regarding message content and communication preferences.

Message Content ❷

Although perceived as informal documents, email messages are business records and archived as a part of the official records of Sudduth and Associates. Follow these effective communication guidelines:

❸
- Write clear, concise sentences, avoiding clichés, slang, redundancies, and wordiness.
- Avoid emoticons and text message jargon or acronyms.
- Break the message into logical paragraphs, sequencing in an appropriate order. White space is important in email messages as well as printed documents, so be sure to add extra space between paragraphs.
- Limit email messages to one idea per message, and preferably limit to one screen.
- Always include a subject line that clearly defines the email message.
- Consider carefully the recipients of the email; do not waste your colleagues' valuable time by sending or copying unnecessary emails.
- Spell-check email messages carefully; verify punctuation and content accuracy.
- Check the tone of the message carefully. If angry, wait at least one hour before clicking the Send button. Review the message, modify if needed, and then send the message.

Preferences

Although email is a common means of communication, other methods include face-to-face communication, telephone, voice mail, and instant messaging. It is important to realize that each person has preferred methods of communication, and the method will vary depending upon the message content. To accomplish tasks more effectively, be aware of individuals' preferred channels of communication and use those channels if appropriate for the business purpose.

Remember that effective communication is essential to be successful in reaching the goals of Sudduth and Associates. Apply these important email acceptable use guidelines as directed in AUP 13.02.

[1] Adopted 1/15/2009; revised 6/30/2014

Margins: Use the default 1" top, side, and bottom margins.

Font size: Use the 11-point default font size.

Spacing: Use the default line spacing for all reports.

Title: ❶

- Position at about 2". (Tap ENTER three times.)
- Capitalize the first letter of all main words.
- Tap ENTER twice after the title.
- Apply Title style. If the title is long, shrink the font so the title fits on one line.

Side heading: ❷

- Key side headings at the left margin.
- Capitalize the first letter of all main words.
- Apply Heading 1 style.
- Tap ENTER once after heading.

Enumerated or bulleted items: ❸

- Use the default 0.25" indention of bulleted and numbered items.
- Tap ENTER once after each item.

LESSON D

Skill Building *Accuracy Emphasis*

Select the Skill Building tab; choose the appropriate emphasis and then Lesson D.

Skill Building *Technique Builder*

DRILL 13

Adjacent Key Review

Key each line once; strive for accuracy.

1 nm many enmity solemn kl inkling weekly pickle oi oil invoice join
2 iu stadium medium genius lk milk talk walks uy buy buyer soliloquy
3 mn alumni hymn number column sd Thursday wisdom df mindful handful
4 me mention comment same fo found perform info le letter flew files

5 The buyer sent his weekly invoices for oil to the group on Thursday.
6 Mindful of the alumni, the choirs sang a hymn prior to my soliloquy.
7 An inmate, a fogger, and a genius joined the weekly talks on Monday.
8 They were to join in the talk shows to assess regions of the Yukon.

Timed Writings

1. Take a 1' writing on each paragraph.
2. Take a 3' writing on both paragraphs.

Writing 26

	gwam 1'	3'
All people, in spite of their eating habits, have two major needs	13	4
that must be met by their food. They need food that provides a	26	9
source of energy, and they need food that will fill the skeletal and	40	13
operating needs of their bodies. Carbohydrates, fats, and protein	53	18
form a major portion of the diet. Vitamins and minerals are also	66	22
necessary for excellent health.	72	24
Carbohydrates make up a major source of our energy needs.	12	28
Fats also serve as a source of energy and act as defense against	25	32
cold and trauma. Proteins are changed to amino acids, which are	38	37
the building units of the body. These, in turn, are utilized to make	52	41
most body tissue. Minerals are required to control many body	64	45
functions, and vitamins are used for normal growth and aid against	77	50
disease.	84	52

1' | 1 | 2 | 3 | 4 | 5 | 6 | 7 | 8 | 9 | 10 | 11 | 12 | 13 |
3' | 1 | 2 | 3 | 4 |

DRILL 4 DELETE FOOTNOTES

1. In the open document (*43-drill3*), delete the second footnote.
2. Proofread and check; click Next Activity. (*43-drill4*)

Communicating Today ▶

Why Styles Cannot Be Overlooked

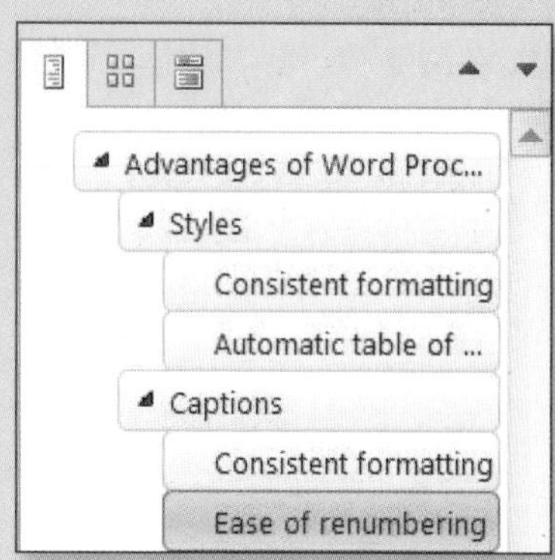

Often it is easy to overlook time-saving word processing features because you are not familiar with them. The styles feature is a command that you cannot afford to overlook.

Styles provide consistent and attractive formatting with a quick click. The Format Painter can even be used to copy a style once it has been applied.

Most importantly, when styles are applied, the headings are listed in the navigation bar for easy movement within a large document. At the right you can see the Level 1 heading displayed at the far left. The two Level 2 headings are indented beneath that and Level 3 headings are indented again. Simply click on the heading to go to that section of the paper. No more time-consuming scrolling is needed.

Another major advantage of using styles, especially in a long report, is the ability to generate an automatic table of contents. Once the proper level of heading styles is applied, one click of the mouse creates a beautifully formatted table of contents. If changes are made in the report, one click updates the table of contents. Why would you want to overlook this time-saving feature?

LESSON E

Skill Building *Accuracy Emphasis*

Select the Skill Building tab; choose the appropriate emphasis and then Lesson E.

Skill Building *Technique Builder*

DRILL 14

Word Beginnings

Key each line once, working for accuracy.

br
1 bright brown bramble bread breath breezes brought brother broiler
2 In February my brother brought brown bread and beans from Boston.

exe
3 exercises exert executives exemplify exemption executed exemplary
4 They exert extreme effort executing exercises in exemplary style.

bt
5 doubt subtle obtains obtrusion subtracts indebtedness undoubtedly
6 Extreme debt will cause more than subtle doubt among my creditors.

ny
7 tiny funny company nymph penny nylon many anyone phony any brainy
8 Anyone as brainy and funny as Penny is an asset to their company.

Timed Writings

1. Take a 1' writing on each paragraph.
2. Take a 3' writing on both paragraphs.

Writing 27

	gwam 1'	3'
Many people believe that an ounce of prevention is worth a pound	14	5
of cure. Care of your heart can help you prevent serious physical	27	9
problems. The human heart is the most important pump ever	39	13
developed. It constantly pushes blood through the body tissues. But	52	17
the layers of muscle that make up the heart must be kept in proper	66	22
working order. Exercise can help this muscle to remain in good	78	26
condition.	80	27
Another important way to maintain a healthy heart is just by	13	31
avoiding habits which are considered to be greatly detrimental to the	27	36
body. Food that is high in cholesterol is not a good choice. Also,	41	40
use of tobacco has quite a negative effect on the function of the	54	49
heart. You can minimize your chances of heart problems by avoiding	67	54
these bad health habits.	72	55

1' | 1 | 2 | 3 | 4 | 5 | 6 | 7 | 8 | 9 | 10 | 11 | 12 | 13 |
3' | 1 | 2 | 3 | 4 |

FOOTNOTES

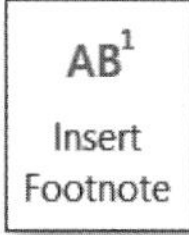
AB1
Insert
Footnote

References cited in a report are often indicated within the text by a superscript number (. . . story.[1]) and a corresponding footnote with full information at the bottom of the same page where the reference is cited. Additionally, content footnotes supplement the information included in the body of the report.

Word automatically numbers footnotes sequentially with Arabic numerals (1, 2, 3), positions them at the left margin, and applies 10-point type.

A footnote is positioned with the same margin widths as the body of the report. Do not indent the footnotes.

To insert and edit footnotes:

References/Footnotes/Insert Footnote

1. From Print Layout view, position the insertion point in the document where the footnote reference is to be inserted.
2. Click the Insert Footnote button. The reference number and the insertion point appear at the bottom of the page. Key the footnote ❶.

   A footnote divider line ❷ is automatically added above the first footnote on each page. Tap ENTER once to add one blank line between footnotes.
3. Click anywhere above the footnote divider line to return to the document.
4. To edit a footnote, click in the footnote at the bottom of the page and make the revision.
5. To delete a footnote, select the reference number in the text and tap DELETE.

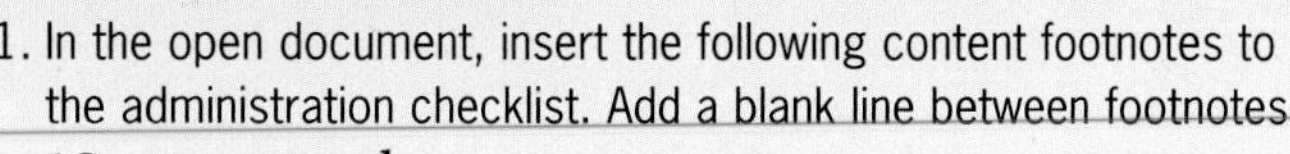
2
1
1 All computers are installed with the Windows 8 operating system and Office 2013.

[2] Instructors must pick up the gift certificate from Mary Katherine Morgan, Office 208.

DRILL 3 FOOTNOTES

checklist

1. In the open document, insert the following content footnotes to the administration checklist. Add a blank line between footnotes.

   18 computers[1]

   [1] All computers are installed with the Windows 8 operating system and Office 2013.

   Door prize—Joey's Steak House Gift Certificate[2]

   [2] Instructors must pick up the gift certificate from Mary Katherine Morgan, Office 208.
2. Proofread and check; click Next Activity. (*43-drill3*)

Formatting and Word Processing Essentials

Learning Outcomes

Keyboarding

+ Key fluently using good keying techniques.
+ Key about 40 words a minute with good accuracy.

Document Design Skills

+ Format memos, letters, tables, and reports appropriately.
+ Apply basic design skills to announcements, invitations, and newsletters.
+ Enhance documents with basic graphics.

Word Processing Skills

+ Learn essential word processing commands.
+ Apply word processing commands to create, edit, and format documents effectively.

Communication Skills

+ Review and improve basic communication skills.
+ Compose simple documents.
+ Use proofing tools effectively.
+ Proofread and edit text effectively.

Remember to proofread and preview each document SOP. You will not be reminded to do this.

STYLES

The Styles feature enables you to apply a group of formats automatically to text, which saves time and ensures a consistent and professional format. When a new document is opened, the Office theme and the Normal style are the default settings. Text keyed using these defaults is 11-point Calibri, left-aligned, 1.08 spacing, 8-point spacing after a paragraph, and no indent. Other styles available include Heading 1, Heading 2, Heading 3, Heading 4, and Title. Each style has its own specific formatting associated with it.

Styles include both character and paragraph styles. The attributes listed in the Font group on the Home ribbon and in the Font dialog box make up the character styles.

Character styles apply to a single character or characters that are selected. In Lesson 27 you learned how to apply character styles using the Font group.

Paragraph styles include both the character style and other formats that affect paragraph appearance such as line spacing, bullets, numbering, and tab stops.

To apply paragraph styles:

Home/Styles

Apply the document theme and desired formatting before applying styles.

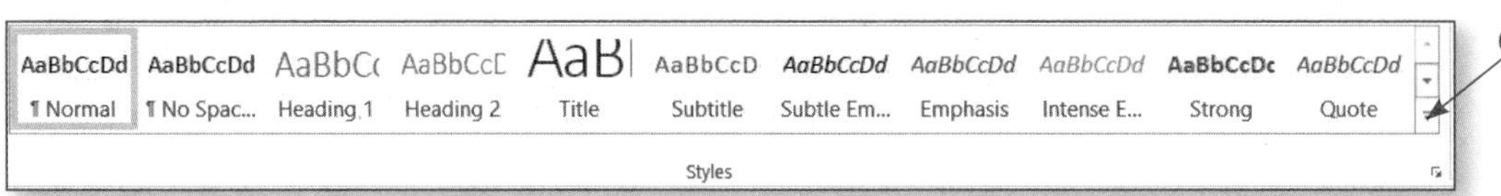

1. Select the text to which you wish to apply a style.
2. Choose a desired style from the Quick Styles gallery.
3. If the desired style does not display, click the More button (1) to expand the Quick Styles gallery.
4. Select the desired style from the expanded list of styles.

DRILL 2 STYLES

schedule

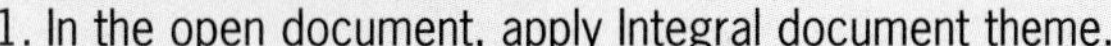

1. In the open document, apply Integral document theme.

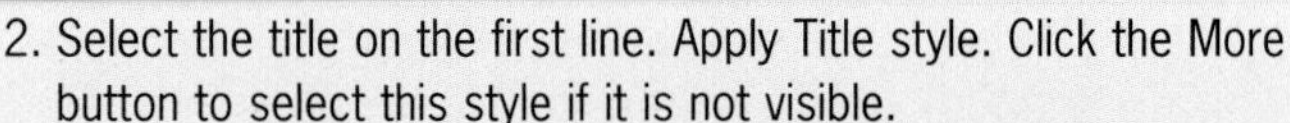

2. Select the title on the first line. Apply Title style. Click the More button to select this style if it is not visible.
3. Select the subtitle on the second line. Apply Subtitle style.
4. Select *Monday;* apply Heading 1 style. **Hint:** Click the scroll buttons to the right of the Styles button to move in the Styles list.
5. Select *Monday* and use Format Painter to copy the Heading 1 style to the remaining days of the week and the heading *Extracurricular Activities.*
6. Proofread and check; click Next Activity. (*43-drill2*)

MODULE 3

Word 2013 Essentials

LEARNING OUTCOMES

- Learn and apply essential *Word 2013* commands.
- Create, save, and print documents.
- Apply text, paragraph, and page formats.
- Navigate, review, and edit documents.
- Build keyboarding skills.

Lesson 26 Getting Started with Word

New Commands

- Launch Word
- Blank Document
- New Folder
- Save As
- Close
- Open
- New
- Print
- Exit

New Commands

26a Getting Started with *Word*

LEARNING THE BASICS

All activities in this lesson will be completed using *Word 2013* software. **Do not access *Keyboarding Pro DELUXE Online* (*KPDO*).** In this lesson, you will learn to use *Word* to create, format, and print documents in the same way that you will use it in your other classes, in a part-time job, or in your personal business activities. You will also learn to manage your own files.

In all other lessons, *KPDO* will perform these activities and will manage your files.

LAUNCH WORD

Word can be launched in several different ways. The first time you launch *Word*, you will probably have to click the *Word* icon on the Start screen or on the taskbar at the bottom of your desktop screen. The illustration on the next page shows you how to launch *Word* using *Windows 8* as the operating system.

If your computer is using *Windows 7*, your screen may look slightly different. Your instructor will provide information on how to launch *Word* with *Windows 7*.

New Commands

43c

DOCUMENT THEMES

Built-in document themes incorporate colors, fonts, and effects that can be applied to a *Word* document or to documents in other *Microsoft Office* applications. The default theme is Office Theme.

To apply a document theme:

Design/Document Formatting/Themes

1. Click the down arrow to display the gallery of Built-in themes. The default theme is Office.
2. Click the document theme you wish to use.

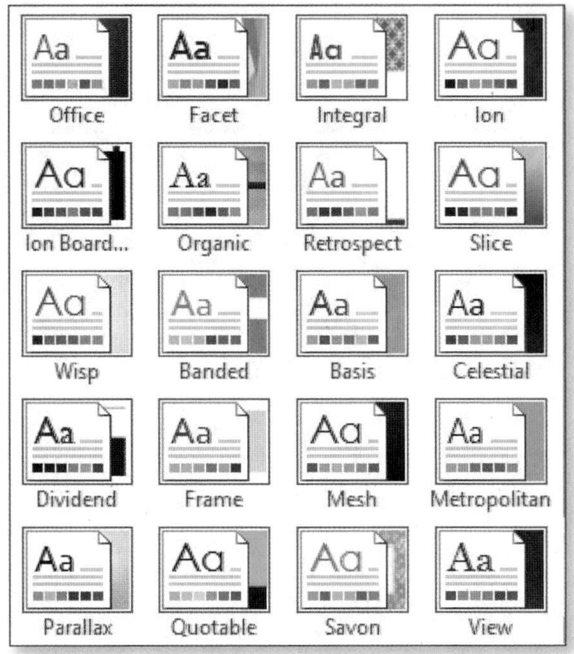

DRILL 1 THEMES

document themes

1. Review the open document; read the information about the headings and Live Preview.
2. Display the Document Theme gallery and use Live Preview to view at least six of the theme options. Note changes in color and font styles.

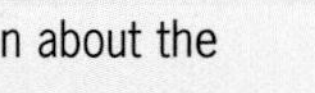

3. Apply Facet document theme.
4. Proofread and check; click Next Activity. (*43-drill1*)

Desktop

When you start your computer, your desktop will look like the illustration shown at the right with the daisies if the defaults were used when *Windows 8* was installed. The other part of the illustration shows the default colors.

To launch *Word* from taskbar:

1. Check the Taskbar at the bottom of the desktop screen to locate the *Word* icon shown at the right.
2. Click the icon to launch *Word*.

If the *Word* icon is not on the taskbar, then check the Start screen.

Start Screen

The Start screen consists of a number of tiles that enable you to access applications from your computer and from the Internet. If you are connected to the Internet, the tiles are dynamic—that is, the information may change. The *Word* icon and icons of other *Office* apps may have been added to the Start screen during the installation.

Once *Word* is open, the *Word* icon displays on the taskbar. Pin it to the taskbar so that it will remain on the taskbar when *Word* is closed.

To pin *Word* to the taskbar:

1. Right-click the icon.
2. Click Pin this program to taskbar.

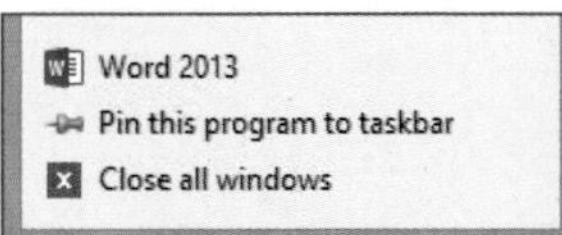

To launch *Word* from the Start screen:

1. Hover your mouse in the lower-left corner of the desktop screen to display the Start screen.
2. Check to see if applications are listed on the right side of your Start screen. If so, click the *Word* icon to launch it.

3. If the icon is not on the Start screen, right-click on the Start screen to display the All apps icon on the bottom right side of the screen. Click the icon.
4. Scroll to locate the *Office 2013 Apps*, and click *Word*.

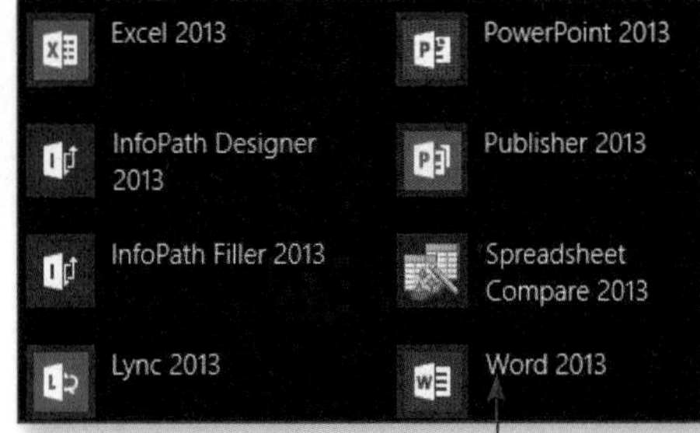

MODULE 6

Reports

Lesson 43 *Unbound Reports*
Lesson 44 *Leftbound Reports*
Lesson 45 *Multiple-Page Reports*
Lesson 46 *Reports in MLA Style*
Lesson 47 *Reports in APA Style*
Lesson 48 *Palmetto Event Solutions, Inc.*
Lesson 49 *Assessment Modules 5 and 6*

LEARNING OUTCOMES

- Format two-page reports with document themes and styles.
- Insert footnotes.
- Insert file.
- Format academic reports in MLA and APA style.
- Find and replace text and formatting in a document.
- Build keyboarding skills.

Lesson 43 Unbound Reports

New Commands

- Themes
- Styles
- Footnotes

Warmup *Lesson 43a Warmup*

Skill Building

A ALL LETTERS

43b Timed Writing

1. Key a 1' timing on each paragraph; work to increase speed.
2. Key a 3' timing on all paragraphs.

The most vital element of a business is its clientele. It is for this reason that most organizations adopt the slogan that the customer is always right. The saying should not be taken literally, but in spirit.

Patrons will continuously use your business if you provide an exceptional product and service. The product you sell must be high quality and last a long time. The product must perform just as you claim. The environment and surroundings must be safe and clean.

Customers expect you to be well groomed and neatly dressed. They expect you to know your products and services and to be dependable. When you tell a customer you will do something, you must perform. Patrons expect you to help them willingly and quickly. Add a personal touch by greeting clientele by name, but be cautious about conducting business on a first-name basis.

OPENING WORD SCREEN

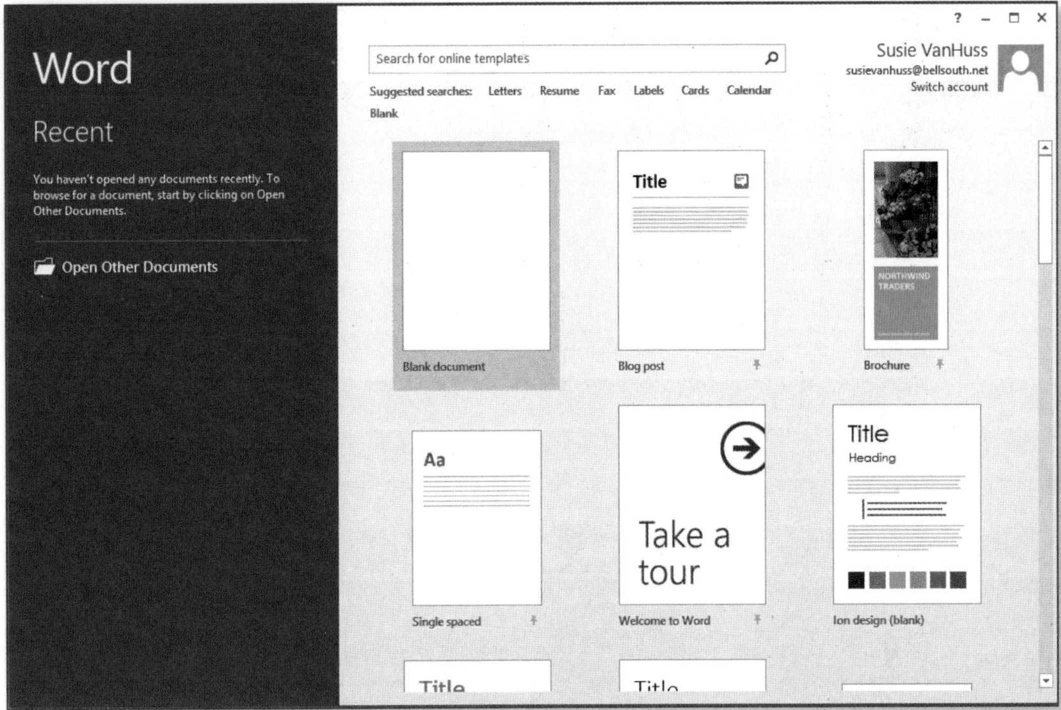

Note the following parts of the screen:

Left pane—contains a list of recently created documents and an option to open other documents that you may have created.

Main pane—provides the option to create a new blank document or create a document using one of the templates. At the top right side of this pane, your name will appear with either a picture or blank icon. If your Windows Live account has a picture, it will automatically appear at the top of your documents. Click the Blank document icon to begin working in *Word*.

Status bar—appears at the bottom of the screen. On the left side, the Start icons for any open applications display. The right side provides the time, date, and information about your system.

BLANK DOCUMENT

The opening screen displays when you launch *Word*. To display the document screen, click the Blank document icon in the main pane. This screen is also referred to as the New Document screen because you use it to create new documents.

42-d3

Table with Table Style

1. Key the table below. Arrange the speakers in alphabetical order according to the speaker's last name.
2. Apply Grid Table 5 Dark – Accent 4 table style. Adjust column widths to display the information attractively.
3. Change the height of row 1 to 0.5". Change the font to 16-point and Align Center the text in row 1.
4. Change the height of row 2 to 0.3". Bold the column heads in columns B and C. Align Center all the columns heads in row 2.
5. Apply Align Center Left alignment to the names in cells A3–A6.
6. Apply Align Center Left alignment to the topics in cells B3–B6.
7. Proofread and check; click Next Activity. (*42-d3*)

WEALTH PROTECTION STRATEGIES SPEAKERS		
Speaker	Topic	Address
James M. Kohn	Estate Protection The Probate Process	Kohn and Crane, Attorneys at Law 325 Munras Avenue Carmel, CA 93923
Lindsey Cunningham, CPA	Estate Taxes Trust Accounts	Certified Public Accounting Services 364 Toro Parkway Lake Forest, CA 92610
William L. Nelson	Wealth Preservation	Gottrocks Financial Planners 6590 Madison Avenue New York, NY 10022
Maria C. Hernandez	Risk Management	Ortega Risk Management Consultants 100 Redwood Avenue, Suite 200 Palo Alto, CA 94304

42-d4

Compose Letter

palmetto letterhead – las cruces

Learn More:
www.cengagebrain.com

1. Compose a letter to William Nelson (see address in table above) telling him that Carlos Torres would like to meet with him to discuss his speech at the opening session. Mr. Torres will be picking him up at the airport and taking him to the hotel. Request the date, time, airline, and flight number of his arriving flight to Orange County Airport so that Carlos can schedule the meeting.
2. Use your name and title (Administrative Assistant) in the closing.
3. Proofread and print. (*42-d4*)

BLANK DOCUMENT SCREEN

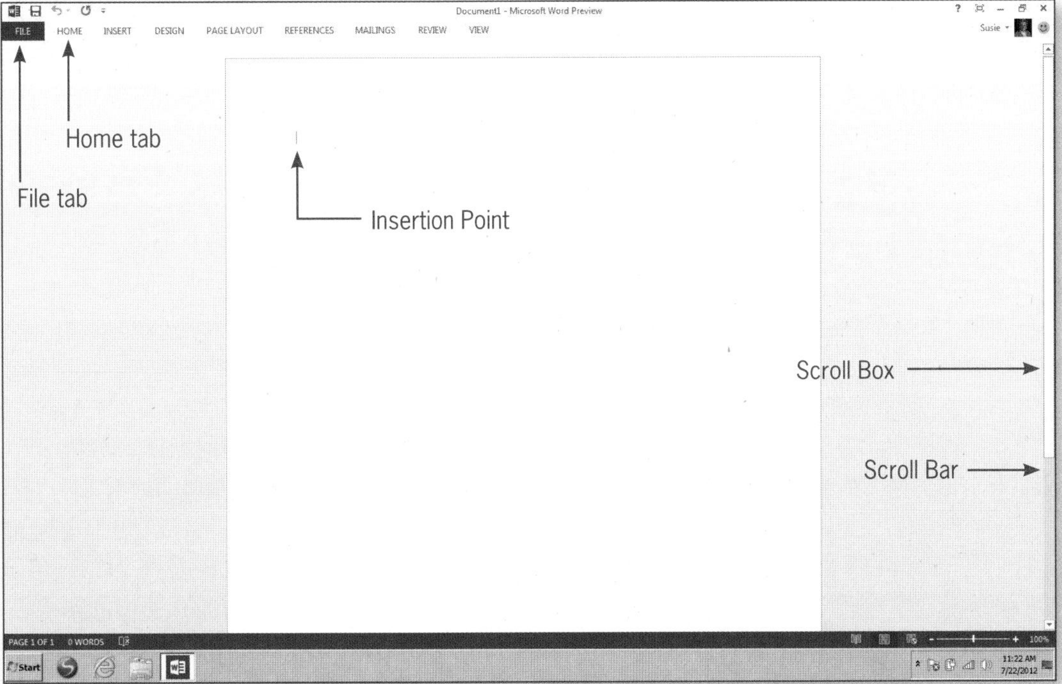

1. The document title, Document1, displays at the top center. When you save the document, you will give it a new name.
2. The Minimize or Maximize buttons appear in the top right corner of the screen. If your *Word* screen does not open large enough to fill the computer screen, enlarge it by clicking the Maximize button.

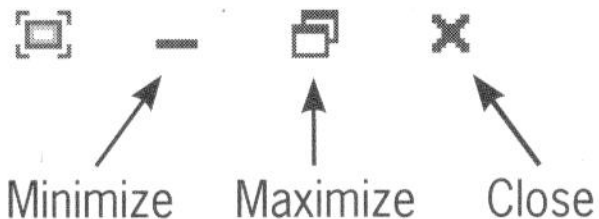

3. A row of tabs displays beginning in the upper-left corner with File tab and then Home tab. These tabs are part of the Ribbon.
4. The center portion is the document screen on which you will key your documents. It resembles a blank sheet of paper. The insertion point indicates the position at which you will begin to key.
5. The status bar appears at the bottom of the page. The page number and the word count are listed on the left side. The right side provides different ways to view the document on the screen.

6. The scroll bar on the right side of the screen provides options for moving through a document.

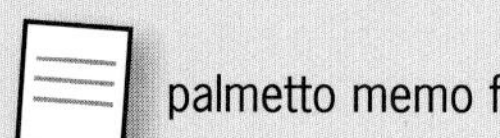

Memo with Table

palmetto memo form

1. Key the memo to **Wealth Protection Strategies Seminar Attendees**, from **Carlos Torres, Regional Manager**. The subject is **Appointment with Seminar Speaker**.
2. Create the table. Change the width of column A to 0.3". Change the width of column B to 3.5".
3. Apply Grid Table 4 – Accent 5 table style. Center the table horizontally.
4. Change the row height to 0.4" for the entire table.
5. Change the font size in row 1 to 12-point. Align Center the text in row 1.
6. Proofread and check; click Next Activity. (*42-d2*)

Your seminar speakers are renowned practitioners in their respective career fields. One of the benefits your participation in the seminar provides you is the opportunity to meet in a one-on-one basis with these noted speakers.

Please indicate the speaker(s) with whom you would like to meet. If you would like to meet with more than one speaker, indicate your first, second, and third choices. We will attempt to honor all requests. Individual sessions will be scheduled for 20 minutes each.

√	**Name**	**Indicate 1st, 2nd, or 3rd Choice**

Complete the form above and return to me no later than September 1, 201-. A list of the speakers, their contact information, and the topics they will be addressing is attached.

xx

Attachment

FILE MANAGEMENT

File management refers to saving documents in an organized manner so that they can be easily located and used again.

Using *KPDO*—*KPDO* manages all of your files for this class. You must manage your own files if you do not use *KPDO*.

Not using *KPDO*—create and name a separate folder for each module, such as Module 3. (Do the same for your classes or projects—English 101b or Scholarship Fundraising Event.) Name files logically so that you will be able to find them easily, such as *business plan*. Use the file name in parenthesis at the end of each drill (*26-drill1*) or document in the Apply It section (*28-d1*).

FILE TAB

File/command

FILE

The File tab located in the upper-left corner of the document screen provides you with all of the commands that you need to work with files. When you click the File tab, the options for things you can do to a document, such as open, close, save, or print it display.

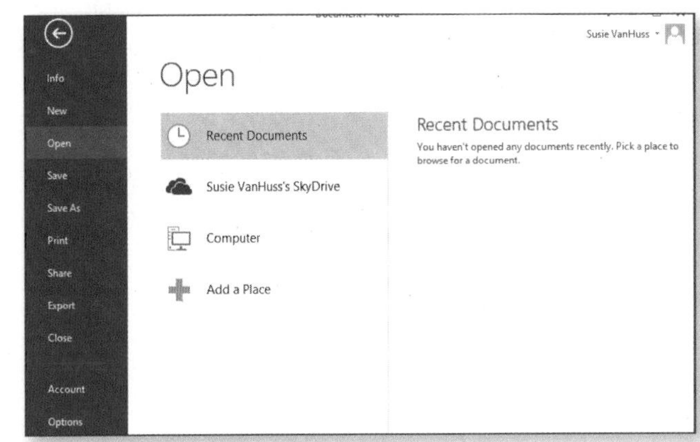

- Commands are on the left pane. The left arrow in the circle at the top takes you back to your open document.
- Places for storing documents are shown in the middle pane.
- Recent documents are shown in the right pane.
- Click the File tab any time you want to use a command to work with files.

TIP

The default in *Word 2013* with *Windows 8* is to save documents to your SkyDrive. Therefore, select the appropriate place on your computer or your flash drive when you save folders or documents.

SAVE AND CREATE NEW FOLDER

The Save and Save As commands on the File menu preserve documents for future use.

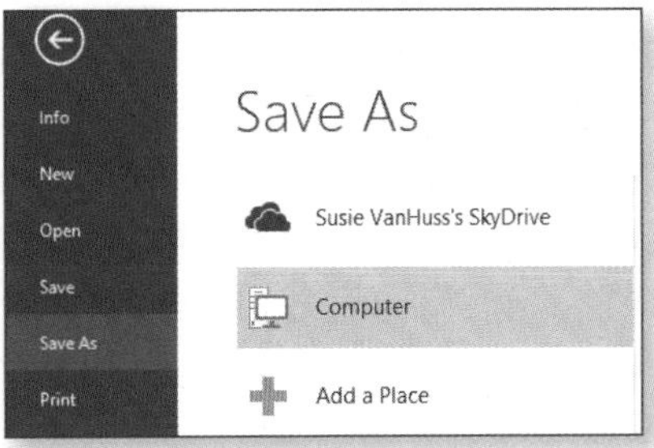

- Save is used to save a document with the same name.
- Save As is used to save a document with a name for the first time, with a different name, or to a different place.

New folders can be created from the Save As dialog box.

42-d1

Seminar Schedule Table

1. Create a 4-column, 12-row table. Key the table below. Merge the cells as needed for row 1 and column A.
2. Apply Grid Table 5 Dark – Accent 6 style. Adjust column widths to display the information attractively.
3. Change the height of row 1 to 0.6". Change the title to 16-point font. Align Center the title.
4. Change the height of row 2 to 0.3". Apply bold to the column heads in columns B, C, and D. Align Center the column heads in row 2.
5. Change the text in cells A3–A5 to 12-point font; change the text to Align Center.
6. Align Center Right the time of the breakout sessions in column B. Align Center Left the room names in column C.
7. Proofread and check; click Next Activity. (*42-d1*)

WEALTH PROTECTION STRATEGIES			
Day	**Time**	**Room**	**Breakout Session**
Monday **To Tax or Not to Tax the Estate**	9:30 a.m.	Harvard	Protect your estate for the family.
	10:30 a.m.	Princeton	The why, what, and how of a Revocable Living Trust.
	1:30 p.m.	Harvard	Resolve probate and conservatorship problems.
	3:30 p.m.	Yale	Solutions to eliminate 37%–45% estate taxes.
Tuesday **Using Trust Accounts to Minimize Estate Taxes**	9:30 a.m.	Princeton	Dynasty Trusts are used to protect family wealth, real estate, and business interests.
	10:30 a.m.	Duke	Use Irrevocable Life Insurance Trusts to protect life insurance from estate taxes.
	1:30 p.m.	Harvard	Wealth Accumulation Trusts and Income Savings Trusts can be used to minimize federal and state taxes.
	3:30 p.m.	Yale	Qualified Personal Residence Trusts can be used to safely transfer your home.
Wednesday **Wealth Preservation**	9:30 a.m.	Duke	Protect your family, business, and assets from the risks of lawsuits.
	10:30 a.m.	Yale	Use limited partnerships and limited liability companies to hold real estate and other investments.

A path similar to the one shown under the heading at the right will be shown each time you use a command on the File tab.

To save a document in a new folder:

File/Save or Save As

1. Click File and then Save As. A shortcut known as a path (File/Save or Save As) lists the File tab and the command to select for this activity.
2. Click the place to store the document, such as Computer, to display the Save As dialog box.
3. Click the New Folder button to create a new folder in which to store the document. The New Folder Name box displays in blue.
4. Click in the New Folder Name box and key the name, such as Module 3.
5. Click open or double-click the new folder (Module 3) to open it.

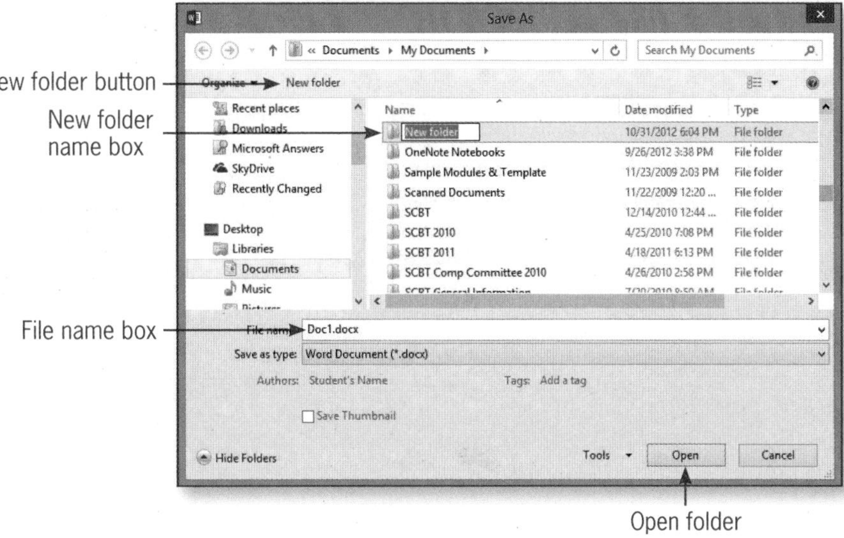

Discover

To save a document to a flash drive, use the same steps shown in this activity except for step 2.

In step 2, scroll down and click the name of your flash drive (or removable disk if the specific name is not listed). Note the Kingston flash drive listed below.

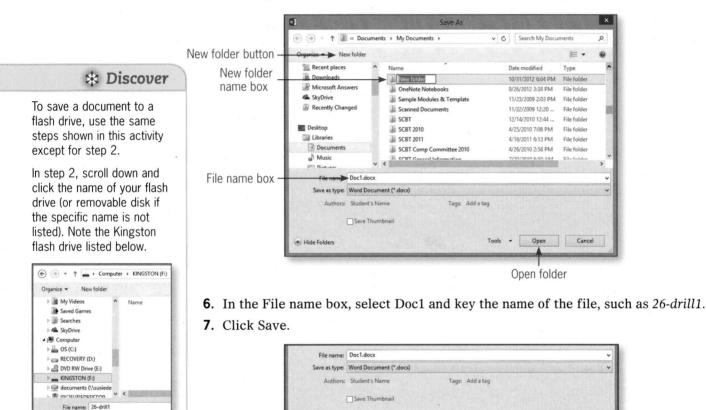

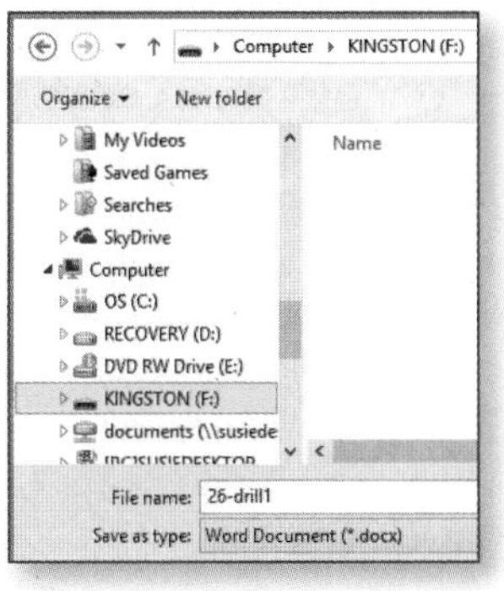

6. In the File name box, select Doc1 and key the name of the file, such as *26-drill1*.
7. Click Save.

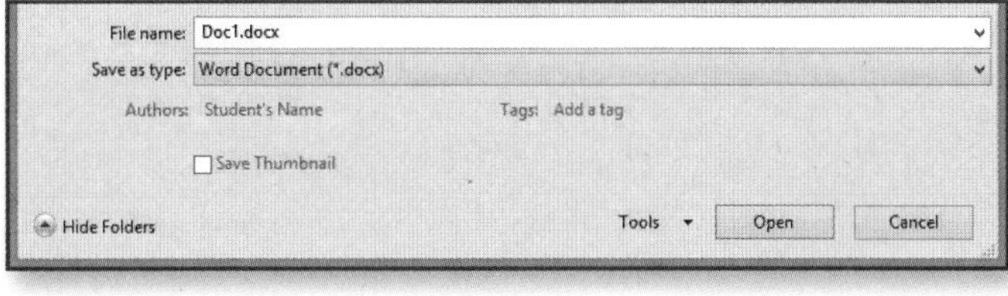

DRILL 1 SAVE DOCUMENT IN NEW FOLDER

1. Launch *Word* and open a blank document.
2. In the new document, key your name; then tap ENTER, and key the text below.
3. Save the document on your flash drive or computer in a folder named Module 3; name the document **26-drill1**.
4. Leave the document open.

An effective way to manage files is to create folders to store related documents. Always name folders and files logically. Typically, folder names are formatted using initial caps and filenames using lowercase.

Lesson 42 Palmetto Event Solutions Inc.

Learning Outcomes

- Apply keying, formatting, and word processing skills.
- Work independently with few specific instructions.

Warmup *Lesson 42a Warmup*

A ALL LETTERS

Skill Building

42b Timed Writing

Key two 3' timed writings.

Whether your company can succeed depends on how well it fits into the economic system. Success rests on certain key factors that are put in line by your management team that has set goals for the company and has enough good judgment to recognize how best to reach these goals. Because of competition, only those companies that are very well organized get to the top.

A commercial enterprise is formed for a specific purpose; that purpose is usually to equip others, or consumers, with whatever they cannot equip themselves. Unless there is only one provider, a consumer will search for a company that returns the most value in terms of price; and a relationship with such a company, once set up, can endure for many years.

Thus our system assures that the businesses that manage to survive are those that have been able to combine successfully an excellent product with a low price and the best service—all in a place that is convenient for the buyers. With no intrusion from outside forces, the buyer and the seller benefit both themselves and each other.

Project Setting

WEALTH PROTECTION STRATEGIES SEMINAR

The Southwest office of Palmetto Event Solutions accepted a contract to promote, set up, and direct the Wealth Protection Strategies Seminar to be held in Newport Beach, California. Renowned speakers from around the country will be presenting at the seminar. The three-day seminar will be held at the Thirty-nine Palms Hotel and Resort.

You will assist Ellen Miller, the Executive Assistant to the President and CEO of Palmetto Event Solutions, Inc. with preparing promotional material, creating the agenda, and scheduling appointments for the speakers.

CLOSE DOCUMENT

If you have only one document open and you click the Close button at the upper-right side of the screen, you will close the document and exit *Word*. If you have more than one document open, only that document will close.

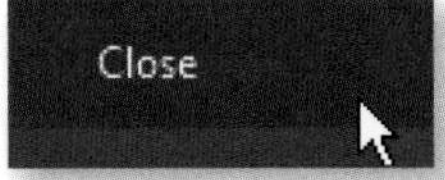

Clicking the Close command on the File menu, closes the document and keeps *Word* open.

To close a document and leave *Word* open:

File/Close

1. Click the File tab.
2. Click the Close command on the File menu.

OPEN EXISTING DOCUMENT

Existing documents can be opened in two ways. When you launch *Word*, recent documents will display in the left pane of the opening screen.

Word 2013

Recent

26-d1.docx

Y: » 19e Solutions » Module 3

If you are working in *Word*, you can open existing documents not listed as recent documents by using the Open command on the File menu.

To open an existing document:

File/Open

1. Click File, Open, and then Computer.
2. Click the Browse icon, and select the folder in which you have stored the document.
3. Double-click the document name, or select it and click Open.

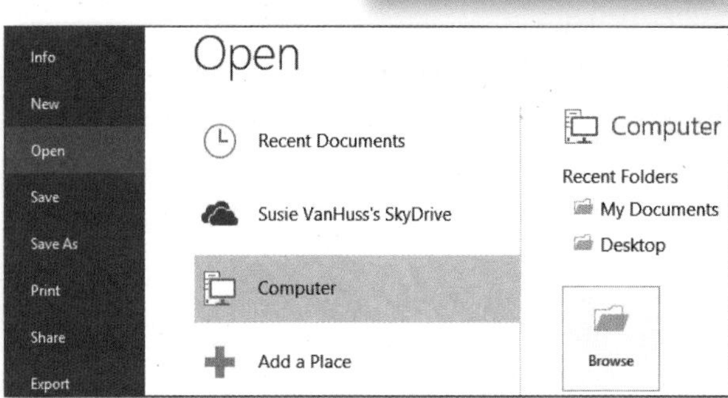

DRILL 2 OPEN AND CLOSE

1. Close the open document. *(26-drill1)*
2. Open *26-drill1* and on the line below your name, key **26-drill2**. (**Note:** Text to be keyed is set off in bold; do not apply bold.)
3. Save as **26-drill2** and close. *(26-drill2)*

Check your document from page 163 against the illustration below.

REGENTS MEMORIAL MEDICAL CENTER February Seminars		
Seminar Title	**Description**	**Registration**
Surgical Weight Loss	Methods of losing weight, including healthy diet, exercise, and medication, will be discussed in detail. Surgical weight loss is an option for those who are motivated and willing to commit to lifestyle changes.	Classes will be held at the Outpatient Surgery Center 75 Pacific Crest Laguna Niguel, CA 92677-5773. Call 949.555.0111 to register.
Life in Motion with Osteoarthritis	Osteoarthritis no longer means that you need to live with a painful disability. Modern medicine, diet, exercise, and surgery can help you enjoy life more fully. Intricate surgical procedures including joint replacement and spinal fusion will be covered.	Register online at www.regents.org/calendar. Materials fee $10.00.
Experts' Cancer Updates	The cancer experts of Regents Medical Center will unveil the results of the latest cancer studies. New breakthrough treatments will be discussed. They will explain what you should know about cancer screenings. Tips on preventing various types of cancers will be provided.	Call 949.555.0100 or register online at www.regents.org/calendar.

41-d4

Composition

1. Key a memo to your instructor. In the first paragraph, request a meeting to discuss the agenda for the next Business Club meeting. Tell your instructor that you are available to meet at any time that you are not scheduled to be in class.
2. Key your class schedule in a table; the table will be the second paragraph.
3. In the third paragraph, ask your instructor to email you with a couple of dates and times that will be convenient to meet. Include your email address.

Power and Versatility of Tables

Communicating Today ▶

Tables have traditionally been used to present data in documents. Today, the table feature is one of the most widely used tools in *Microsoft Word*. A table can be used to create a page layout, forms, newsletters, brochures, flyers, resumes, certificates, and more. Tables often provide the structure for web pages.

The Table feature is one of the most powerful and flexible features available in *Word*. You can use a table to organize a complex page layout. A table can hold text, graphics, or contain a nested table. You can remove the borders so that the table structure is not visible. If you are keying a table that contains numbers, you can perform basic calculations without having to use a calculator. *Word* also allows you to convert regular text to table format and vice versa.

You can always dress up a document by displaying text or data in a table and applying an attractive table style. The colorful table will attract the reader's attention and add some pizzazz to your document.

Shortcut: To go directly to a new *Word* document when you launch *Word*, tap the ESC key or tap ENTER.

NEW DOCUMENT

You have already opened a new blank document when you launched *Word*. If you are already working in *Word*, you can create a new document by using the New command.

To create a new **Word** document:

File/New

1. Follow the path to display the New Document options.
2. Click the Blank document icon to open a new document.

PRINT

Print displays the printing options next to the File menu and provides a preview of the document on the right side of the screen.

To print a document:

File/Print

1. Follow the path to display the Print options. Note the settings that are available.
2. Preview the document.
3. Select the printing options desired.
4. Click Print.

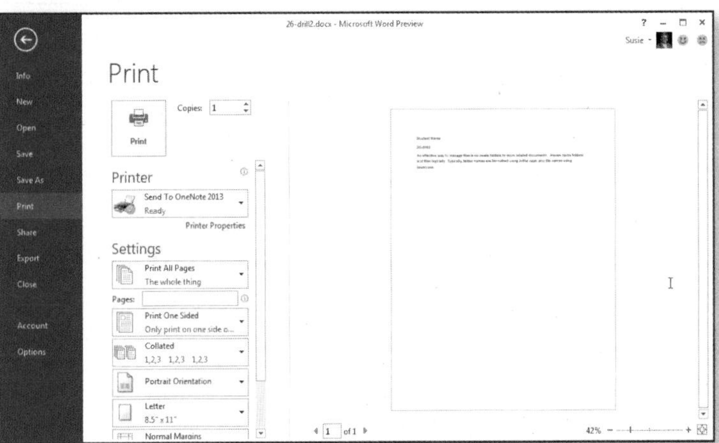

DRILL 3 PRINT AND CREATE A NEW DOCUMENT

1. Open *26-drill2*.
2. Preview and print one copy of the document.
3. Close the document.
4. Open a new document.
5. Key your name on the first line and **26-drill3** on the line below it.
6. Save, close the document, and exit *Word*. *(26-drill3)*

Apply It

26-d1

Create, Save, and Print Document

1. In a new document, key your name on the first line, and then key **26-d1** on the next line. (**Note:** Text to be keyed is set off in bold; do not apply bold.)
2. Save the document as **26-d1** in a new folder named **Applications**.
3. Preview and print the document.
4. Close the document and exit *Word*. *(26-d1)*

41-d2

Memo with Table

 REVIEW

Remember to insert space before the paragraph that follows the table.

Home/Paragraph/Line and Paragraph Spacing/Add Space Before Paragraph

1. Key the memo below to **Roberto Perez** from **Marcia Lewis**. The subject is **Purchase Order 5122**. Insert the current date.
2. Apply the List Table 6 Colorful – Accent 1 table style. (*Hint:* List table styles are located toward the bottom of the list.) Center columns A and C. Adjust column width to remove extra space in each column; center the table horizontally.
3. Proofread and check; click Next Activity. (*41-d2*)

The items you requested on Purchase Order 5122 are in stock and will be shipped from our warehouse today. The shipment will be transported via Romulus Delivery System and is expected to arrive at your location in five days.

Item Number	Description	Unit Price
329-8741	Lordusky locking cabinet	$265.00
336-1285	Anchorage heavy duty locking cabinet	$465.00
387-6509	Lordusky locking cabinet (unassembled)	$195.00

Please call us if we can assist you any further.

41-d3

Block Letter with Table

1. Key the block letter below with open punctuation. The letter is from **Veejah Patel | Collections Manager**. Supply necessary letter parts.
2. Center the data in column A; right-align the amounts in column D. Apply the table style Grid Table 1 Light – Accent 2.
3. Adjust column width and center table horizontally on the page.
4. Proofread and check; click Exit Word. (*41-d3*) Click Log out to exit *KPDO*.

Ms. Beatrice Snow | Collections Manager | Precision Office Products | 2679 Orchard Lake Road | Farmington Hills, MI 48333-5534

Thank you for allowing International Financial Systems to assist you in managing your delinquent accounts. We provide you with the fastest interface to International Systems Collection Services. The activity report for last month is shown below.

Client Number	Last Name	First Name	Current Balance
1487	Rodriguez	Delia	$1,567.00
1679	Kim	Lisa	$954.35
1822	Batavia	Kirsten	$1,034.21
1905	Vokavich	Kramer	$832.09

Please verify the accuracy of the names transmitted by your billing office. If you find any transmission errors, please contact Joseph Kerning at 888.555.0134 immediately. | Sincerely

Lesson 27 Getting Started with KPDO

New Commands

- Font Group commands
- Mini toolbar

Warmup *Lesson 27a Warmup*

A ALL LETTERS

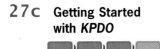

Skill Building

27b Timed Writing

1. Key a 1' timed writing on each paragraph; work to increase speed. Use wordwrap.
2. Key a 3' timed writing on all paragraphs.

Many students and young professionals find it quite difficult to juggle the things they prefer to do with the things they ought to do. Too often the most tempting and desirable things are just distractions from doing the things that should be given priority.

The key is to set priorities and stick with them. Individuals who organize their work effectively and do the most critical things first not only accomplish more, they are the most likely to have sufficient time to do those things they enjoy doing as well.

Choosing friends wisely can help you to stay on target. Individuals who have similar expectations help each other to meet their goals. They know how important goals are to success, and they value their time and try to use it appropriately.

New Commands

27c Getting Started with *KPDO*

WORD IN KPDO

Word 2013 enables you to create and format professional-looking documents that are easy to read. In Lesson 26, you learned the basic commands for using *Word* by itself. Going forward, you will launch *Word* directly in *KPDO*. When you select a *Word* activity, the Document Options box presents various options.

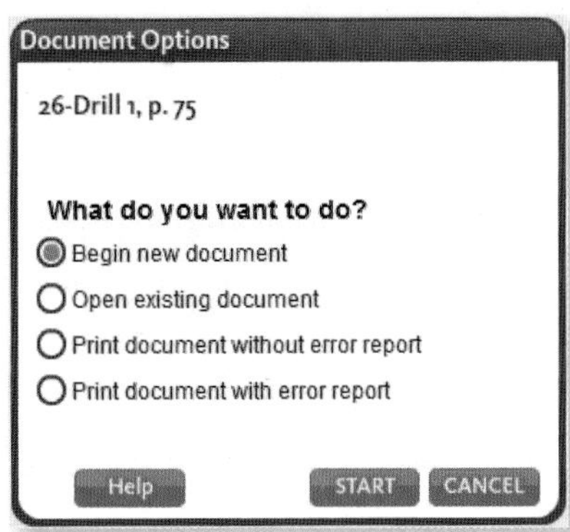

Begin new document: Creates a new document—a new pass.

Open existing document: Opens the existing (saved) document for editing.

Print document without error report: Displays the *Word* document as keyed.

Print document with error report: Displays the *Word* document in checked format.

Apply It

41-d1

Table with Table Style

Grid table styles are displayed in the second group.

Key the text in cell C3 so that the name and address of the Surgery Center is easily readable. Adjust column width so that the ZIP Code fits on the same line as the city and state.

1. Key the table below; tap ENTER twice to double-space between paragraphs beginning in row 3.
2. Format the main heading using 14-point font, uppercase, and bold, and the secondary heading in 12-point bold, capitalizing each word. Align Center the headings in row 1.
3. Change the height of row 1 to 0.75"; change the height of row 2 to 0.3".
4. Apply Grid Table 4 – Accent 5 table style. Adjust column widths to display the information attractively.
5. Use the Quick Check on page 165 to compare your table.
6. Proofread and check; click Next Activity. (*41-d1*)

REGENTS MEMORIAL MEDICAL CENTER **February Seminars**		
Seminar Title	**Description**	**Registration**
Surgical Weight Loss	Methods of losing weight, including healthy diet, exercise, and medication, will be discussed in detail. Surgical weight loss is an option for those who are motivated and willing to commit to lifestyle changes.	Classes will be held at the Outpatient Surgery Center 75 Pacific Crest Laguna Niguel, CA 92677-5773. Call 949.555.0111 to register.
Life in Motion with Osteoarthritis	Osteoarthritis no longer means that you need to live with a painful disability. Modern medicine, diet, exercise, and surgery can help you enjoy life more fully. Intricate surgical procedures including joint replacement and spinal fusion will be covered.	Register online at www.regents.org/calendar. Materials fee $10.00.
Experts' Cancer Updates	The cancer experts of Regents Medical Center will unveil the results of the latest cancer studies. New breakthrough treatments will be discussed. They will explain what you should know about cancer screenings. Tips on preventing various types of cancers will be provided.	Call 949.555.0100 or register online at www.regents.org/calendar.

CREATE WORD DOCUMENT

After you complete the Skill Building activities, *KPDO* automatically opens the Document Options dialog box for the first *Word* activity. If you skip the preliminary Skill Building activities, choose the exercise directly from the Lesson menu.

To create a document in *KPDO:*

1. From the Document Options dialog box, select Begin new document and click OK.
2. *Word* opens with the KPDO Student tab displayed; four commands are available.

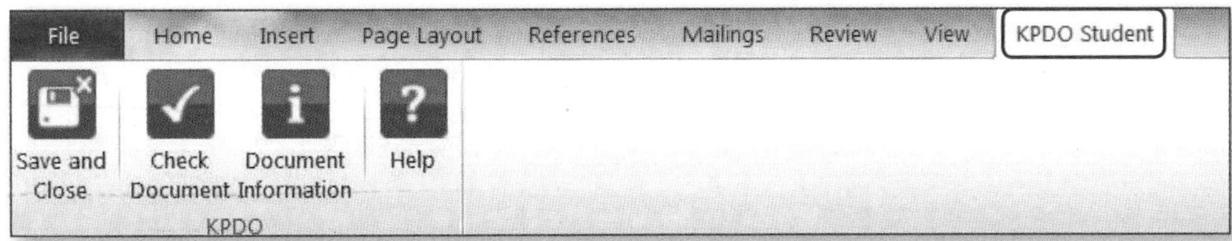

Save and Close: Saves the document without checking it.

Check Document: Checks completed document, reports errors, and displays results.

Document Information: Displays the activity name and page number.

Help: Provides access to global help.

3. The insertion point is positioned in the document and ready for you to begin. To access any *Word* command, select the tab you need and the ribbon for that tab displays.
4. After creating and proofreading the document, select Check Document.

REVIEW CHECKED WORD DOCUMENT

After *KPDO* checks a document, a checked version displays on the screen. The KPDO Student ribbon changes and new functionality is available.

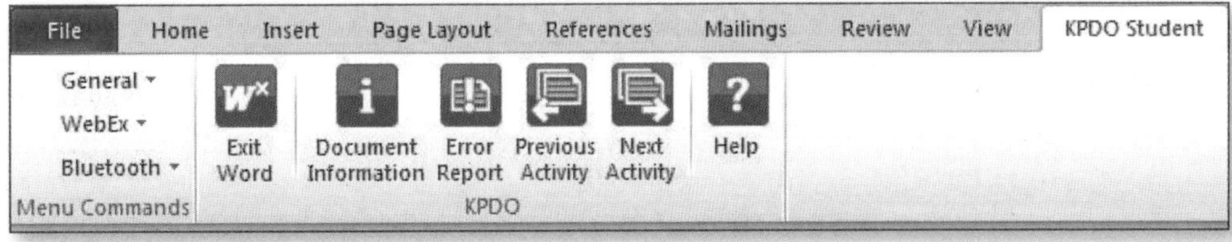

Exit *Word*: Closes *Word* and returns to the Lesson menu.

Document Information: Identifies the document.

Error Report: Lists the reason for each error.

Application Review

POSITION A TABLE IN A DOCUMENT

In previous lessons, you worked with stand-alone tables, or tables that are introduced by a simple heading and/or subheading. In the business world, however, tables are frequently inserted within documents. A table showing sales by quarter may be inserted in a memo on annual sales, for example, or a table showing items ordered may be included with a purchase confirmation.

When inserting a table into a document, care must be taken to provide the same amount of space below the table as above the table. *Word*'s default Normal style inserts an 8-point space after a paragraph and uses 1.08 line spacing. However, *Word* defaults to single spacing in a table with no spacing after a paragraph. Therefore, when a table is keyed within a document, extra spacing needs to be inserted below the table. The extra space can easily be inserted by clicking on the paragraph below the table, clicking the Line and Paragraph Spacing drop-list arrow, and choosing Add Space Before Paragraph.

1.0
1.15
1.5
2.0
2.5
3.0
Line Spacing Options...
Add Space Before Paragraph
Remove Space After Paragraph

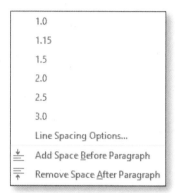

Tables in documents may be formatted with the same design and layout options as stand-alone tables. A table that is less than the full-page width should be centered horizontally.

Default paragraph formats with 1.08 line spacing and 8 points after ¶

The items you requested on Purchase Order 7051 are in stock and will be shipped from our warehouse today.

Item Number	Description	Unit Price
531-8741	Base cabinet	$365.00
596-1285	Hutch	$765.00
542-6509	Shelf unit	$275.00

Click in this paragraph and select Add Space Before Paragraph

Please call us if we can assist you any further.

DRILL 2 POSITION A TABLE IN A DOCUMENT

1. Key the text as shown in the illustration above.
2. Turn on Show/Hide.
3. Click the Line and Paragraph Spacing drop-list arrow and choose Add Space Before Paragraph.
4. Adjust column width and center the table horizontally on the page.
5. Center and bold column heads. Center the data in columns 1 and 3.
6. Proofread and check; click Next Activity. (*41-drill2*)

REVIEW CHECKED WORD DOCUMENT, CONTINUED

Previous Activity: Opens the *Word* activity within the lesson. The Document Options dialog box gives you the option to begin a new pass or open an existing document and edit it.

Next Activity: Moves to the next *Word* activity in the lesson. *Word* stays open.

Help: Provides access to global help.

Mistakes are highlighted in the document, and errors are counted sequentially above each paragraph. If format is being checked, format errors are identified with a blue box. If the format error applies to an entire paragraph, the first word in the paragraph is highlighted in blue. To confirm the reason why an error is being charged, select Error Report.

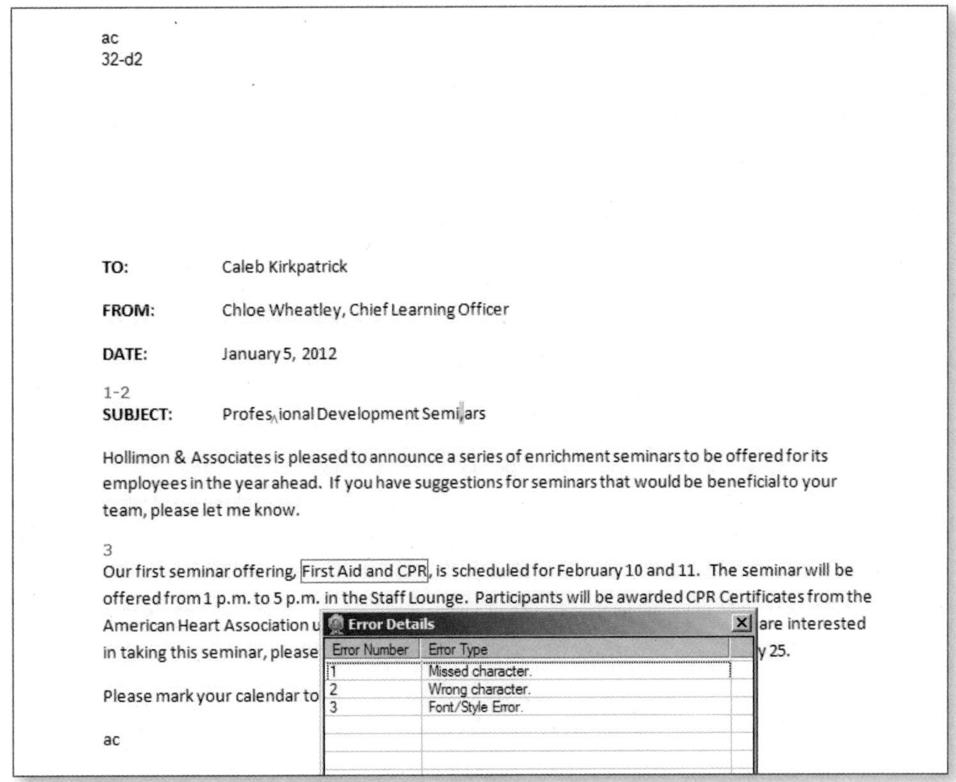

ac
32-d2
TO: Caleb Kirkpatrick
FROM: Chloe Wheatley, Chief Learning Officer
DATE: January 5, 2012
1-2
SUBJECT: Profes ional Development Semi ars
Hollimon & Associates is pleased to announce a series of enrichment seminars to be offered for its employees in the year ahead. If you have suggestions for seminars that would be beneficial to your team, please let me know.
3
Our first seminar offering, First Aid and CPR, is scheduled for February 10 and 11. The seminar will be offered from 1 p.m. to 5 p.m. in the Staff Lounge. Participants will be awarded CPR Certificates from the American Heart Association u
are interested
in taking this seminar, please
y 25.
Please mark your calendar to
ac
Error Details
Error Number
Error Type
1 Missed character.
2 Wrong character.
3 Font/Style Error.

OPEN AN EXISTING DOCUMENT

Open an existing *Word* document to complete or edit it. *KPDO* considers the first completed document as Edit 1 of Pass 1. When you open a checked document, make changes, and then check it again. *KPDO* refers to the second version as Edit 2.

Table styles are located in the Table Styles group on the Design tab. As you move the mouse over each style, you will also see your table formatted in that style. A ToolTip also displays with the name of the style. Click the More button to display the entire list of styles.

The styles are arranged in three groups: Plain Tables display at the top, Grid Tables follow, and List Tables display at the bottom.

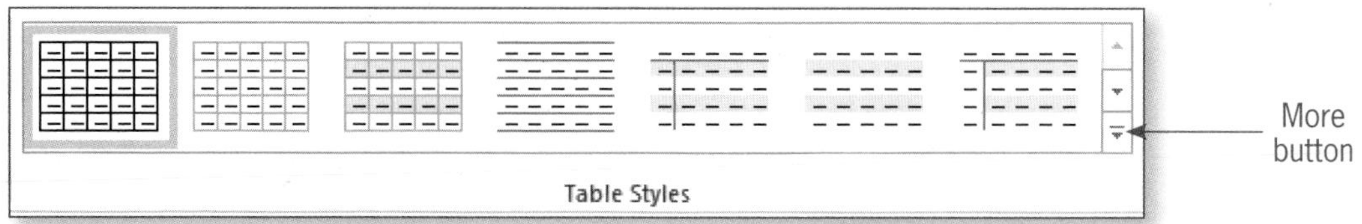

Table styles can be modified by selecting and deselecting options in the Table Style Options group of the Table Tools Design tab. For example, if you choose a table style that places extra emphasis on the header row and you do not want the first row emphasized, you can deselect Header Row to remove the formatting.

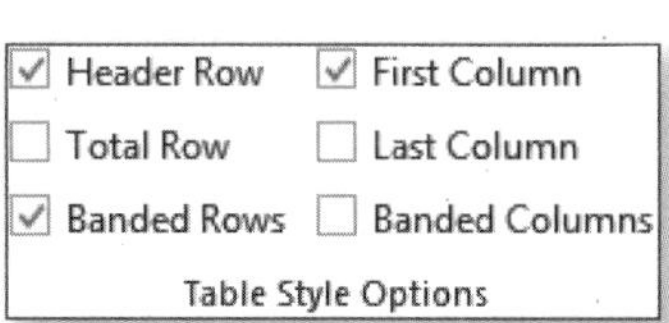

To apply table styles:

Table Tools Design/Table Styles

1. Click in the table to display the Table Tools tabs.
2. Click the More button to display the Table Styles gallery.
3. Move the mouse pointer over each table style until you find the desired one. Use the scroll bar, if needed, to view all available styles.
4. Click a style to apply it to the table.
5. Adjust Table Style options, if necessary.
6. Recenter the table horizontally after applying a style.

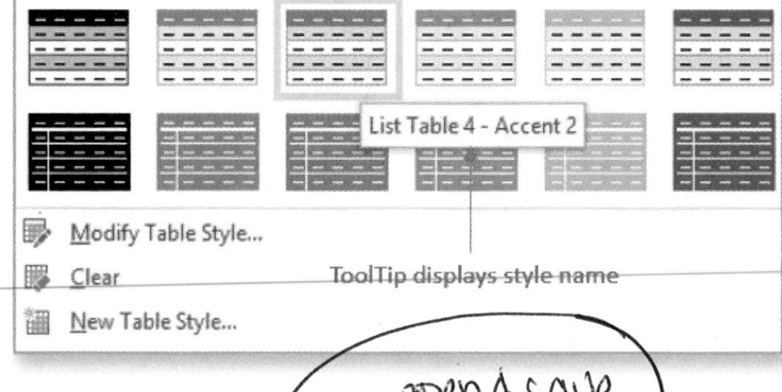

DRILL 1 TABLE STYLES AND STYLE OPTIONS

open & save

styles

1. Click in the table and display the Table Styles gallery.
2. Apply Grid Table 2 – Accent 1 style. (*Hint:* Grid table styles display as the second group.) Blue
3. Insert a row at the end of the table. Key **Total** in cell A8. Key **$581,700** in cell C8.
4. Click the Total Row checkbox in the Table Styles Options group so that additional formatting will be applied to the total row.
5. Remove the check mark from the First Column checkbox to change the look of the first column.
6. Center the table horizontally on the page. Center
7. Proofread and check; click Next Activity. (*41-drill1*)

To open an existing document:

1. Select the document from the Lesson menu at the far right of the screen.
2. Select Open existing document from the Document Options box and OK. You will receive a message that Word is opening.
3. Close the Document Information screen.
4. Edit the document and check it.

DRILL 1 CREATE DOCUMENT IN KPDO

1. The Document Options box displays after you have completed the timed writing. Select OK to accept the option Begin new document.
2. Close the Document Information screen.
3. At the insertion point, key the text shown below.
4. Select Check Document from the *KPDO* Student tab.
5. Mistakes are identified and counted. Select Error Report for a description of your errors. Tap the Page Down key to see your results. If you need to print the checked document, from the File tab select Print.
6. Select Close Word. You will return to the Lesson menu. (*27-drill1*)

KPDO will track my progress on all exercises that I key. My word processing documents will be checked for accuracy, which may help me become a better proofreader.

DRILL 2 OPEN EXISTING DOCUMENT

1. From the Lesson menu, select 27-Drill 1.
2. Choose Open existing document from the Document Options box.
3. After the last sentence, key the sentence below.
4. From the KPDO Student tab, select Check Document. Review your results.
5. From KPDO Student tab, select Next Activity. Notice that *Word* does not close, and you are ready to begin Drill 3.

I look forward to learning to use Word 2013 in this class.

FORMAT TEXT WITH FONT COMMANDS

Text must be selected in order to format it using font commands. To access the text you wish to select, move the insertion point with the mouse or the arrow keys on the keyboard.

Lesson 41 Table Tools—Design

New Commands

- Table Styles
- Memos with Tables
- Letters with Tables

Warmup *Lesson 41a Warmup*

A ALL LETTERS

Skill Building

41b Timed Writing

Key two 3' timed writings.

I have an interesting story or two that will transport you to faraway places, to meet people you have never known, to see things you have only fantasized, to experience things that you thought would only be a figment of everyone's imagination.

I can help you master appropriate skills you desire and need. I can inspire, excite, instruct, challenge, and entertain you. I answer your questions. I work with you to realize a talent, to express a thought, and to determine who you really are and desire to become.

I am your online library. My digital format provides easy and fast access from most places in the world as long as you have a computer and an Internet connection. You can use the library any hour of the day or evening; I do not close. You will never have a problem with a book being checked out, as books in an online library are available to many users simultaneously. You can quickly search for information in my vast collection using my information retrieval software. Use any search term, such as a word, phrase, title, name, or subject, to quickly find needed information.

New Commands

41c

DESIGN TAB

After a table is created, it needs to be formatted to make it more attractive and enhance its readability. Table design features can be accessed by clicking in the table and then clicking the Design tab. The Design tab is divided into three groups: Table Style Options, Table Styles, and Borders.

TABLE STYLES

Microsoft Word has preformatted table styles that you can use to make your tables more attractive. The styles contain a combination of font attributes, colors, shading, and borders to enhance the appearance of a table.

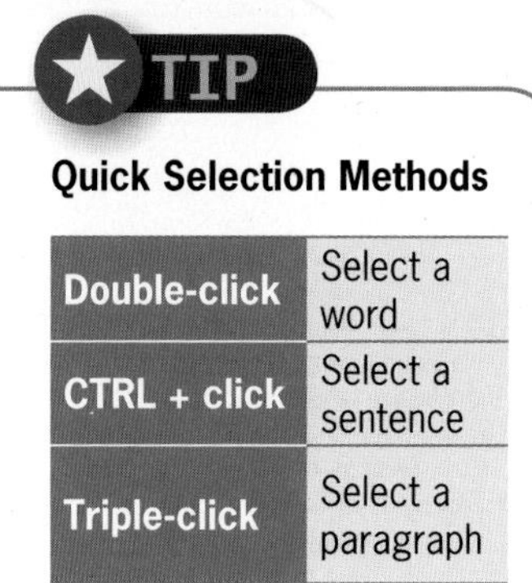

TIP

Quick Selection Methods

Double-click	Select a word
CTRL + click	Select a sentence
Triple-click	Select a paragraph

To select text:

- Move the I-beam pointer to the beginning of the text you wish to select, and click the left mouse button.
- Drag the mouse over the text to highlight it. The selected text is highlighted in blue.

To format text, you will use commands on the Home tab of the Ribbon. Note that when you click the Home tab, the Ribbon displays with a number of commands clustered in groups.

Tabs—located at the top of the Ribbon. The Home tab is selected as shown by the blue text color. The other tabs also have commands that display as a ribbon when the tab is selected.

Groups—contain a number of related commands. Logical names are positioned at the bottom of the Ribbon below each group of commands. See the Font group.

Commands—the icons, the boxes for entering information, and the drop-list menus that provide a variety of options. The Font Color command identified changes the color of text—in this case to red. The small drop-list arrow next to the Font Color command displays the colors available.

To keep the Ribbon open with the commands displayed, click the Pin icon at the far right side of the Ribbon. Click the Unpin icon to display only the Tabs.

40-d3

Insert and Delete Columns and Rows

1. In the open document (*39-d2*), delete column D (*Unit Price*).
2. Insert a new column between columns A and B.
3. Key the text below in the new column. Align Center the column head and align the remainder of the column with Align Center Left.

   Publisher
   Bodwin
   American
   TWSS
   Bodwin
   TWSS

4. Insert a new row above *Law and Ethics in Computer Crimes* and add the following information:

   Digital Data Analysis Tools | American | 2014 | $9,675.95

5. Insert a blank row above row 1; merge the cells in the new row. Key **OXFORD LEARNING SYSTEMS** in 14-point font and apply bold. Change the row height to 0.4" and center the text vertically and horizontally in the cell.
6. Proofread, finalize, and check the document. (*40-d3*)

Communication

ABBREVIATIONS

40d

References/Communication Skills/Abbreviations

abbreviations

1. Complete the Abbreviations exercise in *KPDO*.
2. Review the guidelines on abbreviations in the *abbreviations* data file.
3. In the *Corrected* column, key a corrected copy of the text in the *Original* column, applying the abbreviation guidelines.
4. Add a row above row 1 of the Application table and merge the cells. Key the main heading, **USING ABBREVIATIONS CORRECTLY**, in 14-point bold font. Change the height of row 1 to 0.4". Center the main heading vertically and horizontally in the row.
5. Change the height of row 2 to 0.25" and apply bold to the headings. Center the text vertically and horizontally in the row.
6. Proofread and check; click Exit *Word*. (*40-d*)
7. Click Log out to exit *KPDO*.

FONT COMMANDS

Home tab/Font group/Font commands

Note that the path shown above (Home tab/Font group/Font commands) guides you in the location of commands. To follow the path: Click on the tab (Home); then look for the group label (Font) at the bottom of the Ribbon, and finally select the desired command (such as Font Size or Bold). The path will be provided for most commands throughout this textbook to assist you in locating commands quickly and easily. In this lesson, you will apply the format commands from the Font group to text that you have selected.

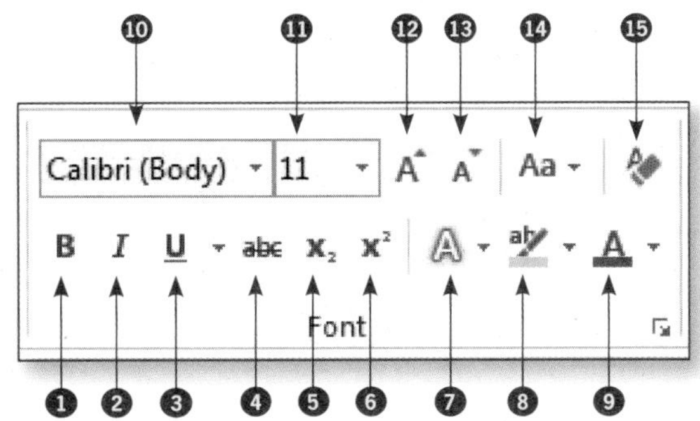

❶ Bold ❷ Italic ❸ Underline ❹ Strikethrough ❺ Subscript ❻ Superscript

❼ Text Effects and Typography ❽ Text Highlight Color ❾ Font Color

❿ Font ⓫ Font Size ⓬ Increase Font Size ⓭ Decrease Font Size

⓮ Change Case ⓯ Clear Formatting

DRILL 3 FORMAT TEXT WITH FONT COMMANDS

1. In a new document, click the Home tab and move the mouse pointer over each of the 15 commands (9 in bottom row; 6 in top row) in the Font group to identify the commands and note the short description of each.
2. Note that some of the commands such as Font and Underline have drop-list arrows on the side of the command. Click the drop-list arrow to see the gallery of options that can be selected.
3. Key the names of the 15 commands in sequential order; tap ENTER after each command. Do not key the numbers.
4. Select each of the first four commands you keyed and apply the format to the name of the command.
5. Key the number **1** at the end of *Subscript* and **2** at the end of *Superscript*; apply the format to the numbers.
6. Select Text Effects and Typography and apply Fill – Gold, Accent 4, Soft Bevel text effect (last icon in first row).
7. Select Text Highlight Color and apply yellow highlight.
8. Select Font Color and change the color to Blue from the Standard Colors palette.
9. Select Font and change to Cambria; select Font Size and change to 14 point.
10. Select Increase Font Size and click the Increase Font Size command twice.
11. Select Decrease Font Size and click the Decrease Font Size command once.
12. Select Change Case and change case to UPPERCASE.
13. Select Clear Formatting and apply Bold and Italic. Click the Underline drop-list arrow; select a double underline.
14. With Clear Formatting selected, click the Clear Formatting command to clear the formatting.
15. From the *KPDO* Student tab, select Check Document.
16. Click Next Activity command to begin Drill 4. *(27-drill3)*

Note: If you are not using *KPDO*, save the file with the name in parentheses. (*27-drill3*)

DRILL 3 MERGE AND SPLIT CELLS

1. Create a 2-column, 5-row table.
2. Merge the cells in row 1; key the main heading in uppercase 14-point bold font. Change the height of row 1 to 0.4".
3. Key **Course Name** in cell A2 and **Enrollment Figures** in cell B2.
4. Select cells B3–B5; split these cells into two columns and three rows. Key **Undergraduates** in cell B3 and **Graduates** in cell C3. Key the rest of the table as shown.
5. Select cells A2 and A3; merge the cells. Select all the headings and apply Align Center. Bold all column heads.
6. Right-align all numbers.
7. Adjust column width and center table horizontally.
8. Proofread and check; click Next Activity. (*40-drill3*)

FINAL SEAT COUNT		
Course Name	**Enrollment Figures**	
	Undergraduates	**Graduates**
English Reading and Composition	12,875	97
Medical Microbiology	782	1,052

Apply It

40-d1

Insert Column/Row and Merge

1. In the open document (*39-d1*), insert the following column between columns B and C.

   Division
   Commercial
   Space Shuttle
   Military
   Commercial

2. Insert a blank row above row 1. Merge the cells in row 1. Key **SAFETY AWARDS** in 14-point font and apply bold.
3. Change the height of row 1 to 0.4". Use Align Center to center the text in rows 1 and 2.
4. Proofread and check; click Next Activity. (*40-d1*)

40-d2

Insert and Delete Rows

1. In the open document (*40-d1*), insert a row after Lorianna Mendez and add the following information:

   Robert Ruiz | Research | Military | $2,250

2. Insert a row at the end of the table and add the following information:

   Frank Cousins | Security | Space Shuttle | $500

3. Delete the row for William Mohammed.
4. Proofread and check; click Next Activity. (*40-d2*)

MINI TOOLBAR

The Mini toolbar simplifies editing text by positioning frequently used commands at the point they are needed. It appears when you select text.

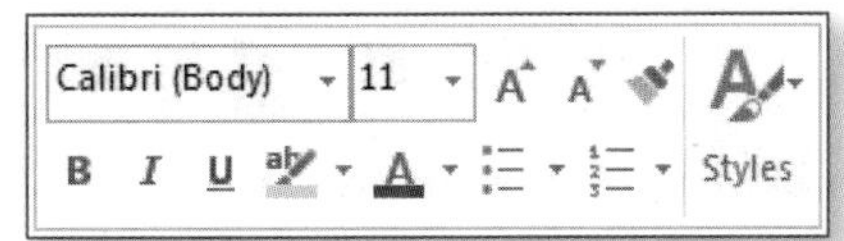

To use the Mini toolbar:

1. Select text to which you want to apply a commonly used format.
2. Move the mouse pointer toward the Mini toolbar when it appears in a faded view.
3. Click the command(s) that you want to apply when the Mini toolbar darkens.

DRILL 4 EDIT USING MINI TOOLBAR

1. Activity 27-drill4 should be open because you clicked Next Activity when you completed 27-drill3. If it is not open, select 27-drill4 from the Lesson menu.
2. Key the document name **27-drill4** at the top of the document, and tap ENTER. (**Note:** Text to be keyed is set off in bold; do not apply bold.)
3. Key the following sentence:

   This is a new document I have created.

4. Select the document name; use the Mini toolbar to change the font to Calibri Light and the font size to 14 point.
5. Select *new document* in the sentence you keyed, and use the Mini toolbar to highlight both words in Bright Green.
6. Proofread and ensure that you followed directions carefully.
7. Check your document and then click Next Activity on the *KPDO* Student tab to continue. (*27-drill4*)

STANDARD OPERATING PROCEDURES

1. Key and format documents as directed in the textbook.
2. Proofread for keying or formatting errors. Check your document against the directions in the textbook.
3. Check the document when you are totally satisified that it is correct.
4. Review the checked document for mistakes; select Error Report to see the reasons for mistakes. See page 90 for an example.
5. Scroll to the end of the document to view the report of errors, *gwam*, etc.
6. Use the commands on the KPDO Student tab to move to the previous or next document without closing *Word*, or choose Exit Word to return to the Lesson menu.

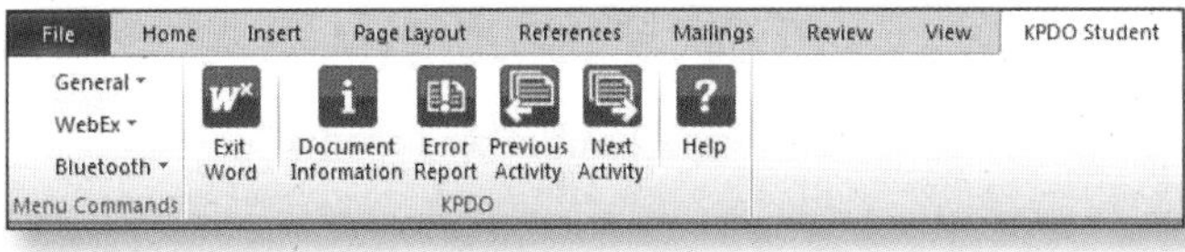

7. Log out of *KPDO* when you are ready to end the session.

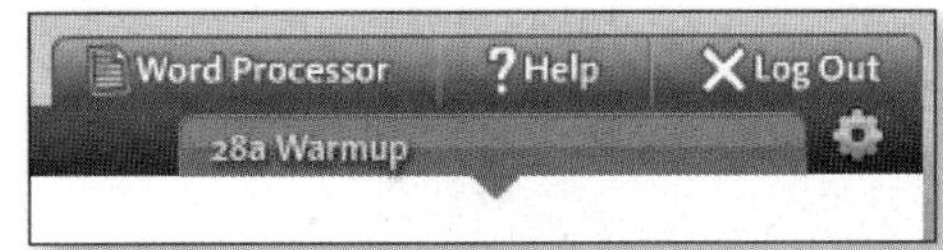

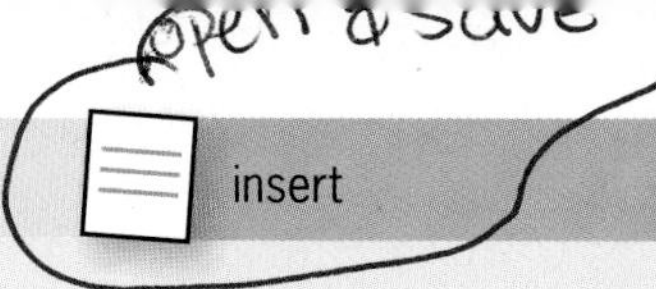

DRILL 2 INSERT ROWS AND COLUMNS

1. In the open document, insert the following rows so that the items are in correct alphabetical order.

Connors, Margaret	**South**	**$87,560**
Roberts, George	**East**	**$97,850**
Zales, Laura	**West**	**$93,500**

2. Delete the row containing Hoang, Thomas.
3. Insert a column between columns B and C and key the following entries in the column.

Office
Wilshire
Toledo
Lake Forest
Tampa
Las Vegas
Boston
Chicago
San Francisco

4. Left-align cells C2–C9. Click in column C and change the column width to 1.3" so that *San Francisco* does not wrap.
5. Proofread and check; click Next Activity. (*40-drill2*)

MERGE AND SPLIT CELLS

Merging is the process of combining two or more table cells located in the same row or column into a single cell. Cells can be joined horizontally or vertically. For example, you can merge several cells horizontally to create a table heading row that spans several columns. A cell or several selected cells can be divided into multiple cells and columns by using the Split Cells feature.

To merge cells:
Table Tools Layout/Merge/Merge Cells

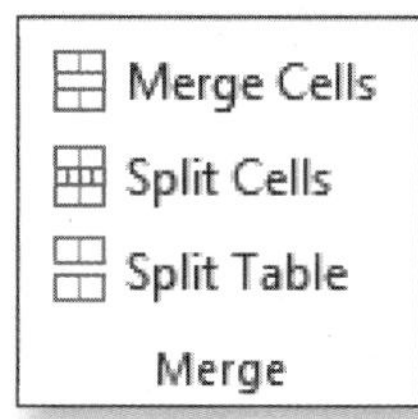

1. Select the cells that are to be merged.
2. Click Merge Cells to merge the selected cells.

To split cells:
Table Tools Layout/Merge/Split Cells

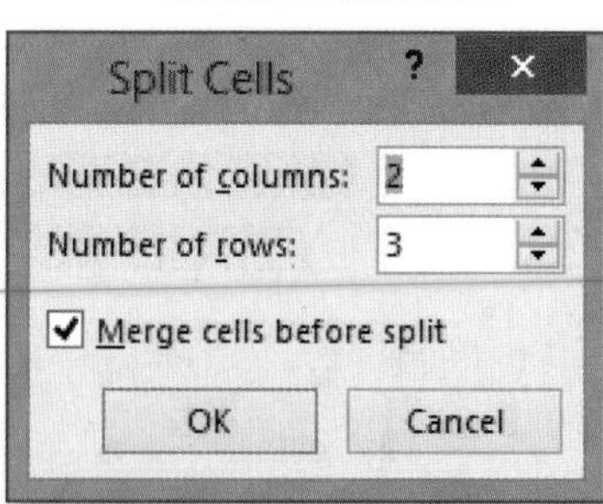

1. Click in the cell that is to be divided into multiple cells. If multiple cells are to be split, select them.
2. Display Split Cells dialog box.
3. Key the number of columns or rows that the selected cells are to be split into.

Apply It

27-d1

Create a New Document

1. In a new document, key **27-d1** on the first line.
2. Key the following sentences. Do not key the letters used to identify the sentences. Tap ENTER after each sentence.

   a. The default for Heading 1 is Calibri Light 16-point font.

   b. I use red font color, yellow highlighting, or orange text effects for emphasis.

   c. This sentence illustrates bold text, italic text, and underline format.

   d. He said, "Revert back to the previous form."

   e. Use text formats to emphasize text in documents, but do not overuse them.

3. In sentence a, apply Calibri Light 16-point font size to Heading 1.
4. In sentence b, apply Red font color to the word *red*, Yellow highlight to the word *yellow*, and Fill - Orange, Accent 2, Outline - Accent 2 text effect (the third icon in the first row of the gallery) to the word *orange*.
5. In sentence c, apply bold format to the word *bold*, italic format to the word *italic*, and underline format to the word *underline*.
6. In sentence d, apply strikethrough to the word *back*.
7. In sentence e, apply bold, italic, and Red font color to the words *emphasize text*.
8. In sentence e, use clear formatting to remove all formats from the words *emphasize text*.
9. Proofread and check. Click Exit Word from the *KPDO* Student tab to close the document. (*27-d1*)
10. Click Log out to exit *KPDO*.

! WORKPLACE SUCCESS

Pixellover RM 7 / Alamy

Social Networks

Social networks are websites designed to foster social interaction among a group of people with common interests. *Facebook* and *MySpace* popularized the idea of social networks and initially appealed to teenagers and college students. Today, many other networks and social media tools have been created and the profiles of those who use them have changed significantly. Millions of adults of all ages are active users of *Facebook*, *LinkedIn*, *Twitter*, *YouTube*, *Flickr*, and a host of other social media tools. Businesses as well as nonprofit organizations active use social media tools to promote their organizations and enhance their businesses. Although using social media is extremely popular and offers many advantages, care needs to be taken to protect against the abuse of the media that is also rampant.

A column can be inserted using the same process. Move the mouse pointer above the table and point to the border where the new column is to be inserted; then click the plus symbol.

Award Winners	Department	Amount
Lorianna Mendez	Accounting	$2,000
William Mohammed	Marketing	$800
Cynthia Khek	Engineering	$1,500
Charles Pham	Purchasing	$1,000

DRILL 1 INSERT ROW AND COLUMN

1. In the open document (*38-drill2*), insert a row following Ms. Man Jin Callentonni.
2. Key **Mr. Frederick Douglas, Compliance Committee Chair** in the blank row.
3. Insert a column between columns A and B.
4. Key: **Extension** | **5278** | **4902** | **2561** | **9302** | **3715.**
5. Center the text in column B.
6. Align Center the column heads in row 1.
7. Apply bold to the column heads.
8. Adjust column width and center the table horizontally on the page.
9. Proofread and check; click Next Activity. (*40-drill1*)

INSERT AND DELETE ROWS AND COLUMNS USING TABLE TOOLS

Rows and columns can also be inserted or deleted by using commands on the Table Tools Layout tab.

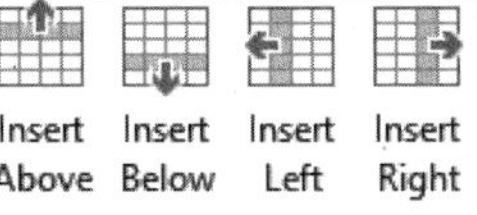

To insert rows or columns in a table:

Table Tools Layout/Rows & Columns

1. Position the insertion point where the new row or column is to be inserted. If several rows or columns are to be inserted, select the number you want to insert.
2. In the Rows & Columns group, click the appropriate command.

To delete rows or columns in a table:

Table Tools Layout/Rows & Columns/Delete

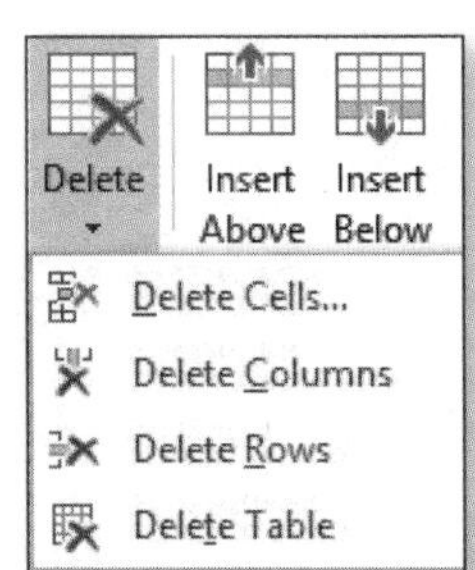

1. Position the insertion point in the row or column that is to be deleted. If more than one row or column is to be deleted, select them first.
2. Display the Delete options and select the appropriate command.

Lesson 28 Paragraph Formats

New Commands

- Alignment
- Show/Hide
- Line Spacing
- Quick Access Toolbar

K P D O **Warmup** *Lesson 28a Warmup*

Skill Building

28b **Textbook Keying**

1. Key each line once, concentrating on using good keying techniques.
2. Repeat the drill if time permits.

one-hand

1 A few treats were served as reserve seats were set up on a stage.
2 In my opinion, a few trees on a hilly acre created a vast estate.

balanced hand

3 Pam and Jake did go to visit the big island and may fish for cod.
4 Ken and six men may go to visit an island with an ancient chapel.

1st/2nd fingers

5 Kimberly tried to grab the bar, but she missed and hurt her hand.
6 My name is Frankie, but I prefer to be called Fran by my friends.

3rd/4th fingers

7 Zola and Polly saw us play polo at Maxwell Plaza; we won a prize.
8 Zack quickly swam past all six boys at a zoo pool on Saxony Land.

New Commands

28c

TIP

From this point forward, *KPDO* will launch *Word* for all activities unless you are specifically directed otherwise.

PARAGRAPH FORMATS

Home/Paragraph/Command

Some paragraph commands are positioned together in subgroups separated from one another by divider bars. The following overview presents the commands by the subgroups.

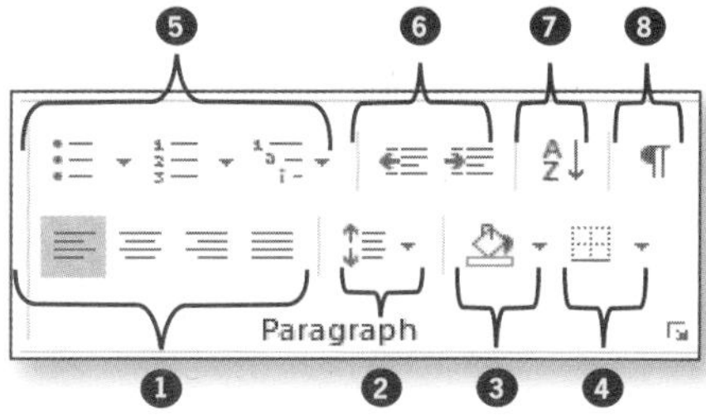

1. **Alignment commands**—Align Left, Center, Align Right, and Justify—specify how text lines up.
2. **Line and Paragraph Spacing**—determines the amount of space between lines of text and before and after paragraphs.
3. **Shading**—applies color as a background for text and paragraphs.
4. **Borders**—apply and remove inside and outside borders and horizontal lines.
5. **Bullets, Numbering, and Multilevel List**—apply formats to lists of information. Bullets and Numbering present information on one level, whereas Multilevel List presents information in a hierarchy.
6. **Decrease and Increase Indent**—move all lines of a paragraph to the right or left.
7. **Sort**—alphabetizes selected text or arranges numerical data in ascending or descending order.
8. **Show/Hide**—displays paragraph markings and other nonprinting characters.

Lesson 40 Change Table Structure

New Commands

- Insert and Delete Columns and Rows
- Merge and Split Cells

Warmup *Lesson 40a Warmup*

Skill Building

40b Textbook Keying

1. Key each line concentrating on good keying techniques.
2. Repeat the drill if time permits.

d 1 do did dad sad faded daddy madder diddle deduced hydrated dredged
k 2 keys sake kicked karat kayak karate knock knuckle knick kilometer
d/k 3 The ten tired and dizzy kids thought the doorknob was the donkey.
w 4 we were who away whew snow windward waterway window webworm award
o 5 on to too onto solo oleo soil cook looked location emotion hollow
w/o 6 Those who know their own power and are committed will follow through.
b 7 be bib sub bear book bribe fiber bombard blueberry babble baboons
v 8 vet vat van viva have over avoid vapor valve seven vanish vanilla
b/v 9 Bo gave a very big beverage and seven coins to everybody bowling.
r 10 or rear rare roar saturate reassure rather northern surge quarrel
u 11 yours undue unity useful unique unusual value wound youth succumb
r/u 12 The truth of the matter is that only Ruth can run a rummage sale.

New Commands

40c

INSERT A COLUMN OR ROW

A row can be inserted in a table by placing the mouse pointer at the left edge of the table and pointing to the position where the new row is to be inserted. If you need to add a row below Lorianna Mendez, in the illustration below, place the insertion on the border between Lorianna Mendez and William Mohammed. Click the plus symbol to insert a new row. If more than one row is to be inserted, first select the number of rows, place the insertion point where the new rows will be inserted, then click the plus symbol.

Award Winners	Department	Amount
Lorianna Mendez	Accounting	$2,000
William Mohammed	Marketing	$800
Cynthia Khek	Engineering	$1,500
Charles Pham	Purchasing	$1,000

Discover

Enhanced ScreenTips—Position the mouse pointer over a command to display its name, a description of it, and the keyboard shortcut to apply (if available).

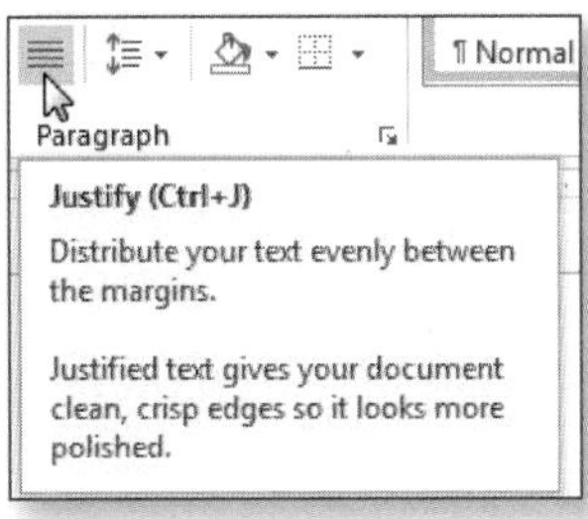

ALIGNMENT

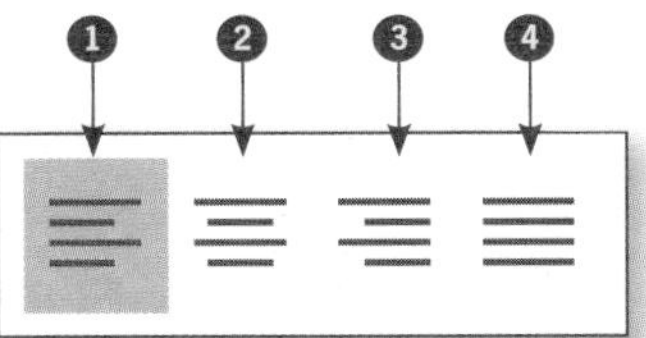

1. **Align Left**—all lines begin at left margin.
2. **Center**—all lines are centered.
3. **Align Right**—all lines are aligned at the right margin.
4. **Justify**—all lines are aligned at both the left and right margins.

To apply alignment formats:

Home/Paragraph/Align Left, Center, Align Right, or Justify

1. Click in a single paragraph or select multiple paragraphs to which a format is to be applied.
2. Click the format to be applied.

Right-aligned text

Centered Text

Left-aligned text is the most frequently used alignment. All lines begin at the left margin. The right margin is uneven when text is aligned at the left side.

Justify aligns text at both the left and the right margins. All lines are even on both sides except that the last line of a paragraph may be shorter and will not end at the right margin. The system allocates additional space as needed to force the right margin to align evenly.

DRILL 1 ALIGNMENT

1. In a new document, move the mouse pointer over each command to view the Enhanced ScreenTips for the format paragraph commands. Click the drop-list arrow on those commands that have a drop-list arrow to view the options.
2. Key the document shown above; do not format as you key.
3. Apply the alignment formats shown above.
4. Proofread and check; click Next to continue. (*28-drill1*)

Apply It

39-d1

Create Table, Adjust Cell Height and Width, and Center Horizontally

1. Key the table below.
2. Adjust the width of column A to 1.95". Adjust the width of column B to 1.5". Adjust the width of column C to 1.15".
3. Center the table horizontally on the page.
4. Adjust the height of row 1 to 0.3". Align Center and bold the column heads.
5. Proofread and check; click Next Activity. (*39-d1*)

Award Winners	Department	Amount
Lorianna Mendez	Accounting	$2,000
William Mohammed	Marketing	$800
Cynthia Khek	Engineering	$1,500
Charles Pham	Purchasing	$1,000

39-d2

Create Table, Adjust Cell Sizes

1. Key the table; adjust column width so that the text does not wrap to a second line.
2. Center columns B and D. Right-align the values in column C.
3. Adjust Cell Size height to 0.3" for the entire table. Center the text vertically in the cells. Align Center and bold the column heads. Center the table horizontally.
4. Proofread and check. (*39-d2*)
5. Click Log out to exit *KPDO*.

Book Title	Publication	Sales	Unit Price
Computer Crimes	2014	$478,769.00	$69.50
Digital Data Forensics	2014	$91,236.00	$63.00
Computer Criminology	2014	$89,412.50	$75.50
Law and Ethics in Computer Crimes	2015	$104,511.00	$93.50
Role of Operating Systems in Computer Forensics	2015	$194,137.50	$83.50

SHOW/HIDE

Home/Paragraph/Show/Hide

¶ Paragraph formats apply to an entire paragraph. Each time you tap ENTER, *Word* inserts a paragraph mark and starts a new paragraph. Thus, a paragraph may consist of a partial line or of several lines. You must be able to see where paragraphs begin and end to format them. Turning on the Show/Hide button displays all nonprinting characters such as paragraph markers (¶) or spaces (..). The Show/Hide button appears highlighted when it is active. Nonprinting characters can be turned off by clicking the Show/Hide button again.

DRILL 2 SHOW/HIDE

1. In a new document, turn on Show/Hide. Tap ENTER three times.
2. Key the text shown below; then apply both the text formats and the alignment formats listed in the following steps.
3. Apply bold format to *My Personal Assistant*; right-align it.
4. Apply Cambria 14-point font and bold to the centered text.
5. Add italic to *KPDO* and in the last line to *personal assistant*.
6. Proofread and check; click Next Activity. (*28-drill2*)

My Personal Assistant

Why Use Show/Hide?

Using Show/Hide will help you format your documents correctly. It can also help you earn better scores on your work as it will display symbols to indicate spacing and other errors before the checker in *KPDO* finds them.

Think of Show/Hide as a personal assistant when you key documents!

LINE AND PARAGRAPH SPACING

Line and paragraph spacing enable you to choose the amount of space between lines and between paragraphs. The illustration at the right shows the options that display when you click the drop-list arrow. To view the default line and paragraph spacing, click Line Spacing Options.

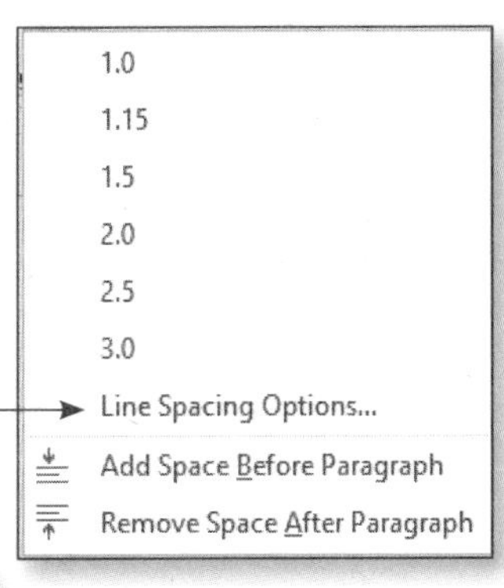

The 1.08 line spacing and 8 points after paragraph defaults are shown in the illustration below.

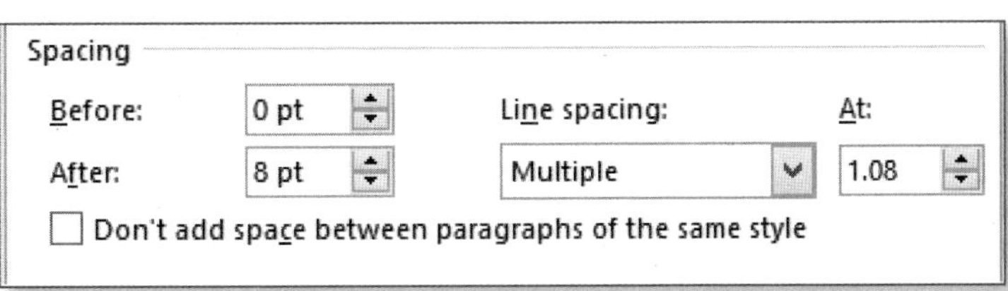

CHANGE CELL SIZE

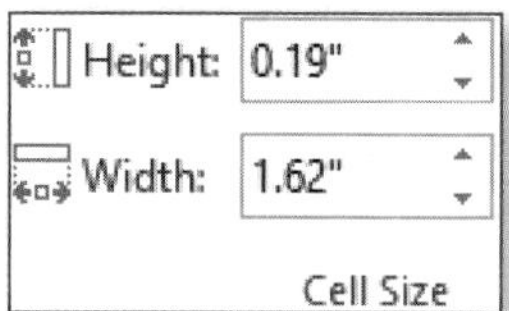

The Cell Size group on the Layout tab allows you to set cell height and width to exact dimensions. The height of a row is often increased to provide some blank space above and below the text to make the contents in the cell easier to read.

To change cell height or width:

Table Tools Layout/Cell Size

- Click in the cell or column and then key the dimension in the Height box or use the spin arrows to set the height dimension.
- Select the cell or row and then key the dimension in the Width box or use the spin arrows to set the width dimension.

CHANGE TEXT ALIGNMENT IN CELL

Table Tools Layout/Alignment

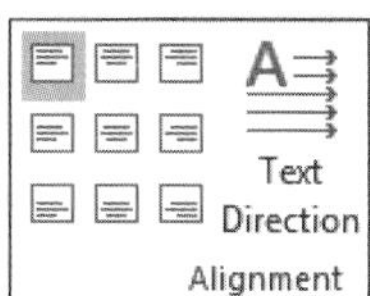

By default, text displays left aligned at the top of the cell. When cell height is increased, text may need to be centered vertically in the cell to make the table more attractive.

Commands in the Alignment group allow text to be aligned at the top, middle, or bottom of the cell. You can also align text at the left, middle, or right of the cell. Select the button that provides the best combination of vertical and horizontal alignment.

To change the alignment of the text in the cell, select the cell(s) and click the appropriate alignment command.

DRILL 3 ADJUST CELL HEIGHT AND WIDTH

1. In the open document (*38-d1*), select column A. Change the width of the column to 2.2".
2. Select column B. Change the width of column B to 1.4".
3. Select column C. Change the width of column C 1.5".
4. Select row 1. Change the height of row 1 to 0.3".
5. Align Center the column heads in row 1.
6. Apply bold to the column heads.
7. Center the table horizontally on the page.
8. Proofread and check; click Next Activity. (*39-drill3*)

To change line spacing:

Home/Paragraph/Line and Paragraph Spacing

1. Position the insertion point in the paragraph whose spacing you wish to change.
2. Click the Line and Paragraph Spacing button and select the desired spacing.

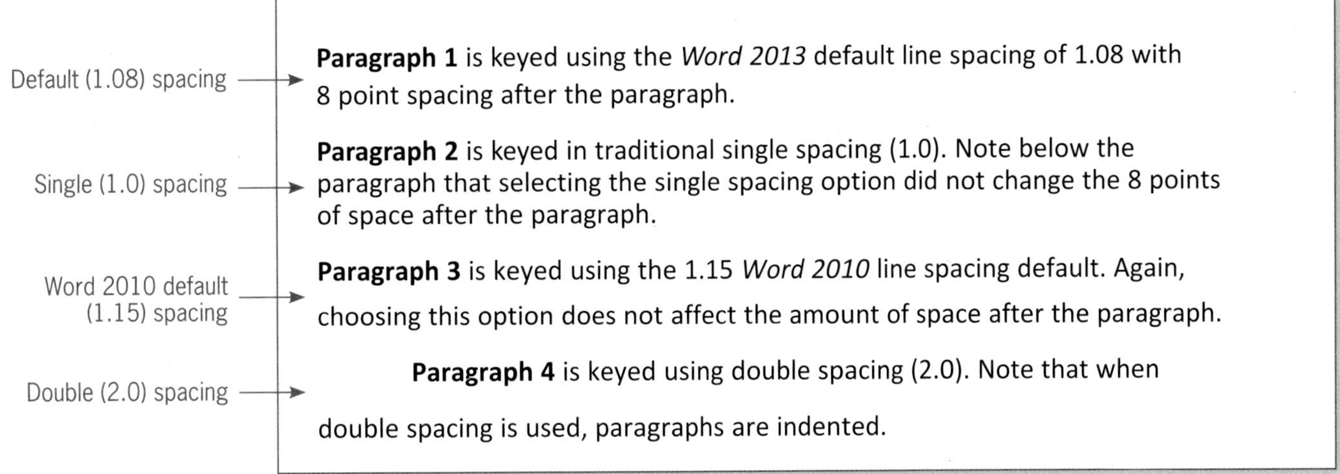
Default (1.08) spacing → **Paragraph 1** is keyed using the *Word 2013* default line spacing of 1.08 with 8 point spacing after the paragraph.

Single (1.0) spacing → **Paragraph 2** is keyed in traditional single spacing (1.0). Note below the paragraph that selecting the single spacing option did not change the 8 points of space after the paragraph.

Word 2010 default (1.15) spacing → **Paragraph 3** is keyed using the 1.15 *Word 2010* line spacing default. Again, choosing this option does not affect the amount of space after the paragraph.

Double (2.0) spacing → **Paragraph 4** is keyed using double spacing (2.0). Note that when double spacing is used, paragraphs are indented.

DRILL 3 LINE SPACING

1. In a new document, key the four paragraphs above; then apply the formatting shown in each paragraph. Remember to apply bold and italics.
2. Note the differences between 1.08 spacing, 1.15 spacing, 1.0 spacing, and 2.0 spacing shown above.
3. Proofread and check; click Next Activity. (*28-drill3*)

Note: The amount of space (8 points) between paragraphs does not change when you change the line spacing. It is 8 points after each paragraph.

The Quick Access Toolbar is available from all tabs on the Ribbon.

QUICK ACCESS TOOLBAR

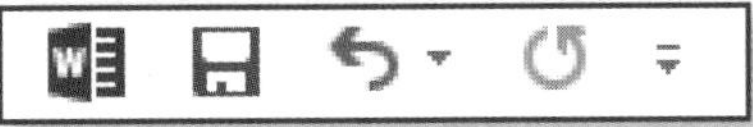

The Quick Access Toolbar is located in the upper-left corner of the screen above the File and Home tabs. It contains icons for three frequently used commands: Save, Undo, and Redo. The Quick Access Toolbar provides a shortcut or one-click option for these frequently used commands. *KPDO* saves documents for you, but the Save command will be useful when you are not using *KPDO*.

To adjust column widths using the mouse:

1. Point to the column border that needs adjusting.
2. When the pointer changes to ⟷, hold down the left mouse button and drag the border to the left to make the column narrower or to the right to make it wider.
3. Adjust the column widths appropriately. Leave approximately 0.5" to 0.75" between the longest line and the border. Use the Horizontal Ruler as a guide.
4. The widths of the columns can be displayed by pointing to the column marker on the Ruler, holding down the ALT key, and clicking the left mouse button.

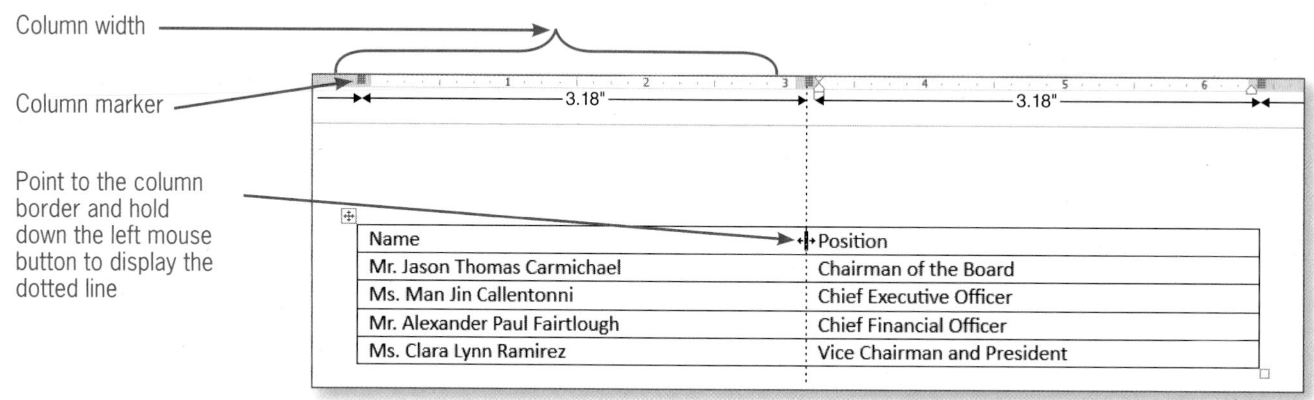

Column width
Column marker
Point to the column border and hold down the left mouse button to display the dotted line
3.18"
3.18"
Name
Position
Mr. Jason Thomas Carmichael
Chairman of the Board
Ms. Man Jin Callentonni
Chief Executive Officer
Mr. Alexander Paul Fairtlough
Chief Financial Officer
Ms. Clara Lynn Ramirez
Vice Chairman and President

CENTER TABLE HORIZONTALLY

Once column widths have been adjusted, a table will no longer be full-page width. Use the Table Properties dialog box to center the table horizontally on the page.

Another method of centering a table horizontally is to click the Table Move handle to select the table and then click the Center button on the Home tab.

To center table horizontally on page:

Table Tools Layout/Table/Properties

1. Click in a table cell.
2. Open the Table Properties dialog box.
3. On the Table tab, select Center.

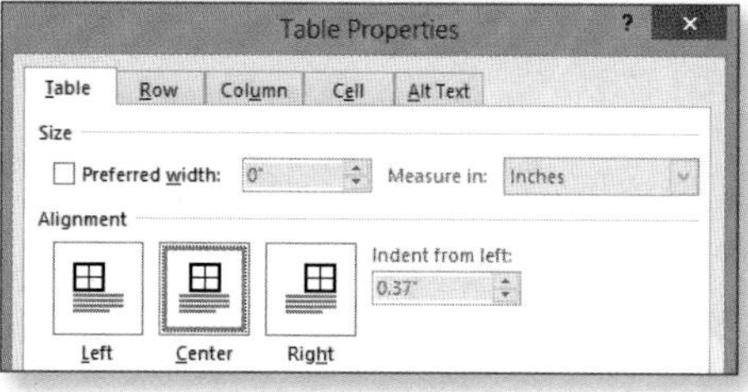

DRILL 2 ADJUST COLUMN WIDTH AND CENTER TABLE

1. In the open document (*39-drill1*), click in the table.
2. Use the mouse to adjust column borders. Leave approximately 0.5" between the longest line and the right border.
3. Center the table horizontally on the page.
4. Proofread and check; click Next Activity. (*39-drill2*)

QUICK ACCESS TOOLBAR, CONTINUED

Save preserves the current version of a document or displays the Save As dialog box to save a new document.

Undo reverses the most recent action you have taken (such as inserting or deleting text or removing formats). The drop-list arrow displays a list of the commands that you can undo. Selecting an item on the list will undo all items above it on the list.

Redo reverses the last undo; it can be used several times to redo the past several actions. You can also select new text and click Redo to repeat the last redo.

DRILL 4 QUICK ACCESS TOOLBAR

1. Key the four sentences below.
2. In sentence 1, apply bold and underline to *Undo/Redo.*
3. Undo the underline in sentence 1.
4. Apply bold to Undo in sentence 2 and to Redo in sentence 3. Then apply italic to both.
5. Remove italic in both sentences 2 and 3.
6. In sentence 4, apply bold to *use.*
7. Select *You can* and then click Redo to repeat the bold command.
8. Key Quick Access Toolbar below the last sentence, and then right-align it. Notice that double-spacing is carried forward from the previous paragraph.
9. Use Undo to remove the right-align; then use Redo to go back to right-align.
10. Proofread and check; click Next Activity. (*28-drill4*)

Keying and formatting changes can be reversed easily by using the Undo/Redo commands.

If you make a change, one click of the Undo command can reverse the change.

If you undo a change and decide that you want to keep the change as it was originally made, you can go back to the original change by clicking the Redo command.

You can use the Redo command as a Repeat command.

You can also select an entire table, a row, or a column by moving the mouse pointer to different locations on or near the table.

To select	Move the insertion point:
Entire table	Over the table and click the Table Move handle at the upper-left corner of the table. To move the table, drag the Table Move handle to a new location.
Column	To the top of the column until a solid down arrow (⬇) appears; click the left mouse button.
Row	To the left area just outside the table until the pointer turns to an open diagonal arrow (↗); then click the left mouse button.

Cells can also be selected by clicking in the cell, holding down the mouse button, and dragging across or down.

ADJUST COLUMN WIDTH

A new *Word* table extends from margin to margin when first created, with all columns the same width regardless of the width of the data in the columns. Some tables, however, would be more attractive and easier to read if the columns were narrower or adjusted to fit the data in the cells.

Use the AutoFit option on the Layout tab to adjust the width of a column to fit the widest entry in each column.

To adjust column width using AutoFit:

Table Tools Layout/Cell Size/AutoFit

1. Click a table cell.
2. Display the AutoFit options.
3. Select the desired option.

You can also change column width manually using the mouse. Using the mouse enables you to adjust the widths as you like. Columns look best when approximately 0.5" of blank space is left between the longest line and the column border.

DRILL 1 ADJUST COLUMN WIDTH USING AUTOFIT

Table Tools Layout/Cell Size/AutoFit

1. In the open document (*38-drill2*), click in the table.
2. Click AutoFit Contents. The columns adjust to fit the data.
3. Click AutoFit Window to restore the table to full size.
4. Place the insertion point in the last cell and tap TAB.
5. Key your name and **Administrative Assistant** in the last row.
6. Proofread and check; click Next Activity. (*39-drill1*)

Apply It

28-d1

Announcement

1. In a new document, key all paragraphs below using default font, size, and spacing. Turn on Show/Hide.
2. Position the insertion point at the beginning of the title, *Standard Operating Procedures*, and tap ENTER three times; apply bold, 16-point Arial font to the title, and center it.
3. Apply bold and 14-point Arial font to the three side headings.
4. Proofread and check; click Next Activity. (*28-d1*)

Standard Operating Procedures

Many companies develop standard operating procedures (SOPs) for virtually every phase of their business. When standard operating procedures are mentioned, most people think of a manufacturing or service business and are surprised to learn that standard operating procedures apply to management and office administration as well. Most companies have SOPs for producing documents in their offices for several reasons.

Quality Control

SOPs ensure that company image is consistent throughout the organization. Guides are presented for using and protecting the company logo, standard colors may be specified, and document formats are standardized.

Training Tools

New and experienced employees both want to do a good job. SOPs provide an excellent training tool to ensure that all employees do their work accurately and meet company expectations consistently. Most employees do not like to be told repeatedly what to do. Having a set of guides to follow enables them to work independently and still meet quality standards.

Productivity Enhancement and Cost Reduction

Documents are very expensive to produce. SOPs are designed to be efficient, and efficiency translates to cost savings.

28-d2

Apply Font and Paragraph Formats

1. Open *28-d1*; turn on Show/Hide. Select the entire title; use the Mini toolbar to decrease the font size to 14 point.
2. Click in the paragraph below the centered title and change the line spacing to double spacing. Tap TAB to indent the first line of the paragraph. Select the entire paragraph and change the font to Times New Roman 11 point.
3. Click in the paragraph below each side heading, and change the line spacing to double spacing. Then tap TAB to indent the first line of the paragraphs. Triple-click to select the entire paragraph and change the font to Times New Roman 11 point.
4. Turn off Show/Hide.
5. Proofread and check; click Exit Word to close. (*28-d2*)
6. Click Log out to exit *KPDO*.

Lesson 39 Table Tools—Layout

New Commands

- Adjust Column Width
- Center Table on Page
- Change Cell Size
- Text Alignment in Cells

Warmup *Lesson 39a Warmup*

Skill Building

39b Textbook Keying

1. Key each line, concentrating on good keying techniques.
2. Repeat the drill if time permits.

t 1 it cat pat to top thin at tilt jolt tuft mitt flat test tent felt
r 2 fur bur try roar soar ram trap rare ripe true rear tort corral
t/r 3 The track star was triumphant in both the third and fourth heats.
m 4 me mine memo mimic named clam month maximum mummy summer remember
n 5 no snow ton none nine ninety noun mini mind minnow kennel evening
m/n 6 Men and women in management roles maximize time during commuting.

New Commands

39c

LAYOUT TAB

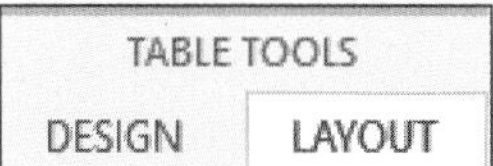

When you click in a table, the Table Tools tab displays with two tabs—the Design tab and the Layout tab. The Design tab contains commands for changing the appearance of the table. The Layout tab contains commands for altering the table structure.

SELECT PORTIONS OF A TABLE

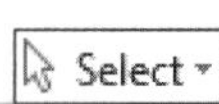

To alter the table structure, select the cells, column, or row that will be altered. Use the mouse to select the cells or the Select command on the Table Tools Layout tab to select parts of the table or the entire table.

To use the Select command to select portions of a table:
Table Tools Layout/Table/Select

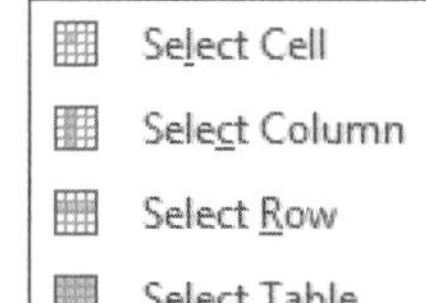

1. Click the insertion point in a table cell; then display the Select options.
   a. Choose Select Cell to select only the cell the insertion point is in.
   b. Choose Select Column or Select Row to highlight the entire column or row that contains the cell.
   c. Choose Select Table to highlight the entire table.

Lesson 29 Format Paragraphs/Navigate Documents

New Commands

- Bullets and Numbering
- Scroll bars
- Slider Zoom
- View
- Spelling and Grammar
- Thesaurus
- Define
- Word Count

Warmup *Lesson 29a Warmup*

Skill Building

29b Textbook Keying

Key each line once, concentrating on using good keying techniques.

balanced-hand words, phrases, and sentences

1 if me to so he is us do go or sod fir for pen may big dig got fix
2 dog jam sit men lap pay cut nap tug lake worn make torn turn dock

3 he is | it is | of it | is it | go to | to go | is he | he is it | for it | she can
4 did he | pay them | she may | is it torn | it is worn | he may go | the lake

5 He may also go with them to the dock or down to the lake with us.
6 Did she go with Keith to the lake, or can she go to town with us?

29c Timed Writing

1. Key a 1' timed writing on each paragraph; work to increase speed. Use wordwrap.
2. Key a 3' timed writing on all paragraphs.

Learning new software applications can be exciting, but it often requires much hard work. However, if you are willing to work hard and to work smart, in a relatively short period of time you can learn very important skills.

If you accept change easily and willingly, you are more likely to learn new things quickly. A person who avoids change has just about the same chance of learning new software applications as a lazy person.

Working smart might be just as important as working hard. Help is easy to use if you will take the time to explore the resources that are provided in your software. Valuable information is also available on the provider's website.

Create Table

1. Key the 3-column, 8-row table below. Your columns will be wider, so your text will not wrap as shown below.
2. Select cells C1–C8 and click Center. When all the items in a column are the same length, the column will look better centered.
3. Select cells A1 and B1 and click Center.
4. Proofread and check; click Log out to exit *KPDO*. (*38-d3*)

TIP

Align column heads at the left or center them in the column, whichever looks better.

Movie Title	Time of Showing	Location
The Amazing Bionic Woman	1:15, 4:10, 7:10	Theatre 1
Global Warming: 3D	1:20, 6:25, 9:10	Theatre 2
The Hourglass	12:00, 2:30, 5:10, 7:45, 10:25	Theatre 3
The Circus Comes to Town: 3D	12:25, 2:40, 5:00, 7:40, 10:10	Theatre 4
Time Marches On	12:30, 3:30, 6:30, 9:30	Theatre 5
Humpty Dumpty's Great Fall	11:00, 1:40, 4:20, 7:10	Theatre 6
The Silver Knight: The IMAX	12:00, 3:30, 7:00, 10:30	Theatre 7

WORKPLACE SUCCESS

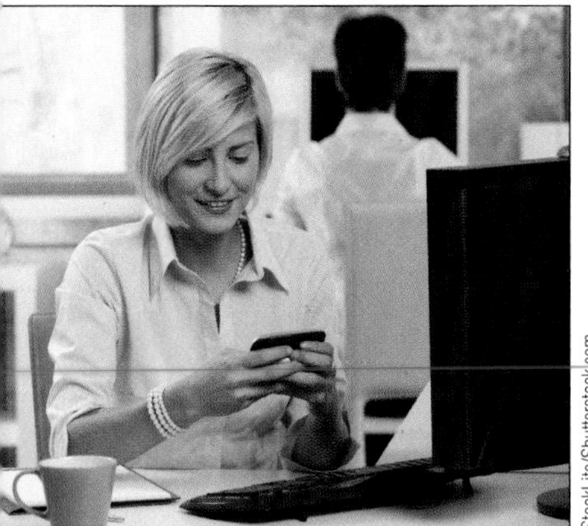

StockLite/Shutterstock.com

High-Tech Etiquette

In today's day and age, high-tech manners can be just as critical as dining etiquette in developing your professional image. Knowing the difference between Bluetooth and houndstooth is just as important as knowing how to host a business luncheon.

Improper or ill-timed use of new high-tech devices can destroy your professional image rather than enhance it. Using a smartphone may make you appear technically savvy; however, continually glancing at your device during a meeting is like checking your watch. It is considered rude and inappropriate behavior.

Cell phone usage should be limited during work hours. Some companies require that employees keep their cell phones in their car. If your company allows you to bring your cell phone to your desk, set it on vibrate. Do not walk around the office building talking on a cell phone; it annoys others and is not professional. If you work in a cubicle environment, be mindful that others can hear your conversation and that what you say may not be appropriate for coworkers to hear.

New Commands

29d

BULLETS AND NUMBERING

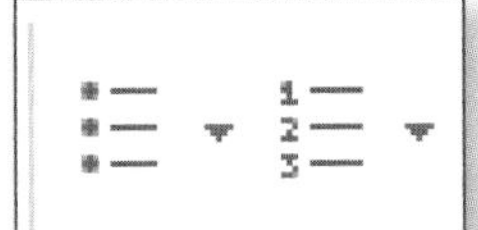

Bullets are used for lists of unordered items, whereas numbering is used for items that are in a sequence. Bullets can be converted to numbers, and numbers can be converted to bullets. The drop-list arrow on bullets and numbering displays a library of styles for each command. If you have recently used bullets or numbering, the style used will display at the top of the library. Bullets and numbering are easier to apply after text has been keyed.

To apply Bullets and Numbering:

Home/Paragraph/Bullets or Numbering

1. Key the list.
2. Select the list and click either the Bullets or the Numbering command.

To select a different format for Bullets and Numbering:

1. Click the drop-list arrow on either the Bullets or the Numbering button to display the library of styles.
2. Select the desired style.

Note: The gallery that displays on your computer may have different bullet styles than the one shown at the right.

DRILL 1 BULLETS AND NUMBERING

1. In a new document, key the two lists below.
2. Bold the headings. Apply bullets to the first list below the heading *Procedures for Completing an Activity*.
3. Apply numbering to the second list, *Things to Do This Weekend*.
4. Convert the first list with bullets to numbering using the number format with right parentheses (Left alignment).
5. Convert the second list with numbering to square bullets.
6. Proofread and check; click Next Activity. (*29-drill1*)

Procedures for Completing an Activity

Preview and proofread the document.

Print the document.

Save document with appropriate name and close it.

Things to Do This Weekend

Complete library research.

Pick up office supplies.

Install new software.

Apply It

38-d1

Create Table

TIP

Text is keyed left-aligned. Numerical amounts are right-aligned.

1. Create and key the table below. Your solution will look different than the table below.
2. Select cells C2–C5 and click Align Right (Home/Paragraph/Align Right) to right-align the numbers in column C. Select row 1 and click Center.
3. Place the insertion point in the last cell and tap TAB to add a row.
4. Key the following copy in row 6:

   Lawrence Jose Gonzalez **East** **$83,479**

5. Proofread and check; click Next Activity. (*38-d1*)

Sales Representative	Region	Amount of Sale
Stephanie Acosta	Northwest	$1,157,829
Mitzi Fujitsu	Central	$99,016
Joanna B. Breckenridge	Southwest	$6,301,625
Jack M. Harrigan	Midwest	$4,245,073

38-d2

Create Table

1. Create the 3-column, 4-row table below.
2. Key column C using wordwrap. Your columns will be wider, so your text will not wrap at the same position as shown.
3. Proofread and check; click Next Activity. (*38-d2*)

The Golden Mile	Boutique Shops	The Golden Mile is one square mile of boutique shops located between Beverly Boulevard and Pacific Coast Highway. You will find many designer-label retail outlets, high-end jewelry stores, and charming sidewalk cafes.
Birds of Paradise	Floral District	The Floral District offers exceptional values on fresh flowers, plants, and floral arrangements. Flowers and plants are locally grown.
Wellington Gardens	Mall	The Wellington Gardens Mall provides a luxury shopping experience with over 200 retail shops and 12 department stores. This mall is noted for its extraordinary boutiques, personal service, and upscale amenities.
Sew and Sew Fabrics	Textile District	Sew and Sew Fabrics houses over 150 vendors of fabrics and notions from around the world. Shoppers will find fabrics for apparel, crafts, and home décor.

NAVIGATE AND VIEW A DOCUMENT

The document window displays only a portion of a page at one time. The keyboard, mouse, and scroll bars can be used to move quickly through a document to view it.

Keyboard options—press CTRL + HOME to go to the beginning of a document and CTRL + END to move to the end of the document. The Page Up and Page Down keys can also be used to move through a document.

Mouse and scroll bar—use the scroll bar located on the right side of the screen to move through the document. Scrolling does not change the position of the insertion point; it only changes your view of the document. You must click in the text to change the position of the insertion point.

Zoom—enables users to view the document with enlarged or reduced text. Zoom is located on the status bar and the View menu.

View tab—provides additional options for viewing documents.

SCROLL BAR

The scroll bar on the right side of the screen provides options to move through the document. The scroll bar at the bottom of the screen allows you to move to the left or right to see the entire line of writing.

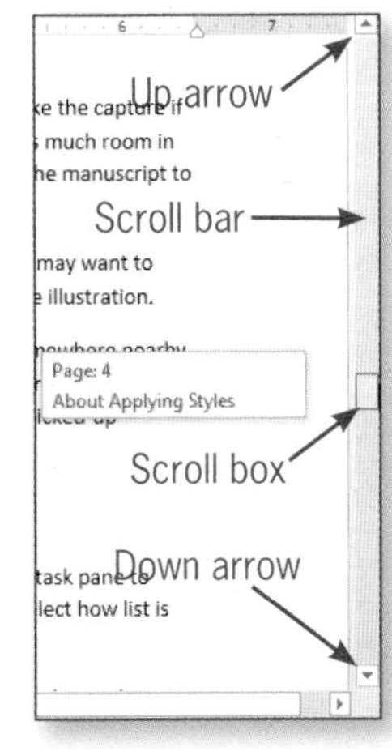

To move through a document:

- Click the up and down arrows. -or-
- Click above or below the scroll box. -or-
- Click the scroll box and drag it to the desired position.

Note the position displays when you drag the scroll box.

ZOOM OR SLIDER

Clicking the plus or minus sign on the Slider changes the settings in increments of 10 percent.

Zoom, located on the status bar at the lower right-side of the *Word* window, controls the magnification of your document. Zoom is positioned in the center of the slider bar, which displays text at 100% of its actual size. It is sometimes called the Slider because Zoom slides to the right or left to increase or decrease text size.

Zoom

USE THE INSERT TABLE COMMAND

The Insert Table dialog box lets you specify the number of columns and rows for the table. This option can be easier to use than dragging over the Table grid if you need a large number of rows or columns.

To create a table using the Insert Table command:
Insert/Tables/Table

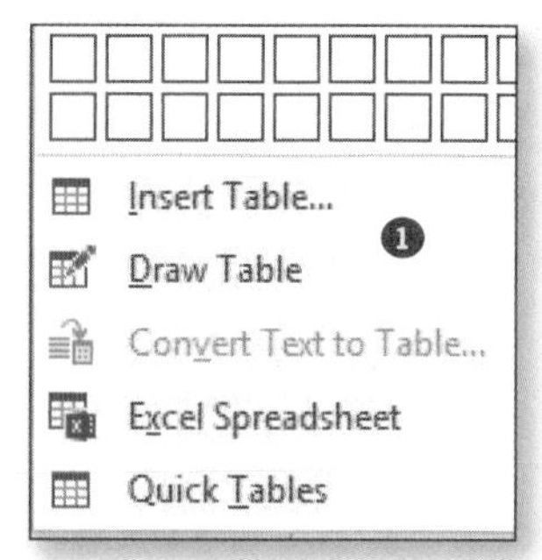

1. Click the insertion point where the table is to be inserted.
2. Display the Insert Table menu.
3. Click Insert Table ❶ to display the Insert Table dialog box.
4. Insert the number of columns by keying the number or using the spin arrows ❷.
5. Insert the number of rows by keying the number or using the spin arrows ❸.

Word automatically creates a table with fixed column widths. You can adjust the column widths in the Insert Table dialog box, or choose an AutoFit option to fit column widths to the longest line or to the current window size.

DRILL 2 CREATE AND FORMAT TABLE

1. Use the Insert Table command to create a 2-column, 4-row table.
2. Key **Name** in cell A1 and **Position** in cell B1. Row 1 contains the column heads and is often called the header row. Key the rest of the table below (your columns will be wider).
3. Place the insertion point in the last cell and tap TAB to add a row at the bottom of the table.
4. Key the following text in cell A4.

   Ms. Clara Lynn Ramirez

5. Key the following text in cell B4.

   Vice Chairman and President

6. Proofread and check; click Next Activity. (*38-drill2*)

Name	Position ← Header row
Mr. Jason Thomas Carmichael	Chairman of the Board
Ms. Man Jin Callentonni	Chief Executive Officer
Mr. Alexander Paul Fairtlough	Chief Financial Officer

To view smaller or larger versions of text:

1. To view a larger version of a segment of text, move Zoom toward the right or positive (+) side. The text will be larger, but you see a smaller segment of it.
2. To see more of the document, move Zoom toward the left or the negative (–) side. To view two full pages, move the Zoom to about 50 percent. Clicking the plus or minus signs increases or decreases size in increments of 10 percent.

VIEW

Document views display a document in different formats. The view that is selected when you save and close a document will be the view that displays when that document is opened again.

Document views can be accessed by clicking the view on the status bar or the View tab. With Outline view, the Close option must be clicked to exit it.

To access document views from the status bar:

1. Click the desired view. Print Layout is the default view.
2. To close the view, click Print Layout.

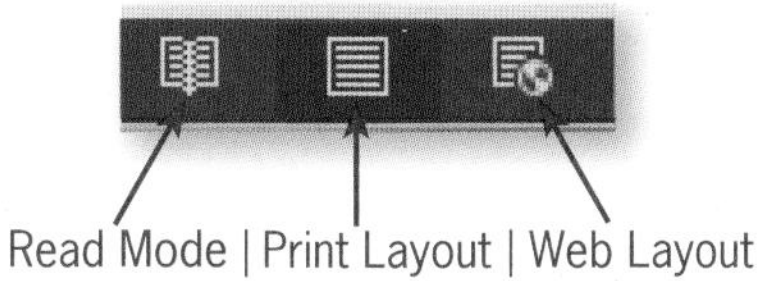

Read Mode | Print Layout | Web Layout

To view documents using Views:

View/Views/Read Mode or other views

1. Click the desired view.

   Hover the mouse over each view and review the Enhanced ScreenTip that describes the view and when it is best used. Two additional views—Outline and Draft—are added to those on the status bar.

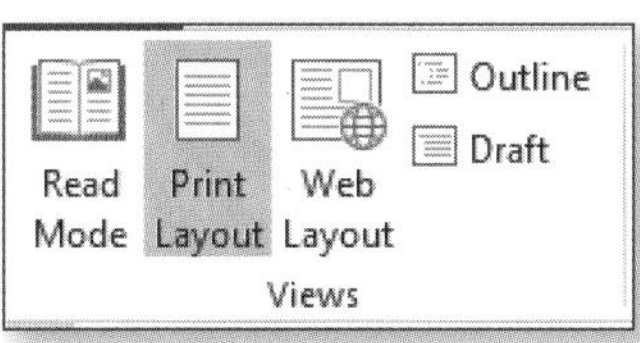

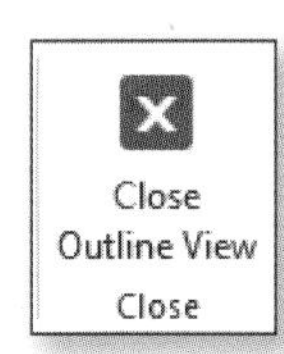

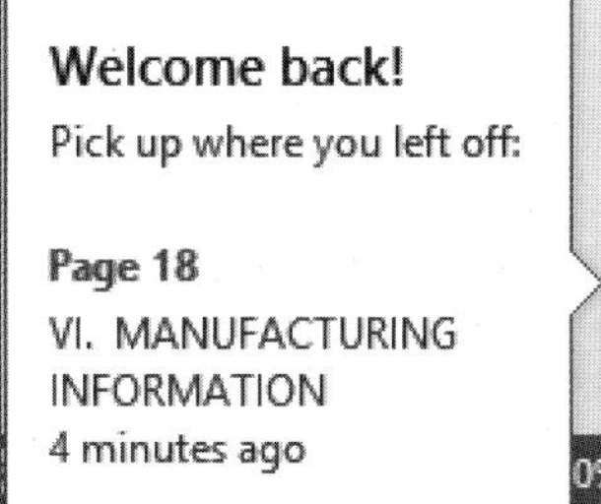

Welcome back!
Pick up where you left off:
Page 18
VI. MANUFACTURING INFORMATION
4 minutes ago

2. Click the Close Outline view button to exit that view.

The Read Mode has additional tools designed to enhance reading. When you close a document and later return to finish reading it, the bookmark shown at the right brings you back to the page you were reading.

To create a table using the Table grid:

Insert/Tables/Table

1. Click the insertion point at the position where the table is to be inserted. Follow the path to display the Insert Table menu.
2. Drag on the grid to select the number of columns and rows needed for the table.
3. Click the left mouse button to display the table in the document.
4. Click in the first cell (A1); key your text. The cell widens as you key to accommodate the length of your text. Tap TAB to move to the next cell, and then key the text. Continue to tap TAB and key until all text has been keyed.

MOVE WITHIN A TABLE

The insertion point displays in cell A1 when a table is created. Tap TAB to move to the next cell, or simply use the mouse to click in a cell. Refer to the table below as you learn to key text in a table.

Press or Tap	Movement
TAB	To move to the next cell. If the insertion point is in the last cell, tapping TAB will add a new row.
SHIFT + TAB	To move to the previous cell.
ENTER	To increase the height of the row. If you tap ENTER by mistake, tap BACKSPACE to delete the line.

DRILL 1 CREATE TABLE USING THE TABLE GRID

1. Create a 3-column, 4-row table using the Table grid. Turn on Show/Hide.
2. The insertion point is in cell A1. Tap TAB to move to cell B1. Tap TAB to move to cell C1.
3. Tap ENTER. Notice the increase in the row height. Delete the ¶ symbol by tapping the BACKSPACE key.
4. Position the mouse pointer on the table to display the Table Move handle and the Sizing handle. Notice the markers at the end of each cell and each row.
5. Drag the Table Move handle down the page. This moves the table. Drag the handle back to the original position.
6. Click in the last cell (C4). Tap TAB to insert an additional row at the bottom of the table.
7. Click Check Document and then Next Activity. (*38-drill1*)

To view documents using Zoom options:

View/Zoom/Zoom or Page Options

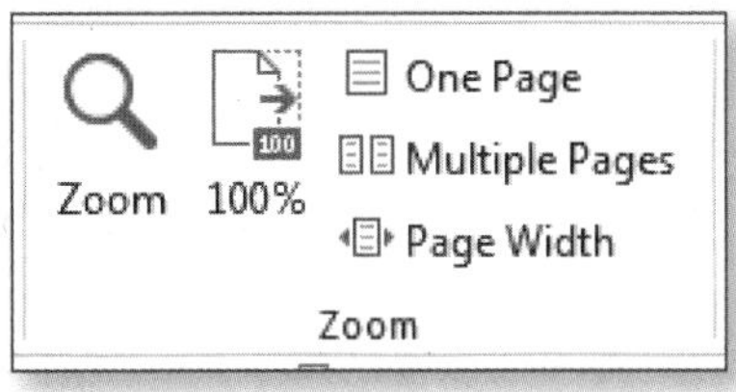

1. To view smaller or larger portions of text, click Zoom and select percentage.
2. To view a full page, two pages, or page width, click the appropriate alternative.

DRILL 2 NAVIGATION AND VIEW

1. In the open document (*28-d2*), move to the end of the document (Ctrl + End). Tap ENTER and key **29-drill2**; right-align the document name.
2. Use the keyboard to move up and down through the document. Press CTRL + HOME to go to the beginning of the document, then CTRL + END to move to the end.
3. Use the mouse, the scroll box, and the up and down arrows to move in the document.
4. Move the Zoom to the left to 50% and view the document; then move it to 200% and view the document.
5. Move the Zoom back to the center at 100%.
6. Use the View tab to change the document view to Page Width.
7. From the View tab, hover the mouse over each document view to display the ScreenTip.
8. Click each view on the View tab. To exit Read Mode, click Print Layout view on the status bar. To exit Outline view, click the Close Outline View button.
9. Return to Print Layout view from the status bar.
10. Click Check Document and then Next Activity. (*29-drill2*)

Communicating Today ▶

Proofing Tools: Technology Assisted Communication

Many errors made while you key are corrected automatically by a feature called AutoCorrect. In addition, *Word 2013* provides four enhanced proofing tools that are designed to help you compose, edit, and proofread documents.

Spelling and Grammar. In addition to marking errors, this feature provides the correct alternative and explains the rule that applies.

Define. A Dictionary application can be downloaded and is available for looking up the definition of words that you do not know.

Thesaurus. An online thesaurus helps you select the best word to express a particular thought and provides synonyms for words that you tend to overuse.

Word Count. In many situations, documents such as articles and resumes are limited to a specific number of pages or words. Document statistics are readily available.

Language tools are also available to help you if you are working with a second language. The **Translate** feature provides the translation for words to many different languages and helps you select the proper word to use.

New Commands

38c

TABLE OVERVIEW

The Table commands make it easy to present data and graphics in a *Word* document. A table helps you easily align columns and rows of text and numbers.

Table: Columns and rows of data—either alphabetic, numeric, or both.

Column: Vertical list of information labeled alphabetically from left to right.

Row: Horizontal list of information labeled numerically from top to bottom.

Cell: An intersection of a column and a row. Each cell has its own address consisting of the column letter and the row number (cell A1).

The table displays with end-of-cell and end-of-row markers. These markers are useful when editing tables. Place the mouse pointer on the table to see the Table Move handle in the upper-left corner of the table. Drag the Table Move handle to move the table to a different location in the document. Use the Sizing handle at the lower-right corner of the table to make the table larger or smaller.

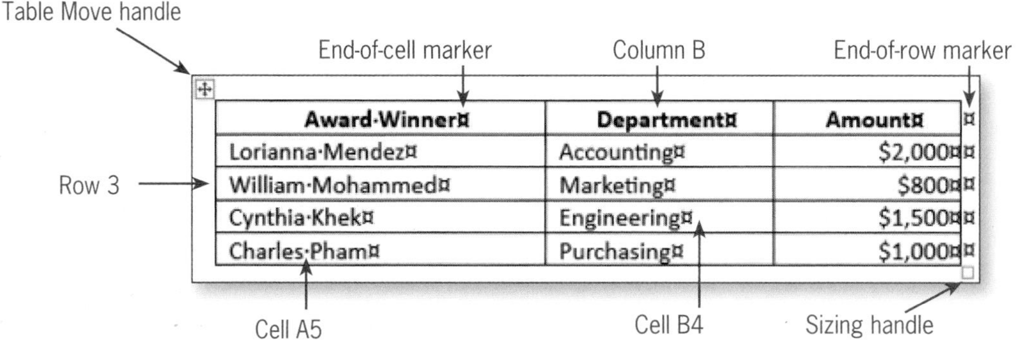

Award·Winner¤	Department¤	Amount¤
Lorianna·Mendez¤	Accounting¤	$2,000¤
William·Mohammed¤	Marketing¤	$800¤
Cynthia·Khek¤	Engineering¤	$1,500¤
Charles·Pham¤	Purchasing¤	$1,000¤

USE THE TABLE GRID

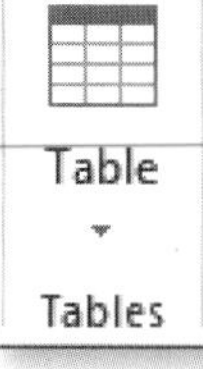

Tables are inserted into existing documents or new documents. Begin creating a table by locating the Tables group on the Insert tab. The Table button contains options for creating various types of tables; you will use two of the options in this module.

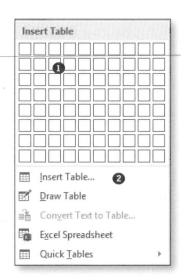

Tables are created by using the grid or the Insert Table command. Click the Table button to display the Insert Table menu, which provides several methods for creating tables. The Table grid ❶ is often used to create tables with a few columns and rows. Larger tables can be created by using the Insert Table command ❷.

Insert Table
❶
Insert Table... ❷
Draw Table
Convert Text to Table...
Excel Spreadsheet
Quick Tables

SPELLING AND GRAMMAR

Review/Proofing/Spelling & Grammar

Errors that are not corrected automatically are marked in the text as you key. Although this feature is helpful, it is not totally accurate. Careful proofreading is still required. Errors are detected in three ways.

1. Color-coded squiggly lines appear in your text as you key.
   - Red indicates spelling or keying errors.
   - Blue indicates grammar or contextual errors. Right-click the errors while you are keying. An option box displays and provides the correct version as shown below. Click Grammar to display the Grammar pane which provides the rule and examples.

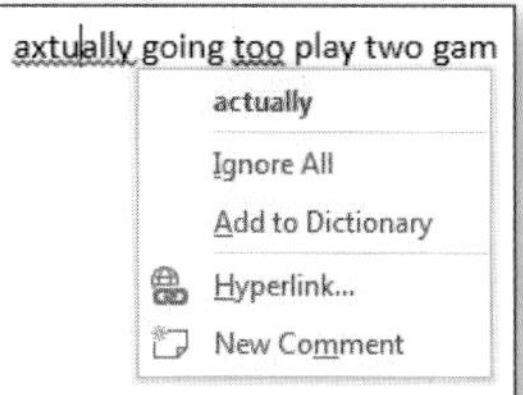

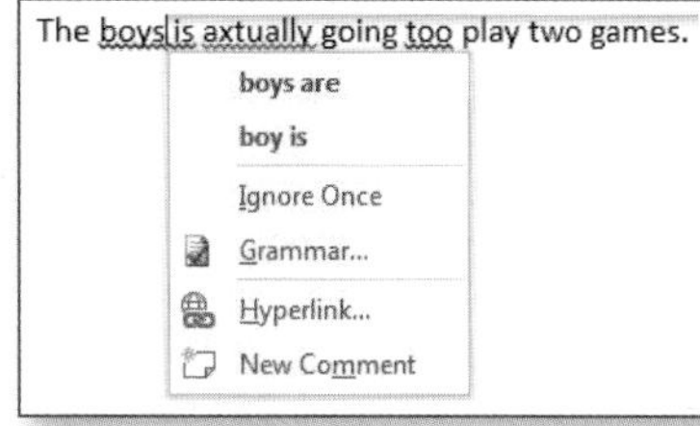

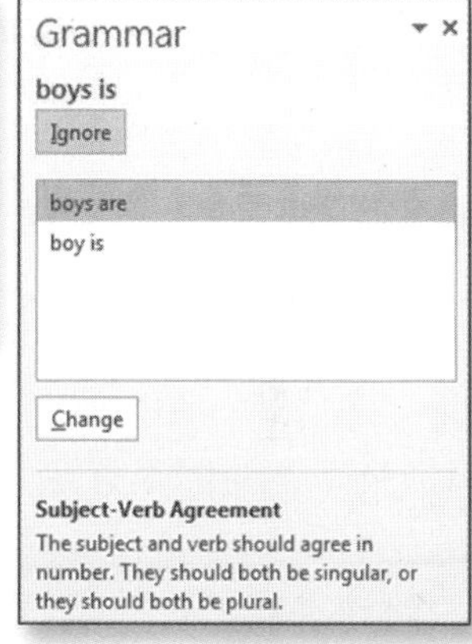

2. The error detection button with an X displays in the status bar when an error is detected. Click the button to display the Grammar or Spelling pane and correct the error. When the document is error free, the button displays a check (✓).

3. The Spelling & Grammar command in the proofing group is generally used to check the entire document at once. Click the command and the Spelling or Grammar pane displays to correct each error. Even if you have corrected errors as they were marked, it is important to run the Spelling & Grammar check after you have completed the document.

DRILL 3 SPELLING AND GRAMMAR

1. Key the paragraph on the right exactly as shown.
2. Correct the three errors.
3. Proofread and check; click Next Activity. (*29-drill3*)

Spelling errors are ofen corrected automatically. If an error are not detected by the software, you should proofread and correct it. To often writers skip the proofreading step.

MODULE 5

Tables

Lesson 38	*Create Tables*
Lesson 39	*Table Tools—Layout*
Lesson 40	*Change Table Structure*
Lesson 41	*Table Tools—Design*
Lesson 42	*Palmetto Event Solutions, Inc.*

LEARNING OUTCOMES

- Create tables.
- Change table structure.
- Format tables.
- Create tables within documents.
- Build keying speed and accuracy.

Lesson 38 Create Tables

New Commands

- Table Grid
- Insert Table

Warmup *Lesson 38a Warmup*

A ALL LETTERS

Skill Building

38b Timed Writing

Key two 3' timings on all paragraphs; work for control.

Your perception of yourself has a strong impact on how others perceive you. The more confidence you have, the more likely it is you will succeed. Having confidence in yourself and your abilities helps you when you are making a difficult decision or adapting to a new situation. A great number of factors that affect self-confidence are beyond your control, but there are many things that you can do to build confidence.

People with confidence are just full of energy and have established goals; they have places to go, people to see, and important work to do. Confident people make a positive impression on others and empower others. They stand up straight, walk quickly, hold their head up high, and make eye contact. They present themselves well by having a good personal appearance and are cognizant of the new styles.

Educating yourself and being prepared are some of the keys to being a confident person. If you are asked to give a speech, for example, research the topic ahead of time. Use the research as supporting evidence in your speech. Finally, practice your speech over and over to make it a polished presentation. So prepare and you will feel more comfortable and confident.

Define uses a dictionary app to provide the definitions requested. When you use it for the first time, you may have to download the app when requested to do so.

DEFINE

The Define command displays the Dictionary pane, which provides the definition of a word.

Merriam-Webster Dictionary

Dictionary

al·be·it

: conceding the fact that : even though : ALTHOUGH

To find the definition of a word:

Review/Proofing/Define

1. Click in the word you wish to define.
2. Click the Close (X) button at the top of the pane.

THESAURUS

The Thesaurus command displays the Thesaurus pane, which provides synonyms and in some cases antonyms.

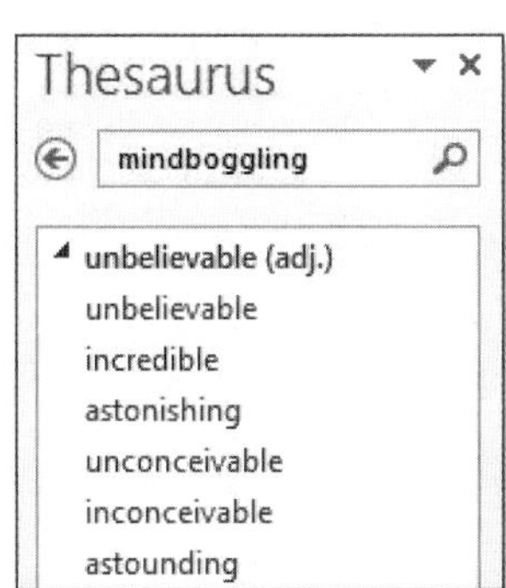

To find the synonym of a word:

Review/Proofing/Thesaurus

1. Click in the word for which you want to locate a synonym.
2. Select the appropriate synonym.
3. Click the Close (X) button at the top of the pane.

WORD COUNT

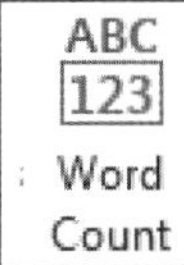

The word count displays by default in the status bar. However, additional statistics can be accessed with the Word Count command.

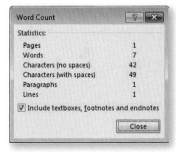

Word Count

Statistics:

Pages	1
Words	7
Characters (no spaces)	42
Characters (with spaces)	49
Paragraphs	1
Lines	1

Include textboxes, footnotes and endnotes

Close

To find document statistics:

Review/Proofing/Word Count

1. Click Word Count to display the Word Count statistics.
2. Click Close (X) at the bottom of the dialog box.

DRILL 4 DEFINE AND THESAURUS

1. Key the sentence shown at the bottom right. Look up the definition and synonyms of the last three words.
2. On the next line, key a new sentence substituting the following synonyms:
   a. mind-boggling—second under *unbelievable.*
   b. albeit—first option.
   c. extravagant—fourth under *exaggerated.*
3. Determine the number of characters with spaces in the two sentences. Key the answer on the next line.
4. Proofread and check; click Next to continue. (*29-drill4*)

My Smart TV is mind-boggling, albeit extravagant.

37-d3

Modified Block Letter

1. Key the following letter in the modified block format with mixed punctuation. Insert the current date. Remove extra spacing as necessary.
2. Supply the correct salutation, a complimentary closing, your reference initials, and an enclosure notation.
3. Create an envelope and add it to the letter.
4. Preview for letter placement, and continue to the next document. (*37-d3*)

Ms. Mukta Bhakta
9845 Buckingham Road
Annapolis, MD 21403-0314

Thank you for your recent inquiry about our wireless pet fence. The Hilton Pet Fence was developed to assist many pet owners like you who desire the safety of their pets without the barrier of a traditional fence.

Hilton Pet Fence also provides a customer support service to assist you in training your pet and a technical support team for providing technical assistance. For additional information, please call:

Customer and Technical Support
Telephone: 410.555.0112
9:00 a.m.-5:30 p.m. EST, Monday-Friday

Please look over the enclosed brochure. I will call you within the next two weeks to discuss any additional questions you may have.

Alexander Zampich | Marketing Manager

37-d4

Memo

1. Key the following memo in correct format.
2. Check the test and close. (*37-d4*) Click Exit *Word*.
3. Click Log out to exit *KPDO*.

TO: All Sunwood Employees

FROM: Julie Patel, Human Resources Director

DATE: Current date

SUBJECT: Eric Kershaw Hospitalized

We were notified by Eric Kershaw's family that he was admitted into the hospital this past weekend. They expect that he will be hospitalized for another ten days. Visits and phone calls are limited, but cards and notes are welcome.

A plant is being sent to Eric from the Sunwood staff. Stop by my office before Wednesday if you wish to sign the card. If you would like to send your own "Get Well Wishes" to Eric, send them to Eric Kershaw, County General Hospital, Room 401, P.O. Box 13947, Atlanta, GA 38209-4751.

Learn More:
www.cengagebrain.com

Apply It

29-d1

Edit and Proofread

1. In a new document, key the 10 sentences; tap ENTER after each sentence.
2. Proofread and correct errors.
3. Use proofing tools as needed.
4. Proofread and check; click Next Activity. (*29-d1*)

TIP

Review proofreaders' marks in Lesson 23, page 62.

Discover

Insert/Delete—To insert text, click in the document at the point you wish to insert text and key the text.

To delete text, select the text and tap DELETE.

Do you assess you writing skills as average, great, or mediocre?

You should also ask your instructor about your writing skills.

Your instructor will know how to greatly improve your writing skills.

Do you always edit and proofread carefully things that you write?

few people who donot bother to edit there work are good writers.

Learning to edit effective may be just as important as writing well.

Another question to ask is: how important are writing skills?

Good writing skills are needed to be successful in most careers.

You can improve your writing skills by making it a priority.

Judge your writing only if you have proofread and edited your work.

29-d2

Compose and Edit

1. In a new document, compose a document by filling in the information indicated. Use the information in 29-d1 to help you with your composition. Use Undo and Redo as well as proofing tools as you compose and edit.
2. Edit and proofread your document carefully.
3. Recheck the document using proofing tools.
4. Proofread and check. Click Exit Word to close. (*29-d2*)
5. Log out of *KPDO*.

Improving my writing skills during my career preparation is important to me because (*complete the sentence*). Proofreading and editing skills are especially important because (*complete the sentence*).

(*In a new paragraph, complete the following introductory sentence using three numbered sentences.*) Three things that I can do to improve my writing skills are:

Lesson 37 Assessment Modules 3 and 4

Warmup *Lesson 37a Warmup*

Apply It

37-d1

Announcement

1. In a new document, key the title centered; apply Calibri Light 72-point font; and apply Fill - Black, Text 1, Shadow text effect.
2. Key the remainder of the text. Apply Calibri Light 36-point font and bold.
3. Center the page vertically.
4. Preview, check with proofing tools, then proofread, correct errors, and continue to the next document. (*37-d1*)

REVIEW

Center Page

Page Layout/Page Setup dialog box launcher/Layout tab, Vertical alignment

Room Change Notice

All classes and laboratories held in Room 250 of Westbrook Hall have been moved to Room 102 of Eastbrook Hall. This change will be in effect from October 10 until October 25.

37-d2

Block Letter

1. Key the letter below in the block letter style with open punctuation. Add an appropriate salutation. Send a copy of the letter to **Olivia Cavenaugh.**
2. Add an envelope to the document.
3. Continue to the next document. (*37-d2*)

Current date | Mr. John Long, Manager | Durrington Electronics Store | 9822 Trevor Avenue | Anaheim, CA 92805-5885

With your letter came our turn to be perplexed, and we apologize. When we had our refund coupons printed, we had just completed a total redesign program for our product boxes. We had detachable logos put on the outside of the boxes, which could be peeled off and placed on a coupon.

We had not anticipated that our distributors would use back inventories with our promotion. The e-book readers you sold were not packaged in our new boxes; therefore, there were no logos on them.

We are sorry you or your customers were inconvenienced. In the future, simply ask your customers to send us their sales slips, and we will honor them with refunds until your supply of older e-book readers is depleted.

Sincerely | Cynthia Wertz | Sales and Promotions Department | xx

Lesson 30 Clipboard Commands and Center Page

New Commands

- Clipboard
- Cut
- Paste
- Format Painter
- Center Page

KPDO **Warmup** *Lesson 30a Warmup*

Skill Building

30b Textbook Keying

1. Key each line once; concentrate on using good keying techniques.
2. Repeat the drill if time permits.

direct reach words, phrases, and sentences

1 hung deck jump cent slope decide hunt serve polo brave cedar pump

2 no way | in tune | many times | jump in | funny times | gold plated | in sync

3 June and Cecil browsed in craft shops and found many funny gifts.

adjacent reach words, phrases, and sentences

4 were pop safe sad quick column tree drew opinion excite guy point

5 we are | boil over | are we | few rewards | short trek | where are we going

6 Bert said he tries to shop where we can buy gas, oil, and treats.

Communicating Today ▶

Clipboard Commands: Editing Reminder

Cut, copy, and paste are excellent editing tools that make it easy to add new text, to delete unwanted text, or to move text to a new location. However, these tools also create special editing challenges. Once the changes have been made, it is very important to determine if the addition or deletion of text had any effect on surrounding paragraphs or on the whole document. Follow these steps:

- Read the entire document to ensure that all necessary information is included.
- Check the flow of information when paragraphs have been deleted or added. Often the transition from one paragraph to another is not smooth when changes have been made.
- Check to see if newly added material duplicates or conflicts with any of the existing document content.

Remember that careful editing can mean the difference between composing excellent documents and mediocre ones.

36-d3

Letter

palmetto letterhead
portland

1. Key the letter below in 11-point Calibri font; do not create an envelope as it will be attached to an email.
2. Send a copy to Garrett Russell, President (of Palmetto Event Solutions, Inc.).
3. Proofread and check; click Next Activity. (*36-d3*)

Mr. Jacob Burch | Tri-City Partnership | 760 Rockdale Street | Portland, OR 97204-0760 | Dear Mr. Burch

We are pleased to have been chosen as your event planner for the upcoming City Center Centennial Gala. Planning for this event is progressing as projected, and listed below are major activities at this point:

- Neil Ferguson with Ferguson Caterers has agreed to cater the food for the event. Ten caterers submitted bids, and five finalists were interviewed. Ferguson Caterers was selected based on five criteria deemed essential for this prestigious event. His creative menu complementing the farm-to-table philosophy and his budget projection were very impressive in the final decision.
- Bids have been solicited from 12 local florists. We are expecting to make this selection in two weeks.
- The entertainment committee is busy scouting available talent and will report their top three choices to me on Friday.

An initial meeting with Neil Ferguson of Ferguson Caterers, Jean Blake, convention center manager, and Tyler Crockett, account associate, is scheduled for September 23, 201-, at 10 a.m. at the convention center offices. You are invited to attend this meeting to meet these key players and to tour the venue. Please let me know if your schedule permits you to attend.

36-d4

Compose Email

1. Compose an email to your instructor, who is posing as Jennifer Anderson. You have been asked to draft an email that Ms. Anderson will send to the nine caterers who were not selected for the event. Key **Draft of Email to Caterers Not Selected for the City Center Centennial Gala** as the subject line.
2. The first paragraph should tell Ms. Anderson that the draft of the email to the nine caterers not selected for the event follows in the email.
3. The remaining paragraphs should be the draft email to the nine caterers. First, thank the caterers for submitting a bid and let them know that the submissions were very competitive. Using a kind tone, state that the bid was not chosen. In a new paragraph, build goodwill by sharing that other events are scheduled in the coming months and encourage the caterer to submit future bids. End with how important excellent caterers are to the success of Palmetto Event Solutions.
4. Proofread and check. (*36-d4*) Click Exit *Word*.
5. Click Log out to exit *KPDO*.

New Commands

CLIPBOARD GROUP

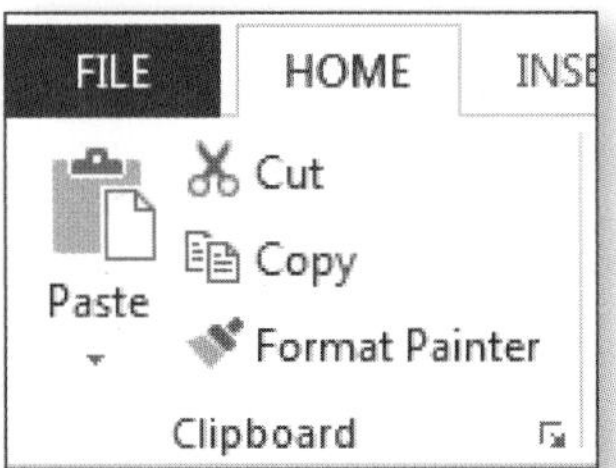

The commands in the Clipboard group, located on the Home tab, enable you to store text or graphics temporarily until you need them.

Cut—removes the selected text from its current location and saves it on the Clipboard.

Paste—positions text that was cut or copied in another location.

Copy—makes a copy of the selected text.

Format Painter—copies formatting from one place to another.

Clipboard pane—displays up to 24 items cut or copied to the Clipboard. The Clipboard pane is opened by clicking the Dialog Box Launcher (the small arrow in the lower-right corner of the Clipboard group).

CUT, COPY, AND PASTE

Home/Clipboard/Cut, Copy, or Paste

Cut

Copy

1. Select the text or graphics to be cut or copied.
2. To remove the text or graphics, click Cut; to copy the text or graphics, click Copy.
3. To paste the text or graphics, position the insertion point in the desired location and click Paste.

To use the following Clipboard shortcuts, select the text and then apply the shortcut:

Cut:	CTRL + X
Copy:	CTRL + C
Paste:	CTRL + V

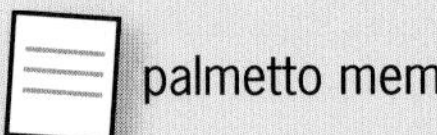

Memo

palmetto memo

1. Prepare the following memo to Susan Walker, Executive Chef. Key the subject line **Menu for City Center Centennial Gala Due Tomorrow**.
2. Proofread and check; click Next Activity. (*36-d1*)

Please send the menu for the City Center Centennial Gala by close of day tomorrow. As always, include all details required for caterers submitting bids.

Bids to the top ten caterers that you recommended will be mailed on Monday with a response required in ten days. You will be called upon to evaluate the bids.

Thank you for your excellent work on the catering needs of this project.

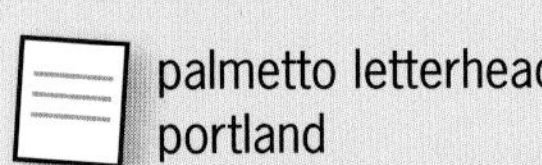

Letter

palmetto letterhead
portland

1. Key the letter below. Create an envelope and add to the letter.
2. Key the writer's name and title on separate lines.
3. Proofread and check; click Next Activity. (*36-d2*)

Current date | Mr. Neil Ferguson | Ferguson Catering | 4535 Lakeview Street | Portland, OR 97204-4535 | Dear Mr. Ferguson

Congratulations! I am pleased to inform you that Ferguson Catering was selected as the caterer for the City Center Centennial Gala. Your bid for $20,000 was well within the budget set by our client, Tri-City Partnership. Your creative menu complements perfectly the farm-to-table philosophy of our organizers.

A contract outlining your responsibilities is enclosed for your review and signature. Please sign both copies and return to me by the end of next week.

I have tentatively scheduled our initial meeting for Thursday, September 23, at 10 a.m. at the convention center offices. Other participants include Jacob Burch of the Tri-City Partnership, Jean Blake, convention center manager, and Tyler Crockett, one of our event planners.

Please contact me if you have any questions about the contract or if we need to plan a different date and time for the meeting.

Paste Options

Paste options determine how the text will look once it is inserted at the target location. Paste options are accessed in two ways: the drop-list arrow at the bottom of the Paste button or the Paste Options button that displays when text is pasted.

To apply options from the Paste button:

1. Click the drop-list arrow on the Paste button to display the paste options.

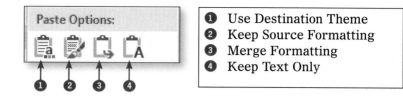

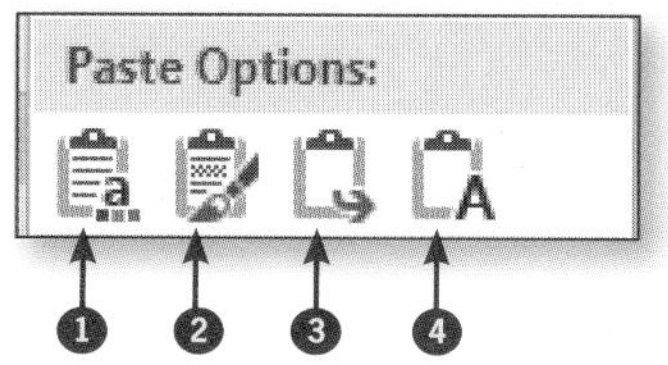

1. Use Destination Theme
2. Keep Source Formatting
3. Merge Formatting
4. Keep Text Only

2. Click the desired option.

The Keep Text Only option does not display when a graphic or object is pasted.

To apply options from the Paste Options button:

1. When the Paste command is clicked to paste text, the Paste Options button displays at the end of the pasted text.
2. Click the drop-list arrow to display the options, and select the desired option.

Note that the results occur whether you use the Paste button drop list options or those from the Paste Options button.

(Ctrl)

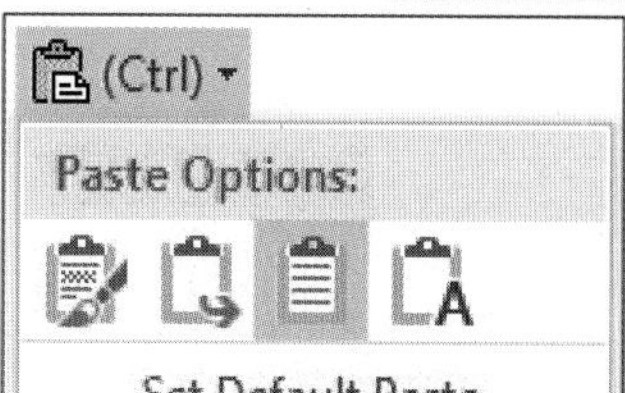

DRILL 1 CUT, COPY, AND PASTE

1. In a new document, key only the first two sentences below.
2. Select *carefully* in the first sentence, cut it, and paste it after *packing*. Use the Merge Formatting option.
3. Select *enclosed* in the second sentence; cut and paste it before *diagram*. Use the Keep Text Only option.
4. Copy the second sentence. Paste it below the second sentence and then key the additional text shown in the third sentence below. Use the Keep Source Formatting option.
5. Use Show/Hide and delete paragraph symbols at the end of the document if any exist.
6. Proofread and check; click Next to continue. (*30-drill1*)

Please try to carefully remove the packing before taking the computer out of the box.

The diagram enclosed provides step-by-step instructions for assembling the computer.

The enclosed diagram provides step-by-step instructions for assembling the computer. A Help number to call for assistance is provided on the diagram.

Lesson 36 Palmetto Event Solutions, Inc.

Warmup *Lesson 36a Warmup*

ALL LETTERS

Skill Building

36b Timed Writing

1. Key a 1' timing on each paragraph; work to increase speed.
2. Key a 3' timing on all paragraphs.

Have simple things such as saying please, may I help you, and thank you gone out of style? We begin to wonder when we observe front-line workers interact with customers today. Frequently their careless attitudes indicate that the customer is a bother and not important. But we realize there would be no business without the customer. So what can be done to prove to consumers that they really are king?

First, require that all workers train in good customer service. They must recognize that their jobs exist for the customer. Also, explain why they should talk to their supervisors about any problem. You do not want workers to talk about lack of breaks or schedules in front of customers. Remember customers must always feel that they are king and should never be ignored.

Project Setting

In this project, you are assigned to the regional office of Palmetto Event Solutions, Inc., located in Portland, Oregon. You report to Jennifer Anderson, Senior Account Executive, who is charged with planning the City Center Centennial Gala, a major fundraising event sponsored by the Tri-City Partnership.

Read the *About Us* section on page 118 to review information about Palmetto Event Solutions. Read the Standard Operating Procedures for the project carefully. You will not be reminded to do these steps. Refer to them as needed during the project.

Standard operating procedures for the project:

1. Use block letter style with open punctuation and the Palmetto letterhead from the data files. Use appropriate opening and closing lines. Use the Date command to add the current date and begin the date at approximately 2".
2. Create envelopes for letters only when directed, as many letters are attached to an email.
3. The data files also contain a Palmetto memo form. Use appropriate subject lines if a subject line is not provided.
4. Add your reference initials, enclosure notations, and copy notations as appropriate.
5. Proofread and check; when you are satisfied with the document, click Next Activity.

DATA FILES

Data files are extra documents you will need to complete an assignment. When a data file is required, an icon and filename are listed after the drill name or document name.

- In *KPDO (Keyboarding Pro DELUXE Online)*, the data file opens automatically when you select the activity. For example, in *36-d1* below, the file *palmetto memo* will open automatically.
- Non-*KPDO* users: Download the data files from www.cengagebrain.com; go to the student companion resources site. Save the data files to your hard drive or flash drive. The files are organized by module.

FORMAT PAINTER

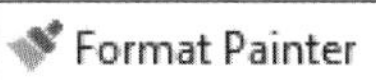

Format Painter copies a format from one paragraph to another or to multiple paragraphs

TIP

1. To copy both text and paragraph formats, select the paragraph including the paragraph marker.
2. Apply to the text you want to format.

To copy a paragraph format to a single paragraph:

Home/Clipboard/Format Painter

1. Click in the paragraph that has the desired format.
2. Click the Format Painter.
3. Drag Format Painter across the paragraph to copy the desired format.

To copy a paragraph format to multiple paragraphs:

1. Click in the paragraph that has the desired format.
2. Double-click the Format Painter to keep it turned on.
3. Drag Format Painter across the paragraphs to copy the desired format.
4. Click Format Painter to turn it off or tap ESC.

DRILL 2 FORMAT PAINTER

Home/Paragraph/Show/Hide

1. In a new document, turn on Show/Hide, tap ENTER three times, and key the document below. Be sure to read the tip below.
2. Apply 14-point Arial font and bold to the title, **HOW MUCH IS TOO MUCH?**, and center it.
3. Use the Format Painter to copy the title format to the subtitle directly below the title.
4. Format the paragraph below the subtitle using 12-point Times New Roman font, and justify.
5. Double-click Format Painter to copy the same format to the last two paragraphs.
6. Proofread and check; click Next Activity. (*30-drill2*)

When you key two hyphens with no spaces before or after, *Word* automatically converts them to an em dash.

HOW MUCH IS TOO MUCH?

Executive Compensation—A Hot Topic!

Many people question the huge salaries paid to top executives. Employees earning less than $50,000 a year do not understand how their company can pay one person millions of dollars each year. The gap between executive pay and employee pay creates problems.

Shareholders clearly want to reward and retain executives who increase shareholder value, but they expect pay to be linked to performance. In many cases, executive compensation has increased at the same time that performance has decreased significantly.

Media coverage about mega-bonuses has caused an outrage among investors. In response, the SEC now requires public companies to disclose the amount and source of all compensation paid to their top executives. This information is readily available to the public and to employees.

Apply It

35-d1

Modified Block Letter

1. Key the model letter on page 137 in modified block format with mixed punctuation.
2. Set a left tab at 3.25". Tap ENTER three times to position the date at about 2". Do not key the letterhead.
3. Press SHIFT + ENTER to remove the added space in the letter address and between the writer's name and title. Use Show/Hide to view paragraph markers to confirm correct spacing between letter parts.
4. Add an envelope to the letter. Omit a return address.
5. Proofread and check; click Next Activity. (*35-d1*)

35-d2

Modified Block Letter

1. Key the following letter in modified block letter style with mixed punctuation. Add all required letter parts. ❊ Remove the hyperlink in the second paragraph. **Note:** Remove the hyperlink if the document is not read on screen.
2. Add an envelope to the letter.
3. Proofread and check; click Next Activity. (*35-d2*)

❊ *Discover*

Remove Hyperlink

Insert/Links/Hyperlink

Click the hyperlink and follow the path above. Then click Remove Link.

Shortcut: Right-click and click Remove Hyperlink.

Current date | Mr. Ricardo Delgado | Wildwood Sports Goods | 1525 South Ash Street | Gainesville, FL 32601-1525 | Dear Mr. Delgado:

Thank you for your generous donation of 100 golf caps for the players in our upcoming Carter Alverston Scholarship Golf Tournament. Your kind contribution will allow us to attract more players, thereby increasing funding for our scholarship program. Last year's tournament raised over $10,000 to assist our students in pursuing distant internships. This year's goal is to attract 100 players and 20 sponsors.

As one of our key sponsors, you are invited to participate with a team in the tournament. All participant fees are waived for sponsors. We also ask you to encourage your business colleagues and personal contacts to join us either as sponsors or players. Sponsor and player forms can be downloaded at www.sw-de.edu/tournament.pdf.

Once again, thank you for your generous support of this important scholarship program.

Sincerely, | Leslie Gregory | Director of Public Relations | xx

35-d3

Edit Letter

 REVIEW

Clear Tabs

Home/Paragraph/Line and Page Breaks Tab/Tabs/Clear All

1. Open *35-d2* and edit to change to a block letter style with open punctuation. *Hint:* Select the entire letter (CTRL + A) and remove the tabs. If necessary, tap Backspace to return date and closing lines to the left margin.
2. In the company name in the letter address, change *Sports* to **Sporting**. Change the house address to **323 Second Street**.
3. Select the letter address, and create a new envelope. Click Change Document to accept the change on the previously created envelope.
4. Proofread and check. (*35-d3*) Click Exit *Word*.
5. Click Log out to exit *KPDO*.

CENTER PAGE

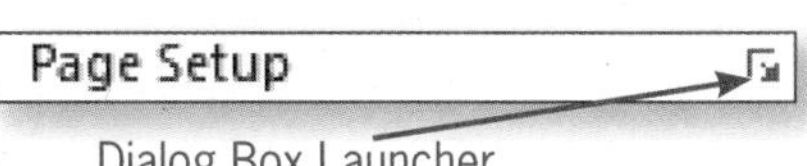

The Center Page command centers a document vertically on the page. Should extra hard returns (¶) appear at the beginning or end of a document, these blank lines are also considered to be part of the document. Therefore, it is important to turn on Show/Hide and delete extra hard returns at the beginning and end of the document before centering a page.

To center a page vertically:

Page Layout/Page Setup/Dialog Box Launcher

1. Position the insertion point on the page to be centered.
2. Turn on Show/Hide and remove any extra hard returns.
3. Display the Page Setup dialog box.
4. Click the Layout tab.
5. Click the Vertical alignment drop-list arrow and select Center.

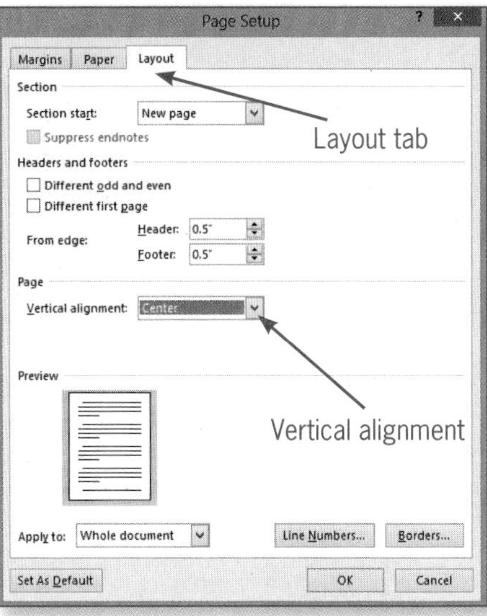

DRILL 3 CENTER PAGE

1. Open *30-drill2* and remove the three hard returns at the top of the page.
2. After the last line, key **30-drill3** and right-align it.
3. Center the page.
4. Proofread and check; click Next Activity. (*30-drill3*)

Communication

30d

References/Communication Skills/Proofreading

1. Complete the proofreading exercise in *KPDO*.
2. Proofread each sentence on the right and then key the sentence correcting the error in it. Do not key the number.
3. Proofread and check; click Next to continue. (*30d*)

PROOFREADING

1. The only way to proofread numbers effectively is too compare the keyed copy to the original source.
2. Concentration is an important proofreading skill, especially it you proofread on screen.
3. May people skip over the small words when they proofread; yet the small words often contain errors.
4. They sole 15 baskets at $30 each for a total of $450. Always check the math when you proofread.
5. Names are often spelled in different ways; there fore, you must verify the spelling to ensure that you use the correct version.
6. Reading copy on a word-bye-word basis is necessary to locate all errors.
7. Checking for words that my have been left out is also important.
8. Of course, you should also check to make sure the content in correct.

About 2"

E-Market Firm
10 East Rivercenter Boulevard
Covington, KY 41016-8765
Telephone: 513.555.0139

Set tab at 3.25" → January 14, 201-

Ms. Kathryn Vanderford
Professional Document Designs, Inc.
P.O. Box 3891
Weatherford, TX 76086-3891

Press SHIFT + ENTER to remove extra space

Dear Ms. Vanderford: ← Mixed punctuation

Your inquiry concerning a comparison of the modified block letter format and the block letter format is one often answered by our document designers. The modified block format differs from block format in that the date, complimentary close, and the writer's name and title are keyed at the center point. For production efficiency, we recommend block paragraphs.

Although modified block format is an accepted letter style, we do recommend the block letter style. The block letter style is more efficient for a standard letter style, requires no additional settings by the user, and is attractive.

For additional formats, please refer to the enclosed report related to formatting with the latest version of *Word* and the *Model Documents Reference Guide*. Our designers are available at 666.555.0197 to assist you with your design needs.

Sincerely, ← Mixed punctuation

Jeremy Gillespie } Press SHIFT + ENTER
Communication Consultant ↓ 2

xx

Enclosures

Modified Block Letter with Mixed Punctuation

Apply It

30-d1

Invitation

1. In a new document, key the text shown below. Apply Lucida Calligraphy 14-point font. Center all lines except the last one, which should be left-aligned. Decrease the font size on the last line to 11 point. Replace 201- with the current year.
2. Apply 3.0 line spacing.
3. Center the page. Verify the page is centered.
4. Proofread and check; click Next Activity. (*30-d1*)

You are cordially invited to attend a reception
Honoring Dr. Fritz H. Schmohe
Honorary Degree Recipient
September 28, 201- at 7:30 in the evening
Koger International Center
Black Tie Optional
RSVP by September 20, 803-555-0174

30-d2

Heading, Indent, Format Painter

1. In a new document, tap ENTER three times, and then key the document below.
2. Apply Verdana 16-point font and bold to the title, *Weekly Report*, and center it.
3. Use the Format Painter to copy the title format to the date shown below the title.
4. In the first sentence, cut *with reporters* and paste it after *spoke*. The sentence should read: *The head football coach spoke with reporters at his weekly news conference.*
5. Apply Verdana 12-point font to the first paragraph below the date. Justify the text.
6. Use Format Painter to copy the first paragraph's format to the last two paragraphs.
7. Proofread, check, and close. (*30-d2*)
8. Click Log out to exit *KPDO*.

WEEKLY REPORT

June 20, 201-

The head football coach spoke at his weekly news conference with reporters. He was asked about the summer workout program and seemed to be very frustrated with some of his student-athletes.

The coach pointed out that summer workouts are voluntary programs, and it is against the rules to require student-athletes to participate. However, the workouts are a good way to judge the commitment level of your players. He indicated that some of our players are very committed and are very likely to get playing time. Others are lazy, and it is doubtful they will be ready to play when the season begins.

In response to a reporter's question, he indicated only about a dozen of the 95 scholarship players did not show up regularly. The goal of the program is to improve conditioning and lessen the likelihood of injuries.

Document Design

MODIFIED BLOCK LETTER

35c

References/Document Formats/Modified Block Letter

In the modified block format, the date line and the closing lines (complimentary close and writer's name and title) begin at the center point of the page. All other guidelines for the block letter style are applied to the modified block letter. Remember to remove the extra spacing between the letter address and other short lines. Review the model modified block letter on the next page.

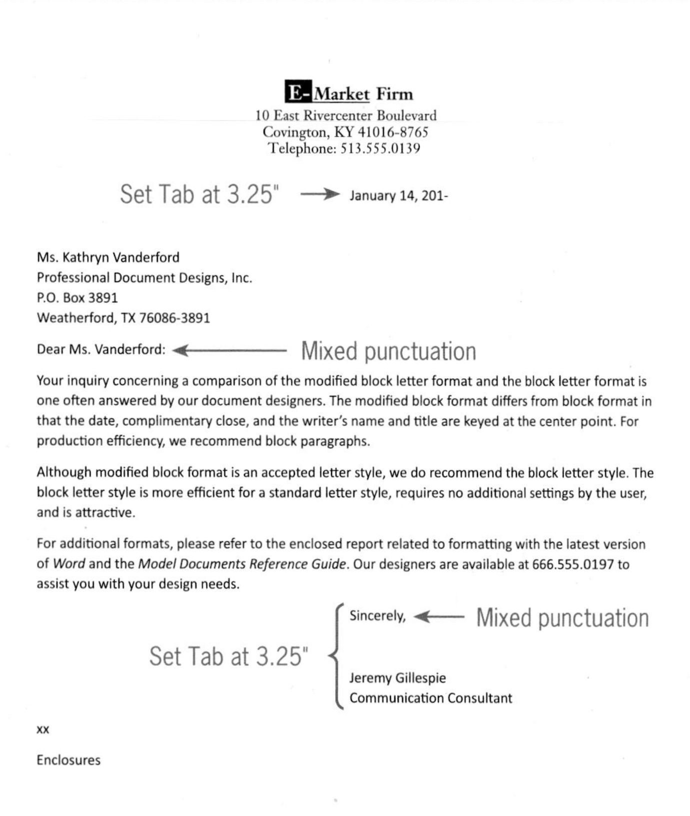

E-Market Firm
10 East Rivercenter Boulevard
Covington, KY 41016-8765
Telephone: 513.555.0139

Set Tab at 3.25" → January 14, 201-

Ms. Kathryn Vanderford
Professional Document Designs, Inc.
P.O. Box 3891
Weatherford, TX 76086-3891

Dear Ms. Vanderford: ← Mixed punctuation

Your inquiry concerning a comparison of the modified block letter format and the block letter format is one often answered by our document designers. The modified block format differs from block format in that the date, complimentary close, and the writer's name and title are keyed at the center point. For production efficiency, we recommend block paragraphs.

Although modified block format is an accepted letter style, we do recommend the block letter style. The block letter style is more efficient for a standard letter style, requires no additional settings by the user, and is attractive.

For additional formats, please refer to the enclosed report related to formatting with the latest version of *Word* and the *Model Documents Reference Guide*. Our designers are available at 666.555.0197 to assist you with your design needs.

Sincerely, ← Mixed punctuation

Set Tab at 3.25"

Jeremy Gillespie
Communication Consultant

xx

Enclosures

Dateline:

- Position at about 2".
- Begin at least 0.5" below the letterhead.
- Set a left tab at 3.25". Determine the position of the tab by subtracting the side margin from the center of the paper.

4.25" Center of the paper
–1.00" Margin
3.25" Tab setting

Complimentary closing: Begin keying at 3.25".

Writer's name and title: Begin keying at 3.25".

MIXED PUNCTUATION

Although most letters are formatted with open punctuation, some businesses prefer mixed punctuation. To format a letter using mixed punctuation, key a colon after the salutation and a comma after the complimentary close.

Dear Mr. Hathorn:

Sincerely,

Lesson 31 Palmetto Event Solutions, Inc.

Learning Outcomes

- Apply keying, formatting, and word processing skills.
- Work independently with few specific instructions.

Warmup *Lesson 31a Warmup*

A ALL LETTERS

Skill Building

31b Timed Writing

Key two 3' timed writings.

Click fraud concerns small business owners who want to place an advertisement on a website and be charged for it based on the number of hits on it. They frequently believe they are getting the most for their advertising dollars because they only pay for those who actually read their advertisement. The problem, however, is that someone may be paid to click on the advertisement many times just to increase the revenue from it.

While business owners are working hard to maximize the impact of their businesses, frequently they are losing money because some individuals are trying to scam them. Many people try to do the right thing, but many others just are not honest. Often it is difficult to determine if you are working with an honest person or not when you use the Internet.

This problem is not a very easy one to resolve, but a few things can be done to minimize the risk. Research shows that late-night advertisements and advertisements in certain countries are the most likely to be targeted. By choosing not to run advertisements at those times and in those locations, you can lower your risk. In addition, a number of very sophisticated and very effective technical tools can be used to help detect click fraud.

Project Setting

Palmetto Event Solutions prefers to use periods rather than hyphens and parentheses to separate units in telephone numbers, which is the current trend in industry.

PALMETTO EVENT SOLUTIONS, INC.

At the end of each module in this book, you will work as an assistant preparing documents for various executives of Palmetto Event Solutions, a national company that specializes in managing corporate events for businesses and organizations. You will apply the formatting and word processing skills that you have developed in the module. The logo and contact information for the headquarters office are shown below.

Palmetto Event Solutions, Inc.

24 Palmetto Bay Road, Hilton Head, SC 29928-3220 | 864.555.0124

www.palmettoeventsolutions.com

Lesson 35 Modified Block Letter

New Commands • Tabs

Warmup *Lesson 35a Warmup*

New Commands

35b

TABS

Tabs are used to indent paragraphs and to align text vertically. The default tab stops are set every half inch. *Hint:* If the ruler is not displayed, go to View/Show and click Ruler.

To set a left tab:

1. Check the tab selector to be sure the left tab is selected.
2. Click the Horizontal Ruler where you want to set the left tab.

When a new tab stop has been set, all default tabs to the left of the newly set tab are automatically cleared. Therefore, if other tabs are needed, simply choose the desired tab alignment, and then click the Horizontal Ruler where the desired tab is to be set.

To move a tab:

Select all of the text that will be affected, and drag the tab to be moved to the new desired location. *Note:* If you do not select all of the text, only the tab that your cursor is on will be moved.

To clear a tab:

Select all of the text that will be affected and drag the tab off the Horizontal Ruler bar.

DRILL 1 SET TABS

1. Set a left tab at 3.25". Insert the current date at 3.25", and tap ENTER twice.
2. Set a left tab at 1". Key the following lines and tap ENTER once. Press SHIFT + ENTER to remove the added space between the items.

   Enclosures: Promissory Note
   Amortization Schedule

3. Set a left tab at 0.5". Key the following lines. Press SHIFT + ENTER to remove the added space between the lines. Be sure to undo automatic capitalization so the *c* in copy notation is not capitalized.

   c Ashley Nobles
   Ethan Vilella

4. Proofread and check; click Next Activity. (*35-drill1*)

31-d1

Standard Operating Procedures

Your first assignment is to work with Ellen Miller, the Executive Assistant to the President and CEO of Palmetto Event Solutions, Inc. Ellen has been working on revising the standard operating procedures (SOPs) that are used in the main office and the four regional offices. This document will be sent to the regional offices for review and will continually be updated.

Pay particular attention to the SOPs and the documents you prepare in this lesson because they will provide you with information that you will use each time you work with Palmetto Event Solutions. You will be directed to review these procedures periodically.

1. Tap ENTER three times, and key the document below; apply the following formats.
2. Center the heading, and apply Calibri Light 14-point heading bold font to both lines.
3. Change the bullets to numbering using Number Alignment Left style and periods.
4. Add **Procedures revised** and today's date using 00/00/0000 format after the last numbered item and apply Align Right format.
5. Use proofing tools, proofread, and correct all errors. Click Next Activity. (*31-d1*)

Standard Operating Procedures

For Document Formatting

These procedures are designed to enhance our image and to ensure that our brand is used consistently and appropriately.

- Use the letterhead and memo form provided digitally for all letters and memos. Letterhead is provided with addresses for each of the five office locations. Use block-letter format with open punctuation.
- Ensure that all documents are error-free. Use proofing tools and then edit, proofread, and correct errors. Verify dates and all numerical data against the source copy.
- Use email for brief communications, which do not contain information needed to work with clients or as a delivery vehicle. Any information that will become a part of our records should be prepared in memo, letter, table, or report format and attached to the email for distribution.
- Additional procedures may be provided by each of the regional offices.

Apply It

34-d1

Block Letter

1. Key the letter below in block style with open punctuation. Tap ENTER three times to begin the date at about 2". Press SHIFT + ENTER to remove the extra space in the letter address, signature line, and enclosures.
2. Add an envelope to the letter.
3. Proofread and check; click Next Activity. (*34-d1*)

May 19, 201- | Ms. Coralia Lopez | Chief Financial Officer | Midland Corporation | 1001 North Tenth Avenue | Chicago, IL 60290-1001 | Dear Ms. Lopez

Thank you for your continuing business with Henderson, Blakney, Hardin, Mayfield CPA Firm. We appreciate the long-term partnership between our organizations.

The audit for Midland Corporation is scheduled for September 1-5, 201-. Ken Smith and Jill Matthews, the on-site auditors, will arrive at 9 a.m. on September 1. They will meet with you for approximately one hour before beginning the audit. Please review the enclosed audit questionnaire prior to this meeting. Also, to ensure security of sensitive financial records, they will require a private office with Internet access.

Ms. Lopez, if you have questions concerning the audit, please call me at 312.555.0138.

Sincerely | John D. Henderson, Partner | xx | Enclosure |
c Ms. Lynda Maxwell, President

34-d2

Edit Letter

1. In the open document (*34-d1*), make the following edits.
2. Change the ZIP Code to 60291-1001; update the envelope.
3. Change the dates of the audit to October 1-5; auditors will arrive on October 1.
4. Ken Smith will not be assigned to this audit. Change to Rory Jones.
5. Move the third sentence of the second paragraph to the end of the paragraph.
6. Send a copy also to Mr. Wendell Havard, Controller. Remember to press SHIFT + ENTER to remove the extra space between the names; tap TAB and key Mr. Havard's name.
7. Proofread and check; click Next Activity. (*34-d2*)

34-d3

Envelope

1. Key an envelope to the following address and add to the document.
2. Proofread and check. (*34-d3*) Click Exit *Word*.
3. Click Log out to exit *KPDO*.

Mr. Jacob Gillespie
1783 West Rockhill Road
Bartlett, TN 38133-1783

31-d2

About Us

Read the information below about Palmetto Event Solutions carefully. This information will become the first webpage of the About Us section of the company website. It will help you understand the type of company you will work for in each module.

1. Tap ENTER three times and key the document as shown.
2. Change the case of the title to uppercase, apply 18-point bold Verdana font, and center.
3. Select paragraph 1; apply double-spacing (2.0), Verdana 12 point. Indent the first line of the first paragraph as recommended by the web developer for draft copy.
4. Then use Format Painter to copy the formats to the remaining paragraphs.
5. Proofread as prescribed in the SOPs. Click Next Activity. (*31-d2*)

About Us

Palmetto Event Solutions was founded by Mrs. Roberta Russell in 1992 in Hilton Head, South Carolina. The initial emphasis was on catered dinners, weddings, and other social events. Many corporate executives attended impressive functions managed by Mrs. Russell and requested her services for corporate events. By 2000, corporate events represented more than 75 percent of the business. Mrs. Russell retired, and her son Garrett Russell became president and CEO.

Many events we managed were corporate reward trips, trade shows, and professional meetings in various sections of the country. Our management team determined that clients could be served better if we focused on corporate events and established offices in other regions of the country. In 2002, four regional offices were established in the Midwest, Northwest, Northeast, and Southwest to complement the Hilton Head office.

Today, our company has more than quadrupled its size and has established key partnerships with service providers in all regions who can provide full services for virtually any type of corporate event requested.

31-d3

Compose and Format an Invitation

1. Ellen Miller asked you to compose, edit, and format a draft of an invitation. Review the instructions for 30-d1 on page 115. Use this same style and format for this invitation.
2. Use the notes below to compose the invitation. (Do not key these notes.) Remember to format the phone number with periods.
   - Ask clients to please join us for a tour of our new reception center, followed by a client appreciation reception.
   - The event will be on Friday, September 10, at 5:30 p.m. in the Palmetto Event Solutions Reception Center. Include an RSVP by September 6 and our telephone number. Tip: The number is contained in the contact information on page 116.
   - The attire for the event is business attire.
3. Proofread and check. (*31-d3*)
4. Click Log out to exit *KPDO*.

Document Design

34e

ADDITIONAL LETTER PARTS

In Lesson 33, you learned the standard letter parts. Listed below are several optional letter parts.

Enclosure notation/Attachment notation: If an item is included with a letter, key an enclosure notation/attachment notation one blank line below the reference initials. If enclosures/attachments are itemized, tap TAB to align the enclosures at 1" using default tabs.

Left tab at 1"

Enclosures: Certificate of Completion
Receipt

Enclosures: 2

Copy notation: A copy notation (c) indicates that a copy of the document has been sent to the person(s) listed. Key the copy notation one line below the reference initials or enclosure notation (if used). Tap TAB to align the names. If necessary, click Undo Automatic Capitalization after keying the copy notation to lowercase the letter c.

Left tab at 0.5"

c Francine Milam
Janet Bevill

When two lines are keyed for either the enclosure notation or the copy notation, press SHIFT + ENTER to remove the extra space after the paragraph.

xx

Enclosures: Certificate of Completion
Receipt

c Francine Milam
Janet Bevill

TIP

Attachment: Commonly used when emailing a letter or memo that references other documents to be included in the mailing.

Enclosure: Used when mailing in an envelope a letter or memo that references other documents to be included in the mailing.

Communicating Today

Business Letters: Then and Now

The delivery of business letters has changed dramatically since the origin of the U.S. Post Office in 1775 and the Internet Protocol Suite (TCP/IP) introduced in 1982. Documents that once took two to three days or longer to deliver are now delivered instantaneously with a reply supplied in the same speed.

Reading a business letter on the computer screen has become the new normal. Default fonts designed for online reading and increased spacing in word processing software address these new approaches to accomplishing our work. Reading online also makes accessing links seamless. When the letter is read and action taken, the recipient can easily store the letter electronically, which also supports today's focus to protect the environment. However, the increased focus on speed of delivery can lead to challenges.

Do remember that sending letters quickly does not change the need for factual accuracy, completeness, appropriate format, correct spelling, proper grammar, and precise punctuation. Write clearly and proofread all documents carefully before sending them by any means of distribution. Your reputation is on the line.

MODULE 4

Memos and Letters

LEARNING OUTCOMES

- Format memo.
- Format block and modified block business letters.
- Create envelopes.
- Edit letters.
- Build keyboarding skills.

Lesson 32 Memos and Email

New Commands

- Date/Time
- Vertical Page Position

Warmup *Lesson 32a Warmup*

A ALL LETTERS

Skill Building

32b Timed Writing

1. Key a 1' timing on each paragraph; work to increase speed.
2. Key a 3' timing on all paragraphs.

Congratulations, you have just learned to key with very little visual help and are moving quickly from one key to the next. As you continue to build speed and become productive, it is always important to continue keying with proper techniques. Because it is easy to become lazy, take a quick check of correct techniques.

Sit up straight with both feet on the floor with back against the chair. Drop hands to your side and allow your fingers to curve naturally; maintain this curve as you key. If hands are in correct position, you can balance a penny on your wrists. Keep your eyes on the copy or screen, and key continuously without any breaks. An excellent method to monitor progress is to record yourself for several minutes. Evaluate your techniques carefully, and make needed changes.

New Commands

34d

ENVELOPES

The Envelopes command can insert the delivery address automatically if a letter is displayed. The default is a size 10 envelope (4⅛" by 9½"); other sizes are available by clicking the Options button on the Envelopes tab.

TIP

To create an envelope without a letter, follow the same steps, but key the address in the Delivery address box.

To generate an envelope:

Mailings/Create/Envelopes

1. Select the letter address and click Envelopes; the mailing address automatically displays in the Delivery address box.
2. Click the Return address Omit box if using business envelopes with a preprinted return address (assume you are).

   To include a return address, do not check the Omit box; click in the Return address box and key the return address.
3. Click Print to print the envelope or click Add to Document to add the envelope to the top of the document containing the letter.

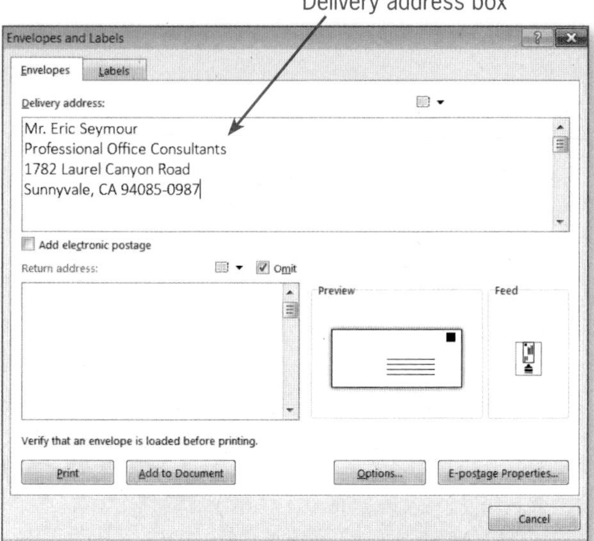

DRILL 1 CREATE ENVELOPE

1. In the open document (*33-d1*), select the letter address. Create an envelope. Omit the return address.
2. Add the envelope to the document.
3. Proofread and check; click Next Activity. (*34-drill1*)

Note: Your instructor may have you print envelopes on plain paper.

DRILL 2 CREATE ENVELOPE

1. In a new document, go to the Envelopes and Labels dialog box without keying a letter address.
2. Key the following letter address in the Delivery address box.

   Mr. Andrew Callais
   993 North Carpenter Lane
   Shreveport, LA 71106-0993
3. Add the envelope to the document.
4. Proofread and check; click Next Activity. (*34-drill2*)

New Commands

32c

DATE AND TIME

Date & Time The Date and Time command allows the selection of the desired format. Often the month/day/year format is used for letters, and the numerical format (00/00/0000) for memos and documents with statistics.

To insert the date and/or time:

Insert/Text/Date and Time

1. Click at the point the date is to be inserted.
2. Select the desired date format ❶ (July 22, 2012) or time format ❷ (17:37).
3. Leave Update automatically ❸ blank unless you want the date/time to update each time the document is opened. Click OK.

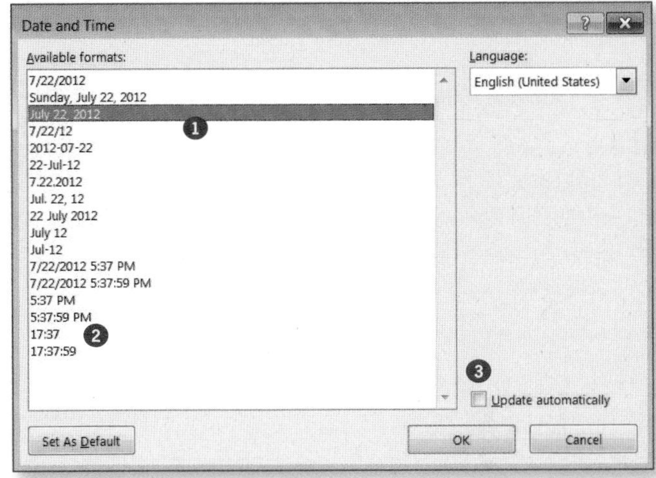

Discover

Automatic Current Date

Key the first four characters of the current month and tap ENTER to accept the date. Tap Space Bar to display the remainder of the current date.

VERTICAL PAGE POSITION

Although the default top margin is 1", not all documents are attractive beginning at the top of the page. To move the insertion point lower on the page, simply tap ENTER.

The status line is located at the bottom left of the screen and displays important information about the page, including the vertical page position when turned on.

To display the vertical page position on the status line:

1. Right-click on the status line located at the bottom of the screen.
2. Click Vertical Page Position. The vertical page position now displays at the bottom left of the status line, showing the default top margin at 1".

PAGE 1 OF 1 AT: 1"

TIP

Remember to proofread and preview each document as standard operating procedure (SOP). You will not be reminded to do this.

DRILL 1 DATE AND TIME

1. In a new document, display the vertical page position on the status line.
2. Tap ENTER three times to position the insertion point at about 2". Key the first four characters of the current date, e.g., Octo for October. Tap ENTER and then the Space Bar to display the current day. Tap ENTER to begin a new line.
3. Insert the date and time in the numerical format 7/15/2012 3:35 PM, and tap ENTER.
4. Print. Verify that the date prints approximately 2" from the top of the page.
5. Proofread and check; click Next Activity. (*32-drill1*)

Lesson 34 Block Letter with Envelope

New Commands

- Envelopes

Warmup *Lesson 34a Warmup*

A ALL LETTERS

Skill Building

34b Timed Writing

1. Key a 1' timing on each paragraph; work to increase speed.
2. Key a 3' timing on all paragraphs.

Many people are sometimes quite surprised to learn that either lunch or dinner is included as part of a job interview. Most of them think of this component of the interview as a friendly gesture from the organization.

The meal is not provided to be thoughtful to the person interviewing. The organization expects to use that function to observe the social skills of the person and to determine if he or she might be effective doing business in that type of setting.

What does this mean as you prepare for a job interview? Spend time reading and practicing social etiquette just as you would on how to answer questions or about what to wear. The time committed to reading about and learning to apply excellent social skills pays off during the interview and also after you accept the job.

34c Textbook Keying

1. Key each drill, concentrating on using good keying techniques.
2. Repeat the drill if time permits.

adjacent reach

1 The people were sad as the poor relish was opened and poured out.

2 Sophia moved west with her new silk dress and poor walking shoes.

direct reach

3 Freddy stated that hurricanes are much greater in number in June.

4 Many juniors decide to work free to add experience to the resume.

balanced hand

5 The eight ducks lay down at the end of right field for cozy naps.

6 Kala is to go to the formal town social with Henry and the girls.

ELECTRONIC MAIL AND MEMOS

32d

Informal communication shared among individuals in a company are prepared as emails, instant messages, text messages, or memos. In a business setting, correct grammar, spelling, capitalization, and professional tone are required in all messages to portray professionalism and to gain/maintain respect among supervisors and peers.

The memo is the most formal type of informal message and may be preferred when a somewhat formal communication with company employees is demanded, such as the announcement of a new policy or participation in a mandatory training program. Often this formal memo is attached to an email as a method of distribution to all employees. *Word*'s Share option allows the user to email the memo as a *Word* attachment or a PDF without even opening the email system.

An email is commonly used to convey casual internal messages that do not demand a more formal tone and presentation. Examples would include an email transmitting a memo or letter, providing the location and time of a meeting, or requesting routine information.

To format a memo:

1. Tap ENTER three times to position the first line of the heading at about 2".
2. Key the memo headings and format them in bold and uppercase. Tap TAB once or twice after each heading to align the information. Generally, courtesy titles (Mr., Ms., etc.) are not used; however, the receiver's name may include a title depending on rank in the company.
3. Single-space (1.08 default spacing) the body of the memo. Tap ENTER once after each paragraph.
4. Add reference initials one line below the body if the memo is keyed by someone other than the sender. Do not include initials when keying your own memo.
5. Items clipped or stapled to the hard-copy memo and electronic files attached to an email are noted as attachments. Items included in an envelope with a memo are noted as enclosures.

   Key enclosure or attachment notations one line below the reference initials.

TO: Sales Managers ↓1

FROM: Miyoko Suno ↓1

DATE: Current date ↓1

SUBJECT: Updated Email Addresses ↓1

We have received new email addresses from several customers. Please change the following addresses in your printed directory: Brenda Jordan (bjordan@alexander.jones.com), Zachary Maillet (zachary.maillet@westwood.com), and Lynn Peterson (lpeterson@rentswellsupplies.com). The changes have already been made in our database. ↓1

New printed directories will be available in about 30 days. ↓1

xx

33-d3

Block Letter

1. Key the following letter in block style with open punctuation. Begin the date at about 2". Remember to remove the extra space by using SHIFT + ENTER.
2. Proofread and check. (*33-d3*) Click Exit Word.
3. Click Log out to exit *KPDO*.

April 4, 201- | Ms. Rose Shikamuru | 55 Lawrence Street | Topeka, KS 66607-6657 | Dear Ms. Shikamuru

Thank you for your recent inquiry about employment opportunities with our company. We are happy to inform you that Mr. Edward Ybarra, our recruiting representative, will be on your campus on April 23–25 to interview students who are interested in our company.

We suggest that you talk soon with your student placement office, as all appointments with Mr. Ybarra will be made through that office. Please bring with you the application questionnaire the office provides.

You will want to visit our website at www.skylermotors.com to find facts about our company mission and accomplishments as well as learn about the beautiful community in which we are located. We believe a close study of this information will convince you, as it has many others, that our company builds futures as well as small motors.

If there is any way we can help you, please email me at mbragg@skylermotors.com.

Sincerely | Margaret K. Bragg | Human Services Director | xx

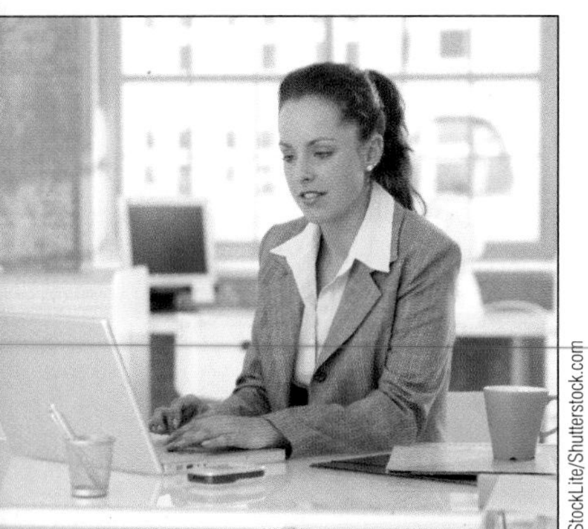

StockLite/Shutterstock.com

WORKPLACE SUCCESS

Organizational Skills

Well-organized employees accomplish daily tasks in a timely manner, avoid stress, and impress their employers and coworkers. Following simple daily time management practices reaps benefits and often even a promotion. How would you rate yourself on the following time management practices?

1. Prioritize tasks to be done each day and the amount of time needed to complete each task. Assign tasks to a specific time on the calendar.
2. Set designated times to answer email and return phone calls.
3. Place calendar/planner on desk in location for easy access to add notes and see priority items.
4. Record notes, phone numbers, addresses in calendar and not on post-it notes.
5. Place phone, notepad, and pen on desk for easy reach.
6. Keep reference books in a designated location—not on the desk.
7. File any materials for which you no longer need immediate access.
8. Prepare folders for pending items, projects, and reading, and file those materials away instead of keeping them piled on the desktop.

To prepare an email:

1. Prepare the email header:

   To: Key the email address of the receiver accurately.

   Cc: Key the email address of individuals who are to receive a copy of the message.

   Bcc: Key the email address of individuals designated to receive a blind copy (meaning the recipient is not aware of the message being sent to the blind recipient/s).

   Subject: Key a specific subject line that is helpful to the busy recipient sorting through important email to read and act upon.

   Attachment: Follow the steps to attach any electronic files referred to in the body of the memo.

2. Prepare the email body:

   a. Single-space (SS) the body of an email and tap ENTER twice between paragraphs. Do not indent paragraphs.

   b. Do not add bold or italic or vary the fonts. Do not use uppercase letters for emphasis. Avoid using emoticons or email abbreviations in business email (e.g., ;- for wink or BTW for by the way).

   c. Write a clear, concise message about one topic. State the purpose in the first paragraph, and then provide the needed details. End with a courteous closing that states the required action, if any.

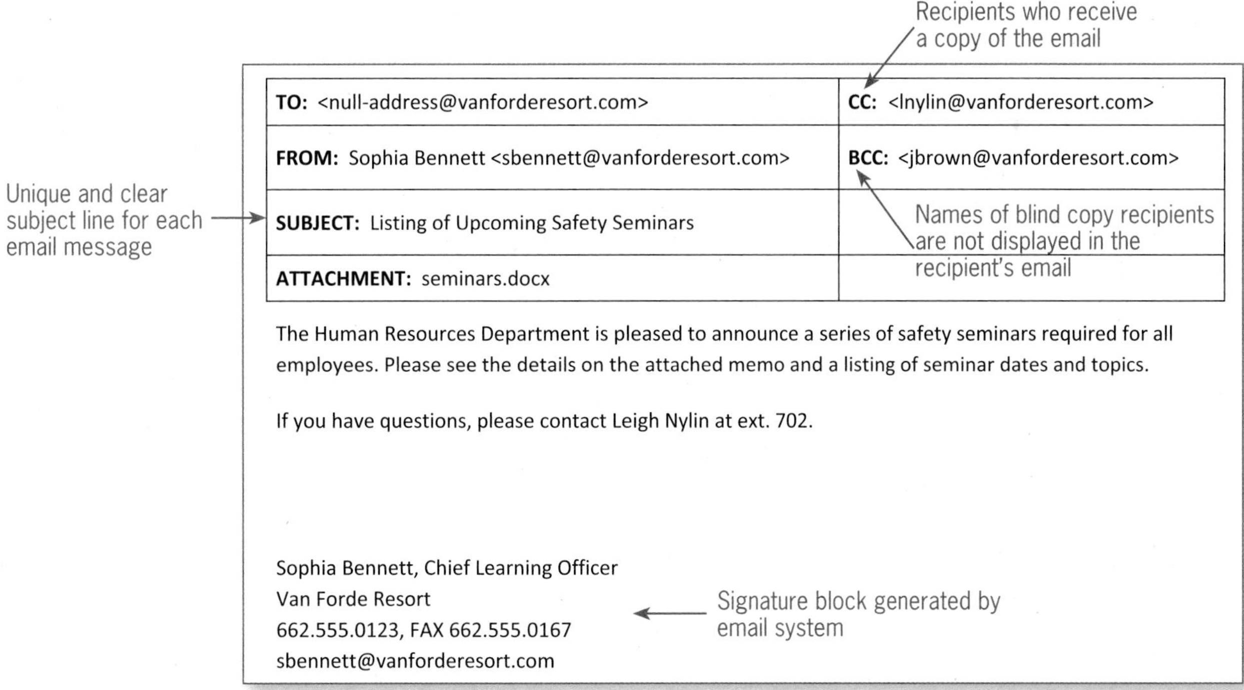

TO: <null-address@vanforderesort.com>	**CC:** <lnylin@vanforderesort.com>
FROM: Sophia Bennett <sbennett@vanforderesort.com>	**BCC:** <jbrown@vanforderesort.com>
SUBJECT: Listing of Upcoming Safety Seminars	
ATTACHMENT: seminars.docx	

The Human Resources Department is pleased to announce a series of safety seminars required for all employees. Please see the details on the attached memo and a listing of seminar dates and topics.

If you have questions, please contact Leigh Nylin at ext. 702.

Sophia Bennett, Chief Learning Officer
Van Forde Resort
662.555.0123, FAX 662.555.0167
sbennett@vanforderesort.com

Apply It

33-d1

Block Letter

1. Tap ENTER three times to position the date at about 2". Key the model block letter on page 128. Do not key the letterhead.
2. Press SHIFT + ENTER to remove the added space in the letter address and between the writer's name and title.
3. Replace the reference initials *xx* with your initials. Be sure to undo automatic capitalization of the first letter of your initials.
4. Follow the proofreading procedures outlined on page 126. Use Show/Hide ¶ to view paragraph markers to confirm that you have correct spacing between letter parts. Use Print Preview to check the placement.
5. Proofread and check; click Next Activity. (*33-d1*)

33-d2

Block Letter

1. Key the letter below in block format with open punctuation. Insert the current date. Add your reference initials in lowercase letters. Remove added space in the letter address and the writer's name and title.
2. Proofread and check; click Next Activity. (*33-d2*)

Current date

Ms. Ramona Vilella
Wicker Hotel and Resort
89 Airport Road
Omaha, NE 68105-0089

Dear Ms. Vilella

Certainly having a web presence is essential, but have you updated your hotel's website recently? Advances in technology and the increased sophistication of your clients are both good reasons for you to meet with our designers at Internet Solutions to discuss advanced hotel web design that will improve your marketing efforts.

Our online reservation system is designed for today's clients; it is easy to navigate and provides many extras such as 360-degree panoramic pictures of the hotel lobby, guest rooms, restaurants, spa, and pool, as well as maps to your beautiful hotel. Two-way communication is also important today as clients are eager to provide review rating and valuable comments to others desiring a pleasant hotel experience. Our design offers seamless means of valuable dialog between you and your clients.

Call today for a consultation with one of our designers and discuss our many innovative website marketing strategies. Give your clients the best when they are shopping for hotel reservations.

Sincerely

Daniel Jankoski
Marketing Manager
xx

1195 Singing Cactus Avenue
Tucson, AZ 85701-0947

About 2" (Tap ENTER three times)

TO: All Employees ↓ 1

FROM: Sophia Bennett, Human Resources Director ↓ 1

DATE: Current date ↓ 1

SUBJECT: Safety Seminars Offered for Certification ↓ 1

The Human Resource Department is pleased to announce a series of safety seminars for all employees. The purpose of the seminars is to provide safety knowledge and procedures included in the certification examination administered at the end of the seminar. ↓ 1

The seminars are offered in two formats to meet the needs of all employees. Face-to-face seminars are scheduled in room 310 on Wednesday afternoons from 1 to 5 p.m. and Thursday mornings from 8 a.m. until noon. Online seminars are also available which can be completed at times that meet your specific schedule.

Please meet with your supervisor to determine the seminars needed for your position. Thank you for your participation in these important seminars. ↓ 1

xx ← Student's first and last initials

Memo

Bennett Community Foundations

3840 Cedar Mill Parkway
Athens, GA 30606-4384

2" (Tap ENTER three times)

Date line October 15, 201- ↓ 2

Letter address
Mr. Jackson Elliott
President and CEO
Elliott Corporation
8333 Fifth Avenue, Suite 203
New York, NY 10028-8333 ↓ 1

Press SHIFT + ENTER to remove extra space

Salutation Dear Mr. Elliott ↓ 1

Body Thank you for agreeing to provide our keynote address for the opening session of the annual Bennett Community Foundations Convention in Dallas, Texas, on Friday, March 20, 201-. Our organization consists of over 10,000 members throughout the world with typically 2,000 members attending the convention each year.

The opening session begins at 3:30 p.m. in the Grand Ballroom of the River Ridge Convention Center. We invite you to join our executive board at a reception in your honor from 2 to 3 p.m. in Suite 2035. We are all eager to meet you and welcome you to our convention.

We look forward to your contributions to our convention, and we invite you to remain for the entire convention if your time permits.

Complimentary close Sincerely ↓ 2

Type on line 3

Writer's name & title
Gerald M. Bailey
Executive Director

Press SHIFT + ENTER to remove extra space

Reference initials xx

Block Letter with Open Punctuation

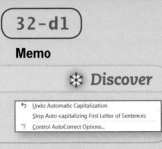

Apply It

32-d1

Memo

Discover

Undo Automatic Capitalization
Stop Auto-capitalizing First Letter of Sentences
Control AutoCorrect Options...

1. Tap ENTER three times and key the memo illustrated on page 123. Do not key the memo letterhead. *Hint:* Select *TO:* and then apply bold; bold the colon. Remember to turn off bold and uppercase. Repeat for remaining heading items. Be sure to insert the date.
2. If the first letter of your reference initials is automatically capitalized, point to the initial until the AutoCorrect Options button appears. Click the button; then choose Undo Automatic Capitalization.
3. Proofread and check; click Next Activity. (*32-d1*)

32-d2

Memo

1. Key the memo below.
2. Proofread and check; click Next Activity. (*32-d2*)

TIP

Numbering

Home/Paragraph/ Numbering

TO: Emily Welch, Brian McKenzie, Olivia von Staden

FROM: Michael Holcomb

DATE: July 18, 201-

SUBJECT: Video Conference Call Scheduled Friday, July 26, 201-

The final video conference call to select the contractor for the Keystone Community Project will be held on Friday, July 26, 201-, from 3:30 to 5:00 p.m. EST. To join the video conference, follow these steps:

1. Call 601.555.0168 and enter the passcode 8103622 when prompted.
2. Go to www.conferences.com/holcomb/PDS/ and join the meeting.

Please review the proposals carefully and be prepared to make a recommendation at the meeting. If you have questions about the proposals, please call me at 601.555.0193 or email me at mholcomb@svdco.com.

xx

32-d3

Compose Email

1. Compose an email to your instructor from you. Key **Email Etiquette** as the subject of the email. Send a copy to one of your classmates.
2. In the body of the email, share three specific email etiquette rules that are important but often abused. Number the three items. Refer to the discussion on email on page 122.
3. Proofread and check; close the document. (*32-d3*)
4. Click Exit *Word*.
5. Click Log out to exit *KPDO*.

References/Document Formats/Block Letter

LETTER PARTS AND BLOCK LETTER STYLE

Businesspeople expect to see standard letter parts arranged in the proper sequence. Letters consist of three main parts: the opening lines to the receiver (letter address and salutation), the body or message, and the writer's closing lines. Standard letter parts and the required spacing using the defaults of *Word* are explained below and illustrated on the following page.

Block letter style is a typical business letter format in which all letter parts are keyed at the left margin. For most letters, use open punctuation, which requires no punctuation after the salutation or the complimentary closing.

Letterhead: Preprinted stationery that includes the company name, logo, address, and other optional information such as telephone number and fax number.

Dateline: Date the letter is prepared. Position at about 2" (tap ENTER three times). Be sure to begin at least 0.5" below the letterhead.

Letter address: Complete address of the letter recipient. Begin two lines below the date (tap ENTER twice).

Generally includes receiver's name, company name, street address, city, state (one space after state), and ZIP Code. Include a personal title, e.g., Mr., Ms., Dr. Press SHIFT + ENTER after each line of the letter address to remove the added space.

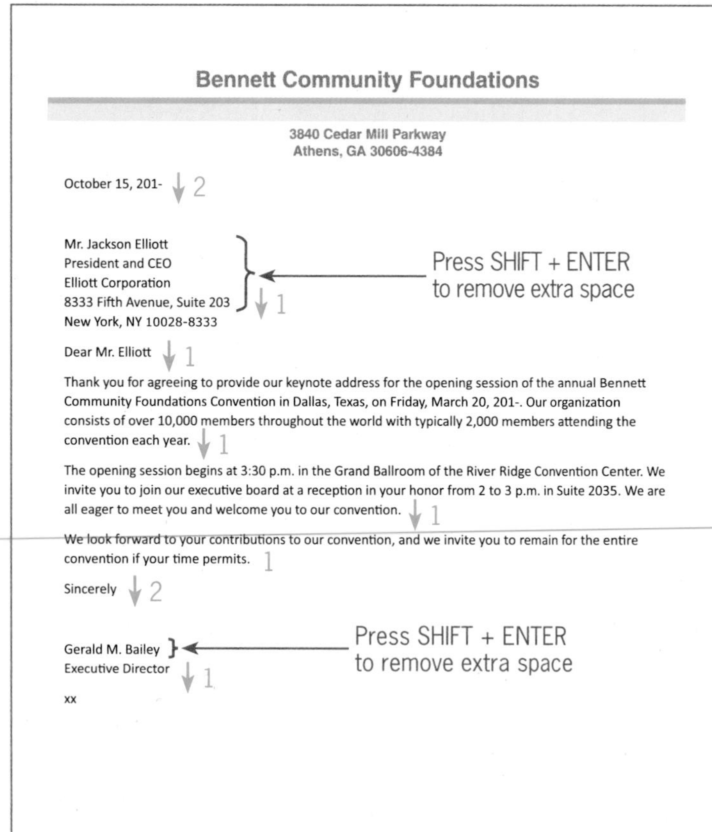

Bennett Community Foundations

3840 Cedar Mill Parkway
Athens, GA 30606-4384

October 15, 201-

Mr. Jackson Elliott
President and CEO
Elliott Corporation
8333 Fifth Avenue, Suite 203
New York, NY 10028-8333

Dear Mr. Elliott

Thank you for agreeing to provide our keynote address for the opening session of the annual Bennett Community Foundations Convention in Dallas, Texas, on Friday, March 20, 201-. Our organization consists of over 10,000 members throughout the world with typically 2,000 members attending the convention each year.

The opening session begins at 3:30 p.m. in the Grand Ballroom of the River Ridge Convention Center. We invite you to join our executive board at a reception in your honor from 2 to 3 p.m. in Suite 2035. We are all eager to meet you and welcome you to our convention.

We look forward to your contributions to our convention, and we invite you to remain for the entire convention if your time permits.

Sincerely

Gerald M. Bailey
Executive Director

xx

Salutation (or greeting): Begin one line below the letter address (tap ENTER once). Include courtesy title with person's name, e.g., Dear Mr. Smith.

Body: Begin one line below the salutation.

Use the default line spacing; tap ENTER once between paragraphs. Use *Ladies and Gentlemen* when addressing a company.

Complimentary closing: Begin one line below the body. Capitalize only the first letter of the closing.

Writer's name and title: Begin two lines below the complimentary closing (tap ENTER twice). Include a personal title to designate gender only when the writer's name is not gender specific, such as Pat or Chris, or when initials are used, such as J. A. Moe.

Key the name and title on either one or two lines, whichever gives better balance. Use a comma to separate name and title if on one line. If two lines are used, press SHIFT + ENTER to remove the added space between the two lines.

Reference initials: Begin one line below the writer's name and title. Key reference initials, e.g., **xx** in lowercase. Replace *xx* with your initials.

Lesson 33 Block Letter

New Commands

- Remove Space after Paragraph

Warmup *Lesson 33a Warmup*

New Commands

33b

REMOVE SPACE AFTER PARAGRAPH

Word automatically adds extra white space after ENTER is tapped to make text easier to read and to save the user time in only tapping ENTER once between paragraphs.

To remove space after a paragraph when the extra space is not needed, press SHIFT + ENTER to begin a new line.

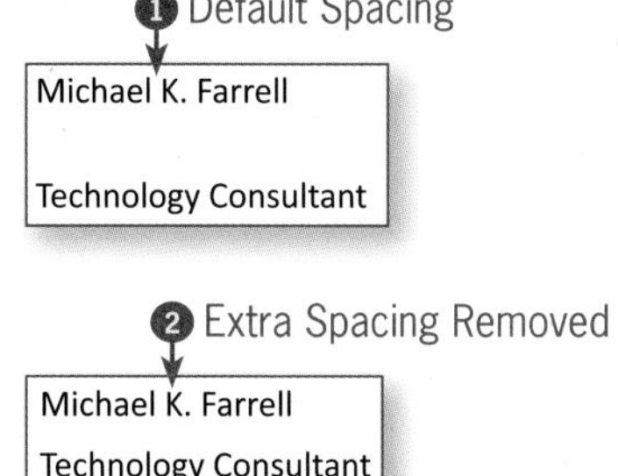

DRILL 1 REMOVE SPACE

1. Key the following letter address; press SHIFT + ENTER at the end of each line.

   Mr. Grayson T. Winston
   Winston & Smith Law Firm, LLC
   389 Main Street
   San Antonio, TX 78229-0389

2. Proofread and check; click Next Activity. (*33-drill1*)

Communication

33c

References/Communication Skills/Spelling

1. Complete the Spelling exercise in *KPDO*.
2. Proofread each statement at the right, and then key the statement correctly using the numbering feature.
3. Proofread and check; click Next Activity. (*33c*)

SPELLING

1. Turkeyes are in the meat department.
2. The locker room for gentlemens is being remodeled.
3. Companys with more than 50 employees have different requirements.
4. Managers are asked to investigate reoccuring tardiness.
5. Only cash or checkes are accepted at the ice cream store.
6. Do you beleive the time is right for you to invest in higher risk investments?
7. Mr. Jones closes his letters with Yours truley or Sincerely yours.
8. The theives were apprehended, and the stolen property was returned.
9. Give the reciept to the accounting manager.
10. Are you refering to Purchase Order #2051?

Document Design

33d

BUSINESS LETTERS

Business letters are used to communicate with persons outside of the business. Business letters carry two messages: the first is the tone and content; the second is the appearance of the document. Appearance is important because it creates the critical first impression. Stationery, use of standard letter parts, and placement should convey that the writer is intelligent, informed, and detail minded.

P P I Park Place International
300 Park Place
Atlanta, GA 30303-1142
404.555.0131 • 404.555.0132

April 9, 2011

Ms. Pamela FoxMeyer
Human Resources Director
Letter Beams, Inc.
2112 Smythe Road, North
Arlington, VA 22201-1201

Dear Ms. FoxMeyer

Mr. Terry Beckett, an employee of Letter Beams, Inc., from 2010-2011, has applied for a position with our company as a computer analyst. He has given us your name and his permission to ask about his work history with Letter Beams, Inc.

Therefore, will you please verify Terry's employment with you and respond as you desire about his performance with your organization? Thank you, Ms. FoxMeyer.

Sincerely

A. Alonzo Cruz
Human Resources Director

xx

Stationery

Letters should be printed on high-quality (about 24-pound) letterhead stationery. Standard size for letterhead is 8½" × 11". Envelopes should match the letterhead in quality and color.

P P I Park Place International
300 Park Place
Atlanta, GA 30303-1142
404.555.0131 • 404.555.0132

Ms. Pamela FoxMeyer
Human Resources Director
Letter Beams, Inc.
2112 Smythe Way, North
Arlington, VA 22201-1201

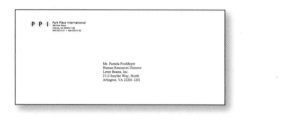

SALUTATIONS AND COMPLIMENTARY CLOSINGS

The salutation, or greeting, consists of the individual's personal title (*Mr.*, *Ms.*, or *Mrs.*) or professional title (*Dr.*, *Professor*, *Senator*, *Honorable*), and his or her last name. Do not use a first name unless you have a personal relationship. The salutation should agree in number with the addressee. If the letter is addressed to more than one person, the salutation is plural.

	Receiver	Salutation
To individuals	Dr. Alexander Gray Dr. and Mrs. Thompson	Dear Dr. Gray Dear Dr. and Mrs. Thompson
To organizations	TMP Electronics, Inc.	Ladies and Gentlemen
Name unknown	Advertising Manager	Dear Advertising Manager

Choose a complimentary closing that reflects the relationship with the receiver. Use *Sincerely* to show a neutral relationship, *Cordially* for a friendly relationship, and *Respectfully* when requesting approval.

PROOFREAD AND FINALIZE A DOCUMENT

Apply these procedures when processing all documents:

1. Use Spelling and Grammar to check spelling when you have completed the document.
2. Proofread the document on screen to be sure that it makes sense.
3. Preview the document, and check the overall appearance.
4. Save the document and compare it to the source copy (textbook).
5. Revise, save, and print if necessary.

Appendix A Numeric Keypad

Skill Building

Keypad Lessons

Keypad instruction is available from the Keypad tab in KPDO. The NUMLOCK key must be on for you to use the software. The Summary Report shows the exercise you have completed and the scores achieved. Complete each lesson before keying the related practice on the next few pages.

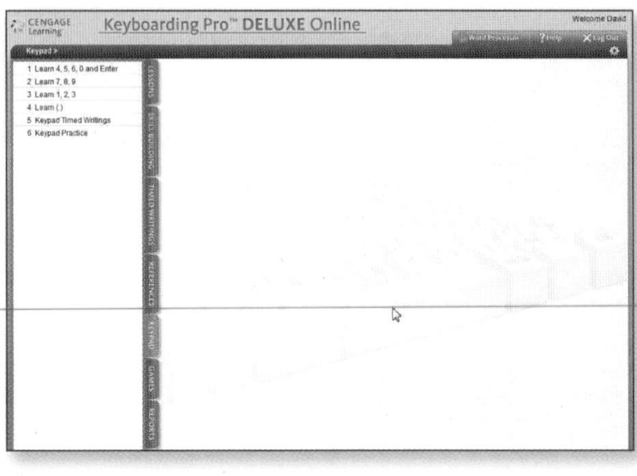

Keypad Timed Writings

Select Keypad Analysis on the Keypad lesson menu for additional keypad practice. Nine activities are available, each of which emphasizes a certain row or number type.

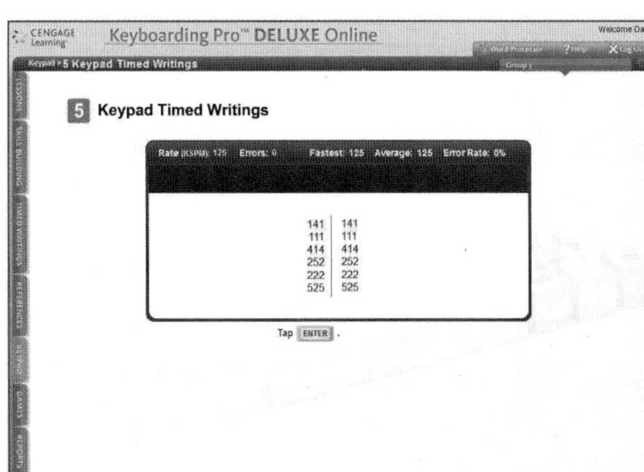

Keypad Practice

Select the Keypad Practice button to practice the exercises on the next few pages. Tap ENTER on the keypad after each number. Tap ENTER twice to sum the amounts keyed. Click the Print button to print the figures.

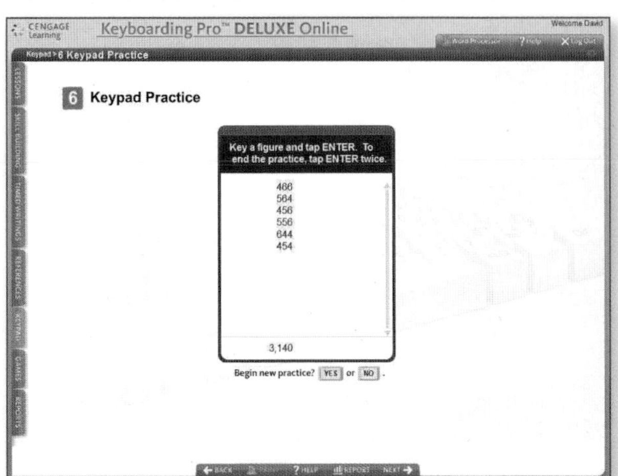

DRILL 1

4, 5, 6, 0

Complete Lesson 1 before keying Drill 1.

1. Turn on NUMLOCK. Click the Keypad Practice button.
2. Tap ENTER after each number.
3. To obtain a total, tap ENTER twice after the last number in a group.
4. Key each problem until the same answer is obtained twice; you can then be reasonably sure that you have the correct answer.

Follow these directions for each lesson.

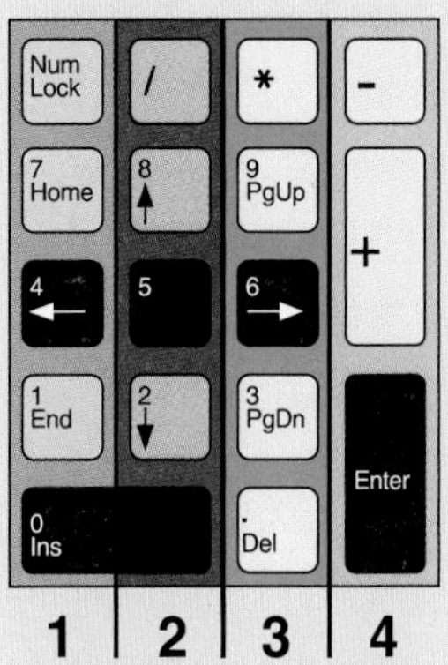

© Cengage Learning

a	b	c	d	e	f
46	55	56	46	55	56
45	64	45	45	64	45
66	56	64	66	56	64
56	44	65	56	44	65
54	65	45	54	65	45
65	54	44	65	54	44
466	445	546	654	465	665
564	654	465	545	446	645
456	464	546	545	564	456
556	544	644	466	644	646
644	455	464	654	464	554
454	546	565	554	456	656
400	404	505	606	500	600
404	505	606	500	600	400
500	600	400	404	505	606
650	506	404	550	440	550
506	460	605	460	604	640
406	500	640	504	460	560
504	640	550	440	660	406
560	450	650	450	505	550
640	504	440	640	450	660
400	600	500	500	600	400
650	505	404	606	540	560
504	404	640	404	406	606

DRILL 2

7, 8, 9

Complete Lesson 2 before keying Drill 2.

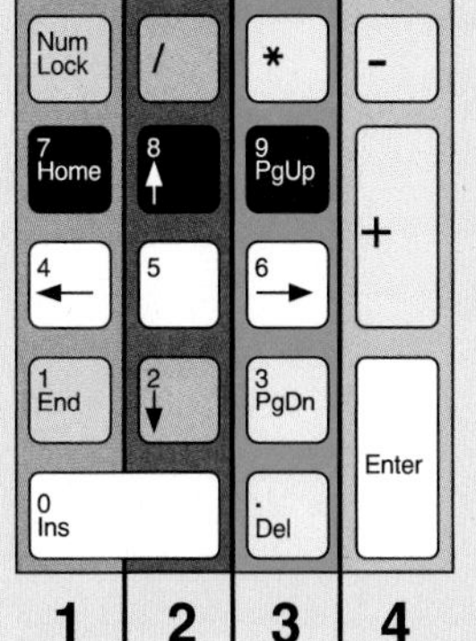

a	b	c	d	e	f
74	85	96	70	80	90
47	58	96	87	78	98
90	70	80	90	90	70
89	98	78	89	77	87
86	67	57	48	68	57
59	47	48	67	58	69

a	b	c	d	e	f
470	580	690	770	707	407
999	969	888	858	474	777
777	474	888	585	999	696

a	b	c	d	e	f
858	969	747	770	880	990
757	858	959	857	747	678
579	849	879	697	854	796
857	967	864	749	864	795
609	507	607	889	990	448
597	847	449	457	684	599

a	b	c	d	e	f
85	74	96	98	78	88
957	478	857	994	677	579
657	947	479	76	94	795
887	965	789	577	649	849
90	80	70	806	709	407
407	567	494	97	80	70

a	b	c	d	e	f
50	790	807	90	75	968
408	97	66	480	857	57
87	479	567	947	808	970
690	85	798	587	907	89
94	754	879	67	594	847
489	880	97	907	69	579

1, 2, 3

Complete Lesson 3 before keying Drill 3.

Keep fingers curved and upright over home keys. Keep right thumb tucked under palm.

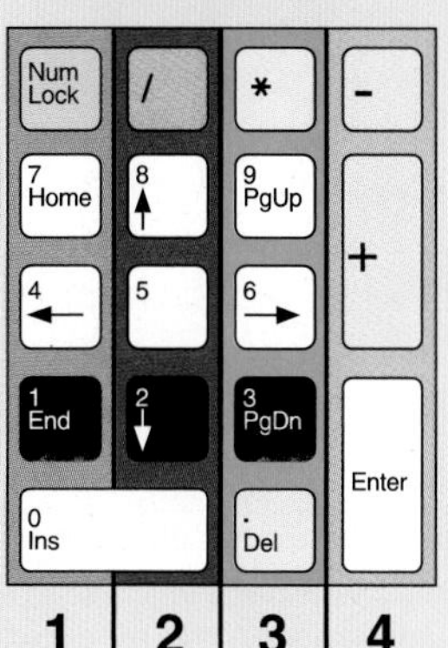

© Cengage Learning

a	b	c	d	e	f
11	22	33	14	15	16
41	52	63	36	34	35
24	26	25	22	42	62
27	18	39	30	20	10
30	30	10	19	61	43
32	31	21	53	83	71

a	b	c	d	e	f
414	141	525	252	636	363
141	111	252	222	363	333
111	414	222	525	333	636

a	b	c	d	e	f
111	141	222	252	366	336
152	342	624	141	243	121
330	502	331	302	110	432
913	823	721	633	523	511
702	612	513	712	802	823
213	293	821	813	422	722

a	b	c	d	e	f
24	36	15	12	32	34
115	334	226	254	346	246
20	140	300	240	105	304
187	278	347	159	357	158
852	741	963	654	321	987
303	505	819	37	92	10

a	b	c	d	e	f
28	91	37	22	13	23
524	631	423	821	922	733
15	221	209	371	300	25
823	421	24	31	19	107
652	813	211	354	231	187
50	31	352	16	210	30

DRILL 4

Decimal

Follow the directions given. The decimal (.) key is usually located at the bottom right of the keypad. Use the third finger to reach down to tap the decimal key.

TECHNIQUE TIP

Tap each key with a quick, sharp stroke. Release the key quickly. Keep the fingers curved and upright, the wrist low and relaxed.

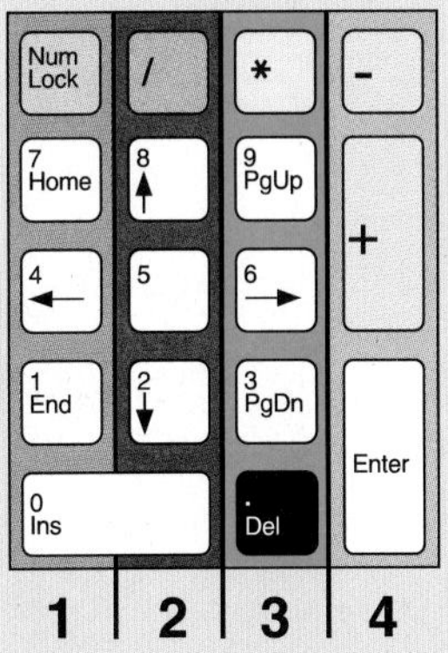

a	b	c	d	e	f
.28	.19	.37	.42	.81	.96
.51	.67	.81	.27	.55	.80
.64	.50	.60	.50	.62	.43

a	b	c	d	e	f
7.10	8.91	5.64	3.12	6.04	5.01
5.32	4.27	9.21	6.47	5.28	3.24
8.94	3.06	7.38	5.89	1.37	6.78

a	b	c	d	e	f
3.62	36.94	86.73	.60	8.21	4.02
8.06	10.31	537.34	5.21	100.89	6.51
321.04	10.55	687.52	164.84	.85	207.65
.75	.26	10.85	627.98	2.57	46.51
687.46	357.95	159.46	85.21	654.32	753.15
20.46	220.48	6.10	3.04	123.54	315.47

a	b	c	d	e	f
761.64	2.82	627.25	196.25	82.99	4.02
285.46	34.60	.29	89.24	512.69	99.80
33.99	739.45	290.23	563.21	701.21	546.78
60.41	52.79	105.87	951.32	357.02	123.94
108.97	211.00	46.24	82.47	61.28	75.61
3.54	5.79	5.41	1.32	8.54	.27

a	b	c	d	e	f
.05	1.19	77.54	112.96	33.68	2.75
112.54	561.34	114.85	.24	647.21	432.89
35.67	22.01	67.90	41.08	71.28	11.00
579.21	105.24	731.98	258.96	741.21	546.21
.34	1.68	.24	.87	.63	.54
21.87	54.89	2.34	5.89	4.68	10.72

Num Lock / * -
7 Home | 8 ↑ | 9 PgUp | +
4 ← | 5 | 6 →
1 End | 2 ↓ | 3 PgDn | Enter
0 Ins | . Del

1 | 2 | 3 | 4

DRILL 5

Review

TECHNIQUE TIP

Keep fingers curved and upright over home keys. Keep right thumb tucked under palm.

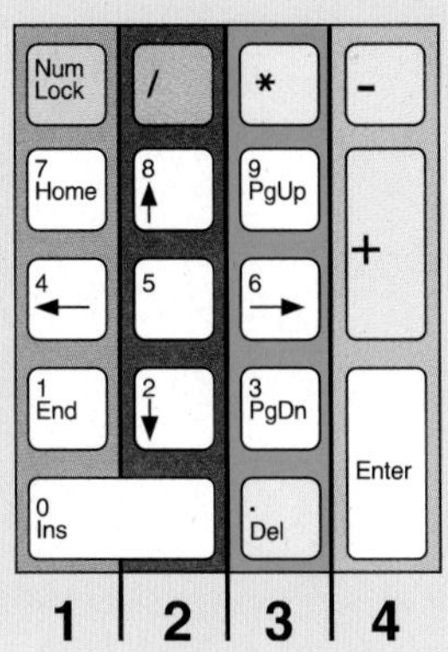

a	b	c	d	e	f
349	854	961	789	631	80
64	97	164	64	972	167
108	326	207	207	803	549
25	40	83	153	54	23

a	b	c	d	e	f
51	467	825	347	901	208
873	54	258	540	467	375
106	208	504	45	95	34
24	13	13	126	238	160
94	648	21	52	178	341
157	72	341	412	57	89

a	b	c	d	e	f
687	645	32	87	461	541
21	58	647	281	38	1,923
2,753	1,002	549	105	20	567
3,054	25	4,008	2,194	3,079	2,089
369	4,770	158	3,066	657	478
1,004	123	2,560	38	2,098	3,257

a	b	c	d	e	f
71.64	2.72	27.59	89.24	4.02	.57
285.36	118.50	438.96	102.46	55.71	6.37
3.79	24.73	4.71	527.90	.64	1.27

a	b	c	d	e	f
42.08	63.87	91.47	159.34	28.47	1.25
31.07	128.46	1.50	.28	374.95	116.00
365.87	.24	163.48	22.84	24.96	514.38
.25	394.28	452.87	349.51	852.43	234.94
147.25	32.54	821.47	164.87	.08	3.54
183.12	20.80	.60	5.07	121.07	.97

Appendix B Windows 8

START WINDOWS 8

Windows 8 is an operating system software released by Microsoft. The operating system software controls the operations of the computer and works with the application software. *Windows 8* works with *Word* in opening, printing, deleting, and saving files. It also allows you to work with photos, play music and videos, and access the Internet.

When you turn on your computer, the *Windows 8* Lock screen displays. Press any key to display the *Windows 8* Sign-in screen. Key your password and press ENTER to display the *Windows 8* Start Screen.

***Windows 8* Lock screen**

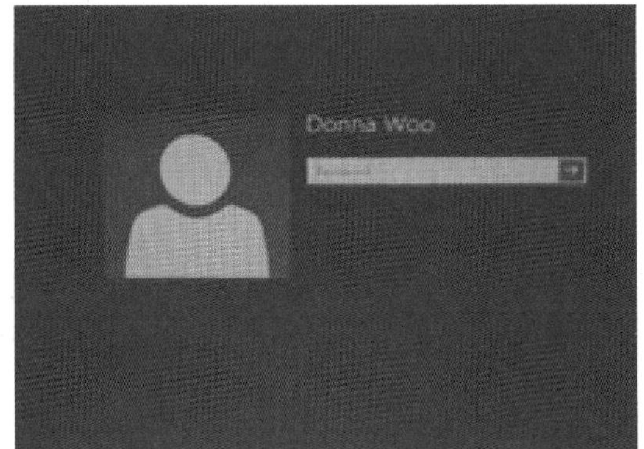

***Windows 8* Sign-in screen**

WINDOWS 8 START SCREEN

The *Windows 8* Start screen contains tiles that represent an application or a *Windows 8* feature; click the tile to start the application. Some tiles are live in that they show updated information, such as the Weather, News, and Finance tiles. If you do not see the tile for the application that you wish to launch, scroll to the right to view more apps, or right-click an empty spot on the Start screen and click the **All apps** button in the lower-right. The Desktop tile, in the lower-left, provides access to the *Windows 8* desktop.

To display the Start screen from any location, tap the Windows key (⊞) or move the mouse to the lower-left corner of the screen to display the Start icon and click on it.

WINDOWS 8 DESKTOP

The *Windows 8* desktop displays when you click the Desktop tile on the *Windows 8* Start screen. To display the desktop from any location, press ⊞ + D. Refer to the illustration below to familiarize yourself with the basic screen elements.

- *Taskbar* ❶. The taskbar displays across the bottom of the window. Use the mouse to point to each item in the taskbar. Look for the ScreenTip that displays identifying each element.
  - *Program and file buttons*. Buttons display for the programs that are open or pinned to the taskbar and allow you to switch between them easily. The *Internet Explorer* ❷ icon is displayed to provide quick access to the Internet. The *File Explorer* ❸ icon provides quick access to your files.
  - *Notification area* ❹. The notification area provides helpful information, such as the date and time and the status of the computer. When you plug in a USB drive, *Windows* displays an icon in the notification area letting you know that the hardware is connected.
- *Icons and Shortcuts* ❺. Icons, small pictures representing certain items, may be displayed on the desktop. The Recycle Bin, shown as a wastepaper basket, displays when *Windows* is installed. Other icons and shortcuts may be added.
- *Desktop* ❻. This is the work area where you will be working on your documents and programs.

SHUT DOWN COMPUTER

Microsoft has made it easy for you to interface with the *Windows 8* features by using either keyboard shortcuts or by moving the mouse to the "hot corners" of the computer screen. Many of the keyboard shortcuts utilize the Windows key (Winkey) and another key. For example, pressing Winkey + D displays the *Windows* desktop, and Winkey + E opens *File Explorer*. The Windows key (⊞) is located to the left of the space bar.

Charms are icons that provide quick access to *Windows 8* launch areas. The five Charms are Search, Share, Start, Devices, and Settings. Point to the lower-right corner of the screen to display the Charms bar. You can also display the Charms bar by pressing Winkey + C.

Charms bar

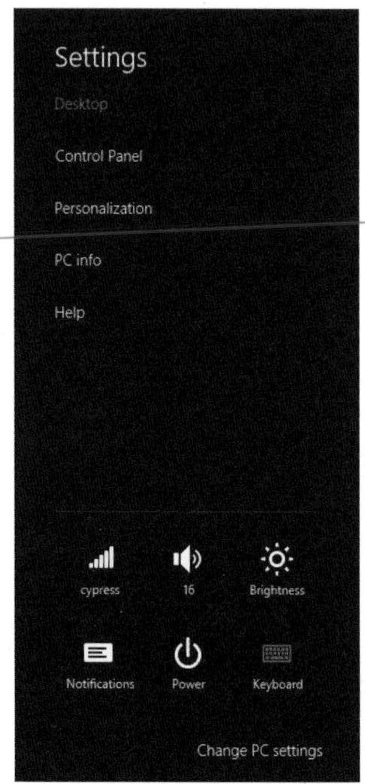

Settings options

To shut down the computer:

1. Display the Charms bar, Winkey + C.
2. Click the Settings charm to display the Settings options.
3. Click Power to display the Power options menu.
4. Click Shut down.

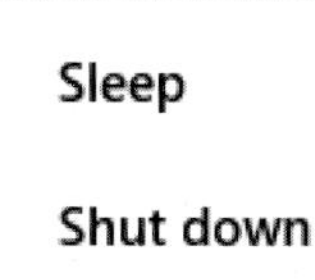

Power options

DRILL 1 START WINDOWS

1. Sign in to *Windows 8*.
2. Display the *Windows 8* Start screen.
3. Click the Weather tile; the Weather app displays full screen.
4. Click the WinKey to display the Start screen.
5. Click the Finance tile to display the Finance app. Click the right arrow in the lower-right corner of the screen to scroll through the Finance app.
6. Move the mouse to the lower-left corner of the screen; click the Start screen icon.
7. Right-click on any empty spot on the Start screen and click the All apps button.
8. Press WinKey + C to display the Charms bar.
9. Click the Settings charm.
10. Click Power, then Shut down.

WINDOWS 8 HELP

The *Windows 8 Help and Support* feature contains documentation on how to use *Windows 8*; this feature is stored on your computer. Additional links are provided that will take you to the Microsoft site for more information, if you are connected to the Internet.

The easiest way to display Windows Help and Support is to press F1 from the Desktop. The Help feature can also be access from Settings options (Charms bar/Settings/Help). To search for help, key your topic in the Search box, then click the Search button. A list of topics will display; click the link to display the information.

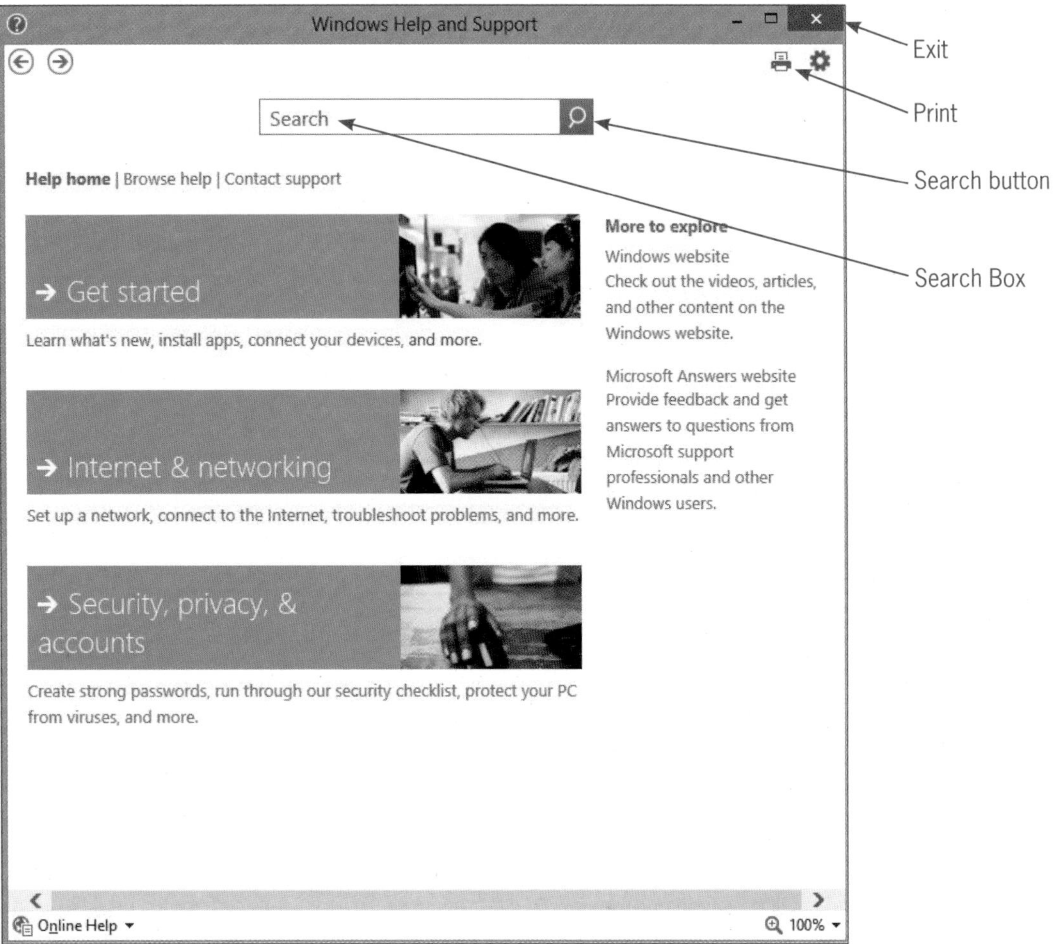

DRILL 2 USING WINDOWS HELP

1. Sign in to *Windows 8*. From the *Windows 8* desktop, press F1.
2. The *Windows 8* Help and Support screen displays.
3. Click Get started.
4. Click the Get to know Windows link.
5. Key **keyboard shortcuts** in the Search box.
6. Click the Search button.
7. Click the link–Mouse and Keyboard: What's new.
8. Read the information that displays. Click the Print button in the upper-right of the screen.
9. Click the exit button in the upper-right of the pane to close the Windows Help and Support screen.

Appendix C File Management

FILE EXPLORER

Data is stored in files on the computer. To use the files, you need to know the name of the file and the location in which the file is saved. *Windows 8* stores related files in folders. Folders can also be stored within folders, called subfolders. *File Explorer* provides the interface for you to manage the file system. Click the File Explorer icon on the Taskbar to display the *File Explorer* window.

The left pane is the Navigation pane, which shows the drives on the computer and the files stored on each drive. If an expand icon ▷ displays to the left of the folder or drive, that means that the folder or drive contains subfolders. You can expand the list to view the subfolders by clicking the ▷ icon. Once the list is expanded, the expand icon changes to a collapse icon; clicking the collapse icon ◢ will hide the subfolders.

The Contents pane lists the contents of the folders. Click on a folder in the Navigation pane to display the contents of the folder in the Contents pane. If you want to get a preview of what a file looks like, click the View tab, then in the Panes group click Preview pane to display an additional pane that shows a preview of your file.

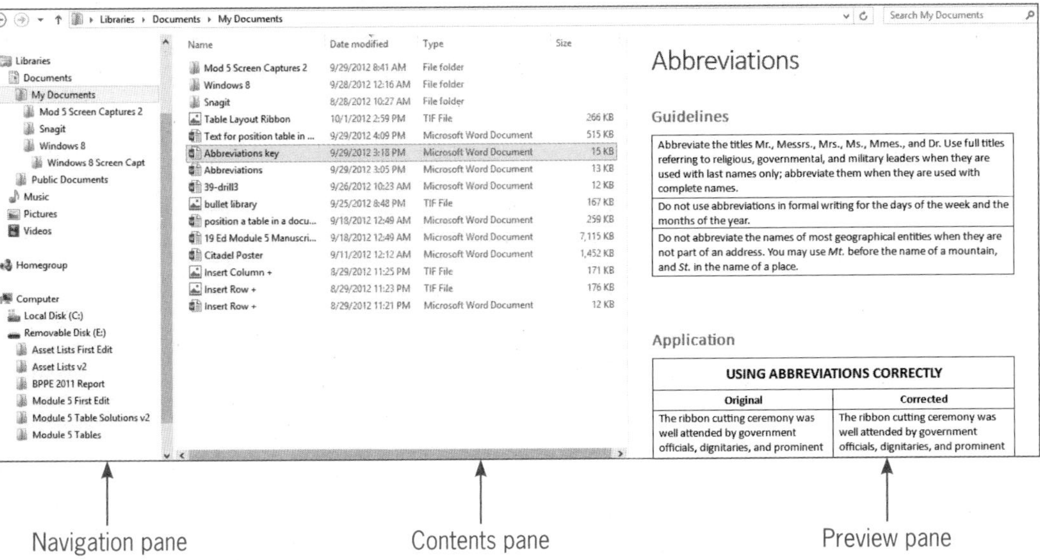

When you open *File Explorer*, it displays four default libraries—Documents, Music, Pictures, and Videos. The libraries display similar types of files regardless of the drive they are stored on. The Pictures Library will list all the pictures stored on the C: drive as well as any that you may have on a USB drive or other external drives that are plugged into the computer. The Documents Library lists all the documents (*Word, Excel, PowerPoint*, etc.) that are stored on drives connected to the computer. This differs from the way the Navigation pane displays the folders, in that the Navigation pane displays according to the contents of each drive.

Documents, by default, save in the My Documents folder. To view the My Documents folder, move the mouse over Documents in the left pane; then click the expand icon. Click the expand icon to the left of the My Documents folder to display its contents.

Files can be stored in various locations or drives on the computer. To view the drives on your computer, click Computer in the Navigation pane. The drives on your computer display in the right pane. The drives are labeled with letters followed by a colon (C:, D:, E:). The hard drive, which stores the software, is usually labeled as drive (C:) If you are using a USB drive to save your files, the USB drive is often designated as drive E: or F:

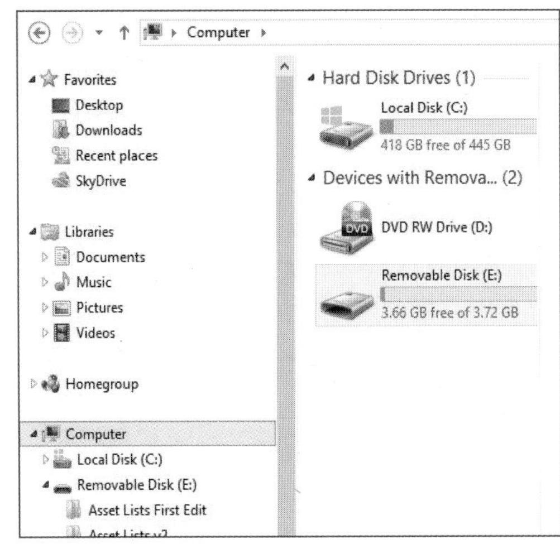

FILE ADDRESSES

The address bar, located above the Navigation and Contents pane, shows the location or address of the file. Each level of the file hierarchy is separated with a ▶ symbol; the highest level display at the left of the address bar. The ▶ symbol indicates the next lower level. The illustration below shows that the selected file, Windows 8 Manuscript, is located in the Windows 8 subfolder ❶, which is located in the My Documents folder ❷, in the Documents Library ❸.

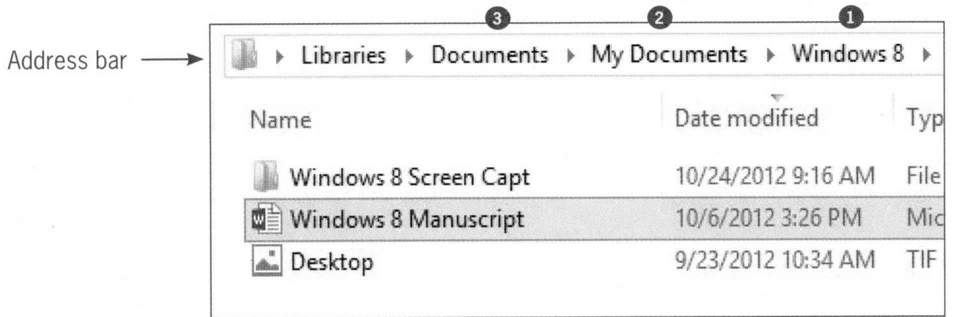

You can move up the hierarchy by clicking on the higher level in the address bar or by clicking on a higher level in the Navigation pane. You can also display the contents of the folder by clicking on the folder name in the address bar.

WORK WITH FILES AND FOLDERS

Folders are extremely important in organizing files. You will create and manage folders and the files within them so that you can easily locate them. A folder can store files; or a folder may contain subfolders which store files. The use of folders and subfolders helps to reduce clutter so that you can find, navigate, and manage your files, folders, and disks with greater speed.

NAMING FILES

Good file organization begins with giving your folders and files names that are logical and easy to understand. A filename should be meaningful and reflect the contents of the file. Filenames can be up to 255 characters long (but in practice you won't use filenames that long). In addition, the following symbols cannot be used in a filename: \ / : * ? " , . The descriptive name is followed by a period (.), which is used to separate the descriptive name from the file extension. The file extension is three or four letters that follow the period. When renaming a file, do not delete or change file extensions as this may cause problems opening the file.

FILE EXPLORER HOME RIBBON

Commands that are commonly used are located on the Home tab. The ribbon is divided into groups, similar to that of other *Microsoft Office* products. The commands to create new folders, rename files and folders, and copy, move and delete files are all located on the Home tab.

To create a file folder:
Home/New/New Folder

1. In the left pane of *File Explorer*, click the drive or folder that is to contain the new folder.
2. Follow the path to create a new folder. A yellow folder icon displays at the top of the right pane with the words *New folder* highlighted.
3. Key the new folder name and tap ENTER.

To rename a file or folder:
Home/Organize/Rename

1. Access *File Explorer* and display the contents of your removable storage drive (or the location where you have been instructed to save your document files or folders).
2. Click the file or folder icon to be renamed.
3. Click Rename on the ribbon.
4. Key the new name and tap ENTER.

COPY, MOVE, OR DELETE FILES OR FOLDERS

The names of the files need to be selected from the Contents pane in order to use the commands in the Home ribbon.

To move a file or folder to a new location, select the file and click the *Move to* command. Select a location from the drop list or click *Choose location* to display the *Move items* dialog box. Select the location the file or folder is to be moved to, then click the *Move* button.

Copy a file to leave it in its current location and make a duplicate of it in another location. To place a copy of a file or folder in a new location, select the file and click the *Copy to* command. Select a location from the drop list or click *Choose location* to display the *Copy items* dialog box. Select the location the file or folder is to be copied to, then click the *Copy* button.

To delete a file or folder, highlight the file or folder icon in the *Explorer* window and click Delete in the ribbon. When you delete a file or folder from the hard drive, it is not removed from the storage immediately. It moves to the Recycle Bin and remains there until the Recycle Bin is emptied. This gives you the opportunity to restore the file to its original location if you discover that it should not have been deleted.

SKYDRIVE APP

Microsoft made the SkyDrive an integral part of the *Windows 8* operating system by placing the SkyDrive app on the Start screen. The SkyDrive is a service that allows you to store documents, photos, videos, and audio files on the *Microsoft* servers. A benefit of storing files on the SkyDrive is the ability to access the files from any computer or *Windows* phone. The files can be shared with family and friends. Co-workers can collaboratively work on *Microsoft Office* documents. You need to have a *Microsoft* account to access the SkyDrive.

Updates are continually made to the SkyDrive. Read your screen carefully as appearance and steps may vary over time.

To access the SkyDrive: *(Internet connection needed with a Microsoft account.)*

1. From the *Windows 8* Start screen, click the SkyDrive app icon.
2. Your SkyDrive Home location displays. Folders display the folder name and the number of files in the folder. Files display the file name and an icon identifying the file type. Picture files contain a preview of the picture file.
3. Click the file or folder to open it.

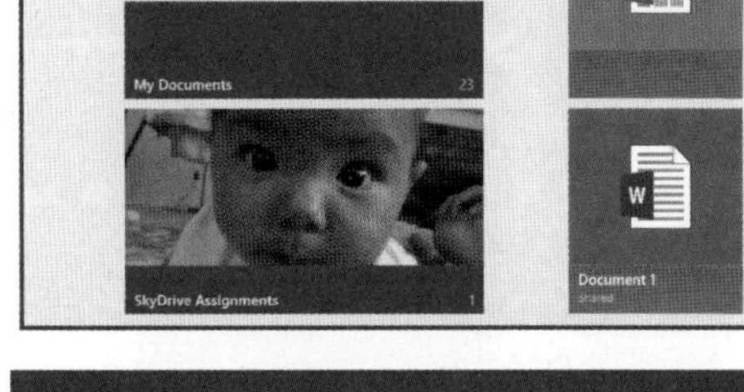

To upload a file to SkyDrive:

1. From the *Windows 8* Start screen, click the SkyDrive app icon.
2. Right-click any blank area to display a toolbar at the bottom of the screen.
3. Click New Folder. Key the folder name in the Create Folder dialog box.
4. Click the new folder to open it.
5. Right-click in the new folder and choose Upload.
6. Browse to select the file(s) to upload. A ✓ displays in the upper-right of each file that is selected. After all files are selected, click the *Add to SkyDrive* button.
7. The status of the upload displays in the upper-right corner of the SkyDrive screen. "Done" displays when the upload is complete.

To download a file to your computer:

1. Select the file(s) to be downloaded.
2. Click the Download button.
3. Choose the location to place the file.
4. Click the *Choose this folder* button in the lower-right; then click OK.

DRILL 3 UPLOADING A FILE TO SKYDRIVE

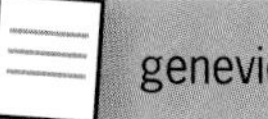

genevieve

1. Click the SkyDrive app on the Start screen.
2. On your SkyDrive home page, right-click and choose New Folder.
3. Name the folder **SkyDrive Assignments**.
4. Click the folder to open it. Right-click in the folder and choose Upload.
5. Navigate to the folder and select the **Genevieve** file.
6. Click the Add to SkyDrive button.
7. Click the down arrow to the right of SkyDrive Assignments; choose your SkyDrive from the list that displays.
8. Press the WinKey to return to the Start screen.
9. Log off or shut down the computer.

Appendix D Reference Guide

Capitalization

Capitalize:

1. First word of a sentence and of a direct quotation.

   We were tolerating instead of managing diversity.
   The speaker said, "We must value diversity, not merely recognize it."

2. Names of proper nouns—specific persons, places, or things.

   Common nouns: continent, river, car, street
   Proper nouns: Asia, Mississippi, Buick, State St.

3. Derivatives of proper nouns and geographical names.

   American history   English accent
   German food   Ohio Valley
   Tampa, Florida   Mount Rushmore

4. A personal or professional title when it precedes the name or a title of high distinction without a name.

   Lieutenant Kahn   Mayor Walsh
   Doctor Welby   Mr. Ty Brooks
   Dr. Frank Collins   Miss Tate
   the President of the United States

5. Days of the week, months of the year, holidays, periods of history, and historic events.

   Monday, June 8   Labor Day   Renaissance

6. Specific parts of the country but not compass points that show direction.

   Midwest   the South   northwest of town

7. Family relationships when used with a person's name.

   Aunt Helen   my dad   Uncle John

8. Noun preceding a figure except for common nouns such as *line*, *page*, and *sentence*.

   Unit 1   Section 2   page 2   verse 7   line 2

9. First and main words of side headings, titles of books, and works of art. Do not capitalize words of four or fewer letters that are conjunctions, prepositions, or articles.

   Computers in the News   *Raiders of the Lost Ark*

10. Names of organizations and specific departments within the writer's organization.

    Girl Scouts   our Sales Department

Number Expression

General guidelines

1. Use **words** for numbers *one* through *ten* unless the numbers are in a category with related larger numbers that are expressed as figures.

   He bought three acres of land. She took two acres.
   She wrote 12 stories and 2 plays in 13 years.

2. Use **words** for approximate numbers or large round numbers that can be expressed as one or two words. Use **numbers** for round numbers in millions or higher with their word modifier.

   We sent out about three hundred invitations.
   She contributed $3 million dollars.

3. Use **words** for numbers that begin a sentence.

   Six players were cut from the ten-member team.

4. Use **figures** for the larger of two adjacent numbers.

   We shipped six 24-ton engines.

Times and dates

5. Use **words** for numbers that precede o'clock (stated or implied).

   We shall meet from two until five o'clock.

6. Use **figures** for times with *a.m.* or *p.m.* and days when they follow the month.

   Her appointment is for 2:15 p.m. on July 26, 2011.

7. Use **ordinals** for the day when it precedes the month.

   The 10th of October is my anniversary.

Money, percentages, and fractions

8. Use **figures** for money amounts and percentages. Spell out *cents* and *percent* except in statistical copy.

   The 16% discount saved me $145; Bill, 95 cents.

9. Use **words** for fractions unless the fractions appear in combination with whole numbers.

   one-half of her lesson   5 1/2   18 3/4

Addresses

10. Use **words** for street names First through Tenth and **figures** or ordinals for streets above Tenth. Use **figures** for house numbers other than number **one**. (If street name is a number, separate it from house number with a dash.)

    One Lytle Place   Second Ave.   142--53rd St.

Use an apostrophe

1. To make most singular nouns and indefinite pronouns possessive (add **apostrophe** and **s**).

   computer + 's = computer's   Jess + 's = Jess's
   anyone's   one's   somebody's

2. To make a plural noun that does not end in s possessive (add **apostrophe** and **s**).

   women + 's = women's   men + 's = men's
   deer + 's = deer's   children + 's = children's

3. To make a plural noun that ends in s possessive. Add only the **apostrophe**.

   boys + ' = boys'   managers + ' = managers'

4. To make a compound noun possessive or to show joint possession. Add **apostrophe** and **s** to the last part of the hyphenated noun.

   son-in-law's   Rob and Gen's game

5. To form the plural of numbers and letters, add **apostrophe** and **s**. To show omission of letters or figures, add an **apostrophe** in place of the missing items.

   7's   A's   It's   add'l

Use a colon

1. To introduce a listing.

   The candidate's strengths were obvious: experience, community involvement, and forthrightness.

2. To introduce an explanatory statement.

   Then I knew we were in trouble: The item had not been scheduled.

Use a comma

1. After an introductory phrase or dependent clause.

   After much deliberation, the jury reached its decision.
   If you have good skills, you will find a job.

2. After words or phrases in a series.

   Mike is taking Greek, Latin III, and Chemistry II.

3. To set off nonessential or interrupting elements.

   Troy, the new man in MIS, will install the hard drive.
   He cannot get to the job, however, until next Friday.

4. To set off the date from the year and the city from the state.

   John, will you please reserve the center in Billings, Montana, for January 10, 2011.

5. To separate two or more parallel adjectives (adjectives could be separated by *and* instead of a comma).

   The loud, whining guitar could be heard above the rest.

6. Before the conjunction in a compound sentence. The comma may be omitted in a very short sentence.

   You must leave immediately, or you will miss your flight. We tested the software and they loved it.

7. Set off appositives and words of direct address.

   Karen, our team leader, represented us at the conference.
   Paul, have you ordered the DVD-ROM drive?

Use a hyphen

1. To show end-of-line word division.
2. In many compound words—check a dictionary if unsure.
   - Two-word adjectives before a noun:

     two-car family

   - Compound numbers between twenty-one and ninety-nine.
   - Fractions and some proper nouns with prefixes/suffixes.

     two-thirds   ex-Governor   all-American

Use italic or underline

1. With titles of complete literary works.

   College Keyboarding   *Hunt for Red October*

2. To emphasize special words or phrases.

   What does *professional* mean?

Use a semicolon

1. To separate independent clauses in a compound sentence when the conjunction is omitted.

   Please review the information; give me a report by Tuesday.

2. To separate independent clauses when they are joined by conjunctive adverbs (*however, nevertheless, consequently,* etc.).

   The traffic was heavy; consequently, I was late.

3. To separate a series of elements that contain commas.

   The new officers are: Fran Pena, president; Harry Wong, treasurer; and Muriel Williams, secretary.

Use a dash

1. To show an abrupt change of thought.

   Invoice 76A—which is 10 days overdue—is for $670.

2. After a series to indicate a summarizing statement.

   Noisy fuel pump, worn rods, and failing brakes—for all these reasons I'm trading the car.

Use an exclamation point

After emphatic interjections or exclamatory sentences.

Terrific!   Hold it!   You bet!   What a great surprise!

Proofreading Procedures

Proofread documents so that they are free of errors. Error-free documents send the message that you are detail-oriented and a person capable of doing business. Apply these procedures after you key a document.

1. Use Spelling & Grammar to check the document.
2. Proofread the document on screen to be sure that it makes sense. Check for these types of errors:
   - Words, headings, and/or amounts omitted.
   - Extra words or lines not deleted during the editing stage.
   - Incorrect sequence of numbers in a list.
3. Preview the document on screen using the Print Preview feature. Check the vertical placement, presence of headers or footers, page numbers, and overall appearance.
4. Save the document again and print.
5. Check the printed document by comparing it to the source copy (textbook). Check all figures, names, and addresses against the source copy. Check that the document style has been applied consistently throughout.
6. If errors exist on the printed copy, revise the document, save, and print.
7. Verify the corrections and placement of the second printed copy.

Proofreaders' Marks

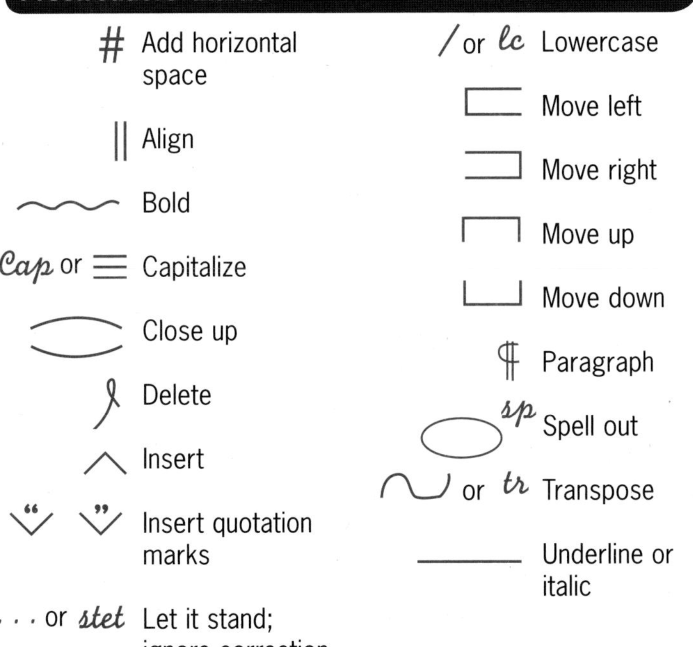

Addressing Procedures

The Envelope feature inserts the delivery address automatically if a letter is displayed. Title case, used in the letter address, is acceptable in the envelope address. An alternative style for envelopes is uppercase with no punctuation.

Business letters are usually mailed in envelopes that have the return address preprinted; return addresses are printed only for personal letters or when letterhead is not available. The default size of *Word* is a size 10 envelope ($4^1/_8$" by $9^1/_2$"); other sizes are available using the Options feature.

An address must contain at least three lines; addresses of more than six lines should be avoided. The last line of an address must contain three items of information: (1) the city, (2) the state, and (3) the ZIP Code, preferably a 9-digit code.

Place mailing notations that affect postage (e.g., REGISTERED, CERTIFIED) below the stamp position (about line 1.2"); place other special notations (e.g., CONFIDENTIAL, PERSONAL) below the return address about line 1".

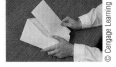

IMAGE MAKERS
5131 Moss Springs Road
Columbia, SC 29209-4768

REGISTERED

Ms. Amy Vreede
Communications Limited
57 Santa Ynez Street
Santa Ana, CA 92708-1537

Folding and Inserting Procedures

Large envelopes (No. 10, 9, 7¾)

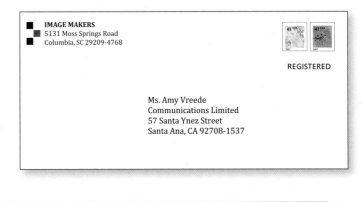

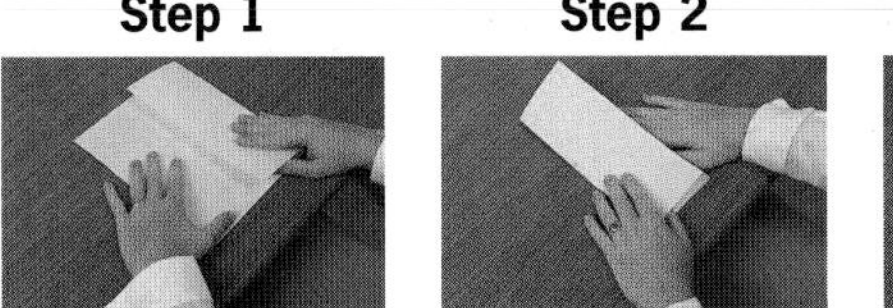

Step 1: With document face up, fold slightly less than 1/3 of sheet up toward top.

Step 2: Fold down top of sheet to within 1/2" of bottom fold.

Step 3: Insert document into envelope with last crease toward bottom of envelope.

Formatting Decisions

Decisions regarding document formats require consideration of four elements: (1) attractiveness of the format, (2) readability of the format, (3) effective use of space on the page, and (4) efficiency in producing the format. Please note several formatting decisions made in this text regarding defaults in *Word 2013*.

Styles

Word 2013 offers a quick gallery of styles on the Home tab. Using these styles results in efficient production of attractive report headings, page number, and table styles.

Default Line Spacing

The default line spacing of 1.08 in *Word 2013* provides readers with an open and readable copy.

Space after the Paragraph

The default space after a paragraph in *Word 2013* is 8 point after the paragraph. This automatic spacing saves time and creates an attractive document.

Remove Space after the Paragraph

While enjoying the benefits of efficiency, it is also necessary to consider the amount of space that is being consumed. For example, extra spacing between the lines of the letter address requires too much space and is not an attractive layout. Note the formats in this book when the extra spacing is removed by simply tapping SHIFT+ENTER after those short lines. Other examples include removing the extra space between the writer's name and title in the closing lines of a letter.

Margins

The default margins for *Word 2013* are 1" top, bottom, left side, and right side. With the side margin default of 1", additional space is needed for the binding of leftbound reports.

Fonts and Document Themes

Microsoft provides true type fonts in *Office 2013* and a number of new document themes that incorporate color and a variety of fonts depending on the theme selected. Many documents presented in the text are based on the default document theme *Office*, and use the default heading font, Calibri Light, and the default body text font, Calibri 11 point. For the initial reports module, the *Word 2013* style set is applied to the document theme. See the illustration below of the default headings and fonts, using the Office theme and *Word 2013* style set.

Title (28 pt. Calibri Light, Automatic—Black)

Subtitle (11 pt. Calibri, Black, Text 1, Lighter 35%)

Heading 1 (16 pt. Calibri Light, Blue, Accent 1, Darker 25%)

Heading 2 (13 pt. Calibri Light, Blue, Accent 1, Darker 25%)

Heading 3 (12 pt. Calibri Light, Blue, Accent 1, Darker 50%)

Heading 4 (11 pt. Calibri Light, Italic, Blue, Accent 1, Darker 25%)

The default body text is Calibri, 11 pt. Color Automatic (Black).

Default Document Theme: Office

Letter Parts

Letterhead. Company name and address. May include other data.

Date. Date letter is mailed. Usually in month, day, year order. Military style is an option (day/month/year).

Letter address. Address of the person who will receive the letter. Include personal title (*Mr.*, *Ms.*, *Dr.*), name, professional title, company, and address. Remove the extra spacing in the letter address.

Salutation. Greeting. Corresponds to the first line of the letter address. Usually includes name and courtesy title; use *Ladies and Gentlemen* if letter is addressed to a company name.

Body. Message. Key in default line spacing; tap ENTER once between paragraphs.

Complimentary close. Farewell, such as *Sincerely*.

Writer. Name and professional title. If the name and title are keyed on two lines, remove the extra spacing between the lines.

Initials. Identifies person who keyed the document (for example, *tr*). May include identification of writer (*ARB:tri*).

Enclosure. Copy is enclosed with the document. May specify contents. If more than one line is used, align at 1" and remove the extra spacing between the lines.

Copy notation. Indicates that a copy of the letter is being sent to person name. If more than one line is used, align at 0.5" and remove the extra spacing between the lines.

Note: To remove extra spacing between lines, press SHIFT + ENTER.

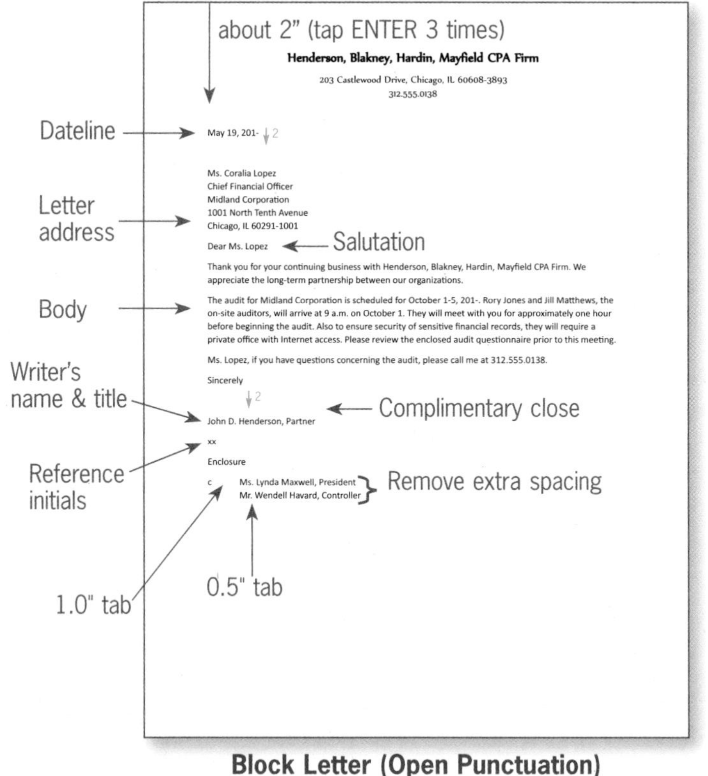

Henderson, Blakney, Hardin, Mayfield CPA Firm
203 Castlewood Drive, Chicago, IL 60608-3893
312.555.0138

May 19, 201-

Ms. Coralia Lopez
Chief Financial Officer
Midland Corporation
1001 North Tenth Avenue
Chicago, IL 60291-1001

Dear Ms. Lopez

Thank you for your continuing business with Henderson, Blakney, Hardin, Mayfield CPA Firm. We appreciate the long-term partnership between our organizations.

The audit for Midland Corporation is scheduled for October 1-5, 201-. Rory Jones and Jill Matthews, the on-site auditors, will arrive at 9 a.m. on October 1. They will meet with you for approximately one hour before beginning the audit. Also to ensure security of sensitive financial records, they will require a private office with Internet access. Please review the enclosed audit questionnaire prior to this meeting.

Ms. Lopez, if you have questions concerning the audit, please call me at 312.555.0138.

Sincerely

John D. Henderson, Partner

xx

Enclosure

c Ms. Lynda Maxwell, President
Mr. Wendell Havard, Controller

Block Letter (Open Punctuation)

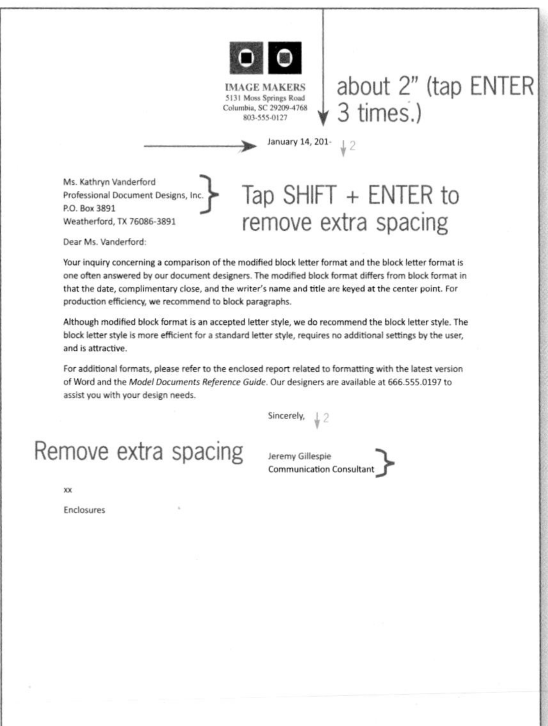

IMAGE MAKERS
5131 Moss Springs Road
Columbia, SC 29209-4768
803-555-0127

January 14, 201-

Ms. Kathryn Vanderford
Professional Document Designs, Inc.
P.O. Box 3891
Weatherford, TX 76086-3891

Dear Ms. Vanderford:

Your inquiry concerning a comparison of the modified block letter format and the block letter format is one often answered by our document designers. The modified block format differs from block format in that the date, complimentary close, and the writer's name and title are keyed at the center point. For production efficiency, we recommend to block paragraphs.

Although modified block format is an accepted letter style, we do recommend the block letter style. The block letter style is more efficient for a standard letter style, requires no additional settings by the user, and is attractive.

For additional formats, please refer to the enclosed report related to formatting with the latest version of Word and the *Model Documents Reference Guide*. Our designers are available at 666.555.0197 to assist you with your design needs.

Sincerely,

Jeremy Gillespie
Communication Consultant

xx

Enclosures

Modified Block Letter (Mixed Punctuation)

IMAGE MAKERS
5131 Moss Springs Road
Columbia, SC 29209-4768

Ms. Kathryn Vanderford
Professional Document Designs, Inc.
P.O. Box 3891
Weatherford, TX 76086-3891

Envelope

Academic Reports in MLA Style

Font: 12-point Times New Roman.

Margins: Side margins 1".

Report heading: Key at 1". Include writer's name, instructor's name, assignment name, and date in DDMMYY order (Ex. 10 April 2014).

Spacing: DS paragraphs and indent 0.5".

Report title: Center one line after the report heading; capitalize all main words.

Headings: Key Level 1 headings in this report at the left margin.

Numbers: Number pages at top right; include the writer's last name and the page number (LName 1).

Internal citations: References cited are indicated within the text in parenthesis. Indent quotes of 40 or more words 1" from left margin.

Works cited: Lists all references in alphabetical order by authors' last names. Format as hanging indent.

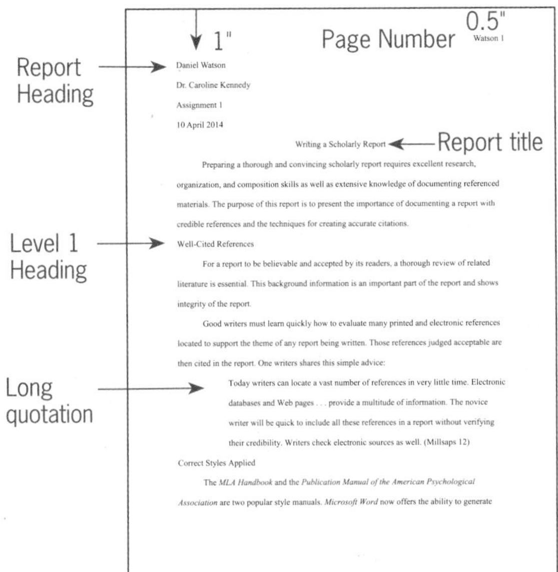

Watson 1

Daniel Watson

Dr. Caroline Kennedy

Assignment 1

10 April 2014

Writing a Scholarly Report

Preparing a thorough and convincing scholarly report requires excellent research, organization, and composition skills as well as extensive knowledge of documenting referenced materials. The purpose of this report is to present the importance of documenting a report with credible references and the techniques for creating accurate citations.

Well-Cited References

For a report to be believable and accepted by its readers, a thorough review of related literature is essential. This background information is an important part of the report and shows integrity of the report.

Good writers must learn quickly how to evaluate many printed and electronic references located to support the theme of any report being written. Those references judged acceptable are then cited in the report. One writers shares this simple advice:

> Today writers can locate a vast number of references in very little time. Electronic databases and Web pages . . . provide a multitude of information. The novice writer will be quick to include all these references in a report without verifying their credibility. Writers check electronic sources as well. (Millsaps 12)

Correct Styles Applied

The *MLA Handbook* and the *Publication Manual of the American Psychological Association* are two popular style manuals. *Microsoft Word* now offers the ability to generate

MLA Report, Page 1

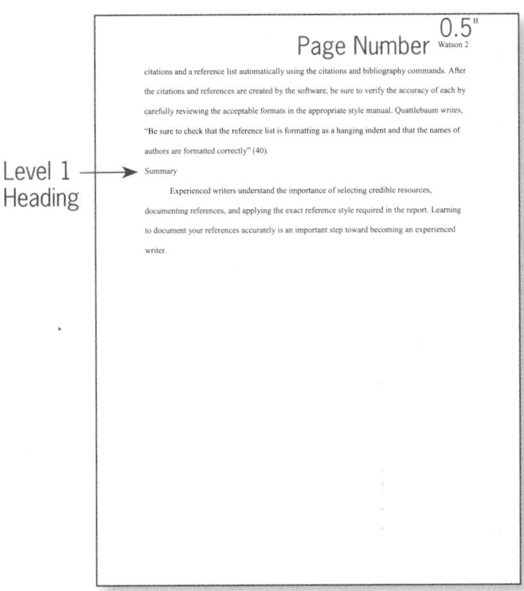

Watson 2

citations and a reference list automatically using the citations and bibliography commands. After the citations and references are created by the software, be sure to verify the accuracy of each by carefully reviewing the acceptable formats in the appropriate style manual. Quattlebaum writes, "Be sure to check that the reference list is formatting as a hanging indent and that the names of authors are formatted correctly" (40).

Summary

Experienced writers understand the importance of selecting credible resources, documenting references, and applying the exact reference style required in the report. Learning to document your references accurately is an important step toward becoming an experienced writer.

MLA Report, Page 2

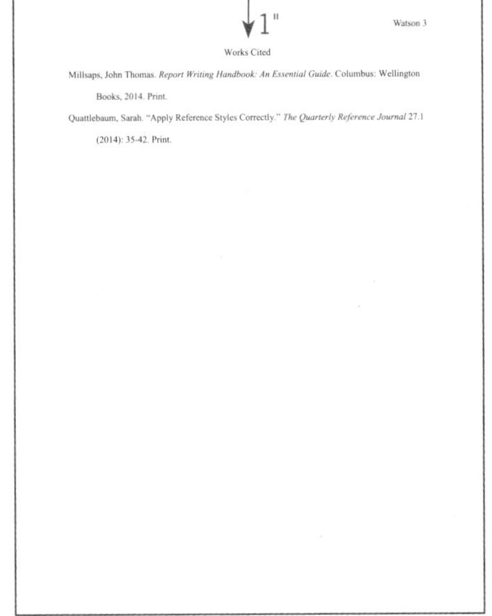

Watson 3

Works Cited

Millsaps, John Thomas. *Report Writing Handbook: An Essential Guide*. Columbus: Wellington Books, 2014. Print.

Quattlebaum, Sarah. "Apply Reference Styles Correctly." *The Quarterly Reference Journal* 27.1 (2014): 35-42. Print.

MLA Works Cited page

Academic Reports in APA Style

Font: 12-point Times New Roman.

Margins: Side margins 1".

Spacing: DS paragraphs and indent 0.5".

Report title: Center one line after the report heading; capitalize all main words.

Headings: Key Level 1 headings in this report at the left margin.

Page numbers: Key a running head that includes the title of the paper (limited to 50 characters) at the left margin and the page number aligned at the right.

Internal citations: References cited are indicated within the text in parenthesis. Indent quotes of 40 or more words 0.5" from left margin.

Bibliography: Lists all references in alphabetical order by authors' last names. Format as hanging indent.

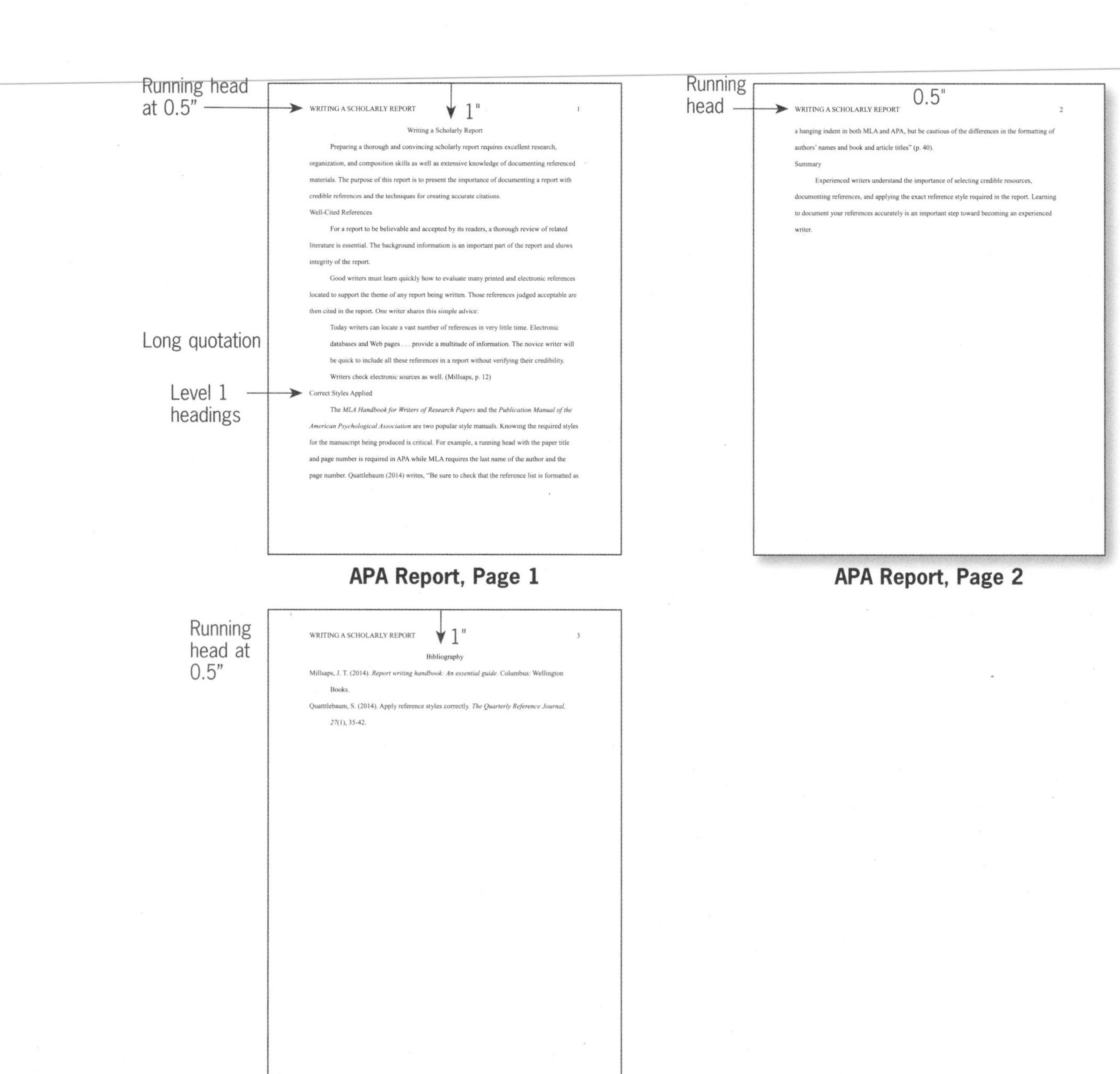

WRITING A SCHOLARLY REPORT 1

Writing a Scholarly Report

Preparing a thorough and convincing scholarly report requires excellent research, organization, and composition skills as well as extensive knowledge of documenting referenced materials. The purpose of this report is to present the importance of documenting a report with credible references and the techniques for creating accurate citations.

Well-Cited References

For a report to be believable and accepted by its readers, a thorough review of related literature is essential. The background information is an important part of the report and shows integrity of the report.

Good writers must learn quickly how to evaluate many printed and electronic references located to support the theme of any report being written. Those references judged acceptable are then cited in the report. One writer shares this simple advice:

> Today writers can locate a vast number of references in very little time. Electronic databases and Web pages . . . provide a multitude of information. The novice writer will be quick to include all these references in a report without verifying their credibility. Writers check electronic sources as well. (Millsaps, p. 12)

Correct Styles Applied

The *MLA Handbook for Writers of Research Papers* and the *Publication Manual of the American Psychological Association* are two popular style manuals. Knowing the required styles for the manuscript being produced is critical. For example, a running head with the paper title and page number is required in APA while MLA requires the last name of the author and the page number. Quattlebaum (2014) writes, "Be sure to check that the reference list is formatted as

APA Report, Page 1

WRITING A SCHOLARLY REPORT 2

a hanging indent in both MLA and APA, but be cautious of the differences in the formatting of authors' names and book and article titles" (p. 40).

Summary

Experienced writers understand the importance of selecting credible resources, documenting references, and applying the exact reference style required in the report. Learning to document your references accurately is an important step toward becoming an experienced writer.

APA Report, Page 2

WRITING A SCHOLARLY REPORT 3

Bibliography

Millsaps, J. T. (2014). *Report writing handbook: An essential guide.* Columbus: Wellington Books.

Quattlebaum, S. (2014). Apply reference styles correctly. *The Quarterly Reference Journal, 27*(1), 35-42.

APA Bibliography page

Margins: Tap ENTER three times to begin first page of report at 2"; default 1" top margin for succeeding pages; default 1" for bottom margin.

Unbound report: Side margins 1"

Leftbound report: Side margins 1.5"

Titles: Title style. Main words capitalized.

Spacing: Default line spacing; paragraphs blocked. Tap ENTER once between paragraphs.

Page numbers: Second and subsequent pages are numbered at top right of the page. One blank line follows the page number.

Side headings: Heading 1 style. Main words capitalized.

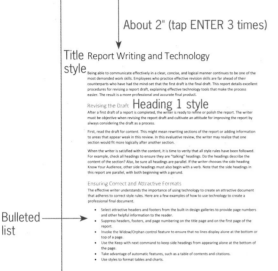

About 2" (tap ENTER 3 times)

Title style

Report Writing and Technology

Being able to communicate effectively in a clear, concise, and logical manner continues to be one of the most demanded work skills. Employees who practice effective revision skills are far ahead of their counterparts who have had the mind-set that the first draft is the final draft. This report details excellent procedures for revising a report draft, explaining effective technology tools that make the process easier. The result is a more professional and accurate final product.

Revising the Draft

Heading 1 style

After a first draft of a report is completed, the writer is ready to refine or polish the report. The writer must be objective when revising the report draft and cultivate an attitude for improving the report by always considering the draft as a process.

First, read the draft for content. This might mean rewriting sections of the report or adding information to areas that appear weak in this review. In this evaluative review, the writer may realize that one section would fit more logically after another section.

When the writer is satisfied with the content, it is time to verity that all style rules have been followed. For example, check all headings to ensure they are "talking" headings. Do the headings describe the content of the section? Also, be sure all headings are parallel. If the writer chooses the side heading Know Your Audience, other side headings must also begin with a verb. Note that the side headings in this report are parallel, with both beginning with a gerund.

Ensuring Correct and Attractive Formats

The effective writer understands the importance of using technology to create an attractive document that adheres to correct style rules. Here are a few examples of how to use technology to create a professional final document.

Bulleted list

- Select attractive headers and footers from the built-in design galleries to provide page numbers and other helpful information to the reader.
- Suppress headers, footers, and page numbering on the title page and on the first page of the report.
- Invoke the Widow/Orphan control feature to ensure that no lines display alone at the bottom or top of a page.
- Use the Keep with next command to keep side headings from appearing alone at the bottom of the page.
- Take advantage of automatic features, such as a table of contents and citations.
- Use styles to format tables and charts.

Unbound Report, Page 1

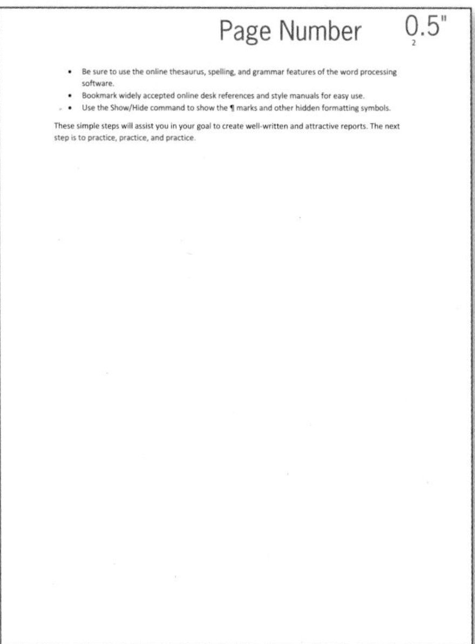
Page Number 0.5"

2

- Be sure to use the online thesaurus, spelling, and grammar features of the word processing software.
- Bookmark widely accepted online desk references and style manuals for easy use.
- Use the Show/Hide command to show the ¶ marks and other hidden formatting symbols.

These simple steps will assist you in your goal to create well-written and attractive reports. The next step is to practice, practice, and practice.

Unbound Report, Page 2 (Plain Number 3 Style)

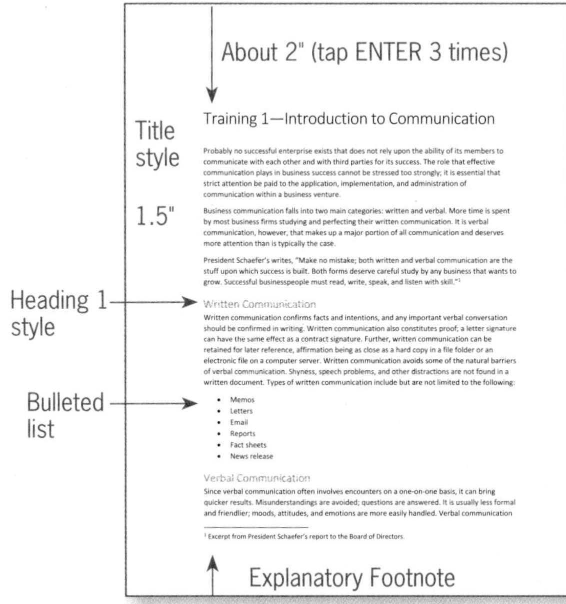
About 2" (tap ENTER 3 times)

Title style

1.5"

Training 1—Introduction to Communication

Probably no successful enterprise exists that does not rely upon the ability of its members to communicate with each other and with third parties for its success. The role that effective communication plays in business success cannot be stressed too strongly; it is essential that strict attention be paid to the application, implementation, and administration of communication within a business venture.

Business communication falls into two main categories: written and verbal. More time is spent by most business firms studying and perfecting their written communication. It is verbal communication, however, that makes up a major portion of all communication and deserves more attention than is typically the case.

President Schaefer's writes, "Make no mistake; both written and verbal communication are the stuff upon which success is built. Both forms deserve careful study by any business that wants to grow. Successful businesspeople must read, write, speak, and listen with skill."[1]

Heading 1 style

Written Communication

Written communication confirms facts and intentions, and any important verbal conversation should be confirmed in writing. Written communication also constitutes proof; a letter signature can have the same effect as a contract signature. Further, written communication can be retained for later reference, affirmation being as close as a hard copy in a file folder or an electronic file on a computer server. Written communication avoids some of the natural barriers of verbal communication. Shyness, speech problems, and other distractions are not found in a written document. Types of written communication include but are not limited to the following:

Bulleted list

- Memos
- Letters
- Email
- Reports
- Fact sheets
- News release

Verbal Communication

Since verbal communication often involves encounters on a one-on-one basis, it can bring quicker results. Misunderstandings are avoided; questions are answered. It is usually less formal and friendlier; moods, attitudes, and emotions are more easily handled. Verbal communication

[1] Excerpt from President Schaefer's report to the Board of Directors.

Explanatory Footnote

Leftbound Report with Footnote, Page 1

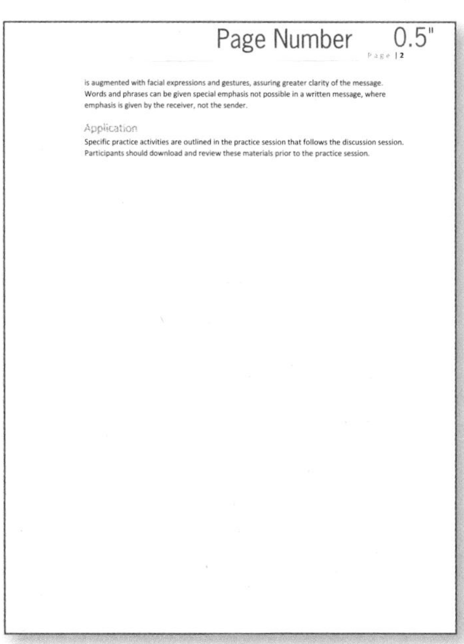
Page Number 0.5"

Page | 2

is augmented with facial expressions and gestures, assuring greater clarity of the message. Words and phrases can be given special emphasis not possible in a written message, where emphasis is given by the receiver, not the sender.

Application

Specific practice activities are outlined in the practice session that follows the discussion session. Participants should download and review these materials prior to the practice session.

Leftbound Report, Page 2 (Page Number Style)

About 2" (tap ENTER 3 times)

Tab (1" from left margin)

TO: Emily Welch, Brian McKenzie, Olivia von Staden

FROM: Michael Holcomb

DATE: July 18, 201-

SUBJECT: Video Conference Call Scheduled Friday, July 26, 201-

The final video conference call to select the contractor for the Keystone Community Project will be held on Friday, July 26, 201-, from 3:30 to 5:00 p.m. To join the video conference, follow these steps:

1. Call 601.555.0168 and enter the passcode 8103622 when prompted.
2. Go to www.conferences.com/holcomb/PDS/ and join the meeting.

Please review the proposals carefully and be prepared to make a recommendation at the meeting. If you have questions about the proposals, please call me at 601.555.0193 or email me at mholcomb@svdco.com.

xx

Memo

REGENTS MEMORIAL MEDICAL CENTER
February Seminars

Seminar Title	Description	Registration
Surgical Weight Loss	Methods of losing weight, including healthy diet, exercise and medication, will be discussed in detail. Surgical weight loss is an option for those who are motivated and willing to commit to lifestyle changes.	Classes will be held at the Outpatient Surgery Center 75 Pacific Crest Laguna Niguel, CA 92677-5773. Call 949.555.0111 to register.
Life in Motion with Osteoarthritis	Osteoarthritis no longer means that you need to live with a painful disability. Modern medicine, diet, exercise, and surgery can help you enjoy life more fully. Intricate surgical procedures including joint replacement and spinal fusion will be covered.	Register online at www.regents.org/calendar. Materials fee $10.00.
Experts' Cancer Updates	The cancer experts of Regents Medical Center will unveil the results of the latest cancer studies. New breakthrough treatments will be discussed. They will explain what you should know about cancer screenings. Tips on preventing various types of cancers will be provided.	Call 949.555.0100 or register online at www.regents.org/calendar.

Table (formatted with Table Style)

Maria J. Rex
2104 Adger Road, Columbia, SC 29204-3253
803.555.0194 | Maria.Rex@wcc.edu | http://www.linkedin.com/in/rex

Current date

Mr. Eric Todd, President and CEO
CunCo Consulting Alliance
416 West Bay Street
Savannah, GA 31401-1115

Dear Mr. Todd

Ben Sullivan, your manager of Business Development, sent me a copy of the job description posted for the office manager position open at CunCo and suggested that I contact you. My qualifications match the requirements for the office manager you are seeking. Please consider me as an applicant for that position.

My education and my two years of experience managing the four-hour evening shift of two teams of trainers and one of nutrition counselors enabled me to develop the team management and the operational management skills that you require. Our teamwork resulted in a significant revenue increase and expense reduction.

My internship in the President's Office of Wexford Community College enabled me to refine my organizational, problem-solving, and soft skills. Both my experience at Pat's Fitness and Wellness Center and in the President's office required extensive Word, Excel, and PowerPoint use and excellent communication skills. I delivered high-quality products and met very tight deadlines consistently. I understand how those skills can be of value to CunCo.

After you have had an opportunity to review the enclosed resume as well as my LinkedIn Profile, I look forward to meeting with you to discuss how my qualifications and my office management career aspirations can be applied to your position at CunCo Consulting Alliance.

Sincerely

Maria J. Rex

Enclosure

Personal Business Letter

Maria J. Rex
2104 Adger Road, Columbia, SC 29204-3253
803.555.0194 | Maria.Rex@wcc.edu | http://www.linkedin.com/in/rex

Qualifications Profile for Office Manager

Highly effective, results-oriented, administrative office professional with AS degree and two years of relevant part-time work experience, including demonstrated effective supervisory, customer service, records management, time management, and project management skills. Create professional documents that enhance company image and productivity using Word, Excel, and PowerPoint. Strong written, oral, and electronic communication skills. Excellent interpersonal skills. Honest, ethical, and possess strong work ethic.

Education

AS degree in Business Administration with majors in Office Administration and Office Management from Wexford Community College, Columbia, SC, May 2012, 3.65 GPA.

High school diploma with career emphasis in English and Business, Maxwell High School, Charleston, SC, August, 2010, 3.85 GPA.

Experience

Wexford Community College, President's Office, Columbia, SC, internship, summer 2012.

- Prepared correspondence, reports, and presentations for senior administrators.
- Scheduled and coordinated special events with high-level constituents.
- Received outstanding evaluation, commending my professionalism, social skills, creativity, reliability, problem-solving skills, and the excellent quality of all work.

Pat's Fitness and Wellness Center, supervisor and promoted to office manager for the 3:30 to 7:30 shift (20-25 hours per week) from June 2010 through May 2012.

- Managed two teams of trainers and one team of nutrition counselors; resolved conflicts for clients. Responsible for correspondence with referring physicians, vendors, and clients.
- Managed facility, records, billing, equipment, and supplies; developed procedures.
- Increased client participation and revenue from my shift over 20 percent while reducing expenses by 12 percent.

Honors and Activities

Named a Dean's Scholar; received the Outstanding Business Student Award. Member of Student Advisory Council, president of the Wexford Honor Society, and president of the Office Management Club.

Resume

The numbered parts are found on most computers. The location of some parts will vary.

1. **CPU (Central Processing Unit):** Internal operating unit or "brain" of computer.
2. **CD-ROM drive:** Reads data from and writes data to a CD or DVD.
3. **Monitor:** Displays text and graphics on a screen.
4. **Mouse:** Used to input commands.
5. **Keyboard:** An arrangement of letter, figure, symbol, control, function, and editing keys and a numeric keypad.

KEYBOARD ARRANGEMENT

1. **Alphanumeric keys:** Letters, numbers, and symbols.
2. **Numeric keypad:** Keys at the right side of the keyboard used to enter numeric copy and perform calculations.
3. **Function (F) keys:** Used to execute commands, sometimes with other keys. Commands vary with software.
4. **Arrow keys:** Move insertion point up, down, left, or right.
5. **ESC (Escape):** Closes a software menu or dialog box.
6. **TAB:** Moves the insertion point to a preset position.
7. **CAPS LOCK:** Used to make all capital letters.
8. **SHIFT:** Makes capital letters and symbols shown at tops of number keys.
9. **CTRL (Control):** With other key(s), executes commands. Commands may vary with software.
10. **ALT (Alternate):** With other key(s), executes commands. Commands may vary with software.
11. **Space Bar:** Inserts a space in text.
12. **ENTER (return):** Moves insertion point to margin and down to next line. Also used to execute commands.
13. **DELETE:** Removes text to the right of insertion point.
14. **NUM LOCK:** Activates/deactivates numeric keypad.
15. **INSERT:** Activates insert or typeover.
16. **BACKSPACE:** Deletes text to the left of insertion point.

Appendix F Command Summary

Command	Path
Align Text	Home/Paragraph/Click desired alignment (Align Left, Center, Align Right, or Justify)
Bullets and Numbering	Home/Paragraph/Bullets or Numbering
Center Page	Page Layout/Page Setup/ Dialog Box Launcher/ Layout tab/Vertical alignment/Center
Close Document	File/Close
Columns—Create	Page Layout/Page Setup/Columns
Cut, Copy, and Paste	Home/Clipboard/Cut, Copy, or Paste
Date and Time—Insert	Insert/Text/Date & Time
Define	Review/Proofing/Define
Document Themes	Design/Document Formatting/Themes
Envelopes	Mailings/Create/Envelopes
Find and Replace	Home/Editing/Find or Replace

Footnotes	References/Footnotes/ Insert Footnote	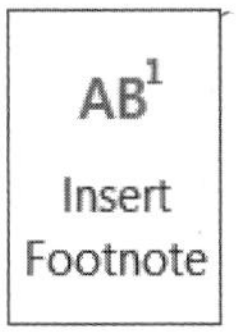 AB[1] Insert Footnote
Format Painter	Home/Clipboard/Format Painter	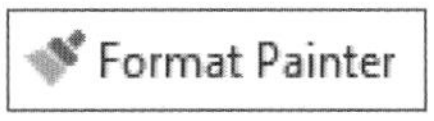 Format Painter
Graphics: Layout Options	Select graphic/Layout options displays	
Hanging indent	Ruler/Indent Markers	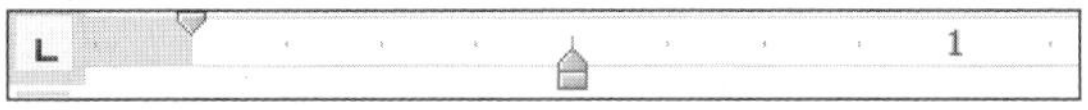 L 1
Header	Insert/Header & Footer/ Header	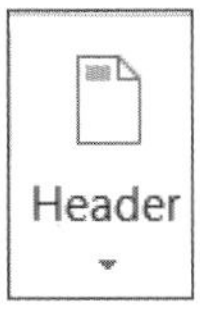 Header
Help	Click Help button	?
Increase/ Decrease Indent	Home/Paragraph/Increase Indent or Decrease Indent	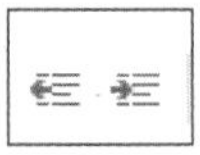
Indent Marker	Ruler/Indent Markers	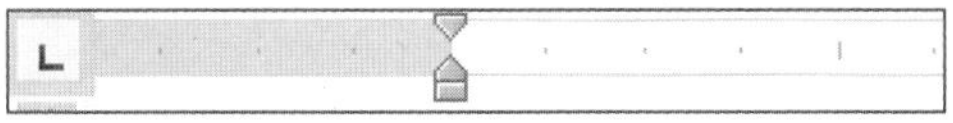 L
Insert File	Insert/Text/Object/ Text from File	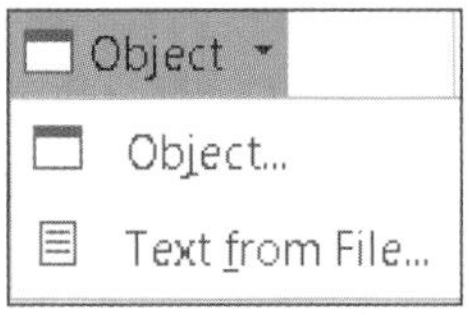 Object; Object...; Text from File...
Line and Page Breaks	Home/Paragraph/Dialog Box Launcher/Line and Page Breaks tab	 Indents and Spacing; Line and Page Breaks
Line Spacing	Home/Paragraph/Line and Paragraph Spacing	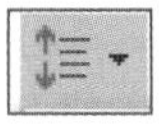
Margins	Page Layout/Page Setup/Margins	 Margins
Mini toolbar	Appears when text is selected	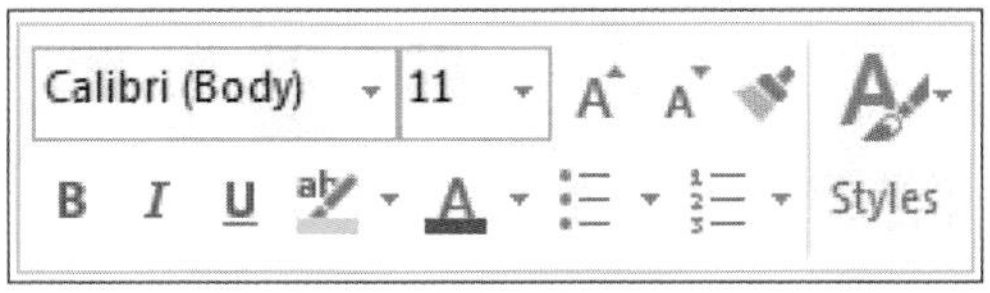 Calibri (Body) 11 A A B I U A Styles

Open Existing Document	File/Open	Open
Open New Document	File/New	New
Page Borders	Design/Page Background/ Page Borders	Page Borders
Page Break	CTRL + ENTER or Insert Pages/Page Break	Page Break
Page Numbers—Insert	Insert/Header & Footer/ Page Number	Page Number
Paste Options	Home/Clipboard/Paste/ Click a Paste Option	Paste Options:
Pictures—Crop	Picture Tools/Format/ Size/Crop	Crop
Picture—Format	Picture Tools/Format	PICTURE TOOLS FORMAT
Picture—Insert	Insert/Illustrations/ Pictures or Online Pictures	Pictures Online Pictures
Pictures—Size	Picture Tools/Format/Size/ Height or Width Arrows	4.88" 6.5" Size
Print	File/Print	Print
Quick Access Toolbar	Upper-left corner of screen/ use down arrow to customize	

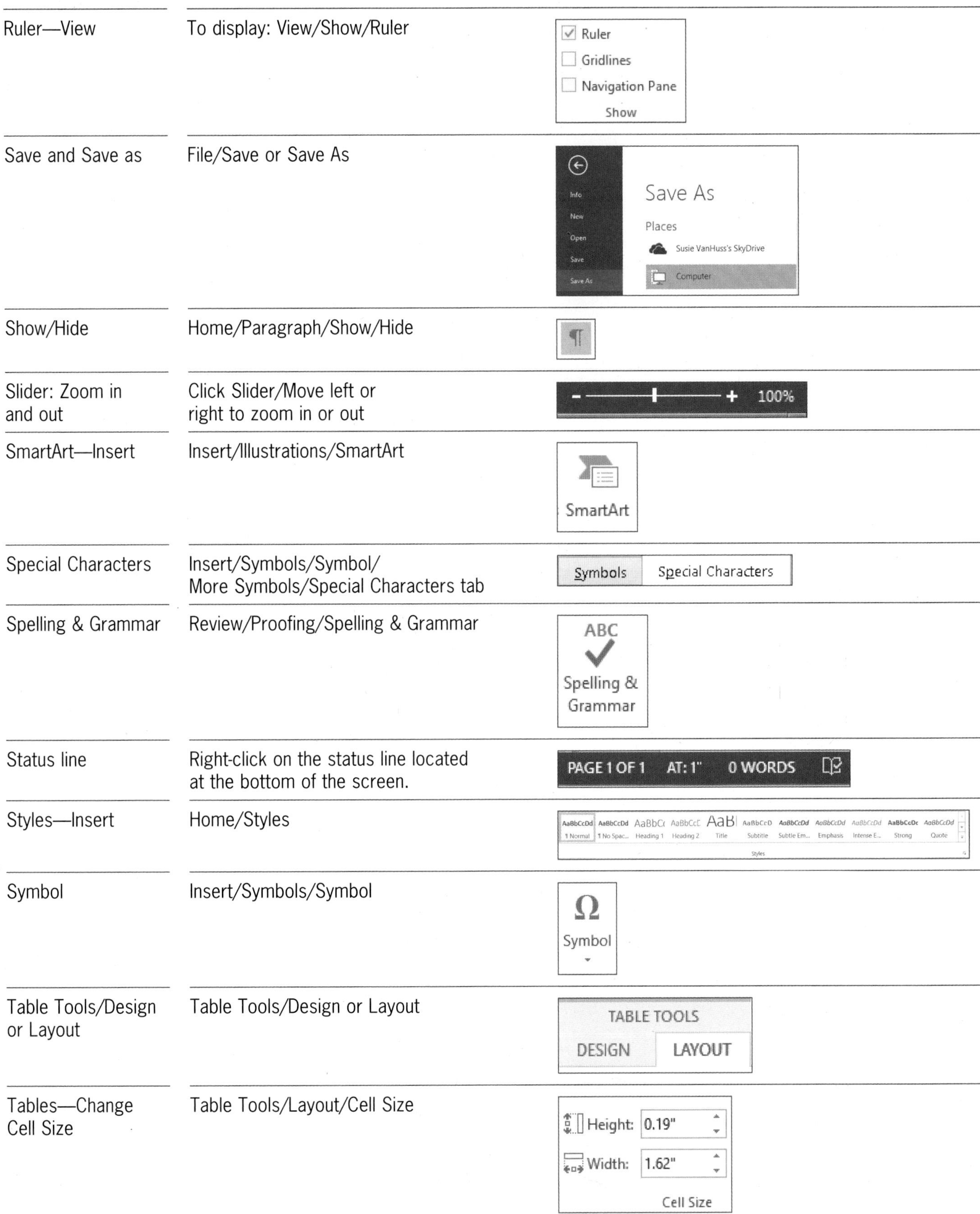

Ruler—View	To display: View/Show/Ruler
Save and Save as	File/Save or Save As
Show/Hide	Home/Paragraph/Show/Hide
Slider: Zoom in and out	Click Slider/Move left or right to zoom in or out
SmartArt—Insert	Insert/Illustrations/SmartArt
Special Characters	Insert/Symbols/Symbol/ More Symbols/Special Characters tab
Spelling & Grammar	Review/Proofing/Spelling & Grammar
Status line	Right-click on the status line located at the bottom of the screen.
Styles—Insert	Home/Styles
Symbol	Insert/Symbols/Symbol
Table Tools/Design or Layout	Table Tools/Design or Layout
Tables—Change Cell Size	Table Tools/Layout/Cell Size

Tables—Change Text Alignment	Table Tools/Layout/Alignment	Text Direction Alignment
Tables—Delete Rows & Columns	Table Tools Layout/Rows & Columns/Delete	Delete · Insert Above · Insert Below Delete Cells... Delete Columns Delete Rows Delete Table
Tables—Insert using the Insert Table command	Insert/Tables/Table/ Insert Table	Insert Table... Draw Table Convert Text to Table... Excel Spreadsheet Quick Tables Insert Table · Table size · Number of columns: 5 · Number of rows: 2 · AutoFit behavior · Fixed column width: Auto · AutoFit to contents · AutoFit to window · Remember dimensions for new tables · OK · Cancel
Tables—Insert Rows & Columns	Table Tools/Layout/Rows & Columns	Insert Above · Insert Below · Insert Left · Insert Right Rows & Columns
Tables—Insert using the Table grid	Insert/Tables/Table/Drag to select number of rows and columns	3x4 Table
Tables—Merge or Split Cells	Table Tools Layout/Merge/Merge or Split Cells	Merge Cells Split Cells Split Table Merge
Tables—Styles	Table Tools Design/ Table Styles	Table Styles
Tabs	View Ruler/Tab Alignment Button/Click on Horizontal Ruler	

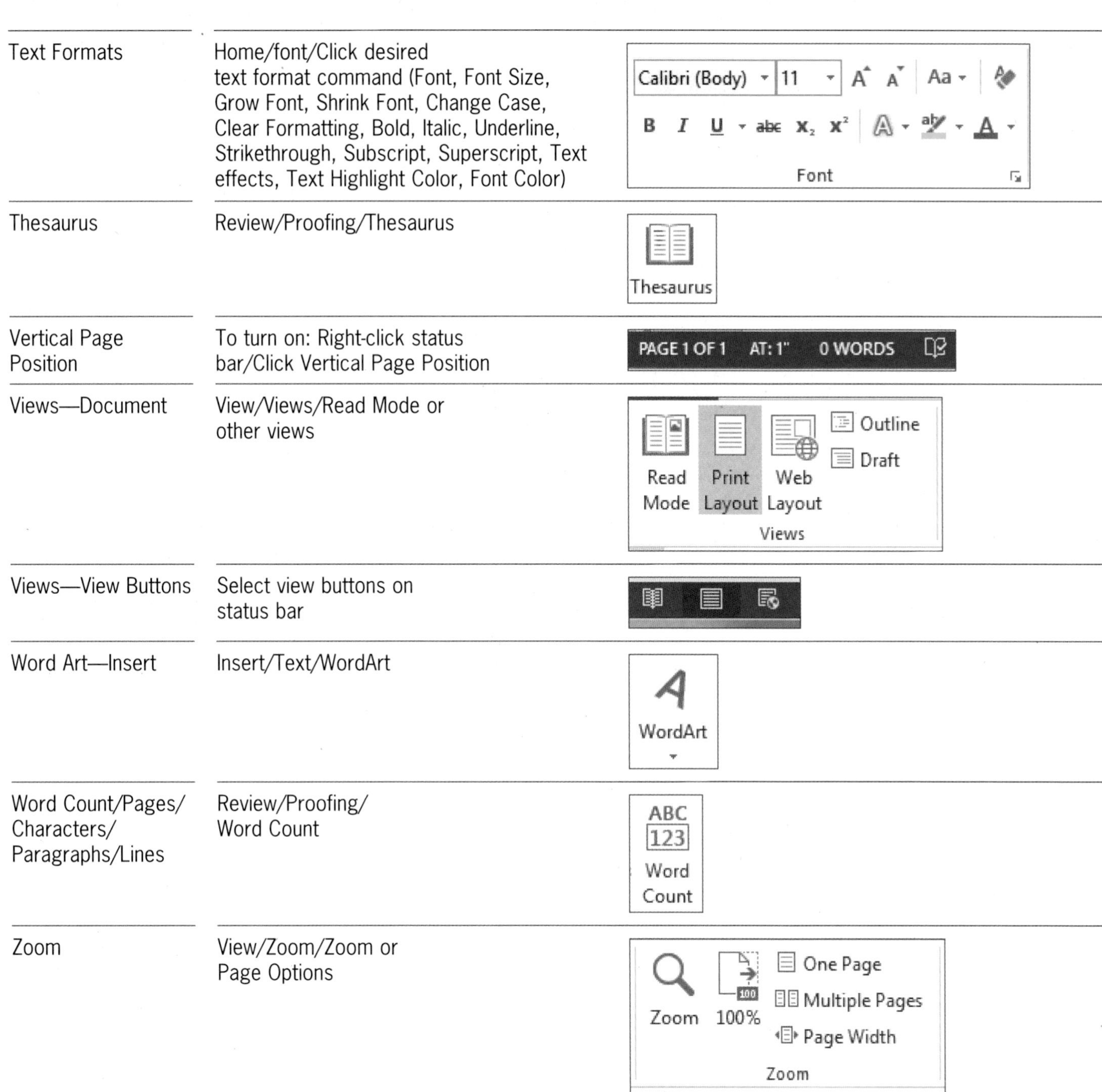

Command	Procedure
Text Formats	Home/font/Click desired text format command (Font, Font Size, Grow Font, Shrink Font, Change Case, Clear Formatting, Bold, Italic, Underline, Strikethrough, Subscript, Superscript, Text effects, Text Highlight Color, Font Color)
Thesaurus	Review/Proofing/Thesaurus
Vertical Page Position	To turn on: Right-click status bar/Click Vertical Page Position
Views—Document	View/Views/Read Mode or other views
Views—View Buttons	Select view buttons on status bar
Word Art—Insert	Insert/Text/WordArt
Word Count/Pages/ Characters/ Paragraphs/Lines	Review/Proofing/ Word Count
Zoom	View/Zoom/Zoom or Page Options

Index

U

V

W

Y

Z

SILVER EDITION

Teacher's Edition with Tests

Interactions 1

LISTENING/SPEAKING

Judith Tanka
Paul Most

Interactions 1 Listening/Speaking Teacher's Edition with Tests, Silver Edition

Published by McGraw-Hill ESL/ELT, a business unit of The McGraw-Hill Companies, Inc. 1221 Avenue of the Americas, New York, NY 10020.

ISBN 13: 978-0-07-329419-3 (Teacher's Edition)
ISBN 10: 0-07-329419-5 (Teacher's Edition)
2 3 4 5 6 7 8 9 10 EUS 11 10 09 08 07

Editorial director: Erik Gundersen
Series editor: Valerie Kelemen
Developmental editor: Terre Passero
Production manager: Juanita Thompson
Production coordinator: Vanessa Nuttry
Cover designer: Robin Locke Monda
Interior designer: Nesbitt Graphics, Inc.

Cover photo: Steve Allen/Creatas Images

www.esl-elt.mcgraw-hill.com

The McGraw·Hill Companies

Table of Contents

Introduction

Student Book Teaching Notes and Answer Keys

Welcome to the Teacher's Edition

The Teacher's Edition of *Interactions/Mosaic* Silver Edition provides support and flexibility to teachers using the *Interactions/Mosaic* Silver Edition 18-book academic skills series. The Teacher's Edition provides step-by-step guidance for implementing each activity in the Student Book. The Teacher's Edition also provides expansion activities with photocopiable masters of select expansion activities, identification of activities that support a Best Practice, valuable notes on content, answer keys, audioscripts, end-of-chapter tests, and placement tests. Each chapter in the Teacher's Edition begins with an overview of the content, vocabulary, and teaching goals in that chapter. Each chapter in the Student Book begins with an engaging photo and related discussion questions that strengthen the educational experience and connect students to the topic.

- **Procedural Notes**
  The procedural notes are useful for both experienced and new teachers. Experienced teachers can use the bulleted, step-by step procedural notes as a quick guide and refresher before class, while newer or substitute teachers can use the notes as a more extensive guide to assist them in the classroom. The procedural notes guide teachers through each strategy and activity; describe what materials teachers might need for an activity; and help teachers provide context for the activities.

- **Answer Keys**
  Answer keys are provided for all activities that have definite answers. For items that have multiple correct answers, various possible answers are provided. The answer key follows the procedural note for the relevant activity. Answer keys are also provided for the Chapter Tests and the Placement Tests.

- **Expansion Activities**
  A number of expansion activities with procedural notes are included in each chapter. These activities offer teachers creative ideas for reinforcing the chapter content while appealing to different learning styles. Activities include games, conversation practice, presentations, and projects. These expansion activities often allow students to practice integrated language skills, not just the skills that the student book focuses on. Some of the expansion activities include photocopiable black line masters included in the back of the book.

- **Content Notes**
  Where appropriate, content notes are included in the Teacher's Edition. These are notes that might illuminate or enhance a learning point in the activity and might help teachers answer student questions about the content. These notes are provided at the logical point of use, but teachers can decide if and when to use the information in class.

- **Chapter Tests**
  Each chapter includes a chapter test that was designed to test the vocabulary, reading, writing, grammar, and/or listening strategies taught in the chapter, depending on the language skill strand being used. Teachers can simply copy and distribute the tests, then use the answer keys found in the Teacher's Edition. The purpose of the chapter tests is not only to assess students' understanding of material covered in the chapter but also to give students an idea of how they are doing and what they need to work on. Each chapter test has four parts with items totaling 100 points. Item types include multiple choice, fill-in-the blank, and true/false. Audioscripts are provided when used.

- **Black Line Masters (Photocopiable Masters)**
  Each chapter includes a number of expansion activities with black line masters, or master worksheets, that teachers can copy and distribute. These activities and black line masters are optional. They can help reinforce and expand on chapter material in an engaging way. Activities include games;

conversation practice; working with manipulatives such as sentence strips; projects; and presentations. Procedural notes and answer keys (when applicable) are provided in the Teacher's Edition.

- **Placement Tests**
  Each of the four language skill strands has a placement test designed to help assess in which level the student belongs. Each test has been constructed to be given in under an hour. Be sure to go over the directions and answer any questions before the test begins. Students are instructed not to ask questions once the test begins. Following each placement test, you'll find a scoring placement key that suggests the appropriate book to be used based on the number of items answered correctly. Teachers should use judgment in placing students and selecting texts.

The Interactions/Mosaic Silver Edition Program

Interactions/Mosaic Silver Edition is a fully-integrated, 18-book academic skills series. Language proficiencies are articulated from the beginning through advance levels <u>within</u> each of the four language skill strands. Chapter themes articulate <u>across</u> the four skill strands to systematically recycle content, vocabulary, and grammar.

- **Reading Strand**
  Reading skills and strategies are strategically presented and practiced through a variety of themes and reading genres in the five Reading books. Pre-reading, reading, and post-reading activities include strategies and activities that aid comprehension, build vocabulary, and prepare students for academic success. Each chapter includes at least two readings that center around the same theme, allowing students to deepen their understanding of a topic and command of vocabulary related to that topic. Readings include magazine articles, textbook passages, essays, letters, and website articles. They explore, and guide the student to explore, stimulating topics. Vocabulary is presented before each reading and is built on throughout the chapter. High-frequency words and words from the Academic Word List are focused on and pointed out with asterisks (*) in each chapter's Self-Assessment Log.

- **Listening/Speaking Strand**
  A variety of listening input, including lectures, academic discussions, and conversations help students explore stimulating topics in the five Listening/Speaking books. Activities associated with the listening input, such as pre-listening tasks, systematically guide students through strategies and critical thinking skills that help prepare them for academic achievement. In the Interactions books, the activities are coupled with instructional photos featuring a cast of engaging, multi-ethnic students participating in North American college life. Across the strand, lectures and dialogues are broken down into manageable parts giving students an opportunity to predict, identify main ideas, and effectively manage lengthy input. Questions, guided discussion activities, and structured pair and group work stimulate interest and interaction among students, often culminating in organizing their information and ideas in a graphic organizer, writing, and/or making a presentation to the class. Pronunciation is highlighted in every chapter, an aid to improving both listening comprehension and speaking fluency. Enhanced focus on vocabulary building is developed throughout and a list of target words for each chapter is provided so students can interact meaningfully with the material. Finally, Online Learning Center features MP3 files from the Student Book audio program for students to download onto portable digital audio players.

- **Writing Strand**
  Activities in each of the four Writing books are systematically structured to culminate in a *Writing Product* task. Activities build on key elements of writing from sentence development to writing single

paragraphs, articles, narratives, and essays of multiple lengths and genres. Connections between writing and grammar tie the writing skill in focus with the grammar structures needed to develop each writing skill. Academic themes, activities, writing topics, vocabulary development, and critical thinking strategies prepare students for university life. Instructional photos are used to strengthen engagement and the educational experience. Explicit pre-writing questions and discussions activate prior knowledge, help organize ideas and information, and create a foundation for the writing product. Each chapter includes a self-evaluation rubric which supports the learner as he or she builds confidence and autonomy in academic writing. Finally, the Writing Articulation Chart helps teachers see the progression of writing strategies both in terms of mechanics and writing genres.

- **Grammar Strand**
  Questions and topical quotes in the four Grammar books, coupled with instructional photos stimulate interest, activate prior knowledge, and launch the topic of each chapter. Engaging academic topics provide context for the grammar and stimulate interest in content as well as grammar. A variety of activity types, including individual, pair, and group work, allow students to build grammar skills and use the grammar they are learning in activities that cultivate critical thinking skills. Students can refer to grammar charts to review or learn the form and function of each grammar point. These charts are numbered sequentially, formatted consistently, and indexed systematically, providing lifelong reference value for students.

- **Focus on Testing for the TOEFL® iBT**
  The all-new TOEFL® iBT *Focus on Testing* sections prepare students for success on the TOEFL® iBT by presenting and practicing specific strategies for each language skill area. The Focus on Testing sections are introduced in Interactions 1 and are included in all subsequent levels of the Reading, Listening/Speaking, and Writing strands. These strategies focus on what The Educational Testing Service (ETS) has identified as the target skills in each language skill area. For example, "reading for basic comprehension" (identifying the main idea, understanding pronoun reference) is a target reading skill and is presented and practiced in one or more *Focus on Testing* sections. In addition, this and other target skills are presented and practiced in chapter components outside the *Focus on Testing* sections and have special relevance to the TOEFL® iBT. For example, note-taking is an important test-taking strategy, particularly in the listening section of the TOEFL® iBT, and is included in activities within each of the Listening/Speaking books. All but two of the *Interactions/Mosaic* titles have a *Focus on Testing* section. Although *Interactions Access Reading* and *Interaction Access Listening/Speaking* don't include these sections because of their level, they do present and develop skills that will prepare students for the TOEFL® iBT.

- **Best Practices**
  In each chapter of this Teacher's Edition, you'll find Best Practices boxes that highlight a particular activity and show how this activity is tied to a particular Best Practice. The Interactions/Mosaic Silver Edition team of writers, editors, and teacher consultants has identified the following six interconnected Best Practices.

* TOEFL is a registered trademark of Educational Testing Services (ETS). This publication is not endorsed or approved by ETS.

Best Practices

Each chapter identifies at least six different activities that support six Best Practices, principles that contribute to excellent language teaching and learning. Identifying Best Practices helps teachers to see, and make explicit for students, how a particular activity will aid the learning process.

Making Use of Academic Content

Materials and tasks based on academic content and experiences give learning real purpose. Students explore real world issues, discuss academic topics, and study content-based and thematic materials.

Organizing Information

Students learn to organize thoughts and notes through a variety of graphic organizers that accommodate diverse learning and thinking styles.

Scaffolding Instruction

A scaffold is a physical structure that facilitates construction of a building. Similarly, scaffolding instruction is a tool used to facilitate language learning in the form of predictable and flexible tasks. Some examples include oral or written modeling by the teacher or students, placing information in a larger framework, and reinterpretation.

Activating Prior Knowledge

Students can better understand new spoken or written material when they connect to the content. Activating prior knowledge allows students to tap into what they already know, building on this knowledge, and stirring a curiosity for more knowledge.

Interacting with Others

Activities that promote human interaction in pair work, small group work, and whole class activities present opportunities for real world contact and real world use of language.

Cultivating Critical Thinking

Strategies for critical thinking are taught explicitly. Students learn tools that promote critical thinking skills crucial to success in the academic world.

Chapter

1

Academic Life Around the World

In this chapter, students will listen to language about academic life, education, and meeting new people. In Part 1, they will hear a conversation in which students meet new people. They will also practice listening for stressed words and listening for reductions. In Part 2, they will listen to a school orientation and practice listening for main ideas and specific information. In Part 3, they will learn two strategies for better listening and speaking: using context clues and using body language. In Part 4, at the end of the chapter, they will learn about listening and giving telephone messages. These topics will prepare students for enrolling in an academic English language program.

Chapter Opener

- Since this is the first chapter, spend a little time at the beginning of each activity explaining its purpose. The goal of the Connecting to the Topic section is to introduce the theme of *Academic Life Around the World* and to help the students think about how the theme relates to their lives.
- Have students look at the photo of university students socializing in their dorm room. Ask them the three questions in the Connecting to the Topic section. Discuss the questions with the class.
- Have the students look at the quote. Ask a volunteer to read the quote. Give them some time to ask for clarification of any words they don't understand. Ask the students as a class to explain what the quote means.

"Teachers open the door. You enter by yourself."

—Chinese proverb

Chapter Overview

Listening Skills and Strategies

Listening for main ideas

Listening for details

Listening to an advisor's presentation

Distinguishing among -*s* endings

Speaking Skills and Strategies

Introducing yourself and others

Leaving telephone messages

Giving telephone messages

Discussing body language

Critical Thinking Skills

Guessing meaning from context

Interpreting a photo

Predicting the content before listening

Distinguishing main ideas from details

Summarizing ideas using key words

Vocabulary Building

Expressions used in introductions

Terms related to arrival and orientation at college or university

Casual expressions for making friends

Instructions (imperatives) used in telephone messages

Pronunciation

Identifying and practicing stressed words

Comparing reduced and unreduced pronunciation

Pronouncing -*s* endings

Focus on Testing

Using context clues to guess the correct answers to questions

Vocabulary

Nouns	Verbs	Expressions
advisor	came over (come over)	call me
facilities	move into	No kidding!
orientation	sound	you guys
placement test	stop by	
schedule	take	

Can You Guess?

- Tell students they are not expected to know the answers to the questions below. Their purpose is to stimulate discussion.
- Ask students to discuss the questions in groups and compare answers with the correct answers.
- Ask students to list subjects that international students want to study in the U.S.

1. What percentage of the world's adults can read and write? *A. Almost 80%.* **2.** How many international students study in the United States? *A. About 1/2 a million.* **3.** Is the number of students studying abroad going up or going down? *A. Going up—about 191,000 U.S. students study abroad per year.*

Before You Listen

Best Practice

Activating Prior Knowledge

The prelistening questions activate students' prior knowledge. This activity will help students relate their own experience of meeting new people to the new language in this chapter. When students activate their prior knowledge before learning new material, they are better able to map new language onto existing concepts, which aids understanding and retention.

1 Prelistening Questions 

- ❑ Have students look at the photo and try to guess what is happening.
- ❑ Have the students read the questions and discuss them in pairs.
- ❑ Compare answers as a whole class.
- ❑ As a whole class, make a list of phrases for introducing someone, for example, *Frank, this is Mary./Kaori, I'd like you to meet Lee.*

2 Previewing Vocabulary 

- ❑ Because this is the first chapter, take some time to explain that doing this activity will help the students understand the conversation that they will hear.
- ❑ Play the recording and ask students to listen to the words.
- ❑ Have students complete the vocabulary preview.
- ❑ Compare their answers as a whole class and write the correct answers on the board.
- ❑ Point out the note at the bottom of the page for *you guys*. Ask the students to give an example of a situation in which you would never use that expression (e.g., talking to your teachers).

ANSWER KEY

1. sounds 2. move into 3. stop by 4. No kidding! 5. (just) call me 6. came over 7. take 8. you guys

Listen

3 Listening for Main Ideas 

(The audioscript follows Activity 5.)

- ❑ Explain that these questions will help students focus on the main ideas in the listening activity. They do not need to understand every word to answer the questions. Tell them to focus on what they *do* understand, rather than worrying about what they *don't* understand.
- ❑ You may want to write the questions on the board.
- ❑ Ask the students if they have any questions.
- ❑ Ask students to close their books as they listen.
- ❑ Play the recording.
- ❑ After listening, have students compare their answers in pairs.

- ❑ Finally, go over the answers to the three questions with the whole class. Ask them for specific words or phrases they heard that support their answers.

ANSWER KEY

1. Jack and Ming already know each other. Peter and Jack have met but forgot each other's names.
2. Ming just moved into the building.
3. Peter will meet his new roommate. Ming and Jack will get something to eat.

4 Listening for Details 

(The audioscript follows Activity 5.)

- ❑ Tell the students to look at the three true-false questions. Make sure that they understand what *true* and *false* mean.
- ❑ Play the recording. Have the students write down their answers.
- ❑ Put the students in pairs to compare their answers.
- ❑ Go over the questions as a group. Ask for additional details from the conversation, e.g., Jack and Peter met last week. Ming doesn't speak Chinese well.

ANSWER KEY

1. F Ming was NOT born in Hong Kong. She was born in San Francisco.
2. F Peter, not Jack, plans to take a Chinese class.
3. F Jack and Peter are not roommates. Peter is now going to meet his new roommate.

STRESS

- ■ Read the instruction box about stress to the students. Ask them questions about stress (e.g., Which words are usually stressed? How are stressed words spoken?).

5 Listening for Stressed Words 

- ❑ Play the recording again. This time tell the students to keep their books open. Have the students repeat the phrase or sentence and then fill in the blanks. Students should fill in the blanks with the words that they hear.
- ❑ After listening, have students check their answers with a partner. Then have each pair check their answers with the audioscript in their books.
- ❑ Next, have students read the conversation with two partners, paying attention to stressed words in their pronunciation and intonation.
- ❑ While the students are reading the conversation, move around the room, giving the students feedback.

AUDIOSCRIPT AND ANSWER KEY

Jack: Hi! How are you doing?

Peter: Hi. You're . . . Jack, right?

Jack: Yeah. And, sorry, you're . . .?

Peter: Peter. Peter Riley.

Jack: Oh, yeah, we met on campus last week. Peter, this is my friend, Ming Lee. She's just moved into the building.

Peter: Hi, Ming Lee.

Ming: Nice to meet you. You can just call me Ming. Lee's my last name.

Peter: Oh. Ming. That sounds . . .?

Ming: Chinese.

Peter: Oh. So, you're from . . .

Ming: . . . from San Francisco. My parents came over from Hong Kong before I was born.

Peter: Oh, that's cool. Actually, uh, I was thinking of taking Chinese this term. Maybe you could help me.

Ming: Well, my Chinese really isn't very good . . .

Jack: Uh, listen, Peter. We're really hungry. Do you want to get something to eat with us?

Peter: Sorry, I can't. I have to go meet my new roommate.

Jack: Oh, OK. Well, stop by sometime. I'm up in 212.

Peter: Hey, I'm on the same floor. I'm in 220.

Jack: No kidding . . .

Peter: Well, nice meeting you, Ming. I'm sure I'll see you guys soon.

Ming and Jack: See you later.

REDUCTIONS 

- Read the *Reductions* box to the students. Ask them questions about reductions (e.g., What words are not stressed in a sentence?).
- Read the unreduced and reduced forms to the students. Have students repeat the two forms after you.

6 Comparing Unreduced and Reduced Pronunciation 

- ❑ Play the recording of the sentences in Activity 6. Ask the students to repeat both forms after the speaker.
- ❑ Put the students in pairs. Have the students take turns reading the unreduced and reduced forms of the sentences.
- ❑ NOTE: If your school has a language lab, this activity (as well as all others that require oral responses/repetition) is particularly suitable for a lab setting, where you can randomly monitor students and give individual feedback.

Content Note

- Some students may think of reduced forms as *incorrect*. Emphasize that these forms are commonly used in spoken English and it is important to be able to understand them. It is not essential for communication to use them, but if they do not use reduced forms, their English may sound too formal.

7 Listening for Reductions 

- ❑ Play the four recorded sentences.
- ❑ Tell the students to fill in the blanks in the activity.
- ❑ Check the answers together as a class.
- ❑ Put the students in pairs. Have the students take turns reading the sentences with reduced pronunciation.

ANSWER KEY

1. How are you feeling?
2. See you in an hour.
3. Jack, do you want to eat at the cafeteria?
4. When do you have to meet your roommate?

After You Listen

8 Reviewing Vocabulary 

- ❑ Review the vocabulary items in this activity.

come over (came over — past tense)

move into	call me ______
sounds	No kidding!
take	you guys*
stop by	

- ❑ Note: *You guys* is an informal expression used only with people you know very well. It's also commonly used to refer to both males and females.

- ❑ Put the students in pairs. Tell them to decide who will be Student A and Student B.
- ❑ Have each student look only at his or her page as instructed in the directions in the Student Book.
- ❑ Have the students ask and answer the questions.
- ❑ Check the answers as a class.

ANSWER KEY

Student A Questions	1.b 2.c 3.a
Student B Questions	1.c 2.a 3.b

Pronunciation

THE -*S* ENDING 

- ■ Read the *Pronunciation* instruction note.
- ■ Play the recording and have students listen and repeat.

9 Distinguishing Among -*s* Endings 

- ❑ Play the recording for Activity 9. Tell the students to write down the words that they hear in the left column.
- ❑ Play the recording a second time. Tell the students to listen carefully to the final -*s*. Tell the students to check the appropriate box at the right.
- ❑ Check the answers as a class.

ANSWER KEY

		/s/	/iz/	/z/
1.	plays	❑	❑	✓
2.	misses	❑	✓	❑
3.	hopes	✓	❑	❑
4.	stops	✓	❑	❑
5.	drives	❑	❑	✓
6.	phones	❑	❑	✓
7.	washes	❑	✓	❑
8.	summarizes	❑	✓	❑
9.	mothers	❑	❑	✓
10.	puts	✓	❑	❑

10 Pronouncing -*s* Endings 

- ❑ Give the students time to read the directions and the questions.
- ❑ Put the students in pairs.
- ❑ Tell the students to take turns asking and answering the questions. The students who are answering the questions should close their books and listen to the questions, not read them.
- ❑ While the students are doing the activity, walk around the room and monitor the pronunciation of /iz/, /s/, and /z/.

Using Language Functions

INTRODUCING YOURSELF AND OTHERS

- ■ Go over the instruction note *Introducing Yourself and Others*.
- ■ Read the expressions and have students repeat and practice them.

11 Making Introductions 

- ❑ Have the students sit in a circle. If they can't sit in a circle, you can try having them stand in a circle.
- ❑ Read directions—steps 1-4—to the students.
- ❑ Give the students cards. Tell the students to write their names on the cards.
- ❑ Tell the students to ask the four questions in Step 3 to a student next to them.
- ❑ Have the students move around the room, introducing their partner to the other students.
- ❑ Now read step 5 to the students.
- ❑ Read through the expressions on page 11 with your students and practice the examples.
- ❑ Tell the students to walk around the room using the expressions to find out the names that they have forgotten.
- ❑ Read the Culture Note on page 11 with the class. Ask the students to paraphrase the information in the box. On the board, write two columns labeled *Dos* and *Don'ts.* Have the students give you items for both columns.

Best Practice

Interacting with Others

The following activity is an example of collaborative learning to encourage fluency and confidence. In these role-plays, based around the topic of students meeting each other, communication is more important than grammar. Students can practice the role-plays in pairs and then improve their performance by switching roles or partners. By the time they perform the role-play for the class, they should feel more confident in the use of the new language.

12 Role-Play: A First Meeting 

- ❑ Have students look at the three-panel illustration in the activity.
- ❑ Ask the students to tell you the story. Help the students with new vocabulary (e.g., *tray, cafeteria*).
- ❑ Read the directions for the activity to the students. Give them some time to ask questions.
- ❑ Have the students work with a partner. Tell the students to write a dialogue for Joe and Meena.
- ❑ Have the students act out their dialogue in front of the class. Ask them to leave their papers at their desks so they don't read them.

REPRODUCIBLE **EXPANSION ACTIVITY**

- Please see Black Line Master "Who Will You Be in 20 Years?" on page BLM 1 of this Teacher's Edition.
- Photocopy and distribute one copy to each student.
- In Part 1, give the students five minutes to write down notes on their future life. They should describe where they will be living and what they will be doing.
- In Part 2, put the students in pairs. Read the directions and the example for the pair interview to them. Give the students five minutes to interview each other.
- Read the directions from Part 3. Have each pair of students walk around the room introducing their partner's future self to other pairs of students.
- After 10 minutes, have the students sit down.
- Tell the students to fill out the chart in Part 4 with information about other students' future lives.

Before You Listen

1 Prelistening Questions 

- ❑ Make three columns on the board. Write the three questions at the top of the columns.
- ❑ Read the questions to the students. Ask the students if they understand the questions.
- ❑ Put the students into groups of three or four. Tell the students to brainstorm a list of items for questions 1 and 2. For question 3, tell the groups that each student has to give a short description of his or her feelings on the first day.
- ❑ After 10-15 minutes, tell the students to write their answers in the appropriate columns on the board.
- ❑ Briefly go over the answers in the first two columns.
- ❑ Discuss the feelings listed in the third column. Ask the students whether there were more negative or positive feelings. Ask the students about their feelings on the first day of your class. Have their feelings changed?

2 Previewing Vocabulary 

- ❑ Play the recording and have students listen to the underlined words.
- ❑ Read the directions to the students. Tell the students to fill in the blanks with the correct definition for the underlined word.
- ❑ Have the students compare their answers with a partner.
- ❑ Check the answers as a class.

ANSWER KEY

1. d 2. a 3. b 4. e 5. c

Listen

Strategy

Hints for Taking Notes

Go over the *Hints for Taking Notes* box on page 13 with the students. Give the students some time to ask questions about the hints.

Best Practice

Organizing Information

This type of activity uses a graphic organizer in the form of note taking to categorize information. Taking lecture notes encourages students to process and organize information while they are listening and also provides a record for them to refer to when they are studying later. This type of graphic organizer emphasizes listing and categorizing skills. Other types of graphic organizers are used throughout this book.

3 Listening for Main Ideas 

- ❑ Have the students look at the photo for this activity. Ask the students to describe what is happening.
- ❑ Tell the students that they are going to listen to a long listening passage. Tell them that they will need to listen carefully and take notes. Tell them to get out a sheet of paper and a pencil.
- ❑ Play the recording of the advisor's presentation. Give the students a few minutes to write their notes. Walk around the room helping the students concentrate only on the main ideas.
- ❑ Play the recording a second time. Give the students a few more minutes to polish their notes.
- ❑ Have the students compare their notes with a partner.
- ❑ Have the students look at the *Main Ideas* box. Tell them to compare their notes to the notes in the box.

AUDIOSCRIPT

Hello, everybody. Welcome to the American Language Center. I'm Gina Richards, your academic advisor. You can all just call me Gina. I know today is your first day at our school, so you're probably a little nervous and maybe a little shy, too. So, I want to tell you right at the beginning: if you don't understand something, please ask questions. OK? And listen very carefully because we're going to give you a lot of important information—information that will make your experience here enjoyable and useful. OK, here we go.

Let me tell you about the plan for today. There are three things on your schedule. First, you will take a placement test. This test will measure your English level. You'll take a reading, grammar, and composition test. Oh, and also listening. A listening test. The whole placement test takes three hours.

Next, you will meet in small groups, with a teacher, for an orientation. This orientation meeting will be about important things you need to know, like where to buy your books, what types of classes you'll have, how to find a roommate, things like that. This is where you can ask a lot of questions.

Then finally, this afternoon, you will take a campus tour. We'll show you the main buildings where your classrooms are; you'll see some of the sports facilities, you know, the tennis courts, the swimming pool, places like that; and you'll also visit the library and the computer lab. I think you'll be surprised how large and how beautiful our campus is. All right. Are there any questions before we begin?

4 Listening for Specific Information 

(The audioscript follows Activity 3.)

- ❑ Show the students the *Main Ideas and Details* note-taking space.
- ❑ Tell the students that they are going to listen to the activity again and fill in the details in the space for note-taking.
- ❑ Play the recording again. Have students fill in the lecture details.

After You Listen

5 Summarizing Ideas 

- ❑ Put the students into pairs. Have them compare their answers.
- ❑ Tell the students to take turns summarizing the presentation to each other. Tell them to use their notes to help them with their summary.

6 Reviewing Vocabulary 

- ❑ Tell the students to read the five questions in this activity and ask questions about anything they don't understand.
- ❑ Put the students in pairs. Tell them to take turns asking each other the questions. Tell them to use the underlined words in their answers.

Best Practice

Cultivating Critical Thinking

The following Expansion Activity is an example of a collaborative team activity resulting in a final product. This type of activity requires students to process the information they have learned and apply it to a new situation. This involves reinterpretation, synthesis, and application of concepts. The process helps students evaluate whether they have understood the new material and helps them remember it better.

EXPANSION ACTIVITY

- Please see Black Line Master "Campus Tour" on page BLM 2 of this Teacher's Edition.
- Photocopy and distribute one copy to each student.
- Read the directions to the students. Tell the students that for homework, they must walk around their campus and list the places on campus that are important for new students. If their language school is not on a college campus, have the students walk around the area near their school.
- Tell the students to write down important details for each item on the list (e.g., Library—Open every day from 9:00 A.M. to 11:00 P.M.).
- When the class meets again, put the students in small groups. Have the students discuss their lists and construct a common list for the group. They should write their common list on a separate sheet of paper.
- At the end of the class, have the students turn in their common lists and details.

Best Practice

Scaffolding Instruction

The next activity raises metacognitive awareness of learning strategies. To understand language, we use surrounding context clues to work out the meanings of unfamiliar words. This activity asks students to use the words that they know in each piece of the conversation to work out the meanings of new words. By asking students to write the context clues, they are guided through the steps of developing this skill.

Focus on Testing

Getting Meaning from Context 

- Tell the students to read the *Getting Meaning From Context* instruction note.
- Point out to the students that this is a *Focus on Testing* activity. The skill taught in this activity will help students with standardized tests, such as the TOEFL® Internet-Based Test (iBT).
- Ask them to summarize the information in the instruction note to you. Clarify the information whenever it is necessary.
- Read the directions to the activity to the students.
- Show the students the chart on page 16. Tell them that they will hear a question and that they have to choose one of the three answers. They must write the context clues in the column to the right.
- Play the first part of the recording. Since this is the first time they are identifying context clues, listen to just the first part of the conversation and have them answer the questions and write down the clues. Elicit the clues from students and write them on the board to make sure students understand the concept of context clues.
- Play the rest of the recording, having students complete the answers and clues.
- After the recording is finished, check answers as a class.

ANSWER KEY

Answers	Clues
1. c. at a pizza restaurant	*cheese, pepperoni, mushrooms, hungry, medium, large*
2. c. teaching assistant	orientation, classes, Professor Murphy, his T.A., spends time answering questions and correcting homework
3. a. It's different from Japan.	surprised, came here, unusual, doesn't look like campus I come from
4. b. telephone, or call, between 8 A.M. and 5 P.M.	need to make a reservation, call tennis center, office open between 8 A.M. and 5 P.M.
5. b. play tennis together	Jack and I have a court for tomorrow, do you want to play doubles? Can you come, Ming?

AUDIOSCRIPT

Part 1

Peter: Let's get a medium with extra cheese and pepperoni on it.

Ming: Can we get mushrooms and tomatoes, too?

Kenji: I don't care. Just get a large one 'cause I'm really hungry.

Question 1: Where are the students?

Peter: This restaurant has got the best pizza on campus!

Part 2

Kenji: Yeah, they told me about this place at the orientation. So, Ming, how are your classes going?

Ming: Pretty good. Well, my chemistry class is a little boring. Professor Murphy knows the subject, but he's not a good teacher. Last week he was sick, and his T.A. was teaching the class. She was much better. This T.A. spends a lot of time answering our questions and correcting our homework.

Question 2: What do you think *T.A.* means?

Kenji: Teaching assistants aren't common in Japanese universities. The professors teach all the classes.

Part 3

Peter: Really?

Kenji: Uh huh. I was very surprised when I first came here. You know what else is unusual for me? All the facilities. I mean, the swimming pool, five tennis courts, the museum, even a post office! Faber College doesn't look like the college campus where I come from.

Question 3: What does Kenji think about the Faber College campus?

Kenji: It's completely different.

Part 4

Kenji: Speaking of tennis courts, I want to play tomorrow. Can I just go there or do I need to . . .

Peter: You need to make a reservation. Just call the tennis center and give them your ID number. You know, your student ID. They'll give you a reservation number. The office is open between 8 A.M. and 5 P.M.

Question 4: How can students make reservations for a tennis court?

Ming: Here's the phone number for reservations.

Part 5

Peter: Hey, Jack and I already have a court for tomorrow afternoon. Do you guys want to play doubles with us?

Kenji: Sounds good to me. Can you come, Ming?

Ming: Yeah. I have a class 'til 2:00. Let's meet there at 2:30.

Question 5: What are the students going to do tomorrow?

Kenji: You mean, meet at the tennis court, right?

Peter: Uh-huh. See you there.

Talk It Over

UNDERSTANDING BODY LANGUAGE

- Read the information about the importance of body language to the students.

1 Using Body Language 

- ❑ Show the students the photograph of the three students meeting on page 4.
- ❑ Put the students in pairs. Tell them to read and answer questions 1 and 2 about body language.
- ❑ Point out the illustrations on page 17. Have the students in small groups discuss the meanings of the eight gestures. Check their answers as a class.
- ❑ If there is time, elicit from the students other gestures that are important in their cultures. Tell the students that you do not want them to give you examples of gestures that have an offensive or bad meaning.
- ❑ Put the students in small groups. Have them act out the situations on page 17 using gestures.
- ❑ After five minutes, have various students come up to the front of the class and act out one of the situations. The class guesses which situation is being acted out.

Part 4 Real-World Tasks: Telephone Messages

Student Book pages 18–19

Best Practice

Making Use of Academic Content

The following activity exposes students to situations that they will face in an academic setting. The phone messages include communications with college friends, university departments, and fellow students.

1 Listening to Telephone Messages 

- ❑ Point to the image of the phone message. Read the message from Dr. Brown's office to the students. Play the sample telephone message.
- ❑ Read the directions and show students the six blank telephone message forms. Tell the students that as they hear the six messages, they must fill out the blank forms.
- ❑ Play the first message. Have the students write down the information.
- ❑ Play the other five messages one at a time, pausing in between each message if necessary.
- ❑ Put the students in pairs. Have them compare and discuss their notes about the messages.
- ❑ Play the six messages one more time without pausing between messages.
- ❑ Check the answers as a class.

ANSWER KEY

1. To: Kenji

From: Nancy from math class

Message: I'm sick and will probably stay home until Monday. Please call me anytime before 11.

Phone Number: 555-0149

2. To: Peter

From: Bud

Message: I want to go to a Latin jazz concert 8:30 Saturday night. I have two free tickets. If you want to go, call today. I'm at Sheri's house.

Phone Number: 555-0126

3. To: Kenji

From: Mrs. Henry of the international student office

Message: We still don't have your papers ready. Please call back next week.

Phone Number: Call the main number. My extension is 4745.

4. To: Peter

From: Research library

Message: We have a biology book with your name on it. If it's yours, pick it up at the front desk. Just show your student identification. Ask for Lisa or Dick.

5. To: Peter

From: Kevin Potter

Message: My advisor gave me your number. She said that you tutor students in math. I need help for my midterm exam. Are you available? How much do you charge?

Phone Number: 555-0118

6. To: Kenji

From: Honda World Service

Message: Your car is fixed. Please pick it up by 5:00 today. The charges came to $175.

AUDIOSCRIPT

Outgoing message

Recording: Hi. You have reached 555-0121. Sorry, but we can't come to the phone right now. If you want to leave a message for Peter, press one. If you want to leave a message for Kenji, press two. We'll call you back as soon as we can.

Example

Linda: Kenji, this is Linda from Dr. Brown's office. I'm calling to change your appointment. Unfortunately, Dr. Brown can't see you at two o'clock on Tuesday. But I can give you an appointment for Wednesday at 2:00. I hope that's convenient for you. Please let us know. Call us at 555-0162.

Message 1

Kelly: Kenji, this is Kelly from your math class. Remember me? I'm calling about this week's homework. I'm still sick and will probably stay home until Monday. So, like, uh, can you call me at 555-0149? Any time before 11:00 is OK. Thanks.

Message 2

Bud: Hi, Peter, it's Bud. Listen, want to go to a concert Saturday? It's a Latin jazz band, I think. My cousin has a couple of free tickets. Give me a call today if you're interested. I'm at Sheri's house, and her number is, uh, 555-0126. Or call me on my cell. The concert starts at 8:30, by the way. Talk to you later.

Message 3

Mrs. Henry: This is Mrs. Henry from the international student office, returning Kenji Suzuki's call. I'm sorry, but we still don't have your papers ready. Please check back next week; just call the main number and, uh, I'm at extension 4745.

Message 4

Don: Uh, yes, uh, this is the research library calling. Peter Riley, we have a biology book with your name and this phone number in it. If it's yours, you can pick it up at the front desk; just show your student identification. Ask for Lisa or Don.

Message 5

Kevin: Hello, Peter? Uh, my name is Kevin Potter. My advisor gave me your number; she said you work with students in math, and I need help studying for my midterm exam. Can you let me know if you're available and, uh, how much you charge for tutoring? My number is 555-0118. Thanks. Bye.

Message 6

Man: Kenji, this is Honda World Service calling. Your car's fixed. Please pick it up by 5:00 today. As we discussed, the charges came to $175.

2 Role-Play: Giving Telephone Messages 

- ❑ Read the directions to the students.
- ❑ Make sure that they understand that they will need to look at the telephone messages notes that they made in Activity 1.
- ❑ Have two students come up to the front of the class and read the sample message from Dr. Brown's office.
- ❑ Put the students into pairs. Tell them to decide which student is Kenji and which student is Peter.
- ❑ Have the students take turns reading their telephone messages to the other student. Kenji will read Peter's messages to Peter. Peter will read Kenji's messages to Kenji.

Strategy

Telephone Numbers

- Read and explain the information in the *Telephone Numbers* strategy box.
- Write several sample telephone numbers on the board. Read the first one. Have the students read it together after you. Explain to the students that sometimes the last four numbers are said individually or in pairs. For example, in 555-4257, the last four numbers may be pronounced *four-two-five-seven* or *forty-two-fifty-seven.*
- Choose individual students to read the remaining sample telephone numbers on the board.

3 Calling for Information 

- ❑ Read the directions.
- ❑ Point to the blank *Parking Permit Application* form.
- ❑ Play the recording of Ming's conversation with the parking office.
- ❑ Have the students fill out the form while they listen.

ANSWER KEY

PARKING PERMIT APPLICATION

FABER COLLEGE

Name: Lee Ming
Last First Middle Initial

Address: 3251 Washington Street

Phone: 555-0103

Car: Toyota Camry 2004
Make Model Year

License Plate: AWJ 130

☑ Fall Semester
❑ Spring Semester
❑ All year

Amount enclosed: $ 210.00

AUDIOSCRIPT

Ming: Hi, I'm calling to get a parking permit. Is parking lot nine available?

Admin: Yes, it is. What's your name, please?

Ming: Ming Lee. My first name is M-I-N-G.

Admin: M-I-N-D?

Ming: No. M as in mother, I as in India, N as in Nancy, and G as in girl. My last name is spelled L-E-E. That's L as in little, E-E.

Admin: OK, got it. Address?

Ming: 3251 Washington Street.

Admin: Daytime phone number?

Ming: Uh, 555-0103.

Admin: OK. What's the year and make of your car?

Ming: 2004 Toyota Camry.

Admin: License plate?

Ming: AWJ 130

Admin: One thirty or one thirteen?

Ming: One, three, oh.

Admin: OK. That'll be $210 for the semester or $420 for the year.

Ming: I just need it for the fall semester.

Admin: All right. So, just send in your payment for $210, and we'll send you a permit for lot number nine.

Ming: Great. Thank you very much.

Admin: You're welcome.

Ming: Bye.

4 Role-Play 

- ❑ Tell the students to read the directions.
- ❑ Put the students in pairs to check their answers in the parking permit application form.
- ❑ Have one student play the role of Ming. The other student will be the administrative assistant.
- ❑ Tell the student playing Ming to call the other student to begin the role-play.
- ❑ Ask for a few pairs of students to perform their role-play.

Self-Assessment Log

- ❑ The Self-Assessment Log at the end of each chapter helps students track their own strengths and weaknesses and also encourages them to take ownership of their own learning.
- ❑ Explain to students that thinking about their learning can help them decide what to focus on in their lessons and homework and help them chart their progress.
- ❑ Read the directions aloud and have students check vocabulary they learned in the chapter and are prepared to use. Have students check the strategies practiced in the chapter (or the degree to which they learned them).
- ❑ Put students in small groups. Ask students to find the information or an activity related to each strategy in the chapter.
- ❑ Tell students to find definitions in the chapter for any words they did not check.
- ❑ If possible, meet privately with each student on a regular basis and review his or her Self-Assessment Log. This provides an opportunity for the student to ask key questions and for you to see where additional help may be needed and to offer one-on-one encouragement.

Chapter 2

Experiencing Nature

In this chapter, students will listen to language about nature, weather, seasons, and vacations. In Part 1, they will hear a conversation about vacation plans. They will also practice listening for weather information and the difference between the words *can* and *can't*. In Part 2, they will listen to a story and practice listening for main ideas and specific information. In Part 3, they will practice talking about weather and the seasons. In Part 4, they will learn how to talk about temperatures in English. They will practice understanding weather forecasts. These topics will prepare students for discussing several common conversation topics with other students. They will be able to talk about weather, seasons, outdoor activities, and vacation plans.

Chapter Opener

- ❑ Have students look at the photo showing a man backpacking in Mount Robson Provincial Park in British Columbia, Canada. Ask the students the three questions in the Connecting to the Topic section. Discuss the questions with the class.
- ❑ Have the students look at the quote. Ask one student to read the quote. Give them some time to ask for clarification of any words they don't understand. Ask the students as a class to explain what the quote means.

" In every walk with nature, one receives far more than he seeks "

— John Muir
American naturalist (1838–1914)

Chapter Overview

Listening Skills and Strategies

Listening for main ideas

Listening for details

Distinguishing between *can* and *can't*

Listening to a story about camping

Listening to weather forecasts

Speaking Skills and Strategies

Discussing vacation plans

Talking about abilities

Talking about the weather and seasons

Using expressions of likes and dislikes

Critical Thinking Skills

Interpreting a photo

Using a T-chart to compare two sides of a topic

Distinguishing main ideas from details

Summarizing ideas using key words

Vocabulary Building

Terms to express abilities

Terms to describe the weather and seasons

Terms to talk about likes and dislikes

Pronunciation

Identifying and practicing stressed words

Comparing reduced and unreduced pronunciation

Pronouncing *can* and *can't*

Focus on Testing

Using context clues to identify seasons

Vocabulary

Nouns	Verb	Adjectives	Expressions
chance of	get a tan	chilly	couldn't wait (can't wait)
degrees		clear	how come
fair skies		extra	it's raining cats and dogs
fall		freezing	
hiking		incredible	
showers		muddy	
spring		overnight	
summer		partly cloudy	
weather forecast		scared	
winter		sick of (verb + *-ing*)	

Can You Guess?

- Tell students they are not expected to know the answers to the questions below. Their purpose is to stimulate discussion.
- Ask students to discuss the questions in groups and compare answers with the correct answers.
- Ask students about their favorite national park, in the U.S. or in any country.

1. What are the highest and lowest recorded temperatures in the world? *A. Highest: El Azizia, Libya; Sept 13, 1922: 136°F/58°C. Coldest: Vostok, Antarctica; July 21, 1983: -129°F/-89°C.* **2.** Where can you see the sun rise and set only once a year? *A. Antarctica.* **3.** Which national park in the United States gets the most Visitors? *A. Great Smokey Mountain National Park (10.25 million visitors/year).*

Before You Listen

Best Practice

Activating Prior Knowledge

The prelistening questions connect new concepts to students' prior knowledge. This activity will help students relate their own experiences of taking outdoor vacations to the new language in this chapter. When students activate their prior knowledge before learning new material, they are better able to map new language onto existing concepts, which aids understanding and retention.

1 Prelistening Questions 

- ❑ Point to the illustration of Ming, Jack, and Peter.
- ❑ Put the students in pairs. Have the pairs discuss the two questions.
- ❑ Have each pair of students report their thoughts to the class.
- ❑ As the students report on their perfect outdoor vacation, write down interesting and important vocabulary that comes up.

2 Previewing Vocabulary 

- ❑ Play the recording and ask students to listen to the words. Remind students that they may not understand all of the words and phrases yet, but they will as they work through the sentences.
- ❑ Have students read the sentences and fill in the blanks with the words and phrases from the list. Encourage them to guess the meanings of unknown vocabulary based on the context of the sentences.
- ❑ Put the students in pairs. Tell them to discuss their answers.
- ❑ Go through the sentences as a class asking students to volunteer the answers.

ANSWER KEY

1. how come; it's raining cats and dogs outside 2. get a tan 3. chance of 4. degrees 5. sick of 6. weather forecast 7. freezing 8. extra

Listen 

3 Listening for Main Ideas

(The audioscript follows Activity 5.)

- ❑ Have the students read the directions silently.
- ❑ Explain that the questions will help students focus on the main ideas in the listening.
- ❑ Tell the students to read the questions in their books, then read the questions aloud.
- ❑ Ask the students if they have any questions.
- ❑ Ask students to close their books as they listen.
- ❑ Play the recording.

- After listening, have students compare their answers in pairs.
- Finally, go over the answers to the three questions as a class. Ask the students for specific words or phrases they heard that support their answers.
- As the students give their answers, write new vocabulary that comes up on the board.

ANSWER KEY

1. Peter wants to go on vacation because he's sick of studying.
2. Ming wants to go to the mountains, especially in the winter. She loves snowboarding.
3. Jack and Peter both want to go to a warm, sunny place. Peter wants to lie on a beach and Jack wants to go swimming and snorkeling.

4 Listening for Details 

(The audioscript follows Activity 5.)

- Go over the Culture Note on page 26. Ask the students to describe the normal school year in their country.
- Keep the students in the same pairs from Activity 3.
- Tell the students to read the three true-false questions. Play the recording again if necessary.
- Have them discuss and answer the questions.
- Go over the questions as a group. Ask for additional details from the conversation (e.g., Ming is going to Bear Mountain in December./ The conversation takes place in October./Jack and Peter like warm weather.).

ANSWER KEY

1. F 2. F 3. T

5 Listening for Stressed Words 

- Play the recording again. This time tell the students to keep their books open.
- Have students write the missing words.
- After listening, have students check their answers with a partner. Then have each pair check their answers with the audioscript in their books.

AUDIOSCRIPT and ANSWER KEY

Peter: Wow. Look. It's raining cats and dogs—again! I hate this weather. When does winter break start?

Jack: Winter break? It's only October.

Peter: I know, but I'm sick of studying. I want to go someplace warm and lie on the beach for a week. Someplace where it's sunny and dry. Florida or Hawaii, maybe?

Jack: Yeah. Where we can go swimming and snorkeling and get a great tan. Now that's my idea of a perfect vacation.

Ming: Not mine. I can't swim very well, and I don't like lying in the sun.

Peter: Oh, yeah? How come?

Ming: I don't know. I just prefer the mountains, especially in winter. I love snowboarding. In fact, I'm planning to go to Bear Mountain with some friends in December. Do you guys want to come?

Jack: No thanks. I went there last year. I was freezing the whole time. Anyway, I don't know how to ski very well. Last year, I fell about a hundred times.

Ming: Peter, how about you?

Peter: Sorry, I'm like Jack. I don't want to go anyplace where it's below 70 degrees.

Jack: By the way, what's the weather forecast for tomorrow?

Ming: The same as today. Cloudy, cold, and a 90 percent chance of rain.

Jack: Oh, no! I left my umbrella at the library.

Ming: You can borrow mine. I've got an extra one.

Reductions

6 Comparing Unreduced and Reduced Pronunciation

- ❑ Read the directions to the students.

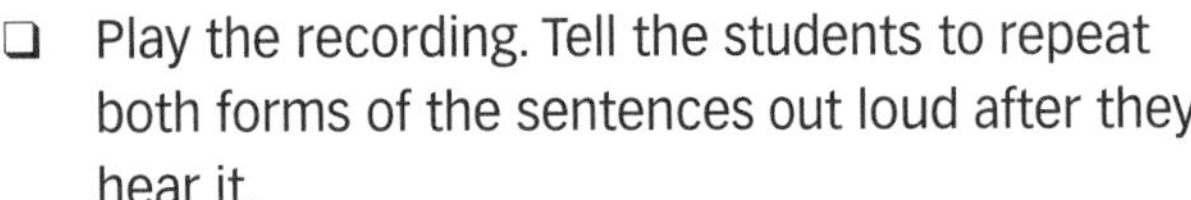

- ❑ Play the recording. Tell the students to repeat both forms of the sentences out loud after they hear it.
- ❑ Listen to the class. Give the students general feedback on their reductions.
- ❑ Ask individual students to volunteer to say each form and give individual feedback.
- ❑ NOTE: As noted in Chapter 1, if your school has a language lab, this activity (as well as all others that require oral responses/repetition) is particularly suitable for a lab setting, where you can randomly monitor students and give individual feedback.

7 Listening for Reductions 

- ❑ Tell the students to read the directions. Give them some time to ask questions about anything that they don't understand.
- ❑ Tell them to look at the conversation with the blanks.
- ❑ Play the recording. Have students write in the answers.
- ❑ Divide the students into groups of three. Have them take parts and read the dialogue. Tell the students to focus on pronouncing the reduced forms correctly.
- ❑ Have the students look at their line, look up, and then say it. Tell them not to read directly from the book.
- ❑ Walk around the room giving pronunciation feedback to the students.

AUDIOSCRIPT

Jack: Hi, Ming. Hi, Peter.

Ming and Peter: Hey, Jack.

Ming: What's happening?

Jack: I'm going to the campus recreation center. Do you want to come?

Ming: What are you going to do there?

Jack: Well, it's a nice day. We can swim and lie in the sun.

Ming: Thanks, but I don't want to go. I'm too tired.

Jack: How about you, Peter?

Peter: I can't. I've got to stay at home and study. Maybe tomorrow.

After You Listen

8 Using Vocabulary 

- ❑ Put the students into pairs.
- ❑ Tell the students to ask each other the questions. The person asking the question should try to look at the other person when asking; in other words, try to read, look up, and then ask the question. The person answering the question should have his or her book closed.
- ❑ Emphasize to the students the importance of using the underlined vocabulary in their answers.
- ❑ As a class, go through the questions. Have several students give answers to each question.

Pronunciation

CAN OR CAN'T 

- Read the *Pronunciation* box.
- Give the students some time to ask questions.

- Say some *can* and *can't* sentences to the students. (e.g., I can't eat a big breakfast. / I can swim. / I can speak two languages. / I can't go to the party on Friday.) Ask them whether you said *can* or *can't*. When they seem to be distinguishing between the two words, move on to the activity.

9 Distinguishing Between *Can* and *Can't* 

- ❑ Read the directions to the students. Make sure that they understand that "affirmative" refers to *can* and that "negative" refers to *can't*.
- ❑ Play the recording.
- ❑ Put the students in pairs to check their answers.
- ❑ If the students are unsure of some of the answers, play the recording one more time.
- ❑ Check the answers as a class, writing the correct answers on the board.

ANSWER KEY

1. Can't	6. Can
2. Can	7. Can't
3. Can	8. Can
4. Can't	9. Can't
5. Can't	10. Can

AUDIOSCRIPT

1. She can't swim very well
2. Michael can drive.
3. The boys can cook.
4. I can't find his phone number.
5. Kenji can't speak Spanish.
6. He can speak Japanese.
7. I can't understand him.
8. Peter can come with us.
9. She can't take photographs in the rain.
10. Herb can play tennis very well.

Using Language Functions

TALKING ABOUT ABILITIES

- Read the information about using *can* and *can't* to talk about abilities.
- Look at the expressions. Give the students examples. Then have students give you sample sentences, e.g., I'm not able to play the violin. / I know how to play the piano. / I wish I could speak many foreign languages. Write them on the board.

Strategy

Graphic Organizer: T-Chart

- Go over the information about T-charts with the students. Show them the example in the next activity.
- Ask the students to give you an additional example of some information that could be effectively organized with a T-chart.

10 Talking About Abilities 

- ❑ Read the directions for the activity. Show the students the chart.
- ❑ Have the students fill in the chart.
- ❑ When they have filled in the chart, put the students in pairs and have them tell their partner about their abilities.

REPRODUCIBLE EXPANSION ACTIVITY

- Please see Black Line Master "Outdoor Activities" on page BLM 3 of this Teacher's Edition.
- Photocopy and distribute one copy to each student.
- Put the students into small groups.
- Read the directions to the students.
- Ask the students to brainstorm words and phrases for each box.

- Give the students ten minutes to fill in the boxes.
- Draw two columns on the board and label them *Outdoor activities that you can do in the summer* and *Outdoor activities that you can do in the winter*. Ask the students to tell you what you can and can't do in the summer and winter.
- Show the students the two questions at the bottom of the sheet. Ask them to write down their answers and then ask each other the questions.

Before You Listen

1 Prelistening Questions 

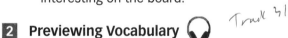

- ❑ Put the students in pairs.
- ❑ Have them read and discuss the prelistening questions.
- ❑ As a class, go through the questions. Write new vocabulary words or phrases that are useful or interesting on the board.

2 Previewing Vocabulary 

- ❑ Play the recording and have students listen to the underlined words.
- ❑ Tell the students to read the directions.
- ❑ Have the students answer the questions individually.
- ❑ Tell the students to compare their answers with a partner.
- ❑ Check the answers as a class, writing the correct answers on the board.

ANSWER KEY

1.d 2.e 3.b 4.f 5.c 6.a

Listen

3 Listening for Main Ideas 

- ❑ Show the students the photo for this listening section. Ask the students to describe what is happening.
- ❑ Tell the students that they are going to listen to a long conversation.
- ❑ Have them read the directions for the activity and ask questions about anything that they don't understand.
- ❑ Read the two questions to the students.
- ❑ Ask the students to make guesses about what will happen in the story.
- ❑ Play the recording.
- ❑ Put the students in groups of three or four and have them discuss the questions.
- ❑ Go over the questions as a class.

AUDIOSCRIPT

Motel Manager: You're all wet and muddy. What happened to you?

Woman: You're not going to believe this! It's the most incredible thing! It all started when we decided to go hiking this morning.

Man: Yeah, the weather was sunny and clear when we got up. So we put on shorts and T-shirts and went hiking. Half an hour later, it started raining cats and dogs!

Woman: So we hiked back to our tent as fast as we could. We couldn't wait to change into dry clothes.

Man: Right. But when we went into our tent, we couldn't find our clothes! So we went back outside to look around. And then we saw the craziest thing. Two great big brown bears came out of the woods, and guess what? They were wearing our clothes!

Manager: Aw, come on. That's impossible! What do you mean, the bears were wearing your clothes?

Man: Well, one bear had my T-shirt around his neck. And the other one had Mary's pants over his head. We still don't know where the rest of our clothes are!

Manager: [laughing]

Woman: I know it sounds funny, but we were so scared! Those bears were big! And now we have a big problem.

Manager: What's that?

Woman and Man: We don't have any dry clothes to wear!

Best Practice

Organizing Information

This type of activity uses a graphic organizer in the form of note-taking to categorize information. In this specific activity, the organizer is a partially completed list of the events in the story. The list encourages students to process and organize information while they are listening and also provides a record for them to refer to when they are summarizing the story later. This type of graphic organizer emphasizes narration. Other types of graphic organizers are used throughout this book.

4 Taking Notes on Specific Information 

- ❑ Read the directions and emphasize that the students are to write down key words only.
- ❑ Show the students the sentences with the blanks. Ask the students what *hr* means. Explain that when people take notes, they often use abbreviations for words (e.g., *w/o* for "without," *e.g.* for "for example").
- ❑ Play the recording.
- ❑ After the recording, give the students several minutes to finish writing down their notes.

After You Listen

5 Summarizing Ideas 

- ❑ Tell the students to read the directions.
- ❑ Put the students in pairs and tell them to take turns summarizing the story.
- ❑ Tell them to look at their notes when they need a reminder of the events.
- ❑ When the summaries are finished, put the students in groups of three.
- ❑ Tell them to role-play the story. Have each group decide who will play the role of the man, the woman, and the hotel manager.
- ❑ After the role-plays are finished, ask for volunteers to do the role-play in front of the class.

6 Reviewing Vocabulary 

- ❑ Play the recording and ask students to listen to the words.
- ❑ Read the directions to the students. Point to the picture that they will be describing.
- ❑ Go over the vocabulary with the students. Make sure that they understand the words.
- ❑ Put the students in small groups. Tell them to take turns telling what is happening in the photo.
- ❑ As a class, have students take turns making sentences about the picture. Write the sentences on the board, underlining the new vocabulary.

Talk It Over

7 Fact or Fiction Game 

- ❑ Bring some index cards to class. Take out enough cards for the number of students in your class.
- ❑ On half of the cards, write *Fact*; on the other half, write *Fiction*. Make sure that the students all understand the meanings of the two words.

- ❑ Read the directions to the students. Give them some time to ask questions.
- ❑ Hand out the cards to the students. Make sure that the other students cannot see the word on their cards.
- ❑ Give them five minutes to think about their stories.
- ❑ Ask for volunteers to tell their stories.
- ❑ After each story finishes, ask the class to vote on whether the story was fact or fiction. For each student's story, count the number of people who guessed incorrectly.
- ❑ At the end, have the student or students with the best scores stand up to be congratulated with a round of applause.

8 Role-Play 

1. Discuss the questions.

- ❑ Put the students in groups of three.
- ❑ Tell the students to read the questions and ask them if they understand them.
- ❑ Show the students the photo in the activity. Explain any words that they don't understand (e.g., footprint).
- ❑ Give the students five minutes to discuss the two questions.
- ❑ Have the groups take turns telling you their answers. If none of the groups understand the sign, tell the students the meaning. You shouldn't take anything from the park (e.g., rocks or plants), and you shouldn't leave anything behind (e.g., garbage).

Best Practice

Cultivating Critical Thinking

This is an example of an authentic problem-solving activity. This type of task-based activity requires students to process the information they have learned and apply it to a real situation. Students must make up their own ending to a story using information from their own experiences. This involves reinterpretation, synthesis, and application of concepts. The process of manipulating language and concepts in this way will create deeper processing of new material which will allow students to evaluate whether they have understood the new material and help them remember it better.

2. Role-play the situation.

- ❑ Read the Culture Note to the students. Give them time to ask questions about the vocabulary. Ask them to paraphrase the Culture Note back to you. This will show you whether or not they have really understood the Culture Note.
- ❑ Read the role-play to the students. Again, ask the students to paraphrase the situation back to you.
- ❑ Tell the students to look at the expressions for *Explaining Rules*. Ask the students to give you one or two sample sentences for each expression, e.g., It's against the rules to leave garbage in the campground.
- ❑ Divide the students into groups of three. Tell the students to decide who is George, Lou, and Rick.
- ❑ Have the students do the role-play. When the groups are all finished, ask a group to volunteer to do their role-play in front of the class.

Getting Meaning from Context

1 Prelistening Discussion 

- Have students look at the four photos of the seasons (spring, summer, fall, winter).
- Read the directions for the activity and the two questions below. Make sure that all of the students understand the words in English for the seasons. Tell them that we also use the word *autumn* to describe fall.
- Ask the students what months are usually associated with the seasons in their city.
- Put the students in pairs. Have them discuss the questions.
- After they have discussed the questions, go over the answers as a class.

Content Note

The concept of "four seasons" is prevalent through much of Europe and North America. Temperature may be the main factor in differentiating the seasons along with trees losing their leaves or flowers blooming. In many parts of the world, however, people may talk about three seasons or five seasons that depend more on the amount of rain than on changes in temperature. Students may talk about "wet" seasons and "dry" seasons.

Best Practice

Scaffolding Instruction

This is an example of an activity that raises metacognitive awareness of learning strategies. In real life, we use surrounding context clues to work out the meanings of unfamiliar words. This activity asks students to use the words that they know in each piece of the conversation to work out the meanings of new words. By asking students to write the clues, they are guided through the steps of developing this skill.

Focus on Testing

Using Context Clues 

- Read the directions to the students.
- Give the students some time to ask for clarification.
- Show the students the table with the columns *Seasons* and *Clues*.
- Play the first conversation. Tell the students to write the name of the season in the *Seasons* column in the table. Tell them to write the clue words in the *Clues* column. Although they did this type of activity in Chapter 1, if you think they need clarification about the concept of context clues, you can go over the first conversation together and elicit the clues from students and write them on the board.
- Play the remaining four conversations and have students complete the table.
- Put the students in pairs. Have them compare their answers.
- Go over the answers as a class.
- If there is time, have the students look at the audioscripts on page 212 and read the dialogues with a partner.

ANSWER KEY

1. fall/autumn 2. winter 3. spring 4. summer 5. summer

AUDIOSCRIPT

Conversation 1

A: Nice weather we're having.

B: Yes. Isn't it a nice surprise? At this time, it's usually much cooler and raining already.

A: Well, this weather will probably end soon; all the leaves on the trees are brown, and the nights are getting cold.

Conversation 2

A: Take your coat; it's freezing outside.

B: Nah, I'm only going to the corner store. I'll be back in five minutes.

A: I'm telling you, it's in the low 30s out there. Do you want to get sick?

Conversation 3

A: How do you like all this rain?

B: Well, it's good for the trees and flowers.

A: Yes, it's nice to see the leaves coming back on the trees again.

B: Yeah, and I'm glad the snow is all gone.

Conversation 4

A: Is it hot enough for you?

B: Whew . . . it sure is. I don't mind the heat so much. It's the humidity that bothers me. Look, I'm all wet.

A: Me too. Let's go get a cold drink somewhere.

B: Yeah, someplace with air conditioning.

Conversation 5

A: Ah, this is the life. No traffic, no worries. Just lie here and enjoy doing nothing.

B: Honey, your back is turning red. If you're not careful, you're going to get sunburned.

A: Could you put some sunscreen on my back?

Talk It Over

Best Practice

Interacting with Others

This type of activity is an example of collaborative learning to encourage fluency and confidence. In this information gap activity, based around the topic of weather and seasons, communication is more important than grammar. In the process of filling out a chart, the students use English to complete a task. They have to practice and develop communication strategies and listen carefully to their partner.

2 Talking About Seasons 

- ❑ Take some time to explain that each student looks at a chart that has missing information. Their partner has the information that they need to complete their chart. They have information that their partner needs.
- ❑ Read the directions to the students. Give them some time to ask questions about the procedure.
- ❑ Read the sample sentences to the students.
- ❑ Put the students in pairs. Have them decide who Student A is and who Student B is.
- ❑ Show the students the two charts. Tell them to look only at the chart that is for them.
- ❑ Give the students at least 15 minutes to do the activity. When the pairs have finished, tell them to look at the other chart to check their answers.

ANSWER KEY

Seasons:	Winter	Spring	Summer	Fall
Months:	December–February	March–May	June–August	September–November
Weather:	cold rainy cloudy snowy wet gray	warm cool rainy	hot humid sunny	cool cloudy windy rainy

EXPANSION ACTIVITY

- The students have just talked about the seasons and the typical weather in each season in New York. Follow up that activity by having the students talk about the real weather in their city.
- Tell the students to make a season chart for their hometown that is similar to the chart that they filled out in the "Talk it Over" activity.
- Put the students into groups.
- Tell the students to take turns telling each other about their hometown. How many seasons are there? What is the weather like in each season? What is the best time of year in their city?
- When the students have finished their discussions, have each student give a brief description of the weather and seasons in his or her city.

Best Practice

Making Use of Academic Content

This is an example of an activity that exposes students to situations that they will actually face in their life in a college or university. The weather is probably the most common topic for small talk. The conversations in this activity include a variety of realistic conversations in different situations.

1 Listening for Temperatures 

- ❑ In this activity, most of the temperatures in the conversations are in Fahrenheit. In one of the conversations, however, the temperature is in Celsius and the word *Celsius* is used. Spend a few minutes at the beginning of the activity making sure that everyone understands the difference between the two systems. Have the students give some Celsius temperatures and the corresponding Fahrenheit temperatures (e.g., 100 degrees Celsius = 212 degrees Fahrenheit). (They can look at the picture of the thermometer for help.) These correspondences don't have to be exact. One other concept that they will need to understand for this activity is *below zero* (e.g., *10 degrees below zero* or more simply *10 below*). Write one or two examples of temperatures that are below zero on the board.
- ❑ Read the directions to the activity. Show the students the temperatures that they will be circling.
- ❑ Read the Language Tip box. Ask the students to use the *in the* construction to tell you the temperature in your classroom. Write the answer on the board.
- ❑ Play the recording and have the students answer the questions.
- ❑ Put the students in pairs to check their answers. If they aren't sure of some of the answers, play the conversations again.
- ❑ Check the answers as a class.

ANSWER KEY

1. 95 2. 80s 3. 30s 4. 40 5. 103 6. 30 7. -13 8. 70s

AUDIOSCRIPT

Conversation 1

A: What's the weather like today?

B: Hot and humid and about 95 degrees.

Conversation 2

A: I'm going to take a swim. Want to come?

B: Is the pool heated?

A: Sure. It's probably over 80 degrees.

Conversation 3

A: How was your skiing holiday?

B: Great! The weather was in the thirties and we had perfect snow conditions.

Conversation 4

A: Let's go for a walk.

B: What's it like out?

A: About 40 degrees, but the wind has stopped.

B: Thanks, but I think I'll stay inside where it's warm.

Conversation 5

A: It's a hundred and three in here! Why don't you turn on the air conditioning?

B: It's broken.

Conversation 6

A: How was the weather in Europe this summer?

B: Just lovely. Hot, but never over 30 degrees.

A: Thirty? Oh, you mean Celsius.

Conversation 7

A: What's wrong?

B: It's 13 below outside and I can't find my gloves.

A: Here. Use mine. I have an extra pair.

Conversation 8

A: Did you check the weather forecast?

B: Yeah. It's supposed to be in the high seventies this weekend.

A: The seventies? I guess we can forget about skiing.

2 Talking About Temperatures

- ❑ The key to this activity is making sure that the students have access to the information that they need. If they have access to the Internet, that will simplify things a great deal. Otherwise, you may have to find a daily newspaper with the temperatures from cities around the world and photocopy the appropriate weather section.
- ❑ This activity can be very simple or you can make it into an elaborate task to find real-world information, bring it back to the class, and report on it. You can have the students report on the weather for the day of the class, or you can have them give a five-day forecast, which will give them an opportunity to practice future tenses.
- ❑ Read the directions to the class. Give them some time to ask for clarification of anything that they don't understand.
- ❑ Read the sample dialogue to the students.
- ❑ Give each student a slip of paper with the name of a major city in the world on it.
- ❑ Give the students time to find the information.
- ❑ Have each student stand up in front of the class and give his or her information on the temperature.

3 Previewing Vocabulary 

- ❑ Play the recording and have students listen to the underlined words.
- ❑ Read the directions to the students. Have the students match the sentences and definitions.
- ❑ Give the students five minutes to complete the activity.
- ❑ Have the students check their answers with a partner.
- ❑ Go over the answers as a class.

ANSWER KEY

1.b 2.e 3.c 4.d 5.a

Best Practice

Activating Prior Knowledge

This is an example of an activity that helps students map what they know about the real world into a framework in English. This activity asks students to use the knowledge that they already have about weather in their native language and the knowledge of vocabulary for weather in English to understand a listening passage in English. By asking students to map concepts about weather onto this chart, we are helping the students put everything that they know about weather together into a coherent whole.

4 Listening to a Weather Forecast 

1. Taking Notes

- ❑ Read the directions to the students.
- ❑ Point out the illustration.
- ❑ Go through the chart with the students showing them the four days at the top and the information categories along the left side. Give the students some time to ask questions.
- ❑ Tell the students to fill in the chart as they listen to the recording. Play the recording.
- ❑ Put the students in groups of four. Have the students go through the chart and compare their answers. If they can't agree on some items, play the recording again.
- ❑ Check the answers as a class.

2. Summarizing

- ❑ Read the directions to the students. Have one student paraphrase the directions back to you to check comprehension.
- ❑ Have the groups of four students take turns summarizing the weather of one of the days.
- ❑ Walk around the room helping students with their summaries.
- ❑ When the groups have finished, choose students to summarize a day's weather for the class, without telling which day they're summarizing. Have the class listen and guess which day the student is describing.

ANSWER KEY

	Friday	Saturday	Sunday	Monday
Sky: (Cloudy? Fair?)	partly cloudy	fair skies	fair	(not stated, but probably cloudy since there's a chance of rain)
Temperature:				
High:	61	sixties	70	---
Low:	mid-fifties	45	below 50	---
Rain: (Yes? No?)	yes	no	no	yes, 50% chance

AUDIOSCRIPT

This is the National Weather Service report at 5:00 in the afternoon, Friday. The forecast for the Bear Mountain area is partly cloudy with some showers through the night, clearing by early morning. The high today was 61 degrees; overnight lows will be in the mid-fifties. Tomorrow's highs will be in the sixties with fair skies continuing throughout the day. Temperatures will drop Saturday night to a chilly low of 45 degrees. Sunday will continue fair, warming up to a high temperature of 70 degrees. Sunday night lows will get down below 50 again. There will be a 50 percent chance of rain on Monday.

Using Language Functions

EXPRESSIONS FOR TALKING ABOUT ACTIVITIES YOU LIKE AND DISLIKE

- Go over the chart with the students.
- Complete the sentences. Then have students give some examples of activities they like and dislike. For example, I like to dance./ I enjoy dancing./ I'm crazy about riding horses./ I don't care for baseball.

5 Interview 

- ❑ Read the directions to the students.
- ❑ Read the sample sentences to the students.
- ❑ Put the students in pairs. Tell the pairs to start asking each other about their favorite activities.
- ❑ When the pairs have finished the interviews, go over the boxes of the chart one by one asking the class to tell you what their favorite activities were.

REPRODUCIBLE

EXPANSION ACTIVITY

- Please see Black Line Master "Class Picnic—It's a Potluck" on page BLM 4 of this Teacher's Edition.
- Photocopy and distribute one copy to each student.
- Ask the students to explain the meaning of the word *picnic*. What kinds of activities and food are there? Explain the expression *potluck*, an event where everyone brings some food that is shared with the group.
- Put the students into small groups.
- Go over the directions with the students. Explain that they must plan a real picnic that the class could possibly have.
- Go over the activities in the first section. Make sure that the students understand all of the vocabulary (e.g., *take a nap*).
- Give the students 15 or 20 minutes in class. Allow them to do some research outside of class. Then give the students some time the next day to discuss their research.
- Have each group stand up in front of the class and present their picnic.
- Have the class take notes and then vote on the best picnic.

Self-Assessment Log

- ❑ The purpose of the log is to help the students reflect on their learning.
- ❑ Read the directions aloud and have students check vocabulary that they learned in the chapter and are prepared to use.
- ❑ Have students check the strategies they understand.
- ❑ Put students in small groups. Ask students to find the information or an activity related to each strategy in the chapter.
- ❑ Tell students to find definitions in the chapter for any words they did not check, or they can look in their dictionaries.

Chapter

3

Living to Eat, or Eating to Live?

In this chapter, students will listen to and use language for food and meals. In Part 1, they will hear a conversation about shopping. They will also practice listening for the pronunciation difference between *teens* and *tens*. In Part 2, they will listen to a show about eating right. Students will also practice listening for main ideas and specific information. In Part 3, they will learn how to talk about different eating places. They will also practice ordering food in a restaurant. In Part 4, they will learn vocabulary and expressions for recipes. These topics will prepare students for a wide variety of situations involving food.

Chapter Opener

- ❑ Have students look at the photo of the family reunion. Ask the students the three questions in the Connecting to the Topic section. Discuss the questions with the students.
- ❑ Give them some time to ask for clarification of anything that they don't understand. Ask the students what they think the quote means.

“ Tomatoes and oregano make it Italian; wine and tarragon make it French. Sour cream makes it Russian; lemon and cinnamon make it Greek. Soy sauce makes it Chinese; garlic makes it good. ”

—Alice May Broc
American author (1941–

Chapter Overview

Listening Skills and Strategies

Listening for main ideas

Listening for details

Distinguishing between *teens* and *tens*

Listening to radio advice on healthy eating

Connecting native foods to their locations

Speaking Skills and Strategies

Interviewing people about food shopping

Using count and non-count nouns in questions

Comparing eating habits at home and when traveling

Ordering food

Refusing food politely

Critical Thinking Skills

Interpreting a photo

Interviewing with possible follow-up questions

Taking notes on causes and effects

Explaining a process

Speculating on the outcome of a situation

Vocabulary Building

Terms used in shopping for food at a market

Terms to talk about healthy eating

Count and Non-count nouns to express quantities of food

Terms for ordering food in a restaurant

Polite refusals

Pronunciation

Identifying and practicing stressed words

Comparing reduced and unreduced pronunciation

Pronouncing *teens* and *tens*

Focus on Testing

Using context clues to guess seasons

Vocabulary

Nouns	Verbs	Expression
aisle	beat	in line
calories	cut down on	
decay	dip	
fiber	fry	
groceries	gain	
ingredients	melt	
pound	serve	
produce	skip	
quart	take checks	
source		
tofu		
vitamins and minerals		

Can You Guess?

- Ask students to discuss the questions in groups and compare answers with the correct answers.
- The price of gold changes. Check the price to see of number 2 is still accurate.

1. What is the most popular food worldwide? *A. Rice.* **2.** Are some foods more expensive (by weight) than gold? Can you name any? *A. Yes. A 35-ounce (1 kilogram) white truffle sold for over US$100,000.** **3.** In the U.S. what percent of all restaurant income comes from fast food sales? *A. 40%.*

Footnotes:
* Source: CNN International, Nov. 22, 2005.

Before You Listen

Best Practice

Activating Prior Knowledge

The prelistening questions activate students' prior knowledge. This activity will help students relate their own experience of shopping for groceries to the new language in this chapter. When students activate their prior knowledge before learning new material, they are better able to map new language onto existing concepts, which aids understanding and retention.

1 Prelistening Questions 

- ❑ Have students look at the photo and describe what is happening.
- ❑ Have the students read the two questions and discuss them in pairs.
- ❑ Compare answers as a whole class.

2 Previewing Vocabulary 

- ❑ Play the recording and ask students to listen to the words.
- ❑ Read through the vocabulary list making sure that the students understand all of the words and phrases. Point out the notes that accompany the asterisked items (see below). Explain the difference between the verb *pro-**DUCE*** and the noun ***PRO**-duce*.
- ❑ Tell students to read through the sentences and ask questions about any words or expressions that they do not understand (e.g., *pretty* as an adverb).
- ❑ Have students fill in the blanks with the words and phrases.
- ❑ Tell them to check their answers with a partner.
- ❑ Go through the sentences as a class asking students to volunteer the answers.

Content Note

* 2.2 pounds equal 1 kilogram.
** A quart is equal to about a liter.
*** Tofu is a soft white food made from soy beans, popular in Asian cooking.

ANSWER KEY

1. pound 2. quart 3. take checks 4. produce 5. groceries 6. aisle 7. in line 8. tofu

Listen

3 Listening for Main Ideas 

(The audioscript follows Activity 5.)

- ❑ Read the directions and the questions aloud. Give the students an opportunity to ask questions about anything they don't understand.
- ❑ Ask students to close their books as they listen.
- ❑ Play the recording.
- ❑ After listening, have students answer the questions. Then have students compare their answers in pairs.

- ❑ Finally, go through the questions as a class comparing their answers.

ANSWER KEY

1. Andrew and Nancy are discussing what food to buy in the grocery store.
2. Andrew always buys too much food when he's hungry.
3. Andrew and Nancy can't use the express line because they have more than ten items. Also, you can't pay with checks in the express line.

4 Listening for Details 

(The audioscript follows Activity 5.)

- ❑ Tell the students to read the three true-false questions.
- ❑ Play the recording.
- ❑ Put the students in pairs to answer the questions.
- ❑ Go over the questions as a group.

ANSWER KEY

1.T 2.F 3.F

Stress

5 Listening for Stressed Words 

- ❑ This is the third time the students have done this type of activity, so little explanation should be necessary. (See Teacher's Edition, page 5 for a full explanation of this activity.)
- ❑ Play the recording and have students fill in the answers.
- ❑ After listening, have students check their answers with a partner. Then have each pair check their answers with the audioscript in their books.

AUDIOSCRIPT and ANSWER KEY

Andrew: Well, I got a few groceries that aren't on the list.

Nancy: I can see that! We're not shopping for an army, you know.

Andrew: I always do this when I'm hungry.

Nancy: Well, let's see what you have here.

Andrew: Some nice, fresh strawberries for only $1.79 a pound.

Nancy: Well, that's fine. They always have nice produce here. But why do you have all these cookies?

Andrew: Don't you like them?

Nancy: Oh, I don't know . . . I hope you got a box of tofu.

Andrew: I think I forgot. Where's the aisle with the Asian foods again?

Nancy: Aisle three.

Andrew: I'll go get it.

Nancy: Wait—this steak you got looks really expensive!

Andrew: Well, it isn't. It's on sale for just $3.99 a pound.

Nancy: And what's this? More ice cream? We already have a quart at home. Why don't you put it back? Meanwhile, I'll get in line right here.

Cashier: I'm sorry, Miss; this is the express line, and it looks like you've got more than ten items. Oh, and we don't take checks here.

- ❑ Tell the students to look at the completed conversation.
- ❑ Put the students in groups of three. Have the students choose a role in the conversation and read it with their partners.
- ❑ Tell the students to focus on stressing the important words correctly.

- Remind the students to read their line, look up, and then say it.
- Walk around the room giving the students feedback on their speaking.

Reductions

6 Comparing Unreduced and Reduced Pronunciation 

- Read the directions to the students.
- Play the recording and listen.
- Play the recording again and have the students repeat both forms of the sentence out loud after they hear it.
- Listen to the class. Give the students general feedback on their reductions.
- Ask individual students to volunteer to say each form and give individual feedback.
- As noted in previous chapters, this activity (and similar activities) can work well in a language lab.

7 Listening for Reductions 

- After reading the directions, tell students to look at the conversation with the blanks. Clarify anything that they don't understand. This is an important step as there several new words (e.g., *fresh* and *canned*).
- Play the recording and have the students write their answers.
- Divide the students into groups of three. Have them check their answers together.
- Check the answers as a class.
- Have the students take parts and read the dialogue. Tell the students to focus on pronouncing the reduced forms correctly.
- Walk around the room giving pronunciation feedback to the students.

AUDIOSCRIPT

Customer:	Waiter?
Server:	Yes sir. Do you know what you want?
Customer:	Do you have the spaghetti with mushroom sauce tonight?
Server:	Yes, we do.
Customer:	Well, are the mushrooms fresh or canned?
Server:	They're fresh, and the sauce has lots of them.
Customer:	Great, I'll have that.
Server:	Do you want something to drink?
Customer:	I don't know. Why don't you recommend something?
Server:	How about some nice Italian mineral water?

After you Listen

8 Using Vocabulary 

- Tell the students to read the questions. Clarify any questions.
- Put the students in pairs. Have the students ask and answer the questions. Have one person ask the question while the other person closes his or her book.
- When the students have finished, go over the questions as a class.

Pronunciation

TEENS OR TENS? 

- Read the information in the *Teens* or *Tens* box.
- Pronounce the numbers in the chart.

9 Distinguishing Between Teens and Tens 

- Read the directions for the activity.

- ❑ Play the recording and have the students write down the answers.
- ❑ Have the students check the answers with a partner.
- ❑ Go over the answers together.

ANSWER KEY

1.30 2.14 3.15 4.60 5.70 6.18 7.90

AUDIOSCRIPT

1. We waited in line for 30 minutes.
2. My sister is 14 years old.
3. We've lived in this city for 15 years.
4. Sixty people came to the party.
5. The groceries cost 70 dollars.
6. There are 18 students in the class.
7. I live 90 miles from my parents.

10 Listening for Teens and Tens 

- ❑ Read the directions to the students.
- ❑ Show them the illustrations with the blanks.
- ❑ Play the recording.
- ❑ Put the students in pairs to check their answers. If necessary, play the recording again.
- ❑ Check the answers as a class.

ANSWER KEY

1.14; 2.10:30; 3.$40; 4.13th; 5.$1.90; 6.15; 7.30; 8.15; 9.70; 10.19

AUDIOSCRIPT

1. This turkey weighs 14 pounds.
2. The market is open until 10:30.
3. We spent $40 on groceries yesterday.
4. This milk is good until November 13th.
5. Those peaches cost $1.90 a pound.
6. Everything in this store is about 15 percent cheaper today.
7. I'm having a big party this weekend. I need 30 bottles of mineral water.
8. The store will close in 15 minutes.
9. By using this coupon, you can save 70 cents on this ice cream.
10. Canned vegetables are in aisle 19.

Talk It Over

11 Interview 

- ❑ Go over the Language Tip box on noncount and count nouns.
- ❑ Ask the students to give you more examples of noncount nouns (e.g., *milk*, *sugar*) and count nouns with quantity words (e.g., *a jar of peanut butter*).
- ❑ Read the directions to the students.
- ❑ Read the sample sentences to the students. Make sure that they understand the difference between *how much* (use with noncount nouns) and *how many* (use with count nouns).
- ❑ Go over the chart with the students. Make sure that they understand the time expressions at the top of the chart and the food vocabulary in the chart.
- ❑ Tell the students to ask you *how much* and *how many* questions. Have them fill in your information in the chart.
- ❑ Put the students in groups of four. Tell them to ask each member of the group the questions. Tell them to fill in all of the information in the chart.
- ❑ Go over the information together. Ask questions about the information. Who drinks the most coffee? Who eats the most candy bars?

Before You Listen

1 Prelistening Questions 

- Tell the students to read the introductory paragraph about the four food groups. Answer any questions that they have about vocabulary.
- Point to the illustration of the man eating junk food. Tell them that they will use this illustration to answer some of the questions.
- Tell the students to read the questions. Answer any questions they have about the vocabulary (e.g., *frozen*, *habits*).
- Put the students into pairs. Have them answer the questions together.
- Walk around the room helping the students with the questions.
- When the students have finished their discussions, go through the questions one by one. Have each pair report their answers.

2 Previewing Vocabulary 

- Play the recording and have students listen to the underlined words.
- Tell the students to read the directions.
- Have the students answer the questions individually.
- Tell the students to compare their answers with a partner.
- Check the answers as a class, writing the correct answers on the board.

ANSWER KEY

1.g 2.e 3.h 4.f 5.a 6.c 7.b 8.d

EXPANSION ACTIVITY

- Put the students in groups.
- Have the students take turns reading the definitions for the words in Activity 2.
- As one student is reading the definition, the other students close their books.
- The other students try to guess which word the definition is for.

Best Practice

Organizing Information

This type of activity uses a graphic organizer to categorize information. Taking lecture notes encourages students to process and organize information while they are listening and also provides a record for them to refer to when they are studying later. This type of graphic organizer emphasizes listing and categorizing skills. Other types of graphic organizers are used throughout this book.

Listen

3 Listening for Main Ideas 

- Read the directions to the students.
- Have the students read the main idea question. Remind them to listen for answers to this question.
- Put the students in small groups.
- Play the recording.
- Have them list all of the things that they can do to eat right.
- Check the answers as a class.

ANSWER KEY

1. Eat a lot of fruits and vegetables. 2. Don't eat too much sugar. 3. Reduce the amount of fat in your diet. 4. Eat more whole grains. 5. Don't drink too much coffee or alcohol.

AUDIOSCRIPT

Bob: Hi, everyone, I'm Bob.

Pam: And I'm Pam, and this show is all about "Eating Right!"

Bob: You know, Pam, with people so busy today, they don't have a lot of time to shop or plan what to eat.

Pam: That's true, but healthy eating might just give you a longer and happier life! So here are some things we all should think about regarding our diet.

Bob: First, eat lots of fruits and vegetables. Why? Well, they're a good source of vitamins and minerals . . .

Pam: Right, and they're a good source of fiber, too. Also, they're almost all low in calories and fat, and eating them may help protect you against cancer. So, put an apple or a banana in your lunchbox, or have a carrot for a snack—skip those potato chips.

Bob: That's right. Fruits make a great desert —you don't need all those sugary sweets and drinks, cookies, cakes, candies, sodas.

Pam: You bet you don't. So a second point to remember: too much sugar in your diets can lead to health problems like weight gain, tooth decay—that's trips to your dentist . . .

Bob: Owww! Or even diabetes, and that's serious!

Pam: Now the third thing we want you to think about is reducing the fat you eat.

Bob: Uh-huh. Cutting down on the fat in our diet would be good for many of us.

Pam: So true. It can help us lose weight.

Bob: Or *not gain* weight in the first place.

Pam: And it can lower our chance of getting heart disease, and cancer, too.

Bob: So cut back on all those hamburgers, cheeseburgers, French fries . . .

Pam: And chips—they're full of fat . . .

Bob: And salt. Oh, I don't want to forget our fourth suggestion: Eat more whole grains. You'll get plenty of fiber, vitamins, and minerals from them.

Pam: You mean, like brown rice and whole wheat bread?

Bob: That's it. They're much healthier than white bread, white rice, and things like that.

Pam: Finally, you don't want to drink too much coffee. Coffee can make you nervous and keep you awake at night. Or even affect your heart—but we'll talk about drinking alcohol on another show . . .

Best Practice

Activating Prior Knowledge

This is an example of an activity that helps students map what they know about the real world into a framework in English. This activity asks students to use the knowledge that they already have about nutrition in their native language and fit it into a framework in English in order to understand a listening passage about nutrition in English. By asking students to map concepts about nutrition onto this chart, we are helping the students put everything that they know about nutrition together into a coherent whole.

4 Taking Notes on Specific Information 

(The audioscript follows Activity 3.)

- ❑ Read the directions to the students.
- ❑ Show the students the chart for the information from the conversation. Make sure that the students understand what *Reasons* are.
- ❑ Play the recording. Tell the students to fill in the chart, working individually.
- ❑ Walk around the room checking to see how the students are doing.
- ❑ If necessary, play the recording again.

ANSWER KEY

Things You Should Eat	**Reasons**	**Examples**
vegetables	*fiber*	*carrots*
fruit	good source of fiber, vitamins, and minerals low in calories and fat	apples, bananas
whole grains	have plenty of fiber, vitamins, and minerals	brown rice, whole wheat bread
Things You Shouldn't Eat	**Reasons**	**Examples**
sugar	can cause weight gain, tooth decay, and diabetes	cookies, cakes, candies, sodas
fat	causes heart disease and cancer	hamburgers, cheeseburgers, French fries, potato chips
coffee	makes people nervous, can keep them up at night or affect the heart	(coffee—If students put coffee here, it should be considered correct.)
alcohol	isn't good for the body or brain	

After You Listen

5 Summarizing Ideas 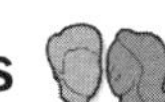

- ❑ After the students have filled in the chart, put them in pairs. Have them compare answers.
- ❑ Read the directions for number 1 to the students.
- ❑ Have pairs summarize the advice. Walk around the room to make sure that they are using complete sentences.
- ❑ Read the directions for number 2.
- ❑ Have the class tell you which ones they have tried and how effective they were.

Best Practice

Interacting with Others

This type of activity is an example of collaborative learning to encourage fluency and confidence. In these discussion questions, based around the topic of nutrition and health, communication is more important than grammar. Students can discuss the questions, exchanging authentic information and opinions. By the time they discuss their answers with the class, they should feel more confident in the use of the new language.

6 Using Vocabulary 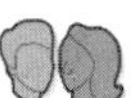

- ❑ Read the directions to the students.
- ❑ Tell them to read all of the questions and to ask questions about anything that they don't understand.
- ❑ Put the students in pairs. Have them discuss all of the questions.
- ❑ Go over the questions as a class.

Talk It Over

7 Comparing Eating Habits 

- ❑ Read the directions to the students. Make sure that they understand the vocabulary (e.g., *customs*).
- ❑ Show the chart to the students and explain the three columns.
- ❑ Make sure that they understand what each row means.
- ❑ Have the students fill out the chart individually.
- ❑ Put the students in pairs. Tell them to compare their eating habits.
- ❑ Go over the charts as a class. Ask the students to look for any general tendencies (e.g., they eat more traditional food when at home than when traveling).

Best Practice

Cultivating Critical Thinking

The following activity is an example of a collaborative team activity resulting in a final product. This type of activity requires students to process the information they have learned and apply it to a new situation. This involves reinterpretation, synthesis, and application of concepts. In this activity, the students will use the information that they have learned about good nutrition and apply it to a realistic situation, the menu in their school cafeteria.

REPRODUCIBLE **EXPANSION ACTIVITY**

- Please see Black Line Master "The Menu at Our School Cafeteria" on page BLM 5 of this Teacher's Edition.
- Photocopy and distribute one copy to each student.
- Put students in small groups.
- Have them read the directions and ask questions about anything that they don't understand.
- Tell the students to fill in the cafeteria menu with suggestions for healthy lunch meals.
- The lunches must be complete, that is, they must have a main dish, either a soup or salad, some choices of drinks, and a dessert.
- When the groups are finished, have them take turns presenting their information to the class.

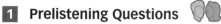

Getting Meaning from Context

1 Prelistening Questions 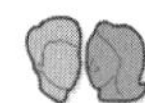

- Read the directions to the students. Show the students the four pictures.
- Have the students read the questions for this activity. Give them an opportunity to ask questions about the vocabulary and grammar (e.g., *the cheapest*).
- Put the students into pairs. Have each pair discuss the questions.
- When the students have finished, go over their responses as a class.

Best Practice

Scaffolding Instruction

The following activity is an example of an activity that raises metacognitive awareness of learning strategies. In real life, we use surrounding context clues to work out the meanings of unfamiliar words. This activity asks students to use the words that they know in each piece of the conversation to work out the meanings of new words. By asking students to write the clues, they are guided through the steps of developing this skill.

Focus on Testing

Using Context Clues 

- Read the directions to the students. Tell them that they will be practicing an important learning strategy for listening.
- Point out to the students that this is a *Focus on Testing* activity. The skill taught in this activity will help students with standardized tests, such as the Internet-based TOEFL®.
- Go over the chart with the students. Since they did this kind of activity in the previous chapters, they should be familiar with the concept of a "clue." If the students need more information about this activity, show them the complete explanation in Chapter 1, *Focus on Testing*, page 15.
- Play each conversation. Have the students circle the correct answer and write down several clues before moving on.
- Put the students in pairs and have them compare their charts.
- Go over the answers and clues as a class.

ANSWER KEY

Answers	Clues
1. c. nice restaurant	appetizers, menus, specials, fresh broiled swordfish, formal waiter (server)
2. b. diner	counter, coffee, waitress is informal.
3. a. cafeteria	Salads, hot dish, "You pay down there at the cashier." The food is directly in front of the speakers.
4. c. fast-food place	"May I take your order?" burritos, Cokes, order of nachos, Cost is only $8.00.

AUDIOSCRIPT

Conversation 1

Server: Good evening. My name is Pierre. Would you like something to drink?

Bob: No, thanks. But we would like to order some appetizers.

Server: Certainly, here are your menus. Our specials tonight are lemon chicken and fresh broiled swordfish.
Question 1: The speakers are in a . . .
Susan: This is such a beautiful restaurant, Bob. Thanks for bringing me here.

Conversation 2

Felipe: Why don't we sit at the counter? There aren't any free tables.
Salim: Fine.
Waitress: Coffee?
Felipe: Yes.
Salim: Yes, please.
Waitress: I'll be right back to take your order.
Question 2: The speakers are in a . . .
Felipe: This is my favorite diner. The prices are low and the service is great.

Conversation 3

A: These salads look great. Do you want one?
B: No, I want a hot dish from over there.
Server: Yes, what would you like?
A: Is that mushroom soup?
Server: No, it's bean soup.
A: How much is it?
Server: It's two dollars a bowl. You pay down there at the cashier.
Question 3: The speakers are in a . . .
B: I hear this cafeteria is open all night.

Conversation 4

Server: May I take your order?
John: I'll have two burritos, no onions, and two small Cokes.
Server: For here or to go?
John: For here. Oh, and an order of nachos.
Server: That'll be eight dollars.
Question 4: The speakers are in a . . .
John: I know fast food is fattening, but I really love it.

Using Language Functions

ORDERING IN A RESTAURANT

- Read the *Ordering in a Restaurant* box to the students.
- Read the expressions for server and customer out loud. Have the students repeat the expressions after you. Give the students time to ask for clarification.

2 Ordering in a Restaurant 

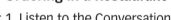

Part 1. Listen to the Conversation

- ❑ Have the students read the restaurant conversation. Ask them to tell you what they don't understand.
- ❑ Play the recording of the conversation.
- ❑ Put the students in pairs. Have the students take the roles of server and customer and practice the conversation. Remind them not to read directly from the book. Have them read, look up, and then speak.

AUDIOSCRIPT

Server: Are you ready to order, ma'am?
Customer: Yes, I am.
Server: What would you like?
Customer: I'd like the grilled salmon dinner.
Server: Would you like soup or salad with that?
Customer: What kind of soup do you have?
Server: We have Japanese miso soup or Italian minestrone.
Customer: I'll have the minestrone.

Server:	And would you like potatoes or rice with your salmon?
Customer:	Rice, please. Does the dinner come with a vegetable?
Server:	Yes, would you prefer green beans or broccoli?
Customer:	Green beans, please.
Server:	What would you like to drink?
Customer:	I'd like a glass of iced tea.
Server:	OK, that's minestrone soup, followed by grilled salmon with rice and green beans, and a glass of iced tea. Would you like an appetizer while you're waiting?
Customer:	No thanks.

Part 2. Role-Play

- Read the directions to the students.
- Put the students in pairs. Tell them to decide which student is the server and which is the customer.
- Have the servers read the *Server's Instructions* and have the customers read the *Customer's Instructions.*
- Give the students time to read the menu. Ask them what they don't understand.
- Encourage the students to practice the role play without reading the conversation and to use the expressions that they have studied. Walk around the room to help get them started.

REPRODUCIBLE

EXPANSION ACTIVITY

- Photocopy a short restaurant review from your local newspaper.
- Pass out copies to your students and quickly read through it.
- Ask the students to tell you what information is in the review.
- See Black Line Master "Restaurant Review" on page BLM 6 of this Teacher's Edition.
- Photocopy and distribute one copy to each student.
- Read the directions to the students. Tell them that they will be reading their reviews to the other students.
- Have them answer the questions individually. Walk around the room helping as necessary.
- When the students have finished, have them read their reviews to their classmates.

Recipes

1 Previewing Vocabulary 

- ❑ Tell the students to read the directions.
- ❑ Play the recording and ask students to listen to the words.
- ❑ Have the students try to write definitions for the words they know and to get out their dictionaries and look up the words that they don't know.
- ❑ Tell the students to give two examples of each of the words. For example, for *ingredients*, the students can say "salt" and "sugar." For *fry*, students can say "chicken" or "French fries."
- ❑ Go over the meaning of the words with the students, checking that they understand them in the context of cooking.

2 Taking Notes on a Recipe 

- ❑ Read the directions to the students.
- ❑ Show the students the lines for ingredients and for the steps of the recipe.
- ❑ Go over the information in the Culture Note with the students. If possible, bring a set of American measuring cups and spoons to class to show the students the measurements used in the U.S.
- ❑ Point to the illustrations in the activity on page 57. Give the students a few minutes to look at them.
- ❑ Play the recording. Stop after Tom lists the ingredients. Give the students some time to write them down. If necessary, repeat this section.
- ❑ Play the rest of the recording. Give the students some time to write down the five steps in the cooking process. If necessary, play the recording again.

ANSWER KEY

Activity 2

Steps:

1. Beat the eggs, milk, and salt for one minute.
2. Melt the butter in a frying pan.
3. Dip eight slices of bread in the egg mixture.
4. Fry the slices bread until they're golden brown.
5. Serve them on a warm plate with butter and syrup or jam.

AUDIOSCRIPT

Tom: To make French toast for four people, here's what you'll need: two eggs, one cup of milk, one-half teaspoon of salt, and about a tablespoon of butter. Have you got all that?

First, beat the eggs, milk, and salt with a fork for a minute until they're well mixed.

Then melt the butter in a frying pan.

While the butter is melting, dip eight slices of bread into the egg mixture.

Then when the butter is hot, fry the bread slices until they're golden brown.

Serve them on a warm plate with butter and syrup or jam.

3 Explaining a Recipe 

- ❑ Put the students in pairs. Tell the students to check their answers from the previous activity with each other.
- ❑ Then have the students take turns playing the role of Tom explaining how to make French toast. Walk around the room helping students as needed.

4 Sharing Recipes

- ❑ Tell the students to read the directions. Give them a few minutes to think of a recipe that they would like to teach the class.
- ❑ Have the students write down the ingredients for their recipe. Then tell the students to write down brief notes on each step of the recipe (e.g., stir in rice).
- ❑ Have the students take turns presenting their recipe to the class. Tell the students to take notes so that they can retell the recipe.
- ❑ After each presentation, choose a student to retell the recipe.

Best Practice

Making Use of Academic Content

The prelistening discussion is an example of a discussion that students may actually encounter in a classroom. This type of activity encourages students to relate the topic to the authentic world of their own experiences. Asking students to talk about the food in their country and other countries creates a framework through which they can interpret the topic. This activity gives students a chance to discuss authentic examples from their own lives.

Regional Foods

5 Prelistening Questions 

- ❑ Read the directions to the students. Have the students read the two questions about regional and foreign food. Have them ask questions about anything that they don't understand.
- ❑ Put the students in pairs. Tell them to discuss the three questions.
- ❑ For the question on North American food, have the students give examples of what they've eaten and liked or disliked.
- ❑ When the students have finished their discussions, go over the answers as a class.

6 Regional Foods 

- ❑ Have the students read the directions. Show the students the map of North America. Make sure they look at the place names with blanks.
- ❑ Play the recording. Have students mark their maps as they listen.
- ❑ Put the students in pairs and have them check their answers.
- ❑ Check the answers as a class.
- ❑ In Part 2, have the same partners discuss the two questions about cities and states.
- ❑ Go over the answers as a class.

ANSWER KEY

Wisconsin—terrific cheese
Maine—seafood, fantastic lobster
Georgia—fried chicken is popular
Florida—the best oranges
Texas—spicy Mexican food
San Francisco—excellent Chinese and Japanese restaurants, special bread
Napa/Sonoma—excellent wine
Vancouver—Chinese food, great fish like salmon
Montreal—the French food is fabulous
Chicago—very good beef

AUDIOSCRIPT

Paula: Vancouver, in Western Canada, has delicious Chinese food because there are many Chinese immigrants in that part of Canada. And Vancouver has great fish—like salmon.

San Francisco also has excellent Chinese and Japanese restaurants. Oh, and the bread in San Francisco is really special. Just north of San Francisco there are two little towns called Napa and Sonoma. That's where they make some wonderful California wine.

Now, if you drive to Texas, be sure to eat some Mexican food. It's very spicy, but so delicious. In the Midwest, the middle of the United States, you can find terrific cheese in Wisconsin. And don't forget to have a steak in Chicago. The beef is very good there.

If you drive to the Northeast, try to visit Maine to taste the seafood. Lobster is fantastic. And nearby, in Montreal, Canada, the French food is fabulous. Oh, and if you decide to go down south to Georgia, fried chicken is very popular. And in Florida, of course, you'll find the best oranges.

Talk It Over

7 Refusing Food Politely 

- ❑ Have the students read Soo Yun's situation. Tell the students to look at the three illustrations for this activity.
- ❑ Tell them to explain it to you so that you can check their understanding.
- ❑ Put the students in pairs. Have them answer the discussion questions.
- ❑ Then tell the partners that they will act out the situation between Soo Yun and Cathy's mother.
- ❑ Go over the expressions for refusing food politely in the chart. Say the expressions for offering food to someone with food items in the blanks. Have the students refuse politely.
- ❑ Have the pairs act out Soo Yun's situation together. When the pairs feel comfortable with the dialogue, have them act out the situation in front of the class. After each skit, have the other students say whether the refusal was polite or not.

Self-Assessment Log

- ❑ The purpose of the log is to help the students reflect on their learning.
- ❑ Read the directions aloud and have students check vocabulary that they learned in the chapter and are prepared to use.
- ❑ Have students check the strategies they understand.
- ❑ Put students in small groups. Ask students to find the information or an activity related to each strategy in the chapter.
- ❑ Tell students to find definitions in the chapter for any words they did not check, or they can look in their dictionaries.

Chapter

4

In the Community

In this chapter, students will learn a great deal of useful language for functioning effectively in a city. In Part 1, they will hear a conversation in which a student is running errands in a variety of shops. They will also practice the language for understanding and talking about locations. In Part 2, students will practice comparing cities, for example, small towns and big cities. In Part 3, they will learn more about using context clues to understand what they're listening to. In Part 4, students will practice reading and discussing a map and will practice understanding and giving directions. These topics will prepare students for the practical aspects of living in a city.

Chapter Opener

- ❑ Have students look at the photo of a man using a cell phone and laptop in a laundromat. Ask the questions from the Connecting to the Topic section. Have students discuss the questions as a class.
- ❑ Have students read the quote from Ibsen. Give them some time to ask for clarification of any words that they don't understand (e.g., *helm*, *community*).
- ❑ Ask the students what they think the quote means. If they don't understand it, tell them that in a good community, all people should be ready to become leaders. Ask the students if they agree with that idea.

" A community is like a ship; everyone ought to be prepared to take the helm. "

—Henrik Ibsen
Norwegian playwright (1828–1906)

Chapter Overview

Listening Skills and Strategies

Listening for main ideas

Listening for details

Following directions

Speaking Skills and Strategies

Talking about running errands

Describing locations in a city

Asking for and giving directions

Describing your neighborhood

Comparing cities and towns

Critical Thinking Skills

Interpreting a photo

Using a concept map to make comparisons

Summarizing ideas using key words

Vocabulary Building

Terms to describe locations in a city

Expressions for giving and asking for directions

Pronunciation

Identifying and practicing stressed words

Comparing reduced and unreduced pronunciation

Focus on Testing

Using context clues to guess seasons

Vocabulary

Nouns	Verbs	Adjectives
advantage	drop off (something or somebody)	conservative
debit card	give (someone) a ride	convenient
disadvantage	have got to	crowded
dry cleaner	run errands	
jaywalking		
laundry		
smog		

Can You Guess?

- Ask students to discuss the questions below in groups and compare answers with the correct answers.

1. Which are the most and least expensive cities in the world? Number them in order. *A. Most: 1. Tokyo, 2. Osaka, 3. London; Least: 1. Asuncion, 2. Manila, 3. Buenos Aires.** **2.** Which country has the most traffic accidents? *A. China (300 deaths/day).*** **3.** Which is the world's cleanest city? *A. Calgary, Canada.*†

Footnotes:
* Source: CNNMoney.com (June 22, 2005)
** Source: Weekend Standard (China's business newspaper, Feb. 12-13, 2005)
† Source: Worldwide Quality of Life Survey (http://www.mercerhr.com)

Before You Listen

Best Practice

Activating Prior Knowledge

The prelistening questions activate students' prior knowledge. This activity will help students relate their own experience of living in a city to the new language in this chapter. When students activate their prior knowledge before learning new material, they are better able to map new language onto existing concepts, which aids understanding and retention.

1 Prelistening Questions 

- Go over the questions with the students. Give them time to ask about any vocabulary that they don't understand. Point out the picture of Kenji and the police officer and make sure that the students understand that they will need to look at that picture for question number 3.
- Have the students discuss the questions in pairs.
- Compare answers as a whole class. For the first question, possible answers are: *to get cash*—a bank, an ATM; *to clean your dirty clothes*—a laundromat, a dry cleaners; *to repair your computer*—a computer store; *to pay a traffic ticket*—the courthouse, online; *to buy medicine*—a pharmacy.
- Write new vocabulary on the board.

2 Previewing Vocabulary 

- Play the recording and have students listen to the words and phrases.
- Go over the vocabulary table with the students. Have them read the words and definitions and then read the sentences.
- Have students fill in the blanks in pairs, guessing from context if they don't know the answer.
- Compare their answers as a whole class and write the correct answers on the board.

ANSWER KEY

1. run errands 2. laundry 3. convenient 4. give (me) a ride 5. have got to 6. dry cleaner 7. debit card 8. drops off 9. jaywalking

Listen

3 Listening for Main Ideas 

(The audioscript follows Activity 5.)

- Read the directions to the students. Give them some time to ask for clarification of anything that they don't understand.
- Tell the students to read the questions in their books, then read the questions aloud.
- Ask the students if they have any questions.
- Ask students to close their books as they listen.
- Play the recording.
- After listening, have students answer the questions and then compare their answers in pairs.

- ❑ Go through the three questions as a class comparing their answers. Ask them for specific words or phrases they heard that support their answers.
- ❑ Finally, answer any questions about vocabulary that they heard but did not understand.

ANSWER KEY

1. Kenji asks Peter to give him a ride downtown.
2. Kenji needs to run some errands.
3. Peter is going downtown to pay for a traffic ticket.

4 Listening for Details 

(The audioscript follows Activity 5.)

- ❑ Tell the students to look at the three true-false questions.
- ❑ Play the recording.
- ❑ Put the students in pairs to answer the questions.
- ❑ Go over the questions as a group. Ask for additional details from the conversation. How are Kenji's ticket and Peter's ticket different? Who doesn't drive?

ANSWER KEY

1. False. Kenji needs to get his laptop repaired, not buy a new computer.
2. True.
3. True.

Stress

5 Listening for Stressed Words 

- ❑ Play the recording again. This time tell the students to keep their books open. Tell the students to fill in the blanks with the words that they hear.
- ❑ After listening, have students check their answers with a partner. Then have each pair check their answers with the audioscript in their books.

AUDIOSCRIPT and ANSWER KEY

Kenji:	Peter, are you going downtown today?
Peter:	Uh-huh. Why?
Kenji:	Can you give me a ride? I have to run some errands.
Peter:	Where do you need to go?
Kenji:	Uh, a lot of places. First, I have to go to the bank. Could you drop me off at the corner of King Boulevard and Second Avenue?
Peter:	King and Second? Oh, sure. I know where that is. But why are you going to the bank? Why don't you use the ATM machine on campus?
Kenji:	'Cause my debit card isn't working; I've got to get a new one. And the cleaner's is next door to the bank. I have to pick up some clothes there anyway.
Peter:	Why don't you use the laundry room here in the building?
Kenji:	I'm not picking up laundry. It's dry cleaning. By the way, is there a computer repair shop near there? I need to drop off my laptop.
Peter:	Computer repair? Oh, yeah. There's a Good Buy across the street from the bank. They fix computers there.
Kenji:	Oh, that's convenient. So what are you going to do downtown?
Peter:	I'm going to the courthouse. I've got to pay a ticket, too.
Kenji:	No kidding! I have to pay a ticket, too. I just got a ticket last week.
Peter:	But, Kenji, you don't drive!
Kenji:	I know. I got a ticket for jaywalking!
Peter:	Really?!

Kenji: Yeah. I didn't know it's illegal to cross in the middle of the street!

- ❑ Read the directions at the bottom of Activity 5.
- ❑ Tell the students to look at the completed conversation above.
- ❑ Put the students in pairs. Have the students choose a role in the conversation and read it with their partner.
- ❑ Tell the students to focus on stressing the important words correctly.
- ❑ Walk around the room, giving the students feedback on their speaking.

Reductions

6 Comparing Unreduced and Reduced Pronunciation

- ❑ Read the directions to the students.
- ❑ Play the recording of the unreduced and reduced forms of the sentences from the conversation.
- ❑ Have the students as a class repeat the two forms.

7 Listening for Reductions 

- ❑ Read the directions to the students.
- ❑ Play the recording and have students write down their answers.
- ❑ When the conversation is finished, put the students in pairs and have them check their answers. Then check the answers as a class.
- ❑ Have the pairs take roles and read the conversation. Walk around the room, reminding the students to practice their reduced pronunciation.

ANSWER KEY

A: Do you know where Central Library is?

B: Sure. You have to take Bus number 9.

A: Could you walk with me to the bus stop?

B: I'm sorry. I don't have time 'cause I've got to do a lot of things.

A: Oh. Then can you just give me directions to the bus stop?

B: Are you kidding? It's right there across the street.

8 Reductions Game 

- ❑ Show the students the box at the end of the activity.
- ❑ Go over the reduced forms and the words and phrases in the *Word Bank*.
- ❑ Read the directions to the students.
- ❑ Divide the students into groups. Have them start saying sentences and repeating the sentences that come before them.
- ❑ When each group has a winner, have the winners stand up for recognition.

After You Listen

9 Using Vocabulary 

- ❑ Tell the students to read the questions. Give them time to ask about anything that they don't understand.
- ❑ Put the students in pairs. Have the students ask and answer the questions.
- ❑ When the students have finished, go over the questions as a class.
- ❑ Many of the questions involve interesting cultural issues (e.g., Who does the laundry in your family?), so you can take this opportunity to practice discussion skills by discussing cultural differences.

Using Language Functions

DESCRIBING LOCATIONS

- Go over the *Describing Locations* box.
- Have the students go back to Activity 5 on pages 66 and 67 and find the locations of the three places.
- Go over the list of location expressions at the bottom of the box.
- Read the Culture Note to the students. Give them time to ask questions about the information in the box.

ANSWER KEY

Bank: at the corner of King Boulevard and Second Avenue

Dry cleaner: next door to the bank

Computer repair shop: across the street from the bank

10 Finding Locations 

- Have students look at the map on page 71. Tell the students that they will be using this map in the activity.
- Read the directions to the students. Read the example to the students. Give them time to ask questions.
- Put the students in pairs. Tell them to start checking the sentences. Walk around the room making sure that they are correcting any incorrect sentences.
- Check the answers as a class. If a location is incorrect, write the student's corrected version on the board.

ANSWER KEY

1. No, that's wrong. The woman in the wheelchair is next to the hot dog stand. She is in the park. She is near the fountain.
2. No, that's not correct. The bus station is the third building from the corner.
3. No, that's wrong. The fountain is in the middle of the park. It's across the street from the medical center.
4. No, that's incorrect. The post office is next door to the bank. It's next door to the bus station. It is between the bank and the bus station. It's the second building from the corner.
5. No, that's not correct. Kinko's is on the corner. It's at the corner.
6. No, that's wrong. The ambulance is in front of the medical center (or hospital).

Best Practice

Making Use of Academic Content

This activity is an example of using a real world example. This type of activity encourages students to relate the topic to the authentic world of their own experiences. Asking students to talk about their neighborhood creates an authentic framework through which they can interpret the topic. This activity gives students a chance to use the language and expressions learned in the chapter to describe their real world to their classmates. It is excellent practice for an actual encounter inside or outside of class.

11 Describing Your Neighborhood 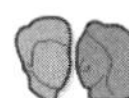

- Put the students in pairs.
- Read the directions for the activity. Read the sample answer to the students.
- Give the students time to ask for clarification.
- While the students are discussing their neighborhoods, walk around the class helping them with grammar and vocabulary.

- ❑ When the students have finished, have them describe their neighborhoods to the class.

Best Practice

Cultivating Critical Thinking

This is an example of a collaborative team activity resulting in a final product. This type of activity requires students to process the information they have learned and apply it to a new situation. This involves reinterpretation, synthesis, and application of concepts. The process of manipulating language and concepts in this way will create deeper processing of new material, which will allow students to evaluate whether they have understood the new material and help them remember it better. In this activity, students must use the language they have learned for describing cities and use it to create an image of an ideal neighborhood. To do this, they must evaluate various criteria for neighborhoods and make a judgment of what is important to them.

EXPANSION ACTIVITY

- Please see Black Line Master "Our Ideal Neighborhood" on page BLM 7 of this Teacher's Edition.
- Photocopy and distribute one copy to each student.
- Go over all of the directions for this activity. It's important for the students to understand all of the steps before they begin.
- For Part 1, tell the students to take some time to think individually about an ideal neighborhood. Have them write down some descriptive words and phrases (e.g., *safe*, *has a lot of trees*) in the first box.
- Encourage the students to dream big, to be imaginative (e.g., have an amusement park).
- For Part 2, put the students in small groups. Have them compare their descriptions and come up with a group idea of an ideal neighborhood.
- When they have finished describing the neighborhood, begin Part 3. Give each group a large piece of poster board or other paper. Tell them to draw a map of their ideal neighborhood on the piece of paper.
- For Part 4, have each group put their map on the board and describe their neighborhood. Remind the students to give reasons for their decisions. For example, we have a large park so that people have a place to exercise and play games.

Before You Listen

1 Prelistening Questions 

- ❑ Tell the students to look at the three illustrations labeled *Village*, *Town*, and *City*.
- ❑ Read the directions to the students.
- ❑ Tell the students to read the two questions. Give them time to ask clarification questions.
- ❑ Put the students into pairs and have them discuss the questions.
- ❑ Go over their answers as a class.

2 Previewing Vocabulary 

- ❑ Tell the students to read the directions. Give them some time to ask questions.
- ❑ Play the recording and have students listen to the underlined words.
- ❑ Have the students answer the questions individually.
- ❑ Tell the students to compare their answers with a partner.
- ❑ Check the answers as a class, writing the correct answers on the board.

ANSWER KEY

1.d 2.e 3.b 4.a 5.c

Listen

3 Listening for Main Ideas 

- ❑ Read the Culture Note on page 73 to the students. Make sure they understand the information in it. Make sure that they understand the words *suburb* and *commute*. If there is time, introduce related words, for example, *urban* and *rural*.
- ❑ Tell the students that they are going to listen to a long listening passage. Tell them that they must focus on the main ideas in the conversation.
- ❑ Read the directions for the activity. Tell the students to read the possible titles for the listening passage.
- ❑ Play the recording.
- ❑ Have the students decide which title is the best for the listening passage.
- ❑ As a class, discuss the different titles. Elicit from the students reasons why the incorrect titles are inappropriate.

ANSWER KEY

No Place Is Perfect—This is the correct answer because the three people do not ever reach an agreement on whether small towns or big cities are better. They list advantages and disadvantages of each. Neither is all positive.

AUDIOSCRIPT

Peter: Phew . . . I'm glad I don't live downtown. The traffic is terrible. I have a headache from the noise and all the smog.

Ming: You think our downtown is bad? Ask Kenji about Tokyo.

Kenji: Yeah, Tokyo is noisier and much more crowded.

Ming: Yeah, and I hear the smog's worse, too.

Kenji: That's right.

Peter: So, I guess you don't miss *that*, huh?

Kenji: Well, I don't miss *those* things. But a big city like Tokyo can be very exciting.

Peter: Yes, I'm sure that's true. But I prefer the peace and quiet of a small town like ours.

Kenji: Yeah, I like it here, too. The people are friendlier and things are cheaper.

Ming: Well, you know, I come from a really small town, and it can be so conservative and boring. When I

	graduate, I want to live in a big city like New York or Chicago. You can make more money there, too.
Peter:	Yeah, but it's more dangerous there.
Ming:	Yeah, that's a disadvantage. But there are also lots of advantages.
Peter:	Like what? The long lines at the bank or in the stores?
Ming:	Waiting in line doesn't bother me. I really love shopping in the city. You can find anything.
Kenji:	Great! Then next time we need something downtown, we'll send *you*.

Strategy

Graphic Organizer: Concept Map

- Read the description of the concept map to the students. Give them time to ask for clarification of anything that they do not understand.
- Point out the concept map in Activity 4. Make sure that they understand where the different types of information will be entered in the map.

Best Practice

Organizing Information

This type of activity uses a graphic organizer to compare and contrast information. Taking notes about the conversation encourages students to process and organize information while they are listening and also provides a record for them to refer to when they are studying later. This type of graphic organizer emphasizes comparing and contrasting skills. Other types of graphic organizers are used throughout this book.

4 Taking Notes on Specific Information 

- ❑ Read the directions for the activity. Have one or two students paraphrase back to you what they are going to do.
- ❑ Play the recording again. Give the students time to write down their ideas in the chart.

ANSWER KEY

Big Cities		Small Towns	
Good Things	Bad Things	Good Things	Bad Things
1. exciting 2. can make more money 3. good shopping	1. traffic 2. noise 3. smog 4. dangerous 5. long lines	1. peace 2. quiet 3. friendlier people 4. things are cheaper	1. conservative 2. boring

After You Listen

5 Summarizing Ideas 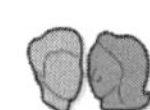

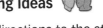

- ❑ Read the directions to the students. Read the example. Give the students an opportunity to ask questions.
- ❑ Put the students in pairs. Tell them to compare their concept maps.
- ❑ Tell the students to summarize what Peter, Kenji, and Ming said. Make sure that they use complete sentences.
- ❑ Walk around the room helping the students.
- ❑ As a class, check the answers.

6 Using Vocabulary 

- ❑ Read the directions to the students.
- ❑ Tell them to read all of the questions and to ask for clarification of anything that they don't understand.
- ❑ Put the students in pairs. Have them discuss all of the questions.
- ❑ Go over the questions as a class.

Reproducible EXPANSION ACTIVITY

- Please see Black Line Master "My Hometown and Where I Live Now" on page BLM 8 of this Teacher's Edition.
- Photocopy and distribute one copy to each student.
- Go over all of the directions with the students.
- For Part 1, have the students work individually and write five sentences comparing the two places.
- For Part 2, put the students in pairs. Have them tell each other their information.
- Tell the students that as they listen, they should fill in their partner's information in the appropriate area in the Venn diagram. Explain that the middle area is for similarities. The right and left areas are for features that are only true for either the hometown or the present town.
- For Part 3, have the students take turns explaining their partner's information to the class.

Getting Meaning from Context

Best Practice

Scaffolding Instruction

This is an example of an activity that raises metacognitive awareness of learning strategies. In real life, we use surrounding context clues to work out the meanings of unfamiliar words. This activity asks students to use the words that they know in each piece of the conversation to work out the meanings of new words. By asking students to write the clues, they are guided through the steps of developing this skill.

Focus on Testing

Using Context Clues 

- Read the directions to the students. Tell them that they will be practicing an important learning strategy for listening.
- Go over the chart on page 76 with the students. Since they have done this kind of activity in previous chapters, they should be familiar with the concept of a "clue." If the students need more information about this activity, show them the complete explanation in Chapter 1, Focus on Testing on page 15.
- Play each conversation, stopping before the answer is revealed. Give the students time to circle the correct answer and write down several clues before moving on.
- Put the students in pairs and have them compare their charts.
- Go over the answers and clues as a class.

ANSWER KEY

Answers	Clues
1. b. in a bank	to cash, sign the back, account, branch, identification
2. c. on a bus	stop at Third and Highland, passengers, move to the rear, get there
3. b. at a dry cleaner	shirts, pants, jacket, pick them up, ready, coffee stain
4. a. getting a driver's license	application, line, eye test, road test, written test, picture
5. c. at a post office	get to New York, express mail, a book of stamps

AUDIOSCRIPT

Conversation 1

A: Next, please.

B: I'd like to cash this.

A: Sure. Don't forget to sign the back. Do you have an account here?

B: Not at this branch.

A: Then I'll have to see your identification.

Question 1: Where are the speakers?

B: By the way, how late is this bank open?

Conversation 2

A: Excuse me. Do you stop at Third and Highland?

B: Yes, ma'am . . . Passengers, please move to the rear.

A: Could you tell me when we get there?

B: Sure. I'll let you know.

Question 2: Where is the woman?

A: Is the bus always this crowded?

Conversation 3

A: Can I help you?

B: Yes, I've got four shirts here and two pairs of pants and a jacket. I'm leaving town in a few days, so can I pick them up tomorrow?

A: We can have the pants ready, but the shirts won't be back until Wednesday morning.

B: Well, OK. Oh, and don't forget to take out this coffee stain.

Question 3: Where are the speakers?

A: No problem. We're the best dry cleaners in town.

Conversation 4

A: Fill out this application and wait in that line for your eye test.

B: About how long will this take?

A: Well, you'll have to take a 15-minute road test, and the written test also takes 15 minutes. But you may have to wait in line a long time for your picture.

Question 4: What is the young man doing?

B: Will you send me my driver's license, or do I have to pick it up in person?

Conversation 5

A: Will this get to New York in two days?

B: Only if you send it Express Mail.

A: OK. I'd like to do that.

B: All right. Anything else?

A: Yes. A book of stamps, please.

B: Fine, that's, uh, sixteen dollars and sixty cents, please.

Question 5: Where are the speakers?

A: Is this post office open on Saturdays?

Talk It Over

1 Role-Play 

- Have students look at the three-panel illustration, or cartoon, of Mr. Kim's story on page 77.
- Show the students the *Useful Vocabulary* section on page 76. Go over all of the words with the students. Give them time to ask for clarification.
- Read the directions to the students.
- Put the students in pairs. Have them take turns explaining what is happening in the illustration.
- Tell the students to prepare a conversation between Mr. Kim and the parking officer. Make sure they understand that they will perform the conversation in front of the class.
- Have the pairs act out the conversation.

Best Practice

Making Use of Academic Content

This is an example of an activity that exposes students to situations that they will actually face in an academic setting. Students at a university will often have to ask for and give directions. This activity will give the students the authentic practice that they will need to develop this skill.

Using Language Functions

EXPRESSIONS FOR ASKING FOR AND GIVING DIRECTIONS

- Go over the expressions in the *Using Language Functions* section.

1 Reading a Map 

- ❑ Have the students look at the map for this activity. Make sure that the students can find the café and the tennis courts.
- ❑ Have the students individually write directions from the café to the tennis courts.
- ❑ Put the students in pairs and have them compare their answers. Have one student read his or her directions as the other student follows on the map. Then switch roles. Did each student end up at the right place—the tennis courts?
- ❑ Go over the answers as a class and write the directions on the board.

ANSWER KEY

Possible answers

From the café to the tennis courts

1. Go north on Lennox Avenue.
2. Go two blocks.
3. You'll pass a market on your left.
4. Turn left on Broadway Boulevard.
5. The tennis courts will be on your left.

From the tennis courts to the movie theater

1. Go east on Broadway Boulevard.
2. Turn right on Lenox Avenue.
3. Go two blocks.
4. Turn left on 4th Street.
5. The movie theater is halfway down the block. It will be on your right.

2 Following Directions 

- ❑ Show the students the map for this activity. Make sure that they find Joe's Diner.
- ❑ Read the directions to the students. Make sure that they understand that they will be labeling buildings on the map.
- ❑ Play the recording. For each segment, stop the recording before the answer is revealed.
- ❑ Go over the answers briefly at the end and check to see if the students had any problems. Understanding directions can be a challenge. If the students are struggling, put them in pairs and have them read the dialogue transcripts in the back of their book.

ANSWER KEY

The bank is location C.

The department store is location A.

King's Books is location F.

Chow's Chinese restaurant is location E.

Lowe Auditorium is location H.

AUDIOSCRIPT

Peter: Excuse me. Is there a bank near here?

Man: There's one four or five blocks from here. Walk north on Newbury Boulevard to First Street; turn right on First. At the second block, turn left, and look for the bank on the right side of Walnut Street just before Cherry Lane.

You are at location C. Continue to the next place from here.

Peter: Excuse me, ma'am. I'm trying to find a big department store nearby.

Woman: Oh, there's one on the corner of Newbury and Cherry. Just walk down Cherry two blocks and turn left. Then you'll see it on the left.

You are at location A. Continue to the next place from here.

Peter: Could you tell me where King's Books is? I hear it's a great bookstore.

Man: King's Books? Oh, yes. They've got great stuff. Do you know how to get to Washington Boulevard?

Peter: I think so. I go out on First Street and turn right.

Man: Nope. Turn left. Washington's the first street. Turn right on Washington and follow it a couple of blocks to Columbus Street. Turn left and cross Walnut Street. On the left side, you'll see a barbershop and then a market. Walk between them, and you'll find the bookstore in back.

You are at location F. Continue to the next place from here.

Peter: Can you recommend a Chinese restaurant near here?

Woman: Sure. Chow's has good Chinese food.

Peter: How do I get there?

Woman: Go out to Walnut Street and go up to Second Street. Walk west, cross Washington Boulevard, and the restaurant is across from Mort's Gym.

Peter: So it's on the south side of the street?

Woman: That's right.

You are at location E. Continue to the next place from here.

Peter: Is there a concert at Lowe Auditorium tonight?

Man: I think so.

Peter: How do I get there?

Man: Are you driving?

Peter: No, I'm walking.

Man: Turn right and walk all the way to McMillan Road. Then make a left and go straight a block or two. The auditorium is on the corner of Cherry Lane and McMillan.

You have arrived at location H. Stop and relax.

Best Practice

Interacting with Others

This type of activity is an example of collaborative learning to encourage fluency and confidence. In this discussion, based around the important skill of giving directions, communication is more important than grammar. While students are focusing on communicating information about how to get from one place to another, they are learning how to use English naturally without worrying about making grammar or pronunciation mistakes.

3 Giving Directions 

- ❑ Put the students in pairs.
- ❑ Read the directions at the top of the activity to the students. Read the example to them.
- ❑ Tell the students to take turns giving directions from and to the places listed.
- ❑ Walk around the room helping the students.

- ❑ When the students are finished with 1–4, have one or two pairs give directions in front of the class.
- ❑ Read the directions at the end of the activity. Tell the pairs that they are now all at Joe's Diner.
- ❑ Have one of the students of each pair give directions to one of the lettered locations on the map to the other student.
- ❑ When the students have finished, ask them how successful they were. What kind of mistakes did they make? Do they feel as if they are mastering this important skill?

GETTING DIRECTIONS ON THE PHONE

- Read the directions with the students.
- Go over the three pieces of information that you need to tell the bus company.
- Read and explain the *Language Tip* to the students.

4 Listening for Directions on the Phone 

- ❑ Read the directions for the listening exercise.
- ❑ Play the short conversations one by one. After each conversation, give the students time to fill in the chart.
- ❑ After the last phone conversation, put the students in pairs. Tell them to check their answers.
- ❑ If the students are having a difficult time, play the recording one more time.
- ❑ Go over the answers as a class. Write the answers on the board.

ANSWER KEY

1. Destination: the airport
   Bus number: 33
   Time to get on: 4:50
   Place to get on: the corner of Main and Grant
   Place to get off: Airport Boulevard
2. Destination: Salem
   Time to get on: 8:50 in the morning
   Place to get on: Hilton Hotel
   Fare: $7.00 one way
   Travel time: about 40 minutes
3. Destination: 1800 Orange Street
   Bus number: 102
   Place to get on: the corner of Hollywood and Temple
   How often bus runs: every six minutes

AUDIOSCRIPT

Conversation 1

A: Metro Bus Company.

B: Hello. I need to go to the airport from Main Street.

A: Main Street and what?

B: Main and Grant.

A: OK. What time do you have to be at the airport?

B: At six o'clock.

A: Take bus thirty-three at four-fifty at the corner of Main and Grant. Get off at Airport Boulevard. That's two blocks from the airport.

B: So it's bus number thirty-three at four-fifty; and I get off at . . .

A: Airport Boulevard.

B: Thank you very much.

Conversation 2

A: Bus information. Tom speaking.

B: I want to go to Salem. Is there a bus at around nine in the morning?

A: Just a minute . . . There's one at eight-fifty, leaving from the Hilton Hotel.

B: I see. What's the fare?

A: It's $7.00 one way.

B: How long does it take?

A: About forty minutes.

B: Thanks.

Conversation 3

A: Metro Bus Company. May I help you?

B: How can I get to 1800 Orange Street?

A: From where?

B: From Hollywood Boulevard. Hollywood and Temple.

A: Get on bus number 102 at the corner of Hollywood and Temple. Get off at Madison Avenue and Orange, then walk two blocks north on Orange.

B: How often does the bus run?

A: Ah, let's see. Bus 102 runs, uh, every six minutes.

B: Every six minutes? That's great. Thanks.

Self-Assessment Log

- ❑ The purpose of the log is to help the students reflect on their learning.
- ❑ Read the directions aloud and have students check vocabulary that they learned in the chapter and are prepared to use.
- ❑ Have students check the strategies they understand.
- ❑ Put students in small groups. Ask students to find the information or an activity related to each strategy in the chapter.
- ❑ Tell students to find definitions in the chapter for any words they did not check, or they can look in their dictionaries.

Chapter

5

Home

In this chapter, students will learn language related to the home. In Part 1, they will hear a conversation about moving to a new apartment. They will also practice listening for and pronouncing *-ed* endings on past tense verbs. In Part 2, students will learn language for renting an apartment and practice listening for main ideas and specific information. In Part 3, they will enhance their knowledge of using context clues. They will also practice language for finding a roommate. In Part 4, students will use the language that they have learned in the context of giving instructions to movers. These topics will prepare students for dealing with authentic housing situations in their life.

Chapter Opener

- ❑ Have students look at the photo of the men loading a sofa into a moving van. Ask the students the three questions in the Connecting to the Topic section. Discuss the questions with the class.
- ❑ Have students read the quote from Joyce Maynard.
- ❑ Ask the students what they think the quote means. If they don't understand it, tell them that a *home* is more than just a "house." People have to work hard together to develop a family atmosphere. You can't buy love and cooperation.

"A good home must be made, not bought."

—Joyce Maynar
American author (1953 –

Chapter Overview

Listening Skills and Strategies

Listening for main ideas

Listening for details

Following directions

Distinguishing among past tense *-ed* endings

Listening to a house tour

Following house-sitting instructions

Speaking Skills and Strategies

Talking about finding somewhere to live

Describing a moving day

Interviewing someone about an apartment

Making and answering requests

Interviewing possible roommates

Critical Thinking Skills

Interpreting a photo

Explaining a process

Taking notes while separating positive from negative details

Using a multi-column chart to fill-in notes and organize a plan

Summarizing ideas using key words

Vocabulary Building

Terms to talk about apartments

Common verbs related to moving

Expressions for making and answering requests

Verbs and frequency expressions to explain homecare

Pronunciation

Identifying and practicing stressed words

Comparing reduced and unreduced pronunciation

Pronouncing past tense *-ed* endings

Focus on Testing

Using context clues to guess what speakers are implying

Vocabulary

Nouns	Verbs	Adjectives	Adverb
closet	fix	available	pretty
fireplace	move (in/out)	furnished/unfurnished	**Expression**
landlord	raise	stressed out	month-to-month
leak			
lease			
studio			
vacancy (vacancies)			

Can You Guess?

- Ask students to discuss the questions in groups and compare answers with the correct answers.
- Ask students how these statistics compare to their culture.

1. What percentage of American homes and apartments are lived in by their owners? *A. 68%.* * **2.** How many times does the average American move in his or her life? How does this compare with people in another culture that you know? *A. 11 times; Americans are more than four times as likely to change residences in the course of a year.* ** **3.** What is the average number of people living in an American home? *A. 2.69 people.* †

Footnotes:
* Source: U.S. Department of Housing and Urban Development (HUD): http://www.hud.gov/news/focus.cfm?content= 2003-01-28.cfm
** Source: Slate: http://www.slate.com/id/2122832/fr/rss
† Source: http://factfinder.census.gov

Before You Listen

Best Practice

Activating Prior Knowledge

The prelistening questions activate students' prior knowledge. This activity will help students relate their own experience of living in different kinds of housing to the new language in this chapter. When students activate their prior knowledge before learning new material, they are better able to map new language onto existing concepts, which aids understanding and retention.

1 Prelistening Questions 

- ❑ Have the students look at the photo of the apartment building with the *vacancy* sign. Ask what the word *vacancy* means.
- ❑ Explain that the prelistening questions will help the students with the conversation that they are going to hear.
- ❑ Have the students read the questions and discuss them in pairs.
- ❑ Compare answers as a whole class.

2 Previewing Vocabulary 

- ❑ Play the recording and ask students to listen to the words.
- ❑ Read the directions to the students.
- ❑ Go over the vocabulary to make sure that the students know what each word means.
- ❑ Have students complete the activity individually.
- ❑ Compare their answers as a whole class and write the correct answers on the board.

ANSWER KEY

1. landlord 2. closet 3. studio 4. unfurnished 5. pretty 6. raised 7. vacancies 8. fireplace 9. move out 10. stressed out

Listen

3 Listening for Main Ideas 

(The audioscript follows Activity 5.)

- ❑ Have different students read the questions.
- ❑ Ask them if they understand the questions.
- ❑ Ask students to close their books as they listen.
- ❑ Play the recording and have students answer the questions.
- ❑ Tell them to compare their answers in pairs.
- ❑ Finally, go over the answers with the class. Ask them for specific words or phrases they heard that support their answers.

ANSWER KEY

1. The landlord raised the rent.
2. There is a one-bedroom apartment available in Ming's apartment building.

4 Listening for Details 

(The audioscript follows Activity 5.)

- ❑ Ask the students to look at the four true-false questions. Have the students take turns reading the questions to the class.
- ❑ Play the recording.
- ❑ Have the students answer the questions individually.
- ❑ Put the students in pairs to compare answers.
- ❑ Go over the questions as a group. Ask for additional details from the conversation (e.g., What other features does the apartment have?).

ANSWER KEY

1. T 2. F 3. T 4. F

Stress

5 Listening for Stressed Words 

- ❑ Have a student read the directions. Respond to any questions.
- ❑ Play the recording again. This time tell the students to keep their books open. Tell the students to fill in the blanks with the words that they hear.
- ❑ After listening, have students check their answers with a partner. Then have each pair check their answers with the audioscript in their books.
- ❑ Read the final instruction about reading the conversation with a partner. Tell the students to look at the completed conversation above.
- ❑ Put the students in pairs. Have the students choose a role in the conversation and read it with their partner.
- ❑ Tell the students to focus on stressing the important words correctly.
- ❑ The students should read each of their conversation turns, but then look up at their partner, not at their book, when they are speaking. Remind the students that eye contact is very important when speaking in English.
- ❑ Walk around the room, giving the students feedback on their speaking.

AUDIOSCRIPT and ANSWER KEY

Beth: I'm so stressed out. My landlord just raised my rent. I think I'll have to move.

Ming: Really? You know, my building has some vacancies. It's a pretty nice place, and it's just ten minutes from campus.

Beth: Oh yeah? How much is the rent for a studio?

Ming: There are no studio apartments in our building. My neighbor just moved out of a one-bedroom. He paid $850 a month, I think.

Beth: That's not bad. Tell me more.

Ming: Well, one-bedrooms come with a bathroom, a kitchen, a fireplace in the living room, pretty big closets, and uh . . . Are you looking for a furnished or unfurnished place?

Beth: Unfurnished. I have all my own stuff. What about parking and laundry?

Ming: There's no garage. You have to park on the street. But there *is* a laundry room downstairs.

Beth: Hmm. I think I'm interested. Could you give me the address?

Ming: Sure. It's 1213 Rose Avenue. The manager's name is Mr. Azizi. Call him up or just stop by and talk to him.

Beth: Thanks, Ming. I'm going to do that tomorrow for sure.

Reductions

6 Comparing Unreduced and Reduced Pronunciation 

- ❑ Have a student read the directions to the class. Ask the class whether they understood the directions.
- ❑ Read and explain the *Language Tip* below the sentence chart about /h/.
- ❑ Play the recording of the unreduced and reduced forms of the sentences from the conversation.
- ❑ Have the students as a class repeat the two forms. Give general feedback.
- ❑ Have individual students volunteer to say the two forms. Give individual feedback.

7 Listening for Reductions 

- ❑ Read the directions to the students.
- ❑ Play the recording and have students write in their answers.
- ❑ When the conversation is finished, put the students in pairs and have them check their answers. Then check the answers as a class.
- ❑ Have the pairs take roles and read the conversation. Remind them to read, look up, then speak.

ANSWER KEY

A: Mr. Azizi, I have to talk to you. I have another problem.

B: Could you call me later? I'm busy now.

A: No, I need the plumber again. Could you call him right now?

B: I have a lot of things to do. I'll call him tomorrow morning, okay?

A: No, I need him right now!

B: Are you having trouble with the toilet again?

A: Yes. Look, just give me the plumber's number. I'll call him.

B: All right, all right. Just give me a minute and I'll do it.

After You Listen

8 Using Vocabulary 

- ❑ Read the directions aloud. Point out the page numbers for Student A and Student B as indicated in the directions of the Student Book.
- ❑ Put the students in pairs. Tell them to decide who will be Student A and Student B.
- ❑ Read the A and B directions in the Student A and Student B boxes. This activity is more complicated than most that they have done. Make sure that the students understand that Student A will ask three questions first. Student B must look at the three choices and choose the appropriate one. The students who are responding must use true information from their life or from their culture. Tell the students that they will have to take the incomplete sentences that they see and use them to say a complete sentence.
- ❑ Have the students ask and answer the questions.
- ❑ Check the answers as a class.

ANSWER KEY

Student A: 1. c 2. b 3. a

Student B: 1. c 2. a 3. b

Since the answers in the parentheses are true information from the students' lives, answers will vary.

Pronunciation

THE *-ED* ENDING IN PAST TENSE VERBS 

- Read and explain the *Pronunciation* instruction note about the *-ed* ending.
- Play the recording. Have students listen and repeat.

9 Distinguishing Among *-ed* Endings 

❑ Read the directions for the activity.

❑ Play the recording and have students write the words in the blanks and check the sound they hear at the end of the word.

❑ If necessary, play the recording again.

❑ Have the students check their answers in pairs.

❑ Write the answers to the activity on the board.

ANSWER KEY

	/id/	/t/	/d/
1. turned	❑	❑	✓
2. rented	✓	❑	❑
3. mixed	❑	✓	❑
4. asked	❑	✓	❑
5. recommended	✓	❑	❑
6. walked	❑	✓	❑
7. tested	✓	❑	❑
8. followed	❑	❑	✓
9. moved	❑	❑	✓
10. changed	❑	❑	✓

AUDIOSCRIPT

1. turned
2. rented
3. mixed
4. asked
5. recommended
6. walked
7. tested
8. followed
9. moved
10. changed

10 Pronouncing *-ed* Endings 

❑ Read the directions to the students.

❑ Give the students time to read the questions and ask questions about them.

❑ Put the students in pairs.

❑ Tell the students to take turns asking and answering the questions. Ask the student who is answering the question to close his or her book.

❑ Tell the students to be careful with the pronunciation of the *-ed* sounds.

❑ While the students are doing the activity, walk around the room and monitor the students' pronunciation.

❑ As a class, go over the answers.

11 Using *-ed* Endings 

❑ Point out the illustrations and the verbs below the illustrations. Tell the students that they will be using these verbs to explain Jennifer's moving experience.

❑ Read the directions to the students. Have a student read the example.

❑ Remind the students that Jennifer has already moved, so all sentences need to be in the past tense.

- Put the students in pairs. Have them take turns making sentences explaining what is happening in the illustrations. Answers will vary.

ANSWER KEY

Possible answers

1. Jennifer watched the movers take her boxes into her apartment. The movers carried the boxes inside.
2. She called her family. They asked her to describe the apartment.
3. She looked at a stack of boxes. She decided where everything should go.
4. She unpacked her dishes.
5. She washed her dishes. She dropped some cups.
6. She dusted her furniture. She sneezed.
7. She painted some rooms in her apartment.
8. She worked in the yard. She planted some flowers.
9. She ordered pizza for dinner.
10. She rested after dinner.

Talk It Over

12 Asking for Information About Apartments

- Have the students look at the three apartment advertisements on pages 90 and 91. Point out the ideas for questions on the right.
- Read the directions to the students. Tell the students to write five questions for each apartment. Explain that they will be doing a role play and will ask these questions to a partner. Because the ads do not answer these questions, the student who plays the manager will have to create answers.
- When the students have finished their 15 questions, go over them with the students. Select students to read their questions. This will give students who struggled with the questions a chance to revise theirs.
- Put the students in pairs. Tell them to decide who will be the manager and who will be the renter. Have the students start the role play.
- When the students have finished, select pairs to act out the role plays in front of the class.

Sample Questions

Apartment 1—How much is the rent? How many rooms are there? Is the apartment noisy? Is there a stove or refrigerator? (Student's own question.)

Apartment 2—How big is the apartment in square feet (or in square meters)? Or How many square feet (or square meters) is it? How long is the lease for? Is there a garage? How many bathrooms are there? (Student's own question.)

Apartment 3—Are male and female roommates both O.K.? How many rooms are there in the apartment? Is smoking allowed? Where is the apartment? How much is the rent?

Best Practice

Interacting with Others

This type of activity is an example of collaborative learning to encourage fluency and confidence. In this information exchange activity, based around the topic of the students' residence, communication is more important than grammar. Students practice the activity in pairs, improving their understanding and performance by switching roles. Each student has the opportunity to present information and to receive information. By the time they explain their partner's information to the class, they should feel more confident in their use of the new language.

EXPANSION ACTIVITY

- Please see Black Line Master "My Home" on page BLM 9 of this Teacher's Edition.
- Photocopy and distribute one copy to each student.
- Read all of the directions to the students.
- Point out the two boxes to the students. Make sure that they understand that they are going to first draw their home in the first box. They will then describe their home to a partner. The partner will draw the home in the second box.
- Give the students time to draw their homes.
- For Part 2, put the students in pairs. Have the students take turns describing their homes.
- Walk around the room helping the students. Make sure that they use only words to help their partner draw their homes.

Before You Listen

Best Practice

Making Use of Academic Content

The prelistening discussion is an example of personalization. This type of activity encourages students to relate the topic to the authentic world of their own experiences. Asking students to talk about their current residence creates a framework through which they can interpret the topic. This activity gives students a chance to discuss authentic examples from their own lives.

1 Prelistening Questions 

- ❑ Read the directions to the students.
- ❑ Tell the students to read the three questions. Give them time to ask clarification questions.
- ❑ Put the students into pairs and have them discuss the questions.
- ❑ Go over their answers as a class.

2 Previewing Vocabulary 

- ❑ Tell the students to read the directions. Give them some time to ask questions.
- ❑ Play the recording and have students listen to the underlined words.
- ❑ Have the students answer the questions individually.
- ❑ Tell the students to compare their answers with a partner.
- ❑ Check the answers as a class, writing the correct answers on the board.

ANSWER KEY

1. d 2. a 3. b 4. e 5. c

Listen

3 Listening for Main Ideas 

(The audioscript follows Activity 5.)

- ❑ Tell the students that they are going to listen to a listening passage. This one is longer than the first one. Tell them that they will need to listen carefully and take notes. Show the students the lines in the book on which they can take notes.
- ❑ Go over the directions with the students.
- ❑ Have a student read the three questions.
- ❑ Play the recording.
- ❑ Tell the students that you will be answering the questions in a later activity.

ANSWER KEY

1. The manager shows Beth the living room, the kitchen, the bedroom, and the bathroom.
2. No it isn't. Clues: There is no air conditioning. The bedroom is small. There was a leak.
3. Beth needs more time to think before making a decision.

Best Practice

Organizing Information

This type of activity uses a graphic organizer to categorize information. Taking notes encourages students to process and organize information while they are listening and also provides a record for them to refer to when they are studying later. This type of graphic organizer emphasizes categorizing information into positive and negative categories. Other types of graphic organizers are used throughout this book.

4 Taking Notes on Specific Information 

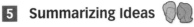

(The audioscript follows Activity 5.)

- ❑ Have the students look at the organization chart for the information from the dialogue. Make sure that they understand what *Good Points* and *Bad Points* are.
- ❑ Read the directions for the activity. Have one or two students paraphrase back to you what they are going to do.
- ❑ Play the recording. Give the students time to write down their ideas in the chart.
- ❑ Put the students into pairs. Have the partners compare their notes.

ANSWER KEY

Rooms Visited	Good Points	Bad Points
living room	just painted, lots of light, fireplace	green walls, no air conditioning, street noises
kitchen	dishwasher, big refrigerator, enough room for a breakfast table	--------
bedroom	new carpeting, lots of closet space	small bedroom
bathroom	shower and bathtub	leak
apartment in general	(Note: there's nothing generally good about the apartment itself, but some students might consider the option of a month-to-month lease or a year's lease a good point.)	raised rent

After You Listen

5 Summarizing Ideas 

- ❑ Read the directions to the students. Give the students an opportunity to ask questions.
- ❑ Put the students in pairs. Tell them to summarize the conversation. Encourage them to look back at their notes from Activities 3 and 4 to help them.
- ❑ Walk around the room, helping the students.

AUDIOSCRIPT

Mr. Azizi: So, here's the living room. Oh, and please don't touch the walls; we just painted them. I hope you like green.

Beth: Well, green is not my favorite color . . .

Mr. Azizi: As you can see, there's lots of light in here. And here's the fireplace. It's great in the winter.

Beth: Whew, it's warm in here, isn't it? Is there any air conditioning?

Mr. Azizi: No, there isn't. Just keep this window open. Oh, it's almost never this noisy.

Beth: I'm sorry, what did you say?

Mr. Azizi: Come this way. Here's your kitchen, an electric stove, a dishwasher . . . This big refrigerator is included, and there's room for a breakfast table here . . .

Beth: That's nice. Could I see the bedroom?

Mr. Azizi: Sure, it's over here. We just put in new carpeting, so . . . uh . . . we raised the rent $25.

Beth: Oh, really? Hmm . . . the bedroom looks a little small.

Mr. Azizi: But look at all the closet space! And here's the bathroom, with a shower and bathtub.

Beth: Oh, what about that leak?

Mr. Azizi:	Hmm. I can't believe it. The plumber just fixed it last week.
Beth:	Uh, if I decide to take this apartment, when can I move in?
Mr. Azizi:	It's available on the first of the month. So that's actually the day after tomorrow.
Beth:	I see. And, uh, do I have to sign . . . I mean, is there a lease?
Mr. Azizi:	It's up to you. You can sign a one-year lease or you can pay month-to-month. So, uh, are you interested?
Beth:	Possibly. I need to think about it a little more. And I have a few more questions.
Mr. Azizi:	No problem. Let's go to my office and talk.

6 Using Vocabulary 

- ❑ Read the directions to the students.
- ❑ Tell them to read all of the questions. Clarify any questions.
- ❑ Put the students in pairs. Have them discuss all of the questions.
- ❑ Go over the questions as a class.

Best Practice

Making Use of Academic Content

This is an example of an activity that exposes students to a situation that they will actually face in an academic setting. They will live in an apartment, house, or dormitory and will sometimes need to discuss problems with a landlord or a residence hall manager. The language for polite requests which they learn and practice in this activity will be extremely useful when they are faced with this kind of situation.

Using Language Functions

MAKING AND ANSWERING REQUESTS

- Go over the expressions in the *Making Requests* chart. Make sure that the students understand the note about "Would you mind" at the bottom of the chart.

7 Role-Play 

- ❑ Go over the directions with the students. Make sure the students understand the five things that Beth will ask about.
- ❑ Put the students in pairs. Tell them to decide who is Beth and who is Mr. Azizi. Make sure the students understand that the student who is Beth must ask the landlord to improve the five aspects of the apartment.
- ❑ Have several pairs perform their role-plays for the class.

Best Practice

Cultivating Critical Thinking

This is an example of a collaborative team activity resulting in a final product. This type of activity requires students to process the information they have learned and apply it to a new situation. The process of manipulating language and concepts in this way will create deeper processing of new material which will allow students to evaluate whether they have understood the new material and help them remember it better. In this activity, student must use the concepts that they have learned about residences and apply them to the creation of a new, *ideal* residence.

EXPANSION ACTIVITY

- Please see Black Line Master "A Perfect House" on page BLM 10 of this Teacher's Edition.
- Photocopy and distribute one copy to each student.
- Put the students in small groups.
- Have a student read the general directions. Give the students time to ask questions about anything they don't understand.
- Read the directions for Part 1 and Part 2. Point out the questions and the lines for their description.
- Tell the students that this is a creative activity. They can let their imaginations go. If they want a Jacuzzi or an exercise room in their house, they can have one.
- Make sure they understand that they will be presenting their perfect house to the class.
- Give the groups time to answer the questions and write a description.
- Have the groups present their houses one-by-one. Every member of the group must have a speaking part in the presentation. Groups may use the board to draw the rooms of the house, but the presentation must depend on the students' oral explanations.

Best Practice

Scaffolding Instruction

This is an example of an activity that raises metacognitive awareness of learning strategies. In real life, we use surrounding context clues to work out the meanings of unfamiliar words. This activity asks students to use the words that they know in each piece of the conversation to work out the meanings of new words. By asking students to write the clues, they are guided through the steps of developing this skill.

Getting Meaning from Context

Focus on Testing

Using Context Clues 

- Read the directions to the students. Tell them that they will be practicing an important learning strategy for listening.
- Point out to the students that this is a *Focus on Testing* activity. The skill taught in this activity will help students with standardized tests, such as the Internet-based TOEFL®.
- Go over the chart with the students.
- Play each conversation, and have students write their answers.
- Put the students in pairs and have them compare their charts.
- Go over the answers and clues as a class.

ANSWER KEY

Answers	Clues
1. b. had a party at the house	couldn't study because of the noise, couldn't sleep, kept me up till 3:00 A.M.
2. a. because she is messy and doesn't clean	dishes still on the table, clothes never in closet, on the floor, on the chair
3. c. There's only one television in the house.	news, favorite comedy show, argument, turn to channel 4
4. a. His roommate should pay more than half.	most of the phone calls, never cook, don't want to pay half
5. b. It's not comfortable for four people.	tiny kitchen, not much privacy, can't even relax, sleep on living room floor

AUDIOSCRIPT

Conversation 1

Sam: Alex, can I talk to you about something?

Alex: Sure, what's up?

Sam: You know, last night I couldn't study because of all the noise. And then I couldn't sleep either. You guys kept me up till 3:00 A.M.

Question 1: What did Alex probably do last night?

Alex: Sorry man, next time I won't have a party on a weeknight.

Conversation 2

Amy: I hate my roommate. Look at this! All the dishes are still on the table from last night! And her clothes! She never puts them in her closet. They're on the floor, on the chair, everywhere.

Susanna: Amy, why don't you talk to her about it?

Amy: I already talked to her about ten times. She won't change.

Question 2: Why does Amy hate her roommate?

Susanna: You know, you should find another roommate who isn't messy and who cleans up after herself.

Conversation 3

Tara: Do you mind if I watch the news?

Kim: Yes, actually I do. My favorite comedy is coming on right now.

Tara: Is that more important than the news?

Kim: Don't start that again. We had the same argument last night. Just turn to channel 4, OK?

Question 3: Which sentence is probably true?

Tara: I think our house needs another television set.

Conversation 4

Joe: Sasha, we need to pay our bills today. The telephone bill is $360 and the gas is $40.

Sasha: OK, so I'll give you $200. We're sharing everything half and half, right?

Joe: Yes, but it's not fair. *You* made most of the phone calls. And I almost never cook. So I don't want to pay half of these bills.

Sasha: But Joe, we agreed to pay everything 50–50!

Question 4: What does Joe think?

Joe: I don't think $200 is enough. This month you need to pay more than half.

Conversation 5

Carol: Alice, you know, your friends have stayed with us for over a month.

Alice: I know, but they haven't been able to find their own place to live yet.

Carol: I understand, but we just have one bathroom, a tiny kitchen, and not much privacy.

Alice: But they're so nice—you really think there's a problem?

Carol: Yeah—we can't even relax, or watch TV when they go to sleep on the living room floor!

Question 5: What is probably true about their apartment?

Alice: I know it's uncomfortable here for four people, but they'll leave soon, I promise.

Talk It Over

1 Finding a Roommate 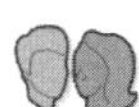

- ❑ Have students look at the three-panel illustration of Nabil and Roberto. Ask the students to tell you what they think is happening in the story.
- ❑ Read the directions to the students. Make sure that they understand all of the information about Nabil and Roberto.
- ❑ Put the students in pairs.
- ❑ Tell the students to prepare a conversation between Nabil and Roberto as they meet each other for the first time. Encourage them to ask a lot of questions that they need to know about this new person to determine if they should be roommates. Make sure they understand that they will perform the conversation in front of the class.
- ❑ Have the pairs act out the conversation.
- ❑ Ask for volunteers to perform a role play in front of the class.

Strategy

Graphic Organizer: Multi-Column Chart

- Read the description of the multi-column chart to the students.
- Go over the information in the sample chart with the students.

1 Preparing to Leave Home for Vacation 

- ❑ Have students take turns reading parts of the directions. Make sure that the students understand the cultural situation of having someone take care of a home in the owners' absence.
- ❑ Go over the chart with the students. Give the students an opportunity to ask questions about anything which they do not understand.
- ❑ Play the recording. Give the students time to write what they have understood in the chart.
- ❑ Play the recording a second time.
- ❑ Put the students in pairs. Have the students compare their charts and discuss differences.
- ❑ Go over the chart as a class.

ANSWER KEY

Homecare Vacation Instructions

Item to Take Care of	What to Do	How Often/ When to Do It	Details, Notes
1. *mail newspaper*	a) get mail b) *pick up from yard*	every day	put them inside the front door in a bag
2. *dog*	a) feed the dog b) walk the dog c) give him water	twice a day around 8:00 A.M. and around 5:00 P.M. walk him after he eats keep water bowl filled up	*dog food will be in bag in kitchen* give a cup of dry dog food
3. *garbage*	a) put garbage can back in the back yard	Tuesday night	*uncle will take garbage to street*
4. *rose bushes*	a) water rose bushes	a) two or three times a week	not necessary if it rains
5. *Swimming pool and house*	a) *clean up*	(no details included)	no wild parties

AUDIOSCRIPT

Uncle: So Beth, you're sure you have time to do some things for us while we're away?

Beth: No problem. Just let me know what you need done.

Uncle: OK. First, can you get our mail from the mailbox and any newspapers in the yard—and just put them inside the front door in a bag?

Beth: Fine. How often do you want that done?

Uncle: Every day, actually. But you'll need to feed and walk the dog twice a day, so you'll be over there anyway.

Beth: I see. What do I feed the dog, and how far should I walk him?

Uncle: A cup of dry dog food around 8:00 in the morning, and another around 5:00 should be fine. I'll leave a big bag of dog food in the kitchen. Walk him around the block when he's done eating. Oh, and keep his water bowl filled up, if you could.

Beth: Sure. Anything else?

Uncle: Well the garbage collector comes Tuesday, and I'm going to leave the garbage can down by the street today, but Tuesday night, can you put it back in the back yard for us?

Beth: I suppose so . . .

Uncle: Oh, and can you water the rose bushes in the front yard?

Beth: How often should I do that?

Uncle: Two or three times a week if it doesn't rain . . .

Beth: So is that all?

Uncle: Just one more thing—you're welcome to enjoy the swimming pool, the house —you know we just got a giant new plasma TV—just clean up, and no wild parties, OK?

Beth: How about the keys to your BMW?

Uncle: Sorry, but the car's not included . . .

2 Listening to Moving Instructions 

- ❑ Go over the illustrations for this activity with the students. Ask them to name the rooms. Ask the students what the room behind the bedroom is.
- ❑ Read the instructions to the students.
- ❑ Go over the seven items below the rooms. Ask the students to predict where Beth will ask the mover to put the items.
- ❑ Tell the students to write each item's number in the correct place in the apartment.
- ❑ Play the recording.
- ❑ Put the students in pairs. Have them compare answers.
- ❑ If necessary, play the recording again.

ANSWER KEY

1. The boxes of dishes should go on the kitchen counter.
2. She wants the TV on the right side of the fireplace.
3. The boxes of books are next to the bed.
4. The towels will go by the bathroom door.
5. Beth wants the couch where she is standing.
6. She wants the bookcase in the bedroom.
7. The clothes are on the bed.

AUDIOSCRIPT

Mover: Where do you want the couch, Miss?

Beth: How about . . . here, where I'm standing.

Mover: What about the TV?

Beth: Just put it to the right side of the fireplace.

Mover: And the bookcase? You want it in the living room, too?

Beth: No—in the bedroom, please.

Mover: What about these towels?

Beth: By the bathroom door would be great.

Mover: Where should I put these boxes? They're really heavy.

Beth: Careful! Those are my dishes. Just leave them on the kitchen counter. Where are the boxes with my books?

Mover: They're next to the bed. And your clothes are there, too. We put them on the bed. Is that OK?

Beth: Sure. Everything is a mess anyway.

3 Comparing Pictures 

- ❑ Tell students that they will look at two similar illustrations and find ten differences between the two illustrations.
- ❑ Have a student read the directions. Give the students some time to ask questions.
- ❑ Have two different students read the two sample sentences.
- ❑ Put the students into pairs. Make sure that the students are looking only at their page in the back of the Student Book.
- ❑ Tell the students to write down ten differences. Answers may vary so check the answers together as a class and write the sentences on the board.

Self-Assessment Log

- ❑ The purpose of the log is to help the students reflect on their learning.
- ❑ Read the directions aloud and have students check vocabulary that they learned in the chapter and are prepared to use.
- ❑ Have students check the strategies they understand.
- ❑ Put students in small groups. Ask students to find the information or an activity related to each strategy in the chapter.
- ❑ Tell students to find definitions in the chapter for any words they did not check, or they can look in their dictionaries.

Chapter

6

Cultures of the World

In this chapter, students will learn and practice language for talking about the world's cultures. In Part 1, the students will practice language for learning new customs. They will hear a conversation in which foreign students talk about adjusting to the culture of the United States. In Part 2, they will listen to a lecture about children becoming adults. They will also practice listening for main ideas and specific information. In Part 3, they will learn language for comparing customs. Students will also receive additional practice in recognizing context clues. In Part 4, they will practice talking about table manners. These topics will prepare students for a variety of real-life situations in which they will be interacting with people from various cultures.

Chapter Opener

- ❑ Have students look at the photo of a traditional Korean wedding ceremony. Discuss with the class the questions in the Connecting to the Topic section.
- ❑ Read aloud the quote from Voltaire.
- ❑ Ask the students what they think the quote means. If the students don't understand the quote, tell them that there is truth and beauty in all cultures and religions in the world.

" No culture has a monopoly on beauty and no religion has a monopoly on truth

—Voltaire (Francois-Marie Afouet)
French writer and philosopher (1694–1778)

Chapter Overview

Listening Skills and Strategies

Listening for main ideas

Listening for details

Listening to a lecture about coming of age ceremonies

Listening to instructions for setting a formal dinner table

Speaking Skills and Strategies

Comparing customs

Discussing minimum age requirements in different cultures

Talking about dining customs and table manners

Apologizing

Critical Thinking Skills

Interpreting a photo

Using a matrix diagram to organize ideas

Summarizing ideas using key words

Vocabulary Building

Adjectives describing feelings

Expressions for apologizing

Correct use of 'I'm sorry' vs. 'Excuse me'

Terms used related to table settings and table manners

Pronunciation

Identifying and practicing stressed words

Comparing reduced and unreduced pronunciation

Focus on Testing

Using context clues to identify culturally incorrect behaviors

Vocabulary

Nouns	Verbs	Adjectives	Expressions
adult	lay	amazed	so far
adulthood	look forward to (something)	exotic	used to
ceremony	serve	logical	
doggie bag	set the table	responsible for (something)	
handle			
impression			
leftovers			
napkin			
passage			
patio			
silverware			
utensil			
the woods			

Can You Guess?

- Ask students to discuss the questions below in groups and compare answers with the correct answers.
- Make sure that the students understand the words *custom* and *culture*. Ask for examples of both words. Customs are practices and behaviors that make up a culture.
- Ask the students what culture(s) they consider themselves to be a part of. Tell the students what culture(s) you consider yourself from.
- Ask the students whether they understand the word taboo.
- Ask the students to list taboos they know about.

1. Which is the second-most common language in the United States? *A. Spanish* **2.** At what age can a person drive in the United States? *A. 16.*

Before You Listen

Best Practice

Activating Prior Knowledge

The prelistening questions activate students' prior knowledge. The following activity will help students relate their own experience of meeting people from a different culture to the new language in this chapter. When students activate their prior knowledge before learning new material, they are better able to map new language onto existing concepts, which aids understanding and retention.

1 Prelistening Questions 

- Have students look at the photo and try to guess what is happening.
- Have the students read the questions and discuss them in pairs. For the first question, the students will have figured out the basic situation looking at the illustration. A woman is being told to stop using her cell phone in a restaurant. In this question, tell them to focus on the cultural issues. Why would she be surprised that she can't use her cell phone in a restaurant?
- Compare answers as a whole class.
- NOTE: This is a rich set of discussion questions dealing with complex cultural issues. For example, the third question asks students about their feelings when they travel and meet people from other cultures. If the students are interested in this topic and are anxious to tell their stories, let the activity go on longer than you usually do at this point in the chapter. The students may want to talk about their experiences.

2 Previewing Vocabulary 

- Play the recording and ask students to listen to the underlined words.
- Read the directions to the students.
- Don't explain the meaning of the underlined words. Tell the students that they must use the context of the sentences to guess the meaning.
- Have students complete the activity individually.
- Put the students into pairs. Have them compare their guesses about the meaning of the words.
- Compare their answers as a whole class and write the correct answers on the board.

ANSWER KEY

1. opinion, judgment 2. accustomed to or familiar with 3. unusual, different from the usual 4. a bag in which people take food home from a restaurant 5. surprised 6. until now 7. the food that was not eaten

Listen

3 Listening for Main Ideas 

(The audioscript follows Activity 5.)

- ❑ Tell the students to read the directions and questions in their books.
- ❑ Ask the students if they have any questions.
- ❑ Ask students to close their books as they listen.
- ❑ Play the recording. Have students write down their answers and then compare them with a partner.
- ❑ Finally, go through the three questions as a class comparing their answers. Ask them for specific words or phrases they heard that support their answers.

ANSWER KEY

1. The people are friendly and the city is beautiful, but the food isn't so good.
2. Salma was surprised about several things. In restaurants, you receive too much food. Beth took the leftovers home. There is air conditioning in restaurants, so it's very cold. They put ice in the water. You can't smoke in restaurants.
3. Ask for permission before you start smoking.

4 Listening for Details 

(The audioscript follows Activity 5.)

- ❑ Tell the students to look at the five true-false statements.
- ❑ Play the recording again if necessary.
- ❑ Put the students in pairs to answer true or false for each statement.
- ❑ Go over the items as a group. Ask for additional details from the conversation.

ANSWER KEY

1. False. Salma doesn't like hotdogs because they are usually made from pork.
2. True. He didn't like it at first, but he's used to it now.
3. False. Yolanda wasn't surprised, Salma was.
4. True. In Lebanon, people use cell phones "almost everywhere."
5. False. Salma uses that expression when she says that it was OK for Beth to make her smoke outside.

Stress

5 Listening for Stressed Words 

- ❑ Have a student read the directions.
- ❑ Play the recording again. This time tell the students to keep their books open.
- ❑ After listening, have students check their answers with a partner. Then have each pair check their answers with the audioscript in their books.

AUDIOSCRIPT AND ANSWER KEY

Kenji: So, Salma, is this your first trip to the United States?

Salma: Yes, it is.

Kenji: And what's your impression so far?

Salma: Well, the people are really friendly, and the city is beautiful. But the food; well, it's not so good.

Kenji: Oh, yeah, that's what I thought too when I first got here. But I'm used to American food now. I actually love hotdogs and French fries.

Yolanda: So last night I took Salma to a Mexican restaurant. I wanted her to try something exotic.

Kenji: Did you like it?

Salma: Yeah, the food was pretty good, but it was too much. I couldn't finish it all.

Yolanda: Salma was amazed when I took the leftovers home in a doggie bag.

Kenji: Yeah, that's funny, isn't it? They call it a doggie bag, but it's for people. Anyway, what else surprised you?

Salma: That the restaurant was so cold! We don't use air conditioning so much in my country. Oh, and the water had ice in it, too. I had to put on my sweater, I was so cold!

Salma: Excuse me. Hello? Oh, hi, Eduardo.

Waitress: Excuse me, Miss, but we don't allow cell phones in the restaurant.

Salma: Oh, sorry. I didn't know... Eduardo, I'll have to call you back. That's strange for me. In Lebanon we use phones everywhere. I mean, we try to talk quietly in a place like this, but...

Kenji: Same in Japan. This kind of rule is getting more popular, though.

Yolanda: I'm sorry, Salma.

Salma: No, no, it's OK. When in Rome, do as the Romans do.

- ❑ Read the directions at the end of Activity 5.
- ❑ Tell the students to look at the completed conversation in their books.
- ❑ Put the students in pairs. Have them choose a role in the conversation and read it with their partner.
- ❑ Tell them to focus on stressing the important words correctly.

Reductions

6 Comparing Unreduced and Reduced Pronunciation 

- ❑ Have a student read the directions to the class. Answer any questions.
- ❑ Play the recording of the unreduced and reduced forms of the sentences from the conversation in their books.
- ❑ Have the students as a class repeat the two forms.

7 Listening for Reductions 

- ❑ Explain to the students that although they may feel reluctant to use reduced forms, they need to be able recognize them when others use them.
- ❑ Play the recording and have students write their answers.
- ❑ When the conversation is finished, put the students in pairs and have them check their answers. Then check the answers as a class.
- ❑ Have the pairs take roles and read the conversation.

ANSWER KEY

Anita: Well, it's time to get back to the office. I'll see you soon, Brenda.

Brenda: OK, see you . . . Wait, Anita, is this your cell phone?

Anita: Oh my goodness, yes, thanks. By the way, I almost forgot: my parents are coming for a visit next week.

Brenda: Really? I'd love to meet them.

Anita: Well, do you want to have lunch with us on Saturday?

Brenda: Saturday? Hmm . . . I promised my roommate I would go shopping with her that day. Could we get together for coffee later in the afternoon?

Anita: I don't know. They might be busy, but I'll ask.

After You Listen

8 Using Vocabulary 

- ❑ Put the students in pairs. Have the students ask and answer the questions. Have the student who is not asking the question close his or her book. Alternate who asks the questions.
- ❑ When the students have finished, go over the questions as a class.
- ❑ Many of the questions involve interesting cultural issues (e.g., Do you remember the first time you visited a foreign country?), so you may want to allow the discussion to continue for some time.

Best Practice

Interacting with Others

This type of activity is an example of collaborative learning to encourage fluency and confidence. In this role-play, based around the topic of dealing with cultural differences, communication is more important than grammar. Students can practice the role-plays in small groups and then improve their performance by switching roles or partners. By the time they perform the role-play for the class, they should feel more confident in the use of the new language.

Talk It Over

9 Discussing Behavior 

- ❑ Go over the directions with the students.
- ❑ Have a student read the two discussion questions. Give the students time to ask for clarification.
- ❑ Put them in small groups and have them discuss the two questions in Part 1.
- ❑ When they have finished, go over their responses as a class.

EXPANSION ACTIVITY

- Please see Black Line Master "My Culture" on page BLM 11 of this Teacher's Edition.
- Photocopy and distribute one copy to each student.
- Go over the situation with the students. Remind them of the aspects of culture that they have discussed in Part 1 of this chapter.
- Have students read the questions in Part 1 of the BLM.
- Give the students 10 or 15 minutes to write down the most important aspects of their cultures, including taboos. Tell the students that they shouldn't write complete sentences. They can write down brief notes to help them speak with their friend (e.g., must take off shoes).
- For Part 2, put the students in pairs. If you have a heterogeneous class, make sure that everyone's partner comes from a different culture. If everyone in your class comes from the same culture, you will have to change the activity so that the pairs work together to create a detailed description of their culture.
- Read the directions to the students. Give them some time to ask questions.
- Tell the students to describe their cultures to each other. The partner who is listening should take notes.
- When the students have finished, ask for volunteers to describe their partner's culture to the class.

Before You Listen

1 Prelistening Questions 

- ❑ Ask the students to read the two questions. Give them time to ask clarification questions.
- ❑ Put the students into pairs and have them discuss the questions.

2 Previewing Vocabulary 

- ❑ Play the recording and ask students to listen to the words.
- ❑ Have the students answer the questions individually.
- ❑ Tell the students to compare their answers with a partner.
- ❑ Check the answers as a class, writing the correct answers on the board.

ANSWER KEY

1.e 2.g 3.b 4.a 5.f 6.d 7.c

Listen

3 Listening for Main Ideas 

- ❑ Read the directions and point out the four blank lines.
- ❑ Play the recording and have the students write down the four cultures. Put the students into pairs and tell them to check to see whether or not they heard the same four cultures.

ANSWER KEY

The four cultures discussed are North American Indian cultures, Jewish culture, Japanese culture, and the culture of the United States.

AUDIOSCRIPT

At what age does a child become an adult? The answer depends on your culture or religion. Here are a few examples.

First, in some North American Indian cultures, a boy becomes a man around the age of 13. At that time, he goes into the woods alone, without food or water, for several days. When he returns safely, he becomes an adult man. Girls become adult women as soon as they are old enough to have babies, also around the age of 12 or 13.

In the Jewish religion, children spend years studying their history and religion. Then at age 13 for boys and 12 for girls, they go through an important religious ceremony. The boys' ceremony is called a *bar mitzvah* and the girls' is called a *bat mitzvah*. From that day, they are adults, and they are responsible for their own religious development.

In Japan today, young people become legal adults at age 20. Each year on the second Monday in January, they celebrate "Coming-of-Age Day," when all the 20-year-olds in a town are invited to attend a special ceremony. They wear traditional clothes, listen to speeches, and visit with old friends.

Finally, in the United States, the passage into adulthood takes several years. American teenagers look forward to their 16th birthday because in most states that is the age when they can get a driver's license. The *legal* age of adulthood is 18, when Americans can vote, get married, and work full-time.

Best Practice

Organizing Information

This type of activity uses a graphic organizer to categorize information. Taking lecture notes encourages students to process and organize information while they are listening and also provides a record for them to refer to when they are studying later. This type of graphic organizer emphasizes listing and categorizing skills. Other types of graphic organizers are used throughout this book.

4 Taking Notes on Specific Information 

- ❑ Show the students the organization chart for the information from the lecture.
- ❑ Read the directions for the activity.
- ❑ Play the recording. Give the students time to write down their ideas in the chart.
- ❑ Put the students into pairs. Have the partners compare their tables.

ANSWER KEY

Culture / religion	Age	Details
1. North American Indian	*12-13*	Boys go into the woods alone at age 13, without food or water, for several days. When the boys return, they are men. Girls become adults when they can have a baby, at age 12 or 13
2. Jewish religion	Boys—13 Girls—12	Boys have bar mitzvah, a religious ceremony at age 13 Girls have bat mitzvah, a religious ceremony at age 12. After these ceremonies, boys and girls are responsible for their own religious development.
3. Japan	20	Both boys and girls celebrate "Coming-of-Age Day." All 20-year-olds attend a special ceremony, listening to speeches and visiting old friends.
4. United States	16, 18, and 21	At 16, in most states, both boys and girls can get a driver's license. At 18, they can vote, get married, and work full-time. At 21, they can drink alcohol. Some people celebrate by going to a bar with friends.

After You Listen

5 Summarizing Ideas 

- ❑ Put the students in groups of four. Have them compare their notes from Activities 3 and 4.
- ❑ Tell the students to choose one of the four cultures from the lecture and summarize the information about that culture.
- ❑ Remind the students to speak in complete sentences.
- ❑ If there is time, have four students summarize the information in front of the class.
- ❑ Tell the students to read the descriptions of their cultures without naming the culture. The class should guess which culture they are talking about.

6 Using Vocabulary 

- ❑ Tell the students to read all of the questions and to ask for clarification of anything that they don't understand.
- ❑ Put the students in pairs. Have them discuss all of the questions.
- ❑ Go over the questions as a class.

Talk It Over

Best Practice

Cultivating Critical Thinking

The following activity is an example of a collaborative team activity resulting in a final product. In this activity, students must decide what the appropriate age is for a variety of rights (e.g., the right to drive). The students must take their knowledge of their own culture's norms and integrate it with what they have just learned about four other cultures. They must decide what their own personal opinions are and find out what the other members of their group think. Finally, the students together will come up with a synthesis of their opinions to present to the class.

7 At What Age . . .? 

- ❑ Read the directions to the students.
- ❑ Have a student read the sample sentences.
- ❑ Go over the chart with the students, making sure they understand all of the items listed.
- ❑ Put the students into small groups. Try to have as much diversity of cultures in each group as possible.
- ❑ Tell the students to read each activity and decide when people should be allowed to do that activity. Have them fill in the *Age* columns of the chart.
- ❑ When the group discussions are finished, discuss each item as a class. Be sure to ask the students for their reasons for the ages that they decided on.

Reproducible — EXPANSION ACTIVITY

- Please see Black Line Master "A New Coming-of-Age Ceremony" on page BLM 12 of this Teacher's Edition.
- Photocopy and distribute one copy to each student.
- Read the directions for Part 1 and Part 2 to the students. Make sure that they understand that they will have to present their new ceremony to the class. Each student must present part of the group's plan.
- Put the students in groups. Have each group answer the questions. Tell them that after answering the questions, they should have enough information to present their new ceremony to the class.
- For Part 2, have them complete the chart by indentifying which portion each person will present. Then have them present their ideas to the class.

Getting Meaning from Context

Strategy

Graphic Organizer: Matrix Diagram

- Read the description of matrix diagrams to the students.
- Point out the matrix diagram used in the next activity.
- Ask the students for a new example of information that could be organized with this kind of graphic organizer.

Best Practice

Making Use of Academic Content

This is an example of an activity that exposes students to issues that they will actually face in an academic setting. They will be engaging in intercultural interactions in a variety of formal and informal settings with friends, colleagues, and strangers. They need to become familiar with possible cultural pitfalls so that they can develop a range of strategies for dealing with people from different cultures.

1 Prelistening Discussion 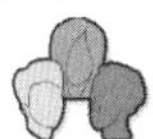

- ❑ Point out the culture chart. Make sure that the students understand the words *polite* and *rude*.
- ❑ Have the students fill out the chart individually.
- ❑ Put the students in small groups. Have them compare their charts.
- ❑ Go over the chart as a class. Write the different polite and rude behaviors on the board.
- ❑ Analyze the results. Are there cultures that are complete opposites in some categories? What cultures are similar?

Best Practice

Scaffolding Instruction

This is an example of an activity that raises metacognitive awareness of learning strategies. In real life, we use surrounding context clues to work out the meanings of unfamiliar words. This activity asks students to use the words that they know in each piece of the conversation to work out the meanings of new words. By asking students to write the clues, they are guided through the steps of developing this skill.

Focus on Testing

Using Context Clues 

- Point out to the students that this is a *Focus on Testing* activity. The skill taught in this activity will help students with standardized tests, such as the Internet-based TOEFL®.
- Read the directions to the students. Tell them that they will be practicing an important learning strategy for listening.
- Play each conversation.
- Put the students in pairs and have them compare their charts.
- Go over the answers and clues as a class.

ANSWER KEY

Answers	Clues
1. a. She didn't call before visiting.	Belinda sounds surprised. Uh . . . Belinda is "a little bit" busy. Come in for a few minutes, anyway.
2. b. He forgot to leave a tip.	Was there a problem? Was the service O.K.? Did I do anything? No, you were great. Excellent service.

3. c. The man did because he came too early.	The beginning was kind of strange. I went there at exactly 8:00. She was still in the shower. The food wasn't ready. There were no other guests.
4. a. He asked about the price of the house.	The woman's speech becomes full of hesitation sounds after he asks the price. Uh, well, I mean, uh, uh...
5. c. That Koreans don't hug people they don't know very well.	She looked uncomfortable and kind of pushed me away.

AUDIOSCRIPT

Conversation 1

Yuka: Hi, Belinda.

Belinda: Hi, Yuka. What are you doing here?

Yuka: Oh, I was in your neighborhood. I just wanted to say hi.

Belinda: Uh, that's nice. Uh . . .

Yuka: Are you busy?

Belinda: Uh, yes, a little bit. But come in for a few minutes, anyway.

Question 1: What mistake did Yuka make?

Yuka: I'm sorry I didn't call before I came. I'll only stay a few minutes.

Conversation 2

Customer: Excuse me, waiter!

Waiter: Yes, are you ready to pay, sir?

Customer: Yes, here you are.

Waiter: Thank you. Uh . . . Excuse me, sir. Was there a problem with your food?

Customer: No. It was delicious, thank you.

Waiter: Uh, was the service OK? I mean, did I do anything . . .?

Customer: No, you were great. Excellent service.

Waiter: Oh, OK. I just, uh, wasn't sure . . .

Question 2: What mistake did the customer probably make?

Customer: Oh, I almost forgot. Here's your tip.

Conversation 3

Woman: So how was your neighbor's party last night?

Man: Fine, but the beginning was kind of strange.

Woman: Oh? What happened?

Man: My neighbor said the party started at eight o'clock. So I went there at exactly 8:00. I couldn't believe it: she was still in the shower, the food wasn't ready, and there were no guests.

Woman: So what did you do?

Man: Oh, I just sat down and waited for about half an hour. Then people began to arrive and the party got started.

Question 3: Who made a mistake?

Woman: I guess you didn't know: in the U.S., people never arrive at parties exactly on time.

Conversation 4

Man: Wow, this is a great house!

Woman: Thanks.

Man: When did you move in?

Woman: We bought it two months ago. We finally moved in last week.

Man: How much did you pay for it?

Woman: Uh, well, it was a good, I mean, uh, a pretty good price, uh . . . Would you like a drink or something?

Man: Yeah, a glass of water would be great, thanks.

Question 4: What mistake did the man make?

Man: It was rude of me to ask how much you paid. I'm sorry.

Conversation 5

Woman: I don't understand my new neighbors from Korea.

Man: What do you mean?

Woman: Well, yesterday was my neighbor Hyun-Ee's birthday. So I told her happy birthday and put my arms around her. You know, to give her a big hug.

Man: Uh-oh. What did she do?

Woman: She looked uncomfortable and kind of pushed me away. Don't you think that's rude?

Man: No. She probably thought *you* were rude.

Question 5: What didn't the American woman know?

Man: In Korea, it's not customary to hug people you don't know very well.

Talk It Over

2 Comparing Customs 

- ❑ Go over the directions and read the sample sentences in numbers one and two. Explain that in numbers three to five, the students must create the complete answers.
- ❑ Put the students in pairs. Have them fill in the blank lines with comparisons between countries. They can get information from the conversations in Activity 1 on page 116 and from their own experiences.
- ❑ Go over the answers as a class.

Using Language Functions

APOLOGIZING

- Read the information about apologizing to the students. Go over the chart with the expressions.
- Make sure that the students see that the apologies and responses become more formal as they go down the chart.
- Tell the students that when Americans apologize, they often give a reason for what they did, e.g., I'm really sorry that I'm late. Traffic was horrible. I should have left earlier.
- Review the Culture Note on the difference between *excuse me* and *I'm sorry*.

3 Role-Play 

- ❑ Point out the illustration of the angry man. Ask the students what they think is happening in the illustration.
- ❑ Have a student read the introductory directions.
- ❑ Have four different students read the four role-play situations.
- ❑ Put the students in pairs. Have them prepare short conversations for each situation in which one person apologizes and the other responds.
- ❑ Ask for volunteers to present the various situations in front of the class.

Culture Note

- Have the students read the culture note to themselves.
- Clarify any questions they might have.
- Point out the photo and discuss the details with the class. Ask them what they see in the picture. You might ask if they would like to be a part of this dinner party. Why or why not? Note: The two people in the photo are part of a bigger dinner party which appears formal.

1 Prelistening Questions 

- ❑ Have students first take turns reading the discussion questions to the class.
- ❑ Put the students into pairs. Tell them to discuss the questions.
- ❑ Go over the questions as a class. On the board, write new vocabulary that comes up in the discussion.

2 Previewing Vocabulary 

- ❑ Play the recording and have students listen to the underlined words.
- ❑ Have the students do the activity individually. Remind them to use context clues to guess the meaning of words that they don't know. For example, for *set the table*, the phrase "before dinner" is a clue.
- ❑ Put the students into pairs to compare their answers.
- ❑ Go over the answers as a class.

ANSWER KEY

1. h 2. d 3. g 4. f 5. b 6. c 7. a 8. e

3 Following Directions for Setting a Table 

- ❑ Read the situation and directions to the students. Make sure that the students understand that they will be writing the numbers from the top picture in the correct location in the bottom picture.
- ❑ Read the names of the items in the top picture. Ask the students if they understand the items and their names.
- ❑ Point out the two items in the bottom picture. Make sure that the students know the word *plate*. Mention that this will be called a *dinner plate*.
- ❑ Play the recording and have the students write their answers as they listen.
- ❑ Put the students in pairs and ask them to compare answers.
- ❑ Go over the answers as a class.

ANSWER KEY

1. napkin: in the center of the dinner plate
2. water glass: above the plate and to the right
3. white wine glass: Note: The white wine glass is not at this place setting because according to the conversation, they're only serving red wine.
4. red wine glass: to the right of the water glass
5. small plate for bread: above the dinner plate to the left
6. soup spoon: to the right of the dinner knife
7. dessert spoon: above the dessert fork with handle pointing to the right
8. dinner fork: to the left of the plate (already placed in illustration)
9. salad fork: to the left of the dinner fork
10. dessert fork: above the dinner plate with handle pointing to the left
11. butter knife: across the top of the bread plate
12. dinner knife: to the right of the dinner plate

AUDIOSCRIPT

Mrs. Riley: OK, so we start by putting the napkin in the center of the dinner plate, like this.

Ming: All right. Now what?

Mrs. Riley: Well, let's put the glasses out. Are you planning to serve wine?

Ming: Yes, of course.

Mrs. Riley: White or red?

Ming: Uh . . . does it matter?

Mrs. Riley: Well, there are different glasses for each kind of wine.

Ming: I see. Well, I plan to serve roast beef.

Mrs. Riley: In that case, you'll need these glasses here. They're for red wine. But first you need to set the water glass. It goes above the plate and a little to the right. And then you put the wine glass to the right of the water glass.

Ming: Like this?

Mrs. Riley: Exactly. Now, this little plate here is for bread. You put it above the dinner plate to the left. And this is a special knife for butter. Lay it across the top of the bread plate.

Ming: All right. What's next?

Mrs. Riley: Silverware.

Ming: Sorry?

Mrs. Riley: Silverware. Knives, forks, and spoons. There are different ones for each course. Are you serving a salad?

Ming: Yes.

Mrs. Riley: And soup?

Ming: Yes.

Mrs. Riley: O.K. Take this dinner knife and put it to the right of the dinner plate. Then put the soup spoon to the right of the knife. Good. Now, to the left of the plate, first put this big fork. That's the dinner fork. And put this smaller fork to the left of that. It's for salad. OK. Now, what are you serving for dessert?

Ming: Chocolate cake.

Mrs. Riley: Then you need a dessert fork. Put it above the dinner plate, with the handle pointing to the left. And then put this small spoon, for coffee, above it, with the handle pointing to the right.

Ming: All these knives and forks! How do people know which ones to use?

Mrs. Riley: Actually, it's quite simple. You always use the utensil that's on the outside, and you serve the food in the same order. So, for example, you'll serve your soup first, your salad second, your main course third, and the dessert last. See?

Ming: Yes. It's really quite logical. Thanks, Mrs. Riley. You've been a great help!

Mrs. R: You're welcome.

Ming: Now I just have to make sure not to burn the food!

4 Using Vocabulary 

- ❑ Read the directions for number 1. Ask a student to read the sample sentence about the napkin.
- ❑ Put the students in pairs. Tell them to make sentences telling where the numbered items should go.

- ❑ Go over the questions with the students.
- ❑ Have the same pairs answer the questions.
- ❑ Go over the questions as a class.

5 Talking About Table Manners 

- ❑ Review the instructions for the first part of the activity.
- ❑ Point out the illustration of the people at a dinner table.
- ❑ Put the students in small groups. Tell them to find the 10 examples of rude behavior.
- ❑ When the students are finished, go over the answers together.

ANSWER KEY

1. reading the newspaper at the table 2. making a face that shows you think the food is disgusting 3. reaching over someone else's dish in order to grab a dinner roll 4. using your finger to pick food from your teeth 5. putting on lipstick/makeup 6. putting your foot on a chair 7. licking food off a knife 8. drinking from a bowl 9. wearing headphones 10. using a napkin to blow your nose

- ❑ Go over the directions for the second part of the activity. Clarify vocabulary (e.g., *behaviors*) as necessary.
- ❑ Put the students back in their small groups. Tell them to discuss the three questions about manners.
- ❑ Go over the answers as a class.
- ❑ Finally, have students take turns reading portions of the Culture Note on page 118. Have them paraphrase the information back to you so that you can check their comprehension.

Self-Assessment Log

- ❑ The purpose of the log is to help the students reflect on their learning.
- ❑ Read the directions aloud and have students check vocabulary that they learned in the chapter and are prepared to use.
- ❑ Have students check the strategies they understand.
- ❑ Put students in small groups. Ask students to find the information or an activity related to each strategy in the chapter.
- ❑ Tell students to find definitions in the chapter for any words they did not check, or they can look in their dictionaries.

Chapter

7

Health

In this chapter, students will listen to language about health. In Part 1, they will hear a conversation about health clubs. They will also learn how to recognize and use tag questions. In Part 2, students will learn language for talking with doctors and will practice listening for main ideas and specific information. In Part 3, they will learn language for talking about general issues related to health. In Part 4, students will practice language for talking with a variety of health care professionals, for example, pharmacists. These topics will prepare students for dealing with a wide variety of health-related situations in their lives.

Chapter Opener

- ❑ Have students look at the photo of the men in a gym. Discuss the questions in the Connecting to the Topic section.
- ❑ Have the students read the proverb.
- ❑ Ask the students what they think the proverb means. If the students don't understand the proverb, tell them that laughing is very good for your health because it relieves stress.

" Laughter is the best medicine. "

—Proverb

Chapter Overview

Listening Skills and Strategies

Listening for main ideas

Listening for details

Listening to a health club tour

Distinguishing between rising and falling intonation in tag questions

Listening to medical advice

Listening to phone messages from healthcare professionals

Speaking Skills and Strategies

Forming and using tag questions with correct intonation

Asking for and giving advice

Discussing smoking –advertising and laws

Talking to healthcare workers: making appointments by phone

Critical Thinking Skills

Interpreting a photo

Using a problem-solution chart to list and clarify symptoms and treatments

Completing a questionnaire on stress and interpreting the score

Summarizing a medical visit using key words

Vocabulary Building

Terms connected with a health club

Terms describing symptoms and remedies

Expressions for giving and accepting advice

Terms used in expressing agreement or disagreement

Pronunciation

Identifying and practicing stressed words

Comparing reduced and unreduced pronunciation

Contrasting rising and falling intonation in tag questions

Focus on Testing

Using context clues to identify unusual details within situations

Vocabulary

Nouns	Verbs	Adjectives	Expressions
aspirin	jog	swollen	eat right
boxing	lift weights	weak	in good/bad shape
cardio	ought to		
discount	show (someone) around		
fever			
headache			
health club			
lane			
locker room			
prescription			
rest			
sore throat			
upset stomach			
yoga			

Can You Guess?

- Ask students to discuss the questions below in groups and compare answers with the correct answers.
- Ask students how life expectancy in their countries compares to the country in question

1. Which countries have the most smokers? *A. East Asia and Pacific region.** **2.** What is the average life expectancy worldwide? Which countries have the longest life expectancy, and about how long do people from these countries live? *A. Avg. worldwide life expectancy: 66 years; Japan has highest – about 81 yrs.*** **3.** What are some of the most common reasons people go to the emergency room of a hospital in North America? *A. Chest pain 4.6%, general pains 4.1%, abdominal pain 4.1%.*†

Footnotes:
* Source: World Health Organization. (http://www.wpro.who.int/media_centre/fact_sheets/fs_20020528.htm)
** Source: US Census Bureau, IDB updated 4-26-05
† Source: ABC News Sacramento (http://www.news10.net.news.er.reasons.htm)

Before You Listen

1 Prelistening Questions 

- ❑ Have students look at the photo and describe what is happening.
- ❑ Have the students read the questions.
- ❑ Put the students in pairs and have them discuss the questions.
- ❑ Compare answers as a whole class.

2 Previewing Vocabulary 

- ❑ Play the recording and ask students to listen to the words and phrases.
- ❑ Show the students the list of words. Tell them that they should try to guess the meanings of the words while doing the activity.
- ❑ Have students complete the activity individually.
- ❑ Put the students into pairs. Have them compare their answers.
- ❑ Compare their answers as a whole class and write the correct answers on the board.

ANSWER KEY

1. health club 2. lift weights 3. in good shape 4. lane 5. discount 6. boxing 7. jog 8. ought to 9. show (you) around 10. yoga 11. aerobics 12. locker room, swim

Listen

3 Listening for Main Ideas 

(The audioscript follows Activity 5.)

- ❑ Ask the students to read the directions and questions in their books.
- ❑ Have the students look again at the photo on page 122. Tell the students that this illustrates one thing that happens in the conversation that they are going to hear.
- ❑ Ask students to close their books as they listen.
- ❑ Play the recording and have the students write down individual answers.
- ❑ Then have the students compare their answers in pairs.
- ❑ Finally, go over the answers to the two questions with the whole class.

ANSWER KEY

1. Peter and Kenji are in a health club. We know that they like it because they say things like, "This is cool!," "Wow," and "I really need to start lifting weights."
2. The purpose of the tour is to give Peter and Kenji enough information that they can decide whether or not to become members. The guide would like them to join before the end of the month.

4 Listening for Details 

(The audioscript follows Activity 5.)

- ❑ Tell the students to read the four questions. Give them some time to ask questions.
- ❑ Play the recording again if necessary.
- ❑ Put the students in pairs to answer the questions.
- ❑ Go over the questions as a group. Ask for additional details from the conversation.

ANSWER KEY

1. Peter and Kenji saw a cardio class.
2. Boxing and yoga
3. Ellen, one of the instructors
4. because there is a student discount

Stress

5 Listening for Stressed Words 

- ❑ Play the recording again. This time, tell the students to keep their books open and write their answers.
- ❑ After listening, have students check their answers in groups of three. Then have each group check their answers with the audioscript in their books.
- ❑ Finally, read the directions that follow the conversation in the book and have the students read the conversation in groups of three. Remind them to stress the words correctly.

AUDIOSCRIPT and ANSWER KEY

Adel: Hi, I'm Adel. I'm sure you're going to like it here. Let me show you around. Here's the weight room. We've got the newest machines, and our instructors can show you how to use them.

Peter: This is cool!

Kenji: Yeah. I really need to start lifting weights.

Adel: And here is a cardio class . . .

Peter: I've never tried cardio. It's just dancing, isn't it?

Adel: Not really. Actually, they're working harder than you think.

Kenji: And cardio is very good for your heart.

Adel: It sure is. But you should do it at least three times a week if you want to be in good shape.

Peter: Well, I already jog three times a week.

Adel: That's terrific.

Kenji: You also have boxing and yoga classes here, don't you?

Adel: Yes. I'll give you a schedule of classes when we finish our tour. Now here's our swimming pool.

Peter: Wow! Look at that woman in the middle lane. She's really fast, isn't she?

Adel: Oh, yeah. That's Ellen, one of our instructors.

Kenji: I'd like to take lessons from her!

Adel: You're not the only one. C'mon, I'll show you the showers and the locker room.

Adel: You know, if you want to join our gym, you ought to do it before the end of the month.

Kenji: Really? Why?

Adel: Well, because we have a special discount for students this month. Let's go to my office and I'll tell you all about it.

After You Listen

6 Using Vocabulary 

- ❑ Ask the students to read the questions.
- ❑ Put the students in pairs. Have the students ask and answer the questions using the underlined vocabulary.
- ❑ When the students have finished, go over the questions as a class.

Pronunciation

INTONATION WITH TAG QUESTIONS

- ■ Read through the information on tag questions. Read the sample sentences with tag questions with a somewhat exaggerated rising and falling voice to emphasize the two different patterns.
- ■ Go over the Culture Note on tag questions. Read the two sample sentences.
- ■ Ask the students to paraphrase the information so that you can check their comprehension. You can also ask them to think of other types of questions, e.g., *It's a beautiful day, isn't it? / She's a good instructor, isn't she? / That was a difficult test, wasn't it?*

7 Pronouncing Tag Questions 

- ❑ Read the directions for this exercise.
- ❑ Play the ten sentences one at a time. Have students repeat them.

AUDIOSCRIPT

1. We need special shoes for cardio, don't we?
2. The pool is warm, isn't it?
3. You play football, don't you?
4. You don't eat junk food, do you?
5. You didn't hurt yourself, did you?
6. My father looks healthy, doesn't he?
7. This exercise is hard, isn't it?
8. Your parents love to dance, don't they?
9. She can swim fast, can't she?
10. It's a beautiful day, isn't it?

8 Understanding Tag Questions 

- ❑ Read the directions to the students.
- ❑ Show the students the two columns.
- ❑ Play the recording through.
- ❑ Have the students do the exercise individually.
- ❑ Play the recording again. After each sentence, ask the students what the answer is.

ANSWER KEY

1. asking a question 2. asking a question 3. making conversation 4. asking a question 5. making conversation 6. asking a question

AUDIOSCRIPT

1. **Peter:** I've never tried cardio. It's just dancing, isn't it?
   Adel: Not really.
2. **Kenji:** You also have boxing and yoga classes here, don't you?
   Adel: Yes.
3. **Peter:** Wow! Look at that woman in the middle lane. She's really fast, isn't she?

	Adel:	Oh, yeah. That's Ellen, one of our instructors.
4.	**Peter:**	The gym is open 24 hours a day, isn't it?
	Adel:	Almost. It's open from 5 A.M. to 1 A.M.
5.	**Kenji:**	The pool is really crowded, isn't it?
	Peter:	Yeah.
6.	**Adel:**	You guys are students, aren't you?
	Peter and Kenji:	Yes, we are.

Using Language Functions

FORMING TAG QUESTIONS

- Go over the information in the box.
- Write some statements on the board, e.g., *It's hot today. (isn't it) / Laura can play volleyball. (can't she) / Kevin doesn't have to work today. (does he)).* Then ask the students to add tag questions.

9 Using Tag Questions 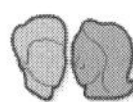

- ❑ Read the directions to the students and go over the dialogue in the footnote about answering tag questions. Emphasize that the students should answer the questions truthfully.
- ❑ Role-play the example with a student.
- ❑ Put the students in pairs and tell them to decide which student is Student A and which is Student B. Tell them to put a piece of paper over their partner's part so they can't see it and they have to listen.
- ❑ Tell the students to take turns asking each other the questions. The intonation patterns will vary according to the situations. There are no correct or incorrect answers.

Talk It Over

10 Talking About Stress 

- ❑ Point out the two photos on page 128. Ask the students to compare and contrast them.
- ❑ Read the questions to the students.
- ❑ Discuss the questions as a class.

11 Completing a Questionnaire About Stress

- ❑ Point out the ratings for stress. Explain to the students that they must read the 18 statements and put one of the numbers in each blank.
- ❑ Tell the students to start answering the questionnaire. Walk around the room answering questions about vocabulary, grammar, or expressions.
- ❑ When the students have finished the questionnaire, go over the rating chart with them answering any questions that they have about the language in the chart.

12 Follow-Up

- ❑ Go through the follow-up questions as a class.

Content Note

Some researchers describe two personality types. Type A people are thought to be tense, very active, concerned with success, and often unable to relax. Type B people are characterized as more relaxed and easy going and less concerned about appearances, success, and money. People sometimes label each other as a "type A" or a "type B" person, and there are types in between. What type do you think you are?

Best Practice

Interacting with Others

This type of activity is an example of collaborative learning to encourage fluency and confidence. In these role-plays, based around the topic of developing a stress-reduction plan, communication is more important than grammar. Students can practice the role-plays in pairs and then improve their performance by switching roles or partners. By the time they perform the role-play for the class, they should feel more confident in the use of the new language.

EXPANSION ACTIVITY

- Please see Black Line Master "A Stress-Reduction Plan" on page BLM 13 of this Teacher's Edition.
- Photocopy and distribute one copy to each student.
- In Activity 12 on page 130, the students talked about two areas that they would like to change in their lives. In this activity, partners will develop those ideas further to help each other create a plan to reduce their stress.
- Read the situation and then the directions for Part 1 to the students.
- Put them in pairs and tell them to show each other the results of their stress questionnaire.
- Have the students answer the six questions together.
- For Part 2, have the students work individually to write five advice sentences for their partner.
- In Part 3, put the students back in pairs. Have them read and discuss their suggestions with their partners.
- As a class, have the students give examples of advice that their partners gave them.

Before You Listen

Best Practice

Activating Prior Knowledge

The prelistening questions activate students' prior knowledge. This activity will help students relate their own experience with the flu to the new language about influenza and other sicknesses in this chapter. When students activate their prior knowledge before learning new material, they are better able to map new language onto existing concepts, which aids understanding and retention.

1 Prelistening Questions 

- ❑ Read the directions to the students.
- ❑ Tell the students to read the three questions. Make sure that the students understand the word *symptoms*.
- ❑ Put the students into pairs and have them discuss the questions.
- ❑ Go over their answers as a class. Write new vocabulary on the board as it comes up in the discussion.

Content Note

The United States does not have universal healthcare insurance for all residents. Many employers pay for all, or a part, of an employee's health care insurance along with partial coverage for family members, if any. Many other people pay for private health care insurance which can amount to $8,000 or more a year for a family of four. There are also large numbers of people without insurance who sometimes find it difficult to obtain adequate medical care.

Strategy

Graphic Organizer: Problem-Solution Chart

- ■ Read the description of the problem-solution chart to the students.
- ■ Point out the problem-solution chart for the flu in Activity 2.

2 Previewing Vocabulary 

- ❑ Play the recording and ask students to listen to the words.
- ❑ Read the directions for the first part of the activity. Give the students time to ask about anything that they don't understand.
- ❑ Point out the two-column table.
- ❑ Put the students in small groups and have them put the words in the table. Tell them to look the words up in their dictionary if it is necessary.
- ❑ Check the answers as a class.

ANSWER KEY

Part 1

Symptoms of the flu

upset stomach, sore throat, headache, fever, weak, swollen

Treatment of the flu

rest, prescription, aspirin, eat right

- ■ For part two of the activity, have the same pairs write short definitions of the words.
- ■ Check the answers as a class.

Part 2

muscle: the body tissue that makes the bones move

forehead: the part of the face above the eyes and below the hairline

throat: the front of the neck between the chin and the chest

Culture Note

- Have a student read the Culture Note on page 131.
- Ask the students to give you an example of a medicine that would require a prescription. This would also be a good place to introduce the phrase *over-the-counter* as the opposite of *prescription*.

Listen

3 Listening for Main Ideas 

- Have students look at the photo. You can ask if this is a typical doctor, or atypical. Are doctors usually men, women, or both in the country you're in? How about in the students' native countries?
- Read the directions for this activity to the students. Show the students the chart with columns for complaints and advice.
- Read the two questions to the students.
- Tell the students that they are going to listen to a long listening passage.
- Play the recording. Put the students into pairs and tell them to answer the questions.
- Briefly check the answers as a class just to make sure that all of the students understand the general situation.

Best Practice

Organizing Information

This type of activity uses a graphic organizer to categorize information. Taking lecture notes encourages students to process and organize information while they are listening and also provides a record for them to refer to when they are studying later. This type of graphic organizer emphasizes categorizing the main ideas of this dialogue into complaints and advice. Other types of graphic organizers are used throughout this book.

4 Taking Notes on Specific Information 

- Point out the problem-solution chart for the details of the conversation. Make sure that the students understand that *complaints* in this case means "symptoms." These are the "problems."
- Advise the students that the recording is quite long, so they should make brief notes in the columns rather than write down complete sentences.
- Play the recording and have students write down their answers.
- Put the students in pairs. Tell them to check their answers.
- If necessary, play the recording one more time.
- Check the answers as a class.

ANSWER KEY

Barbara's complaints

1. headache
2. upset stomach
3. weakness
4. body feels hot
5. muscles hurt
6. sore throat

Doctor's advice

1. stop drinking coffee
2. eat fruits and vegetables
3. take two aspirin four times a day
4. drink a lot of juice
5. get plenty of rest
6. If your throat doesn't get better in a week, call me.

AUDIOSCRIPT

Doctor: Barbara, you're back again! What seems to be the trouble?

Barbara: Well, I woke up this morning with a terrible headache.

Doctor: Yes?

Barbara: And I had an upset stomach, too. I'm feeling really weak, and my whole body feels hot, and my muscles hurt. Oh, and I'm starting to get a sore throat.

Doctor: Well, your forehead feels really warm. You probably have a fever. Let me see your throat.

Barbara: Ahhhh.

Doctor: Ah-hah. It's all red and swollen. I think you've got another case of the flu. You were sick just last month, weren't you?

Barbara: Yeah, I was.

Doctor: Are you taking good care of yourself?

Barbara: What do you mean?

Doctor: Well, do you eat right, and do you get enough sleep?

Barbara: Well, right now I'm studying for some tests and I'm very tired. I've been drinking a lot of coffee and eating pizza and hamburgers.

Doctor: You should stop drinking coffee and eat lots of fruits and vegetables. I want you to take two aspirin four times a day, drink a lot of juice, and get plenty of rest. If your throat doesn't get better in a week, I want you to call me, OK?

Barbara: So I don't need a prescription, do I?

Doctor: Not yet. Well, try to take care of yourself, and don't work too hard.

After You Listen

5 Summarizing Ideas 

- ❑ Read the directions. Read the sample sentence.
- ❑ Put the students in groups and have them summarize Barbara's complaints and the doctor's advice using past-tense verbs.

6 Reviewing Vocabulary 

- ❑ Tell the students to read all of the questions.
- ❑ Put the students in pairs. Have them discuss all of the questions.
- ❑ Go over the questions as a class.

Using Language Functions

GIVING ADVICE

- Go over the *Giving Advice* instruction note with the students.
- Where there is an incomplete sentence, have the students give you a sample sentence with the phrase, e.g., *You'd better get more sleep.*

7 Asking for and Giving Advice 

- ❑ Read the instructions for the three steps in the activity.
- ❑ Point out the list of *Possible Remedies* and the five pictures that correspond to them. Help the students with difficult vocabulary (e.g., *bandage*, *swollen*).
- ❑ Read the sample sentences.

- ❑ Put the students in pairs. Tell them to describe the five problems in the pictures.
- ❑ Go over the answers as a class.
- ❑ Have the students match the pictures with the possible remedies. Check the answers together.
- ❑ Put the students in pairs again for the role-play. Tell the students to take turns describing the problem and giving advice for the problem.
- ❑ Have the pairs act out the role-plays for the class.

ANSWER KEY

Picture

1. sunburned woman 2. swollen or sprained ankle 3. sleeplessness/insomnia 4. stomachache 5. cut finger/hand

Remedy

1. Take a cold shower. 2. Put ice on it. 3.take a sleeping pill. (NOTE: You can add that this is not always advisable and should only be done after seeing a doctor. There are other remedies to insomnia, e.g., doing relaxation techniques, exercising in the day, not drinking coffee late at night.) 4. Drink tea. 5. Bandage it.

Best Practice

Scaffolding Instruction

This is an example of an activity that raises metacognitive awareness of learning strategies. In real life, we use surrounding context clues to work out the meanings of unfamiliar words. This activity asks students to use the words that they know in each piece of the conversation to work out the meanings of new words. Having students write the clues guides them through the steps of developing this skill.

Getting Meaning from Context

Focus on Testing

Using Context Clues 

Part 1

- Point out to the students that this is a *Focus on Testing* activity. The skill taught in this activity will help students with standardized tests, such as the Internet-based TOEFL®.
- Read the directions for Part 1 to the students.
- Emphasize that in this particular activity, they are concentrating on what is "strange."
- Play the recording.
- Go over the clues as a class.

ANSWER KEY

Answers	Clues
1. Person seemed to be on a diet, but ordered a rich dessert of ice cream and cake.	low-fat cottage cheese, no dressing, no butter, unsweetened, ice cream, cake
2. One person seems very health conscious, doing a lot of exercise, but eats junk food	three miles, played tennis, 50 sit-ups, drink water, want a bag of potato chips
3. Person is getting a sunburn, but stays in the sun.	sleeping quite a while, cover up, get in the shade, want to get a good tan, look a bit red, "Don't worry.", do this every summer
4. Andrea is completely stressed out, but thinks that a vacation in Hawaii would be boring.	stressed out, can't eat, can't sleep, going crazy, so many things to do, isn't enough time, vacation, maybe go to Hawaii, "I don't want to do that."

AUDIOSCRIPT

Conversation 1

M: Hello, may I take your order?

W: Yes, I'd like a salad with low-fat cottage cheese no dressing, please. And one slice of bread, no butter.

M: Anything to drink?

W: Do you have unsweetened iced tea?

M: Yes, we do. Will that be all, Miss?

W: Yes . . . oh, wait! For dessert, I'll have a piece of chocolate cake with ice cream.

Question 1: What's surprising about the woman's order?

M: You know, before you ordered that cake, I thought you were on a diet.

Conversation 2

W: So, that was a good workout, wasn't it?

M: Yeah. Let's see . . . what did we do? We ran three miles, we played two sets of tennis, and we did 50 sit-ups.

W: Yeah. I want to get a nice cold bottle of water from the vending machine.

M: And I want a bag of potato chips.

Question 2: What's surprising about what the man says?

Woman: You know, you take such good care of yourself and get so much exercise. I really don't understand why you eat junk like potato chips.

Conversation 3

Woman: Why did you wake me up?

Man: You were sleeping quite a while. I think you should cover up and get into the shade.

Woman: You think so? I really want to get a good tan.

Man: Well you already look a bit red to me.

Woman: Don't worry. I do this every summer at the beach.

Question 3: What's surprising about what the woman says?

Man: You shouldn't lie in the sun so long without protection. You're going to get a *terrible* sunburn.

Conversation 4

Man: Hi, Andrea. How're you doing?

Woman: I am so stressed out! I can't eat, I can't sleep. I feel like I'm going crazy!

Man: Why? What's the problem?

Woman: I've got so many things to do. You know, school, my job, housework, sports—there just isn't enough time for everything.

Man: You really ought to take a vacation. Maybe go to Hawaii for a week.

Woman: Oh, I don't want to do that.

Man: Why not?

Woman: It's so boring there. There's nothing to do.

Question 4: What's surprising about what Andrea said?

Man: I don't get it. You're complaining about how stressed out you are, but you don't even want some time to relax!

Focus on Testing

Part 2

- Read the directions for Part 2. Read the possible answers to the students.
- Play the recording. Have the students answer the two questions individually.
- Put the students in pairs to write down what clues they heard in the dialogues.
- Go over the context clues as a class.

ANSWER KEY

1.b 2.c

AUDIOSCRIPT

Conversation 1

A: So Nancy went into the hospital last night?

B: That's right, and her husband is waiting for the news right now.

A: Is this her first?

B: Yes, so they're both very nervous. Especially Steve.

A: When can Nancy come home?

B: If all goes well, they'll both be home in a couple of days. It's exciting, isn't it?

Question 1: The situation is . . .

A: Yes, having your first baby is always very special.

Conversation 2

A: These carrots are organic.

B: What about your eggs? Are they fresh?

A: Of course. All our eggs come from local farms daily.

B: You sell vitamins, don't you?

A: Yes, they're right next to the nuts over there.

B:	Your stuff looks great, but it's a little expensive.
A:	Well, we sell only the best.
Question 2: The speakers are in a . . .	
B:	Well, I guess this is the best health food store in town.

1 Role-Play 

- ❑ Read the directions to the students. Point out the picture and explain that it illustrates the first situation.
- ❑ Read the information about the other patients.
- ❑ Read the Culture Note for this activity.
- ❑ Put the students in pairs. Tell them to decide which student is the psychologist and which is the patient.
- ❑ Tell the student to start one of the four role-plays. If there is time, have the students do more than one of the role-plays. Tell them to switch roles from psychologist to patient.
- ❑ At the end, invite different pairs to perform the role-plays for the class.

Talk It Over

2 Discussing Your Opinion 

- ❑ Read the directions with the students.
- ❑ Put the students in small groups. Make sure that they know that they must agree or disagree with each statement and give reasons for each opinion.
- ❑ Go over the opinions as a class.

Best Practice

Cultivating Critical Thinking

The following activity requires students to process the information they have learned and apply it to a new situation. This involves reinterpretation, synthesis, and application of concepts. In this activity, students will use the health-related language that they have learned to describe the health situation in the city in which they live. They move from talking about health in language exercises to talking about it in an authentic situation.

REPRODUCIBLE EXPANSION ACTIVITY

- Please see Black Line Master "Improving Health in Our City" on page BLM 14 of this Teacher's Edition.
- Photocopy and distribute one copy to each student.
- Explain to the students that they will be creating a plan to improve the general health level in the city where they are studying English.
- Have the students work in small groups.
- In Part 1, have them discuss the answers to the questions. This helps them identify problems that might be present in their city.
- In Part 2, they will determine how to spend the money to improve health in their city. Possible items are given in the list, but they may come up with their own items. They will make a pie chart showing the percentages for each item.
- Remind them that their group has to agree on how the money is spent.

Best Practice

Making Use of Academic Content

This is an example of an activity that exposes students to situations that they will actually face while studying in a university. The activity develops skills that the students will need to succeed in an English-speaking environment. The phone messages include communications with a variety of health professionals in contexts that the students may experience in the future.

1 Taking Notes on Phone Conversations 

- ❑ Read the directions. Point out the lines where the students are to write their notes.
- ❑ Play the recording and have students write down their notes. Remind the students to make brief notes rather than trying to write in complete sentences.
- ❑ Put the students into pairs to compare notes.
- ❑ If necessary, play the recording one more time.
- ❑ Go over the answers as a class.

ANSWER KEY

Conversation 1

Reason for call: to make an appointment/has broken tooth

Name of dentist: Dr. Jones

Location: 532 Western Avenue, near Third Street

Time of appointment: 2:00 P.M. tomorrow

Conversation 2

Reason for call: to find out if prescription is ready

Name of patient: Ellen Beattie

Price of medicine: $14.95

Special instructions: Take pills every six hours with food. Don't mix with alcohol.

Closing time: 5:00 P.M.

Conversation 3

First reason for call: to change appointment time

Name of baby's doctor: Dr. Stork

Time of baby's new appointment: Monday at 10:00

Second reason for call: her husband needs a checkup

Time of husband's appointment: Tuesday at 6:00

Name of husband's doctor: Dr. Miller

AUDIOSCRIPT

Conversation 1

A: University Dental Clinic. May I help you?

B: Yes, I'd like to make an appointment.

A: Do you have a problem, or is it just for a checkup?

B: I think I've broken a tooth.

A: Well, can you come in tomorrow morning?

B: No, but how about after lunch?

A: Well, let me see . . . Dr. Jones can probably take you at around . . . 2:00. How's that?

B: That's great. Where is your office?

A: We're at 532 Western Avenue. That's near Third Street.

B: OK. I'll see you tomorrow at 2:00.

Conversation 2

A: Drugs R Us. May I help you?

B: Yes, I'd like to know if my prescription is ready.

A: What's the name, please?

B: Ellen Beattie.

A: Spell that, please.

B: B-E-A-T-T-I-E.

A: Oh, yes, here it is. It comes to $14.95.

B: Are there any special instructions?

A: Well, let me see. Take the pills every six hours with food. But don't worry. The instructions are also on the bottle.

B: OK. How late can I pick it up?

A: Today we're open until 5:00.

B: All right. Thanks a lot. I'll be in later.

Conversation 3

A: Family Medicine.

B: Hi, Sherry. This is Penny Berkowitz.

A: Hi. You're bringing your baby in this afternoon, aren't you?

B: Well, our car broke down. So I'd like to change our appointment with Dr. Stork, if that's OK.

A: Sure. What's a good time for you?

B: Can I come in on Monday?

A: How about 10:00?

B: Fine.

A: OK. We'll see you then.

B: Oh, while we're on the phone, my husband needs a checkup. Can you take him one evening next week?

A: I think so. What about Tuesday at 6:00 with Dr. Miller?

B: That's perfect. Thanks. Bye-bye.

2 Making Appointments with Doctors 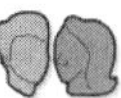

- ❑ Go over the new expressions for symptoms in the *Language Tip* box.
- ❑ Point out the three situations and make sure that the students see the two different roles.
- ❑ Put the students in pairs. Have each pair decide who is the receptionist and who is the patient. Stress the importance of students only looking at the appropriate information for their own role. Encourage them to cover the information for the other role with a piece of paper.
- ❑ Tell the students to choose one of the situations to role-play.
- ❑ If some pairs finish the first role-play early, have them start another. Some pairs may finish all three.
- ❑ At the end, ask for volunteers to do each role-play in front of the class.

Self-Assessment Log

- ❑ The purpose of the log is to help the students reflect on their learning.
- ❑ Read the directions aloud and have students check vocabulary that they learned in the chapter and are prepared to use.
- ❑ Have students check the strategies they understand.
- ❑ Put students in small groups. Ask students to find the information or an activity related to each strategy in the chapter.
- ❑ Tell students to find definitions in the chapter for any words they did not check, or they can look in their dictionaries.

Chapter

8

Entertainment and the Media

In this chapter, students will learn and practice of language about entertainment and the media. In Part 1, they will be introduced to the language that they will need to talk about television and its effect on society. They will also learn expressions for stating an opinion, agreeing, and disagreeing. In Part 2, they will practice the language needed for news reports. In Part 3, they will receive additional practice in recognizing context clues and practice listening to television commercials. In Part 4, students will practice the language needed for discussing different types of television programs. These topics will prepare students for social conversation and serious discussions about media and the role it plays in our modern life.

Chapter Opener

- ❑ Have the students look at the photo. This is from a popular U.S. TV show, "Extreme Home Makeover," which first aired in October, 2005. Host Ty Pennington (left) helps a family celebrate the moment they see their new home for the first time. Ask them the questions in the Connecting to the Topic section. Discuss the answers as a class.
- ❑ Have the students read the quote. Give them some time to ask for clarification of anything that they don't understand.
- ❑ Ask the students what they think the quote means. Make sure that they understand the vocabulary (e.g., *media*, *images*, *controls*). If the students don't understand the quote, tell them that communication media such as television, the Internet, and radio, are extremely powerful. People who control them have tremendous influence in a country's culture.

"Whoever controls the media—the images—controls the culture."

—Allen Ginsberg
American Beat poet (1926–1997)

Chapter Overview

Listening Skills and Strategies

Listening for main ideas

Listening for details

Listening to opinions about television

Listening to a news report

Listening to radio ads

Speaking Skills and Strategies

Expressing, agreeing with, and disagreeing with opinions

Discussing the qualities of good ads

Talking about types of TV programs

Describing favorite TV shows and movies

Critical Thinking Skills

Interpreting a photo

Identifying the four "W's" in a news report

Summarizing news reports using key words

Locating information in a TV guide

Vocabulary Building

Terms for expressing opinions, agreeing and disagreeing

Terms related to TV- watching habits

Terms to describe types of TV programs

Pronunciation

Identifying and practicing stressed words

Comparing reduced and unreduced pronunciation

Focus on Testing

Using context clues to identify products and services in commercials

Vocabulary

Nouns	Verbs
averages week	block
couch potato	change channels
injury	channel surf
passenger	hurt
remote control	land
top story	run out of
the TV	turn down the volume
waste of time	turn on the TV
	turn the TV off

Can You Guess?

- Put the students in pairs and go over the questions below. Have students give the reasons for their opinions and compare answers with the correct answers.

1. Do Americans spend more time watching TV or using the Internet? *A. Using the Internet (Avg. 3 hrs/day online, 1.7 hrs/day watching TV).** **2.** Who usually decides what TV program the family should watch, men or women? *A. Men are twice as likely to decide.*** **3.** Which is the world's most popular newspaper? *A. The Times of India – 2.4 million sold a day.*†

Footnotes:
* Source: http://www.clickz.com/stats/sectors/demographics/article.php/3455061
** Source: http://www.aber.ac.uk/media/Students/crl9501.html
† Source: http://timesofindia.indiatimes.com/articleshow/1152489.cms

Before You Listen

Best Practice

Activating Prior Knowledge

The prelistening questions activate students' prior knowledge. This activity will help students relate their own experience with communication media to the new language in this chapter. When students activate their prior knowledge before learning new material, they are better able to map new language onto existing concepts, which aids understanding and retention.

1 Prelistening Questions 

- Have students look at the photo and describe what the two people are doing.
- Tell the students that this photo will help them understand the conversation that they will hear later.
- Ask the students to name as many of the objects in the photo as they can (e.g., *magazine*, *couch/sofa*, *potato chips*).
- Have the students read the questions. Give them time to ask for clarification.
- Put the students in pairs and have them discuss the questions.
- Compare answers as a whole class. If there is time, ask for more details in their answers. For example, if they get their news from the Internet, what website do they go to? What language is it in?
- As a whole class, make a list of any new words or expressions that come up.

2 Previewing Vocabulary 

- Show the students the list of nouns and verbs for watching TV.
- Play the recording and ask students to listen to the words and phrases.
- Make sure that the students understand that they are only filling in the blanks in the sentences. They should not put anything in the shorter blanks to the left of the sentences.
- Have students complete the vocabulary preview in pairs.
- Compare their answers as a whole class and write the correct answers on the board.

ANSWER KEY

1. turn on the TV 2. turn the TV off 3. change channels (could also be channel surf) 4. turn down the volume 5. the TV 6. channel surf (could also be change channels) 7. couch potato 8. remote control 9. waste of time 10. average week

Listen

3 Listening for Main Ideas 

(The audioscript follows Activity 5.)

- ❑ Tell the students to read the directions and questions in their books.
- ❑ Have the students look again at the photo at the beginning of Part 1. Tell the students that this illustrates some important information about Ming and Jack.
- ❑ Ask students to close their books as they listen.
- ❑ Play the recording.
- ❑ After listening, give the students some time to write down individual answers.
- ❑ Then have the students compare their answers in pairs.
- ❑ Finally, go over the answers to the three questions as a class. Ask them for specific words or phrases they heard that support their answers.

ANSWER KEY

1. Jack and Ming disagree about TV. Ming thinks that watching TV is a waste of time. Jack thinks that news and sports programs are interesting. 2. Ming prefers newspapers and the Internet because they have more news and she can get the news whenever she wants. Also, she hates TV commercials. 3. When commercials come on, Jack turns down the volume or changes channels.

4 Listening for Details 

(The audioscript follows Activity 5.)

- ❑ Tell the students to look at the five true-false questions.
- ❑ Play the recording. Have the students answer the questions individually.
- ❑ Put the students in pairs to compare their answers.
- ❑ Go over the questions as a class. Write the answers on the board.
- ❑ Ask for additional details from the conversation (e.g., Jack thinks that sports and the news are good programs.).

ANSWER KEY

1. False. It's four hours per day, not five. 2. False. She's reading a magazine, not a newspaper. 3. False. Ming doesn't like TV. 4. True 5. True

Stress

5 Listening for Stressed Words 

- ❑ Read the directions to the students.
- ❑ Play the recording again. This time tell the students to keep their books open. Tell the students to fill in the blanks with the words that they hear.
- ❑ After listening, have students check their answers with a partner. Then have each pair check their answers with the audioscript in their books.
- ❑ Read the instruction at the bottom of the activity about practicing the stressed words.
- ❑ Tell the students to look at the completed conversation above.
- ❑ Put the students in pairs. Have the students choose a role in the conversation and read it with their partner.
- ❑ Tell the students to focus on stressing the important words correctly. Tell the students that when they are speaking, they must look at their partner, not at their book. Eye contact is an important part of conversing in English.
- ❑ Walk around the room, giving the students feedback on their speaking.

AUDIOSCRIPT and ANSWER KEY

Ming: Hey, listen to this. The average American watches four hours of TV a day.

Jack: A day? You're joking.

Ming: No, it says so right here in this newspaper. Hmm, I guess *you're* an average American, Jack. You always have your TV on.

Jack: Come on. Are you saying I'm a couch potato?

Ming: Yeah. I really think watching TV is a waste of time.

Jack: Oh, come on. Some programs are bad, like those soap operas. But what about sports or the news? You watch those sometimes, don't you?

Ming: Well, actually, for the news, I prefer the newspaper. Or the Internet.

Jack: Why?

Ming: First, because they give you a lot more information. And I can read them any time I want. Plus, I hate all the commercials.

Jack: I know what you mean. That's why when the commercials come on, I just turn down the volume or change channels.

Ming: Yeah, I noticed that. Channel surfing drives me crazy.

Jack: Okay, next time you come over, I'll let you have the remote control.

Ming: Oh, that's so sweet. But I have a better idea. Next time I come over, let's just turn the TV off.

Reductions

6 Comparing Unreduced and Reduced Pronunciation 

- ❑ Have a student read the directions to the class.
- ❑ Play the recording of the unreduced and reduced forms of the sentences from the conversation.
- ❑ Have the students as a class repeat the two forms.

7 Listening for Reductions 

- ❑ Play the recording and have the students write down their answers.
- ❑ When the conversation is finished, put the students in pairs and have them check their answers. Then check the answers as a class.
- ❑ Have the pairs take roles and read the conversation.

ANSWER KEY

A: Are you calling the movie theater?

B: Uh-huh. Don't you want to go to the movies tonight?

A: To tell you the truth, I'm pretty tired. But we can go to an early show. Do you know what you want to see?

B: Not really. I'll let you choose. *Batman III* is playing at eight and James Bond is at ten.

A: Let's see *Batman*. I'm tired now, and by ten o'clock, I'm going to be dead.

After You Listen

8 Using Vocabulary 

- ❑ Point out the cartoon from the *New Yorker*. Ask the students whether or not they think it's funny.

- ❑ Read the directions. Make sure that they understand that they must look back at Activity 2 to do this exercise.
- ❑ Have the students read the statements in Activity 2 and check the sentences that are true for them.
- ❑ Read the sample sentences to the students.
- ❑ Put the students in pairs. Have them discuss the sentences they didn't check. Those are the sentences that are not true for them. Remind them to speak in complete sentences so that they will use the vocabulary.
- ❑ As a class, go through the sentences and ask the students to raise their hands if a sentence is not true for them.

Using Language Functions

EXPRESSING OPINIONS, AGREEING, AND DISAGREEING

- Go over the information on expressing opinions, agreeing, and disagreeing. Give the students some time to ask for clarification.
- Be sure to look at the expressions on page 149.

9 Expressing Opinions 

- ❑ Read the directions. Tell the students that they will be working together in groups of three.
- ❑ Point out and explain the model for how their conversations will be structured.
- ❑ Choose three students to read the sample sentences from Ming, Jack, and Peter.
- ❑ Help the students form groups of three. Tell them to go through the topics following the sample conversation. Ask them to add one more topic, number nine.
- ❑ When their discussions are finished, go through the nine topics as a class, having the students state their opinions, agree, and disagree.

Best Practice

Interacting with Others

This type of activity is an example of collaborative learning to encourage fluency and confidence. In these role-plays, based around the topic of movie ratings, communication is more important than grammar. Students will create a new rating system together using the language for communication media that they have learned in previous activities in this chapter. By the time they present their new system to the class, they should feel more confident in the use of the new language.

EXPANSION ACTIVITY

- Please see Black Line Master "Guidelines for Children's Television Viewing" on page BLM 15 of this Teacher's Edition.
- Photocopy and distribute one copy to each student.
- Read the *Situation* to the students.
- Talk to the students about the current movie-rating system in the United States. The categories for movies are G (general), PG (parental guidance suggested), PG-13 (parental guidance suggested for children under 13), R (children under 17 must be with an adult), and NC-17 (no one under 17 allowed). Make sure that the students understand that they must come up with a different system for television.
- Read the directions for Part 1 and Part 2.
- Go over the questions with the students. Make sure that they understand what they are to do for each question. For question 1, they may decide that they will start with children under eight, for example.
- Explain the words *profanity*, *mandatory*, and *voluntary*.
- Put the students in groups of three or four. Tell them to discuss the questions and to write down notes about their system.
- Have each group present their ideas to the class. Have the students discuss the similarities and differences between their systems. If your class has students from many different cultures, see if there are any cultural tendencies.
- As a follow-up, direct the students to information on the Internet about the American rating system for TV programs, for example, by going to a search engine like Google and typing in key words such as *TV* and *rating*.

Before You Listen

Strategy

Graphic Organizer: Four (Five) W's

- Go over the description of the graphic organizer. Explain that writing four or five questions with the basic *wh-* question words will help them get prepared for hearing the news report.
- Point out the *why* may not always be appropriate in a news story. There may not be a clear reason for something to have happened.
- Ask the students to describe a recent news event. Help them write five *wh-* questions for the event.

Best Practice

Organizing Information

This type of activity uses a graphic organizer to help the learner prepare for, or anticipate, a long listening passage. By writing down four or five questions before listening, the learner sees the value of predicting the content of a lecture or news report. This type of graphic organizer emphasizes prediction skills. Other types of graphic organizers are used throughout this book.

1 Prelistening Questions 

- ❑ Read the two prelistening questions to the students.
- ❑ Point out the graphic organizer with the spaces for four questions.
- ❑ Put the students in pairs. Have them discuss the first question.
- ❑ Tell the students to write the four *wh-* questions individually. Walk around the room, helping students come up with questions.
- ❑ Tell the students to compare their questions with a partner.
- ❑ Ask the students to volunteer their questions with the class.

ANSWER KEY

Questions will vary. Possible answers:

What: What happened? What crashed?

Where: Where did the crash happen?

When: When did the crash happen?

Who: Who crashed? Who was in the crash?

2 Previewing Vocabulary 

- ❑ Play the recording and ask students to listen to the underlined words.
- ❑ Have the students match the underlined words in the sentences with the definitions.
- ❑ Put the students in pairs to check their answers.
- ❑ Check the answers together as a class.

ANSWER KEY

1. e 2. g 3. a 4. d 5. f 6. c 7. b

Listen

3 Listening for Main Ideas 

- ❑ Have students look at the picture for this activity. Tell them that this picture goes with the news story that they are going to hear.
- ❑ Ask the students to describe what is happening in the picture.
- ❑ Read the directions for the activity.
- ❑ Go over the two questions in this activity. Make sure that the students understand that in the first question, they are only to write down the most important words that will help them understand the main ideas.
- ❑ Play the recording.

- ❑ Have the students individually answer the questions. You can also have students answer the questions from Activity 1 on page 151.
- ❑ Put the students into pairs. Have them compare their answers.
- ❑ Go over the answers as a class.

ANSWER KEY

1. Key words (Answers may vary. These are suggested answers.): hour ago, airplane, six people, landed, safely, Highway 1, injuries, ground, no one hurt, ran out of gasoline, blocked traffic 2. c

ANSWER KEY

Answers from the Graphic Organizer, page 151

What: A small airplane landed.

Where: It landed on Highway 1.

When: It happened about an hour ago.

Who: There were six people in the plane. There were two witnesses on the highway.

AUDIOSCRIPT

Radio Announcer: Good evening. Our top story tonight: about an hour ago, a small airplane carrying six people landed safely in traffic on Highway 1. Two of the passengers received back injuries, and one of the passengers suffered a broken leg. Here's reporter Laura Jones at the scene of the crash.

Reporter: Good evening, Mark. I'm standing here on Highway 1 with two drivers who almost hit the plane as it landed. Could you tell me what you thought as you watched the plane coming down?

Witness 1: Well, at first I wasn't scared. But then I saw it was flying very low. So I drove to the side of the road in a hurry.

Reporter: And you, sir?

Witness 2: I almost didn't see the plane at all. It happened so fast. When I finally heard the plane's engine, I knew something was wrong. And then I hit my brakes. Phew . . . it was really close. I'm still shaking.

Reporter: Fortunately, no one on the ground was hurt, but the plane blocked traffic for over an hour. Officer John McNamara of the local highway police thinks the plane ran out of gasoline. A complete investigation will begin tomorrow. Back to you, Mark.

4 Listening for Specific Information 

- ❑ Go over the questions with the students. Make sure that they understand that they are just taking notes, not trying to write complete sentences.
- ❑ Play the recording.
- ❑ Give the students time to fill in the blanks in the activity.
- ❑ Put the students in pairs to compare their answers.
- ❑ Go over the answers as a class.

ANSWER KEY

1. Highway 1; 2. Six; 3. Three; 4. Two back injuries, one broken leg; 5. None; 6. The plane may have run out of gasoline.

After You Listen

5 Summarizing Ideas 

- Read the directions to the students. Make sure they understand that they are to use their notes from three previous activities—Activities 1, 3, and 4.
- Put the students in pairs. Have them take turns summarizing the news report.
- When they are finished, have one or two students volunteer to summarize the news report for the class.

6 Using Vocabulary 

- Read the directions to the students.
- Tell them to read all of the questions.
- Put the students in pairs. Have them discuss all of the questions and use the underlined vocabulary in their answers.
- Go over the questions as a class.

Talk It Over

7 Summarizing News Reports 

- Read the directions to the students. Make sure that they understand that this report will be about a true news story that they watch.
- Point out the five lines with *wh-* question words. Tell the students that they should fill out these lines after they watch the program and before they come to class.
- In class, put the students in pairs. Give them time to practice summarizing their news reports.
- Have the students take turns presenting their news reports to the class.

REPRODUCIBLE

EXPANSION ACTIVITY

- Please see Black Line Master "An Amazing News Story" on page BLM 16 of this Teacher's Edition.
- Photocopy and distribute one copy to each student.
- Read the directions for Part 1 and Part 2.
- Make sure the students understand that they will be acting out their interview for the class. One member of their group will be a reporter. The others will be witnesses who answer the reporter's questions.
- Put the students in groups of three or four. Give them time to answer the questions in Part 1.
- After 15 minutes, tell the students to begin planning their interview. The reporter should write the interview questions on the lines in Part 2. The witnesses should write notes that will help them answer the questions.
- Tell the students that all members of the group must have a speaking part in the interview.
- Have each group present their interview to the class.
- If you feel that it is appropriate, have the students vote on which group's interview was the best.

Best Practice

Scaffolding Instruction

This is an example of an activity that raises metacognitive awareness of learning strategies. In real life, we use surrounding context clues to work out the meanings of unfamiliar words. This activity asks students to use the words that they know in each television commercial to work out the meanings of new words. By asking students to write the clues, they are guided through the steps of developing this skill.

Getting Meaning from Context

Focus on Testing

Using Context Clues

- Point out to the students that this is a *Focus on Testing* activity. The skill taught in this activity will help students with standardized tests, such as the Internet-based TOEFL®.
- Read the directions to the students. Tell them that they will be practicing an important learning strategy for listening.
- Go over the chart with the students. Since they have done this kind of activity in previous chapters, they will understand it quickly.
- Play each commercial, stopping after the question. Give the students time to circle the correct answer and write down several clues before playing the answer and moving on.
- Put the students in pairs and have them compare their charts.
- Go over the answers and clues as a class.

ANSWER KEY

Answers	Clues
1. b. breakfast cereal	healthy, delicious flavor, time to go to work, no time to cook, healthy breakfast, morning, bowl
2. c. cell phone company	12 midnight, in California, good news, calling for free, 5,000 free nighttime minutes, new calling plan, camera phone
3. b. a used car	sell, fine beauties, 2005 two-door sedan, automatic, low mileage, clean, tires, GPS system, airbags, test drive, $16,000, $500/month
4. c. sleeping pill	midnight, tired, on TV, two o'clock in the morning, breakfast, take some Dreamease
5. b. daytime TV drama	love, secret, destroy a life, Will she tell it? Find out Monday at nine, on KNXT.

AUDIOSCRIPT

Commercial 1

Announcer: Looking for a healthy start and delicious flavor? Time to go to work, but no time to cook a healthy breakfast? Start your morning right with a bowl of *Flakos*!

Question 1: What are *Flakos*?

Announcer: They're my favorite cereal, and they provide all the energy I need for the morning.

Commercial 2

A: Hello?

B: Hi, Marge. Are you asleep?

A: Not anymore. Who is this?

B: It's Bill. I'm on vacation in California.

A: Bill, it's 12:00 midnight.

B: Yeah, but I have some good news! I'm calling for free! I get 5,000 free nighttime minutes on this new calling plan. And I got a great new camera phone!

Question 2: This is an ad for a . . .

Announcer: SureCell—the cell phone company that saves you money all day—and all night!

Commercial 3

Hi! This is Tex Lewis. I'll do anything to sell you one of these fine beauties. Lookie here. We've got a 2005 two-door sedan here, automatic, with low mileage. This baby is clean; got new tires, GPS system, side airbags, the whole works. Take a test drive today. And it can be yours for just $16,000, or $500 per month. Come in and check it out. See you soon.

Question 3: This is an ad for . . .

Announcer: Tex's Used Cars. Quality cars for less.

Commercial 4

A: Honey, make me a sandwich.

B: Henry! It's midnight. I'm tired.

A: Honey, what's on TV?

B: I don't know. It's two o'clock in the morning.

A: Honey, can I have some breakfast?

B: Henry, it's four o'clock in the morning. Why don't you take some Dreamease?

Question 4: Dreamease is a . . .

Announcer: Dreamease, the sleeping pill that helps you get the rest you need.

Commercial 5

Man: Daisy, you must tell me everything. You believe me, don't you?

Woman: I can't, Rob. I just can't.

Man: Don't treat me this way, Daisy. I know you love me. And I love you, too.

Woman: I know. But, but I promised. And I can't break a promise.

Announcer: Her secret can destroy a life. Will she tell it? Find out this Monday at 9:00 on KNXT.

Question 5: This is an ad for a . . .

Announcer: *Daisy*, the most popular drama on television.

Talk It Over

Best Practice

Making Use of Academic Content

This is an example of an activity that exposes students to materials that they will actually face in an academic setting. The authentic advertisements that the students will bring into class will provide the students an opportunity to engage in the kind of analysis that they will face in actual classrooms.

1 Discussing Advertisements 

- ❑ Read the directions for the first part of this activity.
- ❑ Put the students in groups of three or four.
- ❑ Tell the students to make a list of the qualities of a good advertisement. For example, it should be funny, it should have a clear message, it should be short, and it should be graphically interesting.
- ❑ Go over the groups' answers as a class.
- ❑ Point out the advertisement on page 155.
- ❑ Have the students in the same groups compare the ad to the qualities they identified for good ads. How many of the qualities are in the ad on page 155?
- ❑ Discuss the students' opinions as a class.
- ❑ For homework, tell the students to bring into class two advertisements. One should be a very interesting ad and one should be boring.
- ❑ Have the students present their ads in small groups.
- ❑ If there is time, have students present ads to the class.

1 Types of TV Programs

- ❑ Read the directions for part one to the students.
- ❑ Go through the list of program types and make sure that the students understand what they mean. Ask the students to describe each type, e.g., *A drama series is very serious and may have action in it*.
- ❑ Put the students in pairs and have them give examples of each TV program type.
- ❑ As a class, go through the list and check to see if the students' examples are in the correct category.
- ❑ Read the directions for part two to the students. Make sure that they understand that they are to match the actual programs in part two with the program types in part one. The students must put the letter of the program type in the blank in part two.
- ❑ If the students are not familiar with these programs, you can assign part two as homework and tell the students to look up the programs on the Internet. You can also briefly describe each program to the students and have them decide what type of program it is.
- ❑ When the students have completed the activity, go over the answers with them.
- ❑ Ask the students what other popular shows they know. Write the program names on the board with their program type.

ANSWER KEY

Part One (Possible answers)

a. reality show - *American Idol*

b. cartoon - *Pokemon, the Simpsons*

c. game show - *Jeopardy, Wheel of Fortune*

d. drama series - *The Sopranos, The West Wing*
e. sitcom - *Everybody Hates Chris, Malcolm in the Middle*

f. children's show - *Barney, Pokemon*

g. news program - *CBS Evening News, The News Hour*

h. soap opera - *The Young and the Restless, As the World Turns*

Part Two

1. g. news program 2. d. drama series 3. f. children's program 4. e. sitcom 5. c. game show 6. b. cartoon/e. sitcom 7. a. reality show

2 Discussing a Program Guide 

- ❑ Read the directions to the students.
- ❑ Point out the TV guide below and give the students a few minutes to look it over.
- ❑ Put the students in pairs and have them answer the three questions.
- ❑ Go over the answers as a class.

ANSWER KEY

1. Survivor - reality show 2. 9:00 P.M. on channel 7 3. Celebrity couples will be the guests on *The Oprah Winfrey Show.*

- ❑ Read the directions for part two to the students
- ❑ Point out the blanks in the TV guide. Make sure the students see the program types underneath the blanks. They will be circling one of these.
- ❑ Play the recording. Give the students time to fill in the blanks.
- ❑ Put the students in pairs to check their answers.
- ❑ If necessary, play the recording again.
- ❑ Check the answers as a class.

ANSWER KEY

1. Channel 7 — *Who Wants to Be a Millionaire?* (game show) 2. Channel 11 — *The Matrix* (movie)

3. Channel 13 — *Shanghai Knights* (movie)
4. Channel 20 — *Scream* (horror movie)
5. Channel 53 at 8:00 — *Friends* (sitcom) 6. ESPN at 9:00 — basketball/NBA finals

AUDIOSCRIPT

Jennifer: What's on TV tonight?

Raul: Let me check the TV guide. What time is it now?

Jennifer: It's almost 7:30.

Raul: There are probably some game shows on.

Jennifer: Yeah, I think *Who Wants To Be a Millionaire*? is on Channel 7 at seven o'clock.

Raul: *Who Wants to Be a Millionaire?* I'm a little tired of that one.

Jennifer: OK. See if there are any good movies on.

Raul: Well, there are three movies on at eight o'clock.

Jennifer: Which ones are they?

Raul: There's *Shanghai Knights* on Channel 13—you know, the comedy with Jackie Chan.

Jennifer: I've already seen it.

Raul: Then on Channel 11 there's *The Matrix*. But you don't like science fiction, right?

Jennifer: Ugh. I hate sci-fi.

Raul: And then there's the horror movie *Scream* . . . that's on Channel 20.

Jennifer: Oh, wait—what's tonight? Wednesday? My favorite sitcom is on at eight o'clock!

Raul: At eight? You must be kidding—you don't want to watch *Friends again*! Channel 53 should take it off, it's so old.

Jennifer: I don't care. *Friends* is still the funniest.

Jennifer: Come on, let's make a decision.

Raul: OK. We can watch your sitcom at 8:00 if you let me watch basketball at 9:00 on Channel 25.

Jennifer: Basketball? But you played basketball all afternoon!

Raul: But it's the NBA finals!

Jennifer: Fine. But I want to catch the news at 8:30. I want to know about the president's trip to Asia.

Raul: Yeah, me too. I'm sure CNN on Channel 24 will have a good report.

Jennifer: Yeah. I guess we're all set. I'll go make some popcorn.

Best Practice

Cultivating Critical Thinking

This is an example of an activity that requires students to process the information they have learned and apply it to a new situation. This involves reinterpretation, synthesis, and application of concepts. In this activity, students use the language and concepts that they have learned to talk about a specific movie or TV program which they like. The students must think about their reasons for liking it and then explain their reasons to the class.

3 Describing a Favorite Show or Movie 

- ❑ Read the directions to the students.
- ❑ Go over the four lines for the students to take notes on. Ask the students if they have any questions.
- ❑ Have a student read the example about *Desperate Housewives*. Have the students underline the key information from the four questions above the example. They will, for example, begin by underlining <u>soap opera</u> for the first question that asks about the *kind of show*.
- ❑ Give the students 10 minutes to think of their favorite program and to fill in the blanks with their notes.
- ❑ Put the students in pairs and have them describe their programs to each other.
- ❑ When they have finished, ask for volunteers to describe their programs to the class.

Self-Assessment Log

- ❑ The purpose of the log is to help the students reflect on their learning.
- ❑ Read the directions aloud and have students check vocabulary that they learned in the chapter and are prepared to use.
- ❑ Have students check the strategies they understand.
- ❑ Put students in small groups. Ask students to find the information or an activity related to each strategy in the chapter.
- ❑ Tell students to find definitions in the chapter for any words they did not check, or they can look in their dictionaries.

Chapter

9

Social Life

In this chapter, students will listen to language for participating in social events, including dating. In Part 1, they will learn language for meeting old friends. They will also practice understanding and using exclamations and giving and accepting compliments. In Part 2, they will practice language for discussing dating customs. They will also practice listening for main ideas and specific information. In Part 3, they will learn language for parties. In Part 4, they will practice language for entertainment events. These topics will prepare students for informal social situations and for making arrangements to participate in entertainment events.

Chapter Opener

- ❑ Have students look at the photo of people in a cafe. Ask them the questions in the Connecting to the Topic section. Discuss the answers as a class.
- ❑ Have the students read the proverb. Give them some time to ask for clarification of anything that they don't understand.
- ❑ Ask the students what they think the proverb means. If the students don't understand the proverb, tell them that friends are people with whom you have a special relationship. You can't be everybody's friend.

" A friend to all is a friend to none. "

—Greek proverb

Chapter Overview

Listening Skills and Strategies

Listening for main ideas

Listening for details

Interpreting intonation used with exclamations

Listening to a conversation on dating and a marriage match

Listening to phone calls on entertainment

Speaking Skills and Strategies

Discussing dating customs

Giving and accepting complements

Discussing parties

Discussing preferences and experiences in spending free time

Critical Thinking Skills

Interpreting a photo

Comparing alternatives - selecting the best match

Gathering information from entertainment advertisements

Summarizing research on upcoming events

Vocabulary Building

Terms connected with friendship and dating

Exclamations

Expressions used in giving and accepting compliments

Terms to talk about personal qualities and compatibility

Terms connected with parties and common entertainment activities

Pronunciation

Identifying and practicing stressed words

Comparing reduced and unreduced pronunciation

Using appropriate intonation with exclamations

Focus on Testing

Using context clues to guess the nature of interpersonal relationships

Explaining a sport

Vocabulary

Nouns	Verbs	Adjectives	Expression
box office	be up to	good at	on the road
cover charge	keep in touch	terrific	
graduation	make a reservation		
live music	make sense		
pre-med			
sales rep			
sci-fi film			
service charge			
show times			
vacancy			

Can You Guess?

- Put the students in small groups to discuss the questions below and compare their answers with the correct answers.

1. About what percent of American men, age 30-34, have never married? American women? *A. Men: 33%; Women: 23%.** **2.** About what percent of single people use the Internet for dating? *A. 61%.*** **3.** What is "speed dating"? *A. An evening during which each participant has several 3-4-minute "dates".* **4.** What is a "professional matchmaker"? *A. A person or agency paid to find partners or mates for individuals.*

Footnotes:
* Source: Statistical abstract of US table #53: http://www.census.gov/prod/2004pubs/04statab/pop.pdf
** Source: NY Times: http://d8me.blogharbor.com/blog/_archives/2005/3/24/472945.html

Before You Listen

Best Practice

Activating Prior Knowledge

The prelistening questions activate students' prior knowledge. This activity will help students relate their own experience with old friends to the new language in this chapter. When students activate their prior knowledge before learning new material, they are better able to map new language onto existing concepts, which aids understanding and retention.

1 Prelistening Questions 

- ❑ Have students look at the photo and describe what the three people are doing.
- ❑ Ask them if they can guess what the situation is.
- ❑ Ask the students where this conversation is taking place.
- ❑ Tell the students that this photo will help them understand the conversation that they will hear later.
- ❑ Have the students read the questions.
- ❑ Put the students in pairs and have them discuss the questions.
- ❑ Compare answers as a whole class. If there is time, ask for more details in their answers. For example, do many of their old friends still live in the same town or city? Have many moved to a new country?
- ❑ As a whole class, make a list of any new words or expressions that come up.

Best Practice

Organizing Information

This type of activity uses a graphic organizer, in this case a table, to categorize information. Having students write down a sentence that has new vocabulary and then asking them to paraphrase the meaning of the new words helps students process and organize the information while they are listening. This type of graphic organizer emphasizes guessing the meaning of new words in context. Other types of graphic organizers are used throughout this book.

2 Previewing Vocabulary 

- ❑ Play the recording and ask students to listen to the words and expressions.
- ❑ The students haven't done this type of activity yet, so take more time than usual with your explanations.

- ❑ Read the directions to the students. Ask students to look at the sentences with the blanks and the chart with three columns. Make sure that they understand that they should fill in the blanks before starting on the chart.
- ❑ Read the words in the left column of the chart. Have the students repeat the words and phrases after you.
- ❑ Go over the sample phrase *good at* in the first row of the chart. Make sure that they understand that the middle column is taken from the sentences with blanks and the right column is where they paraphrase the meaning of the target word or phrase.
- ❑ Tell the students to fill in the blanks in the sentences under the chart. Then tell them to fill in the middle and right columns of the chart.
- ❑ When they have finished, put them in pairs to check the answers.
- ❑ Go over the answers as a class.

ANSWER KEY

Words and Expressions	**Use of Words and Expressions in the Sentences**	**Meanings as Used Here**
good at	he has always been good at science	He's able to understand science and study it easily.
graduation	celebrate my graduation from high school	the day someone finishes high school or college
keep in touch	I want to keep in touch with them.	not lose contact with
make sense	It doesn't make sense to buy a car.	It's not a smart thing to do.
on the road	I'm on the road most of the time.	traveling
pre-med	She's studying pre-med courses.	courses that prepare people for medical school
sales rep	So you're a sales rep.	salesperson, sales representative
terrific	It really looks terrific.	It looks very good.
be up to	What have you been up to?	What have you been doing?

ANSWER KEY

(Sentences)

1. good at 2. up to 3. terrific 4. on the road 5. pre-med 6. keep in touch 7. graduation 8. make sense 9. sales rep

Listen

3 Listening for Main Ideas 

(The audioscript follows Activity 5.)

- ❑ Remind the students that they should focus only on the main ideas in the first listening. They do not need to understand every word to answer the questions.
- ❑ Tell the students to read the directions and questions in their books. Give the students time to ask questions.
- ❑ Have the students look again at the photo in Activity 1 on page 162. Tell the students that

this illustrates some important information about the conversation.

- ❑ Ask students to close their books as they listen.
- ❑ Play the recording.
- ❑ After listening, give the students some time to write down individual answers.
- ❑ Then have the students compare their answers in pairs.
- ❑ Finally, go over the answers to the three questions as a class. Ask them for specific words or phrases they heard that support their answers.

ANSWER KEY

1. They discuss what they are doing in their lives. They haven't seen each other in a long time, so they are catching up.
2. Ming expresses doubts about Dan's hard work. She says, "Sure you have . . .", which means that she thinks that he is exaggerating.
3. Dan suggests that they keep in touch and gives them his email address..

4 Listening for Details 

(The audioscript follows Activity 5.)

- ❑ Tell the students to read the three questions.
- ❑ Play the recording.
- ❑ Put the students in pairs to answer the questions.
- ❑ Go over the questions as a group. Ask for additional details from the conversation that support their answers.

ANSWER KEY

1. graduation night; 2. computer science;
3. Yolanda is a pre-med student at State College.

Stress

5 Listening for Stressed Words 

- ❑ Read the directions to the students.
- ❑ Play the recording again. Tell the students to fill in the blanks with the words that they hear.
- ❑ During each pause, tell the students to repeat the phrase or sentence to themselves before filling in the blank.
- ❑ After listening, have students check their answers with a partner. Then have each pair check their answers with the audioscript in their books.

AUDIOSCRIPT and ANSWER KEY

Yolanda: Ming, look! I can't <u>believe</u> it! It's Dan. Hey Dan! How are you?

Dan: Yolanda? Ming? Wow! I haven't seen you guys since <u>graduation</u> night!

Ming: I know. You look <u>great</u>!

Dan: Thanks. So do <u>you</u>!

Ming: So what have you been <u>up</u> to?

Dan: Well, I go to Faber College.

Yolanda: <u>Really</u>? Do you <u>like</u> it?

Dan: Yeah, <u>so</u> <u>far</u>. But I've been <u>studying</u> really hard.

Ming: <u>Sure</u> you have . . .

Yolanda: So, what's your <u>major</u>?

Dan: It's <u>computer</u> science.

Ming: Ah-h-h. <u>That</u> makes sense. You always <u>*were*</u> good at <u>math</u> and <u>science</u>.

Dan: Thanks. Anyway, what have <u>*you*</u> guys been up to?

Ming: Well, I'm a <u>sales</u> rep for a publishing company.

Dan: No <u>kidding</u>! How do you like that?

Ming: Oh, I <u>love</u> it! I'm on the road a lot, but I get to meet some interesting people.

Dan: That's <u>terrific</u>. And how about <u>you</u>, Yolanda?

Yolanda: I'm studying pre-med at State College.

Dan: Wow — you can be my doctor! You always were good at science, too. Well, it was great seeing you both. Let's keep in touch from now on. Email me sometime. Here's my address.

After You Listen

6 Using Vocabulary 

- ❑ Tell the students to read the questions. Give them some time to ask about anything that they don't understand.
- ❑ Put the students in pairs. Have the students ask and answer the questions.
- ❑ Remind the students to use the target vocabulary in their discussions.
- ❑ When the students have finished, go over the questions as a class.

Pronunciation

INTONATION WITH EXCLAMATIONS 

- Go over the information about exclamations with the students. Play the recording and have them repeat the expressions.

7 Pronouncing Exclamations 

- ❑ Read the directions to the students. Explain that they are simply going to repeat the key exclamations from this chapter.
- ❑ Play the recording, stopping after each item. Have the students repeat the exclamation with you.

8 Matching Statements and Responses 

- ❑ This is not an activity type that the students are familiar with, so spend a little more time explaining how it works than you usually do.
- ❑ Point out the eight exclamations and the eight numbered blanks.
- ❑ Explain that the students will hear eight statements or questions and must decide which exclamation is the appropriate response.
- ❑ Play the recording and have students write their answers.
- ❑ Put the students in pairs and have them check answers.
- ❑ Check the answers as a class.

ANSWER KEY

1.a 2.b 3.e 4.c 5.e, g, or h 6.f 7.d 8.g or h

AUDIOSCRIPT

1. My sister just had triplets.
2. Guess what? I'm getting married next month.
3. Would you like a job for a dollar an hour?
4. I've been dancing a lot, and I've finally learned the tango.
5. Someone hit my car yesterday. It's going to cost $1,000 to repair.
6. I met the president of the United States yesterday.
7. My sister likes to eat peanut butter and banana sandwiches.
8. I locked the keys in the car.

Best Practice

Interacting with Others

This type of activity, a dialogue, is an example of collaborative learning to encourage fluency and confidence. In this pair activity, based around using exclamations, communication is more important than grammar. Because the students add authentic information to one item and create the final item, the activity becomes personal, thereby increasing its importance to the student.

9 Practicing Exclamations 

- ❑ Put the students in pairs. Tell the students to decide who will be Student A and who will be Student B.
- ❑ Go over the directions with the students. Make sure that they understand that Student A must only look at the Student A page and Student B must only look at the Student B page.
- ❑ Explain that they will be taking turns reading sentences. Their partner will respond with an appropriate exclamation.
- ❑ Point out the special requirements of the items that have blanks. In number 5, the students must write their own sentence.
- ❑ Give the students time to fill in the items that have blanks.
- ❑ Go over the exclamations for the sentences as a class.

Using Language Functions

GIVING AND ACCEPTING COMPLIMENTS

- Read the information in the *Giving and Accepting Compliments* box to the students.
- Give the students some time to absorb the cultural information for receiving compliments.

Content Note: Accepting Compliments

For students from many cultures, it will be difficult to accept that in English-speaking countries, a person receiving a compliment is expected to thank the person who gave it. This thanking does not mean that the person agrees with the compliment. They are thanking the person for their kindness in giving a compliment.

10 Giving and Accepting Compliments 

- ❑ If possible, have the students sit in a circle. If there are too many students, have multiple circles.
- ❑ Read the directions to the students. Make sure that they understand the concept of a chain of compliments that will go around the circle.
- ❑ Go over the list of topics for compliments. Have the students give you an example for each category.
- ❑ Choose one person from each circle to be Student A and start giving compliments.

Before You Listen

1 Prelistening Questions 

- ❑ Read the directions to the students.
- ❑ Tell the students to read the six questions. There is a great deal of culture-specific information in this activity, so you should expect to spend some time explaining these questions. For example, many students won't know what a *blind date* is or what *love at first sight* means.
- ❑ Put the students into pairs and have them discuss the questions.
- ❑ Go over their answers as a class. Write new vocabulary on the board as it comes up in the discussion.
- ❑ If romance is a topic that is uncomfortable for the students in your class, you may choose instead to pass over this activity.

Listen

2 Listening for Main Ideas 

- ❑ Read the directions for this activity to the students.
- ❑ Tell the students that they are going to listen to a long listening passage.
- ❑ Read the three questions to the students.
- ❑ Play the recording and have them answer the questions.
- ❑ Briefly check the answers as a class just to make sure that all of the students understand the general situation.

ANSWER KEY

1. Tanya wants to set Meena up on a date with a handsome man.
2. Meena comes from a very traditional culture in which people do not date. She is not supposed to go out with men before marriage.
3. Yes, she does. She asks many polite questions about Meena's beliefs and compares Meena's culture's practices favorably to her own culture.

AUDIOSCRIPT

Tanya: Listen, Meena, a friend is coming to town next week. He's great looking, and I think you might enjoy going on a date. Would you like to meet him?

Meena: No thanks, Tanya. You know how traditional my family is. Dating just isn't part of our culture. In fact, I'm not supposed to go out with guys at all before marriage.

Tanya: Hmm, I see. How are you going to meet a partner or a husband?

Meena: Oh, my family's always looking for the right kind of person. Or they might even take me to a professional matchmaker.

Tanya: Interesting . . . So what makes a good match?

Meena: Well, he's got to be from a good family from my parents' point of view. And he has to share our religious beliefs.

Tanya: That's just what *my* mother says. And . . .?

Meena: He should be honest and hardworking, be a strong leader, but be kind.

Tanya: Sounds good to me. But what if you don't love the guy your family wants you to be with?

Meena: You know, my parents would never force me to marry someone I really couldn't accept . . . But we believe love is something that takes time—it can grow in the right situation.

Tanya: I think I understand . . .

Meena:	Maybe it doesn't sound very romantic. But our family life is really strong, and all my relatives seem pretty satisfied with their marriages.
Tanya:	I wish I could say the same . . .

3 Taking Notes on Specific Information 

(The audioscript follows Activity 2.)

- Read the directions to the students. Point out the lines below the directions for taking notes.
- Read the phrases in front of the blank lines to the students.
- Play the recording again. Have students write the answers individually.
- Put the students in pairs. Have them compare their notes.
- Go over the answers as a class.

ANSWER KEY

Ways to meet a husband: dating, having the family find someone, hiring a professional matchmaker

For Meena, the right man must be: from a good family, must share her religious beliefs, should be honest, hardworking, a strong leader, kind

Meena's view on love: it takes time; it can grow in the right situation

Possible advantages of this kind of marriage: family life is really strong; all Meena's relatives seem satisfied with their marriages

After You Listen

4 Summarizing Ideas 

- Put the students into pairs. Tell the students to take turns explaining Meena's beliefs about finding a good marriage partner.
- Tell the students to use their notes from Activity 3.
- While the students are talking, walk around the room, helping them with anything that they do not understand.

5 Discussing Dating Customs 

- Start by reading the Culture Note on dating to the students. Give the students time to ask for clarification. No discussion is necessary at this point as the students will have a lot of time to discuss dating in the activity.
- Read the directions to the students.
- Tell them to read all of the questions and to ask for clarification of anything that they don't understand.
- Put the students in small groups. Have them discuss all of the questions. Tell them that one way they can explain their answers (as it asks them to do in the directions) is to give specific examples of their own or their friends' experiences.

Talk It Over

6 Meeting Friends and Dates Online 

- Read the directions with the students. Make sure that they understand that they will be the matchmaker in this activity.
- Tell the students to read over the descriptions of the six people. Give them time to ask for clarification.
- Put the students in small groups. Tell them to decide whether or not any of the people might be a good match.
- Go over their answers as a class. Ask students for reasons for their matches. For example, they may pair Ji Woo (shy, but friendly) and Ali (likes privacy and quiet places) because they aren't big party goers, and they are both serious about business.

7 Filling Out a Questionnaire

- Because this is a multi-step activity, it may take a fair amount of time to explain it.
- Go over the first paragraph making sure that the students understand how an Internet dating service works.
- Point out the Internet dating application on pages 172–173. Make sure that the students understand that they are not really going to apply for an Internet date. Tell them that they will be putting a false name on the application and that they can put things on the application that aren't true.
- Have the students read through the application and ask questions about anything that they do not understand. Don't have them fill it out just yet.
- Read through the steps for the activity.
- Now give the students time to fill out the applications.
- Post the completed forms on the board or wall. Have the women read the men's applications and the men read the women's applications.
- When the students have decided which application is most interesting to them, have them return to their seats. Hold up the applications one by one and read them. Ask the students to guess who the student is.

Best Practice

Cultivating Critical Thinking

This is an example of an activity in which a student must use personal beliefs and desires to produce a final product which will be presented to other students. This type of activity requires students to process the information they have learned and apply it to a new situation. This involves reinterpretation, synthesis, and application of concepts. This process will allow students to evaluate whether they have understood the new material and help them remember it better.

Reproducible

EXPANSION ACTIVITY

- Please see Black Line Master "My Perfect Night Out" on page BLM 17 of this Teacher's Edition.
- Photocopy and distribute one copy to each student.
- Read the situation to the students. Give them time to ask for clarification.
- Go over the procedures for Part 1 and Part 2. Make sure that the students understand that they will be explaining their perfect night out to a partner and then listening to their partner's night out. They will present their partner's night out to the class, so they must listen to their partner very carefully and take detailed notes.
- When the students have finished Part 1, put them in pairs and have them describe their perfect nights out to each other.
- When the students have finished Part 2, have them present their partner's perfect night out to the class.

Getting Meaning from Context

Focus on Testing

Using Context Clues

- Point out to the students that this is a *Focus on Testing* activity. The skill taught in this activity will help students with standardized tests, such as the Internet-based TOEFL®.
- Read the directions to the students.
- Go over the chart with the students.
- Play each conversation, stopping after the question. Give the students time to circle the correct answer and write down several clues before playing the answer and moving on.
- Put the students in pairs and have them compare their charts.
- Go over the answers and clues as a class.

ANSWER KEY

Answers	Clues
1. b. The man is new in town.	seems nice, been so busy, haven't done any sightseeing, show me around
2. c. The man and woman used to work together.	Are you glad you left? Very glad. He (the manager) still is (a pain in the neck). Every day, I hate going to work.
3. a. The woman doesn't want to go out with the man.	difficult for me to get away, very busy, too tired after work, friend is coming from Miami, be out most of the time
4. a. The man is worried about Tony.	took his bike out, it's pitch dark
5. b. The man and woman had a misunderstanding.	where were you, I waited 45 minutes, I thought, wait a minute, you said, that's *not* what I said

AUDIOSCRIPT

Conversation 1

Man: So how long have you lived here?

Woman: I've lived here all my life. I really love it here.

Man: It seems nice, but I've been so busy with my new job and moving in to my new apartment that I haven't done any sightseeing yet. Are you free on Saturday afternoon? Maybe you could show me around a little.

Question 1: Which of these sentences is true?

Woman: Sure. Tell me, how long have you been in town?

Man: Only about three weeks.

Conversation 2

Woman: So, are you glad you left?

Man: Very glad. My salary wasn't great, as you know, and the manager was a pain in the neck.

Woman: He still is. Every day I hate going to work. But I don't know if I could find a better job.

Man: Why don't you start looking around? You might get lucky like me.

Question 2: Which of these sentences is true?

Man: I really enjoyed working with you, of course. I just didn't like the boss.

Conversation 3

Man: I've really enjoyed talking with you. Would you like to have lunch together sometime?

Woman: Thanks, you're very kind. But, well, uh, it's difficult for me to get away from work. I'm very busy.

Man: Well, how about dinner?

Woman: I'm usually too tired to go out after work.

Man: Can I call you over the weekend?

Woman: Well, this weekend my friend is coming from Miami, and I'll probably be out most of the time.

Man: How about next weekend?

Question 3: Which of these sentences is true?

Woman: Actually, I have a boyfriend, so I really can't go out with you.

Conversation 4

Man: Where's Tony?

Woman: I think he took his bike out to get some soda.

Man: Really? Do you think he can see out there? I mean, it's pitch dark.

Woman: I don't know. I'm sure he's fine. It's only been about an hour.

Question 4: Which of these sentences is true?

Man: One hour! The store is just five minutes from here. I hope he's OK.

Conversation 5

Man: One hour! The store is just five minutes from here. I hope he's OK.

Man: I thought you were going to pick me up. I had to take a taxi.

Woman: Wait a minute. You said you wanted to leave your car at my house.

Man: That's not what I said. I said I wanted to leave my car *at home*.

Question 5: Which of these sentences is true?

Woman: Listen, I'm sorry. Let's not fight over this misunderstanding, OK?

Talk It Over

1 Discussing Parties 

- ❑ Go over the directions and the questions with the students. Give the students time to ask for clarification of anything they don't understand.
- ❑ Put the students in small groups and give them time to discuss the questions.
- ❑ Go over their answers as a class.

Best Practice

Making Use of Academic Content

This is an example of an activity that exposes students to materials that they will actually have to deal with when they are in an academic setting. Looking over the entertainment pages from a newspaper or magazine will prepare the students for their social activities after class and in the evening.

1 Prelistening Discussion 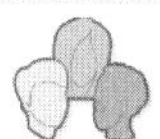

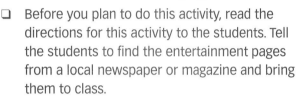

- ❑ Before you plan to do this activity, read the directions for this activity to the students. Tell the students to find the entertainment pages from a local newspaper or magazine and bring them to class.
- ❑ Show the students the sample advertisements and announcements in their textbook. Ask them what kinds of activities are in the samples.
- ❑ In class, put the students into groups of three or four. Have them go through the entertainment pages looking for the types of announcements specified in question 1.
- ❑ Have the students choose activities that they would like to do.
- ❑ Go over the students' answers together. Discuss the results. Are there some activities that attract most of the students? Are there others that no one chose?

2 Previewing Vocabulary 

- ❑ Play the recording and ask students to listen to the underlined words and phrases.
- ❑ Tell the students to read the directions. Give them some time to ask for clarification.
- ❑ Tell the students that they should use the context to help them guess the meanings of words which they do not know.
- ❑ Have the students do the activity individually. Then put them in pairs to check their answers.
- ❑ Go over the answers as a class. Ask students who guessed accurately what words helped give them the correct answer.
- ❑ Put the students in pairs. Have them role-play the first two conversations.

ANSWER KEY

1. sci-fi film — a movie that involves situations that couldn't really happen; situations that are beyond the present limits of scientific knowledge, for example, spaceships invading Earth (clue: fantasy) show times — the times that a theater shows a movie (clues: 4, 7, 10)

2. live music — music that is not recorded (clues: Want to go see . . . tonight?, Who's singing?) cover charge — money that you pay to hear music at a bar or restaurant (clues: $15, expensive)

3. service charge — an extra fee that you pay for a company to do something (clues: on the Internet, two dollars or more) box office — a place that sells tickets (clue: pick the tickets up at the box office)

4. make a reservation — to get a place at a restaurant in advance (clues: before, if not have to wait)

Best Practice

Scaffolding Instruction

This is an example of an activity that gives students a framework which will help them understand what they are hearing. The categories (e.g., *event*) in front of the note lines give the students an understanding of what kind of information they will be dealing with. Later in real situations, before they listen, they will know that they need to listen for the name of the event, the location, the show times, etc.

3 Taking Notes 

- ❑ Read the directions and situation to the students. Go over the categories (e.g., *event*) that they have to listen for.
- ❑ Play the recording.
- ❑ After playing the recording, put the students in pairs so that they can check their information.
- ❑ Go over the answers as a class.
- ❑ If there is time, have the students in pairs read the second and third calls.

ANSWER KEY

Call 1

Event: Movie — *Invasion*
Location: Fox Theater in the Town and Country Shopping Center
Show time(s): two, six, and ten o'clock
Price of tickets: $10 for adults; $5.50 for students, senior citizens, and children under 12

Call 2

Place: Blue Note Jazz and Supper Club
Entertainment tonight: singer — Bebel Gilberto
Cost: $20 cover charge unless you come for dinner
Menu: Italian food, but they have salads and hamburgers
Reservations: two people, 8:00, will stay for the 9:00 show

Call 3

Place: Gallery Shibuya
Band: Buffalo Daughter, rock band
Date: August 4
Price (total): $19.00
Remember to bring: student I.D.

AUDIOSCRIPT

Call 1

Hello. This is the Fox Theater, located in the Town and Country Shopping Center. Today we're proud to present Nicole Kidman in the thrilling sci-fi film, *Invasion*. Show times for Saturday are two, six, and ten o'clock. Tickets are $10 and $5.50 for students, senior citizens, and children under 12. For more information, please hang up and call 555-0183. See you at the movies!

Call 2

Manager: Hello. Blue Note Jazz and Supper Club.
Ming: Hi. I'd like some information.
Manager: Sure, what would you like to know?
Ming: First, is there any live music tonight?
Manager: Yes, we have a terrific Brazilian singer named Bebel Gilberto. There are shows at nine and eleven.
Ming: How much is the show?
Manager: We have a $20 cover charge. But if you come for dinner, the show is free.
Ming: What's your menu like?
Manager: Our specialty is Italian food, but we serve salads and hamburgers too.
Ming: Fine. I'd like to make a reservation for two for dinner at eight, and we'll stay for the nine o'clock show. My last name's Lee – that's L-E-E.
Manager: Very good Ms. Lee, we'll see you at eight.

Call 3

You have reached the information line for Gallery Shibuya, which features live rock music nightly. The gallery is proud to present Buffalo Daughter, now through August 6. For show times, press 1. For directions to gallery Shibuya, press 2. For ticket information and ticket orders, press 3.

Clerk: Hi, this is Sherry speaking. Can I help you?
Ming: Yes, uh, do you still have tickets for the August 4th Buffalo Daughter show?
Clerk: How many tickets?
Ming: Two.
Clerk: I'll check.

Clerk:	Yes, we have tickets for $20.00.
Ming:	Is there a special price for students?
Clerk:	Yes, student tickets are $8.50.
Ming:	OK, that's good.
Clerk:	All right, two student tickets at $8.50 each, that's $17.00. There is also a service charge of $1.00 per ticket, so your total comes to $19.00. And how would you like to pay for your tickets?
Ming:	Can you hold them for me for 10 minutes — I'm just a block away from you?
Clerk:	I can do that — and then there's no service charge. May I have your full name please?
Ming:	Ming Lee.
Clerk:	Ming—M-I-N-G?
Ming:	Right.
Clerk:	And we need your phone number please, Ms. Lee.
Ming:	310-555-0176.
Clerk:	OK, so we'll see you soon, all right? And remember to bring your student ID with you, for the student price.
Ming:	Thank you very much.
Clerk:	You're welcome. Bye-bye.
Ming:	Bye.

4 Using Vocabulary 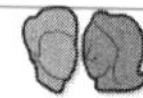

- ❑ Tell the students to read the questions.
- ❑ Put the students in pairs. Have the students ask and answer the questions using the underlined vocabulary in their answers.
- ❑ When the students have finished, go over the questions as a class.

5 Role-Play 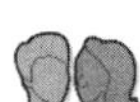

- ❑ Read the directions to the students.
- ❑ Put the students in pairs. Have them decide which student is Student A and which is Student B.
- ❑ Make sure that the students understand that this is a two-part activity. In the first part, Student A is a customer. In the second part, Student B is the customer.
- ❑ Tell the students to open their books to the appropriate pages, depending on whether they are A or B.
- ❑ Tell the students to read all of the *Useful Expressions* in their boxes.
- ❑ Have the students begin the role-plays. Walk around the room, helping the students get started.
- ❑ When the role-plays are finished, ask for volunteers to do the role-plays in front of the class.

EXPANSION ACTIVITY

- Please see Black Line Master "Student Socializing Guide" on page BLM 18 of this Teacher's Edition.
- Photocopy and distribute one copy to each student.
- Read the situation to the students. Give them some time to ask for clarification.
- Go over the procedure for this activity. Make sure that they understand that in Part 1, they will generate their individual ideas. In Part 2, they will work with a group. At the end, each group will present their ideas to the class.
- Give the students 10 minutes to brainstorm ideas in Part 1.
- Put the students in groups of four or five. Tell them to tell each other their ideas from Part 1 and then write at least eight sentences that give information or advice on socializing to new students.
- When the discussions are finished, have each group present its ideas. Tell the groups that each member must have a speaking part.

Self-Assessment Log

- ❑ The purpose of the log is to help the students reflect on their learning.
- ❑ Read the directions aloud and have students check vocabulary that they learned in the chapter and are prepared to use.
- ❑ Have students check the strategies they understand.
- ❑ Put students in small groups. Ask students to find the information or an activity related to each strategy in the chapter.
- ❑ Tell students to find definitions in the chapter for any words they did not check, or they can look in their dictionaries.

Chapter 10

Sports

In this chapter, students will learn a great deal of language to talk about sports. They will also practice listening to people talking about sports. In Part 1, they will hear a conversation in which people discuss martial arts. They will also practice listening for and pronouncing dropped *h* sounds and the *t* between two voiced sounds that is used by North Americans. In Part 2, they will listen to a speech about a female wrestler. They will also practice listening for main ideas and specific information. Finally, they will practice talking about sports. In Part 3, they will practice listening for context clues in conversations about sports. In Part 4, they will practice listening to sports broadcasts. They will also learn to give and understand instructions. These topics will prepare students for a wide range of situations in which sports is the main focus.

Chapter Opener

- ❑ Have the students look at the photo of a soccer match between Charlton Athletic and Manchester United in London in November, 2005. In this shot, Manchester United's Ruud van Nistelrooy narrowly misses as he shoots past Charlton's goalkeeper, Stephan Anderson. Ask them the questions in the Connecting to the Topic section.
- ❑ If the students don't mention it, remind them that in the United States, this game is called soccer, not football.
- ❑ Have the students read the quote. Give them some time to ask for clarification of anything that they don't understand.
- ❑ Ask the students what they think the quote means. If the students don't understand the quote, tell them that very often failing at something early in life is beneficial. It makes people stronger so that they can succeed later in life.

" I've failed over and over and over again in my life and that is why I succeed. "

—Michael Jordan
American basketball player (1963-)

Chapter Overview

Listening Skills and Strategies

Listening for main ideas

Listening for details

Listening to a conversation about martial arts

Listening to a talk by a woman wrestler

Listening to a sportscast

Speaking Skills and Strategies

Explaining a sport

Giving and understanding instructions

Playing "Twenty Questions"

Using correct nouns and verbs to describe sports and athletes

Critical Thinking Skills

Interpreting a photo

Organizing notes into an outline

Summarizing a speech using key words

Vocabulary Building

Nouns vs. verbs to describe sports and athletes

Terms used in a sportscast

Terms for giving instructions

Terms to ensure comprehension

Terms to ask for clarification

Pronunciation

Identifying and practicing stressed words

Comparing reduced and unreduced pronunciation

Pronouncing the North American *t*

Dropping the *h* sound in unstressed words

Focus on Testing

Using context clues to identify different sports

Vocabulary

Nouns	Verbs	Adjective	Expressions
balance	beat	close	It was a close game.
confidence	compete		It was a tie!
flexibility	focus	**Adverb**	What was the score?
individual	get in shape	overtime	
loser	get into		
match	lose		
opponent	score		
rival	stretch		
score	warm up		
set	win		
tennis match			
tie			
winner			

Can You Guess?

- Put the students in small groups to discuss the questions below and compare their answers with the correct answers.
- Ask students a few related questions.

1. Where is the biggest soccer stadium in the world? *A. Salt Lake Stadium in Kolkata, India (120,000 capacity).** **2.** When and where were the first ancient Olympic Games? *A. About 2700 years ago, in Ancient Greece.*** **3.** Who is the Greek goddess of victory, Hermes or Nike? *A. Nike* †

Footnotes:
* Source: http://www.en.wikipedia.org/wiki/List_of_football_stadiums_by_capacity
** Source: http://www.museum.upenn.edu.new/olympics/olympicorigins.shtml
† Source: http://www.museum.upenn.edu/new/olympics/olympicglossary.shtml

Before You Listen

Best Practice

Activating Prior Knowledge

The prelistening questions activate students' prior knowledge. This activity will help students relate their own experience or knowledge of martial arts to the new language in this chapter. When students activate their prior knowledge before learning new material, they are better able to map new language onto existing concepts, which aids understanding and retention.

1 Prelistening Questions 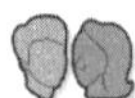

- ❑ Have students look at the photo and describe what is happening.
- ❑ Have the students read the questions and discuss them in pairs.
- ❑ Compare answers as a whole class. Ask the students to name as many martial arts as possible.

2 Previewing Vocabulary 

- ❑ Play the recording and have students listen to the words and phrases.
- ❑ Have students complete the vocabulary preview.
- ❑ Compare their answers as a whole class and write the correct answers on the board.

ANSWER KEY

1. get in shape; 2. stretch; 3. balance; 4. confidence; 5. flexibility; 6. get into; 7. focus; 8. warm up

Listen

3 Listening for Main Ideas 

(The audioscript follows Activity 5.)

- ❑ Tell the students to read the directions and the four questions in their books. Give the students time to ask for clarification.
- ❑ Have the students look at the three photos in this activity. Tell the students that they illustrate some important information about the conversation.
- ❑ Ask students to close their books as they listen.
- ❑ Play the recording.
- ❑ After listening, give the students some time to write down individual answers.
- ❑ Then have the students compare their answers in pairs.
- ❑ Finally, go over the answers to the questions as a class. Ask them for specific words or phrases they heard that support their answers.

ANSWER KEY

1. They will practice Tae Kwon Do. 2. Korea
3. Tae Kwon Do uses hundreds of kicking moves. Karate uses kicks, but karate also uses a lot of punches and blocks. 4. Tae Kwon Do has helped Ming get in shape and develop more confidence.

4 Listening for Details 

(The audioscript follows Activity 5.)

- ❑ Tell the students to look at the four true-false questions.
- ❑ Play the recording.
- ❑ Have the students answer the questions.
- ❑ Go over the questions as a group. Ask for additional details from the conversation.

ANSWER KEY

1. F—Ming is trying to teach her friends Tae Kwon Do.
2. T
3. F—He explains that Karate uses more punches and blocks and that he learned it in school. He demonstrates some Karate punches.
4. F—He shows interest by saying, "Cool," "that's great," and that he wishes he could do it. Also, he asks questions about it which shows he's interested.

Stress

5 Listening for Stressed Words 

- ❑ Read the directions to the students.
- ❑ Play the recording again. Tell the students to fill in the blanks with the words that they hear.
- ❑ During each pause, tell the students to repeat the phrase or sentence to themselves before filling in the blank.
- ❑ After listening, have students check their answers with a partner. Then have each pair check their answers with the audioscript in their books.

AUDIOSCRIPT and ANSWER KEY

Ming: OK guys. Let's warm up and stretch. We've got to work on balance and flexibility.

Peter: So, Ming, when did you get into this Karate stuff?

Kenji: Karate's Japanese. Ming's showing us Tae Kwon Do, and it's Korean.

Peter: Cool. So, what's the difference?

Ming: Tae Kwon Do uses hundreds of different kicking moves. But Karate . . . well, Kenji, sounds like you know something about Karate.

Kenji: Yeah – Karate uses more punches and blocks, too. Maybe you've seen guys break wooden boards with punches. You know, like . . . I learned that when I was in school.

Peter: That's great. I wish I could do that. So, Ming, why did you get into Tae Kwon Do?

Ming: I had a Korean friend in middle school, and he said it could help me get in shape and build my confidence. So I tried it, and I really liked it.

Peter: It looks like you succeeded.

Ming: Well, I'm still working on it. I've really improved my speed and power. It also helps you focus—you'll see.

Peter: Awesome! Let's get started.

Reductions

DROPPING THE /H/ SOUND

- Read the instruction note on *Dropping the /h/ Sound* to the students.
- Read the examples at the bottom of the note.

6 Listening for the Dropped *h*

- Point out the chart with the reduced and unreduced words.
- Play the recording of the sentences to the students.
- Finally, read either the reduced or unreduced sentence to the class. Ask the students to tell you which you read.

7 Comparing Unreduced and Reduced Pronunciation

- This activity is very similar to the previous activity. Make sure that the students understand that in the previous activity, they were only practicing the "*h*" sounds. In this activity, they are practicing a wide variety of reduced sounds that they learned throughout the book.

8 Listening for Reductions

- Play the recording of the conversation to the students.
- Tell the students to fill in the blanks with the unreduced form of the words.
- Put the students in pairs so that they can compare their answers.
- If necessary, play the recording again.
- Go over the answers as a class.

AUDIOSCRIPT

Jane: Hi Helen. Are you going out?

Helen: Yeah, I'm going to the football game. My brother's playing and I thought I'd watch him. Do you want to come?

Jane: I really can't . . . I have to study. But can you do me a favor?

Helen: OK.

Jane: Could you get me tickets for the girls' soccer game next Saturday? My cousin Sue just made the team.

Helen: Sure—that's so cool. What's her position?

Jane: I'm not sure—I'm going to call her, and I can ask her, if you want.

Helen: You don't have to—just wish her luck.

After You Listen

9 Reviewing Vocabulary

- Play the recording and ask students to listen to the underlined words.
- Read the directions to the students.
- Tell them to read all of the questions and to ask for clarification of anything that they don't understand.
- Put the students in pairs. Have them discuss all of the questions.
- Go over the questions as a class.

Pronunciation

THE NORTH AMERICAN "T"

- Read the *Pronunciation* box about the pronunciation of *t* used by North Americans and Australians. Check with the students to see that they have understood the information.

- Play the recording for the information in the box.
- Ask the students if they have noticed this difference between North American and British English. Give them additional examples and ask the students to pronounce them in North American and British English (e.g., *potato/potado, butter/budder*).
- Pronounce the examples again, this time not telling the students whether you're using North American or British pronunciation. Have the students guess which it is.

10 Listening for the North American *t* 

- ❑ Read the directions.
- ❑ Play the recording. Have the students repeat the sentences as a class.

11 Pronouncing the North American *t* 

- ❑ Read the directions for this activity and point out the pages for Student A and Student B.
- ❑ Put the students in pairs. Tell them to decide which student will be Student A and which student will be Student B.
- ❑ Tell the students to look only at their page. Have them read all of the information and ask questions about anything that they do not understand. Make sure that they see that there are five questions and five answers. They must decide which answer is the correct one for the question.
- ❑ Remind the students to pronounce the answer words with the American *t*.
- ❑ While the students are doing this activity, walk around the room, checking their pronunciation.

Best Practice

Interacting with Others

This type of activity is an example of collaborative learning to encourage fluency and confidence. In this discussion, based around the topic of sports, communication is more important than grammar. Students must concentrate on fluency and the use of expressions that they have learned in this and previous chapters to convince the other members of their group that their idea of the best sport is the correct one.

REPRODUCIBLE **EXPANSION ACTIVITY**

- Please see Black Line Master "What is the Best Sport?" on page BLM 19 of this Teacher's Edition.
- Photocopy and distribute one copy to each student.
- Go over the directions for the three parts so that the students understand the complete process of this activity. Emphasize that the pupose of Part 1 is just to help them start thinking about what is important in sports. Have them rank the qualities individually. Then have them compare their answers with a partner.
- After the students have individually finished Part 2 and are ready to talk about the best sport, have them turn back to pages 148–149 in Chapter 8 to review the expressions for giving an opinion, agreeing, and disagreeing. That language will be very useful in this activity.
- Put the students in groups of three or four. Tell them to take turns telling each other what sport they chose and why they chose it.
- Tell the students to finish their presentations before beginning the discussion. Make sure that they understand that they don't all have to agree at the end of the discussion.
- Let the students discuss the question for 10 or 15 minutes.
- When they have finished, have each group tell you how many students chose each sport. Write their choices on the board. Is there a clear winner? If so, what were the reasons for it being the best sport?

Before You Listen

1 Prelistening Questions 

- ❑ Read the directions to the students.
- ❑ Put the students into pairs and have them discuss the questions.
- ❑ Go over their answers as a class. Write new vocabulary on the board (e.g., *Greco-Roman*) as it comes up in the discussion.
- ❑ If there is time, extend the discussion with new questions. For example, you can ask the students if colleges should spend equal amounts of money on men and women or if there are sports that women should not be allowed to play.

2 Previewing Vocabulary 

- ❑ Play the recording and ask students to listen to the underlined words.
- ❑ Read the directions to the students.
- ❑ Make sure that they understand that they are to write the letter of the correct definition in the blank to the left of the sentence. They have completed this activity type in previous chapters, so they should understand what they are to do quickly.
- ❑ Give the students time to complete the activity.
- ❑ Put the students in pairs. Tell them to compare their answers.
- ❑ Go over the questions together.

ANSWER KEY

1.d 2.f 3.a 4.b 5.c 6.g 7.e

Listen

3 Taking Notes on Main Ideas 

- ❑ Have students look at the photo for this activity. Ask the students to describe what is happening. Read the photo caption to the students. Give them time to ask for clarification.
- ❑ Read the directions for this activity to the students.
- ❑ Point out the lines below the directions.
- ❑ Tell the students that they are going to listen to a long listening passage and take notes. Remind them to focus on writing down only the main ideas of the listening passage.
- ❑ Play the recording. Give the students some time to complete their notes.
- ❑ Put the students into pairs and tell them to compare their notes.
- ❑ Briefly have the students summarize the main ideas of the conversation just to make sure that all of the students understand the general situation.

AUDIOSCRIPT

Hi, my name is Terri Whitmore. I'm 21 years old, I major in psychology, I have a boyfriend, and I love movies and shopping and cats. Yeah, most people think I'm a typical college student. That's until they find out that I'm a champion wrestler. Then of course, they're surprised because in most parts of the United States and the world, the idea of women's wrestling is still new. What people don't know is that women's wrestling is growing very quickly, especially since the 2004 Olympics. That's when women's wrestling was finally included as an Olympic sport. Imagine: the sport of wrestling is one of the oldest in history, but women wrestlers couldn't compete until recently.

Anyway, people always ask me, "Why did you choose wrestling?" Well, to me it was natural. I became interested when I was eight because my brothers were on wrestling teams. They let me participate, and I did very well. I mean I won a lot of matches and beat most of the guys. But when I turned 12, they didn't want me on the team anymore just because I was a girl. When I went to college, I started to wrestle again, this time on girls' teams.

Another thing people ask is about the rules. Are they the same as for men? Sure. Basically, the main goal in wrestling is to pin your opponent. That means you try to hold their shoulders to the floor for about one-half second. If you do that, you win right away. But there are other ways to win a match, too. You can score points; I mean points for different moves and holds. The wrestler with the most points is the winner. But you need at least three more points than the other guy. If not, then you go into overtime.

Oh, and then there are all kinds of rules about the parts of the body. You know, the parts that are OK to touch or hold, and things like that. And also, it's important to know that we compete against wrestlers in the same weight group.

Anyway, I'm really glad I chose wrestling. I like competing as an individual. In team sports, you can always blame someone else for not scoring a goal or not catching a ball. But my success or my failure depends only on me, not on a teammate. Sure, it's a lot of pressure, but it's made me stronger and more confident.

Best Practice

Organizing Information

This type of activity uses a graphic organizer to categorize information. Taking lecture notes encourages students to process and organize information while they are listening and also provides a record for them to refer to when they are studying later. This type of graphic organizer, an outline, emphasizes a traditional system for taking academic lecture notes involving the use of Roman numerals and letters. Learning this system will give the student a valuable academic tool as well as insight into academic culture. Other types of graphic organizers are used throughout this book

Strategy

Hints for Taking Notes

Go over the information on *Hints for Taking Notes*. Ask the students to paraphrase the information in the note so that you can see whether or not they really understood it.

4 Reviewing Notes

- ❑ Read the directions to the students. Point out the outline framework below the directions. Make sure that the students understand that they will be writing information from their notes in the blanks.
- ❑ Give the students time to fill in the blanks.

ANSWER KEY

Answers will vary. Possible answers:

I. Introduction

A. Info about Terry: 21 years old, majors in psychology, has a boyfriend, loves movies, shopping, and cats, is a champion wrestler

B. Info about wrestling: women's wrestling is new, but growing very quickly, in 2004 Olympics, women's wrestling was included as an Olympic sport, wrestling is one of the world's oldest sports

II. Why chose wrestling: interested at eight years old, brothers were wrestlers, let her wrestle, she did well, beating most of the boys, at 12, boys didn't want her on the team, in college joined women's teams

III. Rules: same for girls and boys, goal is to pin your opponent (hold his/her shoulders to the floor for 1/2 second), can also score points for moves and holds, wrestler with most points wins, but must have at least 3 more points than opponent or match goes to overtime, many rules about parts of body, some parts are OK. to touch or hold, always compete against wrestlers in the same weight category

IV. Why likes it: likes competing as individual, in team sports you can blame others for mistakes, her success depends only on her, there is a lot of pressure, but it has made her stronger and more confident

5 Listening for Specific Information 

- ❑ Play the recording one more time.
- ❑ Tell the students to look at their outline while listening to check for mistakes and to fill in missing information.

After You Listen

6 Summarizing Ideas 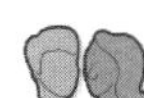

- ❑ Put the students in pairs and have them compare their notes.
- ❑ Tell the students to summarize the information in parts II, III, and IV of their outlines.
- ❑ While the students are summarizing the information, walk around the room, helping them with grammar and vocabulary.
- ❑ Write the basic outline for the interview from Activity 4 on the board. Tell the students to give you the information to fill in the outline. This will act as an answer check.
- ❑ Tell the students to decide which of them is Terri and which is an interviewer.
- ❑ Tell the students to create an imaginary interview with Terri. Tell the students to do the role-play.
- ❑ When the students have finished, ask for volunteer pairs to do their interview in front of the class.

7 Reviewing Vocabulary 

- ❑ Read the directions to the students.
- ❑ Tell them to read all of the questions and to ask for clarification of anything that they don't understand.
- ❑ Put the students in pairs. Have them discuss all of the questions, using underlined vocabulary in their answers.
- ❑ Go over the questions as a class.

Using Language Functions

TALKING ABOUT SPORTS

- Go over the *Talking About Sports* box with the students.
- Ask the students to give you some examples of word forms that aren't in the box (e.g., *skate, skating, skater; hike, hiking, hiker; dive, diving, diver*).

8 Talking About Sports 

- ❑ Read the directions to the students.
- ❑ Point out the four photos and read the example to the students.
- ❑ Put the students in pairs. Have them complete the exercise.
- ❑ Check the answers as a class.

ANSWER KEY

1. playing hockey
2. diving *or* going diving
3. snowboarding
4. doing yoga

Getting Meaning From Context

1 Prelistening Questions 

- Read the directions and the questions to the students. Point out the five sets of three photos in the Focus on Testing section. Give the students time to ask for clarification.
- Put the students in pairs. Tell them to discuss the questions.
- Go over the answers as a class. There will be a good deal of variation in the answers.

Best Practice

Scaffolding Instruction

This is an example of an activity that raises metacognitive awareness of learning strategies. In real life, we use surrounding context clues to work out the meanings of unfamiliar words. This activity asks students to use the words that they know in each passage to work out the meanings of new words. Having students write the clues guides them through the steps of developing this skill.

Focus on Testing

Using Context Clues 

- Point out to the students that this is a *Focus on Testing* activity. The skill taught in this activity will help students with standardized tests, such as the Internet-based TOEFL®.
- Read the directions to the students. Tell them that they will be practicing an important learning strategy for listening.
- Go over the chart with the students. Since they have done this kind of activity in previous chapters, they will understand it quickly.
- Play each conversation, stopping after each description of a sport. Give the students time to circle the correct answer and write down several clues before moving on.
- Put the students in pairs and have them compare their charts.
- Go over the answers and clues as a class.

ANSWER KEY

Answers	Clues
1. a—swimming	outside in summer, inside in winter, no special equipment—just bathing suit, can do by yourself, can't do without water
2. b—boxing	looks like fighting, gloves, special protection for teeth and sometimes for their heads, usually only men do this sport, only sport women don't do at Olympics
3. c—snowboarding	not very old, started as fun activity different from skiing, mix between surfing and skiing, called extreme sport
4. a—gymnastics	old sport, one of most popular Olympic events, beautiful to watch, need flexibility, balance, strength, perform exercises on the floor or on special equipment
5. c—baseball	team of 9 or 10 players, throw the ball, hit it with a stick, gloves, catch the ball, popular in North America and Japan

AUDIOSCRIPT

1. You can do this sport all year: outside in the summer and inside in the winter. You don't need any special equipment, just a bathing suit. You can do it by yourself, but you can't do it without water.
2. This sport looks like two people are fighting. They wear gloves and special protection for their teeth and sometimes for their heads. Usually only men do this sport. But in the past few years, woman have been participating in this sport, too.
3. This sport is not very old. It started as just a fun activity for young people who wanted to try something different from skiing. It's kind of a mix between surfing and skiing. Sometimes it's called an extreme sport, but in 1998 it became part of the Winter Olympics. Some people think this sport will be more popular than skiing in the future.
4. This sport is thousands of years old. Today it's one of the most popular Olympic events because it's very beautiful to watch. Men and women need to have great flexibility, balance, and strength as they perform exercises on the floor or on special equipment.
5. This sport is a game between two teams of nine or ten players. One player throws the ball to another, who tries to hit it with a stick as far as possible. Other players use gloves to catch the ball. This sport is especially popular in North America and Japan.

Talk It Over

Best Practice

Cultivating Critical Thinking

This is an example of a competitive team activity that requires students to process the language that they have learned and apply it to a new situation. This involves reinterpretation, synthesis, and application of concepts. The process of manipulating language and concepts in this way will create deeper processing of new material which will allow students to evaluate whether they have understood the new material and help them remember it better.

2 Twenty Questions

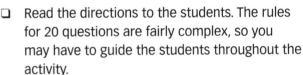

- ❑ Read the directions to the students. The rules for 20 questions are fairly complex, so you may have to guide the students throughout the activity.
- ❑ Make sure that the students know they have to ask *yes/no* questions. Also make sure they understand that they must choose a sport or famous athlete that is truly famous internationally.
- ❑ Have two students read the short sample dialogue.
- ❑ Divide the students into two teams.
- ❑ You can use a coin toss or other method to decide which team chooses someone or something to guess. The team chooses one person to represent the team and to think of a sport or famous athlete.
- ❑ The other team can ask 20 *yes/no* questions. If after 20 questions, the guessing team can't get the answer, the other team gets a point.
- ❑ When a team wins a point, it comes up with the sport or athlete for the next round.
- ❑ You will have to decide how much class time you have for this activity. At the end of the time, the team with the most points wins.

1 Prelistening Questions 

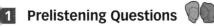

- ❑ Read the directions to the students.
- ❑ Give the students time to read the questions and ask for clarification of anything that they don't understand.
- ❑ Put the students into pairs. Tell them to discuss the questions.
- ❑ Go over their answers as a class.

2 Previewing Vocabulary 

- ❑ Read the directions to the students. Play the recording and ask students to listen to the words and expressions.
- ❑ Point out the two pictures at the bottom of the activity.
- ❑ Put the students in pairs. Tell the pairs to use the vocabulary words to describe the photos. Emphasize to the students that they should try to use as many of the words as possible.
- ❑ Go over the photos as a class. Help the students use all of the new vocabulary to describe the photos.

Best Practice

Making Use of Academic Content

The following is an example of an activity that exposes students to language that they will actually face in an academic setting. The radio broadcast of college sports scores will prepare students for informal discussions with their fellow students about their schools' teams.

3 Sports News on the Radio 

- ❑ Go over the directions for the activity. Point out the photo for the activity.
- ❑ Point out the chart. Show the students the first row of the chart that is filled out.
- ❑ Show the students some places where there are either blanks to be filled or parts of the table that are completely blank.
- ❑ Make sure that the students understand that they are to fill in the missing information.
- ❑ Play the recording.
- ❑ After the recording is finished, give the students another minute or two to complete the chart.
- ❑ Put the students in pairs so that they can check their answers. If necessary, play the recording again.
- ❑ Check the answers as a class.

ANSWER KEY

Sport	Players or Teams	Results / Scores
Men's basketball	*Faber vs. State College*	*Faber lost: 76-72*
Women's basketball	*Faber vs. Hamilton College*	Faber won: 61-43
Men's volleyball	Faber vs. Washington Junior College	*Won all 3 games:* *1: 21-15* *2: 21-18* *3: 21-12*
Tennis tournament	*Mary Johnson* vs. Tina Lewis	Won 6-3, 6-2
Tennis	Susan Johnson vs. *Lisa Kim*	Won 6-4, 4-6, 7-5
Women's soccer	Faber College vs. College Club Rio	Tie 3-3

AUDIOSCRIPT

Announcer Bill:	And now, to Yao Lam and Kristin Fox for Faber College Weekend Sports!
Kristin:	Thanks, Bill. Well it was a busy weekend in sports, wasn't it Yao?
Yao:	Sure was, Kristin. Well, Faber college men's basketball lost a big game to State College, 76–72.
Kristin:	Yeah, it was too bad—it was really close down to the last few seconds . . . On the other hand, our <u>women's</u> basketball team won their game easily. They beat Hamilton College 61 to 43.
Yao:	They get stronger every game. Now turning to volleyball, the women got a rest this weekend, but the men's team played down at Washington Junior College, and they were just <u>unbeatable</u>!
Kristin:	That's right—they won all three games: 21–15, 21–18 and 21–12. In the state college tennis tournament, we can be very proud of our own Johnson sisters.
Yao:	Yeah, the twins are playing really well. Mary Johnson won her match without any trouble: 6–3, 6–2. It took her just half an hour to finish her opponent, Tina Lewis.
Kristin:	Her sister Susan Johnson had to work a little harder, but also was a winner against her rival Lisa Kim. The scores for the sets were 6–4, 4–6, 7–5. It was the longest match of the day.
Yao:	And finally, our women's soccer team is playing matches on a tour down in Brazil.
Kristin:	I wish I was down there reporting on that!
Yao:	Me too. I understand they just finished their first game, and they almost beat the girls from College Club Rio.
Kristin:	Really, what was the score?
Yao:	Actually, it was a 3–3 tie, so no losers. Well, that's it, for Weekend Sports.
Kristin and Yao:	Go Faber!!

Using Language Functions

GIVING AND UNDERSTANDING INSTRUCTIONS

- Point out the photos for this activity. Ask the students to guess what the people are doing.
- Read the headings for each of the three groups of expressions. Go over the new expressions with the students. Give the students time to ask for clarification of anything that they don't understand.
- Make sure that the students understand the differences among the three groups of expressions.

4 Sports Instructions 

- ❑ Read the general directions to the students. Make sure that they understand that they will be using the expressions for giving and receiving instructions in these games.

Game 1

- ❑ Read the directions for Game 1. Give the students time to ask for clarification. Ask one student to read the example.
- ❑ Have one or two students paraphrase the instructions back to you so that you can check their comprehension. This will also give the students another chance to practice some of the target language, e.g., *First, we have to write instructions for playing a sport.*
- ❑ Put the students into groups of three or four.
- ❑ Tell each group to write instructions for playing a sport. Each sentence must be on a separate line.
- ❑ When the students are finished, have them cut the instructions into strips that have one sentence on each strip.
- ❑ Tell the students to give the scrambled strips to another group.
- ❑ Give the groups some time to put the instructions back together. Have the groups check the answers with the groups that wrote the instructions.

Game 2

- ❑ Read the directions and the example to the students.
- ❑ Put the students in small groups.
- ❑ Tell each group to write instructions for playing a sport, as in Game 1. Make sure that the students know that they must not include the name of the sport in their instructions. Also, encourage them to try to be as general as possible, particularly in the first few sentences so they don't give the sport away too quickly.
- ❑ Select one group to read their instructions to the other groups. Tell them to read the instructions slowly.
- ❑ Tell the other groups to listen carefully and guess the name of the sport. When a group guesses correctly, it receives one point. After all of the groups have finished their instructions, the group with the highest number of points is the winner.

5 Teaching or Coaching Your Classmates: Homework Project

- ❑ Read all of the instructions to the students.
- ❑ Make sure that they understand that they should plan their presentation at home and that they can bring props to class to help illustrate their presentation.
- ❑ Remind the students to use the language for giving instructions that they have learned.
- ❑ After the students have planned their presentations at home, give them time to present their instructions in front of the class.
- ❑ Remind the other students to ask questions when the instructions are not clear.

EXPANSION ACTIVITY

- Please see Black Line Master "The Greatest Athlete" on page BLM 20 of this Teacher's Edition.
- Photocopy and distribute one copy to each student.
- Read the directions to the students. Explain the overall structure of the activity.
- Read Part 1. Explain each of the characteristics in the table (e.g., strength).
- Make sure that the students understand the rating system for the chart. Have them complete the chart.
- Have the students do Part 2 individually.
- For Part 3, put the students in small groups. Have them give and defend their choice for greatest athlete.
- Tell the groups to come up with one choice for greatest athlete. If they absolutely cannot agree on one person, tell them that they will have to explain to the class why they could not all agree.
- When the groups have finished, have each group give and explain its choice.
- Analyze the groups' choices as a class. What characteristics were the most important to the students? Did different groups choose the same person?

Self-Assessment Log

- ❑ The purpose of the log is to help the students reflect on their learning.
- ❑ Read the directions aloud and have students check vocabulary that they learned in the chapter and are prepared to use.
- ❑ Have students check the strategies they understand.
- ❑ Put students in small groups. Ask students to find the information or an activity related to each strategy in the chapter.
- ❑ Tell students to find definitions in the chapter for any words they did not check, or they can look in their dictionaries.

Name ______________________ Date ______________

Chapter 1 Part 1: Who Will You Be in 20 Years?

Part 1: Answer the questions below. Write your answers on the lines.

Who will you be in 20 years? Will you have a job? What will you do? Where will you live?

____

____

Part 2: Find a partner. Introduce yourself. Then interview your partner. Ask many questions.

Example: A: Hi, I'm Jorge.
B. Nice to meet you. I'm Lee.
A: What do you do, Lee?
B: I'm a musician. I work in Seoul. What do you do?
A: I'm the president of Mexico. I live in Mexico City.

Part 3: Walk around the room with your partner. Introduce your partner to other pairs. Take turns doing the introductions.

Example: Jorge: Hi, I'm Jorge and this is Lee. Lee is a famous musician.
Kaori: Nice to meet you. I'm Kaori and this is my partner Sasha. Sasha is a doctor in Russia.
Lee: Jorge is president of Mexico. He lives in Mexico City.
Sasha: No kidding! That's cool!

Part 4: Fill out the chart below with information from your introductions.

Name	Personal Information
Jorge	*president of Mexico, lives in Mexico City*

BLM 2

Name ______________________ Date ______________

Chapter 1 Part 2: Campus Tour

Directions: This is a homework assignment. Sometime after this class, walk around your campus. You are going to create a campus tour or a tour of the area around your school. Make a list of the places that a new student needs to know about. For each place, list important details. Put your information in the chart below.

Place	Detailed Information
library	*open every day from 9 a.m.-11 p.m.; use student ID to check out books*

In class, you will be in a group. Discuss your lists together. Then create a new list for the group on a new piece of paper. Include a lot of details about the places that you chose. Give the new list to your teacher.

BLM 3

Name ______________________________ Date ____________________

Chapter 2 Part 1: Outdoor Activities

Directions: With your group, fill in the two boxes below with words for outdoor activities.

Outdoor activities that you can do in the summer
You can go swimming.

Outdoor activities that you can do in the winter
You can snowboard.

Now answer the two questions below:

What is your favorite outdoor activity in the summer? ______________________________

What is your favorite outdoor activity in the winter? ______________________________

Name ______________________ Date ______________

Chapter 2 Part 4: Class Picnic—It's a Potluck!

Directions: Your class is going on a picnic! With your group, plan the details—activities, location, date, time, and food. You may have to do some research on outdoor recreation areas near your city. Begin by answering the questions below.

1. What do you want to do during your picnic? Circle all items that apply.

have a barbecue	play tennis	relax	swim
play card games	lie on a beach	chat with friends	hike
play volleyball	ride horses	take a nap	
ride bicycles	play games	eat a lot of good food	

Other: ______________________

2. Where will the picnic be? Suggest several locations.

____

____

____

3. When should the class have the picnic?

____

4. What kind of food do you want to eat at the picnic?

____

____

____

5. Invite the class to your picnic. Give them the details. They will vote on the best picnic plan.

Name ______________________ Date ______________

Chapter 3 Part 2: The Menu at Our School Cafeteria

Directions: Last week, the staff of your school asked the students to help it plan cafeteria meals. They want to know what food the students would like to eat. You are going to create sample meals for the cafeteria. These meals must be nutritious. They must include food that the students like to eat. Your school wants five complete meals. Each meal must include a main dish, a soup or a salad, a dessert, and a selection of drinks. Look at the chart below. With your group, fill in the two columns.

Day	Meal	Why is this a good meal?
Monday		
Tuesday		
Wednesday		
Thursday		
Friday		

BLM 6

Name ______________________________ Date ________________

Chapter 3 Part 3: Restaurant Review

Directions: You will be writing a review of a restaurant near your school. You are writing this review for the other students in your class. Begin by answering the following questions. Just make notes for answers, not complete sentences.

1. What is the name of the restaurant? ________________
2. How expensive was the restaurant? ________________
3. Who are typical customers at this restaurant (e.g., single adults)? ________________
4. What was the atmosphere in the restaurant (e.g., noisy, bright)? ________________
5. What kind of food does the restaurant serve? ________________
6. What dishes did you eat there? ________________
7. How was the food (e.g., delicious, so-so, bland)? ________________
8. How was the service? ________________
9. What did it look like inside? Was it attractively decorated? ________________
10. Write your review on the lines below:

____

____

____

____

____

____

____

____

____

 BLM 7

Name ______________________ Date ______________

Chapter 4 Part 1: Our Ideal Neighborhood

Directions: You are going to work in a group to describe an "ideal" neighborhood. This is a neighborhood that you would like to live in. You will present this ideal neighborhood to your class.

Part 1: Before you meet with your group, write down some words and phrases (e.g., *busy, has cheap restaurants*) to describe an ideal neighborhood. Use the box below for your words and phrases.

Part 2: With your group, discuss your words and phrases from Part 1. Make a group list of characteristics for your ideal neighborhood. Write a description in the box below.

Part 3: As a group, draw a map of your ideal neighborhood on a large piece of paper. Each member of the group should mark on the map where he or she would live. Draw in any shops, government buildings, and recreation areas. You will present this neighborhood map to your class, so mark the buildings clearly.

Part 4: Prepare your presentation to the class. In your presentation, you must show the locations of important buildings. You must also give the class an idea of your general principles (e.g., safety) for the neighborhood. Be sure to tell the class *why* the buildings are in particular locations. Each member of the groups must speak part of the time. Decide who will present what information.

BLM 8

Name ______________________ Date ______________

Chapter 4 Part 2: My Hometown and Where I Live Now

Directions: Think about your hometown. How is it different from where you are living now? How is it similar?

Part 1: Write five sentences comparing the two places. Include at least two similarities and two differences.

Example: *My hometown, Odawara, is smaller than Tokyo, where I live now.*

1. ______________________
2. ______________________
3. ______________________
4. ______________________
5. ______________________

Part 2: Tell a partner about the differences between your hometown and where you live now. When your partner gives you his or her information, write the information in the appropriate area of the Venn diagram.

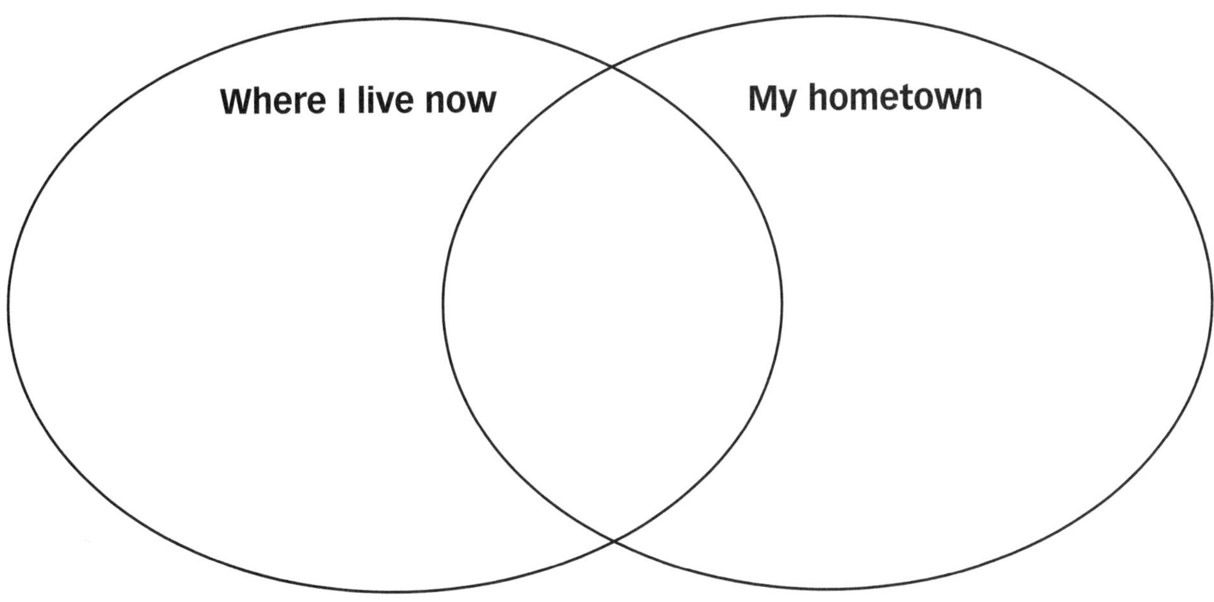

Part 3: Tell your class about your partner's hometown and how it is different from where he or she is living now.

Name ______________________ Date ______________

Chapter 5 Part 1: My Home

Directions: Think about your home now. You will be describing it to a partner.

Part 1: Draw your home in the box below. Draw all of the rooms with the furniture.

Part 2: You and a partner will describe your homes to each other. Describe the number of rooms, the location of the rooms and other details. Use the location language from Chapter 4. Listen carefully and draw your partner's home in the box below.

Example: *The front door leads to the living room. The kitchen is to the right of the living room. The bedroom is behind the living room.*

BLM 10

Name ______________________________ Date ____________________

Chapter 5 Part 2: A Perfect House

Directions: With other students, you are going to design a perfect house. You will present your design to the class at the end of this activity.

Part 1: With your group, read and discuss the questions below.

1. How many rooms are there in your house? Describe the rooms.
2. What furniture is in the house?
3. What is outside the house (e.g., a garden, a lawn)?
4. What facilities does the house have (e.g., a tennis court, a gym)?
5. Describe the neighborhood that the house is in.
6. What makes this a perfect house?

Part 2: Describe your house in detail on the lines below.

____

____

____

____

____

____

____

____

____

Name ______________________________ Date ______________

Chapter 6 Part 1: My Culture

Situation: A friend of yours from a different country is going to your native city or town to work for one year. Your friend knows nothing about your city.

Part 1: You must tell your friend about your city so that he or she will be able to adjust to a new life. Before you meet your friend, write down answers to the questions below.

1. How many different cultures are there in your city?
2. Is there a dominant or majority culture? List all of the cultures in your city.
3. List important customs for all of your city's cultures below. What will your friend need to know about customs for the food, daily living, clothes, music, greetings, and religion?

   ____

   ____

   ____

   ____

4. What taboos in your city should your friend know about? Write several "dos" and "don'ts" for things that your friend should and shouldn't do.

   ____

   ____

   ____

   ____

Part 2: Talk about your city and its cultures with a partner. Tell your partner everything that he or she needs to know before going to your city. Take notes below. You will describe your partner's culture to the class.

____

____

____

____

BLM 12

Name ______________________ Date ______________

Chapter 6 Part 2: A New Coming-of-Age Ceremony

Directions: You have discussed four coming-of-age ceremonies in Part 2 of this chapter. Now, your group is going to design a new coming-of-age ceremony.

Part 1: Begin by answering the questions below.

1. At what age will children become adults? ______________________

2. What rights will adults have that children don't have?

____

____

____

____

3. What will children have to do to become adults? What kind of task or trial will there be? Describe it.

____

____

____

____

4. What kind of ceremony will there be after the task or trial? Describe it in detail below.

____

____

____

____

Part 2: Your group will present your new coming-of-age ceremony to the class. Everyone in your group must present part of your information.

Name	Portion to present

Name ______________________ Date ______________

Chapter 7 Part 1: A Stress-Reduction Plan

Situation: In an earlier exercise in the book, you completed a questionnaire about your stress. You received a stress score. Now you are going to use that information to help a classmate create a stress-reduction plan for you.

Part 1: Share your stress score with a partner. Then discuss your answers to the questions below. Ask follow-up questions to get additional information. Listen carefully and take notes on your partner's answers. You'll need them for Part 2.

1. How many hours of exercise did you get in the last week?
2. How many hours did you work in the last week? Include class work, homework, and work that you did for a job.
3. What was the average number of hours of sleep that you got in the last week?
4. List the top three things that you worry about.
5. Do you have people you can really talk to about very personal issues in your life? Who are they?
6. How many hours did you spend last week doing something fun or relaxing?

Part 2: Use the information about your partner to make at least five suggestions for him or her to reduce stress. Write your suggestions on the lines below. Use expressions for giving advice, such as *You ought to . . .*, *You should . . .*, and *You need to . . . .*

1. ______________________________
2. ______________________________
3. ______________________________
4. ______________________________
5. ______________________________

Part 3: Present your suggestions for reducing stress to your partner. Does he or she agree with your suggestions?

Name ______________________________ Date ____________________

Chapter 7 Part 3: Improving Health in Our City

Situation: The mayor of your city has asked your group to come up with recommendations for improving the health of the citizens. The city has a budget of $1,000,000 for the next year. You will advise the city on how to spend the money.

Part 1: Before you begin discussing how to spend the money, discuss the following questions with your group.

1. How much air pollution is there in your city?
2. Are there enough parks in your city?
3. Does your city have enough public transportation?
4. Are many exercise or sports facilities available to the public?
5. Do many people in your city smoke cigarettes? Is smoking restricted in some places?
6. Does everyone in your city have health insurance?
7. Is there a lot of noise in your city?
8. Does your city have a problem with drug abuse (including alcohol)?

Part 2: With your group, decide how to spend the $1,000,000 in your city. Below are listed a few possibilities. You may also add your own ideas to the list. When you have decided how to spend the money, fill in the pie chart below with the percentages (%) for each item.

reducing pollution   opening a health clinic   health education

building a new park   making a new sports field   buying health insurance for the poor

Name ______________________ Date ______________

Chapter 8 Part 1: Guidelines for Children's Television Viewing

Situation: The mayor of your city has asked your group to create guidelines for children (under 17 years of age) and television. These guidelines are for parents of children at various ages.

Part 1: Begin by answering the following questions.

1. How will you divide the children into groups by age? How many age groups will you have?

   ____

2. How many different ratings will you have for TV programs? ______________

3. What factors (e.g., profanity) will you consider in your ratings? ______________

4. Should your ratings be mandatory or voluntary? ______________

Part 2: Write down notes about your new ratings system below. You will use these notes to present your ratings system to your class. During the presentation, each member of the group must talk part of the time.

____

____

____

____

____

____

____

____

____

____

____

____

Name ______________________ Date ______________

Chapter 8 Part 2: An Amazing News Story

Part 1: You and your group must create a news story. This story should not be true. Use your imagination to come up with a story that is amazing! Before you begin, answer the questions and write down notes on the lines below. These notes will help you plan your presentation in Part 2.

1. What happened? ______________________

2. Where did your story happen? ______________________

3. Who was involved? ______________________

4. When did your story happen? ______________________

5. Why did this happen? ______________________

Part 2: You will present your story to the class. One of you will be a reporter who interviews witnesses. As a group, you all have to decide what questions the reporter will ask and write the witnesses' answers. The reporter should write questions on the lines below. The witnesses should write their answers to the questions on their pages.

____

____

____

____

____

____

BLM 17

Name ______________________ Date ______________

Chapter 9 Part 2: My Perfect Night Out

Situation: You will be going out next Saturday night. It can be a romantic date or you can go out with two or three of your friends. You have unlimited money, but only six hours, from 6:00 P.M. to midnight. You must plan the night out alone. Then you will present it to a partner. Finally, you will present your partner's perfect night out to the class.

Part 1: Answer the questions below. Give as many details for each question as you can.

1. What would you like to do on your perfect night out? ______________________

____

2. Where would you like to go? ______________________

____

3. Who will go with you? ______________________

____

4. How will you travel on your night out? ______________________

____

Part 2: Describe your perfect night out to a partner. When you are finished, listen to your partner's perfect night out. Take notes about your partner's night out on the lines below. You can use these notes when you present your partner's night out to the class.

____

____

____

____

____

____

____

____

____

BLM 18

Name ______________________________ Date ____________________

Chapter 9 Part 4: Student Socializing Guide

Situation: You and a group of classmates are going to write and present to the class a short guide to social activities for new students at your school. The guide will be a list of advice and information.

Part 1: Answer the following questions by yourself. You will share your ideas with your group in Part 2.

1. What are good ways for new students to meet people at your school? ____________________

____

2. Where are good places to go to meet people? ____________________

____

3. Where do students at your school go out? What are the best places? What are the worst places?

____

____

4. What other information or advice can you give new students about socializing? ____________________

____

Part 2: With your group, take the information and advice that you all wrote in Part 1 and write at least eight statements that will help new students understand social activities at your school.

1. ____

2. ____

3. ____

4. ____

5. ____

6. ____

7. ____

8. ____

 BLM 19

Name ______________________ Date ______________

Chapter 10 Part 1: What is the Best Sport?

Part 1: Look at the qualities of sports below. Rank them from 1 to 7 in order of their importance to you. Number 1 represents the most important and 7 is the least important. Compare your answers with a partner.

______ builds your strength

______ makes you flexible

______ is a team sport

______ doesn't require much equipment

______ builds your lungs and heart

______ improves your speed

______ builds confidence

Part 2: Now decide what sport is the best sport. Write the name of the sport on the line below. Give three reasons why you think that it's the best sport.

The Best Sport: ______________________

Reason #1: ______________________

Reason #2: ______________________

Reason #3: ______________________

Part 3: You will now meet in a small group. Tell the group which sport you chose as the best sport. Tell the group why you chose that sport. Write down the sports that your group members chose.

BLM 20

Name ______________________________ Date ______________

Chapter 10 Part 4: The Greatest Athlete

Directions: You are going to choose one athlete as the greatest athlete who ever lived. You can choose an active player, a retired player, or someone from the past.

Part 1: To begin, look at the list of characteristics for greatness. Rate each characteristic by circling a number from 1 (not important) to 5 (very important).

Strength	1	2	3	4	5
Skill	1	2	3	4	5
Influence as a Role Model for Young People	1	2	3	4	5
Personal Character (e.g., honesty)	1	2	3	4	5
Intelligence	1	2	3	4	5

Part 2: Decide on your choice for the greatest athlete in history. Give reasons for your opinion.

Who is the greatest athlete in history? ______________________________

Reasons: ______________________________

____

____

____

____

____

Part 3: Present your choice to your group. Explain why this is your choice. Write your group members' choices below.

Name ____________________ Date ____________ Score __________

Chapter 1 Test

Section I Listening to a Conversation Choose the best answer to each question. **(4 points each)**

1. Which people don't already know each other?
- (A) Kareem and Mary
- (B) Antonio and Kareem
- (C) Mary and Antonio

2. Which of the following is true about Kareem?
- (A) He is a new student in the engineering program.
- (B) He works in the international student office.
- (C) He is from Brazil.

3. What is Mary studying?
- (A) library science
- (B) engineering
- (C) English

4. What is Kareem going to do now?
- (A) He is going to take a test.
- (B) He is going out to eat with Mary.
- (C) He's going to study English.

5. Where is Mary from?
- (A) Oman
- (B) Brazil
- (C) Boston

Section II Listening to a Lecture Listen to the lecture. Choose the best answer to each question. Listen to the lecture again. **(4 points each)**

1. What was the purpose of this lecture?
- (A) to inform students about becoming professional athletes
- (B) to introduce the university sports coordinator
- (C) to introduce the university's sports programs and facilities

2. The university has a new ____________.
- (A) fitness center
- (B) swimming pool
- (C) yoga class

3. In an intramural sports program, ____________.
- (A) the students play against students from a different university
- (B) the students play against students from the same university
- (C) the students only do non-team activities like yoga

4. The university sports program focuses on ____________.
- (A) making good grades in physical education classes
- (B) helping people get good at sports to win more games
- (C) helping people get in good health for their whole life

5. The university's sports facilities are ___________.
   (A) mostly outdoors in the center of the campus
   (B) in many different places on the campus
   (C) all in one corner of the campus

Section III New Words Look at the list of words below. Use the words to fill in the blanks in the sentences. **(4 points each)**

advisor	call me	came over	facilities	move into
orientation	placement test	schedule	stop by	take

John: Hi, Martina! How are you doing?

Martina: Fine, thanks! It's my first day here, but I'm doing OK. I really want to start my English classes.

John: Martina, this is Joseph Park.

Joe: Please, ___________(1) Joe. I don't like the name Joseph.

Martina: Nice to meet you, Joe! John said that you were from Korea.

Joe: Yes, my family ___________(2) to the U.S. about four years ago.

John: Joe and I just rented an apartment near the university. We're going to ___________(3) it tomorrow.

Joe: It's a nice place. Please ___________(4) for a visit.

Martina: I'd love to come see you guys.

John: Martina, are you already in English classes?

Martina: No. I just had my ___________(5) this morning. It was two hours long, but they gave us a lot of important information for foreign students. Then we took a tour of the campus.

John: This university has excellent ___________(6). There's a post office, a museum, tennis courts, and a new swimming pool.

Joe: Martina, your English is excellent! Are you going to be an advanced student in the English program?

Martina: I don't know yet. I'm a new student, so I have to take the ______(7)______. That will tell me my English level.

Joe: I'm sure that you'll be advanced.

Martina: After I get the results, I'll get my ______(8)______. Then I'll know when and where my classes are. I'm really excited! Joe, what do you want to study?

Joe: I'm actually going to see my ______(9)______ right now. She will suggest good classes for me.

John: I want to ______(10)______ two mathematics classes this semester.

Martina: That sounds difficult!

Section IV Using Language Use the five expressions below to fill in the blanks in the sentences. **(4 points each)**

I'd like you to	nice to meet you	this is
same here	what's your name again	

1. Ibrahim, ______________ meet Arnold. He's from Austria.
2. Frank: It's a pleasure to meet you.

   Margarita: ______________.
3. Choi: Hi! My name is Choi.

   Penny: ______________, Choi.
4. Excuse me, ______________?
5. Sheila, ______________ my friend Jin Lei.

TOTAL ____/100 pts.

Name ______________________ Date ______________ Score ______________

Chapter 2 Test

Section I Listening to a Conversation Choose the best answer to each question. **(4 points each)**

1. What is the main topic of this conversation between Cho and Freddy?
(A) their families
(B) their countries
(C) their vacations

2. What season is it in the conversation?
(A) winter
(B) summer
(C) spring

3. Can Cho snowboard?
(A) Yes, but not very well.
(B) Yes, she is really good at it.
(C) No, she can't.

4. Why doesn't Cho go with Freddy?
(A) She doesn't have enough money.
(B) She doesn't like the snow.
(C) Her brother is going to visit her.

5. Freddy says that snowboarding is like ____________.
(A) scuba diving
(B) surfing
(C) skiing

Section II Listening to a Lecture Listen to the lecture. Choose the best answer to each question. Listen to the lecture again. **(4 points each)**

1. What is the best title for this presentation?
(A) American College Students Go to the Beach!
(B) Spring Break, an Important American Tradition
(C) Spring Break in Mexico

2. Which of the following places is now the most popular for college students during spring break?
(A) Fort Lauderdale, Florida
(B) Galveston, Texas
(C) Acapulco, Mexico

3. How did the people in Fort Lauderdale and Daytona Beach feel about the vacationing students?
(A) They got tired of them because of the big parties and the noise.
(B) They loved them because they were polite and were good for business.
(C) They wanted them to come in the fall, not the spring.

4. How many students go on spring break each year?
(A) thousands
(B) millions
(C) billions

5. Spring break is usually in ___________.
   (A) February
   (B) March
   (C) April

Section III New Words Look at the list of words below. Use the words to fill in the blanks in the sentences. **(4 points each)**

chance of	clear	cloudy	degrees	forecast
freezing	how come	sick of	weather	winter

1. The ___________________ is terrible today. It's rainy and cold.
2. I just saw the weather ___________________ on TV. It will probably rain tomorrow.
3. ___________________ you aren't outside? It's beautiful today!
4. I'm ___________________ cold weather! Let's go to Florida.
5. In New York, it's very cold in the ___________________.
6. The sky is ___________________ today. There isn't even one cloud!
7. It's about 90 ___________________ right now. I hate that kind of heat!
8. In my hometown, it's rarely clear and sunny. It's usually ___________________.
9. I'm from Minnesota. In the winter, it's ___________________ cold.
10. On TV, a woman said that there is a good ___________________ showers tonight.

Section IV Using Language Complete the following sentences using your own ideas. **(4 points each)**

1. I can't ____
2. I'm not able ____
3. I wish I could ____
4. I'm good at ____
5. I don't know how ____

TOTAL ____ /100 pts.

Name ______________________ Date ______________ Score ____________

Chapter 3 Test

Section I Listening to a Conversation Listen to the conversation. Choose the best answer to each question. **(4 points each)**

1. Where are the two people?
- (A) in a cafeteria
- (B) in a restaurant
- (C) in a diner

2. The man ___________.
- (A) is a vegetarian
- (B) is unhappy with the waiter
- (C) orders lemon chicken

3. What does the woman order?
- (A) grilled salmon
- (B) a vegetarian dish
- (C) some wine

4. How many vegetarian dishes does the restaurant have?
- (A) one
- (B) two
- (C) three

5. What is the woman's main course?
- (A) lemon chicken
- (B) onion soup
- (C) buttered carrots

Section II Listening to a Lecture Listen to the lecture. Choose the best answer to each question. Listen to the lecture again. **(4 points each)**

1. Where is Jane Martin talking?
- (A) at the Corona Theater
- (B) on the television
- (C) on the radio

2. What is true about Burt's?
- (A) It is a new restaurant.
- (B) It has been open for a long time.
- (C) It is moving to a new place.

3. What is Jane's opinion of Burt's?
- (A) She likes Burt's a lot.
- (B) She likes Burt's a little bit.
- (C) She doesn't like Burt's.

4. What does Jane say about the food from Burt's?
   (A) All of the vegetables come from a food market.
   (B) Burt and Maria only serve meat from their ranch.
   (C) Burt and Maria use a lot of chemicals on their farm.

5. What will vegetarians think about the food at Burt's?
   (A) They will be disappointed at Burt's.
   (B) They have a lot of choices at Burt's.
   (C) They can only eat salads at Burt's.

Section III New Words Read the sentences on the left. Choose a word on the right to complete each sentence. Write the letter of the correct word in the blank. **(4 points each)**

Sentence	Word
1. This grocery store has wonderful ___________. Their lettuce and tomatoes are the best in town!	a. aisle
2. A ___________ is about the same as a liter.	b. take checks
3. The doctor told Mary to ___________ meat and cheese. She was eating too much fat.	c. calories
4. Juices are over there in ___________ six.	d. pound
5. At that store, you have to pay with cash or a credit card. They don't ___________.	e. cut down on
6. Fruits and vegetables are a good source of ___________.	f. minerals
7. If you are trying to lose weight, nutritionists say it is best not to ___________ meals. You just overeat later!	g. produce
8. I can't eat any of that cream pie. It has too many ___________.	h. skip
9. That supermarket is really crowded. I always have to wait ___________.	i. in line
10. I need to buy a ___________ of steak and some carrots for dinner tonight.	j. quart

Section IV Using Language Use the five expressions below to fill in the blanks in the dialogue. **(4 points each)**

May I please	I'll	Would you like
I'd	Are you ready to	

Waiter: ________________ order?
1

Caroline: Yes, ________________ like the lemon chicken.
2

Waiter: ________________ a soup or a salad with that?
3

Caroline: ________________ have the soup.
4

Waiter: Anything to drink?

Caroline: Yes. ________________ have a glass of wine?
5

TOTAL ____/100 pts.

Name ______________________ Date ______________ Score ____________

Chapter 4 Test

Section I Listening to a Conversation Listen to the conversation. Then choose the best answer to each question. **(4 points each)**

1. Where does Lin live now?
- (A) in a different city from Mark
- (B) in a different neighborhood from Mark
- (C) in the same neighborhood as Mark

2. What was Lin's old neighborhood like?
- (A) It was noisy.
- (B) It was boring.
- (C) It was quiet.

3. Who is Lee?
- (A) Lee is Mark's wife.
- (B) Lee is Lin's husband.
- (C) Lee is Lin's sister.

4. What does Lin think of her new neighborhood?
- (A) She likes it better than her old neighborhood.
- (B) She thinks that it's too quiet and boring.
- (C) She doesn't like living near the bus station.

5. What does Mark want to celebrate?
- (A) Lin's move to Mark's neighborhood
- (B) Lin's 30th birthday
- (C) Lin's wedding anniversary

Section II Listening to an Introduction Listen to the introduction. Choose the best answer to each question. Listen to the introduction again. **(4 points each)**

1. What is the best title for this introduction?
- (A) Come and Visit Centerville!
- (B) Centerville, a Good Place for Your Business!
- (C) Basic Facts About Centerville

2. How would you describe Centerville?
- (A) It's a village.
- (B) It's a small town.
- (C) It's a large city.

3. Which of the following is NOT in the introduction?
- (A) The education level in Centerville is very high.
- (B) Centerville has a busy downtown area.
- (C) Centerville is a safe and quiet place to live.

4. What runs through Centerville's downtown?
(A) a river
(B) a highway
(C) a bicycle path

5. What is the median price for a three-bedroom house in Centerville's suburbs?
(A) $1,200,000
(B) $120,000
(C) $250,000

Section III New Words Read the sentences on the left. Choose a word on the right to complete each sentence. Write the letter of the correct word in the blank. **(4 points each)**

Sentence	Word
1. I'm going to ___________ this afternoon. I have to go to the bank and do some shopping.	**a.** advantage
	b. have got to
2. My grandmother is very ___________. She has very traditional ideas about dating and marriage.	**c.** conservative
3. One ___________ of living in a small town is that the people are friendly.	**d.** crowded
	e. dry cleaner
4. You're going downtown! So am I. I'd be happy to give you ___________.	**f.** a ride
5. I'm sorry, but I can't stay. I ___________ go to work.	**g.** jaywalking
6. This is a very ___________ location. It's near great stores and my office is only two blocks away.	**h.** run errands
	i. smog
7. In big cities, the air is really bad. There is too much ___________.	**j.** convenient
8. My city is too ___________! There are people everywhere.	
9. I got a ticket for ___________. I didn't know that you couldn't cross the street in the middle.	
10. My jacket has a big coffee stain on it. I have to take it to the ___________.	

Section IV Using Language Use the five expressions below to fill in the blanks in the conversation. **(4 points each)**

could you tell me where	go past	go straight
on the corner of	turn left on	

Joe: Excuse me. ________________ the bank is?
1

Kim: Sure. Let me see. OK. ________________ down this street. This is Oak Street.
2

Joe: OK. And then what?

Kim: ________________ Second Avenue. You'll see a large supermarket
3

________________ Second and Oak.
4

Joe: Uh-huh.

Kim: ________________ the post office. The bank will be on the right.
5

TOTAL ____/100 pts.

Name ______________________ Date ______________ Score ____________

Chapter 5 Test

Section I Listening to a Conversation Listen to the conversation. Then choose the best answer to each question. **(4 points each)**

1. What did Nick think of the apartment?
- (A) He thought that it was pretty.
- (B) He thought that it was just O.K.
- (C) He didn't like it at all.

2. Who is looking for an apartment?
- (A) Nick
- (B) Antonio
- (C) both Nick and Antonio

3. How much is the rent for the apartment?
- (A) $1,200 a month
- (B) $2,000 a month
- (C) $2,500 a month

4. Which of the following sentences about the apartment is NOT true?
- (A) There is no carpet.
- (B) The landlord is raising the rent.
- (C) The apartment is unfurnished.

5. What color are they painting the walls?
- (A) light pink
- (B) dark brown
- (C) bright white

Section II Listening to Apartment Information Listen to the information. Choose the best answer to each question. Listen to the information again. **(4 points each)**

1. Brentwood Apartments has ____________.
- (A) one small apartment building
- (B) ten small apartment buildings
- (C) a total of 500 apartments

2. Which of the following sentences is NOT true?
- (A) Students can receive a rent discount in the next two weeks.
- (B) Students rarely rent apartments from Brentwood Apartments.
- (C) Brentwood Apartments is near Sonora State University.

3. This information is ____________.
- (A) on a telephone
- (B) on the Internet
- (C) on television

4. All apartments have ___________.
   (A) two bathrooms
   (B) new carpet
   (C) a free Internet connection

5. Brentwood Apartments does not have ___________.
   (A) many sports facilities
   (B) an underground garage
   (C) studio apartments

Section III New Words Look at the list of words below. Use the words to fill in the blanks in the sentences. **(4 points each)**

available	closet	fireplace	fix	leak
move in	pretty	stressed out	unfurnished	vacancy

1. I'm upset at my landlord. My door is broken and he won't ___________ it.
2. I love my living room because it has a ___________. It really keeps us warm in the winter.
3. I want an apartment that is ___________ because I have a lot of furniture.
4. I'm really ___________! I can't find an apartment and school starts next week!
5. There must be a ___________ in the bathroom. There's water all over the floor.
6. There are three apartments ___________ in that building. I may take one of them.
7. There was only one small ___________ in that apartment. Where would I put my clothes?
8. I'd like to live in that apartment building, but there's no ___________. The landlord said that he would call me if someone left.
9. I got an apartment! I have to ___________ next week.
10. I looked at a ___________ nice apartment this afternoon. It's very close to my school and the rent is cheap.

Section IV Using Language Use the five expressions below to fill in the blanks in the sentences. **(4 points each)**

I would be happy to	I'm afraid I can't	Would you mind
I'd like you to	I'm sorry	

1. ______________________ replacing my refrigerator?

2. ______________________ put in air conditioning. It's too expensive.

3. ______________________, but I can't do that.

4. ______________________ fix that leak for you.

5. ______________________ paint my living room.

TOTAL ____/100 pts.

Name ______________________ Date ______________ Score __________

Chapter 6 Test

Section I Listening to a Conversation Listen to the conversation. Choose the best answer to each question. **(4 points each)**

1. Where is Kim from?
- (A) The United States
- (B) Korea
- (C) China

2. Why is the food in the American family strange for Kim?
- (A) Kim likes to eat a lot of salad and vegetables, but the family doesn't.
- (B) Kim is a vegetarian and the family eats a lot of meat.
- (C) The people in the family are vegetarians and Kim eats meat.

3. How is Kim feeling lately?
- (A) She misses her family in her own country.
- (B) She has been feeling a little sick lately.
- (C) She is angry that she has to live with a family.

4. What does Kim dislike about living in the family's house?
- (A) The family is always smoking outside.
- (B) She has to go outside to smoke.
- (C) She has to go outside on the weekends.

5. Which of the following is *not* an advantage of living with the family?
- (A) They take Kim to museums.
- (B) They help Kim with her English.
- (C) They don't eat meat.

Section II Listening to a Lecture Listen to the lecture. Choose the best answer to each question. Listen to the lecture again. **(4 points each)**

1. Who is listening to this lecture?
- (A) American university students
- (B) foreign college students
- (C) all students in the United States

2. What are carcinogens?
- (A) chemicals that cause cancer
- (B) smoke from someone else's cigarette
- (C) a dangerous chemical in tobacco

3. What state in the U.S. that has strict anti-smoking laws does the speaker mention?
- (A) Oregon
- (B) California
- (C) Maine

4. What is generally true about smoking laws in the U.S.?
(A) You can't smoke in restaurants in any state.
(B) You can always smoke in bars.
(C) The laws change from place to place.

5. About how many people may die each year from secondhand smoke?
(A) 60,000
(B) 6,000
(C) 600

Section III New Words Look at the list of words below. Use the words to fill in the blanks in the sentences. **(4 points each)**

adults	amazed	ceremony	exotic	impression
leftovers	logical	look forward to	silverware	utensils

1. Most kitchen ______________ have handles.

2. When my sister got married, she had a beautiful ______________.

3. Customs sometimes seem very strange. They are rarely ______________.

4. I was ______________ when she lit up a cigarette in the office!

5. In the United States, it's OK to take home the ______________ after a meal in a restaurant.

6. On vacations, I really like to go to ______________ places. I don't want to go anywhere ordinary.

7. I really ______________ my mother's visit next December.

8. Almost all Americans use ______________ to eat with, although some use chopsticks.

9. My first ______________ of her wasn't very good, but now I like her a lot!

10. In my culture, children become ______________ at age 16.

Section IV Using Language Use the five expressions below to fill in the blanks in the sentences. **(4 points each)**

all right	don't worry	excuse me
forgive	sorry	

1. Oh, I spilled coffee on your pants! Please ______________________ me.

2. A: I apologize for being late yesterday.

B: ______________________ about it! I understand.

3. I'm really ______________________ about the loud music last night.

4. ______________________. Do you know where the bus station is?

5. A: It was my fault for missing that appointment. I really apologize for that.

B: That's ______________________. It wasn't a problem.

TOTAL ______/100 pts.

Name ______________________ Date ______________ Score ____________

Chapter 7 Test

Section I Listening to a Conversation Listen to the conversation. Choose the best answer to each question. **(4 points each)**

1. Which of the following sentences about Ken's back is true?
- (A) This is the first time that his back has hurt.
- (B) Ken has had back problems in the past.
- (C) Ken's back started hurting yesterday.

2. What is ibuprofen?
- (A) It is an effective drug for back pain.
- (B) It is another name for lower back pain.
- (C) It is the name of Ken's company.

3. What does the doctor think might be the cause of Ken's back pain?
- (A) He isn't stretching enough during work.
- (B) He bends over too much when he types.
- (C) His keyboard might be too high or too low.

4. What did Ken do for his pain?
- (A) He took some pain medicine.
- (B) He put ice on his back.
- (C) He went home and rested.

5. What advice about his back does the doctor *not* give Ken?
- (A) Ken should rest for a day or two.
- (B) Ken should take some pain medicine.
- (C) Ken should take a yoga class.

Section II Listening to an Orientation Listen to the orientation. Choose the best answer to each question. Listen to the orientation again. **(4 points each)**

1. Who is listening to this orientation?
- (A) teachers and administrators
- (B) business executives
- (C) university students

2. What are the three important areas for fitness?
- (A) strength, flexibility, cardio fitness
- (B) muscle strength, aerobic fitness, cardio fitness
- (C) stretching, flexibility, cardio fitness

3. What advice does Jerry give his listeners?
- (A) You should take a cardio class.
- (B) Always stretch before lifting weights.
- (C) It's good to work out three times a week.

4. What does the center have for cardio fitness?
Ⓐ exercise machines and aerobics classes
Ⓑ treadmills, stationary bicycles, and yoga classes
Ⓒ free weights and aerobics classes

5. What is the main idea of this lecture?
Ⓐ Fitness includes exercising, diet, and lifestyle choices.
Ⓑ You have to exercise regularly if you want to be fit.
Ⓒ To be healthy, you have to think about total fitness.

Section III New Words Look at the list of words below. Use the words to fill in the blanks in the conversation. **(4 points each)**

cardio	discount	health club	ought to	prescription
rest	shape	sore	upset	yoga

Tom: Hey, Mary. I'm going to the ____________ (1) to lift weights. Do you want to come?

Mary: Not today, Tom. I'm not feeling well. My throat is ____________ (2) and I have an ____________ (3) stomach.

Tom: I'm really sorry to hear that. You ____________ (4) go home. You need to ____________ (5) in bed.

Mary: I will, but first I'm going to the pharmacy. My doctor gave me a ____________ (6) for medicine. So, do you just lift weights for exercise?

Tom: No, I also take a ____________ (7) class to strengthen my heart and lungs. It's really hard, but I love the fast music during class.

Mary: That's great! I take a ____________ (8) class. It's very relaxing! It's a really great place!

Tom: It's a little expensive. I'm glad that we get a student ____________ (9).

Mary: Yeah. It's important for students to stay in good ____________ (10).

Section IV Using Language Use the five expressions below to fill in the blanks in the sentences. **(4 points each)**

advise you to	should	try to
what do you think	why don't you	

Tom: I have a fever and a sore throat. ____________ (1) I should do?

Maya: Well, you ____________ (2) take some aspirin. And ____________ (3) get some rest.

Tom: But I have a big test tomorrow! I need to study.

Maya: Well, ____________ (4) email your teacher? Tell him that you're going to miss class because you're sick.

Tom: OK. That's a good idea.

Maya: And I ____________ (5) go to bed now.

TOTAL ____/100 pts.

Name ______________________ Date ______________ Score ______________

Chapter 8 Test

Section I Listening to a Conversation Listen to the conversation. Choose the best answer to each question. **(4 points each)**

1. What is Marta watching on TV?

(A) She's changing channels looking for something interesting.
(B) She's watching a movie that she wanted to see.
(C) She's watching a news program on CNN.

2. What does Joe's friend Harry tell him?

(A) A rerun of *Friends* is on Channel 10.
(B) A great movie is on at 10:00.
(C) A really good movie is on at 9:00.

3. Which of the following is *not* true about the movie?

(A) It takes place in Las Vegas.
(B) It won an award for Best Picture.
(C) It has Sandra Bullock in it.

4. What time is it in this conversation?

(A) 6:00
(B) 7:00
(C) 8:00

5. What does Marta want to do before the movie?

(A) She wants to watch *Friends*.
(B) She wants to eat something.
(C) She would like to cook dinner.

Section II Listening to a News Report Listen to the news report. Choose the best answer to each question. Listen to the news report again. **(4 points each)**

1. What is the main idea of this story?

(A) The Waterman building has a problem.
(B) Traffic is blocked on Interstate 280.
(C) There is a terrible fire in Oakland.

2. What condition is the building in?

(A) The bottom and top floors are OK, but the middle was destroyed.
(B) The building will not be used again because it's a total loss.
(C) The owners of the building will have to spend a lot of money on repairs.

3. Where did the fire start?

(A) on the 16th floor
(B) on the 60th floor
(C) on the 36th floor

4. How many people were killed or injured?
   (A) Five people died; about 50 were injured.
   (B) No one died; about 50 were injured.
   (C) One person died; about 15 were injured.

5. What's happening on the highway?
   (A) The traffic is terrible.
   (B) There are no drivers on the highway.
   (C) The drivers are stopping to watch the fire.

Section III New Words Look at the list of words below. Use the words to fill in the blanks in the sentences. **(4 points each)**

blocked	channel surf	injuries	landed	passengers
remote control	run out of	top story	turn down the volume	waste of time

1. I don't like TV. I think that it's a ______________.
2. The TV's too loud. Can you ______________?
3. The airplane ______________ on the highway, but everyone was OK.
4. I don't like to read a TV guide. I just ______________ until I find a good program.
5. There were 85 ______________ on that airplane.
6. Where is the ______________? I want to change the channel.
7. The automobile crash ______________ the highway for two hours.
8. We should stop at a gas station. We don't want to ______________ gas.
9. The ______________ in the news tonight is the president's visit to China.
10. There were 15 ______________ when the plane crashed.

Section IV Using Language Use the five expressions below to fill in the blanks in the conversation. **(4 points each)**

disagree	good point	in my opinion
strong opinion	think that	

Erica: What did you think of the movie last night?

Sasha: Well, ______________ (1), it was a great movie! I loved the acting and the scenary.

Terry: I ______________ (2). I didn't like it at all. I thought that the story was really boring.

Sasha: But Harrison Ford was excellent!

Terry: That's a ______________ (3), but I still didn't like the movie.

Sasha: What did you think of it, Erica?

Erica: Well, I don't have a ______________ (4) really. It was just OK.

Terry: I ______________ (5) we should watch another movie tonight.

Sasha: That's a great idea!

TOTAL ____/100 pts.

Name ______________________ Date ______________ Score ____________

Chapter 9 Test

Section I Listening to a Conversation Listen to the conversation. Choose the best answer to each question. **(4 points each)**

1. How did Juyu enjoy her date?
(A) She didn't enjoy it at all.
(B) It was OK but not great.
(C) She had a good time.

2. Which of the following sentences is *not* true about Tom?
(A) He likes Kung-Fu movies.
(B) He likes to go to steakhouses.
(C) He likes to eat French food.

3. What does Juyu say about Tom?
(A) He's very violent.
(B) He's very quiet.
(C) He's an American.

4. Where is Juyu from?
(A) China
(B) Korea
(C) Japan

5. What did Juyu drink in the restaurant?
(A) milk
(B) soda
(C) mineral water

Section II Listening to a Lecture Listen to the lecture. Choose the best answer to each question. Listen to the lecture again. **(4 points each)**

1. According to Annette, what do you have to do on the first date?
(A) You must talk to your date to find out who he or she is.
(B) You have to have fun to build your relationship with your date.
(C) You have to go to a restaurant or on a relaxing walk in a park.

2. What advice did Annette *not* give about dating?
(A) You and your clothes must be clean.
(B) Eye contact is really important.
(C) You should compliment your date.

3. What is punctuality?
(A) being friendly
(B) being on time
(C) being polite

4. What does Annette say you should *not* talk about?
   (A) yourself
   (B) other dates
   (C) sports

5. What would be a good title for this lecture?
   (A) Advice for Having a Fun Date
   (B) Conversation Advice for Dating
   (C) Great Places for Great Dates

Section III New Words Look at the list of words below. Use the words to fill in the blanks in the sentences. **(4 points each)**

box office	cover charge	good at	graduation	keep in touch
make a reservation	on the road	pre-med	sci-fi	show times

1. We'd better ______________________ for that restaurant. They're always busy!
2. I don't want to be in sales. I hate being ______________________. I like being at home every night.
3. I just called the theater. The ______________________ for that movie are 3, 5, and 7 o'clock.
4. I don't want to go to that nightclub. There's a $20 ______________________.
5. If we're going to play football, let's invite Harry. He's ______________________ all sports.
6. I didn't like that ______________________ film. I don't like fantasy films with a lot of spaceships and planets in it.
7. Lee is going to be a doctor, so he's taking ______________________ courses at college.
8. I bought the tickets for the movie on the Internet, but we have to pick them up at the

   ______________________.
9. My parents gave me a big party for my ______________________ from high school.
10. I tried to ______________________ with my old friends, but now I don't know where they are.

Section IV Using Language Use the five expressions below to fill in the blanks in the sentences. **(4 points each)**

Congratulations!	I really like your	Thanks!
That's awful!	That's great!	

1. A: I lost my wallet. It had $200 in it!

B: ________________________________

2. A: Jenny, I love to hear you sing! You're so good!

B: ________________________________

3. A: ________________________________ hair! It's beautiful!

B: You're very kind.

4. A: I just graduated from college.

B: ________________________________

5. A: My company made a $4,000,000 profit last year!

B: ________________________________

TOTAL ____/100 pts.

Name ______________________ Date ______________ Score ____________

Chapter 10 Test

Section I Listening to a Conversation Listen to the conversation. Choose the best answer to each question. **(4 points each)**

1. Where is Ibrahim going now?
- (A) to Peterson Park
- (B) to the gym
- (C) to the soccer field

2. What is true about the last soccer game between Ibrahim's team and Central University?
- (A) Central University won.
- (B) It was a tie.
- (C) Ibrahim's team won.

3. What does Susan tell Ibrahim about the hike next weekend?
- (A) She will definitely go.
- (B) She might be able to go.
- (C) She won't be able to go.

4. How long is the hike that Ibrahim and Susan discuss?
- (A) ten miles
- (B) five miles
- (C) two miles

5. Who is going on the hike with Ibrahim?
- (A) Sofia and some other people
- (B) Alberto and some other people
- (C) only Ibrahim

Section II Listening to a Lecture Listen to the lecture. Choose the best answer to each question. Listen to the lecture again. **(4 points each)**

1. What would be the best title for this lecture?
- (A) How to Win at Lacrosse
- (B) A Short Introduction to Lacrosse
- (C) The History of Lacrosse

2. Which statement is true about lacrosse?
- (A) It is the oldest sport in North America.
- (B) It is the most popular sport in Canada.
- (C) It is not played professionally.

3. Which of the following is true about lacrosse?
- (A) Women wear more protective padding.
- (B) Women's teams sometimes play men's teams.
- (C) Men's and women's rules are very different.

4. Where are there now lacrosse teams?
   (A) South America and East Asia
   (B) East Asia and Europe
   (C) Africa and Europe

5. Scoring in lacrosse is similar to what other sport?
   (A) soccer
   (B) basketball
   (C) baseball

Section III New Words Look at the list of words below. Use the words to fill in the blanks in the sentences. **(4 points each)**

beat	close	confidence	flexibility	get in shape
individual	opponent	tie	warm up	win

1. The score was 4-4. It was a ____________ game.
2. I like Tae Kwon Do because the stretching increases my ____________.
3. We really wanted to ____________ Washington College, but we lost the game.
4. I'm taking a yoga class and I'm running twice a week. I really want to ____________.
5. I used to be really shy about doing sports, but after playing on a soccer team, I have a lot more ____________.
6. I prefer ____________ sports to team sports. I like to play alone.
7. It's very important to ____________ before starting to play.
8. We lost last time, but this time I think that we will ____________.
9. The score is 3-4. It's a ____________ game.
10. I'll play against Harry tomorrow. He's my ____________.

Section IV Using Language Use the five expressions below to fill in the blanks in the sentences. **(4 points each)**

after that	first	get that
last step	say that again	

Carlos: OK, everybody, we're going to do a hike today. The ____________ thing we'll do is go up that hill over there.

Aki: Wait a minute. We can't hear back here. Can you ____________?

Carlos: Sure. Look over there. There's a hill. We're going to walk up it. Did you ____________?

Aki: Yes, we understood.

Carlos: OK, ____________, we're going to hike north.

Aki: OK.

Carlos: The ____________ is to come back down here to the parking lot.

TOTAL ____/100 pts.

Chapter 1 Test Answer Key

Section I Listening to a Conversation

1.a 2.c 3.b 4.a 5.c

Section II Listening to a Lecture

1.c 2.a 3.b 4.c 5.c

Section III New Words

1. call me 2. came over 3. move into 4. stop by 5. orientation 6. facilities 7. placement test 8. schedule 9. advisor 10. take

Section IV Using Language

1. I'd like you to 2. Same here 3. Nice to meet you 4. what's your name again? 5. this is

Chapter 2 Test Answer Key

Section I Listening to a Conversation

1. c 2. a 3. a 4. c 5. b

Section II Listening to a Lecture

1. b 2. c 3. a 4. b 5. b

Section III New Words

1. weather 2. forecast 3. How come 4. sick of 5. winter 6. clear 7. degrees 8. cloudy 9. freezing 10. chance of

Section IV Using Language

Answers will vary, but correct form of verbs are:
1. I can't + base of verb 2. I'm not able + infinitive
3. I wish I could + base of verb 4. I'm good at + gerund
5. I don't know how + infinitive

Chapter 3 Test Answer Key

Section I Listening to a Conversation

1. b 2. a 3. c 4. b 5. a

Section II Listening to a Lecture

1. c 2. a 3. a 4. b 5. b

Section III New Words

1. g 2. j 3. e 4. a 5. b 6. f 7. h 8. c 9. i 10. d

Section IV Using Language

Waiter: Are you ready to order?
Caroline: Yes, I'd like the lemon chicken.
Waiter: Would you like a soup or a salad with that?
Caroline: I'll have the soup.
Waiter: Anything to drink?
Caroline: Yes. May I please have a glass of wine?

Chapter 4 Test Answer Key

Section I Listening to a Conversation

1. c 2. a 3. b 4. a 5. c

Section II Listening to an Introduction

1. b 2. b 3. c 4. a 5. c

Section III New Words

1. h 2. c 3. a 4. f 5. b 6. j 7. i 8. d 9. g 10. e

Section IV Using Language

1. Could you tell me where 2. Go straight 3. Turn left on 4. on the corner of 5. Go past

Chapter 5 Test Answer Key

Section I Listening to a Conversation

1. c 2. c 3. b 4. a 5. a

Section II Listening to Apartment Information

1. c 2. b 3. a 4. b 5. c

Section III New Words

1. fix 2. fireplace 3. unfurnished 4. stressed out 5. leak 6. available 7. closet 8. vacancy 9. move in 10. pretty

Section IV Using Language

1. Would you mind 2. I'm afraid I can't 3. I'm sorry 4. I would be happy to 5. I'd like you to

Chapter 6 Test Answer Key

Section I Listening to a Conversation

1. b 2. c 3. a 4. b 5. c

Section II Listening to a Lecture

1. b 2. a 3. b 4. c 5. a

Section III New Words

1. utensils 2. ceremony 3. logical 4. amazed 5. leftovers 6. exotic 7. look forward to 8. silverware 9. impression 10. adults

Section IV Using Language

1. forgive 2. Don't worry 3. sorry 4. Excuse me 5. all right

Chapter 7 Test Answer Key

Section I Listening to a Conversation

1. b 2. a 3. c 4. b 5. c

Section II Listening to an Orientation

1. c 2. a 3. b 4. a 5. c

Section III New Words

1. health club 2. sore 3. upset 4. ought to 5. rest 6. prescription 7. cardio 8. yoga 9. discount 10. shape

Section IV Using Language

1. What do you think 2. should 3. try to 4. why don't you 5. advise you to

Chapter 8 Test Answer Key

Section I Listening to a Conversation

1. a 2. c 3. a 4. b 5. b

Section II Listening to a Lecture

1. c 2. b 3. a 4. b 5. a

Section III New Words

1. waste of time 2. turn down the volume 3. landed 4. channel surf 5. passengers 6. remote control 7. blocked 8. run out of 9. top story 10. injuries

Section IV Using Language

1. in my opinion 2. disagree 3. good point 4. strong opinion 5. think that

Chapter 9 Test Answer Key

Section I Listening to a Conversation

1. a 2. c 3. b 4. a 5. c

Section II Listening to a Lecture

1. a 2. c 3. b 4. b 5. a

Section III New Words

1. make a reservation 2. on the road 3. show times 4. cover charge 5. good at 6. sci-fi 7. pre-med 8. box office 9. graduation 10. keep in touch

Section IV Using Language

1. That's awful! 2. Thanks! 3. I really like 4. Congratulations! or That's great! 5. That's great! or Congratulations!

Chapter 10 Test Answer Key

Section I Listening to a Conversation

1. c 2. a 3. b 4. b 5. a

Section II Listening to a Lecture

1. b 2. a 3. c 4. b 5. a

Section III New Words

1. tie 2. flexibility 3. beat 4. get in shape 5. confidence 6. individual 7. warm up 8. win 9. close 10. opponent

Section IV Using Language

1. first 2. say that again 3. get that 4. after that 5. last step

Chapter 1 Test Audioscripts

Section I Listening to a Conversation

Antonio: Hey, Mary. How are you doing?

Mary: Antonio, it's nice to see you.

Antonio: Mary, this is my friend Kareem. He's going to study English here.

Mary: Nice to meet you, Kareem. Where are you from?

Kareem: I'm from Brazil. My parents moved there from Oman about 30 years ago.

Mary: I'm from Boston.

Antonio: Mary works in the library.

Mary: Yeah, but only part time. I'm studying engineering full time. [pause] Hey, do you want to get something to eat?

Antonio: Sorry Mary, but Kareem and I have to go. Kareem has a placement test in 30 minutes.

Mary: Good luck!

Section II Listening to a Lecture

Good morning everyone and welcome to the university sports orientation. I'm Jenny Johnson, the coordinator of our sports program. I'll be telling you about our sports facilities and about our intramural program.

In this university, all of our sports facilities are in the northeast corner of our campus, just north of the science center. We have six multi-purpose athletic fields. They can be used for football, soccer, rugby, baseball, or even for playing Frisbee. We also have four basketball courts and two swimming pools, one indoor pool and one pool that's outside. We also have a brand new fitness center with all of the exercise equipment that you need to get in good shape and stay that way. We also have three studios in the fitness center for exercise and dance classes. You can take yoga, karate, jazz dancing, and many other classes.

Next, I'd like to talk about our intramural sports program. There's one important thing for you to know. Anyone can join an intramural team. Intramural teams don't play teams from other colleges; they only play teams from this university. We have teams at different levels, so don't worry about your ability. There is a team for you. Right now, we have intramural teams for basketball, baseball, volleyball, tennis, and touch football. There are sign-up sheets outside my office in the fitness center. Just come by and we'll find a team for you!

Remember that our goal at this university is to focus on life fitness. We want to help you strengthen your heart and lungs and build up strong bones and muscles. You can do it by starting a fitness program today!

I'll be happy to answer any of your questions now.

Chapter 2 Test Audioscripts

Section I Listening to a Conversation

Cho: Freddy, what are you going to do over break?

Freddy: Well, I was thinking of going snowboarding at Bear Mountain. Can you snowboard?

Cho: Not very well. I'm from Southern China near the coast. It's really warm there. We swim a lot, go scuba diving, and go surfing, but we never have the chance to do winter sports.

Freddy: I'll be glad to teach you how to do it. It's really not difficult. It's just like surfing, but with snow.

Cho: I'd love to, but I really can't. My brother has a vacation also, and he's coming to visit me. I'm going to take him around the city.

Freddy: That's too bad, but I understand.

Section II Listening to a Lecture — Spring Break

At almost all colleges and universities in the United States, students have a two-week vacation called spring break. For most students, spring break is two weeks in March. During that time, millions of college students leave their college campuses and go somewhere else to have fun.

Because there are so many college students taking a vacation at the same time, it has become a very important business. Travel agents, airlines, resorts, hotels, and restaurants all want the students to spend money with them. On the Internet, there are many websites just for spring break. Spring break advertisements start appearing in the winter in college newspapers.

The most popular places with college students are beaches, although a few students may try to get in one more ski trip before the last of the snow melts. For students in colleges on the East Coast of the United States, Florida was a popular destination. In the 1970s and 80s, thousands of students went to Fort Lauderdale and Daytona Beach, Florida, for spring break. Those two cities on the Atlantic Ocean were popular because of the warm weather, beautiful beaches, and good surfing. After many years, however, those cities passed laws that made it difficult for the students to have big parties and make noise. Most students stopped going to Fort Lauderdale and Daytona Beach. Now, more students spend spring break on the Gulf of Mexico, in Panama City, Florida, or on South Padre Island in Texas.

Foreign cities have become very popular with students also. The biggest destinations outside of the United States are Cancun and Acapulco in Mexico and the island of Jamaica. Travel experts estimate that over one million students go to Florida, Texas, Mexico, and Jamaica each year for spring break.

Chapter 3 Test Audioscripts

Section I Listening to a Conversation

Waiter: Are you ready to order?

Pam: Yes. I'd like the lemon chicken. Does that come with a vegetable?

Waiter: Yes. And you also get a soup or a salad.

Pam: That's great. I'll have the onion soup and the buttered carrots.

Waiter: And you sir?

Harry: I don't eat meat or fish. What do you recommend?

Waiter: Well, we have two excellent vegetarian dishes: spaghetti with a tomato and mushroom sauce and a vegetable casserole.

Harry: I'll have the spaghetti. And a small salad.

Waiter: And would you like some wine?

Pam: Yes, could we have just some water, please?

Section II Listening to a Lecture

Jane Martin: Good evening, everyone. I'm Jane Martin and this is *Food Talk*. Thank you so much for taking time out of your busy day to listen to my program. Tonight, I'm going to talk to you about a new restaurant in town. It's called Burt's. It's on the west side on Fifth Street, next to the Corona Theater. It has only been open for three months, but it's already very crowded every night, so if you want to go there, be sure to make a reservation.

My husband and I went there last Monday, and I have to tell you, the steaks are really fabulous. The owners, Burt and Maria Gonzalez, have their own ranch and they only cook meat from there. They feed their cows only organic grain and grass. The cows have a lot of land to walk around on. As a result, the steaks have very little fat. They're also surprisingly tender. I had a sirloin steak and my husband had filet mignon. Both were delicious and not tough at all.

The Gonzalez family also has an organic farm. They grow all of their fruit and vegetables without any chemicals or fertilizers. Burt's is basically a steakhouse, but their menu is full of healthy choices for vegetarians. With my steak, I had a very large mixed salad with a nice oil and vinegar dressing. The greens were all very fresh and crisp. The tomatoes were sweet and juicy. My husband had a baked potato with green beans. Both were excellent. For dessert, we had their special chocolate cake and some very strong Brazilian coffee.

All in all, it was a very enjoyable dining experience, and I can recommend Burt's to all of my listeners.

Chapter 4 Test Audioscripts

Section I Listening to a Conversation

Mark: Lin, how are you doing?

Lin: Fine, thanks, Mark. Hey, I'm living in your neighborhood now. I just moved into that apartment building across the street.

Mark: Really? How do you like it here?

Lin: Well, it's much quieter than my old neighborhood, and I think that it's safer, which is great!

Mark: That's good, but isn't it a little boring here? There's nothing to do on Saturday night.

Lin: I don't mind at all. Lee and I are ready for some peace and quiet. I hated being near the bus station. Sometimes the buses woke me up in the middle of the night.

Mark: That's hard. Hey, isn't your wedding anniversary coming up?

Lin: Yeah. It's next week. Lee and I were married one year ago.

Mark: We have to get together to celebrate.

Lin: Great idea!

Section II Listening to an Introduction

Welcome to the Centerville Business Information website. Please take the time to view this introductory video. It will show you why we think that Centerville is the best town for business in the United States.

First, let's look at some basic facts about Centerville. We have a population of about 15,500 people. We're a small community, but we are very diverse. Because we are the home of Johnstone Technical Institute and Jackson County Junior College, we have people from all over the world. About eight percent of our residents are from outside the United States.

Centerville has everything that your business needs. We have the lowest property taxes in the state and an educated workforce. Almost 90 percent of our citizens have graduated from high school and about 50 percent have college degrees. Our two high schools have won numerous awards for academic excellence.

Centerville has an exciting downtown full of cafes, restaurants, and office buildings. We now have two movie theaters with a total of eight movie screens. The city has just finished the beautiful River Walk, along the scenic Pocawee River. At the Centerville Sports Center, employees can work out in the gym before or after work. The center also has basketball courts and an Olympic-size swimming pool.

In Centerville's suburbs, the median price for a three-bedroom house is currently only $250,000, far below the norm for this region. If your company decides to move to Centerville, our city government will be happy to help your employees find a place to live.

In conclusion, there is no better place for business than Centerville. If you are interested in our beautiful community, contact the Centerville Development Office at the email address at the bottom of your computer screen. We will be happy to talk to you about our lovely town.

Chapter 5 Test Audioscripts

Section I Listening to a Conversation

Antonio: Hey, Nick. How was the apartment?

Nick: Well, I guess it might be OK for someone else. For me, it was pretty bad.

Antonio: Really? Why?

Nick: Well, they're painting the walls a light pink, and the carpet is dark brown.

Antonio: That sounds pretty ugly.

Nick: Yeah, and the landlord said that they're raising the rent to $2,000 a month.

Antonio: That's way too high for us. You and I can't pay that much. Is the apartment at least furnished?

Nick: No, and it doesn't even have a refrigerator or stove.

Antonio: We'll have to find something else. I don't want to buy appliances.

Section II Apartment Information

Thank you for calling the Brentwood Apartments information line. Our apartment buildings are located on 19th Avenue, near Highway 74. Brentwood Apartments is now leasing one-, two-, and three-bedroom apartments. Apartments are available for viewing Tuesday through Sunday from 8 A.M. to 6 P.M. With a total of 500 apartments in ten different buildings, Brentwood Apartments has an apartment for you.

Brentwood Apartments is conveniently located near major bus lines and is just down the street from

Sonora State University. All apartments have two spaces in our underground garage and there is plenty of street parking for guests.

All apartments are unfurnished. However, all apartments come with stoves and refrigerators. All available apartments have been painted and have new carpet. All apartments have one bathroom with a shower. Apartments come with cable access, and Brentwood Apartments has wireless Internet connections available for only $25.00 per month.

All apartment buildings are surrounded by wide green lawns, large flower beds, and wooded groves. Brentwood Apartments have two swimming pools, four tennis courts, and a fitness center. We also have two party rooms that are available for special occasions.

All apartments require a one-year lease with a deposit of one-month's rent. Currently, one-bedroom apartments are renting for $1,000 per month. Two-bedroom apartments are $1,500 per month, and three-bedroom apartments are $1,800 per month. Sonora State University students who rent an apartment in the next two weeks will receive a 10 percent discount. Brentwood Apartments has years of experience helping students from Sonora State University. We look forward to working with them in the future.

If you are interested in talking with a representative of Brentwood Apartments, press three now or just stay on the line. We will be happy to talk with you.

Chapter 6 Test Audioscripts

Section I Listening to a Conversation

Mary: Kim, how are you doing?

Kim: Oh, OK, I guess, but I've been a little homesick lately.

Mary: I'm sorry to hear it. What's going on?

Kim: Well, I'm living with a really nice American family. They try their best to make me feel comfortable, but it's just so different from my home in Korea.

Mary: How is it different?

Kim: Well, the food is still a bit strange for me. They're vegetarians, so I have to eat a lot of salads and vegetables.

Mary: That would be a little hard for me also.

Kim: And they don't smoke, so I have to go outside. (pause) On the other hand, they're very kind. On the weekends, they take me to museums and sometimes we go hiking in the mountains. And they help me with my English every night!

Mary: That's great!

Section II Listening to a Lecture

OK, let's begin our class.

Today, we're talking about smoking in the United States. Specifically, I'm going to talk about the effect that scientific research on smoking has had on our culture.

First, I need to talk about an important term, *secondhand smoke*. That's smoke from someone else's cigarette. When you're sitting next to someone who is smoking, you are breathing in his or her smoke. Secondhand smoke has about 60 carcinogens in it. Carcinogens are chemicals that cause cancer. Some medical researchers estimate that as many as 60,000 nonsmokers die each year because of secondhand smoke.

I think that you can understand why a lot of nonsmokers are angry about this. They have pushed states and cities to ban smoking in all public places. Many places in the United States now have very strict anti-smoking laws for businesses, restaurants, hotels, and bars. All air flights in the United States must be non-smoking flights.

Although there are strict nonsmoking laws in many cities across the United States, some regions are clearly stricter than others. The anti-smoking movement tends to be strongest on the West Coast, for example in California, and in the Northeast. Anti-smoking laws vary considerably. In some cities, you can smoke in bars, but not in restaurants. In other cities, you aren't allowed to smoke in any public place.

For all of you as foreign university students, this information is extremely important. Smoking is a very emotional topic for thousands and thousands of Americans. It may also be very emotional in other countries as well. If you smoke cigarettes, be very careful where you light up. Ask about the local laws and customs first. If you don't smoke, it's a little easier for you, but be careful in conversations. You still could get into a big argument about smoking.

Chapter 7 Test Audioscripts

Section I Listening to a Conversation

Doctor: So, Ken. You hurt your back again. That's not good. When did it happen this time?

Ken: It went out this morning. I was at work typing on my computer. I stood up and suddenly my back really hurt. [pause] The pain is down near my waist.

Doctor: Lower back pain is very common among people who spend a lot of time with computers. What have you done for the pain?

Ken: Well, I put ice on it right away. That's all that I did.

Doctor: That's good. I'll give you some ibuprofen for the pain. Ibuprofen isn't a strong drug, but it's effective. You'll have to rest for a day or two. And you really have to talk to your company about adjusting your chair and your keyboard height. Your hands may be too high or too low.

Ken: Thank you, doctor!

Section II Listening to an Orientation

Hi, everybody. Welcome to the University Fitness Center. I'm Jerry, and I'll be giving you your student fitness orientation. Before I begin, however, I want to talk a little about total fitness.

Here at the fitness center, we help you develop in three areas: strength, flexibility, and cardio fitness. To increase your strength, you have to work out with weights. For flexibility, you need to stretch your muscles. For cardio fitness, you have to do some kind of aerobic exercises. I'll talk in more detail about each of these.

For increasing your muscle strength, we have many different kinds of free weights and weight machines. You will receive a weight card. Every time you lift weights, you write down how much you lifted. That way, over time, you can see your progress. There is one thing that you need to understand, however. Before you can use any of the machines, you have to go through another orientation. We will teach you how to use each of the weight machines in the fitness center.

Next, to increase your flexibility, we recommend yoga. We have yoga classes every day of the week. We will also help you learn a very basic series of yoga stretches. You should always stretch before lifting weights or running.

Finally, we have exercise machines for building up your cardiovascular system. The cardiovascular system is your heart, lungs, and blood vessels. We have treadmills for walking and running and we have stationary bicycles. We also have aerobics classes.

OK, to sum up, you need to think about total fitness if you want to be healthy. You need to build up your muscles, you need to be flexible, and you need to have a strong heart. Do you have any questions before we move on?

Chapter 8 Test Audioscripts

Section I Listening to a Conversation

Joe: What are you watching? I thought that you wanted to see a movie.

Marta: I'm just channel surfing. I watched that new cooking show for a while. Then I turned on the news on CNN. Now I'm watching a rerun of *Friends*. I can't find anything good.

Joe: My friend Harry said that there's a great movie on Channel 10 at 9:00 tonight. It's *Crash* with Matt Dillon, Don Cheadle, and Sandra Bullock.

Marta: Matt Dillon? I've heard of it. That's a drama, isn't it?

Joe: Yes, it takes place in Los Angeles. It won the Best Picture Oscar.

Marta: That sounds really great. It's 7:00 now. Let's go get something to eat before the show.

Joe: Great idea!

Section II Listening to a News Report

Announcer (Margaret): Good evening, everyone. Welcome to the Channel 7 news. Our top story tonight is the big fire in Oakland, California. The Waterman Building, one of the most beautiful buildings in the city, caught fire around noon today. Let's go to Martin Brockman at the scene of the fire.

Martin: Well, Margaret, it's really terrible here. There's so much smoke that we can't really see the building. Firefighters are saying that the building will be a total loss. They are still bringing people out of the building. They have their ladder trucks up next to the building and also have helicopters rescuing people from the roof.

Announcer: Martin, where did the fire start?

Martin: Well, unfortunately, it started in the middle stories of the building. It's a 30-story building and the fire started on the 16th floor. That means that a number of people were trapped in the top of the building. I talked to a police officer a little bit ago. She said that everyone was out of the building now. There are a number of people with severe burns and problems with smoke inhalation. They are on their way to the hospital now.

Announcer: How many people were injured do you think?

Martin: Well, honestly, I think that it's too early to tell. I heard a firefighter say about 50 people would need medical treatment. I think that all of those were because of burns and from breathing in smoke.

Announcer: And Martin, what is the traffic like on Interstate 280 now?

Martin: It's really awful, Margaret. The smoke is blowing right across the highway. The police aren't letting anyone drive anywhere near here.

Announcer: Thank you, Martin. We'll have hourly updates on this important story throughout this evening.

Chapter 9 Test Audioscripts

Section I Listening to a Conversation

Antonio: Juyu, how was your date with Tom?

Juyu: Well, I didn't have a good time. He was too quiet. I don't think that he said more than five things all night.

Antonio: That's too bad. What did you do together?

Juyu: Well, I took him to my favorite French restaurant, but he didn't eat much. He prefers to go to steakhouses. I had some French mineral water, but he likes soda.

Antonio: Oh, well, what did you do then?

Juyu: He took me to a terrible Korean film. It was really violent with a lot of Kung-Fu action. He really likes that kind of movie.

Antonio: Maybe he thought that you'd like Kung-Fu because you're Chinese. So are you going to go out with him again?

Juyu: I think that one time was enough.

Section II Listening to a Lecture

Good evening! Welcome to Etiquette with Annette. I'm Annette de Courtois and tonight I will talk about dating etiquette. Let's start with the basics.

Dating is supposed to be fun. We go on dates to be with nice people. For a first date, you must go somewhere you can have a conversation. You have to find out who your date is. Meeting for lunch in a nice café is a good idea.

Punctuality is a key ingredient for a good date. You must be on time. Your clothes are important because they communicate information about you. Don't wear old, wrinkled, dirty, or torn clothes. And be sure to take a nice shower before your date.

Now let's move on to behavior. First, eye contact is extremely important. Look at your date's eyes often. Your eyes will communicate that you are interested in the conversation.

Next, you should take turns talking and listening. When your date says something interesting, respond. You can say, "Oh, really?" or just "Uh, huh," but say *something*. Spend some time talking about yourself. Your date will want to know some basics about you, but don't tell him or her every little detail about your life. Don't talk about other dates you've had. Definitely don't talk about your ex-wife or ex-husband. And be careful with controversial topics like religion and politics. You want to find out if you share important beliefs, but you don't want to get into an argument. You may want to start by talking about music and movies. That will give you an idea about shared values.

Well, those are the basics. Be polite, be kind, and have fun! Good night everyone.

Chapter 10 Test Audioscripts

Section I Listening to a Conversation

Ibrahim: Susan, are you going to the gym?

Susan: Oh, hi, Ibrahim. Yes, I'm going to meet Alberto. We have a tennis match today. How about you?

Ibrahim: I'm headed to the soccer field. We have a game against Central University today. They beat us 4-3 last month, but we practiced every day last week, so maybe we can win today.

Susan: Good luck!

Ibrahim: Thanks! And hey, uh, Sofia and I are going on a five-mile hike next weekend with some friends. Would you and Alberto like to come?

Susan: That sounds great! Where are you going?

Ibrahim: We're going up to Peterson Park. There's a great trail there that goes up into the mountains.

Susan: I'll talk to Alberto about it. I'll call you tomorrow to let you know.

Section II Listening to a Lecture

Everyone knows about soccer, basketball, and baseball. Many people, however, don't know much about North America's oldest sport, lacrosse. North American Indians developed lacrosse over hundreds of years. French and English settlers learned about it from them. Now, it is the fastest-growing sport in North America. Lacrosse is the national summer sport of Canada. In the United States, it is especially popular in the Northeast, but it is quickly spreading west. There are lacrosse teams at all levels of competition from elementary school to university and even to the professional level.

Today, lacrosse is very different from the many versions played by Native Americans. There are 10 players on men's teams and 12 players on women's teams. All players carry long sticks with a basket on the end. There is a rubber ball that is carried in the basket. Players can pick up the ball from the ground and run with it. They can also throw the ball to other players.

In the men's game, players can hit each other with their bodies and their sticks, although there are strict rules for this. Men wear heavy helmets and protective padding. Women wear much less protective equipment because they are not allowed to hit each other.

Scoring in lacrosse is very similar to soccer. Each team has a goal with a goaltender or goalie. The attacking team must throw the ball into the goal. In men's lacrosse, the players are also allowed to kick the ball.

Lacrosse is an exciting game that is now also spreading through the world. There are now lacrosse teams in East Asia and Europe. There is a lacrosse world championship every four years. For each championship, there are more teams competing.

Name ______________________ Date ______________ Score __________

Interactions/Mosaic
Listening/Speaking Placement Test

Directions: Read these directions before listening to the recorded test.

There are four sections in this test, each with a different type of listening and questions. There are a total of fifty questions to answer. You will hear the test questions only once; they will not be repeated.

Sections:

1. Ten question items – after you hear each question, choose the best response. (questions 1–10)
2. Ten statement items – after you hear each statement, select the best conclusion. (questions 11–20)
3. Ten short conversations – after each conversation there is one question to answer. (questions 21–30)
4. Four longer selections – after each longer listening selection, there are five questions to answer about the listening. (questions 31–50)

Section 1 Listen to the question and choose the best response. **(2 points each)**

Example: (You hear:) Where's your sister gone?

(You read:)

- (A) to Canada (filled in)
- (B) without her friends
- (C) because she was late
- (D) yesterday

Choice "a" is the best answer.

1.
- (A) tomorrow
- (B) to visit his sister
- (C) just this morning
- (D) the train

2.
- (A) Yes, I must go there.
- (B) About five hundred dollars
- (C) I'll have a good time.
- (D) A few days

3.
- (A) He's been once.
- (B) She's been there for three months.
- (C) No, she's still there.
- (D) She was there as a child.

4.
- (A) It's not very fair.
- (B) It takes an hour.
- (C) It's two dollars.
- (D) It's not very far from here.

5. (A) Yes, they can.
(B) The bus stops near the theatre.
(C) There is no way we could make it in time.
(D) It's too bad we missed the eight o'clock show.

6. (A) It's a little too casual.
(B) Yes, the pants fit.
(C) They have three different sizes.
(D) It's a bit tight.

7. (A) They prefer going to the movies.
(B) I haven't really thought about it.
(C) I have no references.
(D) It's either black or white.

8. (A) I would be pleased if she finds a job that she enjoys.
(B) My mother hopes she will go on to college.
(C) I took her on a trip last year.
(D) I want my legs to stop hurting.

9. (A) Yes, the doctor told me to start drinking it more often.
(B) Yes, I needed something to eat.
(C) No, I still drink milk every day.
(D) Sorry, I don't have time.

10. (A) I'm sorry I was late.
(B) I couldn't have come earlier.
(C) Would you like me to come back in a while?
(D) Sorry we left so late.

Section 2 Listen to each statement and then choose the best conclusion. **(2 points each)**

11. (A) Peter's lawyer likes his mother.
(B) Peter likes his mother.
(C) Peter is a liar.
(D) Peter's mother is a lawyer.

12. (A) The flight arrived at 2:30.
(B) The flight took off at 2:30.
(C) The flight will arrive in an hour and a half.
(D) The flight arrived at 1:30.

13. (A) Sixty students went on the sailing trip.
(B) No students went on the sailing trip.
(C) Only a few students arrived to go on the sailing trip.
(D) Nobody signed up for the sailing trip.

14. (A) Judy has to plan something for her birthday.
(B) Someone gave Judy flowers on her birthday.
(C) Judy intends to do something special on her birthday.
(D) Judy bought some plants as a gift.

15. (A) Peter is a fair player.
    (B) The match was relatively short.
    (C) Peter won the match.
    (D) Steve hit the ball fast.

16. (A) Mary was losing her eyesight.
    (B) John won the argument with Mary.
    (C) Mary forgot why she and John were arguing.
    (D) Mary and John argued because it was very hot.

17. (A) Gary preferred Robert to Peter.
    (B) Gary preferred Peter to Robert.
    (C) Robert liked Peter better than Gary.
    (D) Peter liked Gary better than Robert.

18. (A) It's time to plant things in the garden.
    (B) Soon it will be warm enough to start planting seeds.
    (C) You ought to visit the garden at the sea.
    (D) You should be considerate of the garden.

19. (A) The dinner was very good in general.
    (B) Dinner was at a restaurant.
    (C) Everyone thought the dinner was very good.
    (D) Dinner was very good every night.

20. (A) John's brother lives near the club.
    (B) John's brother owns the club.
    (C) John has never invited his brother to the club.
    (D) John's brother has never invited John to the club.

Section 3: Listen to each conversation. Answer the question you hear after each conversation. **(2 points each)**

21. (A) It hasn't rained for many years.
    (B) It has rained an unusual amount this year.
    (C) It hasn't rained much here.
    (D) It hasn't rained this year.

22. (A) He thought the restaurant could have been better.
    (B) He agreed with the woman.
    (C) He thoroughly enjoyed the restaurant.
    (D) It was impossible for the restaurant to be nice.

23. (A) The wind hurt the man's house.
    (B) The wind hurt the woman's son.
    (C) Paint in the woman's basement was ruined.
    (D) Flood water damaged artwork in the woman's house.

24. (A) The man's brother is not strong enough to lift things.
(B) The man's brother is not making any effort to find work.
(C) The brother is unlucky.
(D) The woman is surprised the man's brother is still not working.

25. (A) It's not unusual for him to play in hot weather.
(B) At an earlier time in his life, he played tennis in such weather.
(C) Playing tennis in hot weather uses up his energy.
(D) He's concerned about playing in the heat.

26. (A) It's contradictory.
(B) She doesn't agree.
(C) She wants the man to look at the ducks.
(D) She's angry.

27. (A) He's not planning to purchase anything.
(B) He doesn't need to get anything at this store.
(C) He doesn't agree about the prices.
(D) He doesn't like to buy cheap things.

28. (A) The city nearly burned down.
(B) The mayor was rescued from a burning building.
(C) The mayor was hurt and moved.
(D) The mayor was criticized and left his job.

29. (A) He thinks she should buy a large pizza.
(B) He thinks she should ask for extra mushrooms and cheese.
(C) He likes the mushroom and cheese pizza best.
(D) He thinks the pizzas are too big.

30. (A) The judge was very sure about handling the case.
(B) The judge gave the man a severe punishment.
(C) The judge was difficult to understand.
(D) The judge couldn't decide the theif's punishment.

Section 4 Listen to each longer selection and answer the five questions for the selection. Listen to the first selection. Then answer questions 31–35. **(2 points each)**

31. What do you think T-A-L-K is?
(A) a radio station
(B) a TV station
(C) an animal rescue service
(D) a movie studio

32. What animals are missing?
(A) one dog and two cats
(B) two dogs and one cat
(C) two dogs and two cats
(D) one dog and one cat

33. Which of the animals were taken from a backyard?

(A) None of the animals
(B) All of the animals
(C) Oxen the German Shepherd
(D) Winston the wire-haired terrier

34. Who had a seeing-eye dog?

(A) Mr. Wilson
(B) Mrs. Lincoln
(C) Mrs. Thompson
(D) Oxen

35. What are the listeners supposed to do if they find one of the pets?

(A) Call the T-A-L-K phone line.
(B) Call the police station.
(C) Call the local animal shelter.
(D) Wait a week to call.

Directions: The following selection is a lecture in two parts. Listen to Part 1 and answer questions 36–40. **(2 points each)**

36. In what situation does this talk probably take place?

(A) nutrition class
(B) business or marketing class
(C) supermarket training
(D) a one-day seminar

37. According to the speaker, what is true about product placement?

(A) It's only important in supermarkets.
(B) The concept is hardly used in the United States.
(C) Children are not affected by it.
(D) It's an extremely important selling tool.

38. The speaker said that children often "pester their parents" in a supermarket. What does *pester* mean?

(A) nagging and begging
(B) petting or touching
(C) wanting candy
(D) grabbing food

39. What's the speaker's focus?

(A) product placement outside of the United States
(B) product placement both in and out of the United States
(C) product placement in the United States
(D) products you shouldn't buy

40. What specific examples did the speaker use?

(A) Candy was the only example.
(B) Candy was one of the examples.
(C) The examples were taken directly from the textbook.
(D) The examples would be on the test.

Directions: Listen to Part 2 of the lecture and answer questions 41–45. **(2 points each)**

41. What products did the speaker talk about?
- (A) expensive products
- (B) headache medicine
- (C) tropical shampoo
- (D) shampoo for oily hair

42. What did the speaker say about U.S. stores?
- (A) All U.S. stores follow the same process for placing items on shelves.
- (B) Most U.S. stores place pricey items at eye level.
- (C) Many U.S. stores place inexpensive items at eye level.
- (D) No U.S. stores place items at eye level.

43. What position was stated by the speaker?
- (A) Inexpensive items are better than expensive ones.
- (B) Expensive items are better than inexpensive ones.
- (C) He didn't endorse inexpensive items or expensive ones.
- (D) He doesn't like candy or shampoo.

44. What did the speaker tell the participants?
- (A) They didn't have any homework.
- (B) They had to get ready for a test.
- (C) They had to do some research.
- (D) They had to finish an assignment in class.

45. When does the class probably meet?
- (A) Tuesday and Thursday nights
- (B) Tuesday nights
- (C) Tuesday mornings
- (D) every other week

Directions: The following selection is a lecture. Listen to the lecture and answer questions 46–50. **(2 points each)**

46. What best describes folk wisdom?
- (A) American folklore
- (B) jokes
- (C) sayings that give advice about life
- (D) different means of expressing oneself

47. Which expression of folk wisdom is *not* mentioned?
- (A) myths
- (B) fairy tales
- (C) songs
- (D) poetry

48. What will the speaker probably focus on in the lecture?

(A) humorous sayings
(B) legends
(C) songs of joy and sorrow
(D) famous American Presidents

49. What source of folk wisdom will be used in the talk?

(A) Abraham Lincoln
(B) Mark Twain and Benjamin Franklin
(C) students in this class
(D) All of the above

50. Which is not mentioned about Ben Franklin?

(A) He loved to eat and drink.
(B) People admired his wit.
(C) He took the bitter medicine.
(D) He told others not to overdo things.

Listening/Speaking Placement Test Audioscripts

Narrator: Number 1. When did Steve get in?

Narrator: Number 2. How much time will you have to spend in Boston?

Narrator: Number 3. Has she ever been there before?

Narrator: Number 4. How much is the subway fare?

Narrator: Number 5. Should we try to get to the eight o'clock movie?

Narrator: Number 6. Do you think that this jacket fits?

Narrator: Number 7. What are your preferences in art?

Narrator: Number 8. What are your hopes for your niece?

Narrator: Number 9. On the way home from the doctor, did you stop for some milk?

Narrator: Number 10. Couldn't you have arrived an hour later?

Narrator: Number 11. Peter is a lawyer like his mother.

Narrator: Number 12. Mary's flight was due at one, but it was delayed an hour and a half.

Narrator: Number 13. Sixty students signed up for the sailing trip, but most of them failed to show up.

Narrator: Number 14. Judy's got big plans for her birthday.

Narrator: Number 15. Peter was beaten fairly quickly by Steve in the tennis match.

Narrator: Number 16. In the heat of the argument, Mary lost sight of her original disagreement with John.

Narrator: Number 17. Although Gary liked his uncle Robert, he was fonder of his cousin Peter.

Narrator: Number 18. Considering the season, you really should plant the seeds in the garden before the frost.

Narrator: Number 19. On the whole, the dinner was great.

Narrator: Number 20. John's never been invited to the club by his brother.

Narrator: Number 21.

Man: The weather has been so hot this summer . . .

Woman: And we haven't had rain like this in years.

Narrator: What does the woman mean?

Narrator: Number 22.

Woman: The restaurant wasn't very good in my opinion.

Man: I thought it couldn't have been nicer.

Narrator: What does the man mean?

Narrator: Number 23.

Man: The storm sounded like it would blow the roof off my house.

Woman: Wasn't it terrible? The flood in our basement ruined my son's paintings.

Narrator: What did the storm do?

Narrator: Number 24.

Man: My brother is having a lot of trouble finding a job.

Woman: What a surprise. I haven't seen him lift a finger.

Narrator: What does the woman mean?

Narrator: Number 25.

Woman: Your serve. Whew. It's gotten very hot.

Man: I know, but I'm used to playing tennis in weather like this.

Narrator: What does the man mean?

Narrator: Number 26.

Man: The less I try to whack the ball, the farther it goes.

Woman: Hmm, that's quite a paradox!

Narrator: What does the woman mean?

Narrator: Number 27.

Woman: Richard told me about this store. He said they have the lowest prices in town.

Man: You think? I don't necessarily buy that.

Narrator: What does the man mean?

Narrator: Number 28.

Man: Did you hear that city hall almost burned down?

Woman: Right, and then the Mayor was removed under fire.

Narrator: What does the woman mean?

Narrator: Number 29.

Woman: How's the pizza here?

Man: Good, by and large, especially the mushroom and cheese.

Narrator: What does the man mean?

Narrator: Number 30.

Woman: That young man got 20 years for stealing a bicycle.

Man: Hmm. The judge sure handed down a hard sentence.

Narrator: What does the man mean?

Female Announcer: This is the T-A-L-K "Lost Pet Watch." Tonight we are telling you about three missing pets.

Blacky is a black-and-white kitten, six months old, who ran away from her owner, Mrs. Lincoln. Her house is next to the high school.

Male Announcer: And then, Oxen, a large German Shepherd, is a guide dog for John Wilson who's been blind since birth. Mr. Wilson cannot get around without his dog. Oxen was last seen running through the Green Acres neighborhood. He's wearing a black collar and has a big scar over his left eye.

Also, Winston, a wire-haired terrier, was taken from Mrs. Thompson's back yard. Winston is a prize-winning purebred worth about $3,000.

Female Announcer: If you have any information, please call our studio at 1-800-PET-HELP. The police station no longer handles missing animal reports. The animal shelter's phone is broken and won't be repaired for a week.

Stay tuned for news here at 103.7.

Narrator: Part 1.

Male Professor: This evening I am going to talk about product placement. Product placement is probably one of the most important concepts I will cover this semester. In the United States special care is taken when placing items in different parts of the supermarket. For example, candy is generally placed next to the cashier or check-out counter. This is because customers are often likely to grab a candy bar while waiting in line. Children, who are waiting in line with their parents, often pester their parents to buy candy for them. Another example has to do with the placement of expensive products.

Oh – Let me turn that off......

Narrator: Part 2.

Male Professor: Now where was I... Right —

Well, many stores in the U.S., not all, will place expensive products at eye level. Imported shampoos, for example, are placed at a level where they are clearly visible and people can easily reach for them. Please note that I am not supporting or endorsing cheap items over expensive ones. Before we end this evening, I want to talk about your next assignment.

Though you might not think of it as homework, I expect each of you to go to a large supermarket before next Tuesday to see where the over-the-counter medicine is placed. I look forward to hearing about your findings in a week.

Narrator: The final selection.

Female Professor: Hello, class. Today we're going to be talking about folk wisdom.

Every culture has many sayings that give advice about life. These sayings are part of what is commonly called "folk wisdom." Of course, folk wisdom is also expressed in other ways, such as myths, fairy tales, legends, and songs. Often, however, folk wisdom is shared in the form of short sayings about the best ways to approach life's joys and sorrows.

Today, we'll look at some of the humorous sayings of three famous Americans: Benjamin Franklin, Abraham Lincoln, and Mark Twain. Then I'll ask you to share some examples of folk wisdom from your own communities.

One characteristic of American folk wisdom is its humor. Humor makes the bitter medicine of life easier to swallow.

Ben Franklin was the first of many Americans to be admired for his humorous folk wisdom. Franklin himself loved to have fun. He liked to eat a lot, drink a lot, and be merry, but he always told others to practice moderation.

Interactions Listening/Speaking Placement Test Answer Key

Section 1

1. c 2. d 3. d 4. c 5. c 6. d 7. b 8. a 9. a 10. c

Section 2

11. d 12. a 13. c 14. c 15. b 16. c 17. b 18. a 19. a 20. d

Section 3

21. b 22. c 23. d 24. b 25. a 26. a 27. c 28. d 29. c 30. b

Section 4

31. a 32. b 33. d 34. a 35. a 36. b 37. d 38. a 39. c 40. a 41. a 42. b 43. c 44. c 45. b 46. c 47. d 48. a 49. d 50. c

SCORING FOR INTERACTIONS/MOSAIC LISTENING/SPEAKING PLACEMENT TEST	
Score	**Placement**
0–27	Interactions Access
28–46	Interactions 1
47–65	Interactions 2
66–84	Mosaic 1
85–100	Mosaic 2

This is a rough guide. Teachers should use their judgment in placing students and selecting texts.